CANADIAN
CRIME CONTROL POLICY

CANADIAN
CRIME CONTROL POLICY

SELECTED READINGS

Timothy F. Hartnagel
University of Alberta

HARCOURT
BRACE
CANADA

Harcourt Brace & Company, Canada
Toronto Montreal Fort Worth New York Orlando
Philadelphia San Diego London Sydney Tokyo

Requests for permission to make copies of any part of the work should be mailed to: Permissions, College Division, Harcourt Brace & Company, Canada, 55 Horner Avenue, Toronto, Ontario M8Z 4X6.

Every reasonable effort has been made to acquire permission for copyright material used in this text, and to acknowledge all such indebtedness accurately. Any errors and omissions called to the publisher's attention will be corrected in future printings.

Canadian Cataloguing in Publication Data

Main entry under title:

Canadian crime control policy : selected readings

ISBN 0–7747–3604–6

1. Crime prevention – Canada.   2. Criminal justice, Administration of – Canada. I. Hartnagel, Timothy F., 1941 –.

HV7431.C345 1998   364.4'0971   C97-932190-5

Senior Acquisitions Editor: Heather McWhinney
Senior Developmental Editor: Laura Paterson Pratt
Production Editor: Stacey Roderick
Assistant Production Co-ordinator: Shalini Babbar

Copy Editor: Joyce A. Funamoto
Cover Design: Sonya V. Thursby/Opus House Incorporated
Interior Design: Sonya V. Thursby/Opus House Incorporated
Typesetting and Assembly: Carolyn Hutchings
Printing and Binding: Webcom Limited

Cover Art: William Ronald, J'Accuse (1956). Oil on canvas, 152 x 176cm. Reproduced by permission of the artist and the Robert McLaughlin Gallery, Oshawa, Ontario.

This book was printed in Canada.

1 2 3 4 5   02 01 00 99 98

For Patti, for her support and commitment to the common good.

Preface

[handwritten annotation: doesn't necessarily mean actual crimes decreased eg: people may not trust police]

Although the rate of crime reported to the police dropped 13.1 percent between 1991 and 1995 (Statistics Canada, 1996), many Canadians remain very concerned about crime. In a May 1996 poll, 43 percent believed that violent crime in their community was increasing (Gallup Canada, 1996). In fact, the violent crime rate experienced its third consecutive annual decline in 1995, although this rate was still 36 percent higher than in 1985 (Statistics Canada, 1996). This same Gallup poll found that 75 percent thought the courts were not harsh enough in their dealings with criminals. It's clear from research that public officials' beliefs about public opinion influence criminal justice policy (Roberts, 1992). So crime and the policies that respond to it are important issues in Canada today.

However, controversy rages concerning what policies should be adopted. Many Canadians are reacting with calls for tougher penalties, apparently believing that harsher treatment will deter both actual and potential criminals. There have been calls for the elimination of parole and for lengthier incarceration of "dangerous offenders" in order to better protect society from further victimization. Some advocate far greater attention to the needs and rights of victims of crime while others call for an extension of victim–offender mediation programs. Gun control has been extensively debated as a policy to reduce violent crime, while some argue that early identification of high-risk offenders and the implementation of social prevention programs hold the most promise to reduce crime.

When I first began teaching a university course dealing with these and other crime control policy issues in Canada, I naturally looked for material from Canadian authors and researchers to include as part of the course material. The circumstances of crime and the organization of government and the criminal justice system are different in Canada than in the United States, Great Britain, or other European countries. While we can gain a better insight into our own situation by becoming knowledgeable about the crime control policies and practices of other countries, it is crucial to begin with an understanding of these issues as they have been framed in Canada. But the texts and collections of readings that were appropriate for this course focussed on the United States or Great Britain.

So while continuing to use some of this material, I put together a collection of Canadian articles to use in this course. Since the topic of juvenile justice is typically covered in a specialized course dealing with young offenders, I restricted my coverage to generally deal only with policy issues concerning adult criminality.

The articles are drawn from a variety of sources and were selected to reflect a diversity of approaches and theoretical perspectives found in the criminology literature. Several of the original articles included in this collection have been edited for length or to exclude certain technical or methodological material. While all of these articles have been previously published, they appear in a number of sources; their collection together in a single volume should facilitate their use as required or supplemental reading in undergraduate and graduate courses.

It is not feasible to cover all of the possible crime control policy topics in one collection. However, this collection does bring together recent writing by criminologists, lawyers, psychologists, and other social scientists, that addresses a number of the major contemporary controversies. Part Two looks at issues of sentencing, particularly with respect to the purposes of punishment and the consequences of using the criminal sanction. Readings dealing with differential sentencing of certain categories of offenders and the role of victims in sentencing are also included. Part Three examines the current interest in community policing as an allegedly more appropriate, effective, and cost efficient response to crime problems than the previous emphasis upon law enforcement with rapid response to calls for service. Policing Aboriginal communities is also considered. Part Four examines three specific issues of crime control policy: gun control, drug policy, and street prostitution. The readings in Part Five discuss various aspects of correctional policy, including both imprisonment and community-based alternatives. The first two readings in this section focus on female and Aboriginal inmates. The remaining selections discuss various intermediate sanctions in the community, for example, electronic monitoring, the possible extension of the correctional "net" by various community programs, and the future of parole. Finally, Part Six shifts attention to the social prevention of crime by addressing its underlying causes. The first two readings review the social development approach to crime prevention and the risk factors for the development of delinquent and criminal careers. Reading Twenty-five describes and evaluates the effectiveness of an early intervention program for disruptive children. The final reading discusses situational crime prevention.

Part One attempts to situate the discussion of these various substantive crime control policy issues within the broader subject of the construction of public policy. The four readings in this section describe various aspects of the policy process, including the various stages and actors involved, as well as the role of interests and values in policy-making. Reading Three examines the impact of a specific change in criminal justice policy, the legislation dealing with the processing of sexual assault cases, and discusses some of the difficulties in implementing this policy change. Reading Four discusses some of the ideological aspects of crime control policy focussing upon the first Mulroney Progressive Conservative government.

ACKNOWLEDGEMENTS

I would first of all like to thank the authors who were willing to have their work included in this collection. Without them there would be no book. I hope that with the publication of this book of readings their work will be brought to the attention of a larger audience. The students in my Crime and Public Policy course who worked their way through a previous version of these readings contributed to the final selection of articles through their comments and reactions. Francis Donkor assisted me in the collection of potential articles.

I am grateful to Heather McWhinney, Laura Paterson Pratt, and Stacey Roderick at Harcourt Brace for their excellent help in guiding me through the editorial and production processes.

Finally, I wish to thank the reviewers for their helpful comments on the outline for this text: Donald Clairmont, Dalhousie University; Irwin Cohen, Simon Fraser University; Al Erdahl, Mount Royal College; Anne Morris, Memorial University; David Osborne, Langara College; Kerri Reid, Malaspina University College; Vickie Ryckman, Lambton College; Jean Trepanier, Université de Montréal; Brian Young, Camosun College.

A NOTE FROM THE PUBLISHER

Thank you for selecting *Canadian Crime Control Policy: Selected Readings*, by Timothy F. Hartnagel. The author and publisher have devoted considerable time to the careful development of this book. We appreciate your recognition of this effort and accomplishment.

We want to hear what you think about *Canadian Crime Control Policy*. Please take a few minutes to fill in the stamped reader reply card at the end of the book. Your comments and suggestions will be valuable to us as we prepare new editions and other books.

Contents

PART ONE
Crime Control Policy: Process and Politics

Before turning to the substantive topics of crime control policy discussed in this text, some general issues pertaining to public policy need to be considered. To begin with, what exactly is public policy? One frequently quoted definition is "whatever governments choose to do or not to do" (Dye, 1978:3). This definition emphasizes two elements: that public policy involves state authorities; and that it is constituted by a deliberate decision to act or, occasionally, not to take action on some problem. Public policy is distinguished from the policies of other social organizations by its basis in law and support by the coercive power of the state. But it shares with these other policies a purposeful character: action or inaction is deliberately chosen to accomplish some intent, although this initial intent may be substantially modified by those involved in the process of implementing the policy (Pal, 1987). When we examine particular crime control policies, then, we need to be aware that they may have consequences or effects other than those intended by the authors of the policy. The purposeful character of policy suggests that it is intended to deal with some problem. The official statements, laws, regulations, programs, and other resources make up the substance of a public policy. They represent the means chosen to attempt to achieve the goals identified by public authorities for dealing with the problem as they have defined it. These goals are often likely to include political elements related to public support and re-election, along with the technical solutions proposed to deal with specific problems (Pal, 1987). The influence of the symbolic meaning of issues on policy is particularly applicable to crime control. In fact, most public policy analysts argue that the policy process of defining and responding to public problems is inherently political, involving choice among different ideas, values, and interests. Leslie Pal (1987) summarizes these various aspects of public policy by defining it as the framework of ideas and values within which a course of action or inaction is chosen by public authorities to address a given problem or interrelated set of problems.

Policy problems are socially constructed out of the conflicting views put forward by different groups when they compete for something that cannot be shared so as to satisfy all of them fully (Brooks, 1993). Only certain social or economic conditions are identified as public problems on the political agenda. Their recognition as relevant public problems, how the issues are defined, whose views are taken seriously, what policy goals should be sought, and what sort of "solutions" are seen as tenable, depend upon the particular forces shaping the political agenda at a given time in a specific society (Brooks, 1993). The different values, beliefs, and interests of the different sets of actors or "players" in the policy process result in conflicting formulations of the problem and choice of policy instrument or means for responding to it. Both the choice of policy goals and the "best" instruments of public policy are therefore subject to debate and conflicting evaluations. So although the policy-making process is often described as moving through several clearly identified stages—such as problem definition, priority-setting, policy formulation, and implementation—this suggests that the process is more orderly and logical than it is in reality (Pal, 1987). Rather, the process is characterized by conflict among multiple players, who try to influence the process in their favour, overlapping stages and feedback loops, and a series of decisions that rarely "solve" the problem, often leading to a further round of policy conflict.

Different theories or approaches have been developed in an attempt to explain public policy-making, such as the pluralist, public choice, and neo-marxist perspectives (see, for example, Brooks, 1993; Doern and Phidd, 1992; Dyck, 1993). These theories can be distinguished by their portrayal of the major actors involved in policy-making, their assumptions concerning the nature of society and the role of the state, and their evaluation of the interests served by public policy outputs (Jackson and Jackson, 1994).

Simeon (1976) has grouped the different factors influencing public policy-making into a funnel of causality ranging from very broad forces to the more specific. These include the resources and constraints of the social and economic environments; the political institutions, power relations, and dominant cultural values and beliefs of the society; and the policy-making process itself. This categorization suggests that a wide variety of potential influences on crime control policies should be considered. These could include such factors as the level of unemployment, Aboriginal culture and history, federal–provincial relations and the division of powers among jurisdictions, the Charter of Rights and Freedoms and Supreme Court interpretations, developments in other societies, particularly the United States, treaty and United Nations obligations, the media and public opinion, dominant beliefs concerning the causes of criminal behaviour, electoral politics and political parties, professional associations and other interest groups including various government ministries and officials, and so forth. While the relative importance of factors will vary depending upon the particular issue under consideration, the choice of any policy goal and instrument is likely to result from the interplay of a variety of influences.

Policy instruments must be implemented in order for the goals of the policy to be attained. The implementation of policy used to be assumed to occur more or less automatically toward the end of the policy process. However, it is increasingly recognized that putting policy into practice is itself a problematic process (Brooks, 1993). Public officials charged with implementing policy decisions typically possess a fair amount of discretion in their decision-making about the application of rules, interpretation of regulations, enforcement of laws, and delivery of programs. In fact, the policy goals may be vague and conflicting, and so require a fair amount of revision and interpretation by the implementing officials (Brooks, 1993). Furthermore, officials may distort the policy by implementing it in ways designed to protect their own bureaucratic interests and conform to their local organizational culture, and informal norms and relationships (Walker, 1994). In some cases organizational goals may change if not actually replace the policy goals in the daily operations of the implementing agencies. It is important to recognize, then, that implementation is not merely a technical matter of selecting the best means to achieve a policy goal at the least cost (Brooks, 1993). New policy may be created by administrative agencies through the implementation process, producing results different from the intentions of the original policy-makers.

The evaluation of the impact of programs designed to accomplish a policy goal is sometimes identified as a stage in the policy process. However, measuring the success of programs is not a simple matter, partly due to the often vague and conflicting goals of a policy (Brooks, 1993). The success of a given policy is likely to be a matter of degree rather than absolute and to depend upon the value attached to the goals of the policy (Pal, 1987). Furthermore, the evaluation of a policy's impact should take into account the unintended, hidden consequences along with its manifest, intended effects. However, program evaluation is often at the periphery of the policy-making process since various powerful actors, such as government officials and implementing agencies, frequently have a political interest in ambiguous measures of success.

* * *

Since public policy is purposeful, ideas about the desired goals that individuals and groups seek through state action or inaction play an important role in public policy formation. These ideas range from very broad, general ideologies such as liberalism and conservatism to much more specific objectives such as hiring a more diverse police force (Doern and Phidd, 1992). While policy ideas may often reflect the interests of those who advocate them, debate about public policy usually must address the public interest or good and therefore has a logic beyond mere self-interest (Pal, 1987). In fact, apparently technical arguments about the choice of policy instruments sometimes turn out to be disagreements over political or moral values. Policy ideas, then, provide the normative or value content to public policy.

Walter Miller (1973) has discussed the issue of ideology in crime control policy. Miller defines ideology as "a set of general and abstract beliefs or assumptions about the correct or proper state of things, particularly with respect to the moral order and political arrangements, which serve to shape one's positions on specific issues" (1973:20). He notes that ideological assumptions are generally unexamined presumptions underlying more explicitly expressed positions; that they have a strong emotional charge, particularly when challenged; and that they are relatively resistant to change. Miller contends that ideology and its consequences exert a powerful, but largely unrecognized, influence on criminal justice policies and procedures. He contrasts the general assumptions and "crusading issues" of crime control policy of those on the "right" (conservative) and "left" (liberal) of the spectrum of ideological positions. He argues that the paramount value for the right is order — a society based on a pervasive and binding morality — and the paramount danger is disorder. For the left the paramount value is justice — a society based on a fair and equitable distribution of power, wealth, prestige, and privilege — and the paramount evil is the concentration of valued social resources in the hands of a privileged minority. In criminal justice policy the two sides disagree over the relative priority of these two valuable conditions: whether *order* with justice, or *justice* with order should be the guiding principle.

A similar distinction between two normative models or value systems competing for priority in criminal justice was previously made by Herbert Packer (1968). The crime control model presumes that the suppression of crime is the most important function of criminal justice since failure here leads to the breakdown of public order, the precondition for individual freedom. Therefore, primacy is accorded to efficient law enforcement with minimal restrictions on the informal procedures of police and prosecution. Packer contrasts this assembly line model of the criminal justice process with the obstacle course view of the due process model. This latter model aims to maximize the reliability of criminal justice decision-making to protect the innocent as much as to convict the guilty. The possibility of error requires that limitations be placed upon the powers of officials. Therefore, the due process model insists upon formal, adjudicative, adversarial fact-finding procedures that require that legal, not merely factual, guilt be established. The primary rights of the accused individual require limitations upon the way official power is exercized.

These two contrasting ideological positions result in the crusading issues of the right and left with respect to crime and how to deal with it (Miller, 1973). Crusading issues furnish the basic impetus for action or policy changes. Miller identifies the right's crusading issues as: excessive leniency toward lawbreakers; favouring the welfare and rights of lawbreakers over those of their victims, law enforcement officials, and law abiding citizens; erosion of discipline and of respect for authority; the cost of crime; and excessive permissiveness. In contrast, he claims that the left's crusading issues are: overcriminalization; labelling and stigmatization of offenders; overinstitutionalization; overcentralization in crime control organizations; and discriminatory bias by the agencies of crime control.

These crusading issues derive from the general assumptions of the contrasting ideological positions about the nature of criminal behaviour, the causes of criminality, responsibility for crime, appropriate measures of response to crime, and, more broadly, the nature of human nature, and the proper kind of society. While we can't review all of these assumptions here, an important contrast concerns responsibility for criminal behaviour. While the right assumes that individuals are responsible for and choose their own behaviour, the left attributes responsibility to conditions of the social order. These underlying beliefs about the causes of criminal behaviour are linked to corresponding views regarding the appropriate responses to crime. Those on the right believe that offenders deserve punishment and they, along with potential offenders, will be deterred by it. In contrast, the left emphasizes rehabilitation of offenders and prevention of crime in an attempt to change the conditions that cause criminal behaviour. The general point, then, is that beliefs and ideas, often held implicitly as unexamined presuppositions, can influence the choice of policy objectives and the means for attempting to achieve them.

One set of ideas that can influence the public policy agenda concerning crime control is public opinion. There is the widespread perception that the public favours more punitive sentencing than the courts. This view is part of the rationale for increased incarceration rates. Legislators passing mandatory sentencing legislation, judges imposing harsher sentences, and more restrictive parole release decisions claim to be responding to the public's demand for a more punitive response to crime. However, public knowledge of crime and criminal penalties is often inaccurate. For example, a recent poll (Globe and Mail, 28 July 1997) indicates that most Canadians believe crime in their communities is increasing despite studies showing a significant drop in violent crime across the country. Furthermore, research by Roberts and Doob (1989) demonstrates how the public is misinformed about actual sentencing practices, statutory maxima, recidivism rates, and parole release rates. Most studies have used a single, simple, and abstract question ("In general, would you say that sentences handed down by the courts are too severe, about right, or not severe enough?") to measure punitiveness and conclude that the public is more punitive than the courts. However, Roberts and Doob's (1989) research comparing the public's views concerning the use of imprisonment with actual incarceration rates contradicts this conclusion. In fact, when taking into account the actual number of offenders sent to prison, following the views of the public would, for many offences, result in fewer, not more, admissions to prison. Roberts and Doob claim that when more sophisticated questions concerning sentencing are posed the results indicate both greater leniency toward offenders and greater flexibility in terms of the purposes of sentencing.

The public lacks information about different sentencing alternatives. When this information is provided, opinions change and support for incarceration declines significantly. Research by the Canadian Sentencing Commission (1987) shows that Canadians appear willing to invest more money in nonpunitive, nonrepressive

responses to crime. When given a choice between spending money on prison construction or developing better alternatives to incarceration, 70 percent chose the latter. The respondents were also asked to choose from among a list of alternatives the
single most effective way to control crime. The most popular solution (43 percent)
was to reduce the level of unemployment. Increasing the number of social programs
was chosen by another 11 percent, and the increased use of alternatives to incarceration by 14 percent. Twenty-eight percent thought sentences should be made harsher
while only 4 percent wanted an increased number of police. In a more recent poll
(Globe and Mail, 28 July 1997) a majority (51 percent) of respondents thought a
much higher priority should be placed on social development, attacking the roots of
crime through economic and social programs.

Furthermore, the more information given the public concerning the offender and
the offense, the less punitive they become. For example, in one study (Doob and
Roberts, 1983) 80 percent of those given only a brief description of a manslaughter
case thought the sentence was too lenient. But of those who read a more comprehensive account, only 15 percent thought the sentence given by the court was too lenient.
This finding is important since most sentencing stories in the news media — the primary source of information for the public — are brief and lack much detail, as well as
being biased toward the more sensational and atypical crimes. In fact, research
(Roberts and Doob, 1990) has demonstrated media influences on public attitudes
toward sentencing. Subjects who were randomly assigned to read a news media
account of a sentencing decision were much more likely to feel the sentence was too
lenient than were those who read a summary of the actual court document on the case.

Policy-makers underestimate the amount of public support for reform strategies
in the area of crime control (Gottfredson and Taylor, 1984). There is ample evidence
that the public is not as punitive as their responses to simple poll questions suggest
(see, for example, Roberts, 1992). Therefore, policy initiatives in the area of crime
control and sentencing reform should not be inhibited by concern with a backlash of
public opinion (Roberts and Doob, 1989).

READINGS

The articles in this section examine selected aspects of the process and politics
involved in Canadian crime control policy. The first reading by Solomon provides an
overview of the policy process in Canadian criminal justice. Solomon emphasizes the
point that policy-making is a political process and as such requires more than simply
the examination of substantive issues. Central to the study of the policy process is an
identification of the categories of actors attempting to influence particular policy proposals, and an understanding of the several phases or stages of policy-making.
Solomon distinguishes four stages of policy-making — agenda setting, decision-making, implementation, and evaluation. However, he emphasizes that the notion of
stages paints a too simple, static, uni-decisional, and rational picture of policy-making. Most policy-making is more likely to evolve through a series of decisions and
develop through various sequences. Solomon categorizes policy actors as amateurs — the public and politicians — and professionals, both operational officials and
those engaged in planning and research. He then proceeds to discuss the policy-
making role and relative influence of each category. Having distinguished the actors
and stages in policy-making, Solomon considers two questions: what conditions are

necessary for policy innovation to occur; and how does and should social science contribute to policy development. Both questions require a consideration of actors and their involvement at different stages of policy-making. The reading concludes with a call for more case studies of particular policy issues for a better understanding of the whole policy-making process in Canadian criminal justice.

The second reading considers aspects of the political process that led to Bill C-49 dealing with street prostitution. It is a type of case study focussing on the relative influence of local interest groups on the enforcement of prostitution laws and the development of Bill C-49. Larsen concludes that the socio-economic status and class background of groups affect their ability to influence the policy process concerning control of street prostitution. Mainstream feminist groups rarely regarded the situation of prostitutes as a feminist issue or questioned the legitimacy of prostitution laws themselves.

Criminologists and policy-makers have increasingly recognized the importance of the evaluation stage of policy development. The third reading examines some of the effects of the legislation changing the rape laws in Canada in 1983. After identifying the purposes of this new legislation, the authors describe their study of the processing of sexual assault cases through the criminal justice system in Winnipeg before and after the new legislation. The results indicate that while reports of sexual assault by victims to the police did increase, the legislative changes did not appear to increase convictions, and extra-legal variables reflecting the character of the victim still had a significant impact on the laying of charges and the likelihood of conviction. So Gunn and Linden conclude that this rape reform legislation made only a small impact, and go on to discuss some of the possible reasons for these weak results. This study underlines the difficulties in accomplishing intended policy changes through legislation.

The fourth reading examines the record of criminal justice policy in the first six years of the Mulroney government. The authors compare this record with that of the previous Liberal government to determine if a neo-conservative, law and order policy approach is evident. The analysis is based on the author's model of governing style called "managing consent." The legislative evidence suggests that a law and order approach was not evident but its strategy in criminal justice policy did reflect this government's broader neo-conservative agenda nonetheless. According to the authors, this strategy involves the reaffirmation of justice and security as the primary goals of the criminal justice system; increases the scope of provincial government power in this area; provides the appearance of being tough on crime, while emphasizing efficient management of the system.

QUESTIONS FOR DISCUSSION

1. Do you agree with Hatt et al.'s conclusion that a law and order approach has not been evident in criminal justice policy under Mulroney? Why or why not?
2. Describe some examples of implementation problems with crime control policy. Discuss some possible ways of overcoming these problems.
3. Give some examples of interest groups involved in crime control policy debates. Discuss their possible interests and/or values.
4. Discuss the possible relationship between different categories of actors and their involvement and/or influence at different stages of the crime control policy process.

REFERENCES

Brooks, Stephen. 1993. *Public Policy in Canada*. Toronto: McClelland and Stewart.

Canadian Sentencing Commission. 1987. *Sentencing Reform*. Ottawa: Ministry of Supply and Services Canada.

Doern, G. Bruce and Richard W. Phidd. 1992. *Canadian Public Policy*. Scarborough: Nelson Canada.

Doob, Anthony and Julian V. Roberts. 1983. *An Analysis of the Public's View of Sentencing*. Ottawa: Department of Justice.

Dyck, Rand. 1993. *Canadian Politics*. Scarborough: Nelson Canada.

Dye, Thomas R. 1978. *Understanding Public Policy*. Englewood Cliffs, New Jersey: Prentice-Hall.

Gallup Canada. 1996. *The Gallup Poll*. 56(43): June 13, 1996.

Gottfredson, Stephen and Ralph B. Taylor. 1984. "Public policy and prison populations." *Judicature* 68: 190–201.

Jackson, Robert J. and Doreen Jackson. 1994. *Politics in Canada*. Scarborough: Prentice-Hall.

Miller, Walter B. 1973. "Ideology and criminal justice policy." *The Journal of Criminal Law and Criminology* 64: 141–62.

Packer, Herbert L. 1968. *The Limits of the Criminal Sanction*. Stanford: Stanford University Press.

Pal, Leslie. 1987. *Public Policy Analysis*. Toronto: Methuen.

Roberts, Julian V. 1992. Public opinion, crime, and criminal justice. In M. Tonry (ed.), *Crime and Justice: A Review of Research*. Chicago: University of Chicago Press.

Roberts, Julian V. and Anthony N. Doob. 1989. "Sentencing and public opinion." *Osgoode Hall Law Journal* 27(3): 491–514.

_____. 1990. "News media influences on public views of sentencing." *Law and Human Behavior* 14: 451–68.

Simeon, Richard. 1976. "Studying public policy." *Canadian Journal of Political Science* 9(4): 548–80.

Statistics Canada. 1996. *Juristat*. July, 1996 16(10): 1–21.

Walker, Samuel. 1994. *Sense and Nonsense about Crime and Drugs*. Belmont, California: Wadsworth.

ONE

The Policy Process in Canadian Criminal Justice: A Perspective and Research Agenda[1]

PETER H. SOLOMON, JR.

In a recent paper Denis Szabo urged analysts of criminal justice policies to transfer part of their attention from substantive issues to the politics responsible for

Source: Peter H. Solomon, Jr., "The Policy Process in Canadian Criminal Justice: A Perspective and Research Agenda," *Canadian Journal of Criminology*, 23, 1 (1981): 5–25. Copyright by the Canadian Criminal Justice Association. Reproduced by permission of the *Canadian Journal of Criminology*.

shaping policies.[63] If criminologists want to become more effective in helping to reform criminal justice and law enforcement, Szabo reasoned, they need to understand how the political process deals with proposals for changes in policy and what constraints it places upon the translation of ideas and analysis into action. I heartily agree with Professor Szabo's message and would like here to explore some ways of going about this task.

As Szabo explains at length, the extent to which various actors influence the movement of policy proposals through the phases of decision-making should serve as a central focus of investigation. Toward this end he urges the mounting of a series of case studies. Case studies of the distribution of influence in decision-making are nothing new to the discipline of political science, where they have been a favorite mode of study for more than a generation. As a rule, however, political scientists have studied influence on decisions for a specific reason. They have done so not to better understand policy development, but to determine the structure of power in the political system or society as a whole. In contrast, Professor Szabo proposes studies of political influence that will elucidate how policy-making shapes policies, or more concretely, how politics determines what is and can be adopted and implemented.

Naturally, this different purpose in studying the structure of influence in policy-making affects the concepts and methods used in the exercise. It also leads to the posing of different questions, some of which are just as intriguing as questions relating to the structure of power. Two such questions that we shall discuss here are (1) the problem of innovation in policy — what conditions have to be fulfilled before major changes are adopted and implemented; and (2) the relationship of social science to policy development — how does social science contribute to the development of policy and how can that contribution be enlarged.

There have been very few studies undertaken thus far of the politics of Canadian criminal justice,[15,25,53,14] but the difficulties of working in a near-vacuum can be reduced by using a comparative perspective. Scholars have studied policy-making in Canada for other policy realms[9,43,65,54,17,18] and the formation of justice policy in other countries.[38,16,8,68,60,58] With the help of these works, one can begin to determine in what ways, if any, criminal justice policy differs from other policy realms. Does criminal policy tend to change more slowly than the others? Are there greater obstacles to innovation, and if so, why? How would the answers to these questions vary from one country to another? In what ways do political structure and culture tradition affect policy-making in criminal justice?

Before turning to examine more closely questions raised by the study of the policy process in criminal justice, it is well to discuss what one means by policy and how one may most usefully conceptualize policy-making, both in terms of its stages and the actors who take part in it.

CRIMINAL POLICY AND ITS SOURCES

By a policy I mean the main thrust of an actor's approach to a problem, where the actor might range from a government to a ministry, an agency, or a person, and the problem might vary from a broad area of concern (like law enforcement) to a narrow one (like how the police should handle drunks on the street). Policies may be explicit or implicit, purposeful or accidental, decided at one time or evolve gradually. Policies may constitute the sources of regularities in practice, but they may also represent initiatives that never get implemented.

In many realms of public policy in modern states the policies adopted by politicians in the centres of power and expressed in legislation are decisive in setting the course of action for officials at lower levels in government. Criminal policy, however, is not always one of those policy realms. Especially in Canada (but also in other states) the practice of law enforcement and criminal justice is shaped not only by decisions taken in the centre but also by policies issuing from other levels of government. There are two basic reasons for the fragmentation of criminal policy among multiple levels of government in Canada. First, in Canada as in the USA, formal responsibility for crime control is divided between two levels of the federal system. Criminal law and procedure belong to federal jurisdiction; the provinces administer justice and supervise policing, although some of them use federal police on contract; both levels of government operate correctional institutions.[2,27] Secondly, much of the actual administration of courts and police has remained in the hands of local officials within those institutions and is effectively beyond the reach of federal and provincial governments.

The large local role in law enforcement policy results from the commitment, particularly strong in Anglo-American legal tradition, to keep the actual administration of justice free from political interference. Thus, judges are expected to have a free hand in deciding individual cases (the doctrine of judicial independence), and in Canada, the police claim that as servants of the law they too require freedom from political direction (the doctrine of police independence).[62] This commitment to insulating justice from politics has allowed officials to keep control over aspects of judicial and police administration which are unconnected with the impartiality of justice. Thus, judges have administered their courthouses as well as justice, and police chiefs have determined the tactics and the target of policing. And both groups jealously guard their prerogatives from encroachment. Judges have been reluctant to hand over court administration to the provinces, and police chiefs have resisted attempts by activist police boards to take policy initiatives.[70,62] With important features of judicial and law enforcement policy set locally, it is not surprising that scholars studying criminal justice in the USA and Canada have found wide variations in practices from one locality to another; for example, in the amount and type of plea bargaining and in the activities stressed in police work.[21,39,78] The variations have been so striking that "local legal culture," as opposed to centrally determined policy, has been cited as a major source of judicial and police practice.[29]

A sensitivity to the local component in Canadian criminal policy should take nothing away from the roles played by federal and provincial governments. The higher levels of government are, after all, the sources of the definitions of crimes and punishments and of the relationship between them, and they are dealing more than before with those issues of administration that have traditionally been in the hands of the local officials. This article deals with the policy process in Canadian criminal justice at the federal and provincial levels. The reader is invited to speculate about what modifications in the framework of analysis would be required for studying policy-making at the local level.

THE STAGES OF POLICY-MAKING

Denis Szabo has suggested a set of five phases through which a policy proposal might pass: *formation* (generation of an idea); *formulation* (elaboration and gradual acceptance of the idea by relevant actors); *mise au point* (specification of detail accompanying a decision to adopt); *mise en oeuvre* (implementation), and *evaluation* (assessment of the program's effectiveness). This scheme differs from those commonly used by political scientists in its emphasis on ideational rather than political categories (e.g., formation, formulation, and *mise au point* rather than demands, supports, and decision; or alternatively interest articulation, interest aggregation, and decision.)[63,20,6] Szabo's approach has much merit when the purpose of studying the policy process is to trace the fate of ideas and proposals. Nevertheless, I would modify his scheme in two ways: first, by combining the first and second stages into one stage, "agenda-setting," and secondly, by substituting "decision-making" for *mise au point*. The advantage gained is a clear demarcation between two phases of policy-making prior to adoption, each of which serves a distinct function and is likely to have a distinctive pattern of politics associated with it. Agenda-setting describes the period of social learning that must take place before a new policy idea becomes an acceptable option. Decision-making refers to the period of accommodation and adjustment associated with the policy's adoption. I would, of course, retain Szabo's other two phases, implementation and evaluation.

The idea of agenda-setting as a stage in the political process has an interesting history. It originated among scholars who were dissatisfied with their colleagues' reliance upon visible influence in decisions as an indication of political power. These critics argued that the students of decision-making had failed to pay heed to another kind of power, the power to determine which issues were to be considered and which options became legitimate alternatives. This power to shape the political agenda before decision-making began mattered a lot; for at that earlier stage, the critics continued, the bias in policy was "mobilized" by the really powerful people, who had the capacity to prevent challenges to their interests from being considered.[7] The proposition that some power elite behind the scenes manipulates the political agenda in the modern state is barely plausible and even harder to show.[80] But the idea of a stage of the policy process prior to decision-making, in which proposals for radical changes in policy are either screened out of consideration or accepted as legitimate alternatives, is a useful one (as some scholars have already demonstrated).[44]

The other, more familiar stages of policy-making require less comment. Decision-making is the period when acceptable proposals are debated, considered by persons in authority, and adopted or set aside. When policy proposals are adopted they have to be put into effect, but implementation involves more than a simple translation of goals into action. Implementing policy choices typically requires making further decisions, writing guidelines, determining exceptions to rules—all of which affect the content of policy. It is also possible that opponents of a policy choice will try to obstruct its execution. And, there is the universal problem that policies are easier to adopt than to effect; all the good will in the world may not be sufficient.[55] Evaluation, the last stage, refers not only to formal "scientific" study but to the appraisals of the policy in action that feed back into the making of future decisions. All too often the evaluations are made by the very persons who implement the program, rather than impartial outsiders.

Some outline of the stages of the policy process is a necessary heuristic tool, but one must not forget that any scheme is also a simplification of the reality of policy development. This is because in treating policy-making as decision-making such a scheme assumes that policies are chosen or adopted at a particular moment in time.

A unidecisional, static picture of policy-making closely approximates the "rational" or "optimal" model that remains the normative ideal of some policy analysts. But most students of public administration agree that this mode of policy development does not predominate in practice. In reality, policies are less likely to result from a single choice as from an evolution through a series of decisions. In practice policies are not chosen; they develop incrementally.[41,19,75] The evolution of policies may take various forms. Policy changes may be introduced slowly or rapidly, and they may be modest or innovative in scope. One decision in a series may outrank the rest in importance, but that decision may come at any point in the sequence. For example, a decision of principle may be followed by smaller correctives; or small steps, such as experiments, may lead to a sweeping decision.

Recognition of the developmental nature of policy-making prompts the analyst to extend his horizons beyond the comfortable unidecisional model. He must imagine policies developing through a chain of decisions, each of which may involve some or all of the stages included in our version of the model. And he must allow for the possibility that some policy proposals will follow a smooth path of development which can be easily analyzed with reference to the model, while others take an intricate path which requires a more flexible approach.

ACTORS IN POLICY-MAKING

Szabo identifies more than a dozen kinds of actors in criminal policy-making, locates them in their institutional settings (e.g., scholars in universities, judges in courts), and then groups them according to the type of power those institutions possess (legislative, judicial, executive, and "political").[63] This approach assumes that institutional differences play a major, if not decisive, part in the role and influence of the various actors in criminal policy-making, but the professionalization of governmental activity (which accompanied its growth, increased scope, and specialization) suggests that the distinction between amateur and professional may be more significant. Let me propose an alternative scheme for grouping the actors in policy-making, which is based on this distinction.

One can speak of three types of actors in criminal policy-making — politicians, professionals, and the public (see Figure 1.1). *Politicians* include the elected officials with ultimate authority in policy-making, in Canada the members of Parliament with ministerial responsibilities — the leaders — and also the parliamentary backbenchers and the members of opposition parties in Parliament. By *professionals*, I mean all actors who are regularly involved either with the operation or the evaluation of criminal justice and law enforcement. The professionals divide into two subgroups: those persons with operational responsibilities, including ministerial officials, police chiefs, Crown attorneys, judges, defense counsel, correctional authorities, and probation officers; and those persons concerned with planning and research, including the members of ministerial policy and research units (e.g., secretariats), the members and staffs of commissions (law reform, penal, etc.), and scholars and researchers outside of government. *The public* includes general and elite public opinion, as measured by polls, the media (which express and mould public opinion), and public interest groups, especially issue-oriented groups such as those for and against capital punishment. This way of grouping the actors in criminal justice policy-making enables one to ask about the role and relative influence of the public and of its

FIGURE 1.1 *Actors in Criminal Justice Policy-Making (Federal or Provincial)*

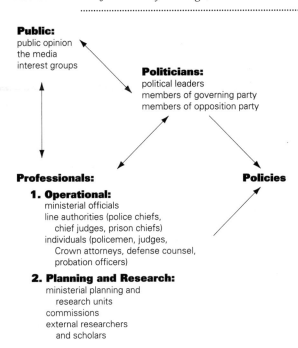

political representatives—i.e., the amateurs—and of the complex of professionals who deal with justice and law enforcement.

Consider first the role of politicians. Except in time of political crisis (such as the FLQ-War Measures Act Crisis of 1970), law enforcement occupies the attention of politicians only intermittently. One is prompted to ask: when do politicians become involved and why (e.g., only when legislation has to be passed or when a controversial issue becomes a matter of heated public debate)? How do politicians relate to the other sets of actors? It seems that when an issue is in the public spotlight, they tend to be particularly responsive to public concerns and pay correspondingly less attention to views of policy professionals. (Was this the case with recent legislation on capital punishment, long-term imprisonment, and gun control—and the so-called Peace and Security Program?) When there is no public perception of an issue, however, politicians appear to defer more readily to recommendations from professionals, including policy planners and researchers (assuming that they are not divided among themselves).

Another question for examination is when, if at all in Canada, issues of criminal justice and law enforcement become matters of partisan politics. Although the conventional wisdom holds that these issues are not usually the focus of inter-party conflicts in the Anglo-American political world, they seem to be becoming so with increasing frequency.[48] Law and order issues played a part in the U.S. Presidential Campaigns of 1964 and 1968; and the British Labor party in opposition produced a report *Crime—A Challenge to Us All* (June 1964), which served as a basis for policy changes introduced after the party came to power (in the *Criminal Justice Act of 1967*).[16,48] In England in the 1970s the major parties continued to differ over matters of penal policy, and in the 1979 electoral campaign, law and order issues were again prominent. The relative lack of inter-party conflict over such issues in Canada during the 1970s requires further explanation.[64] A related issue is the role that non-government members of the party in power may play. Although often assumed to be impotent, the backbenchers became the focus of pressure on the part of the opponents of reforms during the recent debate over gun-control legislation in Canada. The opponents of gun control used party organizers in the home districts to reach the backbenchers, who in turn approached the government ministers.

The role of the public in the politics of criminal justice also raises interesting questions. What kinds of issues provoke public involvement? To what extent do the media create public perceptions and reactions (or merely reflect them)? What conditions account for periodic "law and order" moods, and what constraints do swings in public attention and mood place upon the reform of criminal justice? Until now involvement by the general public has usually been limited to dramatic issues like capital punishment and gun control, but the practice of polling may extend the public's role to other issues besides. The resulting snapshots of public mood and perceptions on issues may have limited validity, but they are easy to produce and much the fashion in government circles. The dangers of relying upon polls are underscored by the fact that public opinion is as much something to be mobilized as to be read. The media, on their own and in response to the initiatives of interest groups, often perform this function, as government leaders are well aware. Thus, during the gun control debate of 1976 the Minister of Justice took advantage of a well-timed shooting of a police officer by proceeding to the scene of the crime with full media coverage.[25,28] Another dimension of public involvement in criminal justice policy-making is the role played by public interest groups (to be distinguished from bodies of professionals in criminal justice). It is worthwhile exploring, as Martin Friedland did so well for gun control legislation, the range and the basis of these groups (it is often easier for one side of an issue to organize than another), the tactics these groups use, their capacity to form coalitions, their points of access to politicians and professionals, and their capacity to exert influence on decisions.[25]

Professionals play a large role in the development of criminal justice policy, but to assess this role one must ask first about the patterns of division and cohesion among those professionals. When we speak of judges, police chiefs, defense counsel, parole boards, RCMP authorities, and criminologists, are we speaking of one set of actors or of many? Jack Walker has suggested that the policy professionals in a particular realm may constitute a "policy community." A policy community exists when the various policy professionals interact regularly (through reading the same journals, attending conferences, etc.) and as a result develop a set of commonly held "core assumptions" about the goals and means that are acceptable for policy. These core assumptions, Walker supposes, act as a screen through which proposed changes in policy must pass before they reach the political agenda, a screen that poses special difficulties for innovations. Walker further hypothesizes that the policy community has its own internal power structure, in which a loosely defined but recognizable set of "cosmopolitan" members have strong influence over the maintenance and modification of the core assumptions, and hence the community's positions on policy proposals.[67,3]

Walker's concept of a policy community and of its critical role as "the patron and arbiter of change" is attractive, but it remains to be seen how well it fits with reality in particular policy realms and in particular countries. Walter Miller's analysis of the ideological stances of actors in American criminal justice — of police, judges, and academic criminologists — suggests that no such community exists there. As Miller sees it, the basic premises and political attitudes of the different professionals in criminal justice vary so greatly and systematically that they react independently to policy proposals and often divide in their evaluations.[46] And, the one relevant case study, Lemert's account of the "revolution" in juvenile justice in California, supports the Miller portrait of divisions within the world of criminal justice professionals.[38]

Does either of these views of professionals apply to Canadian criminal justice? Do police chiefs, judges, officials, policy planners, and scholars in Canada form a community and act in concert when faced with the challenge of reform, or are they a divided lot with hopelessly differing perspectives, which pit one group against the other? Again, the bits of available evidence suggest that the image of fragmentation is closer to the truth. To begin with, the various professionals belong to separate organizations and have their own journals, and some of the groups are further subdivided by province and/or by function. Thus, while lawyers in general may belong to the Canadian Bar Association, there are separate provincial bar associations, provincial Crown attorneys associations, and provincial defense counsel groups — each with their own publications. A similar portrait could be drawn for judges, for police officers, and for correctional officials, not to speak of academic criminologists. Of course, the bonds needed to produce a policy community in Walker's sense might result from the various professionals reading each others' publications and meeting in joint forums. It is not certain how much this happens in Canada, but Hogarth's study of Ontario magistrates suggests that judges at least take a limited part in any such cross-fertilization. Hogarth found that most judges confined their reading to the *Ontario Magistrates Quarterly* and the *Criminal Law Quarterly*; less than half read the *Canadian Journal of Corrections* and only a handful looked at *Federal Probation* or at criminology journals.[30] The signs of divisions among professionals within criminal justice did not mean that the Walker portrait of a policy community might not apply to them in some circumstances. There may be issues on which professionals in law enforcement and criminal justice show a strong degree of cohesion. It is also possible that there are significant alignments within the larger community, for example, among the lawyers in various roles or among researchers and planners.

There are also questions worth posing about the role of particular professionals in criminal justice in policy-making. One may inquire, for example, about the relationships of various groups to politicians. What is the relative importance for those professionals who are government employees (police chiefs, Crown attorneys, judges, probation officers, correctional officials) of hierarchical relationships and of contacts through their professional associations? One should also ask about the role of ministerial research and planning bodies, like the Secretariat of the Federal Solicitor-General's Department, and the comparable units in the Federal Ministry of Justice and in various provincial ministries. The 1970's witnessed a rapid growth of such inhouse intellectual and planning capability, not only in Canada but also in the USA, Great Britain, and elsewhere.[69,23,48] What role do these units and their members play in policy-making? Do they serve as independent sources of policy ideas or are they more often conduits for communications from others? To what extent do they perform an agenda-setting function for federal and for provincial policy-making in criminal justice and law enforcement? Informal discussion with persons working in the Ottawa secretariats suggest that the role of these bodies is not yet institutionalized, but this impression requires confirmation. Another related line of inquiry concerns the role of commissions and advisory bodies in criminal policy-making, past and present. In addition to posing many of the same questions about commissions as about internal research units, one wants to inquire into the relationships between commissions and inhouse analysts, and into the broader political functions commissions often seem to serve.[56,34,31,81]

Distinguishing among politicians, professionals, and the public, and among their various components, raises interesting questions, but the scheme is not perfect. It can be applied most easily to a unitary system of government, such as that of Britain or of France. It is harder to use for a federal system like Canada because the cleavages introduced by federalism may cut across the lines drawn by our circles of actors. Politicians from different levels of government may have competing interests and be engaged in jurisdictional conflicts; and even professionals may divide along federal-provincial lines on some issues. Even for issues that do not arouse conflicts, the potential involvement of actors from different levels of government can complicate the story. Thus, planning and research staff from the federal ministries might contribute to provincial policy-making, quite apart from their counterparts at the provincial level. Generally speaking, the federal system of government in Canada requires further distinctions among actors from different levels of government; and it demands flexibility in the analysis of the roles played by the various types of actors.

Let us now turn to two questions that the study of the policy process in criminal justice can illuminate.

THE PROBLEM OF INNOVATION IN POLICY

How often do reformers, researchers, and commissions stretch their imaginations and promote innovations in criminal justice policy, only to find their proposals neglected, or if considered, later discarded or endlessly delayed? Some of these proposals fail on their merits, but many others fall victim to political expediency. Reformers know instinctively that the more far-reaching a proposal for change, the more difficulties the political process places in its path. This regularity may stem from a natural conservatism in large organizations or systems, but the roots of the problem seem to be more complex. As a rule, innovations in policy face intellectual and structural obstacles that smaller changes do not. The intellectual obstacles tend to be associated with agenda-setting; the structural ones with decision-making.

The first obstacle to the adoption of an innovation is getting the proposal onto the political agenda. Usually this requires a change in thinking or of basic assumptions. Independently, both Donald Schon, a philosopher, and James Q. Wilson, a political scientist, have observed that such a change in thinking tends to occur either in time of crisis or after a long period of difficulties and gradual assimilation of reform perspectives.[59,77] In the absence of such conditions, innovative proposals do not often gain serious consideration, and if promoted vigorously, are opposed with equal vigor by the "guardians" of the agenda.

One crucial part of this picture remains unclear. Just who are the "guardians" of the political agenda? Whose thinking or whose assumptions about policy must change before proposals for innovation are placed on the agenda? The observers have paid little attention to this question, but even so, are divided in their answers, however tentative. Some refer to "the public," perhaps begging the question; others point to segments of the public, such as the highly educated or attentive, or the powerful elites whose opinion matters. In contrast, Jack Walker has directed our attention away from the public to the policy professionals, suggesting that the policy community screens out proposals for innovation that conflict with its core assumptions.[67] Empirical study of the fate of innovations in agenda-setting may help to determine the relative importance of the public (or parts therefore) and of the policy community (or its several parts, including the ministerial policy planners and researchers.) Do all of these actors have to accept the legitimacy of a proposal before it can be considered or only some? Does any hold a veto power? The answers may not be clearcut and might entail variation with the types of issues or circumstances under which they arise.

Once an innovative policy idea becomes sufficiently acceptable to receive consideration, it must still face the hurdles associated with its being adopted. At this stage the feasibility of innovative change becomes the crucial problem and any of a number of structural obstacles may intervene.[42] One is resources. A major shift in policy often incurs new financial costs, and even if no new costs are required, redeployment of spending may be required. A second structural obstacle that faces many innovative programs is their implications for policies in other realms. Increasingly policies of governments are becoming interrelated, so that changes in one sphere require changes in another, or possibly even, cooperation from the latter's policy professionals.[79] Thus, proposals to divert large numbers of delinquents out of the criminal justice system have important consequences for welfare policies in that the case loads of community welfare organizations are bound to increase. A third structural obstacle to innovation with particular relevance for Canada is its effects on intergovernmental relations. Even in a unitary system a policy may disturb divisions of responsibility among levels of government. When it threatens to change the pattern of sharing of functions or resources in a federal system, it will likely provoke opposition, particularly in a highly conflictual federal system like Canada.

If innovations in policy meet with all these obstacles in gaining acceptance onto the political agenda and in the course of adoption, it is not surprising that major changes are adopted only infrequently. But there may be ways of easing the path of innovative change through short-circuiting or endrunning parts of the cycle of innovation. One tactic, almost conventional wisdom in public administration, consists of presenting large changes in policies as small ones, sometimes by dressing them up in technical clothes and hoping that less attention is paid to them. Another approach, apparently on the increase, is to launch innovations in policy at the bottom, sometimes in the form of experiments, and to present them formally as new directions in policy only after they have become policy in fact. An example of this pattern is the development of pretrial diversion in Canada. A wide variety of experimental programs have been launched locally, and the Federal Solicitor-General Department has monitored their performance and done much background analysis preparatory to proposing a federal policy.[12,10,22] Such an "inversion" of the normal pyramid of power in policy-making may be the only way that some changes can enter policy, when the processes of agenda-setting and decision-making are blocked at the top.

Our picture of the conditions under which innovations in policy occur, of the obstacles that may arise, and of the means used to circumvent them — though based upon impressions of the "real world" of policy-making—has only the status of hypothesis. To what extent the handling of proposals for innovations in criminal policy, in Canada and elsewhere, conforms to this pattern or is explained by it, is a topic for research.

SOCIAL SCIENCE AND POLICY-MAKING

Another problem that can be addressed in a study of how policy-making affects criminal justice policy is the difficulties inherent in the use of social science, or more broadly in the translation of ideas into policies. Social scientists, including criminologists, who have done policy-related research or served as consultants to politicians, officials, or commissions, all too often have unhappy experiences, and their reports and *post mortems* result in a jaundiced, if not downright pessimistic view of the possibilities for using social science in policy-making. In part, the disappointments stem, I suspect, from assessment of particular experiences against the background of an idealistic picture of how policies are formed and adopted. Examining the use of social science and the role of social scientists in the context of a detailed study of the whole policy process—from agenda-setting through implementation and evaluation—and including the full range of actors involved, should make clearer where social science fits into policy-making and how it can have a greater impact in the future.

It is helpful to picture social scientists as performing two main functions in policy-making: solving policy problems and providing new perspectives on policy for politicians, officials, and the public. The problem-solving function brings social scientists into decision-making; the "enlightenment function" draws them into agenda-setting as well.[73] Solving policy problems has until recently been regarded by most commentators as the main contribution of social science to policy-making.[37,73] But, in reaction to the frustrations social scientists have experienced in this role, some scholars have begun to treat the enlightenment function as primary.[57,72,41] There is a need for improved understanding of both functions, and there are many research questions worth posing.

The dilemmas associated with the use of social science to solve or alleviate policy problems are as fundamental as they are familiar. One source of difficulty is the nature of social science. Even high-quality research usually cannot answer the questions that politicians as clients may pose—because of the value dimensions inherent in policy choices and because the questions of fact cannot be answered by social science, at least not within the time constraints under which the consulting researcher must labor.[71,31] Not only does research usually not solve problems, it often has the opposite effect of introducing further complexities. In answering one question, good research is likely to raise new ones, thereby adding to the uncertainties with which the politicians must deal.[75,5] Another equally important source of difficulty in the use of social science in policy-making stems from the nature of the decision-making process in public settings. No matter how much social scientists or policy planners might wish, decision-making in government does not even approach the rational model. By the nature of their job, politicians must be concerned with trade-offs among values and with the resolution of conflicts. As a result, they decide issues most often not through an abstract weighing of the substantive pros and cons but through the use of other mechanisms of choice, such as voting, bargaining, and compromise. In these exercises politicians need to mobilize support for courses of action they favor, and they are often pleased to use social science, along with other kinds of knowledge, toward this end.[57,41] Researchers who decry this behavior as misuse or abuse of social science fail to acknowledge the nature and mechanisms of political choice.

Recent studies of the problem-solving role of social science have suggested strategies for improvement. Two observers of the recent history of criminology and public policy in the USA call for modesty and urge researchers to concentrate on what they can do best, namely the evaluation of the operation of current programs and policies. If they did this, the observers claim, researchers would have more to offer to politicians than when they try to translate their theories about crime and its causes into practice.[50,76] A different approach has been suggested by other commentators. Rather than abandon for the time being studies aimed at reforms, the latter contend, scholars who are inclined to such work should add an explicitly political dimension to their work. Thus, the researcher might analyze not only the substantive merits but also the political feasibility and consequences of reform proposals, and they might take an active part in spreading their messages and in overcoming obstacles to change.[75,82,61] Both of these approaches to improving the contribution of social science to solving policy problems are plausible, but will they make a difference? It would be useful to find and study examples of each, in Canada if possible, and to assess their effects.

There may be even more room for improvement in the role social science performs as a source of new ideas and approaches to policy, that is in its enlightenment function. Only in the last few years have observers started to pay attention to the contribution social science might make to agenda-setting, and some of the most thoughtful of them now place much emphasis on this function.[47] For example, Carol Weiss writes that

> Social research can be "used" in reconceptualizing the character of policy issues, or even redefining the policy agenda. Thus, social research may sensitize decision-makers to new issues and turn what were nonproblems into policy problems.... In turn it may convert existing social problems into nonproblems (e g , marijuana use). It may drastically revise the way that a society thinks about issues, (e.g., acceptable rates of unemployment), the facets of an issue that are viewed as susceptible to alteration, and the alternative measures it considers.[72]

Martin Rein agrees that the key function of research is the identification of problems as a step toward putting them on the agenda.[57] Lindblom and Cohen go even further to suggest that the main impact of applied social research may be through its contribution to a "cumulating set of incentives for a general reconsideration by policy makers of their decision-making framework, their operating political or social philosophy or their ideology."[41]

If social science does serve to enlighten other actors in the policy process and helps to shape the policy agenda, how does this happen? Observers have usually assumed that social scientists influence policy-making in this basic way not through their direct contacts with politicians and officials but indirectly. Thus, the most influential social scientist of the century, John Maynard Keynes, reshaped government economic policies not as a consultant, but after a generation of economists accepted his teachings. In like manner, criminological theory and research of the 1950s and 1960s that employed the labelling or interactionist perspective may have influenced public thinking in the USA and Canada toward such issues as decriminalization, decarceration, and diversion — not through commissioned research, but through a "diffuse, undirected seepage" of thought.[73] Some social scientists have come to believe that this kind of indirect influence was the only channel through which they could influence agenda-setting and thereby promote major changes in policy. More direct approaches seemed less effective because of the nature of the consulting role, which like that of the bureaucratic intellectual, seemed to demand a posture of conformity.[45] Successful consultants kept their advice consistent both with the current political agenda and with their client's biases. This conception of the limitations associated with the role of consultant may have been too uniformly pessimistic. A recent study of the receptivity of officials in one U.S. government agency to social science revealed unexpectedly that the personal views of the officials there extended well beyond the current policy and the agenda of changes then under consideration.[74] This result implies that the attempt to familiarize officials with new ideas may be pursued through direct means and that a more activist approach to the enlightenment function of social science may be in order.

The possibility that the role of social science as a source of ideas could be improved raises questions about social scientists as actors in policy-making. One would like to know how, if at all, criminologists divide the problem-solving and enlightenment function? Do researchers working in settings inside government contribute mainly to problem-solving, and scholars on the outside more to enlightenment? To be sure, the research topics that researchers inside government perform tend to be narrower and more applied than some of those pursued by those on the outside. But just as many outside scholars devote themselves to problem-solving, so researchers on the inside may serve to educate officials with whom they have contact. My own interviews with researchers working in the Home Office Research Unit, England (1968), in the Procuarcy Institute, USSR (1970), and in the Research Division of the Solicitor General, Canada (1979), revealed that the researchers themselves thought that their greatest influence on crime policy lay not in their contribution to particular measures but in their influence upon the climate of decision-making. In all three countries, researchers sensed in the officials a new rationality and a new inclination to ask for empirical studies when taking stands.[60] Since the three government research units I visited were all relatively new (they ranged from seven to eleven years old), it is not surprising that they should have this effect, but there was no reason to suppose that the inside researchers would not continue to influence the perspectives of the officials. Such influence might even increase as the units became more established and the researchers developed closer contacts with operational officials.

An equally important question concerns what social scientists on the outside have been doing to promote the enlightenment function of their research. No doubt some, perhaps the bulk, of social scientists merely publish their work for academic audiences and allow the indirect processes of changes in public thinking to take their course. Others, however, may do more to promote their ideas and perspectives, and it would be interesting to learn with what success. One audience worth reaching is the researchers and planners who work inside of government, who in turn may influence the thinking of politicians and officials. To a degree this is the easiest audience to reach, since the inhouse intellectuals read the scholarly publications, but more direct contacts may also be helpful. They will become more important if governments come to give more responsibility to inhouse planning groups and correspondingly less to semipublic commissions and advisory groups. For social scientists to influence immediately the thinking of practitioners in criminal justice may require greater effort, say in the form of writing articles for the journals of particular groups. It would be interesting to compare the effectiveness in communicating to professional groups of scholars who take the initiative and of their counterparts who addressed these audiences only in reply to criticism of their studies.[4] Under some circumstances it may also be important for social scientists to bring their messages to the general public, say when they are dealing with issues that are bound to have a public dimension in any case. To reach firm conclusions about how social scientists might enhance their contribution to policy-making through enlightening other actors requires better understanding not only of the effects of social scientists' actions but also of the agenda-setting process as a whole. The questions we posed earlier, about who could screen innovative proposals from the agenda, and whose thinking mattered most in getting ideas legitimated, must be answered in order to learn how social scientists should distribute their efforts.

CHOOSING CASE STUDIES

The study of policy-making in Canadian criminal justice could proceed by a number of methods. One approach, used in a recent set of studies of penal policy-making in England, focuses upon the various actors in the policy process. Thus, in that collection one finds articles on the role of pressure groups, of advisory bodies, of the news media, of Parliament, of the prison service, of the probation and aftercare service, of the Judiciary, and of the Home Office.[68] While this approach is informative, and more studies of this sort are needed for Canada (the Friedland article is a model),[25] I believe that there is much benefit to be gained from case studies on particular policy issues. Through case studies one could try to view the whole policy-making process and raise a number of the questions that have been developed in this paper.

The benefits from case studies are partly cumulative. Let me, therefore, discuss the criteria I would employ in choosing issues for study and then give brief illustrative comments on a number of candidates. Because of my concern with innovations in policy, and with agenda-setting, I favor issues where major changes in approach were proposed and either adopted or rejected. Issues that underwent a lengthy period of agenda-setting and decision-making tend to be more attractive than those handled with dispatch (although examples of the latter might be included for contrast). Moreover, issues where key decisions, such as to adopt reforms, were taken sometime in the past serve better than current or unresolved ones, for only these issues afford an opportunity to examine the implementation and evaluation of policies adopted. In addition to meeting these general criteria an optimal series of case studies would include; (1) examples of successful and of unsuccessful promotion of policy change; (2) issues with and without complications for federal-provincial relations; (3) proposals with and without implications for other policy realms; (4) proposals for policy change introduced at provincial as well as the federal level of government; and (5) cases of policy changes introduced through legislation and of changes which developed through administrative practice.

Choosing a judicious combination of case studies is a precondition for fruitful generalizations, and will require preliminary investigation of the recent history of Canadian criminal justice policy. Here are a few issues which I find attractive even now, before having made this inquiry:

1. *Juvenile Justice.* For fifteen years Canada has been reconsidering its way of handling juvenile offenders. At first, there was much disagreement about what direction reforms should take, disagreements that caused the failure of the first legislative proposals. Later, after agreement on fundamentals had been achieved, legislation was blocked by structural obstacles such as its implications for resource allocation, for federal-provincial relations, and for adjacent policy realms. A series of commissions was involved, and social science evidence considered. Juvenile justice makes an almost ideal case study. Its main drawback is that the story remains incomplete. Even so, it could serve as a classic study of the failure to adopt innovation in policy at the top. Meanwhile, policy has advanced in administration through experiments, especially in diversion at the local level (e.g., in British Columbia).[53,22]

2. *Pretrial Detention and Bail.* Here is a controversial issue, much studied by social scientists, in regard to which major legislation was passed a few years ago. The time is ripe to assess the implementation of the reforms and the consequences that their "evaluation" by some law enforcement officials are having (is there a backlash against the reform?).[35,36,66]

3. *Reform Penal Measures.* (parole, probation, etc.) From the late 1950s to the late 1960s Canada saw a marked increase in the use of these measures and a proportional reduction in the time average prisoners spent in prison. The 1970s saw a typical turn in the cycle toward some limitations on these non-custodial measures. While public attention tends to force retrenchments, professionals seek the expansion of alternatives to imprisonment, and the economics of the situation tends to favor the latter position. This is a controversial policy issue, in which gradual, small changes have predominated over dramatic or innovative ones.[13,33,11]

4. *Death Penalty.* Another controversial issue. Since capital punishment was abolished some years ago, one can examine the effects of its absence and efforts to revive it. This is one of the issues allowing for a consideration of the role of the public and public interest groups, and its effects on politicians and policy professionals.[32,14]

5. *Decriminalization of Status Offenses.* This process represents the most significant trend in the content of the criminal code. Homosexuality was decriminalized in the late 1960s. The 1970s saw a major commission urge elimination of many drug-related offenses and growing public and political acquiescence to the idea. Legislation is expected shortly.

6. *Gun Control.* After a period of study, proposals for controlling firearms have moved from private members' bills into the most recent omnibus criminal reform bill (C-21, 1978). An issue that provokes intense reactions and sharp political conflict in the U.S.A., gun control is a natural issue for study in Canada. Is it also controversial here, and if not, why not?[24,25,49,62]

In addition to these issues, all which involve federal government policies, it would be useful to have studies of policies adopted wholly at the provincial level.

One good candidate would be the development of new ways of handling summary offenses, in particular the Ontario Provincial Offenses Act of 1980.[51] Other promising subjects include the politics of court administration in various provinces and the attempts by some provinces to undertake closer regulation or control of local police departments (e.g., New Brunswick; British Columbia).[52,70,26,62]

There is so little literature exploring policy-making in criminal justice — in Canada and elsewhere — the door is wide open for studies of almost any issue, present or past. I invite fellow scholars to start to fill this void.

NOTES

1. The paper on which this article is based was presented to a seminar at the Research Division of the Solicitor-General's Department and discussed at a workshop at the Centre of Criminology, University of Toronto. I would like to express particular thanks to Michael Stein, Philip Stenning, and Mike Heumann for thoughtful criticism of the paper, and Judith Osborne for research assistance.

2. A leading constitutional law scholar proposed eliminating much of the division of responsibilities in criminal justice by shifting criminal law and procedure and corrections to provincial jurisdiction. See Abel, Albert: "A Chart for a Charter." *University of New Brunswick Law Journal*, 1976, *20*, 50–51.

3. Along similar lines Hugh Heclo has suggested the concept of "issue networks" to describe "shared knowledge groups having to do with an aspect ... of public policy." The networks have a large number of participants with valuable degrees of mutual commitment and dependence on each other. Though somewhat amorphous, they seem to Heclo both to generate and control some areas of policy. Heclo, Hugh. "Issue Networks and the Executive Establishment." in *The New American Political System*, ed. by A. King. Washington, DC: American Enterprise Institute, 1979, pp. 87–124.

4. For example, William Felstner and Ann Drew explained their studies of European alternatives to American criminal procedure in the *Judges Journal*; but the authors of the major police studies — George Kelling, *et al.*, on preventive patrol, and Peter Greenwood, *et al.*, on criminal investigation, did not write in *The Police Chief* until their studies had been challenged. Felstiner, W., and Drew, A.B. "European Alternatives to Criminal Procedure." *The Judges Journal*, 1978, *17*(3) 18–24, 50–53, and *17*(4), 16–19, 55–56. Kelling, G., and Pate, A. "Response to the David-Knowles Critique of the Kansas City Preventive Patrol Experiment." *The Police Chief*, June 1975, 32–38; Greenwood, P., *et al.*, "Response to an Evaluation of the Rand Corporation's Analysis of the Criminal Investigation Process." *The Police Chief*, December 1976.

5. Aaron, Henry. *Politics and the Professors: The Great Society in Perspective*, Washington: Brookings, 1978.

6. Almond, Gabriel, and Powell, G. Bingham, *Comparative Politics*. Boston: Little Brown, 1966.

7. Bachrach, Peter, and Baratz, Morton. "Two Faces of Power." *American Political Science Review*, 1962, *56*, 947–52.

8. Bottoms, A.E. "On the Decriminalization of English Juvenile Courts." In *Crime, Criminology and Public Policy*, ed. by R. Hood. London: Heinemann, 1974, pp. 319–46.

9. Bryden, Kenneth. *Old Age Pensions and Policymaking in Canada*. Montreal: McGill-Queen's University Press, 1974.

10. Canada Department of Justice and Ministry of the Solicitor General. "Federal Discussions Paper on Diversion." Unpublished, Ottawa, 1979.

11. Canada. House of Commons Standing Committee on Justice and Legal Affairs. Subcommittee on the Penitentiary System in Canada. *Report to Parliament*. Ottawa: Supply and Services, 1977.

12. Canada, Ministry of the Solicitor General. *National Inventory of Diversion Projects — An Update.* Ottawa: Ministry of the Solicitor General, 1979.

13. Canada, Ministry of the Solicitor General. *Selected Trends in Canadian Criminal Justice.* Ottawa: Ministry of the Solicitor General, 1979.

14. Chandler, David. *Capital Punishment in Canada.* Toronto: McClelland and Stewart, 1976.

15. Cook, Shirley. "Canadian Narcotics Legislation, 1908–1923: A Conflict Model Interpretation." *Canadian Review of Sociology and Anthropology*, 1969, 6(1), 36–46.

16. Cronin, Thomas. "The War on Crime and Unsafe Streets." In *America in the Seventies*, ed. by A. Sindler, Boston: Little Brown, 1977.

17. Doern, Bruce, and Aucoin, Peter. *Public Policy in Canada: Organization and Management.* Toronto: Macmillan, 1979.

18. Doern, Bruce, and Wilson, V.S., (eds.). *Issues in Canadian Public Policy.* Toronto: Macmillan, 1974.

19. Dror, Yehezkel. *Public Policy-Making Re-examined.* San Francisco: Chandler, 1968.

20. Easton, David. *A Systems Analysis of Political Life.* Chicago: University of Chicago Press, 1979.

21. Eisenstein, James, and Jacob, Herbert. *Felony Justice.* Boston: Little Brown, 1977.

22. Elton, Tanner. "The Diversion Controversy." In *New Directions in Sentencing*, ed. by B.A. Grosman. Toronto: Butterworths, 1980, pp. 194–212.

23. Ewing, B.G. "Change and Continuity in Criminal Justice Research: A Perspective from N.I.L.E.C.J." *Journal of Research in Crime and Delinquency*, 1978, 15(2), 266–78.

24. Friedland, Martin L. "Gun Control: The Options." *Criminal Law Quarterly*, 1975, 18, 29ff.

25. Friedland, Martin L. "Pressure Groups and the Development of the Criminal Law." In *Reshaping the Criminal Law*, ed. by P.R. Glazebrook. London: Stevens and Sons, 1978, pp. 202–39.

26. Gregory, G.F. "Police Power and the Role of the Provincial Minister of Justice." *Chitty's Law Journal*, 1979, 27, 13–18.

27. Grosman, B.A., and Finley, Michael. "Law Enforcement: Restoring the Balance." In *Canadian Confederation at the Crossroads*, ed. by M. Walter. Vancouver: The Fraser Institute, 1979, pp. 297–317.

28. Hall, S., Critcher, C., Jefferson, T., Clarke, J., and Roberts, B., *Policing the Crisis: Mugging, the State, and Law and Order.* London: McMillan, 1978.

29. Heumann, Milton. "Thinking about Plea Bargaining." In *The Study of Criminal Courts: Political Perspectives*, ed. by P. Nardulli. Cambridge: Ballinger, 1979, pp. 201–25.

30. Hogarth, John. *Sentencing as a Human Process.* Toronto: University of Toronto Press, 1971.

31. Hood, Roger. "Criminology and Penal Change: A Case Study of the Nature and Impact of Some Recent Advice to Governments." In *Crime, Criminology and Public Policy*, ed. by R. Hood. London: Heinemann, 1974, pp. 395–418.

32. Jayewardene, C.H.S. "The Canadian Movement Against the Death Penalty." *Canadian Journal of Criminology and Corrections*, 1972, 14, 366–90.

33. Jobson, Keith B. "Reforming Sentencing Laws: A Canadian Perspective." In *New Directions in Sentencing*, ed. by B.A. Grosman. Toronto: Butterworths, 1980, pp. 73–96.

34. Komarovsky, Mirra, (ed.) *Sociology and Public Policy: The Case of Presidential Commissions.* New York: Elsevier, 1975.

35. Koza, P., and Doob, A.N. "Police Attitudes Toward the Bail Reform Act." *Criminal Law Quarterly*, 1977, 19, 405–14.

36. Koza, P., and Doob, A.N. "The Relationship of Pretrial Custody to the Outcome of a Trial." *Criminal Law Quarterly*, 1975, 17, 391–400.

37. Lazarsfeld, Paul, and Reitz, Jeffrey. *An Introduction to Applied Sociology.* New York: Elsevier, 1976.

38. Lemert, Edwin. *Social Action and Legal Change: Revolution Within the Juvenile Court.* Chicago: Aldine Press, 1972.

39. Levin, Martin. *Urban Politics and the Criminal Courts.* Chicago: University of Chicago Press, 1977.

40. Lindblom, Charles. *The Policy-Making Press*. Englewood Cliffs, NJ: Prentice Hall, 1968.
41. Lindblom, Charles, and Cohen, David. *Usable Knowledge: Social Science and Social Problem Solving*. New Haven: Yale University Press, 1979.
42. Majone, Giandomerico. "On the Notion of Political Feasibility." *Political Studies Review Annual*, 1977, *1*, 80–95.
43. Manzer, Ronald. "Public School Politics in Canada: A Comparative, Developmental Perspective." Paper read to the International Studies Association, Toronto, 1976.
44. Marmor, Theodore. *The Politics of Medicare*. Chicago: Aldine Press, 1973.
45. Merton, Robert K. "The Role of the Intellectual in Public Bureaucracy." In *Social Theory and Social Structure*. New York: Free Press, 1968, pp. 261–78.
46. Miller, Walter. "Ideology and Criminal Justice Policy." *Journal of Criminal Law and Criminology*, 1973, *LXIV*(2), 141–62.
47. Moore, Barrington, Jr. *Political Power and Social Theory*. Cambridge: Harvard University Press, 1958.
48. Moriarty, M.J. "The Policy-Making Process: How It Is Seen from the Home Office." In *Penal Policy-Making in England*, ed. by N. Walker. Cambridge: Institute of Criminology, 1977.
49. Moyer, Sharon. "Firearms Ownership and Use in Canada: A Report of Survey Findings." Unpublished Report submitted to Solicitor-General of Canada, Ottawa, 1978.
50. Moynihan, Daniel P. *Maximum Feasible Misunderstanding*. New York: Free Press, 1970.
51. Ontario. "An Act to Establish a Code of Procedure for Provincial Offences." Bill 74, 3rd Session, 31st Legislature, 28 Elizabeth II, 1979.
52. Ontario. Ministry of the Attorney General. *White Paper on Courts Administration*. Toronto: Queen's Printer, 1976.
53. Osborne, Judith. "Juvenile Justice Policy in Canada: The Transfer of the Initiative." *Canadian Journal of Family Law*, 1979, 2, 7–32.
54. Phidd, R.W., and Doern, Bruce. *The Politics and Management of Canadian Economic Policy*. Toronto: Macmillan, 1977.
55. Pressman, Jeffrey and Wildavsky, Aaron. *Implementation*. Berkeley: University of California Press, 1973.
56. Reich, Robert. "Solving Social Crises by Commissions." *Yale Review of Law and Social Action*, 3(3): 234–71.
57. Rein, Martin, and White, Sheldon. "Can Research Help Policy" *The Public Interest*, 1977, 49, 119–36.
58. Scheerer, Sebastien. "The New Dutch and German Drug Laws: Social and Political Conditions for Criminalization and Decriminalization." *Law and Society Review*, 1977–78, 12, 585–606.
59. Schon, Donald, *Beyond the Stable State*. New York: Norton, 1971.
60. Solomon, Peter H., Jr. *Soviet Criminologists and Criminal Policy*. New York: Columbia University Press and London: Macmillan, 1978.
61. Solomon, Peter H., Jr. "Reforming Canadian Criminal Justice." Unpublished, Toronto, 1980.
62. Stenning, P.C. "The Role of Police Boards and Commissions as Institutions of Municipal Police Governance." Paper read to the Canadian Political Science Association, Montreal, 1980.
63. Szabo, Denis. "L'Évaluation des politiques criminelles: quelques reflexions préliminaires." *Archives de politique criminelle*, 1981, *1*. (in press).
64. Taylor, Ian. "The Law and Order Issue in the British and Canadian General Elections of 1979: Crime, Populism and the State." *Canadian Journal of Sociology*, 1980, 5, 285–311.
65. Taylor, Malcolm. *Health Insurance and Canadian Public Policy*. Montreal: McGill-Queen's, 1978.
66. Thomas, Wayne. *Bail Reform in America*. Berkeley: University of California Press, 1976.
67. Walker, Jack. "The Diffusion of Knowledge and Policy Change: Toward a Theory of Agenda-Setting." Paper read to the American Political Science Association, 1974.

68. Walker, Nigel, (ed). *Penal Policy-Making in England.* Cambridge: Institute of Criminology, 1977.

69. Waller, Irvin. "Organizing Research to Improve Criminal Justice Policy: A Perspective from Canada." *Journal of Research in Crime and Delinquency*, 1979, 16(2), 196–217.

70. Watson, G.D. "The Judge and Court Administration." In *The Canadian Judiciary*, ed. by A.M. Linden. Toronto: Osgoode Hall Law School, 1977.

71. Weinberg, Alvin. "Science and Transcience." *Minerva*, 1972, 209–333.

72. Weiss, Carol. "Introduction." In *Using Social Research in Public Policy-Making*. ed. by C. Weiss. Lexington, MA: D.C. Heath, 1977.

73. Weiss, Carol. "Research for Policy's Sake." *Policy Studies Review Annual*, 1978, 2, 67–81.

74. Weiss, Carol and Buculava, Michael. "The Challenge of Social Research to Decision-Making." In *Using Social Research in Public Policy-Making*, ed. by C. Weiss, Lexington, MA: D.C. Health, 1977.

75. Wildavsky, Aaron. *Speaking Truth to Power*. Boston: Little Brown, 1979.

76. Wilson, James Q. *Thinking about Crime*. New York: Basic Books, 1975.

77. Wilson, James Q. *Political Organizations*. New York: Basic Books, 1973.

78. Wilson, James Q. *Varieties of Police Behavior*. New York: Atheneum, 1970.

79. Wilson, James Q., and Rachal, Patricia. "Can Government Regulate Itself." *The Public Interest*, 1977, 46, 3–14.

80. Wolfinger, Raymond. "Non-Decisions and the Study of Local Politics." *American Political Science Review*, 1971, 65, 1063–80.

81. Wooton, Barbara. "Official Advisory Bodies." In *Penal Policy-Making in England*, ed. by N. Walker. Cambridge: Institute of Criminology, 1977.

82. Zander, Michael. "Promoting Change in the Legal System." *Modern Law Review*, 1979, XLII, 489–507.

TWO

The Politics of Prostitution Control: Interest Group Politics in Four Canadian Cities[1]

E. NICK LARSEN

INTRODUCTION

The existence of street prostitution has always engendered controversy and conflict in cities where it has been prevalent. This has been particularly true in several of Canada's largest urban centres during the past decade. The origins of the controversy and conflict can be traced to the 1978 *Hutt* decision, in which the Supreme Court of

Source: E. Nick Larsen, "The Politics of Prostitution Control: Interest Group Politics in Four Canadian Cities," *The International Journal of Urban and Regional Research*, 16, 2 (1992): 169–89. Reproduced by permission.

Canada rules that public soliciting was only illegal if it was "pressing and persistent."[2] This decision appeared to stipulate that soliciting was only an offence when it created a public nuisance. As a result, it caused an immediate uproar and initiated a protracted and bitter debate that eventually embroiled the police, courts, prostitutes, residents' groups, and local, provincial, and federal politicians in an intensely partisan political process over the best way of dealing with street prostitution. This political process ultimately led to the enactment of Bill C-49, which contained what is undoubtedly one of the toughest approaches to the control of street prostitution currently existing in the western world. This legislation effectively criminalized any public communication for the purpose of prostitution and contrasted sharply with the previous law.[3]

The intent of this article is to analyse the political process that led to the development of Bill C-49, with particular emphasis on the urban political scene. The major focus will be on identifying the various local interest groups involved in the street prostitution issue and assessing their degree of influence over the enforcement of prostitution laws and the development of Bill C-49. These issues are important because the participation of local interest groups in controversial issues represents one of the most basic examples of "grass roots democracy" in action. In addition, the ability of different interest groups to influence events serves as an indicator of both the nature of local politics and the extent of local power structures. In this respect, the analysis will be conducted within a combined class and feminist framework, involving a consideration of several specific issues. First, it is intended to explore the degree to which the socio-economic status of the various groups affected their ability to influence the political process, and the degree to which other broadly defined class variables impacted on the control of street prostitution. In addition, an assessment will be made of the degree to which feminist issues were raised in the prostitution debate, and the role played by identified feminist groups in the political process will be examined.

Although local interest groups were active in most large Canadian cities, this discussion will focus on Vancouver, Toronto, Edmonton, and Winnipeg. These cities were selected because they all adopted different approaches to the common problem of street prostitution in residential areas. Toronto and Vancouver experienced the greatest problems and adopted the most controversial and confrontational approaches, whereas Winnipeg and Edmonton applied more conciliatory approaches to proportionately smaller problems. These cities also differ greatly in terms of their social and economic bases and thus represent a wide cross-section of Canadian cities.

METHODOLOGY FOR THE PRESENT STUDY

This paper is based on a qualitative research study carried out in the cities of Vancouver, Toronto, Winnipeg, and Edmonton during 1989. The following specific methodological steps were utilized in conducting this study:

1. An in-depth media search was conducted of the issue in all four cities. This search was based on the citations provided in the *Canadian News Index* and was used to provide detailed information on the development of street prostitution as a political issue. While the main data-gathering technique was to review the contents of the articles themselves, the overall tone and media stance were also analysed.

2. A series of in-depth unstructured interviews were conducted with selected individuals who played significant roles in the prostitution debate. This survey included police officials, officials in the federal Ministry of Justice and the appropriate provincial Ministries of the Attorney-General, municipal politicians and local interest groups. An attempt was made to maximize the representativeness of the sample by employing a modified quota sample that included informants from all categories of groups in proportion to their numbers and perceived importance. However, because of the small sample size and the tendency of potential informations to "self select" out of the interviews, it was not always possible to maintain the quotas.[4] In keeping with the principles underlying qualitative research, the interviews were kept unstructured and the questions were largely open-ended during the initial part of each interview. However, towards the end of each interview, an attempt was made to structure the overall content, using a prepared questionnaire as a guide. In addition, the following steps were included as part of this survey:

   a. The prepared questionnaire was mailed to those potential informants who had expressed a willingness to participate in this study but who were unavailable for personal interviews.

   b. Follow-up questions were directed at certain individuals who had been identified as particularly reliable and/or helpful sources. These follow-up questions generally involved issues that had come to light as the research progressed, and had thus been omitted from the initial interviews. In certain instances, selected individuals were treated as "key informants" and used to verify and/or cross-check information obtained from other sources.

3. Existing documents were analysed to provide detailed information on the events that contributed to the development of Bill C-49 and the positions of various groups and organizations. This information was used to cross-check and verify the information obtained from the interviews. In addition, the results obtained from each type of document were compared to those obtained from other types wherever possible. The following types of documents were included in this step: the minutes of municipal council meetings; position papers published by community groups; research reports; committee reports (including the Fraser Committee); Hansard (Reports of Parliamentary Debates).

LOCAL POLITICS IN VANCOUVER

In order to adequately analyse the political dynamics that occurred in Vancouver over street prostitution, it is necessary to begin the discussion prior to the *Hutt* decision. During the 1970s, street prostitution in Vancouver was centred in three basic areas: (1) the Downtown business district near Georgia Street and Hornby Street, (2) the West End along Davie Street, between Bute Street and Cardero Avenue, and (3) the skid row area around Main and Hastings, near the harbour. The prostitutes in this latter area were older and less attractive than in the other areas, and their numbers remained constant throughout the time period under discussion. The residents and businesses in this area appeared to coexist peacefully with prostitution and there was little conflict during this period.[5] Thus, this area will not be discussed further in this article.

The major focus of the prostitution debate during the late 1970s and early 1980s was centred in the West End and the Downtown business areas. The

Downtown business district had been frequented by prostitutes for many years prior to the *Hutt* decision without serious problems. This was probably because the prostitutes in this area consisted of limited numbers of higher-class streetwalkers who serviced the patrons of the many luxury hotels located there, and both the prostitutes and their clients wished to conduct business as discreetly as possible. In addition, there was a high degree of cooperation between hotel security and the police, in which the Vancouver police made it a priority to respond quickly to calls from the hotels. This also helped deter unruly conduct, since the prostitutes realized that the police would respond quickly to any calls from the hotels.[6]

The above situation started to change after the Penthouse Cabaret closed in early 1976, largely as a result of the activities of the Vancouver Police Vice Squad. The Penthouse Cabaret had catered mainly to prostitutes and their customers, and its closure displaced many prostitutes onto the streets, where they attempted to follow their clients to the West End and Georgia and Hornby areas. This drastically increased the numbers of prostitutes working in both areas but appeared to exert a greater effect in the Downtown business area. As a result, conflict developed between the hotels and prostitutes, and the hotel owners and other business groups lobbied publicly for action. During the early months of 1977, the Vancouver media devoted considerable attention to the increased numbers of prostitutes working in the Downtown area, and a police report released in September estimated that over 700 prostitutes were working in the Georgia and Hornby and West End areas. This prompted Vancouver City Council to consider ways of addressing the problem, and ultimately led to the formation of a high-profile police squad to attack prostitution in the Downtown area (*VS*, 8 Sept. 1977: 1).

The West End, a high-density residential area bordering English Bay, had been a prostitution stroll for several years prior to the events described above. This area contained a greater mix of prostitutes, including adults of all ages, many juvenile females, and almost all of the male prostitutes in Vancouver. Despite this mix, there was remarkably little conflict in the area prior to the late 1970s (Kohlmeyer, 1982). While the closure of the Penthouse Cabaret resulted in larger numbers of prostitutes working the Davie Street strip, the West End situation took longer to develop into a political issue than the Georgia/Hornby area. This initial lack of conflict was probably due to the size and population dynamics of the area. Because the West End was much larger than the Georgia and Hornby area, it was able to absorb more prostitutes without becoming saturated. Further, the prostitutes initially remained on the north side of Davie, in a much less-developed part of the West End.[7] This area contained many older homes, rooming-houses and cheaper "low rise" apartment buildings, whose residents were probably less likely to complain about the presence of prostitutes. However, during the late 1970s and early 1980s this started to change as developers either demolished many of the older buildings and replaced them with newer buildings or renovated existing buildings.[8] Since this resulted in more expensive housing, the new residents were less likely to tolerate street prostitution in the area. This demographic shift ultimately led to the creation of several residents' groups who wanted prostitution out of "their" neighbourhood.

An additional set of factors revolving around the previously mentioned *Hutt* decision also contributed to the development of street prostitution into a high-profile political issue in the West End. In this respect, it is generally agreed that the *Hutt* decision did not significantly influence the numbers of prostitutes, as several sources have noted that the numbers of prostitutes in this area increased steadily in the years immediately prior to the *Hutt* decision, and particularly after the 1976 closure of the Penthouse Cabaret (Lowman, 1986; Fraser, 1985). While it is commonly believed that the *Hutt* decision encouraged street prostitutes to become more aggressive, there is little independent evidence to establish that the decision itself caused the more aggressive behaviour. In this respect, it appears that a major catalyst behind the development of street prostitution into a high-profile issue was the failure of the Vancouver police to attempt to control the noise and harassment associated with street prostitution. Many different sources have argued that the Vancouver police refused to intervene in the events unfolding in the Davie Street area, even though they clearly could have charged customers for traffic violations and/or noise by-law offences.[9] Thus, the Vancouver police clearly wanted tougher laws dealing with street prostitution, and it appears that their "hands off" attitude was designed to instigate public pressure on politicians.

The stance of the Vancouver police after the *Hutt* decision immediately brought them into conflict with West End residents, Downtown business groups, and Vancouver City Council. As early as 30 March 1978, the Vancouver media were criticizing the Vancouver police for not doing enough to protect the residents and businesses from harassment (*VS*, 30 Mar. 1978: D12). However, the previous good relationship between the police and the Downtown hotels gave the hotel owners an edge in combatting the increased levels of prostitution. The Vancouver Chamber of Commerce, the Downtown Vancouver Association, the BC Hotels Association, and other business groups lobbied the Vancouver Police Department on behalf of the hotel owners. These groups were helped by pressure from Vancouver City Council, which was becoming increasingly concerned about the negative civic image presented to tourists and other visitors by the rampant street prostitution in the city's Downtown business district.

This pressure caused the police to place increased emphasis on the area, and the public protest appeared to decline (as evidenced by a lack of media attention during the latter part of 1978). The police activity ultimately led to the creation of a 30-member Task Force on Prostitution in early 1979. This task force was remarkably successful at controlling the level of prostitution-related activity in the Downtown area, and prompted many people to question why the police had not acted previously, since the existing laws seemed adequate (*CH*, 28 June 1979: 10). In response to public concern, the Assistant Attorney-General, Neil McDairmid, argued that it was necessary to clean up the streets prior to the start of the tourist season. However, he also noted that it required too much police manpower to control prostitution under the existing law, and that the police needed a tougher law to do the job properly (ibid.). While this may have been true, there are two other reasons why the Vancouver police chose that particular time to institute a crackdown. The most obvious reason for the concerted police action was that a major international police convention was scheduled to be held in Vancouver that summer and the Vancouver police clearly did not want to be embarrassed by the presence of rampant street prostitution. An even more important reason involved the fact that the federal government had introduced tough new prostitution legislation into the Canadian Parliament in the spring, and the police may have resumed their anti-prostitution activity because they felt that they had achieved their goal.[10] In any event, police activity during the latter part of 1979 appeared to decrease the level of prostitution activity in the Downtown business area and there was little media attention paid to the area after 1980.

Unfortunately, the task force was less successful in the West End and the prostitution problem in this area increased drastically during the early part of the 1980s. West End residents began to lobby the Vancouver Police Department and Vancouver City Council for assistance. Two main residents' groups evolved in the West End during this period. The better organized of these was the Concerned Residents of the West End (CROWE), headed by community organizers Gerry Stafford and Gordon Price. This organization was formed in late 1981 (approximately) and was composed mainly of middle-class professionals who had moved into the area after the development boom previously described. CROWE styled itself as a political lobby group dedicated to making politicians take responsibility for the street prostitution problem in Vancouver, with particular reference to the West End (Gordon Price). Accordingly, it quickly launched an extensive and well-organized lobbying campaign, targeting all levels of politicians as well as the Vancouver police. CROWE presented a petition to Pat Carney, the federal Member of Parliament for the area. Ms. Carney subsequently tabled this petition in the House of Commons, where she demanded that the Liberal Minister of Justice take action to deal with the problem. CROWE also made several presentations at city council meetings, asking for increased police activity in the West End.

CROWE conducted extensive research into the numbers of cars circling the West End, the numbers of prostitutes on the streets, the levels of noise and other relevant factors. This research was incorporated into elaborate position papers that were submitted to city council members, the police, and other officials. CROWE also encouraged and assisted other groups and individuals in launching protests, although they were careful to distance themselves from some of the more radical groups.[11] CROWE's high degree of organization and middle-class membership base gave it a degree of local influence "all out of proportion to their level of public support," and was largely responsible for Vancouver City Council taking a tough stance towards street prostitution. While almost one-half of all presentations to the council were opposed to tougher legislation, the council nevertheless passed a resolution urging that the tougher laws be enacted as soon as possible.[12] CROWE also precipitated the establishment of permanent traffic diverters to disrupt the traffic patterns of potential customers and was also influential in prompting the Vancouver civic administration to reconsider drafting a by-law aimed at street prostitution (Libby Davies). In fact, when the City Solicitor, Terry Bland, announced the proposed by-law, he suggested that the police would tolerate prostitution in bars and clubs as long as it was kept off the street (VS, 13 Jan. 1984: A1). This statement exemplifies the degree of influence wielded by CROWE.

A second group that appeared somewhat later in the political campaign by West End residents was Shame the Johns (STJ). This group focused on the customers as the source of the problem and was formed in March of 1984 in response to a media article deploring the middle-class customers who exploited very young prostitutes (VS, 25 May 1984: A3).[13] From the outset, STJ took a much more radical approach that disdained any hope of reaching a negotiated solution. One of their first tactics involved targeting a middle-class male from the wealthy suburb of West Vancouver and descending on his home complete with television cameras (ibid.).[14] While there was some membership overlap between STJ and CROWE, STJ contained a much larger proportion of radicals. For this reason, CROWE attempted to distance itself from Shame the Johns, whose tactics were also criticized by the city council and the Vancouver police. As time progressed, these tactics became increasingly aggressive, and started to involve physical confrontations between the residents and customers (and sometimes the prostitutes and pimps as well). Brian Smith, the Attorney-General of British Columbia, became alarmed at what he perceived as an increasingly "vigilante" atmosphere in the West End. As a result, he decided that he could not wait for the federal government to remedy the situation and applied to the BC Supreme Court for a civil injunction banning prostitutes from the West End (*WFP*, 10 May 1984: 15). An interim injunction was granted on 5 July 1984, and prostitutes were prohibited from operating west of Granville Street (*VS*, 5 July 1984: 12).[15]

The interim injunction cleared the prostitutes out of the West End and Downtown areas almost as if someone had waved a magic wand. The Davie Street strip became deserted overnight, as the prostitutes attempted to find alternate locations to ply their trade. They quickly settled on two areas near the city centre. The first area was along Seymour and Richards Street, near where the Penthouse Cabaret had been located. In some respects, it is ironic that the problem was pushed back to the area where it had started. Because this area was primarily a business area that was deserted at night, relatively little conflict was caused by the move. The second area chosen by the prostitutes was located on the south shore of False Creek between the Main and Cambie Street bridges. Known as "Mount Pleasant," this area was primarily a working-class residential area that was slowly being taken over by warehouses and light industry. In this respect, it was hoped that the low population density and mixed land-use patterns would allow the prostitutes to coexist peacefully with the residents.

Unfortunately, the expected peaceful coexistence did not materialize. The same problems that had plagued the West End immediately surfaced in the Mount Pleasant area, where the police were even less responsive to residents' complaints than they had been in the West End. As a result, several residents' groups were organized to lobby City Hall and the police. The two most important of these groups were the Mount Pleasant Committee on Street Prostitution (MPCSP), headed by Timothy Agg, and the Mount Pleasant Action Group (MPAG), headed by Phyllis Alfeld. Both of these groups were dedicated to political action as a means of solving the problem; however, MPAG was much more radical in its political approach. It engaged in the same confrontational activities as STJ had tried in the West End, and routinely carried out "hooker patrols" armed with baseball bats (Phyllis Alfeld). MPCSP, on the other hand, attempted to interact with politicians and prostitutes in a conciliatory fashion, and lobbied for a compromise solution that would legalize soliciting in non-residential areas but prohibit it in residential areas. As well, MPCSP attempted to consult with the prostitutes in a non-threatening manner and induce their cooperation in keeping the noise down.[16] In general, however, the problem was basically insoluble and the police soon refused to respond to prostitution-related calls.

This stalemate continued until well into 1985, despite the fact that the police were increasingly criticized by many groups and individuals, including many local politicians. One of the most vociferous critics of police inaction was Alderman Harry Rankin, who argued that the police had "gone on strike," and insinuated that the situation would be different if Mount Pleasant was a middle-class area. This particular question is interesting in light of the response of another politician to the Mount Pleasant problem. One of the people whom the Mount Pleasant residents had appealed to for help was Gary Lauk, New Democratic Party Member of the

Legislative Assembly for the areas of False Creek and the West End. According to several residents' group representatives, Mr. Lauk was completely uninterested in their problem, and declined to get involved in any way (Phyllis Alfeld; Tim Agg). Considering that he had been extremely vocal in support of CROWE and had publicly lobbied the Social Credit Attorney-General over prostitution in the West End, the Mount Pleasant residents were almost certainly justified in feeling abandoned. In this respect, Mr. Rankin may well have been correct in his assertion that there was class bias evident in the way street prostitution was handled.

In October of 1985, frustrated Mount Pleasant groups organized an overnight "occupation" of City Hall, which incidentally was only a few blocks away from the Mount Pleasant stroll (G & M, 5 Oct. 1985: A8). This finally prompted some police action and the politicians began to search for a solution. One of the first courses of action was to explore the possibility of another injunction. When the Attorney-General ruled this out, Vancouver City Council began to consider establishing an informal "red light" district in a non-residential area. They identified a warehouse area on the shores of False Creek and installed street lighting to make the area safer for prostitutes. While the prostitutes initially agreed to move, they later changed their mind after the Vancouver Police Vice Squad continued to arrest prostitutes who made the move (Marie Arrington). This situation arose because of a lack of communication between the patrol division responsible for Mount Pleasant (Team 6) and the Vice Squad. While Team 6 had agreed not to arrest prostitutes in the assigned area, vice had not been party to the deal and refused to honour it.[17] This brought the situation back to its original stalemate. However, the police began responding to calls and adopted a policy of moving the prostitutes from one block to another so that one area was not constantly subjected to increased traffic and other forms of harassment (Tim Agg). They also began charging drivers with traffic violations and by-law infractions where possible.[18]

The final category of interest groups involves individuals and groups primarily identified with the interests of women. (This category will include female politicians.) In this respect, there were numerous such groups in the Vancouver area, and many did express support for the feminist position that prostitutes were also victims in the prostitution debate. However, their support was only nominal in most cases, and few groups attempted any extensive lobbying on behalf of prostitutes. This did not deter prostitutes from taking action on their own behalf. As early as 1980-1, Vancouver prostitutes were actively lobbying on behalf of prostitutes' rights, and were instrumental in establishing a hostel for young prostitutes. Further, in June 1982, the Alliance for the Safety of Prostitutes (ASP) was formed by Sally De Quadros and Marie Arrington. The stated purpose of this organization was to represent Vancouver prostitutes and to attempt to negotiate with residents' groups such as CROWE. However, it soon became obvious that CROWE was not interested in negotiating with prostitutes. While ASP representatives did attend several community meetings, they were denied the right to participate and were subjected to abuse (VS, 16 Jan. 1984).[19] As a result, ASP attempted to lobby politicians and other groups directly, and organized a march on Vancouver City Hall in April of 1983. However, with two major exceptions, the prostitutes were largely ignored by politicians and other groups.

One exception was the Vancouver Multi-Cultural Women's Association, which lobbied local politicians against taking a tough stand against the prostitutes, and advocated going after the customers instead. A second major exception was Libby Davies, a Committee of Progressive Electors (COPE) alderperson,[20] who attempted to convince the city council that tougher laws were not the answer to what was primarily a social problem. However, neither the Multi-Cultural Women's Association nor Libby Davies were able to completely swing the women's lobby, and many women's groups sided with the residents and businesses in demanding tougher laws.[21] It is significant that these groups were more effective than the groups supporting prostitutes. This was used to great advantage by the anti-prostitution forces who were able to argue that prostitution was not really a feminist issue.

One of the most important of the anti-prostitution women's groups was the West End Traffic Committee, headed by Carole Walker. This group lobbied for a "get tough" approach to prostitution control. Ms Walker later joined COPE and was influential in convincing the party to adopt a policy against legalizing prostitution. She also crossed party lines to support alderpersons May Brown and Marguarite Ford of The Electors Action Movement (TEAM), who were leading a campaign to have Vancouver City Council endorse Mayor Mike Harcourt's tough anti-prostitution stand (*VP*, 17 May 1983: B1). May Brown was instrumental in convincing the Vancouver Council of Women, an umbrella organization representing nearly all Vancouver women's groups, to endorse tougher laws against prostitution (*VS*, 23 April 1983). This endorsement was important because Pat Carney used it in convincing her cabinet colleagues to support Bill C-49, even though it was not unanimously supported by all the member groups. In fact, Jillian Riddington of the National Action Committee on the Status of Women wrote a letter to the *Vancouver Sun* criticizing May Brown, arguing that many groups were opposed to tougher laws and that Ms Brown only consulted those members whom she knew supported her viewpoint.

LOCAL POLITICS IN TORONTO

This discussion will now address the local political scene in Toronto. Interestingly enough, the development of street prostitution into a political issue in Toronto exhibited many similarities to Vancouver. During the early 1970s, street prostitution in downtown Toronto was centred in two main areas: (1) an area along Yonge Street and some of the side streets to the east of Yonge Street, (2) an area to the west of Yonge Street near the YMCA and the Downtown financial district, which was occupied primarily by male prostitutes serving male clients. (There were also small amounts of street prostitution in other areas of Toronto, notably along Lakeshore Drive in Etobicoke and along Queen Street West in west Toronto. However, these areas did not precipitate any political controversy during this period and are excluded from this discussion.) The first hint of friction between the prostitutes and other groups occurred in the aftermath of the murder of Emanuel Jacques in July of 1977. This murder touched off a wave of protests against the entire "Yonge Street strip," including the prostitutes who worked there.[22] These protests led to a campaign to clean up the area, and in July of 1980, many Yonge Street businessmen began to pressure the police and civic officials to "drive away the hookers" (*TS*, 29 July 1980: A3). The police consequently forced most prostitutes off Yonge Street, where they migrated east into the Wellesley area.

This eastward migration of prostitutes initially created little conflict as the Wellesley areas was a "trendy" neighbourhood of art galleries, discos, bars and "bohemian" restaurants, whose residents and habitués were disinclined to get upset about "a few hookers" (Peter Maloney).[23] The prostitutes continued their eastward migration until they infiltrated the Gloucester and Sherbourne area. Because this area contained large numbers of rooming-houses and other decrepit housing, the residents did not immediately object to the increased presence of street prostitutes.[24] However, both of these areas had been targeted for a dramatic "gentrification" programme, which saw large numbers of middle-class professionals move into the area between 1982 and 1984, and begin renovating much of the older housing stock.[25] Up to this point, the chain of events had essentially paralleled the situation which had occurred in Vancouver's West End a few years earlier. In this respect, Toronto's new "gentry" were decidedly unimpressed with the prospect of sharing their neighbourhood with street prostitutes, and began to lobby for their removal.

At this point, the similarity to the Vancouver situation ended. There were two major differences between Vancouver and Toronto regarding the evolution of street prostitution into a political issue. The first major difference involved the approach taken by Toronto residents. The middle-class people moving into the Wellesley and Sherbourne areas included a large number of academics, doctors, lawyers, and other professionals who generally subscribed to a liberal moral philosophy and were cognizant of some of the background factors in the prostitution issue. They were more sympathetic to the plight of the prostitutes and wished to avoid being characterized as "narrow-minded" conservatives. Thus, from the outset, the residents' groups avoided the type of anti-prostitution rhetoric that was so evident in Vancouver, and instead lobbied for a solution that would accommodate the needs of the prostitutes (William MacGill).

The second major difference between Vancouver and Toronto was that the Toronto Police Department was much more responsive to the demands of area residents. The Toronto police had persisted in charging prostitutes after the *Hutt* decision until subsequent court decisions made it impossible in 1980. This attitude also characterized the police reaction to the complaints that started to emanate from residents in 1982. When a group of residents from the Sherbourne area lobbied for increased policy action in May of 1982, the Toronto police almost immediately instituted a crackdown and also lobbied the Police Commission and Toronto City Council to petition Parliament for tougher laws. While this approach may not have accomplished a great deal, it reassured the residents that the police were on their side. The police also experimented with "creative" solutions to the prostitution problem, such as posting uniformed officers on the streets in problem areas (Toronto Police Commission, 1982). These tactics further reassured the residents and also helped alleviate the worst aspects of the street nuisance.

The police approach described above was able to keep the residents relatively appeased throughout 1982 and 1983, such that there were virtually no organized residents' groups until well into 1984. The first such group was the Earl Street Residents Association (ESRA), which was formed in June 1984. This group was composed almost entirely of middle-class professionals, and was headed by a University of Toronto sociology professor who had recently bought a town house on Earl Street. This group immediately established contact with the aldermanic representatives for the area, and enlisted their aid in convening a public meeting to discuss the issue. This meeting was held on 18 June 1984, and was attended by aldermen Jack Layton and Dale Martin. Numerous residents and organizations located in the area attended or sent representatives. In addition to organizing public meetings, ESRA also undertook an extensive and sophisticated lobbying campaign aimed at the Metropolitan Toronto Police and all three levels of government. In order to back up their position, they conducted research into and documented such factors as traffic patterns, levels of noise and the numbers of prostitutes on the street.

Generally, the substantive response of Toronto City Council was similar to that in Vancouver, i.e., to lobby other levels of government and experiment with traffic diverters. These tactics were marginally effective at best, and were sometimes opposed by groups who felt that the "solution" created more problems than it solved. For example, Dr. John Provan, chief surgeon of Wellesley Hospital, wrote a strongly worded letter to Alderman Jack Layton demanding that the traffic diverters be removed because they inhibited the free flow of traffic in the area. In order to counter this and other criticisms, the Toronto government[26] maintained a sophisticated public relations campaign, in which civic politicians attended community meetings and even participated in "hooker patrols" (*TS*, 28 July 1984: A6). This willingness to get involved, combined with a much higher level of police involvement than in Vancouver, kept residents' groups fairly quiet during the period prior to the enactment of Bill C-49.

Another category of interest groups involves those identified with women's issues and/or the interests of the prostitutes themselves. In this respect, Toronto contained many groups organized to advocate the interests of women and the feminist position in general. However, most of these groups concentrated their efforts at the national level, and many restricted their involvement to media pronouncements and testifying before federal committees studying street prostitution. Two notable exceptions were the Canadian Organization for the Rights of Prostitutes (CORP) and the Toronto Elizabeth Fry Society. CORP had been active in Toronto since the early 1980s and was primarily involved in lobbying politicians with respect to the problems faced by prostitutes. Among their "demands" were an attempt to negotiate informal red light districts and a request that Toronto City Council support legalized bawdy houses (*G & M*, 21 Oct. 1983: 5). While the Elizabeth Fry Society was also active in lobbying for the welfare of prostitutes, its main emphasis was on providing support services aimed at helping prostitutes leave the profession. In this respect, Ms Nancy Quinn, a criminologist employed by the Elizabeth Fry Society, criticized the Toronto area governments for not providing enough funding for counselling programmes and other ameliorative services to prostitutes (*G & M*, 15 June 1984: M3).

The emphasis of the Elizabeth Fry Society on helping prostitutes leave the profession (as opposed to lobbying for decriminalization) occasionally created conflict with the CORP objective of decriminalization. This conflict limited the degree of cooperation between the only two groups who were actively lobbying on behalf of prostitutes at the local level in Toronto. Nevertheless, there is no evidence to suggest that any women's groups actually lobbied in favour of tougher laws as occurred in Vancouver. Further, most of the female politicians were at least nominally sympathetic to the plight of the prostitutes. In this regard, Barbara Hall, a Toronto alderperson, attempted to press the feminist position at city council meetings. At the provincial level, Susan Fish, MPP (Member of the Provincial Parliament) for St. George, circulated a questionnaire that solicited support for the legalization of prostitution. The results of this questionnaire generally supported legalized prostitution, and Ms Fish attempted to lobby this position at the federal and provincial levels. However, this was the extent of the feminist involvement in the prostitution issue in Toronto, and when Bill C-49 was announced, most feminist groups were conspicuous by their silence.

LOCAL POLITICS IN EDMONTON

The appearance of street prostitution as a local political issue in Edmonton first occurred in March 1980. At this time, a group of Arlington Street residents[27] complained that prostitutes had started operating south of Jasper Avenue, and lobbied the city council to have them pushed back to the north side of Jasper. The city council refused this request, arguing that such a course of action would be tantamount to sanctioning a red light district on the north side of Jasper (*CH*, 31 March 1980: A3). Nevertheless, the police increased patrols in the area, and the problem appeared to disappear. Interestingly enough, the stated policy strategy was one of promoting "peaceful coexistence" between the residents and the prostitutes (*EJ*, 1 Apr. 1980: B1). This strategy, more than any other factor, may have been responsible for the relative lack of conflict over street prostitution in Edmonton.

Despite the fact that the immediate problem was quickly solved, the incident generated a debate over the feasibility of establishing a red light district in Edmonton. The "pro forces" were led by George Kiado, Director of Social Planning for the City of Edmonton, who argued that this course of action would minimize the nuisance effect of street prostitution and give the police greater control over prostitutes. Robert Lunney, Edmonton police chief, lobbied against a red light district, arguing that it would not solve the problem, and that it would be unwelcome no matter where it was located. However, this did not deter many Downtown residents and business owners from presenting a petition to the city council demanding that the prostitutes be pushed out of the Downtown area into a lower-class area along the CNR tracks (*WFP*, 1 Apr. 1980: 28). Ultimately, however, the Edmonton Police Department vetoed the possibility of a red light district, and began experimenting with other solutions, including traffic diverters (*EJ*, 19 Aug. 1980: B1). This approach apparently solved the problem in the short term, as there was no further mention of it in the media during 1980-1. In fact, when the possibility of a municipal by-law was raised at city council in 1981, the Edmonton Police Department asserted that it was not necessary as they had the problem under control (*EJ*, 3 July 1981: A2).

While the issue of street prostitution continued to surface periodically in Edmonton, the debate never heated up to the same extent as in Vancouver and Toronto. In this respect, the political discussion in Edmonton was noteworthy for several reasons. First, Edmonton was the only city included in this study where the police attempted to negotiate with prostitutes. In so doing, the police resisted attempts to have them "harass prostitutes off the streets," and instead attempted to mediate between prostitutes, residents, and business owners (*EJ*, 1 Aug. 1982: B2).[28] This mediation was relatively successful, in as much as it minimized conflict between prostitutes and other groups. When this is compared to the ineffectiveness of the "hands off" strategy employed by the Vancouver police, and the relative ineffectiveness of Toronto's approach, it would appear that negotiating with prostitutes might well be a key factor in successful prostitution control.

The Edmonton political situation was also remarkable for the apparent willingness of the Edmonton City Council to consider establishing red light districts and licensing prostitutes at an early stage of the process. While both of these alternatives were eventually ruled out as being unconstitutional,[29] they exemplify the degree to which Edmonton was willing to take a practical, commonsense approach to street prostitution. Indeed, this attitude often extended to the general population as well. While media reports indicate that there were mixed feelings about a red light district, a poll taken at a public debate held during early 1983 found that a slight majority of the participants were in favour of legalized prostitution (*EJ*, 26 Apr. 1983: B4). Interestingly enough, there were never any well-organized interest groups active during this period. While the Alliance of Concerned Residents on Street Soliciting (ACRSS) did appear on the scene in 1984, its position was never made clear, and it is unlikely that it exerted any significant effect.

The liberal attitude taken in Edmonton can be partly attributed to the position taken by the Edmonton media, and in particular by the *Edmonton Journal*. Unlike the emotional, anti-prostitution diatribes published by the Vancouver and (to a lesser extent) Toronto media, the *Edmonton Journal* generally took a restrained, analytical position that attempted to consider all sides in the debate. As a result, it often took the lead in analysing the various proposals, and on more than one occasion castigated the police and city council over their action or lack of it. Even more significantly, the editorial stance taken by the *Journal* generally favoured decriminalization and opposed tougher sanctions as being both unnecessary and ineffective. In this respect, it expressed support for the Fraser Committee recommendations regarding legalized bawdy houses.[30] This consistent approach probably served a "watchdog" function over the activities of police and city council, while also shaping public opinion.

The final category of interest groups to be discussed with respect to the Edmonton political scene involves those individuals and groups that were primarily identified with the interests of women. (This category will include female politicians.) In this respect, the Alberta Status of Women Action Committee (ASWAC) actively promoted the rights of prostitutes from a very early stage in the debate. For example, the ASWAC coordinator, Mary Smith, immediately rejected the 1980 call for a red light district in a lower-class area. She argued that this proposal would make it easier for the police to harass the prostitutes, and instead advocated cracking down on the customers as a means of solving the problem (*WFP*, 1 Apr. 1980: A3). In a similar fashion, Mary Burlie, director of the Boyle Street Community Service Coop, also lobbied on behalf of juvenile prostitutes, and frequently criticized the police for their failure to concentrate on the male customers of juvenile prostitutes. This position was also taken by Tricia Smith, executive director of the Elizabeth Fry Society, who lobbied against Bill C-49, arguing that it discriminated against women (*EJ*, 17 Nov. 1985: A11). One final group that attempted to advocate the rights of prostitutes was the Alberta Human Rights and Civil Liberties Association. While not a feminist organization, AHRCLA actively advocated the feminist position and consistently opposed any attempts to establish red light districts on the grounds that such a course of action would unfairly restrict the right of prostitutes to earn a living in a "legal" occupation (*EJ*, 26 Apr. 1983: B4).

While the above feminist groups were influential in keeping Edmonton Council from adopting the type of approach taken in Vancouver, many prominent feminists either remained silent on the prostitution issue or advocated conservative positions. In this respect, most of the female members of Edmonton City Council refused to become involved in the prostitution debate, and some lobbied actively for tougher laws. For example, Alderperson Bettie Hewes, consistently sided with residents and business owners, and had advocated a "get tough" approach to prostitution as early as 1980 (*WFP*, 1 Apr. 1980: 28). This approach was followed by another female alderperson, Olivia Butti, who argued that Jasper Avenue businesses were suffering because of the "unsafe streets" created by the prostitutes (*EJ*, 12 Sept. 1985: E8). (This was despite the fact that other polls had indicated that most potential customers were unconcerned about the presence of street prostitution.) In addition, the Alliance of Concerned Residents on Street Soliciting, headed by Shirley Krause, favoured a more restrictive approach to controlling street prostitution. Finally, there was no real attempt by Edmonton prostitutes to lobby on their own behalf. While a group calling itself The Friends of Jezebel was organized in 1984 to fight for the rights of prostitutes, this group was never very active and appeared to disappear after one brief media announcement (*EJ*, 1 Mar. 1984: D8).

LOCAL POLITICS IN WINNIPEG

During the late 1970s and early 1980s, street prostitution in Winnipeg was practised in three main areas: (1) the "hi track" along Albert Street in the Exchange District, (2) the "lo track" centred on Austin Street in Point Douglas, a lower-class housing area east of Main Street, and (3) the "hill," an area behind the Legislative Buildings along the Assiniboine River, and extending eastward along Kennedy Street. (This latter area was populated almost exclusively by male prostitutes.) It should be noted at the outset that Winnipeg had experienced few problems with street prostitution during the late 1970s and early 1980s simply because there was little demand for prostitutes in Winnipeg compared to other centres (*WFP*, 5 July 1979: 3).[31] This situation did not appear to increase immediately after the *Hutt* decision, and in fact may have decreased. In this respect, at least one senior Winnipeg police officer has suggested that the decision may have caused many Winnipeg prostitutes to move to Toronto and Vancouver (S/Insp. Tony Cherniak). This lack of conflict appeared to prevail during the next few years, and there was little media attention or other indications of conflict between the prostitutes and other groups, i.e., residents and business owners.

The Winnipeg Police Department asked Winnipeg City Council for an anti-soliciting by-law in the early part of 1982, arguing that larger numbers of prostitutes working in Winnipeg made it necessary (*WFP*, 8 Apr. 1982: 3). It is possible that this request was motivated by the success that the Calgary police were having with their by-law, as there was no other indication that Winnipeg had a serious problem with street prostitution at that time. Winnipeg City Council refused to enact such a law on the grounds that it would probably be ruled unconstitutional by the courts. Later in August of 1982, the Winnipeg police again expressed concern about street prostitution. In this instance, the police were worried about rumours that the Los Bravos motorcycle gang was about to move in on the Albert Street prostitutes, and that a gang war between the bikers and the existing pimps was imminent. While these rumours never materialized, the police reaction did serve to raise the visibility of street prostitution in the media. Interestingly, public opinion failed to rally behind the police, and most people appeared unconcerned about the issue. In fact, many Albert Street merchants appeared to like the presence of the prostitutes, as they "were good for business" and were not offensive to either customers or people working in the area (*WFP*, 31 Dec. 1982: 3). This turn of events surprised the police, and the issue was allowed to drop for several years.

This situation lasted until the middle of 1984, when street prostitution began to acquire a much higher "political" profile in Winnipeg. The development of the issue emanated from two separate areas. First, a group of residents from the streets surrounding the "hill" area behind the Legislative Buildings began to complain about the male prostitutes in the area. This particular scenario is interesting for several reasons. First, the "hustlers" had occupied the territory for at least ten years without problems arising. In fact, the police noted that it had been one of the quieter areas of the city up to that point. Similarly, the Lieutenant-Governor, Pearl McConigal, whose official residence was located on the Legislative grounds in the heart of the area, said that she was not bothered by the presence of the prostitutes (*WFP*, 23 June 1984: 1). In fact, both the police and the Lieutenant-Governor were unable to explain the sudden change, as they were unaware of any sudden increase in the level of activity in the area.

A closer examination of the scenario described above does suggest a possible explanation for the "sudden" development of prostitution as a political issue. When one examines the population demographics of the area, a familiar pattern emerges. Up to 1982–3, this area had been a mixture of "run-down" housing, interspersed with a few newer buildings that were occupied mainly by young single people (including a high proportion of "gays"). These people coexisted peacefully with the prostitutes and the area was also well known as a trendy residential area and a "gay meeting place." However, commencing in approximately 1983–4, developers renovated many buildings and replaced much of the other housing with newer buildings. This resulted in a demographic shift as many middle-class professionals moved into the area. As occurred in Toronto and Vancouver, the new residents were not happy with the presence of the prostitutes. In this case, there was a double stigma in that the prostitutes and their customers were gay, which many residents objected to as well.

Prostitution also developed into a political issue in the Exchange District, when several businessmen complained in July 1984 that prostitutes and their clients were creating problems. This led Winnipeg City Council to consider asking the Attorney-General, Roland Penner, to pursue an injunction similar to the one granted in Vancouver. While they ultimately decided against this course of action, a closer analysis of the situation reveals that the only businessmen who complained were the owners of several expensive nightclubs that had located in the Exchange district during the preceding two years. While the nightclub owners were apparently upset because their customers were being propositioned by prostitutes and their prospective customers, other business owners were unconcerned about the problem (*WFP*, 28 Apr. 1985: 1). Nevertheless, this situation brought about a debate in the city council regarding the possibility of dispersing prostitution throughout the city, with some council members arguing that it was unfair to leave all of the "sin" concentrated in the core area. This may well have been a valid argument, but one wonders why the concern for the core area only surfaced after several wealthy businessmen lobbied City Hall. Although the debate broadened to include proposals for the licensing of prostitutes, positive action was never taken on the suggestion to disperse the prostitutes.

The final category of interest groups to be discussed are those associated with the interests of women or who lobbied on behalf of prostitutes. The first group to become involved in this manner was a "gay" community organization that supported the male prostitutes on "the hill." When the residents of the area were complaining about the male "hustlers," Chris Vogel, president of Gays for Equality, attempted to mediate and has been credited with helping to defuse the situation.[32] It must also be noted that feminist organizations in Winnipeg did not shy away from defending prostitutes' rights when the occasion demanded it. In this respect, the Manitoba Action Committee on the Status of Women (MACSW), was quick to criticize the Winnipeg police for their treatment of prostitutes. For example, in April 1984, MACSW spokesperson Carolyn Garlick accused the police of extorting money from the prostitutes under threat of arrest.

While the allegations noted above were never proven, MACSW and other feminists continued to speak up on behalf of prostitutes. In June 1985, Lydia Gyles, wife of the chief Provincial Court judge, organized a public debate between herself, several prostitutes and S/Insp. Tony Cherniak, OIC of the Winnipeg Vice Division. The extent of her influence was such that S/Insp. Cherniak actually went on the record as favouring "mutual tolerance" between residents, business groups, and prostitutes (*WFP*, 16 June 1985: 7). Winnipeg feminists went even further in supporting the prostitutes, and MACSW was instrumental in the creation of the prostitutes' lobby group known as Prostitutes and Other Women for Equal Rights (POWER). This was the first instance of a "mainstream" feminist organization becoming involved with prostitutes in such a "hands on" fashion. In addition, MACSW helped POWER organize a seminar on legal rights for prostitutes and convinced feminist lawyers to donate their time and talents. The effect of this support was such that the creation of POWER was applauded by other social service organizations, and even the Winnipeg police (although their approval was limited to the "bad tricks sheet" compiled by POWER).

SUMMARY AND CONCLUSIONS

The discussion in this article has attempted to provide a detailed analysis of the political activity that occurred over street prostitution in four Canadian cities between 1977 and 1986. The major focus of analysis was on interest-group activity, and specific attention was placed on assessing the degree to which class and feminist frameworks could be applied to the analysis. In this respect, the four specific issues identified in the introduction were used to guide the analysis in this article. The intent of this conclusion is to provide a comparative summary of the political activity in the four cities as it relates to these four issues.

The first issue involves the degree to which the socio-economic status of the different interest groups affected their ability to influence the political process. In this respect, the existence of a class bias in the control of street prostitution was most obvious in Vancouver, where business and hotel interest groups in the Downtown area were clearly more successful than other groups at lobbying the police and politicians. In contrast, the West End was largely ignored until the emergence of middle-class residents' groups prompted local, provincial, and federal politicians to pressure the police into taking action. While the success of groups such as CROWE was partially due to their organizational skills, the lack of success experienced by the equally well-organized working-class groups in Mount Pleasant indicates that social class was an important variable. While this pattern was less well defined in Toronto, it is clear that street prostitution did not become a political issue until middle-class residents' groups made it a priority. In this instance, the movement of prostitutes into residential areas occurred when business interests pressured the police to move them off Yonge Street. While there was no lower-class area to use as a comparison in Toronto,[33] the middle-class residents were successful in pushing their own agenda even when it conflicted with the interests of other people in the area.

The socio-economic class of the interest groups was also a factor in Winnipeg, where the wishes of certain business interests clearly influenced the amount of media attention and political debate on the issue. In this respect, the fact that the Albert Street businesses initially approved of the presence of prostitutes was a major factor in directing public and political attention away from the issue. Similarly, the late lobbying efforts of a few wealthy nightclub owners were instrumental in directing political attention to the issue, despite the fact that other groups were unconcerned about the issue. Further, the middle-class residents of the "hill" were more successful than other groups in attracting media attention, even though prostitution was also common in the lower-class Point Douglas area. In Edmonton, the middle-class residents of the "stroll" area were supported by some politicians and civic officials in their efforts to have the prostitutes pushed into a lower-class area north of the city centre. However, the police were able to successfully resist this pressure, arguing that it would simply move the problem without solving it. Despite this partial exception, it nevertheless appears clear that the socio-economic status of the interest groups was an important factor in determining their political influence over the control of street prostitution.

The second issue involves the degree to which other "broadly defined" class variables affected the control of street prostitution. There were two factors that illustrate this question. First, the "gentrification" of existing inner-city neighbourhoods was an important factor in all cities except Edmonton. In most instances, street prostitution had existed in the problem neighbourhoods for years without serious conflict until the areas were "rehabbed" by middle-class professionals. It can further be argued that the nuisance levels rarely increased, and that the conflict was primarily due to the fact that the new residents simply did not want to share their neighbourhoods with prostitutes, no matter how quiet or discreet they were. This factor adds support to the previous analysis in so far as it suggests that prostitution will primarily be defined as a "problem" when it impacts on middle-class areas.

The second class-related factor which affected the control of street prostitution was the desire of municipal governments to ensure that the urban areas most frequented by visitors were kept relatively free of street prostitution. This was most apparent in Vancouver, where Vancouver City Council became alarmed at the negative image being projected by the prostitution-related activity in the Downtown business area. This caused the politicians to join forces with several business organizations to pressure the Vancouver police (who had their own political agenda) to clean up the Downtown area. This desire to ensure that their cities projected a respectable image also spurred debates in Winnipeg and Edmonton, and was at least partially behind the Toronto police decision to clean up Yonge Street. Inasmuch as this activity usually benefited the business classes more than other groups, it suggests that the interests of the business sector will often override other variables in so far as the actual control of street prostitution is concerned. In this respect, it is instructive that the police responded to the pressure in an efficient fashion, despite their earlier claims that they lacked the legal power to deal with the problem.

In assessing the degree to which feminist frameworks can be applied to the analysis, it is appropriate first to outline several of the feminist stances that are taken towards prostitution.[34] In general, mainstream feminist views can be divided into one of the following three approaches, (1) Prostitution is an extension of patriarchy and thus should be eliminated; the role of feminists in this case should be directed at helping prostitutes leave the profession. (This is broadly referred to as the "social welfare" approach.) (2) Prostitution should be regulated in a non-discriminatory fashion against males and females; thus, feminists should direct their attention to ensuring that male customers and female prostitutes are treated equally by the criminal justice system. (This is sometimes referred to as the "liberal-feminist" approach.) (3) Prostitution is an occupation followed by lower-class women who are forced into it by economic pressure, and the illegality of prostitution activities makes it easier for the police and other males to harass and exploit female prostitutes. The solution, according to these feminists, is to decriminalize all prostitution-related activities and regulate prostitution like any other legitimate occupation. This approach would give prostitutes greater control over their lives and reduce their exploitation by pimps and customers. (This is considered the most radical of the feminist approaches and is the one subscribed to by prostitutes.)

In considering the two issues identified in the introduction, it is obvious that feminist issues rarely dominated the prostitution debate despite the chauvinist bias evident in the political process. Further, even when they were raised, it was usually in the context of the social welfare and liberal-feminist approaches. In this respect, there was particular concern expressed for young prostitutes and a greater emphasis was placed on male customers in some cities as a result of the lobbying efforts of some feminist organizations. However, the debate rarely questioned the legitimacy of prostitution laws themselves or considered the effect of tougher laws on the lifestyles of prostitutes. This failure was probably due to the fact that the activities of mainstream feminist groups also generally represented either the social welfare or liberal-feminist approaches. Indeed, the efforts of some feminist groups in this regard sometimes created tension with prostitutes' organizations, who considered them condescending and counter-productive of their own goals (this was particularly true of Vancouver and Toronto).

The only exceptions to this situation occurred in Winnipeg and Edmonton, where many mainstream feminists actively lobbied on behalf of prostitutes. In Edmonton, ASWAC opposed any course of action that would potentially increase police power to harass prostitutes. In Winnipeg, MACSW openly supported decriminalization and worked directly with prostitutes to establish POWER, a prostitutes' rights organization. Despite these partial exceptions, most women's organizations took a low profile with respect to prostitution, and few groups supported the right of prostitutes to freely practise their trade. This situation was exacerbated by the fact that many female politicians and women's groups actively supported the anti-prostitution positions taken by residents and businesses. This general lack of feminist support is important, inasmuch as it indicates that mainstream feminists rarely considered the plight of prostitutes as a legitimate feminist issue. In this respect, many prostitutes argue that they will continue to lack significant political influence unless mainstream feminists accept that decriminalization is the only way of minimizing the chauvinist exploitation that currently characterizes the control of prostitution.

NOTES

1. The author would like to acknowledge a research grant from the Criminology Research Centre at the University of Manitoba that helped defray some of the expenses associated with the empirical research conducted for this article.
2. *Hutt v. the Queen* (1978), 32 C.C.C. (2d) 418.
3. The provisions of Bill C-49 are as follows:
   1. Every person who in a public place or in any place open to public view
   a. stops or attempts to stop any motor vehicle,
   b. impedes the free flow of pedestrian or vehicular traffic or ingress to or egress from premises adjacent to that place, or
   c. stops or attempts to stop any person or in any manner communicates or attempts to communicate with any person for the purpose of engaging in prostitution or of obtaining the sexual services of a prostitute is guilty of an offence punishable on summary conviction.
   2. In this section, "public place" includes any place to which the public have access as of right or by invitation, express or implied, and any motor vehicle located in a public place or in any place open to public view.
4. In general, politicians were the most likely to decline to participate while the local interest groups were the least likely to opt out.
5. While conflict ultimately did develop in this area, it occurred in the late 1980s and is outside the time frame of this article.
6. This information was obtained in a telephone interview with the director of security for the Georgia Hotel. It was also confirmed by Insp. Don Keith, OIC of the Vancouver Police Vice Squad. It should be noted that much of the information for this article was obtained from direct interviews. Each respondent will be identified in detail (either in the text or in a footnote) the first time they are mentioned. Subsequent references will be indicated by citing the respondent's name in brackets in the text.
7. This assertion is based on the writer's own observations as a resident of the West End during the 1976–82 period. It was also confirmed by other residents of the area.
8. This process is referred to as "gentrification" and became commonplace across North America, as many middle-class professionals became attracted to the conveniences of living downtown. While popular with property owners in these areas, it has led to the widespread displacement of the traditional residents of these areas.
9. One of the individuals who has made such an assertion is Tony Serka, a Vancouver lawyer who defended Debra Hutt. He informed this writer that he personally observed assaults occurring in full view of Vice Squad detectives taking notes in cars, who did not intervene. Other informants have suggested (annonymously) that the Vancouver police even went so far as to encourage the prostitutes to harass West End residents. This was also confirmed by Marie Arrington, founding member of ASP, and current president of POWER.
10. This legislation ultimately failed to pass when one of the political parties withdrew its promised support for the legislation.
11. This information is based on an interview with Mr. Chris Harris, West End resident and member of the NDP Civil Rights Committee.
12. This assertion is based on information and documents provided by Ms Libby Davies, a Vancouver alderperson.
13. The article in question was entitled "Shame the Men who buy our Children" (*VS*, 5 March 1984: A5), and was written by columnist Rick Ousten. It precipitated an

enormous outpouring of emotion, and for the first time the customers were identified as major villains.

14. Other tactics included copying the licence numbers of customers and publishing them in a newsletter, taking pictures of customers picking up prostitutes, sending letters to the families of men seen on the strip, and outright physical intimidation.

15. The injunction application had only asked that prostitutes be banned from the West End (i.e., Burrard Street), but the Supreme Court Justice suggested extending it to Granville Street. A subsequent attempt by a group of businessmen to extend it to Richards Street was unsuccessful (*Montreal Gazette*, 20 September 1984: B4).

16. Tim Agg described an incident in which he was able to quiet a group of noisy hookers by mentioning that there were children trying to sleep in a nearby apartment building.

17. An alternative explanation for this situation involves the possibility that the businesses in the new "red light" area disliked the proposal and lobbied the Vice Squad to kill the deal. This is borne out by some media articles dealing with the proposed plan (*VS*, 9 October 1985: A3).

18. This information was provided by Sgt Thompson of the Vancouver Police Department (Team 6), Oak Ridge Substation. It was also confirmed by Mr. Tim Agg, who emphasized that the police had had plenty of power, even after the Hutt case, to control the worst aspects of prostitution.

19. This information was contained in letters written to Alderperson Libby Davies. It was also confirmed by Marie Arrington in a 1989 interview.

20. COPE (Committee of Progressive Electors) was considered the "social-democratic" party in Vancouver civic politics, and traditionally championed the interests of the lower classes and other minorities. Up until this point, COPE had not articulated a formal policy on prostitution, but many COPE alderpersons had sympathized with the prostitutes (of these Harry Rankin, Libby Davies, and Bruce Erikson were the most prominent).

21. It should be noted that Libby Davies expressed the opinion that the feminist groups were able to delay and moderate council reaction to the prostitution issue, and may have even influenced Bill C-49 in this respect. In addition, there were several feminist organizations that lobbied at the national level. The most prominent of these was the National Association of Women and the Law. The Vancouver chapter of this organization, headed by Vancouver lawyer Gayle Raphael, was active in this regard.

22. While Emanuel Jacques was ostensibly a 12-year-old shoeshine boy, it was generally believed that he had also been a male prostitute. In any event, there was little doubt that he had been killed by four male homosexuals who had picked him up for sexual purposes.

23. Peter Maloney is a defence lawyer whose practice includes numerous prostitutes. He is also politically active in lobbying on behalf of the rights of prostitutes.

24. It should be noted that there had always been small numbers of prostitutes in both of these areas. Valerie Scott, president of CORP, informed this writer that "the Wellesley and Sherbourne areas had been a whores' stroll for a hundred years without any major problems." Thus, what happened was simply that the numbers of prostitutes increased dramatically over a three- to four-year period.

25. Letter from Doreen Campbell to Mayor Eggleton, 11 June 1984.

26. It should be noted that, at the time this article was written, Toronto utilized a two-tier system of government consisting of a "Metro" council superimposed over various municipal governments. Generally, Metro council took little interest in street prostitution, and any references to "Toronto government" apply to the Toronto municipal government.

27. This area was in the heart of the "stroll." It should be noted that there are two main areas in which street prostitution is practised in Edmonton. The "stroll" is located in the Downtown business district along Jasper Avenue between 103 St and 107 St, and is

a largely middle-class area. The lower-class "drag" area is located near the railway tracks in the Boyle and MacCauley Street areas. In addition, a few male prostitutes operated along McDougall Drive overlooking the Saskatchewan River and the Alberta Legislature.

28. This attitude frequently extended to other forms of cooperation as well. For example, the Edmonton Police Department and the prostitute community cooperated with regard to identifying certain prostitutes who were robbing clients (*EJ*, 27 October 1982: C1).

29. Canadian law stipulates that only the federal government can pass criminal legislation. While provinces and cities can regulate businesses, they are restricted to businesses that are clearly legal.

30. The Fraser Committee was a non-parliamentary committee established to hold public hearings and research the street prostitution issue. Among other recommendations, it suggested that prostitutes be allowed to operate out of their own homes without police interference.

31. This was also confirmed by S/Insp. Tony Cherniak, OIC of the Winnipeg Police Vice Division during this period.

32. This information was provided by Ms Jane Runner, a former prostitute and currently a counsellor with "Children's Home," a private social service agency in Winnipeg.

33. While political activity did develop later in the Etobicoke area, it occurred after 1986 and is outside the time frame of this article.

34. Bell (1987) provides a discussion of the approaches taken towards prostitution by feminists and the reasons for much of the tension that exists between prostitutes and mainstream feminists.

REFERENCES

Bell, L. (1987). *Good girls/bad girls: sex trade workers and feminists face to face*. The Women's Press, Toronto.

Calgary Herald (*CH*) Various issues.

Edmonton Journal (*EJ*) Various issues.

Fraser, J. (1985). *Report of the Special Committee on Pornography and Prostitution*. Supply and Services, Ottawa, Canada.

Globe and Mail (*G & M*) Various issues.

Kohlmeyer, K. (1982). *An ethnography of prostitution in Vancouver*. Unpublished Master's thesis, Simon Fraser University, Burnaby, BC.

Lowman, J. (1986). Prostitution in Vancouver: some notes on the genesis of a social problem. *Canadian Journal of Criminology*, 28, 1–16.

Toronto Police Commission (1983). *Report on Prostitution*. Unpublished internal document, City of Toronto, Toronto.

Toronto Sun (*TS*) Various issues.

Vancouver Province (*VP*) Various issues.

Vancouver Sun (*VS*) Various issues.

Winnipeg Free Press (*WFP*) Various issues.

THREE

The Impact of Law Reform on the Processing of Sexual Assault Cases[1]

RITA GUNN AND RICK LINDEN

In her analysis of the history of rape laws, Christine Boyle (1984) has shown how these laws reflected a significant conflict in values. Society strongly condemned sexual attacks upon women, particularly those perceived as chaste and virtuous, and the laws provided harsh penalties for offenders. At the same time, legislators (virtually all of whom were male) seemed to fear innocent men being convicted and provided the accused with extraordinary protection against false charges of rape that many felt women were likely to make (Boyle, 1984).

Critics had identified many problems with the law (Clark and Lewis, 1977; DeKeseredy and Hinch, 1991: Hinch, 1996; Los, 1994), among them the criminal justice system's seeming greater concern for the complainant's credibility than for the innocence or guilt of the accused, which allowed degrading and stressful examination of a victim's previous sexual history. The law applied procedural and evidentiary standards to sexual offences such as corroboration and recent complaint, which were not applied to other offences. Rape was defined as a crime that could not apply to a spouse.

These critics felt the law reinforced stereotypes of rape that have long hampered efforts to prosecute and convict rapists. These stereotypes include myths such as: a woman cannot be raped unless she wants to be; evidence of injury is necessary to prove that a woman really resisted her attacker; women who "lead men on" are themselves responsible for the outcome; women who engage in risky behaviour such as hitchhiking or drinking alone in bars deserve to be raped; and, a woman who has had prior sexual relations with a man or with his friends has implicitly consented to further intercourse even if she says no.

BILL C-127: LEGISLATIVE REFORM

In response to these problems, the Parliament of Canada proclaimed Bill C-127 on January 4, 1983.[2] Included in this new legislation were significant changes such as:

- the reclassification of the crime of "rape" to three levels of sexual assault based on aggravating factors;
- disqualification of evidence concerning the complainant's background that is not pertinent to the case (rape shield law);

Source: Rita Gunn and Rick Linden, "The Impact of Law Reform on the Processing of Sexual Assault Cases," *The Canadian Review of Sociology and Anthropology*, 34, 2 (1997): 155–74. Reproduced by permission.

- removal of spousal immunity;
- making sexual assault gender-neutral; and
- changing the rules of evidence concerning consent, corroboration, and recent complaint.

This change in legislation was intended to redefine sexual assault as a crime of violence rather than as a sexual act, and to reduce the harassment and degradation of victims by the justice system. Proponents hoped the new legislation would encourage more victims to report sexual assaults, ensure that victims were treated more fairly, and increase the conviction rate for sexual assaults, thereby enhancing the deterrent effect of the law.

RESEARCH ON THE IMPACT OF RAPE LAW REFORM

Several researchers have evaluated the impact of C-127. Using national police statistics, Renner and Sahjpaul (1986) compared the treatment of sexual assaults from 1973 to 1982 with post-legislation, 1983 data. The number of reported sexual assaults increased significantly in 1983, while the number of most other types of crime declined. There was no change in the percentage of cases reported as "founded," and small statistically significant increases in the percentage cleared and percentage changed. Roberts (1990) looked at national rates of reported sexual assaults before and after the legislation. He found that the number of complaints of sexual assault remained relatively stable in the six years prior to the implementation of Bill C-127, but that it increased 127 percent in the six years after implementation. There was also a relative decrease in the severity of offences, which suggests that there has been a move away from the former emphasis on penetration (Department of Justice, 1990). However, there was no increase in either the proportion of cases classified as founded (Roberts, 1990) or in conviction rates (Department of Justice, 1990). Roberts and Gebotys (1993) conclude that the legislation

> was successful in achieving one of the goals that inspired it. Ironically, its success has been in attracting more victims into the system, rather than in changing the way that the system responds to complaints of criminal sexual aggression (1993: 168).

The Department of Justice carried out a study of the impact of the legislation in six cities — Vancouver, Lethbridge, Winnipeg, Hamilton, Montreal and Fredericton–Saint John (Clark and Hepworth, 1994). While there was considerable variation from one city to the other, the findings were consistent with those of other studies. There was virtually no change in the proportion of cases reported as founded or in rates of clearance by charge. Conviction rates were higher in some cities, but lower in others: the net impact was therefore minimal.

Researchers have also assessed the impact of rape reform legislation in the United States. Among these have been studies in Michigan (Marsh et al., 1982), Washington (Loh, 1980), California (Polk, 1985; LeBeau, 1987); and a recent comparative study done in six U.S. jurisdictions (Spohn and Horney, 1992). The legislative changes evaluated in these studies were similar to those made in Canada, although the Canadian reforms were broader than those in most states. Effects reported in the American studies were modest at best, suggesting that the legal reform had a very limited impact on the operation of the criminal justice system.

The study carried out by Spohn and Horney is worthy of note because of its scope. Their comparison of the impact of rape law reform in six different states allowed for comparative analysis among states with different degrees of reform. Legislative change ranged from reforms enacted in Michigan and Illinois, which were similar in scope to those introduced in Canada, to those in Georgia and Washington, D.C., which made some changes relating to corroboration and prior sexual history, but that, in both cases, still required evidence of genital penetration and some evidence of resistance. The study used data covering 15 years to show long-term trends. The effect of "history" on the dependent variables was controlled to some extent by the fact that different jurisdictions had different intervention points (different dates of legislative change) while "history" factors such as an increased social concern for rape victims were likely to have been relatively constant from one jurisdiction to another.

Spohn and Horney conducted a time-series analysis using the date of legal change as the independent variable and several dependent variables, including offences reported to the police, number of indictments and number of convictions. Their results showed that the reforms had little effect. Only one jurisdiction showed changes that could be attributed to the legislative reform. That jurisdiction (Detroit) had significant increases in reports and in the ratio of indictments to reports. However, there was no increase in the proportion of cases resulting in conviction or in the likelihood of incarceration. Thus, with one partial exception, the effects of rape law reform in the United States appeared to be minimal.

THE STUDY

In this paper, we present the results of an evaluation of the impact of Bill C-127 on the processing of sexual assault cases through the criminal justice system in Winnipeg, Manitoba. This research was part of the multi-city study discussed by Clark and Hepworth (1994). Other research using national police statistics has shown that the law had a limited impact on charges and convictions. The use of police and court file data in this study allowed us to see if there were changes that were not evident in the national data. Because the law was clearly intended to change the way in which sexual assault cases were treated by the courts, we used logistic regression to examine the impact of several independent variables on charges and convictions before and after the new legislation. Logistic regression allowed us to determine if the rape reform legislation led to changes in the way in which these variables affect charge and conviction. For example, we have been able to determine whether variables reflecting the character of the victim have diminished in importance following the implementation of Bill C-127.

DATA SOURCES

FILE DATA

For this evaluation, information was taken from police records, Crown files, and court documents. The study years consisted of the two years prior to the enactment of Bill C-127 (1981–1982) and the two years after (1984–1985). The two study periods were compared to analyse the extent to which any changes occurred that might be attributed to the implementation of the new legislation.

a. *Police Files* — Police reports signify the first *official* stage of a sexual assault complaint. It is at this level that a case is deemed to be "founded" or "unfounded." A classification of unfounded suggests that the officer receiving the complaint does not believe the complainant. This may be due to lack of evidence, or to other factors, which are often discretionary (e.g., the officer believes the complainant is too intoxicated to recall details; there are contradictions in the complaint; the complainant has a history of unfounded complaints). The officers handling the complaint decide whether they think the complaint is credible. Charging also occurs at this level, although advice may be sought from the Crown on the advisability of proceeding with a case.

The Winnipeg police received approximately 740 sexual assault complaints in 1981–1982 and 1180 in 1984–1985. These totals included all sexual offences, including incest and other offences not relevant to this evaluation. A 50 percent random sample of sexual offences was drawn manually (every second card) from the card files of the Bureau of Police Records.

From the random sample, cases that were not relevant to the evaluation were selected out. The 1981–1982 sample included the crimes of rape, attempted rape, indecent assault, sexual intercourse with a female between 14 and 16, sexual intercourse with a female under 14, gross indecency, and buggery. To permit a comparison with the post-reform sexual assault data, we excluded incest cases except when combined with any of the above offences. The 1984–1985 sample was drawn from all cases that involved a complaint classified as sexual assault (*Criminal Code*, 246.1), sexual assault with a weapon, threats, or causing bodily harm (*Criminal Code*, 246.2), and aggravated sexual assault (*Criminal Code*, 246.3). As in the pre-reform sample, incest was included only when combined with one of the three levels of sexual assault. The 1981–1982 sample consisted of 315 incidents involving 317 complainants and 306 accused persons. The 1984–1985 sample consisted of 523 incidents involving 528 complainants and 469 accused persons.

Incidents that were one-time events and involved more than one complainant or more than one accused were classified as a single incident of sexual assault. Ongoing offences that had multiple complainants and involved one accused or, alternatively, multiple accused and one complainant were classified as separate incidents. Because multiple accused and/or multiple complainants were involved in several cases, the total number of complainants and accused differs from the total number of incidents.

Information obtained from police files included sociodemographic details of the complainants and accused persons, description of the incidents (time, location, resistance, injuries sustained, medical treatment, accomplices, witnesses, etc.), victim/accused relationship, promptness of reporting, accused's prior record, methods of classifying complaints, subjective data (i.e., personal comments reported in files), and any information about the police processing of cases. Reports dropped at the police level were examined to determine whether the complainant or the police made the decision, and the reason for termination.

b. *Crown Files* — Crown attorneys determine whether a complaint should be prosecuted, decide how the case should be prepared, and assess the likelihood of conviction. The Crown has the option of altering or reclassifying charges as they decide which charges to proceed with to obtain a conviction. They can also negotiate with defence counsel to secure a guilty plea from the accused in exchange for a reduction in the number or seriousness of the charges, or a recommendation for a lenient sentence.

Crown files provided details on charging, evidence, witnesses, plea-bargaining, preliminary hearings, and preparation of complainants for court. Information regarding the termination of charges at this level was collected, including details on whether this decision was initiated by the Crown prior to a preliminary hearing, by a judge at a preliminary hearing, or by the complainant, and why this decision was made. Crown files were also used to obtain information concerning the trial process, including the nature of final charges, disposition, sentencing, and appeals. Seventy-eight cases in the pre-reform period and 230 cases in the post-reform period were tracked at the Crown level. Juveniles, who made up 17.6 percent of the 1981–1982 accused and 17.9 percent of the 1984–1985 accused, were not tracked beyond the police level as these cases are handled by Youth Court.

c. *Court Files*—Most sexual assaults are handled as indictable offences, which allows the defendant to elect trial by Provincial Court Judge, Queen's Bench Judge, or Queen's Bench Judge and a Jury. The last two are favoured because the defendant is then entitled to a preliminary hearing. Often, the defendant agrees to plead guilty in exchange for a reduction in the number or seriousness of the charges, or for recommendation for a lenient sentence by the Crown. If the defendant pleads guilty prior to a trial, the plea is heard at a sentencing hearing. If a case proceeded to a sentencing appearance, preliminary hearing, and/or trial, it was tracked to the appropriate Court office (Provincial or Queen's Bench), and court documents were used to supplement information concerning the nature of final charges, dispositions, sentencing, and appeals. Fifty-three cases at the pre-reform level and 178 at the post-reform level were tracked at the Court level.

FINDINGS

Analysis of the filtering of cases through the Winnipeg justice system showed that the number of cases reported to the police increased by 66 percent following the implementation of C-127.[3] The conviction rate increased from 12.7 percent of the pre-reform cases to 29.1 percent of those post-reform cases that resulted in conviction (Gunn and Linden, 1993). While this increase seems to show that the legislation has had a significant impact on conviction rates, earlier research casts doubt on this conclusion. A study of the processing of sexual assault cases during 1976 and 1977 (Minch et al., 1987) showed a conviction rate of 28.9 percent, one almost identical to that found in the post-reform period. This would suggest that the 1981–1982 sample is atypical. This interpretation is supported by the fact that the only substantial difference between the two years is in the proportion of offenders not apprehended by the police. This was 27.9 percent of the pre-reform sample and 10.7 percent for the post-reform cases. In 1976–1977, the proportion not apprehended was 10.9 percent. Thus it does not appear that the revised sexual assault law has reduced the attrition in case processing in the courts, since the only difference occurred at the police level.

These data and the research cited earlier suggest that rape law reform has had a minimal impact on conviction rates. However, even if conviction rates have not increased, the legislation may have led to other changes in the fairness of the system by reducing the influence of legally irrelevant descriptions of the victim. The inclusion of clauses such as the rape shield law in the legislation makes it clear that one purpose of Bill C-127 was to reduce the impact of the victim's character on the outcome of a sexual assault case. The literature contains many examples of rape victims whose testimony was discredited by judges or juries who felt that they were responsible for their own victimization (Comack, 1992). Cases involving victims who dress inappropriately, who get picked up in bars, who hitchhike, who are prostitutes, who use drugs, or who engage in other behaviours departing from the norm of the stable, middle-class married woman often result in acquittals (Gunn and Minch, 1988; LaFree, 1989).

There are two quite different reasons why the success of rape prosecutions often depends on these character issues. First, rape laws have historically been devised to protect male sexual property. The more valuable the property and the more powerful the property owner, the greater the penalty for rape. According to this patriarchal ideology, women only deserve protection if they fit the image of a dutiful wife or daughter raped by a stranger. Second, there are rarely witnesses in rape trials, so a judge or jury must decide the case on the basis of two conflicting versions of the event. If a defence lawyer can portray the defendant as a trustworthy, respectable person, and the victim as an immoral person whose story cannot be believed, a jury could have reasonable doubts about the guilt of the accused. This is particularly true when the defendant does not have to testify or be subjected to cross-examination, while the victim may be subjected to very tough questioning by the defence. The section of C-127 that restricts questioning concerning the past sexual history of the victim was intended to make this process more equitable.

Thus in addition to looking at the impact of Bill C-127 on conviction rates, we can also evaluate the legislation by comparing the processing of pre- and post-reform cases to determine whether extralegal variables involving the character of the victim made a difference in the founding, charging, prosecuting, and convicting of sexual assault cases. This type of analysis has not been conducted in previous evaluations of the impact of rape reform legislation: it is important because even if conviction rates have not changed, the legislation may be considered at least partially successful if it results in the more equitable treatment by the courts of sexual assault cases.

CONCLUSION

The results presented here show that the impact of Canada's rape reform legislation has been modest. The conviction rate does not appear to have increased, and variables reflecting the character of the victim still have a significant impact on the laying of charges and on the likelihood of conviction.

Why did the legal change have such little impact? A major reason is that changing the law does not necessarily mean that the criminal justice system can or will quickly alter the way in which it operates. Boyle points out that "one of the key functions of law reform is the exertion of control over the decision makers at various levels of the criminal justice system" (1984: 127). However, these functionaries may resist change; the decision-making context remains the same and discretion is still in the hands of the same actors who were responsible for the criminal justice system before the legislation was enacted. Boyle also notes that the legal change was aimed at the trial stage, and that it may have had little impact on victim reporting, police and prosecutorial discretion, or sentencing. Since very few sexual assault cases actually go to trial, the impact of the legislation was not likely to be great.

The success of rape law reform may also have been limited by the fact that sexual assault cases are inherently difficult to prosecute, as the crime typically takes place in private and there are rarely witnesses other than the victim and the accused. Since the prosecution must establish proof beyond a reasonable doubt when evidence may consist simply of one person's word against another's, factors such as corroboration and recency of complaint are important in presenting a strong case even if they are not legally required.

In looking at the low rates of conviction for sexual assault, we should keep in mind that the criminal justice system does not efficiently prosecute criminals. Too often, critics look at the low conviction rate for sexual assault and assume that this offence is atypical. However, conviction rates are low for almost all offences. Based on their comparison of the processing of rape cases with homicide, robbery, assault, and burglary in several California counties, Galvin and Polk concluded that while there is a high rate of attrition for rape cases, it is not unique, as attrition is "a distinctive feature of American justice across offences" (1983: 152). In Canada Renner and Sahjpaul (1986) found that the percentage of reported cases resulting in charges was almost identical for physical assault and sexual assault. The percentage of cases cleared that were also charged, however, was considerably higher for sexual assault (64 percent) than for physical assault (42 percent).

The situation was not, however, entirely negative. As we have reported elsewhere, the legislation did have a positive impact on attitudes and practices toward sexual assault victims (Gunn and Linden, 1988). More complainants in the post-reform period were reporting cases that differed from the stereotype of violent attacks by strangers. For example, more prostitutes reported being victimized (though 70 percent of them later refused to cooperate or did not show up in court) and a smaller proportion of cases involved offenders who were strangers to the victims. Physical force was reported less often in the post-reform sample. Interviews with criminal justice personnel and victims showed positive attitudes toward Bill C-127. Police, prosecutors, judges, and sexual assault counsellors all felt the legislation was an improvement, and victims generally felt they had been treated fairly by the system.

Respondents agreed that the courts were following the new law. This perception was supported by our court observation: victims were not questioned about their previous sexual behaviour, and when the defence attempted to pursue this line of questioning, the Crown and judge intervened.

Despite the limited impact the legislation had on the processing of sexual assault cases, we would argue that its passage was still important. The law recognizes the complaints that had been raised about the treatment of rape victims. The feminist critique that the law served as a mechanism for controlling the behaviour of women, particularly those whose conduct did not conform to middle-class standards, was a legitimate one. The previous practice was degrading and unresponsive to victims and was clearly unfair. The law assumed that women were likely to lie about being raped and that special legal restrictions were needed to ensure that accused rapists received a fair trial. Although the statistical impact shown here was small, legislative change was a necessary step in shifting the focus in sexual assault cases from the reputation and behaviour of the victim to the criminal actions of the offender.

The passage of Bill C-127 is an affirmation of the rights of women in the criminal justice system, but legislation cannot solve the problem of violence against women. The only real solution lies in changing communities to ensure they are just, fair, and safe for all citizens (Macleod, 1989; 1994). However, Bill C-127 does provide a formal recognition of social change, which can contribute to the long-term shift in attitudes that is necessary in moving toward a safer society for all.

NOTES

1. This is a revised version of a paper presented at the annual meeting of the American Society of Criminology. Funding for this research was provided by the Department of Justice and by the Solicitor General's Contributions Grant to the Criminology Research Centre, University of Manitoba. The authors would like to thank Don Sabourin for his assistance and the reviewers for their very helpful comments. The manuscript of this article was submitted in April 1994 and accepted in August 1995.
2. Bill C-127 was a response to many years of lobbying by women's organizations and to the 1982 enactment of the Charter of Rights and Freedoms. Los (1994) provides a fascinating account of the development of this legislation.
3. This is consistent with the findings of Renner and Sahjpaul and those of Roberts. Roberts and Gebotys (1993) have shown that this increase is likely due to the impact on public attitudes of the passage of the 1983 legislation and the publicity surrounding the new law. They tested a variety of other hypotheses, including the possibility of changes in police recording patterns, and found that none could have accounted for a change of this magnitude.

REFERENCES

Boyle, C.L.M. 1984. *Sexual Assault*. Toronto: The Carswell Company.

Clark, L. and D. Lewis. 1977. *Rape: The Price of Coercive Sexuality*. Toronto: The Women's Press.

Clark, S. and D. Hepworth. 1994. "Effects of reform legislation on the processing of sexual assault cases." In *Confronting Sexual Assault: A Decade of Legal and Social Change*. J.V. Roberts and R.M. Mohr (eds.). Toronto: University of Toronto Pr., pp. 113–35.

Comack, E. 1992. "Women and crime." In *Criminology: A Canadian Perspective*. 2d ed. R. Linden (ed.). Toronto: Harcourt Brace, pp. 127–62.

DeKeseredy, W. and R. Hinch. 1991. *Women Abuse: Sociological Perspectives*. Toronto: Thompson Educational Publishing.

Department of Justice. 1990. *Sexual Assault Legislation in Canada: An Evaluation — Overview*. Ottawa: Department of Justice.

Galvin, J. and K. Polk. 1983. "Attrition in case processing: Is rape unique?" *Journal of Research in Crime and Delinquency*, Vol. 20, pp. 126–53.

Gunn, R. and R. Linden, 1988. *Evaluation of Bill C-127: Synthesis Report*. Winnipeg: Prairie Research Associates.

———. 1993. "Evaluating the impact of legal reform: Canada's new sexual assault laws." In *Evaluating Justice: Canadian Policies and Programs*. J. Hudson and J. Roberts (eds.). Toronto: Thompson Educational Publishing, pp. 135–54.

Gunn, R. and C. Minch. 1988. *Sexual Assault: The Dilemma of Disclosure, the Question of Conviction*. Winnipeg: University of Manitoba Pr.

Hinch, R. 1996. "Sexual violence and social control." In *Social Control in Canada*. B. Schissel and L. Mahood (eds.). Toronto: Oxford Univ. Pr.

LaFree, G.D. 1989. *Rape and Criminal Justice: The Social Construction of Sexual Assault*. Belmont, CA: Wadsworth.

LeBeau, J.L. 1987. "Statute revision and the reporting of rape: An associational or causal relationship." Paper presented at the Annual Meeting of the American Society of Criminology, Montreal.

Loh, W.D. 1980. "The impact of common law and reform rape statutes on prosecution." *Washington Law Review*, Vol. 55, pp. 543–625.

Los, M. 1994. "The struggle to redefine rape in the early 1980s." In *Confronting Sexual Assault: A Decade of Legal and Social Change*. J.V. Roberts and R.M. Mohr (eds.). Toronto: University of Toronto Pr., pp. 20–56.

MacLeod, L. 1989. *The City for Women: No Safe Place*. Ottawa: Secretary of State.

———. 1994. *Understanding and Charting our Progress Toward the Prevention of Women Abuse*. Ottawa: Family Violence Prevention Division, Health Canada.

Marsh, J.C., A. Geist, and N. Caplan. 1982. *Rape and the Limits of Law Reform*. Boston: Auburn House.

Minch, C., R. Linden, and S. Johnson. 1987. "Attrition in the processing of rape cases." *Canadian Journal of Criminology*, Vol. 29, pp. 389–404.

Polk, K. 1985. "Rape reform and criminal justice processing." *Crime and Delinquency*, Vol. 31, pp. 191–205.

Renner, K.E. and S. Sahjpaul. 1986. "The new sexual assault law: What has been its effect?" *Canadian Journal of Criminology*, Vol. 28, pp. 407–13.

Roberts, J.V. 1990. *Sexual Assaults Legislation in Canada: An Analysis of National Statistics*. Ottawa: Department of Justice.

Roberts, J.V. and R.J. Gebotys. 1993. "Evaluating criminal justice legislation: Effects of rape reform in Canada." In *Evaluating Justice: Canadian Policies and Programs*. J. Hudson and J. Roberts (eds.). Toronto: Thompson Educational Publishing, pp. 155–69.

Spohn, C. and J. Horney. 1992. *Rape Law Reform: A Grassroots Revolution and Its Impact*. New York: Plenum Press.

FOUR

Criminal Justice Policy Under Mulroney, 1984–90: Neo-Conservatism, Eh?

KEN HATT, TULLIO CAPUTO, AND BARBARA PERRY

The rise of neo-conservative[1] regimes in the United States and Great Britain during the 1980s had a marked influence on the nature of criminal justice policy in these countries.[2] Law and order campaigns and the manipulation of the public's fear of crime have figured prominently in the American "heroic" idiom with its war on crime and more recently, on drugs. The need for American political leaders to appear

Source: Ken Hatt, Tullio Caputo, and Barbara Perry, "Criminal Justice Policy under Mulroney, 1984–90: Neo-Conservatism, Eh?" *Canadian Public Policy*, 18, 3 (1992): 245–60. Reproduced by permission.

"tough on crime" is especially evident during election campaigns when politicians of all stripes seek to curry political favour with promises of harsher, and more punitive criminal justice measures (Cullen, Clark and Wozniak, 1985).[3] In Great Britain, the Thatcher regime used an authoritarian approach to law and order as a cornerstone of its broader neo conservative agenda (Hall, 1988; Kinsey, Lea and Young, 1986; Taylor, 1981). In particular, the "moral panic"[4] around "mugging" was used to legitimate a series of repressive practices, and to portray Mrs. Thatcher as a defender of "law and order" (Hall et al., 1978; Lea and Young, 1984; Matthew and Young, 1986). The use of force in putting down the miners' strike, in quelling the Brixton riots, and in response to the Poll Tax riots in London represent clear examples of the Thatcher regime's authoritarian law and order stance.

In Canada, Brian Mulroney and the Progressive Conservative Party (the PCs) won a massive electoral victory in 1984. Since coming to power, the Mulroney government has introduced many political and economic initiatives that are consistent with a neo-conservative agenda. Several examples of this are Mulroney's monetarist economic policies, privatization, deregulation, and such major initiatives as the Free Trade Deal with the United States, the Goods and Services Tax, and the Meech Lake Accord. The Mulroney record in the area of criminal justice policy, however, is less clear. Potentially volatile issues concerning Canada's laws on pornography, prostitution, and abortion have afforded the Conservatives ample opportunity to adopt a law and order approach to criminal justice. However, the Mulroney government has not appeared eager to do so. There has been little evidence of the type of moralistic posturing on criminal justice issues that has characterized neo-conservative politics in Great Britain or the United States.

What then is the record of the Mulroney government on criminal justice policy? Is there any evidence of a systematic agenda in this area? In this paper, we address these questions through a detailed analysis of the criminal justice legislation introduced by the Mulroney administration from 1984 to 1990. Our analysis is based on a theoretical model of the style of governing of successive Canadian federal governments that we have characterized as "managing consent" (Hatt, Caputo and Perry, 1990).

MANAGING CONSENT: UNDERSTANDING CANADIAN NEO-CONSERVATIVISM

A vigorous debate has taken place during the last few years over Canada's experience with neo-conservatism. In this debate, Canada has been variously characterized as a "thoroughly bourgeois" social formation and a "peaceable kingdom" (Taylor, 1985; 1987); as a nation dominated politically by "new establishment ideologies" (Havemann, 1987); and as a political system distinguished by "permanent exceptionalism" (Jenson, 1989; Ratner and McMullan, 1985; 1987).

Our recent contribution to this debate (Hatt, Caputo and Perry, 1990) includes the development of a model of managing consent that facilitates a multi-dimensional analysis of Canada's experience with neo-conservatism. This model avoids the theoretical extremism to which Carroll (1990) has recently drawn attention, while taking account of the historical and cultural realities of Canada's political economy. These include such features as Canada's colonial past, federal-provincial jurisdictional divisions, regionalism, and the role Canada plays in the international community.

Managing consent involves the use by the federal government of a number of strategies for governing such a diverse nation as Canada. The most dominant of these has been to employ the legitimizing power of the institutional order. This strategy emphasizes the generation of public support while avoiding direct, open, and hostile confrontation. When conflict does occur, steps are taken to restore the situation to "normal" as quickly as possible. An effort is made to institutionalize conflict and turn political problems into technical and administrative ones. Thus, whenever possible, problems are defined as procedural anomalies in the actions of individuals or bureaucracies, and solutions tend to avoid addressing underlying structural causes. When problems are acknowledged by the federal government, they are often attributed to the faulty management style of previous administrations, to the intransigence of provincial governments, to the actions of disruptive elements in society, or to the pressures of the world system.

According to our model of managing consent, the federal government is constrained in its actions by both domestic and external forces. In the current period, these constraints have limited the ability of the Progressive Conservative Party to move too quickly or significantly to the right. This explains at least in part, why neo-conservatism in Canada has been characterized by a preoccupation with monetarist economic policy characterized by a practical, administrative style rather than one that is moralistic. The nature of these constraints is discussed in greater detail below.

The external constraints on Canada are related to the role it plays in the international community. This role conditions and limits the types of actions that the federal government can take. For example, in the economic sphere, it is important that Canada be in harmony with its foreign trading partners, especially the United States. As Smiley (1987: 186) points out, the "thrust of the free trade proposals is towards the harmonization within Canada and the United States of policies involving benefits or burdens on private economic activity." Ultimately this calls into question Canadian policies such as Unemployment Insurance, and wage and benefit packages, which may be interpreted as unfair subsidies. Internally, there are also a number of factors that constrain the actions of the federal government. The political culture, for example, inhibits extreme moves either to the right or left. This was evident when the public's response to a PC proposal to deindex pensions caused the government to retract its policy. Although this has not been the case with the recently passed Goods and Services Tax, considerable opposition has been generated and this may contribute to further difficulties for the government.

Another internal factor that limits the actions of the federal government is the traditional role it has played in mediating competing interests in the country: the centre versus the periphery; federal versus provincial powers; competing regional interests; and French versus English aspirations. The federal-provincial dynamic, in particular, has assumed an increasingly important role during the Mulroney era. The practice of devolving responsibilities to lower levels of government has resulted in much more visible and volatile expressions of neo-conservative politics at provincial and local levels. The federal government has used federal-provincial relationships to insulate itself from criticism by shifting frustrations and concerns from its own terrain onto that of the provinces. This has been especially evident in the reduction of provincial transfer payments for health, welfare, education, and regional development. The financial shortfall has resulted in provincial and municipal tax hikes as well as concomitant cuts in social spending.

Politically, federal decentralization of decision-making engenders localized rather than nationally-based opposition to federal initiatives. This further fragments a populace that is naturally diverse by reason of geography, culture, and population density. The form of Canadian federalism characterized by a strong central government, is being recast by the Conservatives in favour of one in which the provinces are faced with the task of assuming a more significant role in meeting social and economic needs.[5]

MANAGING CONSENT: ANALYSING CRIMINAL JUSTICE POLICY

Our model of managing consent provides a useful framework for understanding the approach that the Mulroney government has adopted in the economic and political realms. Several aspects of the model, however, make it especially useful for an analysis of criminal justice policy in Canada. Chief among these is the emphasis that the model places on the division of powers between federal and provincial governments. This is particularly salient in the criminal justice field since the federal government has sole jurisdiction over criminal legislation, while provincial governments have jurisdiction over the administration of justice (except prisons for inmates serving sentences greater than two years, parole, and the RCMP). Control over criminal legislation could easily be used to facilitate a law and order campaign if one were desired by the federal government. Additionally, since the previous Liberal government was defeated shortly after introducing a mammoth piece of criminal justice legislation (Bill C-19), we are able to compare Liberal initiatives with bills introduced by the PCs subsequent to their coming to power. This allows us to examine the nature and extent of any changes that have taken place in the area of criminal justice policy under the Mulroney regime.

Our central purpose in this study is to examine PC criminal justice initiatives to determine whether a neo-conservative agenda is visible in the legislation they have introduced. We would define a neo-conservative agenda in criminal justice as one which reflects a law and order approach (Hall, 1980; Hall et al., 1978).[6] This consists primarily of four key elements:

1. support for more extensive law enforcement practices;
2. the introduction of increasingly harsher, and more punitive measures;
3. the manipulation of public fear of crime; and
4. an ideological emphasis on individual responsibility, traditional values, morality, and the sanctity of the family.

Our research consisted of a clause by clause examination of the major criminal justice legislation introduced by the PCs directly since coming to power in 1984. This included 13 pieces of legislation and the recommendations of three PC initiated commissions. We then compared the PC legislation and commission recommendations to three criminal justice bills and the recommendations of the three commissions introduced by the previous Liberal government. The PC commissions include the Deschenes Commission on War Criminals, the Daubney Commission on Sentencing, Corrections and Parole, and the 1990 Green Paper on Sentencing, Corrections, and Conditional Release. The Liberal Commissions include the Badgley Commission on Sexual Offences Against Children, the Fraser Commission on

Pornography and Prostitution, and the Archambault Commission on Sentencing. In sum, the material we examined includes 13 PC bills and three PC commissions as well as three Liberal bills, (one of which was the omnibus Bill C-19) and three Liberal commissions.

It should be noted that the PC legislation deals with such topics as impaired driving, prostitution, victims of crime, detention for violent offenders, young offenders, child sexual offences, pornography, and parole. For the most part, these were adapted from the Liberal's omnibus Bill C-19. The two pieces of legislation introduced by the PCs that were not derived from previous Liberal initiatives include: a capital punishment bill, and a bill that authorizes search and seizure of proceeds from crime. All of this legislation has been introduced in the House of Commons and has been given first reading. In some cases the legislation was not passed because the House adjourned before it could be addressed, or because there were oppositional problems. The specific bills included in this study and their outcomes are outlined in Figure 4.1 below.

FIGURE 4.1 *Genealogy of Canadian Criminal Justice Legislation, 1984–90*

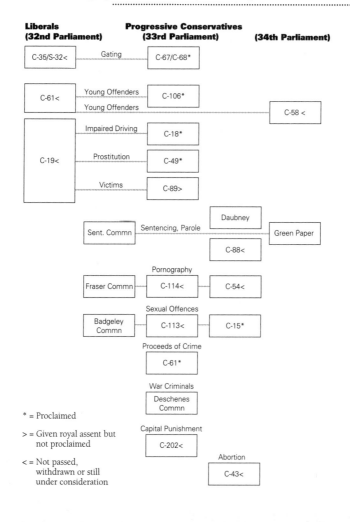

The 13 PC Bills contained a total of 399 clauses. The wording of each clause in the PC legislation was examined and compared with that of its Liberal counterpart. This consisted of a clause by clause comparison of the PC legislation with that introduced by the Liberals in 1984 just prior to their electoral defeat. Where no Liberal legislation existed, the PC legislation was compared to the recommendations of commissions appointed by the Liberal government. As can be seen in Figure 4.1, all of the PC legislation during the Mulroney administration was derived from legislation or commission recommendations previously introduced by the Liberals with the exception of Bill C-202 (Capital Punishment), Bill C-61 (Proceeds of Crime), and Bill C-43 (Abortion). Of the 399 clauses examined in the PC legislation, only 35 were found to differ significantly[7] from those introduced by the Liberals.

Our next step was to analyse the 35 clauses in which there were differences to determine the nature and extent of the changes. This was done by applying the definition of law and order approach outlined above. The four broad criteria outlined in this definition were used to determine whether or not the difference represented a law and order approach. Three distinct outcomes were possible: 1) the difference was in the direction of a law and order approach, 2) the difference was not in the direction of a law and order approach, and 3) the difference was ambiguous or neutral. The results of this analysis are presented in Table 4.1 below.

It became obvious as we carried out our examination of Liberal and PC criminal justice legislation that the Mulroney regime has not taken a law and order approach to criminal justice policy. This was unexpected given their neo-conservative approach in the economic arena to which we previously alluded. What was striking was the way in which the PCs simply re-introduced Liberal criminal justice legislation that had died in the previous parliamentary session. This is especially noteworthy given that the federal government has sole jurisdiction over criminal justice legislation.

The particular approach of the Mulroney government to criminal justice policy becomes clear through an examination of the way in which they reconstituted the Liberal omnibus bill of 1984 (C-19). This bill was broken down by the Conservatives into C-18 dealing with changes in court procedure and impaired driving, C-49 on prostitution, and C-89 concerning victims. There were other topics in the Liberal omnibus bill that still have not been developed; however, the 1990 Green Paper introduces several of these. For example, the Green Paper discussion of fines, community service orders, and the sentencing hearing, follows relevant passages in the Liberals' 1984 bill almost verbatim.

In most cases, the PCs brought forward the same legislation as the Liberals but used a decidedly different tone and rhetoric in their introduction and discussion of it. This can be illustrated through an extended example of impaired driving legislation. For example, the Liberal Justice Minister introduced legislation on impaired driving in February of 1984 by saying,

> these proposed amendments are the best possible balance between legitimate concerns for individual rights and the urgent requirement to prevent needless carnage on Canada's highways (Press release, February 7, 1984).

By December, the PC Minister of Justice was describing essentially the same legislation in the following terms:

TABLE 4.1 *Significant Differences between Liberal and Progressive Conservative Legislation*

		Legislation Changes by the Progressive Conservatives	Law and Order
1.	C-18	did not drop the dangerous offender legislation	yes
2.	C-18	previous conviction counted on sentence	yes
3.	C-18	specified maxima	?
4.	C-49	widened definition, "attempt to communicate"	yes
5.	C-49	widened definition to include "tricks"	yes
6.	C-89	ban on publication	no
7.	C-89	photos as evidence of recovered property	no
8.	C-89	imposed restitution	yes
9.	C-89	victim fine surcharge proposed	yes
10.	C-106	eased separate detention requirements	yes
11.	C-106	eased restriction on publication ban	yes
12.	C-106	eased restriction on records destruction	yes
13.	C-106	breach of probation became a summary offence	yes
14.	C-58	sentence for youth who murder (youth court)	?
15.	C-58	sentence for youth who murder (ordinary court)	no
16.	C-58	limited judicial discretion in transfer decisions	yes
17.	C-58	suggested criteria for decisions on transfer	?
18.	C-58	established conditional release for youth	yes
19.	C-58	established gating system for youth	yes
20.	C-67	detention system for adults (gating)	yes
21.	C-54	revised definitions of pornography	yes
22.	C-54	sex proposed as criteria of hate propaganda	no
23.	C-54	less stringent defences	no
24.	C-54	more severe punishments	yes
25.	C-15	revised definitions	?
26.	C-15	weakened defence	no
27.	C-15	child evidence accepted	?
28.	C-15	sentence for juvenile prostitution increased	yes
29.	C 15	living off of avails of prostitution ambiguous	?
30.	C-88	rejected abolition of parole	no
31.	C-88	guidelines for sentencing not explicit	?
32.	C-88	did not define sentencing as correct decision	?
33.	C-88	earned remission became statutory	?
34.	C-88	increased PED date	yes
35.	C-88	increased DPED date	yes

I am particularly determined to meet the strong public demand for stiffer penalties against impaired driving. This legal regime of stiffer penalties is a strong signal to Canadian drivers that the Federal government is serious about reducing alcohol-related traffic accidents (Press release, December 19, 1984).

But what were the actual differences in the legislation introduced by the two Ministers? In order to provide a thorough comparison, it is important to outline the common elements in both bills on impaired driving. Both defined two forms of offence: impaired driving and dangerous driving. The distinction between dangerous and impaired driving turned on whether or not the concentration of milligrams of alcohol to millilitres of blood exceeded the .08 level. If driving was erratic and the blood-alcohol level was below .08, a charge of dangerous driving would be laid. If the blood-alcohol level was above .08, it would be defined as impaired driving. From these criteria, additional offences were created: impaired driving causing bodily harm, and impaired driving causing death. The sentence for the former offence was a maximum of ten years and for the latter, 14 years imprisonment. Both bills made these activities applicable to aircraft and marine vehicles as well as automobiles. They also contained extensive procedures for obtaining breathalyzer tests or blood samples for determining the level of blood-alcohol concentration. On all of these items, the bills agreed.

A clause by clause examination shows that the PCs differed from the Liberals on two points. First, the PCs made it clear that conviction of a similar offence under the previous legislation would count toward a more severe sentence, where the Liberal wording was vague about this matter. The second difference pertained to what the maximum sentence would be for the charge of impaired driving. On this matter, the Liberals made no changes to the existing maximum sentence. By contrast, the PCs proposed that a conviction for impaired driving per se, would have a maximum sentence of six months imprisonment as a summary conviction and five years as an indictable offence.

As this example shows, the PCs differed marginally from the Liberals in the legislation they introduced on impaired driving. What was different was the tone and rhetoric used by the PC Minister in introducing and describing essentially the same legislation brought forward by the Liberals. Where the Liberal Minister stressed a balance between individual rights and the need to prevent accidents, the PC Minister projected a tough stance that he justified on the basis of the public's demand for stiffer penalties.

The example of the impaired driving legislation reflects a broader pattern we discovered throughout our investigation. In a vast majority of cases, there is no significant difference between the legislation introduced by the PCs and that introduced by the previous Liberal government. This was the case in 364 of 399 clauses that were examined. In the 35 clauses where differences exist, evidence of a law and order approach was found in 19 cases. The differences in nine cases were ambiguous or neutral, while in the remaining seven cases the differences did not reflect a law and order approach. Thus, in only 19 of the 399 clauses of PC criminal justice legislation that we examined was there a difference between the PCs and the Liberals that represented a change toward a law and order approach to criminal justice.

A brief discussion of each of the three types of differences we discovered in our analysis is presented below. This includes differences that do represent a law and order approach; differences that do not represent a law and order approach; and differences that are ambiguous or neutral.

I. DIFFERENCES THAT REPRESENT A LAW AND ORDER APPROACH

1. The Liberals had proposed in C-19 that a section that specified indeterminate imprisonment for persons designated "dangerous offenders" should be taken out of the Criminal Code. The PCs did not remove it and the dangerous offender section is still in the Criminal Code.

2. The Liberals had attempted to address the area of prostitution in C-19 following a Supreme Court decision that solicitation by a prostitute must be "pressing and persistent" in order to get a conviction. The PCs re-defined prostitution in terms of "every person who ... stops or attempts to stop or in any manner communicates or attempts to communicate with any person ..." [for the purpose of prostitution] (C-49, 1986). This enhances the discretion of police, a position consistent with a law and order approach.

3. In Bill C-89, the PCs devised a Victim Fine Surcharge that is to be levied against persons convicted of selected offences who have the ability to pay. In addition, they increased the role of victim impact statements at the sentencing hearing. Judicial discretion is still predominant in the use and consideration of these documents.

4. Besides Bill C-19, a second important piece of Liberal legislation was the *Young Offenders' Act*. This has been a major site of PC legal reconstruction. The PCs have eased a number of restrictive sections on enforcement agencies. These include dropping major provisions on separate detention for offenders, the ban on publication if the youth is being sought by police, and on destruction of records and information. The House of Commons is presently considering a second bill amending the *Young Offenders' Act* (Bill C-58). In this bill, judicial discretion to transfer youths to ordinary court is much more limited, and the criteria for the transfer decision have been changed to place greater emphasis on the protection of society. In addition, a system of parole and a "gating" mechanism for youth who are convicted of murder are proposed.

II. DIFFERENCES THAT DO NOT REFLECT A LAW AND ORDER APPROACH

1. Where youth who murder are dealt with in ordinary court, the PCs proposed that the more onerous normal sentences of life imprisonment with a minimum mandatory parole ineligibility period of ten years for second degree murder and 25 years for first degree murder be changed. As an alternative, the PCs proposed a sentence of life imprisonment with a minimum mandatory parole ineligibility period of between five and ten years.

2. In legislation relating to victims of crime, Bill C-89, the PCs extended power to judges to protect the identity of victims and witnesses by ordering non-publication for certain offences.

3. The (Liberal initiated) Archambault Commission recommended the abolition of parole. However, in Bill C-88, the PCs have opted to retain parole, albeit with some changes.

4. In legislation pertaining to pornography (Bill C-54) the defences relating to whether a work was of artistic merit, or served an educational, medical, or scientific purpose were relaxed. This involved a shift from requiring proof beyond reasonable doubt to proof based on a balance of probabilities.

III. DIFFERENCES THAT ARE AMBIGUOUS OR NEUTRAL

There are several changes introduced by the PCs that are difficult to classify. For example, how should the specification of a maximum sentence for impaired driving be evaluated if the previous legislation did not specify a maximum sentence? What evaluation should be made of a proposal to replace earned remission that could amount to one-third of a sentence, with a statutory form of remission of the same length? In these cases, it is difficult to assess the nature of the changes introduced by the PCs since they reflect an ambiguous or neutral stance.

In sum, our classification of the 35 cases where differences exist between Liberal and PC legislation, indicates that in 19 of the cases, the differences represent a move toward a law and order approach. In seven of the cases, the differences do not involve such a move, while the remaining nine are ambiguous or neutral. From these results, it is difficult to conclude that the PCs have attempted to introduce a law and order approach. In the overwhelming majority of the cases (364 out of 399 clauses) the PCs simply re-introduced Liberal legislation. Given this evidence, we began to consider how the PC strategy in the area of criminal justice compared to their neo-conservative approach in the areas of economic and social policy.

CRIMINAL JUSTICE POLICY UNDER MULRONEY

We anticipated that some additional insight into the PC approach to criminal justice policy could be garnered from those items that came from the PCs without a Liberal origin. The Deschenes Commission represents somewhat of an anomaly yet it will be considered here, since it provides additional information. This commission was initiated by the PCs, however, the impetus for it had come from the Liberal Solicitor General who introduced legislation on this topic as a private member prior to becoming Solicitor General. The Deschenes Commission has not been included in Figure 4.2 because the Liberal government did not introduce legislation in this area, instead, it came from a private member. Furthermore, the Deschenes Commission did not lead to any PC legislation.

The Deschenes Commission undertook an exploration of the moral panic (connected with the former Liberal Solicitor General) regarding the possible entry of the Nazi war criminal, Joseph Mengele, into Canada. Deschenes considered nearly 900 cases and concluded that perhaps 29 persons were even worthy of investigation. Deschenes documented how estimates of war criminals in Canada had grown from several hundred in 1971 to 6,000 by 1986. His basic message was that "[the] matter has lasted long enough: those individuals deserve to be advised that, insofar as Canada is concerned, they can finish their last days in peace" (Canada, 1986: 827).

There are three additional items introduced by the PCs that did not originate with the Liberals: the Proceeds of Crime Bill C-61; the Capital Punishment Bill C-202; and the Daubney Committee report. The first of these, Bill C-61, was introduced in May, 1987 by the Minister of Justice. It created several new offences related to "enterprise crime" or drug trafficking. These included no less than 22 separate offences ranging from bribery, procuring, and extortion, to robbery, counterfeiting, and a myriad of offences based on possession of property related to crime. Special procedures for search warrants, restraint orders, as well as the seizure and forfeiting of goods were set out in the bill. The Minister of Justice stated that his government intended "to take the profit out of crime" (Press Release, May 29, 1987, p. 2). The RCMP were quite pleased with this and announced that they would be using these new legislative powers to mount an aggressive attack against powerful drug trafficking organizations that have hitherto been able to accumulate significant wealth with impunity (RCMP, 1988: 98).

This legislation appears to follow similar bills prepared in the United States in relation to a United Nations initiative on "enterprise crime."

The second bill introduced by the PCs that was not based on previous Liberal initiatives was Bill C-202, on capital punishment. This was not a government bill, but a private members' bill that was put on the House of Commons Order Paper for debate. The PC member from Peterborough, Mr. Domm, had been introducing a bill to reinstate capital punishment since being elected. Like all bills of this type, almost none get consideration or action in the House of Commons. However, when Mulroney was elected, he had such a large majority that there were difficulties maintaining the traditional operations of the House. Mulroney decided to hold a random selection of Private Members' bills to be debated. By chance, Mr. Domm's bill on capital punishment was chosen.

The Prime Minister, and the leaders of the other parties, declared themselves opposed to capital punishment, but the new PC backbenchers, and a number of people across Canada, saw this as an opportunity to re-introduce the death penalty. Opponents of capital punishment mobilized, fearing the beginning of an expected law and order approach by the Conservative government. After extensive debate on the bill, it was not passed.

The third PC initiative not derived from the Liberals was the Daubney Commission. As the capital punishment debate was coming to a close, the government assigned the Standing Committee on Justice and Solicitor General to conduct an inquiry into the areas of sentencing, corrections, and parole. The Archambault Commission (appointed by the Liberals) had just released its lengthy study of sentencing. At the same time, a series of inquests were underway in Canada that were examining cases of death involving criminal justice personnel, and complaints about the miscarriage of justice in Nova Scotia, Ontario, Manitoba, and Alberta. Travelling to seven major metropolitan areas and considering over 200 briefs, the all-party committee submitted a report in 1988. Among the ten members on the committee were Mr. Domm and two of his political colleagues.

The Daubney report was over 300 pages in length and contained 97 recommendations. There were six major areas: 1) the personal responsibility of offenders for their acts; 2) selected restraints and programs for dangerous offenders; 3) community-oriented justice programs; 4) improved information systems in criminal justice; 5) an increased consideration for victims; and 6) increased funding of special programs for dangerous offenders, Native people, and women.

The Daubney report (House of Commons, 1988) represents an attempt to devise a new and more comprehensive PC strategy in criminal justice. While it undoubtedly reflects the neo-conservative philosophy of the PCs, it is more concerned with articulating practical criminal justice strategies. These include the blending of cheaper (but increased) community corrections, electronic management systems, and a populist sense of justice based on individual responsibility and accountability. However, it stops short of recommending a law and order campaign or a declaration of a war on crime.

In considering these bills and commissions in conjunction with the legislation discussed above, the PC strategy in criminal justice becomes more discernible. It includes the following:

1. allowing changes in provincial administration of criminal justice (for example, as found in bills C-58, C-89, C-106, and C-88, among others).
2. finding ways to minimize apparent increases in federal spending on criminal justice.
3. cultivating public support by appearing to be both tough on crime, and efficient in the management of the criminal justice system.

How do the differences between the Liberals and the PCs discussed above reflect this strategy? Several examples can be given as illustrations. First, the administration of criminal justice (a provincial responsibility) is facilitated through the wider definition of prostitution and the amendments to the *Young Offenders' Act*. Similarly, the limited increase in sentence lengths for youths who murder was probably more a result of the increasing cost of imprisoning people for the ten or 25 years specified in the previous legislation. Much of the same could be said for the expensive process of obtaining evidence internationally to prosecute two dozen, 70-year-old war criminals. A decision to switch to statutory remission rather than earned remission may be primarily due to the cost of calculating the dates for earned remission. But what about the abolition of parole that had been recommended by the Archambault Commission? Why wouldn't that be pursued by the PCs? The enormous expense of keeping people in prison for longer periods if parole were abolished may be one factor behind this decision. Additionally, the fact that this was proposed by a Liberal commission may have caused the PCs to postpone action on this matter. As will be shown shortly, the PCs had their own response to the question of parole.

Retaining a dangerous offender legislation, the increased role for victim impact statement, the changes in parole eligibility dates, and the powers of search and seizure in "enterprise crime" reflect the PC interest in maintaining a high public profile that demonstrates that they are "tough" on crime. Perhaps the quintessential PC measure is the victim fine surcharge. This is a program in which persons who have been convicted are required to pay a sum or have a portion added to their fine in order to pay for services to victims. It appears to have popular support and is to be administered by the provinces.[8]

DESCRIBING THE PC STRATEGY FOR CRIMINAL JUSTICE POLICY

Our findings indicate that there has not been a law and order approach in the PC initiatives in criminal justice. However, a distinct PC strategy in this area is apparent. Several factors help to explain the nature of PC activity in the area of criminal justice. For example, wider economic and political issues such as the Free Trade Deal with the United States, the Meech Lake proposal, and current constitutional debate have occupied much of the Mulroney government's agenda. This has reduced the time available on the parliamentary calendar for criminal justice matters. Moreover, much of the time devoted to criminal justice issues has been taken up dealing with the consequences of Supreme Court decisions based on the Charter of Rights and

Freedoms. In this regard, the PCs have had to address matters such as abortion, "gating" legislation, the *Young Offenders' Act*, and prostitution. As a result, little time has been available for new PC criminal justice initiatives.

Another factor is the nature of the leadership by various ministers in the two positions that are central to criminal justice policy, the Minister of Justice and the Solicitor General. In the Liberal government, those ministers had extensive experience and comprehensive agendas. The former facilitated no less than a complete re-writing of the Criminal Code, while the latter matched those ambitions with a revision of criminal legislation on youth and regionalization of federal corrections. By contrast, the PCs have had a series of ministers whose goals or agendas have been much less ambitious.[9] The priority on economic and political re-structuring, the limited time available for criminal justice issues in Parliament, and ministerial leadership, have all contributed to the muted role that criminal justice issues have played during the Mulroney era.

The overall approach of the Liberal and PC regimes can be further characterized by comparing the two most central criminal justice documents of these parties. In 1982, the Liberals published a document entitled *The Criminal Law In Canadian Society* (1982, hereafter known as CLICS). This represented the Liberal statement on the purpose and principles of criminal justice. The strategy involved a statement which would link the newly established Charter of Rights and Freedoms with future legislation and organizational mandates of the federal government. The central statement of purpose called on criminal law to

> contribute to the maintenance of a just, peaceful, and safe society through the establishment of a system of prohibitions, sanctions, and procedures to deal fairly and appropriately with culpable conduct that causes or threatens serious harm to individuals or society (CLICS, 1982: 57).

Thus, it created the "twin purposes" of justice and security in criminal justice. Associated with this was the commitment to achieving a balance between individual interests and those of society (CLICS, 1982: 49–50). Hence, the Liberals attempted to achieve propriety through a commitment to the concept of balance and compromise — recall the comments of the Liberal minister upon introducing impaired driving legislation. It was this same notion that they argued was central in their *Young Offenders' Act*.

Since coming to power in 1984, the PCs had not developed a statement comparable to the CLICS document until the release of the Green Paper in 1990. In it, we see that the basic purpose of criminal justice as proposed by the Liberals has not changed. The Green Paper cites with approval the CLICS document which set "justice and security" as central objectives. The PCs agree that protection of citizens is the central purpose of criminal justice.

We have suggested that the PC strategy in criminal justice involves increased provincial activity, efficient management and the appearance of being tough on crime. The best example of this is found in the proposals in the Green Paper concerning parole. Under the Liberals, parole continued to operate in terms of the contradictory objectives of rehabilitating the offender and at the same time assuring public safety. In the PC approach, the objectives have shifted to a concern with public safety through risk assessment. The decision-making focus of the National Parole

Board (NPB) will be offence based, for it will be guided by whether or not the offender was convicted of a "violent" offence. The NPB previously had to consider each case more broadly to ascertain if a person showed evidence of rehabilitation or prospects for reintegration. The emphasis has now changed such that presumptive release dates are established for non-violent offenders and release dates for violent offenders can be shifted by judges. That is, judges will have the discretion to set actual parole eligibility dates from one-third to one-half of the sentence length for violent offenders. There are two changes involved here: first, in the decision-making source; and second, in the nature of the decision rule. The Green Paper would shift responsibility for determining the eligibility date for parole from statute to the courts. Secondly, the decision rule is made explicit that violent offenders can have a parole eligibility date from one-third to one-half of the sentence.

In addition, PCs are proposing changes to earned remission. Earned remission, which is time off of the sentence for good behaviour, can reduce the time served in prison to two-thirds of the sentence. In place of earned remission, the PCs are proposing a form of statutory remission in which the person will be assumed to serve two-thirds of the sentence unless detained and required to serve the entire sentence. The primary role of the NPB will be to review every person and decide who should be detained to the end of their sentence. Hence the focus of the NPB has shifted considerably. The Archambault Commission on Sentencing recommended the abolition of parole in Canada, but this has been rejected in favour of a re-definition such that the NPB is now oriented to decisions of detention rather than to decisions of release.

DISCUSSION

We have analysed the criminal justice legislation introduced by the Mulroney Progressive Conservative government since coming to power in 1984. A clause by clause comparison was made of the PC legislation with that which had been introduced by the previous Liberal government. The most significant findings of this study are: 1) almost all of the PC criminal justice legislation is a replication of the Liberal initiatives; 2) the differences between the PCs and the Liberals do not represent a law and order approach; 3) the PC strategy in criminal justice does reflect this government's broader neo-conservative agenda and is consistent with their approach to economic and social policy.

These findings reflect the complex nature of criminal justice politics for a neo-conservative government in the Canadian context. The continuity between the PCs and the Liberals is emphasized by their adoption of the justice and security themes of the Liberal CLICS document. Moreover, despite an ideological kinship with the regimes in the United States and Great Britain, we have not experienced the type of law and order campaigns that have been the hallmark of neo-conservatism in those countries. Instead, the PC strategy in criminal justice is consistent with their approach to economic and social policy. They have emphasized efficient management of the criminal justice system and where possible, they have transferred increasing responsibility to the provinces. At the same time, they have projected the image of being tough on crime.

As noted in our model of managing consent, both external and internal factors constrain the activities of the federal government. In our discussion above, we described a number of these including: an emphasis on economic priorities; lack of time on the parliamentary agenda; the need to respond to Supreme Court decisions; and the role of ministerial leadership. In this paper, we also placed particular emphasis on the federal-provincial dynamic, since it is so integrally involved in criminal justice.

Other political and cultural factors also influence the actions of the government. Among these are a relatively low crime rate that inhibits the development of law and order campaigns. In addition, an already harsh system of justice limits the possibility of significant shifts to the right. The traditional orientation of the criminal justice system in Canada is seen in enforcement practices, in sentencing, and in corrections, where Canada has the second highest imprisonment rate among western industrialized nations (Correctional Service of Canada, 1990: 10).

Lobby groups may also play a role in constraining government action. For example, some of the more regressive revisions proposed for the *Young Offenders' Act* in 1986 (C-106) and 1989 (C-58) were greeted by opposition from a broad spectrum of social groups. The amended legislation that was eventually introduced was somewhat more moderate than originally proposed. The role of lobby groups was also evident during the capital punishment debate.

Public mobilization is another conditioning factor in Canadian criminal justice politics. Public concern over crime may result in demands for government action. However, as noted above, it may also limit activity when the government engages in what is seen to be inappropriate action. Mediating this relationship between the government and the public are the media who perform a "watch-dog" function in Canada. That is, rather than stress the "moral decay" of which crime is a symptom, the Canadian media tend to focus on the failure of the state to deal with crime, i.e., the failure of the state to fulfil its role in protecting the public (Ericson, Baranek and Chan, 1987; 1989).

This analysis suggests that the demands on the Canadian federal government in criminal justice politics are contradictory. On the one hand, it must respond to its task of protecting the public in a way that is seen to be tough and effective. On the other hand, it must do so within publicly and economically acceptable bounds, and also within its own political jurisdiction.

Each government operates within this milieu and brings its own political and philosophical orientation to bear on these contradictions. While affirming the twin goals of justice and security, the Liberals attempted to deal with these contradictory demands by striking a balance between the individual and society. For their part, the PCs deal with the contradictory demands of the criminal justice system by applying their own brand of neo-conservatism. The Liberal goals of justice and security are reaffirmed by the PCs and then translated into the need to protect the public by being tough on crime and efficient managers of the criminal justice system. Thus, Canada is neither a law and order society nor a "peaceable kingdom." The major concern in Canadian criminal justice policy remains justice and security.

NOTES

1. Neo-conservative is defined in this paper as a political philosophy and practice characterized by monetarist economic and fiscal policies, an emphasis on traditional moral values associated with fundamentalist religious beliefs, the sanctity of the family

and individual responsibility. This is reflected in a call for "less" government, a dismantling of Keynesian welfare state policies, and a reversion to a free market economy.

2. For example, this was evident in the United States in the Congressional debates over parole and capital punishment legislation. For a detailed analysis of the parole debates, see Cooley (1990).

3. In the 1988 Presidential election, for example, much was made of the signing of a parole order by then Massachusetts governor Dukakis for Willie Horton, a violent criminal. Dukakis suffered politically for appearing "soft on crime."

4. The use of "moral panics" is discussed in greater detail by Brannigan (1989) and Taylor (1982).

5. Even before Mulroney initiated his program of decentralization, British Columbia and Saskatchewan had begun to respond to their own difficulties by introducing neo-conservative principles of government, e.g., privatization, rollbacks in welfare provisions, and budgetary restraint. Increased provincial autonomy would only exacerbate this development.

6. For a more extensive discussion of various models in criminology, see Empey (1982); Horton (1966); Reid and Reitsma-Street (1984); Young (1986).

7. Differences based on wording referring to gender, subsequent renumbering of sections, or similar technical adjustments were not considered significant changes.

8. It is not clear whether every section of this legislation has been proclaimed. It appears that the section pertaining to victim fine surcharges has not been proclaimed. Nevertheless, it is being used in several jurisdictions.

9. The fact that the Conservatives have introduced a Green Paper, as opposed to a White Paper or the actual declaration of policy, is further evidence of the tentative approach of the Mulroney government in this area.

REFERENCES

Brannigan, Augustine (1989) "Moral Panic and Rationality in Criminal Law." Pp. 146–58 in T.C. Caputo, M. Kennedy, C.E. Reasons and A. Brannigan (eds.), *Law and Society: A Critical Perspective* (Toronto: Harcourt, Brace, Jovanovitch).

Canada (1982) *The Criminal Law In Canadian Society* (CLICS) (Ottawa: Department of Justice).

—— (1984) *Sexual Offences Against Children In Canada: Report of the Committee On Sexual Offences Against Children and Youth* (Badgley Report) (Ottawa: Minister of Supply and Services).

—— (1985) *Pornography and Prostitution In Canada: Report of the Special Committee On Pornography and Prostitution* (Fraser Report) (Ottawa: Minister of Supply and Services).

—— (1986) *Commission of Inquiry On War Criminals, Part One, Public* (Deschenes Commission) (Ottawa: Minster of Supply and Services).

—— (1987) *Sentencing Reform: A Canadian Approach. Report of the Canadian Sentencing Commission* (Archambault Commission) (Ottawa: Minster of Supply and Services).

—— (1989) *The Young Offenders Act. Proposals For Amendment* (Ottawa: Department of Justice).

—— (1990) *Directions For Reform In Sentencing, Corrections, and Conditional Release* (Green Paper) (Ottawa: Minister of Supply and Services).

Carroll, William K. (1990) "Restructuring Capital, Reorganizing Consent: Gramsci, Political Economy, and Canada," *The Canadian Review of Sociology and Anthropology*, 27: 3: 390–416.

Cooley, Dennis (1990) "Criminal Justice Policy in Canada and the United States: A Comparative Analysis of Parole Debates between 1970 and 1988." Ottawa, Carleton University, M.A. Thesis, Department of Sociology and Anthropology.

Correctional Service of Canada (1990) *Basic Facts About Corrections in Canada* (Ottawa: Minister of Supply and Services).

Cullen, F.T., G.A. Clark, and J.F. Wozniak (1985) "Explaining the Get Tough Movement: Can the Public Be Blamed?" *Federal Probation*, 49: 16–24.

Department of Justice (1987) "Minister of Justice Takes Action Against Proceeds of Crime." Ottawa, Press Release, May 29, p. 2.

Empey, Lamar T. (1982) *American Delinquency: Its Meaning and Construction* (Homewood, IL: The Dorsey Press).

Ericson, Richard, P.M. Baranek, and J.B.L. Chan (1987) *Visualizing Deviance: A Study of News Organizations* (Toronto: University of Toronto Press).

—— (1989) *Negotiating Control: A Study of News Sources* (Toronto: University of Toronto Press).

Hall, Stuart (1980) "Drifting Into a Law and Order Society," Cobden Trust Human Rights Day Lecture, UK.

—— (1988) "Thatcher's Lessons," *Marxism Today*, March, 1988, pp. 20–27.

Hall, Stuart, Chas Critcher, Tony Jefferson, John Clarke, and Brian Roberts (1978) *Policing the Crisis: Mugging, the State, and Law and Order* (London and Basingstoke: The Macmillan Press Ltd).

Hatt, Ken, T.C. Caputo, and Barbara Perry (1990) "Managing Consent: Canada's Experience with Neo-Conservatism," *Social Justice*, 17: 30–48.

Havemann, Paul (1987) "Marketing the New Establishment Ideology in Canada," *Crime and Social Justice*, 26: 11–37.

Horton, John (1966) "Order and Conflict Theories of Social Problems As Competing Ideologies," *American Journal of Sociology*, (May): 71: 701–13.

House of Commons (1988) *Taking Responsibility: Report of the Standing Committee On Justice and Solicitor General On Its Review of Sentencing, Conditional Release and Related Aspects of Corrections* (Daubney Report) (Ottawa: Minister of Supply and Services).

Jenson, Jane (1989) "'Different' but Not 'Exception': Canada's Permeable Fordism," *The Canadian Review of Sociology and Anthropology*, 26: 1: 69–94.

Kinsey, Richard, John Lea, and Jock Young (1986) *Losing The Fight Against Crime* (London: Blackwell).

Lea, John and Jock Young (1984) *What Is To Be Done About Law and Order?* (London: Penguin).

Matthew, Roger and Jock Young (eds.) (1986) *Confronting Crime* (London: Gage).

Ratner, R.S. and J.L. McMullan (1985) "Social Control and the Rise of the 'Exceptional' State in Britain, the United States, and Canada." In T. Fleming (ed.), *The New Criminologies in Canada: State, Crime and Control* (Toronto: Oxford University Press).

—— (1987) *State Control: Criminal Justice Politics In Canada* (Vancouver: University of British Columbia Press).

Reid, Susan A. and Marge Reitsma-Street (1984) "Assumptions and Implications of the New Canadian Legislation for Young Offenders," *Canadian Criminology Forum*, 7: 1–19.

Royal Canadian Mounted Police (1988) *Drug Intelligence Estimate*, 1987–88 (Ottawa: Department of Supply and Services).

Smiley, Donald (1987) *The Federal Condition in Canada* (Toronto: McGraw-Hill Ryerson Ltd.).

Taylor, Ian (1981) *Law and Order: Arguments for Socialism* (London: Macmillan).

—— (1982) "Moral Enterprise, Moral Panic, and Law and Order Campaigns," In M.M. Rosenberg, R.A. Stebbins, and A. Turowitz (eds.), *The Sociology of Deviance* (New York: St. Martin's).

—— (1985) "Criminology, the Unemployment Crisis and the Liberal Tradition in Canada: The Need For Socialist Analysis and Policy." Pp. 327–43 in I. Fleming (ed.), *The New Criminologies in Canada* (Toronto: Oxford University Press).

—— (1987) "Theorizing the Crisis in Canada." Pp. 198–224 in R.S. Ratner and J.L. McMullan, *State Control* (Vancouver: University of British Columbia Press).

Young, Jock (1986) "Thinking Seriously About Crime: Some Models of Criminology." Pp. 248–309 in M. Fitzgerald, G. McLennan, and J. Pawson (eds.), *Crime and Society: Readings in History and Theory* (London: Routledge and Kegan Paul).

STATUTES

....

An Act to amend the Criminal Code (prostitution) (1985) (Can.) First Session, Thirty-third Parliament (Bill C-49).

An Act to amend the Criminal Code (victims of crime) (1987) (Can.) First Session, Thirty-third Parliament (Bill C-89).

An Act to amend the Criminal Code and the Canada Evidence Act (1986) (Can.) First Session, Thirty-third Parliament (Bill C-113).

An Act to amend the Criminal Code and the Canada Evidence Act (1986) (Can.) Second Session, Thirty-third Parliament (Bill C-15).

An Act to amend the Criminal Code and the Customs Tariff (1986) (Can.) First Session, Thirty-third Parliament (Bill C-114).

An Act to amend the Criminal Code and other Acts in consequence thereof (1987) (Can.) Second Session, Thirty-third Parliament (Bill C-54).

An Act to amend the Criminal Code, the Food and Drugs Act and the Narcotic Control Act (1987) (Can.) Second Session, Thirty-third Parliament (Bill C-61).

An Act to amend the Criminal Code, to amend an Act to amend the Criminal Code and to amend the Combines Investigation Act, the Customs Act, the Excise Act, the Food and Drugs Act, the Narcotic Control Act, the Parole Act and the Weights and Measures Act and to make other consequential amendments (1984) (Can.) Second Session, Thirty-second Parliament (C-19).

An Act to amend the Criminal Code, to amend an Act to amend the Criminal Code and to amend the Combines Investigation Act, the Customs Act, the Excise Act, the Food and Drugs Act, the Narcotic Control Act, the Parole Act and the Weights and Measures Act, to repeal certain other Acts and to make other consequential amendments (1984) (Can.) First Session, Thirty-third Parliament (C-18).

An Act to amend the Parole Act and the Penitentiary Act (1985) (Can.) First Session, Thirty-third Parliament (C-67).

An Act to amend the Parole Act and the Penitentiary Act (1988) (Can.) First Session of the Thirty-fourth Parliament (C-88).

An Act to amend the Parole Act, the Penitentiary Act, the Prisons and Reformatories Act and the Criminal Code (1985) (Can.) First Session, Thirty-third Parliament (C-68).

An Act to amend the Penitentiary Act, the Parole Act and certain other Acts in consequence thereof (1984) (Can.) Second Session, Thirty-second Parliament (Bill C-35).

An Act to amend the Young Offenders Act and the Criminal Code (1989) (Can.) Second Session, Thirty-fourth Parliament (Bill C-58).

An Act to amend the Young Offenders Act, the Criminal Code, the Penitentiary Act and the Prisons and Reformatories Act (1986) (Can.) First Session, Thirty-third Parliament (C-106).

PART TWO

*Sentencing Issues:
The Purposes and
Consequences of
Punishment*

Sentencing issues have been prominent in recent crime control policy debates in Canada. This is no doubt, at least partly, the result of the perception that the courts are too lenient in their sentencing. In addition, various interest groups, such as the police and certain victim advocacy organizations, have been vocal in calling for increased severity of punishment for convicted offenders. Several federal commissions and committees in the 1980s undertook a fundamental reappraisal of the nature and functions of sentencing, and the Government of Canada has responded with new legislation. There has also been evidence of disparity in sentencing and concern about its possibly discriminatory impact on certain categories of persons. A number of high-profile cases of violent crimes committed by released offenders has also focussed concern on the sentencing of high-risk offenders. As a result of these ongoing debates, the traditional purposes or goals of sentencing have been subject to reevaluation.

Five goals or functions of punishment have traditionally been identified: protection or incapacitation, deterrence, rehabilitation, retribution, and denunciation. The goal of protection or incapacitation is to render the criminal, at least temporarily, incapable of repeating an offence. A sentence to imprisonment can thus be justified on the grounds that while incarcerated the offender will not be able to victimize the public and so society is protected by a reduction in crime. This purpose has been emphasized by those advocating selective incapacitation of particular offenders thought likely to commit a disproportionately large number of or particularly violent crimes. Such selective incapacitation requires the knowledge to predict future conduct and to identify with a high degree of accuracy the individual offenders to be incapacitated. Aside from the generally low accuracy of such predictions (Morris and Miller, 1987), their use in sentencing raises questions of justice (Von Hirsch, 1984). Selective incapacitation represents punishment for what someone may do in the future, resulting in a more severe sentence than would be received by another offender convicted of the same offence.

According to the theory of deterrence, the purpose of punishment is to inhibit offenders (individual deterrence) or potential offenders (general deterrence) from committing offences. Deterrence assumes that the threat of future punishment will inhibit the rational individual from choosing to commit crime if the costs in punishment exceed the rewards anticipated from crime. Increasing the certainty, swiftness, and severity of punishment should increase the costs of criminal behaviour, thus reducing the amount of crime in society. This justification for punishment assumes that the potential offender knows the penalties and potential risks, perceives them as unpleasant, and acts rationally, assumptions that can be questioned (Walker, 1994). The research literature supports the conclusion that the threat of punishment, particularly its certainty or likelihood, has some deterrent effect (Miller and Anderson, 1986; Paternoster, 1987). However, informal sanctions, such as shame and guilt, and socialization into law-abiding behaviour are likely to have more effect on behaviour (Grasmick and Bursick, 1990).

Rehabilitation means that sentencing should attempt to reform or correct the offender by identifying and changing the conditions causing the criminal behaviour. Thus rehabilitation is any planned intervention that reduces an offender's further criminal activity (Sechrest, et al., 1979). This purpose assumes that criminal behaviour is caused by biological, psychological, and/or social conditions over which the individual has little or no control or choice. Punishment should fit the criminal rather than the crime; sentences should be individualized. However, this has led to injustices such as unusually lengthy or indeterminant sentences. Furthermore, there has been a growing skepticism regarding the effectiveness of correctional treatment (Sechrest et al., 1979; Doob and Brodeur, 1989). Although some programs may have some positive effects for some offenders (Gendreau and Andrews, 1990), no correctional program has been shown to substantially reduce recidivism rates. However, to change criminal behaviour may require a greater focus on the actual life circumstances of offenders, such as their opportunities in the community for work and family life (Walker, 1994).

Punishment for retribution attempts to balance the harm done by the crime. Justice requires that offenders pay for their wrongdoing to offset the harm caused to the victim and society. Therefore, the punishment must fit the crime or be proportionate to the harm created by it. However, this principle is difficult to implement since there is no way to calculate precisely how much punishment is required to balance the harm (Blumstein, 1982). But retributive punishment is justified on moral rather than utilitarian or pragmatic grounds, in contrast to incapacitation, deterrence, or rehabilitation. Punishment is imposed for its own sake, because it is deserved, rather than for any particular result it is supposed to achieve (Griffiths and Verdun-Jones, 1994).

Finally, punishment can also serve to denounce the criminal behaviour as contrary to the basic values of society. As such, punishment reaffirms these fundamental, collective values, and may serve to educate people regarding what constitutes acceptable behaviour. However, there may be conflict over whether particular behaviours are contrary to societal values, or what those values are or should be.

In addition to these traditional goals of sentencing and punishment, restitution or reparation has in recent years sometimes been advocated as a purpose. Restitution attempts to restore circumstances to their original state or condition prior to the crime. It strives to reconcile victim and offender, and to provide some compensation to the victim for the harm experienced.

Three points should be made concerning these goals of sentencing. Firstly, they may conflict with one another such that a specific sentence may have to emphasize one over another. For example, incapacitation might require a lengthier term of imprisonment than can be justified on the basis of retribution. Secondly, the first three goals are utilitarian; they are justified by their presumed usefulness in attaining some future benefit. However, retribution and, to some extent, denunciation, are moral objectives, expressing certain values. Thirdly, these purposes reflect different assumptions about why people commit crimes, their individual responsibility for their behaviour, and what public policy can and should do in response.

In view of these conflicting purposes of sentencing and the fact that the Criminal Code gives a large amount of discretion in sentencing to the courts, variation in sentencing within and between courts is probable. However, there have been no national sentencing data published since 1978 to document the extent of such variation. But in 1993 the Canadian Centre for Justice Statistics released a special study of sentencing practices in six adult provincial/territorial courts during 1991–92. Comparisons were reported for five provinces and one territory, as well as for six large cities, in terms of incarceration rates and median sentence lengths for 65 offences. The results document variation in punishment for specific offences in different jurisdictions. For example, incarceration rates for sexual assault convictions ranged from 50 percent to over 80 percent; and the median sentence length imposed for offenders sentenced to prison ranged from one and a half months to nine months. Incarceration rates for break and enter convictions ranged from 64 percent to 78 percent and median sentence length from four to ten months. While it appears from these data that there is unwarranted disparity in the sentencing of similar cases, more detailed analysis with additional information is required to explain this variation. For example, there were no data available on recidivism, or other aggravating or mitigating circumstances. Furthermore, there is little agreement on what criteria should be used to establish if cases can be considered similar prior to determining if they have been treated differently by the courts (Griffiths and Verdun-Jones, 1994).

However, other research has examined the characteristics of cases and offenders in an attempt to determine if extra-legal factors, such as race, income, or gender have influenced sentencing decisions. The limited Canadian research on this topic has produced mixed conclusions. For example, Brantingham (1985) found that facts related to the case and the prior record of the defendant were the most important factors influencing sentencing decisions. However, Debicki (1985) reported evidence of differential sentencing on the basis of employment status. But additional research on sentencing disparity is required before more definite conclusions can be reached.

Several federal commissions and committees have evaluated sentencing practices in Canada and recommended fundamental changes. Major reports were issued by the Canadian Sentencing Commission (1987) and the House of Commons Standing Committee on Justice and Solicitor General (Daubney Report, 1988). The Sentencing Commission called for fundamental changes in the orientation and operation of the current system of sentencing, pointing in particular to unwarranted disparity in sentences and an overreliance on imprisonment. The Commission recommended that a statement of purpose and principles of sentencing be added to the Criminal Code. In addition, a number of specific recommendations were made, including a call for a set of presumptive sentencing guidelines, a new structure of maximum penalties, the elimination of full parole, an increase in the use of community sanctions, and the creation of a permanent sentencing commission. The intent of the Commission's recommendations is to make sentencing more equitable, understandable, predictable, and proportionate to the gravity of the offence and the responsibility of the offender.

One year later the House of Commons Standing Committee on Justice and Solicitor General, chaired by David Daubney, M.P. (1988), issued its report on sentencing, conditional release, and related aspects of corrections. Its recommendations were in many cases similar to those of the Sentencing Commission, calling, for example, for more limited use of imprisonment and greater use of community alternatives, proportionality in sentencing, and the establishment of a permanent sentencing commission. However, the Daubney Committee concluded that public protection should be the fundamental purpose of sentencing. Also, it did not agree that parole should be abolished, and argued that any sentencing guidelines should be merely advisory rather than presumptive. It concluded that the rehabilitation of offenders requires a more individualized approach to sentencing than allowed by presumptive guidelines. The Committee also suggested that reparation to the victim and reconciliation with the community should be a purpose of sentencing, requiring offenders to accept and demonstrate responsibility for their crime and its consequences.

The then Conservative government responded to these reports by publishing a consultation document entitled Directions for Reform: A Framework for Sentencing, Corrections and Conditional Release (Government of Canada, 1990). It subsequently introduced Bill C-90 to Parliament in June 1992, proposing to amend the Criminal Code by incorporating some of the recommendations in these reports. However, there was a change in government before this legislation was passed. A number of the recommendations of the Commission and the Committee were eventually enacted into legislation amending the Criminal Code by Bill C-41, and given Royal Assent in July 1995. It specified the fundamental principle that a sentence must be proportionate to the gravity of the offence and the degree of responsibility of the offender. This act also stated that the fundamental purpose of sentencing "is to contribute, along with crime prevention initiatives, to respect for the law and the maintenance of a just, peaceful and safe society by imposing just sanctions that have one or more of the following objectives ..." (Section 718). The Act then proceeds to identify the goals of denunciation, deterrence, incapacitation, rehabilitation, and reparation. However, it remains to be seen whether these legislative changes reduce unwarranted sentencing disparity and the use of imprisonment.

There has been a substantial growth of interest in the victims of crime since the 1970s. Attention has focussed both on their potential rights — to compensation, restitution, and participation in criminal justice decision-making — and to their needs and the provision of programs to assist them in dealing with the effects of crime. A Federal–Provincial Task Force on Justice for the Victims of Crime (Government of Canada, 1983) issued a report with many recommendations, including increasing the use of restitution and providing criminal injuries compensation, as well as allowing the participation of victims at the sentencing stage. The Criminal Code was amended in 1988 to allow criminal courts to accept victim impact statements, either in writing or in person. While there appears to be widespread support for such participation, relatively few victims choose to become involved. Furthermore, the limited evidence suggests that a victim impact statement has only a small influence on judges' choices of sentence (Erez and Tontodonato, 1990).

READINGS

The first reading in this section is a commentary on the rationale behind the proposals of the Canadian Sentencing Commission. After reviewing the different principles of punishment, Gabor argues that retribution or "just deserts" is the dominant principle in these proposals, although the Commission justifies this retributive system through its utilitarian features. Gabor is critical of the "just deserts" principle and discusses a number of problems with it. His fundamental objection, however, is that there is no rational, quantifiable way to determine the exact sentence proportional to a particular crime. While supportive of the Commission's goal of reducing disparities in sentencing, he is opposed to mandatory sentencing guidelines since, in his view, not all variation in sentencing is unjustified.

The paper on restorative justice by the John Howard Society of Alberta argues that the justice system has failed to accomplish its traditional goals and has become less concerned with the victims of crime. This has led to a search for an alternative system of justice. The paper contrasts the retributive and restorative models of justice, the latter emphasizing crime as a violation of one person by another, requiring the offender, victim, and community to participate in a process of restitution and reconciliation to accomplish the restoration of justice and harmony. This article also describes several types of programs aimed at restorative justice.

Mohr briefly describes the gender-neutrality of sentencing reform, reforms that ignore the role of gender in shaping judicial behaviour. In contrast, seeing sentencing as a gendered process suggests that the gender of both the sentencer and the one sentenced is crucial in understanding the roots of unwarranted sentencing disparity. Mohr then discusses the results of a consultation conducted with the Canadian Association of Elizabeth Fry Societies to respond to the report of the Canadian Sentencing Commission. She explores the limitations as applied to gender of the just deserts rationale proposed by the Commission. Mohr concludes that, although this rationale for sentencing may be the best solution to unwarranted disparity in a society where there is true equality, until that goal is attained we must continue to search for an approach that does more than treat unequals equally.

The reading by LaPrairie considers the role of sentencing in contributing to the overrepresentation of Aboriginal offenders in correctional institutions. She first considers both the meaning and causes of overrepresentation, with a detailed look at the evidence concerning differential processing of Aboriginals in the criminal justice system. She concludes that the data concerning the role of judicial discretion in causing the alleged statistical overrepresentation of Aboriginal people in correctional institutions remain contradictory and unclear. LaPrairie distinguishes between systemic discrimination— "treating unequals equally"—and preferential treatment— "treating unequals unequally"—as two different policy responses to the social and economic marginality and inequality of many Aboriginals. She calls for sentencing reform to correct the apparent disproportionate sentencing of Aboriginals to periods of incarceration in the absence of other sentencing options.

The final reading in this section examines the role of victims in the sentencing process. Despite increased attention to the rights and needs of victims in the criminal process, the contribution of victims to the sentencing process remains controversial. Renke reviews the objections to such participation, but argues that compelling interests are served by such participation without unduly impairing offenders' interests. He discusses the variety of interests served by victim participation in sentencing, current legal policy regarding such participation, and how the law might be further developed on this topic.

QUESTIONS FOR DISCUSSION

1. Describe some conflicts among the purposes of punishment. Can any of these conflicts be resolved?
2. Can "just deserts" be calculated? How would you develop a system of graduated penalties for a set of offences according to the principles of "just deserts?"
3. Can the principles of restorative justice be applied to all offences? Should they be? What obstacles are there to the implementation of restorative justice? Discuss what differences this approach might make in the operation of the criminal justice system.
4. Should socio-economic circumstances, gender, or ethnicity be taken into account in sentencing? What constitutes unjustified disparity in sentencing? Discuss these questions in terms of LaPrairie's distinction between systemic dis-

crimination and preferential treatment.

5. Should victims have the right to make sentencing recommendations? How should the rights of victims be balanced by the rights of the accused/convicted?

REFERENCES

Blumstein, Alfred. 1982. "Research on sentencing." *Justice System Journal* 7: 307–30.

Brantingham, Patricia L. 1985. "Sentencing disparity." *Journal of Quantitative Criminology* 1: 281–305.

Canadian Centre for Justice Statistics. 1993. *Sentencing in Adult Criminal Provincial Courts.* Ottawa: Statistics Canada.

Canadian Sentencing Commission. 1987. *Sentencing Reform.* Ottawa: Minister of Supply and Services Canada.

Daubney, David. 1988. *Taking Responsibility.* Ottawa: Queen's Printer.

Debicki, M. 1985. "Sentencing and socio-economic status." In D. Gibson and J.K. Baldwin (eds.), *Law in a Cynical Society.* Calgary: Carswell Legal Publications.

Doob, Anthony N. and J.P. Brodeur. 1989. "Rehabilitating the debate on rehabilitation." *Canadian Journal of Criminology* 31: 179–92.

Erez, Edna and Pamela Tontodonato. 1990. "The effect of victim participation in sentencing on sentence outcome." *Criminology* 28: 451–74.

Gendreau, Paul and D.A. Andrews. 1990. "Tertiary prevention." *Canadian Journal of Criminology* 32: 173–84.

Government of Canada. 1983. Report, Federal–Provincial Task Force on Justice for the Victims of Crime. Ottawa: Supply and Services Canada.

———— 1990. *Directions for Reform.* Ottawa: Minister of Supply and Services Canada.

Grasmick, Harold G. and Robert J. Bursick, Jr. 1990. "Conscience, significant others, and rational choice." *Law and Society Review* 24: 837–61.

Griffiths, Curt T. and Simon N. Verdun-Jones. 1994. *Canadian Criminal Justice.* Toronto: Harcourt Brace Canada.

Miller, J.L. and A.B. Anderson. 1986. "Updating the deterrence doctrine." *Journal of Criminal Law and Criminology* 77: 418–38.

Morris, Norval and Marc Miller. 1987. *Predictions of Dangerousness in the Criminal Law.* Washington, D.C.: Government Printing Office.

Paternoster, Raymond. 1987. "The deterrent effect of the perceived certainty and severity of punishment." *Justice Quarterly* 4: 173–217.

Sechrest, Lee B., Susan O. White, and Elizabeth Brown. 1979. *The Rehabilitation of Criminal Offenders.* Washington, D.C.: National Academy of Sciences.

Von Hirsch, Andrew. 1984. "Selective incapacitation: a critique." *National Institute of Justice Report* 183: 5–8.

Walker, Samuel. 1994. *Sense and Nonsense about Crime and Drugs.* Belmont, California: Wadsworth.

FIVE

Looking Back or Moving Forward: Retributivism and the Canadian Sentencing Commission's Proposals[1]

THOMAS GABOR

In this paper, I will comment on the rationale underlying the proposals of the Canadian Sentencing Commission, as well as some other matters. In commenting on the rationale, I recognize that some scholars, including those on the Commission, distinguish between justifications for legal sanctions in general and justifications relating to the allocation of sanctions. I believe that such a distinction is somewhat artificial as these rationales are not independent. According to the Commission's sentencing guidelines, "the sentence should be proportionate to the gravity of the offence and the degree of responsibility of the offender for the offence" (Canadian Sentencing Commission 1987: 154). Thus, in the Commission's view, the allocation of sanctions should be based, in part, on the blameworthiness of the offender. Such a system of sanctions rests on the notion that offenders are to blame for their conduct and hence deserve to be punished. Thus, proportionality in allocating sentences is clearly tied to a legal system founded on the principle of desert. Despite the interdependence of these rationales, where appropriate, I will indicate whether I am referring to the Commission's general rationale for penal interventions or to the sentencing guidelines they have proposed.

My remarks must also be qualified by the fact that, at this point, any discussion of the Commission's proposals is purely hypothetical. Even assuming that these proposals are accepted by Parliament and incorporated in the *Criminal Code*, the manner in which the sentencing guidelines would be implemented in practice is difficult to foresee. Judges would be empowered to override the presumptive sentences in any case provided they give reasons for so doing. It is unknown whether such departures from the guidelines would occur in very exceptional cases only or whether judges would use this authority as a means of reclaiming their pre-eminent role in sentencing.

The effects on prison populations of changing sentencing practices also cannot be foreseen, although the experience of some American states with presumptive sentencing systems indicates that overpopulation may be the result. While such an outcome is highly speculative, if it does materialize, sentencing practices may be affected as a consequence. Furthermore, where sanctions become more circumscribed, as

Source: Thomas Gabor, "Looking Back or Moving Forward: Retributivism and the Canadian Sentencing Commission's Proposals," *Canadian Journal of Criminology*, 32, 3 (1990): 537–46. Copyright by the Canadian Criminal Justice Association. Reproduced by permission of the *Canadian Journal of Criminology*.

they would be with the institution of the Commission's sentencing guidelines, it is possible that prosecutors may compensate for some of their lost leverage when exercising their discretion about the charges to proceed with and those to dismiss. As an example, a woman who has killed her abusive husband while being battered might ordinarily be charged with manslaughter. In their guideline prototypes, the Canadian Sentencing Commission (1987: 519) suggests that manslaughter should generally carry a prison term of between four and six years. The Crown counsel might believe that this is an exceptional case warranting a far lighter sentence. If judges in that jurisdiction tend to show a reluctance to deviate from the prescribed sentences, the Crown may not want to risk proceeding against the woman and may drop charges altogether.

All the aforementioned forms of adjustment, whether initiated by judges, Crown attorneys, or even the police, can undermine the objectives of sentencing reform pursued by the Commission. They all constitute what Singer (1979: 123) has referred to as "hydraulic discretion":

> A particularly depressing criticism against any proposal for sentencing reform is that it is irrelevant, since it tinkers with only one part of an entire system, blindly ignoring the effect that such reform will have on the other parts. Specifically, the argument is that to opt for affecting judicial sentencing rather than parole decisions is to opt for sentencing by plea bargain ... the presence of plea bargaining is especially anathema to the desert model of sentencing, since the model seeks consistent sentencing not only because equality is basically a desirable goal, but because all persons who commit the same offence should receive both the sanction and social stigma of having committed that offence. If plea bargaining allows some offenders to incur reduced stigma, the goal of equality of desert will have been seriously undermined.

Having made these preliminary remarks, let us examine the rationale for sentencing of the Canadian Sentencing Commission (1987: 151):

> It is recognized and declared that in a free and democratic society peace and security can only be enjoyed through the due application of the principles of fundamental justice. In furtherance of the overall purpose of the criminal law of maintaining a just, peaceful, and safe society, the fundamental purpose of sentencing is to preserve the authority of and promote respect for the law through the imposition of just sanctions.
>
> The proposed purpose is not to be confused with deterrence. It rests on the premise that the majority of the population need to be spared more from the outrage and demoralizing effect of witnessing impunity for criminal acts than to be deterred from indulging in them ... the fundamental purpose of sentencing is to impose just sanctions to impede behaviour denounced by the criminal law. Promoting respect for the values embodied in the law would then strengthen the conviction in citizens that they can be made to account for unlawful behaviour, and that the costs of such behaviour outweigh the anticipated benefits.

I believe that the eclecticism of the Commission's statement of purpose is laudable. Rather than recommending that sanctions be based on one rationale, an attempt is made to blend retributive (the Commission prefers the less pejorative term "justice") and utilitarian goals. The system of sentencing guidelines proposed is also a compromise between mandatory or fixed sentences on one hand and indeterminate or highly variable sentences on the other.

The utilitarian objectives of rehabilitation and selective incapacitation are discarded as primary objectives of legal sanctions. Only very few people consider offender reform as justifying legal interventions. Andrews, in this issue, argues that rehabilitation ought to be the cornerstone of corrections and that parole be maintained. Although I agree with his point that the Commission's treatment of rehabilitation was perfunctory, I disagree with his overly optimistic view of the potential of treatment and a "human science" perspective. The imposition of rehabilitative programs, whether psychotherapeutic, educational, vocational, or social, is practically unfeasible and ethically objectionable. The re-emergence of neo-classical thinking in criminology in the 1970s was a response, in part at least, to the sentencing disparities produced by a system with a greater emphasis on treatment.

The Commission laudably dismisses selective incapacitation as a goal of sentences. The nascent state of risk assessment and prediction technologies, as well as what I consider to be the inherent indeterminacy of human behaviour (Gabor 1986), would seem to preclude the ascendance of this approach to the level of a primary sentencing objective. Even if risk assessments could be shown to be fairly accurate, sentences based on them would create such disparity that the credibility of such a legal system would be rapidly undermined in the eyes of victims and the general public. This is so because many of those committing the most serious crimes (e.g., murder or manslaughter) might be assessed as unlikely to re-offend and, hence, may receive light sentences whereas chronic property offenders, for example, might receive stiff sentences. The Commission has recognized that vigilantism may arise in response to such perceived "injustices."

Also sensible, in my view, is the Commission's emphasis on the need to impose sanctions to promote respect for the law (Canadian Sentencing Commission 1978: 151). The failure to impose sanctions, according to the Commission, has a demoralizing effect on the public. Witnessing repeated violations of the law committed with impunity may weaken the inhibitions that keep members of society from breaking the law. While I believe that such a position constitutes more of a justification for sanctions in general than for the Commission's specific proposals, it is firmly grounded in empirical research.

The social learning theorist's concept of disinhibition can be useful here. Bandura (1977), in explaining the effects of media violence on the behaviour of the viewer, contends that witnessing others behave aggressively lowers the inhibitions of the viewer in relation to such behaviour. Seeing others commit transgressions without being held accountable may, therefore, legitimize such actions.

Studies of progressive vandalism show that property destruction is more likely to occur where property is already in a state of disrepair or has been defiled (Zimbardo 1973; Wilson and Kelling 1983; Samdahl and Christensen 1985). Wilson and Kelling (1983: 31) have shown, for example, that buildings in which windows are broken and left unrepaired are more likely to have other windows broken. Signs of incivility, disorder, and decay have a demoralizing effect on people and lead to the release of otherwise inhibited aggressive behaviour. Thus, while one may question the dissuasive effect of legal sanctions on those already contemplating crimes, it may be more difficult to argue the repeated assaults upon society's legal norms, with the absence of enforcement, cannot unleash a widespread pursuit of self-interest with all its socially harmful ramifications. It can be argued, however, that promoting conformity can be done more effectively by rewarding virtue than by punishing the violation of norms (Walker 1980: 35). Even if this argument were correct, establishing a system of such reinforcements would be a bureaucratic nightmare.

The Commission's sentencing guidelines are likely to be perceived as less capricious by the public than current practices as they involve more realistic sentences. The abolition of parole, while controversial and having some liabilities, ensures that the length of a prison sentence can be reduced by only 25 percent for good behaviour. The current situation, in which an inmate can receive a full parole after one-third of his sentence is served and day parole after only one-sixth is served, creates a sham of the entire sentencing process, seriously undermining the authority of the courts. Since members of the public seem to overestimate the proportion of inmates being paroled (Hanna and Harman 1986) and the damage they do (Roberts and Doob 1989), their loss of confidence in the judicial system comes as little surprise. One wonders whether offenders, too, lose respect for a system in which one part imposes one penalty only to see another part, the Parole Board, roll back a substantial part of it. This "schizoid" characteristic of the justice system lends itself to disrepute, as decisions are neither irrevocable nor comprehensible.

Some have argued that abolishing parole will increase the prison sentences actually served (Dozois, Fréchette, Lemire, Normandeau and Carrière 1989) — such an outcome would not necessarily occur. For one thing, the Commission's emphasis on exercising restraint in sentencing is supported by its proposals to reduce the maximum penalties for a number of offences. Secondly, it would be naive to believe that judges today are unaware, when passing sentence, of the possibility that the offender will be paroled. It is well known that they tend to compensate for early release by passing harsher sentences. When an offender fails to gain early release, he may actually serve more time than under the system proposed by the Commission.

SOME DIFFICULTIES WITH THE PROPOSALS

The reader may infer, at this juncture, that my intention is not to bury the Commission but to praise it. The Commission's proposals have been carefully formulated and their limitations acknowledged. There is an attempt to take into account different principles of punishment, as well as recent empirical research. It would be erroneous to either condemn or embrace, in their totality, the multitudinous proposals that have been advanced. Having mentioned some of the areas in which I believe the proposals are well-founded, I wish now to tackle matters that cause me some concern. Foremost among these is the role of the desert principle and the manner in which it would be applied.

THE PROPOSALS: RETRIBUTIVE OR UTILITARIAN?

Although I have commended the Commission for its attempt to blend retributive and utilitarian goals, there are many ways to do this and the Commission tries to achieve this objective in a curious way. Its sentencing scheme is purely retributive, as it is based on the offender's past conduct — the offence under consideration — as well as his/her degree of culpability. So as not to be perceived as endorsing the intrinsic merits of punishment or pure retribution, however, the Commission justifies this retributive system of sanctions by its utilitarian features. Thus, we are told that "just" sentences will promote respect and, hence, compliance with the law. The Commission clearly wants to have its cake and eat it too. Although, as I have mentioned, such a utilitarian goal has an empirical foundation, the fact remains that the sentencing system being proposed is a retributive one and I shall critique it on that basis. Any retributive system of sanctions will undoubtedly carry some utilitarian benefits through deterrence, incapacitation, and the reinforcement of social norms; however, they are incidental by-products of such a system. On the basis of these by-products, the Commission casts its system as largely utilitarian. Presumably, they do not wish to be branded retributive. In fact, they cite Von Hirsch when making the point that "the pursuit of penal justice for its own sake appears purposeless" (Canadian Sentencing Commission 1987: 131). Since it is hard to conceive of any retributive system that is without some utilitarian benefits, do they mean to say that any ancillary crime preventive effects qualify the system as other than strictly retributive? To be considered as other than strictly retributive, shouldn't the proposed guidelines have to expressly incorporate utilitarian considerations? Rhetoric underscoring the utilitarian benefits of justice-oriented sentences is not sufficient. The model the Commission has advanced tries to make sentences proportional to the harm done and the perceived responsibility of the offender.

Even the list of aggravating and mitigating factors that is to serve as the basis for departures from the guidelines contains no references to the risk the offender poses to the community nor any other preventive considerations. In fact, some of the actors clash directly with preventive objectives. The Commission considers youth a mitigating factor, whereas most predictive studies show that a young person, other things being equal, poses a greater threat to the community than an older one (Gabor 1986). The sentencing guidelines do not, in any way, explicitly consider preventive goals.

Despite the retributive sentencing model it proposes, the Commission repeatedly asserts that utilitarian goals are worth pursuing. At several junctures, the point is made that legal sanctions have at least some deterrent effect. While this statement is undoubtedly true, it provides no justification for the particular system of sentencing proposed by the Commission.

THE FOCUS ON THE EXTERNAL EFFECTS OF SENTENCING

As for the assertion that "the fundamental purpose of sentencing is to impose just sanctions to impede behaviour denounced by the criminal law" (Canadian Sentencing Commission, 1987: 151), the Commission turns on its head the idea that "justice must not only be done but must be seen to be done." Despite the cursory attention paid to the denunciative role of sentences, the Commission is suggesting that the paramount objective in sentencing lies in its effect on society in general. The communication of society's vigilance in relation to lawbreaking seems to have a considerable denunciative component to it.

The perception by the public that justice is done is accorded primary importance by the Commission. The effects of the sentence on the offender receive less attention. It might be argued that distributive justice entails an individualization of sentencing—this point will be discussed more fully below. The reform and deterrence of the offender, too, has been given short shrift. The role given to the effects of sentencing on the *external* audience rather than on those implicated in a criminal case is curious in light of the Commission's position that "there is a wide discrepancy between the public's knowledge of criminal sanctions and their actual features" (Canadian Sentencing Commission, 1987: 142). If the public's perception of actual sentences is so distorted, is it justified to place such a pre-eminent emphasis on the impact of sentencing on the public? Does the Commission feel that its reforms would suddenly enlighten the public about the sentencing process? The Commission cannot regulate the media's coverage of criminal justice issues. Nor can much be done about the tendency of the public to develop stereotypic images of criminals and over-simplified views of sanctions.

The excessive focus on the external effects of the system leaves the offender out in the cold. Although Commissioners stress that their sentencing model does not preclude rehabilitative efforts within the correctional system (Doob and Brodeur 1989), both the sentencing guidelines and the formal Declaration of Purpose and Principles of Sentencing (Canadian Sentencing Commission 1987: 153) make no specific reference to the welfare of offenders. The point is well taken that the philosophy of sentencing to which the Commission subscribes can foster a brutal and vindictive system (Grygier 1988). Sentences that pinpoint blame for past deeds, while ignoring compassion in the present and both offender risk and reform in the future, signal to correctional personnel that their efforts are futile. I am not arguing for a treatment or risk-based system, merely that the Commission's proposals cannot easily accommodate such considerations.

THE FALLACY OF "JUST DESERTS"

A sentencing system based on desert might not be so objectionable were commensurate or proportional sentences as readily quantifiable as justice-oriented sentencing guidelines suggest. These highly systematized schemes promote the illusion that there is a fairly precise penalty fitting each type of offence. In this context, Monahan (1984: 12) has asserted that while "the prediction of recidivism is a Herculean task, the assessment of culpability is a divine one." Indeed, there are many shortcomings of sentencing based on the desert principle.

For one thing, most legal systems, when allocating blame do consider the offender's state of mind (*mens rea*), so, one might ask, why not consider other characteristics of the offender, such as a disadvantaged background, personal stresses prior to the offence, and his motives for the offence (Singer 1979: 21). The proposed presumptive sentences may be able to accommodate such considerations but only within the narrow range allowed by the guidelines. The argument for the individualization of sentences can be made on retributive rather than merely utilitarian grounds as very unequal offenders may be sentenced equally due to similarities in the offence itself. In his dessenting opinion regarding the proposed presumptive guidelines, Commissioner Pateras indicated that "the actual restraint imposed by presumptive guidelines is the restriction of a sentencing judge's discretion to impose the sentence (type, range, etc.) which he or she believes is the just and appropriate one for that offence and that offender" (Canadian Sentencing Commission 1987: 339).

Another problem in establishing a sentencing system based on desert is whether the sentence should reflect the offender's intent or merely the outcome of an offence.

Whether the victim of an assault dies, suffers serious injuries, or escapes injury altogether is partly beyond the offender's control. The physical condition and attributes of the victim, the intervention of third parties, the response of emergency medical services, and many other extraneous factors can affect the outcome of an offence. A fortuitous element can also enter into property crimes such as, for example, the crime of theft. The proposed sentences are different for theft over and under $1000 although chance may determine the amount of money an offender finds in, say, a wallet he has stolen.

Any rating of offences on the basis of seriousness must take into account the psychological harm to the victim (Singer 1979). In sexual assaults and robberies, for example, the emotional effects tend to be more acute and enduring than the physical injuries incurred. The sentencing guidelines are silent about this factor, which is also relevant to some property crimes (e.g., break and enter). Here again, the difficulties in measuring harm and in using it as a criterion in sentencing are evident.

What of the so-called victimless crimes, such as drug trafficking and the sale of pornography? If there is no definable harm, should these be offences at all if desert is based on harm? If so, how do we measure the amorphous injuries inflicted on society by these offences?

Another issue that proponents of sentencing on the basis of desert must wrestle with is that of forseeable harms (Singer 1979: 26–27). Suppose A rapes B who then commits suicide as a result of the disgrace she feels; or A robs B who shoots at A, but instead kills C, a bystander. Should offenders be responsible for these additional consequences of their crimes? Should offenders be held accountable for still other effects on third parties such as the disintegration of a family after a mother is sexually assaulted or after the breadwinner has been disabled following an assault or a robbery?

The desert philosophy also assumes that what appears to be the same punishment will be objectively the same and will be perceived in the same way. Suppose two robbers receive five-year prison terms. The first, a gang leader, has many contacts in the institution and, upon entering, is greeted as though the event was some form of homecoming. The other robber, serving his first penitentiary sentence, is carefully sized up when he enters the prison. The objective experiences of these two individuals in prison will be very different, as the neophyte is far more likely to be attacked and intimidated by both fellow prisoners and guards. Even if one could hold these objective experiences constant, the impact of incarceration would differ from one person to the next depending on such things as one's social status, one's habituation to institutional life, marital status, the proximity of one's family to the institution, and many other factors. The sentencing guidelines offered by the Canadian Sentencing Commission camouflage the fact that neither legislators nor the courts have any control over the application of sanctions and what these sanctions mean to different offenders.

Yet the Commission speaks of fundamental justice. With all the intangibles involved in both crime and punishment, the most "equitable" and proportional system of sanctions constitutes an extremely crude representation of what is "deserved." My greatest objection to the type of guidelines formulated by the Commission is the pretense that one can somehow quantify what is a "just" sentence in a given type of case. Or, is the Commission prepared to reverse Oliver Wendell Holmes's famous aphorism by asserting that the perception of justice is more important than that justice is actually done?

The fact is there is no rational method of determining the exact sentence that is proportional to a particular crime. Decisions based on desert will be more subjective than those based on utilitarian aims as they cannot be validated by agreed upon criteria. One can at least attempt to ascertain whether sentences based on some utilitarian consideration (e.g., deterrence) are achieving their objectives.

HYDRAULIC DISCRETION

Furthermore, a system of sentencing guidelines can be undermined by adjustments at earlier phases of the criminal justice system. The police and the Crown can decide not to lay charges or to drop charges where they feel the prospective sentence would be too harsh. The Crown would have more leverage in extracting plea bargains as this would be the final point at which considerable discretion would remain. Alschuler (1978: 577) writes:

> Eliminating or restricting the discretionary powers of parole boards and trial judges is likely to increase the powers of prosecutors, and these powers are likely to be exercised without effective limits through the practice of plea bargaining. The substitution of fixed or presumptive sentences for the discretion of judges and parole boards tends to concentrate sentencing power in the hands of officials who are likely to allow their decisions to be governed by factors irrelevant to the proper goals of sentencing — officials moreover, who typically lack the information, objectivity, and experience of trial judges.

Even members of the public, if they were as informed about the sentencing guidelines as the Commission hopes they would be, may be reluctant to report offences carrying a presumption of a prison sentence where they may for some reason wish to protect the offender. Aggravated assault, for example, may be perpetrated by a spouse. The victim, under the current system, may report the offence and testify against her husband in order to "shock" him. If she is aware that a serious assault can result in a certain and fairly lengthy prison term, she may be more reluctant to come forward.

THE SELECTIVE USE OF PUNISHMENT

Case attrition in the criminal justice system also seriously undermines the desert principle. According to the Commission's own figures, at best, only three percent of all offenders committing a criminal offence during any given year end up before a sentencing court in that same year (Canadian Sentencing Commission 1987: 119). Chance, skill in crime, economic clout, and other factors having little to do with justice play a major role in whether one is punished for one's transgressions. Such a state of affairs, which is largely beyond the control of the justice system, renders more credible the common refrain of convicted offenders that their plight is due to simple bad luck or harassment by the authorities.

A related issue concerns the type of people who come before the courts and populate our prisons. Since they derive disproportionately from the lowest economic strata of society, from the ranks of aboriginal Canadians, and "street" criminals, the argument can easily be made that the filtering of criminal cases through the criminal justice system is not based exclusively on objective behaviour. That the rich and the powerful, those polluting the environment, marketing dangerous products, or abusing the public's trust are subject to preferential treatment is a truism requiring little documentation here. Until these different standards exist for members of different social groups and for different types of offenders, any system based on the desert principle will have limited credibility.

How many of the Mulroney cabinet officials violating conflict of interest guidelines are serving time in our prisons? Until such large-scale injustices are rectified, measures designed to promote respect for the criminal law, such as those proposed by the Sentencing Commission, will have limited value. Nowhere in its 600 page report does the Commission address the fundamental inequities in our justice system. Its goal, it would appear, is to promote equity in sentencing among the highly selective group of Canadians who appear before a court, rather than among all citizens of this country. An illustration of this point is the rejection of the Swedish model of fines, whereby the amount of fines levied are proportional to the offender's income. Developing sanctions that have equal impact on all Canadians, regardless of their means, is long overdue.

DANGEROUSNESS OF OFFENDERS IS NOT CONSIDERED

Through the retributive system it proposes, the Commission is remarkably silent about employing risk as a criterion in sentencing. Although, as mentioned, the danger posed to the community by the offender should not be the *primary* concern of sentencing, nor need it be completely ignored. While I agree that the prediction of future criminality is precarious, blanket dismissals of prediction grossly oversimplify the subject.

For one thing, the accuracy of prediction is contingent on the outcome one is trying to predict: crime or recidivism in general, violent crime, the rate of offending, or the timing or seriousness of future criminal behaviour. In general, the more precise or rare the outcome that is being predicted, the less accurate the prediction will be (Gabor 1986). Predictions can be made through clinical assessments of individuals, the application of statistical probabilities to groups, or through a combination of these two methods. An amalgamation of the two will tend to produce the best results. Also bearing on the prediction is the "base rate" issue. Where one is trying to predict unlikely events such as particularly heinous crimes, overpredictions of dangerousness may abound. On the other hand, predicting simply that all penitentiary inmates will be re-arrested at some point for some offence may be accurate in three-quarters or more of the cases. Applying predictions to an undifferentiated group will not yield predictions as accurate as those based on a more homogeneous subsample of offenders (Gabor 1986). Recidivism approaches certainty for those with an early onset of criminality and a long history of antisocial and criminal behaviour (Wolfgang, Figlio and Sellin 1972; Hamparian, Shuster, Dinitz and Conrad 1978).

The chronic offender, who may single-handedly be a significant menace to a community, would fall through the cracks of the system proposed by the Sentencing Commission. Both the aggravating conditions that could lead to a departure from the guidelines and the exceptional sentences proposed by the Commission are based primarily on the characteristics of the most recent offence rather than on the characteristics and record of the offender. While it is true that the Commission's guidelines and list of aggravating factors include the presence of a criminal record, this factor would be taken into account differently in retributive as opposed to utilitarian sentencing. As an example, a retributionist would consider the length of time elapsing between a previous conviction and the most recent offence as a potential aggravating factor. Von Hirsch (1976: 87) writes that "The greater the time between the preceding offense and the current one, the harder it becomes to argue that the prior offense bears on the ascription of culpability for the current one." The utilitarian, on the other hand, would likely consider short intervals between offences as meriting a longer sentence due to the offender's high rate of criminal activity. Protection of the community from hardcore offenders who, in some cases, may be responsible for hundreds of crimes a year, again takes a back seat to retribution.

CONCLUSION

The establishment of sentencing guidelines is useful in structuring sentencing decisions. The issue is whether such guidelines should merely guide judicial decisions or be imposed on judges as in the case in the Commission's recommendations, where judges must state the reasons for departures from them. A principal goal of the Commission is to deal with sentencing disparity. Disparity can be defined in two ways. First, it can mean that people convicted of similar offences receive widely varying sentences. A second and tighter definition views disparities as variations in sentences for cases that are very similar, resulting from the different principles subscribed to by judges or personal prejudices. To consider all variation in sentencing as unjustified misses the idiosyncratic features of each criminal case and fails to take into account offender-related factors. Equity can mean similarity in the sentencing criteria used from case to case rather than identical sentences.

The Commission is of the view that there is considerable "unwarranted variation" in sentencing in this country (Canadian Sentencing Commission 1987: 77). Rather than establish guidelines that could be imposed optionally by the courts, their guidelines would limit the discretion of the sentencing judge. The Commission therefore has little faith in the fairness of Canadian judges even if sentencing guidelines were made available to them. The guidelines must therefore be more coercive than a mere nudge or prompt. The irony is that while placing such little faith in the judiciary, the Commission consolidates judicial authority over sentencing by abolishing parole and therefore reducing correctional input. Judicial discretion would presumably be reduced in absolute terms through the adoption of the sentencing guidelines but, in relative terms, would be expanded as judges would have more say in the *formal* discretion that would remain.

The desire of the Sentencing Commission to reduce disparities and enhance fairness in sentencing is to be commended. My fear is that the implementation of the Commission's proposals would engender an inertia in the criminal justice system, signalling to both convicted persons and criminal justice personnel that their efforts are fruitless. The implementation of these proposals would have a symbolic effect, marking the end of efforts to reform and show compassion towards offenders, many of whom have already been victimized by abuse, neglect, and economic privations. A system focusing exclusively on blame for past deeds would be morally and operationally bankrupt, fostering negativity and vindictiveness. Just as many current forms of psychotherapy advise clients not to dwell on the past but rather to face present realities, sentences that look only backwards will be unable to adapt to the ever-changing realities of a dynamic society.

NOTE

1. I am grateful to my colleague, Julian Roberts, for his comments and for engaging me in some animated discussions on various points made in this paper.

REFERENCES

Alschuler, David 1978 Sentencing reform and prosecutorial power: A Critique of recent proposals for "fixed" and "presumptive" sentencing. *University of Pennsylvania Law Review* 126: 550–577.

Bandura, Albert 1977 Mechanisms of aggression. In Hans Toch (ed.), *Psychology of Crime and Criminal Justice*. New York: Holt, Rinehart and Winston.

Canadian Sentencing Commission 1987 *Sentencing Reform: A Canadian Approach*. Ottawa: Supply and Services.

Doob, Anthony N. and Jean-Paul Brodeur 1989 Rehabilitating the debate on rehabilitation. *Canadian Journal of Criminology* 31: 179–192.

Dozois, Jean, Marcel Fréchette, Guy Lemire, André Normandeau and Pierre Carrière 1989 La détermination de la peine au Canada: bilan critique de la Commission Archambault. *Canadian Journal of Criminology* 31: 63–80.

Gabor, Thomas 1986 *The Prediction of Criminal Behaviour: Statistical Approaches*. Toronto: University of Toronto Press.

Grygier, Tadeusz 1988 A Canadian approach or an American band-wagon? *Canadian Journal of Criminology* 30: 165–172.

Hamparian, Donna, Richard Schuster, Simon Dinitz and John Conrad 1978 *The Violent Few*. Lexington, MA: Lexington Books.

Hann, Robert G. and William G. Harman 1986 *Full Parole Release: An Historical Descriptive Study*. Ottawa: Solicitor General Canada.

Monahan, John 1984 The prediction of violent behavior: Toward a second generation of theory and policy. *American Journal of Psychiatry* 141: 10–15.

Roberts, Julian V. and Anthony N. Doob 1989 Sentencing and public opinion: Taking false shadow for true substances. *Osgoode Hall Law Journal* 27: 491–515.

Samdahl, D. and H. Christiansen 1985 Environmental cues and vandalism. *Environment and Behavior* 14: 446.

Singer, Richard G. 1979 *Just Deserts: Sentencing Based on Equality and Desert*. Cambridge, MA: Ballinger.

Von Hirsch, Andrew 1976 *Doing Justice*. New York: Hill and Wang.

Walker, Nigel 1980 *Punishment, Danger and Stigma: The Morality of Criminal Justice*. Totowa, NJ: Barnes and Noble.

Wilson, James Q. and George Kelling 1983 Broken windows. *The Atlantic Monthly*.

Wolfang, Marvin E., Robert F. Figlio, and Thornsten Sellin 1972 *Delinquency in a Birth Cohort*. Chicago: University of Chicago Press.

Zimbardo, Philip 1973 A field experiment in auto shaping. In Colin Ward (ed.), *Vandalism*. London: Architectural Press.

SIX

Briefing Paper on Restorative Justice

JOHN HOWARD SOCIETY OF ALBERTA

INTRODUCTION

Over the last two decades, criminal justice authors have been gradually shifting their attention toward a new concept: restorative justice. Restorative justice offers an alternative to the punishment oriented justice system of today. Umbreit and Coates (1995, p. 47) explain that restorative justice differs from the current justice system by emphasizing that "crime is a violation of one person by another, rather than a violation against the state." Proponents of restorative justice argue that through the use of various techniques, the victim, the offender, and the community can be restored to their pre-crime status (Austin & Krisberg, 1982). They favour a return to offender/victim-centred conflict resolution using community mediation and resulting in some form of mutually acceptable reparation.

Restorative justice arose mainly from the growth of restitution through the 1970s but is also based in a historical perspective. Several factors, including a dissatisfaction with the present system and a lack of concern for crime victims, have caused us to look to alternative models of justice. As the restorative model grows in popularity, community mediation centres and restitution programs are growing in number across North America.

THE NEED FOR CHANGE

There are two major problems fuelling the growth of the restorative model. The first of these is the inability of our justice system to reduce crime rates. Our current practices and philosophies have done little to relieve overwhelming fear of crime. A second motivation is that the legal process has become less and less concerned with the victim. Focus is no longer on the person who is affected the most by an offender's wrongdoing; instead focus is placed on the state. Victim satisfaction with the overall outcome has been ignored. The restorative model proposes to resolve these issues using techniques that involve the victim and contribute to offender rehabilitation and reintegration.

THE FAILURE OF THE JUSTICE SYSTEM

Section 718 of the Criminal Code deals with the purpose and principles of sentencing. The section is intended to provide direction to the courts in making sentencing decisions. The following is the text of the purpose of sentencing:

Source: John Howard Society of Alberta, Briefing Paper on Restorative Justice (1993). Used by permission of the John Howard Society of Alberta.

718. The fundamental purpose of sentencing is to contribute, along with crime prevention initiatives, to respect for the law and the maintenance of a just, peaceful and safe society by imposing just sanctions that have one or more of the following objectives:

(a) to denounce unlawful conduct;
(b) to deter the offender and other persons from committing offence;
(c) to separate offenders from society, where necessary;
(d) to assist in rehabilitating offenders;
(e) to provide reparations for harm done to victims or to the community; and
(f) to promote a sense of responsibility in offenders, and acknowledgment of the harm done to victims and to the community.

The fundamental principle of sentencing is as follows:

718.1 A sentence must be proportionate to the gravity of the offence and the degree of responsibility of the offender.

Other sentencing principles include the following:

718.2 A court that imposes a sentence shall also take into consideration the following principles:

(a) a sentence should be increased or reduced to account for any relevant aggravating or mitigating circumstances relating to the offence or the offender, and, without limiting the generality of the foregoing,
    (i) evidence that the offence was motivated by bias, prejudice or hate based on the race, nationality, colour, religion, sex, age, mental or physical disability or sexual orientation of the victim, or
    (ii) evidence that the offender, in committing the offence, abused a position of trust or authority in relation to the victim
    shall be deemed to be aggravating circumstances;
(b) a sentence should be similar to sentences imposed on similar offenders for similar offence committed in similar circumstances;
(c) where consecutive sentences are imposed, the combined sentence should not be unduly long or harsh;
(d) an offender should not be deprived of liberty, if less restrictive sanctions may be appropriate in the circumstances; and
(e) all available sanctions other than imprisonment that are reasonable in the circumstances should be considered for all offenders, with particular attention to the circumstances of aboriginal offenders.

Notably absent from this list is retribution, a goal that the government has always held central to the process (The Canadian Sentencing Commission, 1987). An examination of our success at accomplishing these goals is disconcerting.

RETRIBUTION
Bazemore and Umbreit suggest that while "retributive justice" is focussed on determining guilt and delivering appropriate punishment ("just deserts") through an

adversarial process, restorative justice is concerned with the broader relationship between offender, victim, and the community (Bazemore & Umbreit, 1995, p. 302). A justice system based on retribution is troublesome for both philosophical and practical reasons.

Cragg (1992) argues that religions often denounce the practice of punishment. In one example, the New Testament (John 8: 1–11) contends that a system of justice based on punishment is not possible since only people free from sin should impose punishment. Since nobody can ever fully live up to moral law, a sinless imposer of punishment does not exist.

In addition, most forms of punishment are actually acts that have been determined to be unlawful (i.e., confinement and corporal punishment). To impose harm in response to harms done is revenge, not resolution.

Beyond the philosophical arguments, there are several practical concerns with retribution. First, retribution is difficult to distinguish from vengeance (which suggests excessiveness). Even without the element of emotionality and revenge, the use of punishment is both morally impractical and practically immoral, given the existence of a feasible alternative. Furthermore, in order to justify imposing punishment, one must be absolutely certain of guilt and intent. Imposing pain upon someone who is innocent or unaware is impractical and illogical. Beyond this concern, the development of appropriate sanctions has been next to impossible. Codes that outline punishments for offences rarely take into consideration the vast differences that exist between cases.

DETERRENCE

A significant problem with justice based on punishment is that it tries to invoke a fear of the law in the general public. As opposed to retribution, deterrence is the forward-looking use of punishment. We try to discourage people from committing crime by making them aware of punishments and their severity. Whether discussing specific deterrence or general deterrence, the evidence overwhelmingly suggests that this practice is pointless. Specific deterrence "occurs when a convicted offender is deterred from committing further offence as a consequence of his or her personal experience of punishment" (Griffiths & Verdun-Jones, 1994, p. 407). The system imposes sanctions in the hope of making offenders fearful of re-exposure to those sanctions. General deterrence, on the other hand, "is acheived when the threat of legal sanction prevents the commission of potential crimes by people other than punished offenders" (Griffiths & Verdun-Jones, 1994, p. 407).

There are several arguments against adopting deterrence as a goal of the legal process. First, legal sanctions will not have a general deterrent impact unless they are widely known. Few people are aware of present day sanctions. In addition, deterrence cannot affect every person the same; some people have more to lose than others. A recent study clearly showed that individuals who are incapacitated actually have a higher risk of reoffending than those who are not (Bridges & Stone, 1986). Based on these arguments, the authors caution against the adoption of deterrence as a goal of justice administration (Griffiths & Verdun-Jones, 1994).

DENUNCIATION

The denunciation of behaviours is closely tied to the concept of retribution. Punishment serves as a statement of society's conviction against certain actions. The severity of penalties, therefore, needs to reflect the degree to which society condemns that specific act. The law exists as a statement of society's values. With the growth of the "get tough" mentality toward criminal justice reform, lengthier sentences are increasingly being called for. Under the restorative model, the amount of reparation would also tend to represent a scale of denunciation. As opposed to denouncing the offenders, however, it proposes to denounce the act. The more damaging a behaviour, the greater the redress will be.

REHABILITATION

The 1950s witnessed the growth of an ideology based on "treating" the offender. Criminal behaviour was seen as some form of sickness. Therefore, the reasonable solution was to subject an offender to treatment that generally took the form of psychological therapy, education, and training. Many programs have been aimed at rehabilitating the offender over the last 45 years.

In 1974, Robert Martinson coined the phrase "nothing works." He based this conclusion on the weight of evidence that showed that rehabilitation programs have not been successful. Since that time, there has been renewed faith in rehabilitation. In more recent years, numerous authors have revived the notion that correctional rehabilitation can be effective given certain conditions. Appropriate types of intervention involve the use of behavioural and social learning principles of interpersonal influence, skill enhancement, and cognitive change. The Correctional Service of Canada (CSC) continues to pursue traditional means of rehabilitation (i.e., nondirective counselling), which have proven ineffective.

INCAPACITATION

The only goal that the present Canadian criminal justice system can truly accomplish is incapacitation. Imprisonment removes the offender from the community and prevents further offending during the period of incarceration. This is, however, a "band-aid" solution. Ignoring problems does not solve them.

REPARATION

The goal of redressing harm highlights the shift to a restorative model. The idea of making reparations for harm done is central to restoring pre-crime states. The implementation of this goal has been difficult and at present is limited to moderate restitution, community service orders, and compensation. But the inclusion of such a goal will certainly pave the way for future reforms based on restorative concepts.

COSTS

The cost of incarcerating and treating offenders is enormous. In 1994/95, the average annual cost for keeping an inmate in a federal penitentiary was $44,344. That same year, over $1.9 billion was spent on adult correctional services (Canadian Centre for Justice Statistics, 1996, p. 1). With an overwhelming pricetag, the government and the public need a cost-effective alternative.

Success is usually assessed by the ability of the system to fulfil the above-mentioned functions. Our system has consistently failed to make identifiable improvements toward meeting these goals, and, consequently, there is growing disillusionment among the general public. Given the strength of the arguments and the evidence that illustrates the extent to which our present system has failed to viably prevent crime, practitioners have been forced to examine other alternatives.

IGNORING THE VICTIM

In 1977, Nils Christie published an article entitled *Conflicts as Property*. This article was one of the first attempts to question the operation of the criminal justice system. Christie identifies two recurring features of most western legal systems. First, the parties who are in conflict are represented by attorneys. Second, the victim, who is to be represented by the state, "is so thoroughly represented that she or he for most of the proceedings is pushed completely out of the arena" (Christie, 1982, p. 299). Christie expresses the opinion that disputes need to be returned to the main parties, namely the victim and the offender.

The crime victim is almost always allocated a peripheral position within the framework of the legal process. While it would be impossible to operate without the cooperation of the victim, once they are no longer useful, the process tends to neglect and ignore them. Several studies have shown that the system can be a weary and tedious experience for the victim (Ash, 1972; Chelimsky, 1981; Knudten, Meade, Knudten, & Doerner, 1976; Rosenbaum, 1977).

Some authors have described the criminal justice process as a dual victimization (Christie, 1982; Symonds, 1980); there is the actual crime, which can include monetary loss, physical injury, and psychological stress, and there is neglect and traumatization brought on by the legal process. Victims often suffer through unfamiliar situations, loss of time, humiliating testimony, and lack of input. The victim is rarely given the opportunity to express opinions, to confront the offender, or to address the issue of reparations (Griffiths & Verdun-Jones, 1994). Restorative justice provides an alternative that not only allows victims to voice opinions, but gives them the opportunity to resolve issues.

WHAT IS RESTORATIVE JUSTICE?

Restorative justice differs completely from the retributive model that is the basis for Canada's criminal justice system. The following chart summarizes many of the differences between the two models.

	Retributive	Restorative
Definition of a Crime	the breaking of rules (laws)	harm done to a person
Aims	to punish offenders for their crimes	to restore victim, offender, and community to their pre-crime status
Offender's Role	to be determined guilty or innocent and to be punished	to make amends to victim and community; to "right the wrong"
Offender's Rights	due process rights	right to express concerns and to negotiate reparation
Nature of Victim	the state	the individual

	Retributive (con't)	Restorative (con't)
Victim's Role	periphery; to report offence and to testify in court when required	central; to reconcile with offender and to negotiate reparation
Victim's Rights	none	to confront offender and to receive restitution
Community Role	none	to mediate reconciliation
Community Rights	to be protected from crime	to be involved in restoration
Court's Role	to determine guilt and to impose a sentence	to help mediation process
Prosecutor's Role	to represent state and to provide evidence	administrative
Standard of Proof	beyond a reasonable doubt	balance of probabilities
Administrative Process	adversarial	negotiation/mediation
Focus	past; determination of guilt and administration of pain	future; search for solutions and promotion of reconciliation
Concept of Guilt	guilt is absolute and permanent	guilt removable through acceptance of responsibility and reparation
Concept of Debt	paid by being punished and owed to the state	paid to victim by making reparations
Concept of Justice	"right-rules," tested by process and intent	"right-relationships," tested by the outcomes
Outcomes	punishment	reparation and reconciliation (based on Zehr, 1990)

Three key principles form the foundation of the restorative justice paradigm:

1. Crime results in injuries to victims, communities, and offenders; therefore, the criminal justice process must repair those injuries;
2. Not only government, but victims, offenders, and communities should be actively involved in the criminal justice process at the earliest point and to the maximum extent possible;
3. In promoting justice, the government is responsible for preserving order, and the community is responsible for establishing peace. (Van Ness, 1990, p. 9)

Restorative justice emphasizes that crime is a violation of one person by another, rather than merely a crime against the state (Umbreit, 1990; Morris, 1992; Bazemore & Umbreit, 1995). The restorative model of justice involves the offender, the victim, and the community in negotiation and dialogue aimed at restitution, reconciliation, and restoration of harmony. Offenders take an active part in the restorative process, with remorse, repentence, and forgiveness being important factors. The stigma arising from an offence may be removed through conforming behaviour on the part of the offender. The restorative model also looks at the social, economic, and moral context of the criminal behaviour, while still holding the offender responsible for his or her actions. Restorative justice places victims and offenders together in problem-solving roles and impresses upon offenders the actual human impact of their behaviour (Umbreit, 1991).

Restorative justice is the concept of restoring a community and its specific members back to their lifestyles prior to the commission of an offence. Although reparations cannot entirely compensate for the physical and emotional costs of crime, partial restoration would be better than the existing situation. The specific elements of restorative justice take many forms and encompass several areas. There are some identifiable broad groups of activities that are central throughout. It is first important to identify restorative justice goals.

RESTORATIVE JUSTICE GOALS

Restorative justice attempts to accomplish several goals. First of all, justice needs to be served in respect to both the victim and the offender. Each party should feel that he or she has received fair treatment. Second, the relationship between the two needs to be addressed; the opportunity for reconciliation must be given. Third, the process must also take into consideration the concerns of the community. Last, directions for resolution must be achieved.

JUSTICE FOR THE VICTIM

Several things must occur in order for victims to feel a sense of justice. Victims need to be able to express facts, opinions, and concerns to the offender. They need to receive directly proportional compensation for their harms. Beyond that, they need to participate and they need support. After these tasks are completed, the victim is more likely to feel a sense of rightness.

JUSTICE FOR THE OFFENDER

Offenders also need to be able to feel that the legal process has treated them fairly. A drunk-driving study revealed that 22 percent of the offenders who participated in regular court proceedings felt they were disadvantaged. However, only 4 percent of offenders who participated in the restorative justice model felt disadvantaged (Sherman & Barnes, 1997, p.3). Offenders need to be given the opportunity to accept responsibility for their actions. They need the chance to challenge any wrong assumptions. Finally, they need the occasion to redress victims.

ADDRESSING VICTIM–OFFENDER RELATIONS

Any successful restorative justice system should encourage interaction between the offender and the victim. Both parties need the opportunity to address issues, ask questions, and hear answers from one another. Reconciliation and forgiveness are essential to the healing process.

COMMUNITY CONCERNS

Different restorative justice programs attempt to include the community in varying degrees. It is widely acknowledged in the literature that society must take responsibility for crime. Communities have an obligation to correct social factors that contribute to crime and to allow offenders to rehabilitate and reintegrate. In order to do so, the public must be aware of crimes, their causes, and their outcomes. Furthermore, the needs of the community must be addressed during dispute resolution. If it is appropriate for the community to receive reparations, then that must be discussed. The community needs to be responsible for crime and represented in resolution.

RESTORATIVE JUSTICE TECHNIQUES

Restorative justice ideals have been manifested in the creation of different types of programs including restitution, victim-offender reconciliation, and community mediation. While most programs have grown out of different movements (e.g., the victim's movement), they are all interconnected by underlying value systems. As the entire restorative movement grows, each of these programs gains popularity.

RESTITUTION

The concept of restitution is ancient and existed long before the creation of formal justice systems. Bruce Jacob (1977) highlights six stages of development that the criminal justice system has undergone. In the first stage, response to crime was one of personal vengeance. People simply took revenge on any person who harmed them. During the second stage, collective vengeance (in the form of kin groups) was the focus. Families of the victim and the offender would seek revenge. Due to the potential for never-ending blood feuds, a third stage evolved. A process of negotiation between families became commonplace. During the fourth level of development, societies adopted codes that contained preset levels of compensations for various crimes (i.e., lex talionis — "an eye for an eye, a tooth for a tooth"). Over the years, lords and rulers gradually became involved in the mediation process and would receive a given percentage of the resulting compensation. The adversarial system became entrenched in resolution. During the final stage, the state made all offences crimes against the state and displaced the victim. The resulting system was contemporary criminal justice.

It is important to differentiate between restitution and compensation. Restitution is "an offender-oriented sanction involving offender payments to the crime victim or some substitute victim" (Hudson & Galaway, 1977, p. 1). Compensation, on the other hand, is a process whereby the state compensates the victim using tax monies. Restitution is generally imposed with property crimes wherein there is obvious financial loss. Compensation is usually assessed and given in cases involving violence and resulting in physical harm or death. It is also important to identify community service work as a form of representative restitution. As opposed to making financial payments to the victim, the offender is sometimes required to perform a specified number of hours of work either for the community or for non-profit organizations within the community.

Restitution programs regained popularity during the 1970s. Over the last two decades, Galaway and Hudson have traced and interpreted the growth of restitution programs across North America. Restitution orders and community service work are now common practices in most jurisdictions in Canada and the United States.

One major issue surrounding restitution is over who has the right to impose it. Legally, the only person who can order restitution is the presiding judge. Any other restitution order must be made through a contract that is enforceable in civil court. Because the amounts of restitution are generally small, the cost of pursuing civil court action would be detrimental. Other people have suggested that parole boards should also be empowered to provide for restitution. To date, there are no provisions under the Corrections and Conditional Release Act whereby the Board can make restitution a condition of release.

VICTIM PARTICIPATION

During the 1980s, the attention of reformers was being drawn toward the issue of victim involvement in the criminal justice process. Early reforms have been criticized for giving victims only marginally improved status with the hope of gaining their cooperation as witnesses. Contemporary reforms, however, try to truly involve the victim. Different programs centre on different stages of the justice system but all attempt to improve victim satisfaction with the process and the outcome.

Pre-trial stage There have been three main attempts to improve victim participation at this stage. First, the police have attempted to increase ties with the community and to make themselves more approachable. It is felt that this will increase the reporting of crime and will stimulate exchange of information thereafter. In order to accomplish this, several police forces across Canada have created Victim Services Units, which provide both information and first contact, crisis management services. These programs are still strongly criticized for simply pursuing the aim of encouraging victims to testify.

Another major reform has been to include victims in plea bargaining. Task forces in both the United States and Canada have concluded that victims deserve to be involved in this process. By allowing victims to participate, they will have the opportunity to express their concerns and to ensure that any bargain represents their interests. The actual integration of victim participation in plea bargaining has yet to be effectively introduced.

Independent victim services programs are yet another attempt to increase victim participation. These groups have several focus areas: they provide crisis services for victims in conjunction with police forces; they act as lobby groups for victims' issues, and they educate the public in matters that concern victims' rights.

Trial stage If a criminal case goes to trial, the testimony of the victim will almost always be required. Testifying in court can, however, be a traumatic and frightening experience. For example, in sex offence trials, defense attorneys may try to establish that the victim has a questionable background. Having one's sexual history examined in court is undoubtedly a humiliating experience. Unfortunately, under a retributive model, little can be done to improve their position. Recently, the government of Canada enacted Bill C-49, an amendment to the Criminal Code guaranteeing some protection to victims against intrusive cross-examination.

Another major reform recommendation is community mediated victim/offender conflict resolution that directly reflects the goals of restorative justice. Most programs are known as Victim-Offender Reconciliation Programs (VORP). The idea for VORPs can be traced back to Kitchener, Ontario, when Probation Officer Mark Yantzi made an in-court recommendation that two vandals would benefit from having to meet their victims (Woolpert, 1991). The presiding judge agreed and the concept became established. This court decision allowed for the creation of several non-profit organizations who facilitate reconciliation.

Essentially, VORPs offer an alternative to the formalized criminal justice system. They are designed to improve conflict resolution, to provide material reparations to victims, to prevent recidivism, and to offer a speedier and less costly alternative to formal processes (Woolpert, 1991). There is a general pattern of procedures that most VORP programs adhere to. They usually involve non-violent offenders at a post-conviction stage (The Church Council on Justice and Corrections, 1996). After the initial screening and assignment of a mediator, separate meetings are arranged with the victim and the offender. These first meetings provide the mediator with an opportunity to introduce himself/herself, to explain the concept behind VORP, and to make arrangements for the main meeting. Once the arrangements are made, the victim and the offender are brought together. Chupp (1989) describes three stages during the reconciliatory meeting: "facts, feelings, and restitution." Both participants are given the opportunity to state the facts from their point of view, then they are allowed to voice their opinions and emotions regarding the events. Once the venting of emotions is done, a verbal negotiation is worked out regarding reparations. Once a restitution contract is agreed upon, there is a period of evaluation and follow-up to determine if restitution has been made. Studies indicate that victims are generally willing to partake in such programs (Galaway, 1991; Reeves, 1989).

In terms of success, Umbreit and Coates (1992, p. 2) indicate that "high levels of client satisfaction (victims, 79 percent; offenders, 87 percent) and perceptions of justice (victims, 83 percent; offenders, 89 percent)" were attained through the mediation process. Given the potential of these programs to relieve the congestion of the formal justice system while at the same time effecting positive and acceptable resolutions, VORPs deserve attention.

Sentencing stage Several reforms have been aimed at involving victims in the sentencing process. Across North America, Victim Impact Statements (VIS) and Victim Statements of Opinion (VSO) have been instituted (Griffiths & Verdun-Jones, 1994). These documents generally provide the presiding judge with information regarding either the objective losses or subjective harm that has been caused to the victim. Taking into account statement information, judges are presumably better able to have sentences reflect the losses of victims. In order to protect the due process rights of offenders, overt victim involvement has been avoided. Mark Umbreit (1990) concluded from a study of victim participation that, although most victims feel that they should have direct involvement in determining restitution, many felt that ultimate sentencing decisions should be left up to the judge.

As opposed to having a sentencing stage, VORPs have negotiations that result in reparation contracts between offenders and victims. This process leaves both parties satisfied with the results. Having voiced their opinions and having heard those of the other party makes the resulting "punishment" seem positive. In fact, lack of information is a major cause of dissatisfaction with the criminal justice system. A study done by Doob and Roberts (1983) indicated that when presented with complete information regarding a criminal case, victim and general public agreement with sentences increased. Reconciliation programs make people aware of extenuating circumstances, which helps to satisfy participants and observers.

Post-sentencing stage Under a true restorative model, post-sentencing involvement would be superficial. Victims would receive reparations in some form. However, trying to incorporate aspects of restorative justice into the present system limits the forms of reparation available.

Some advocates might conclude that the institution of post-sentencing VORPs would be beneficial, but this poses certain problems. The most significant problem would be in motivating the offender to participate. The offender might feel that she or he has nothing to gain. One solution to this problem may be to include VORP participation as a prerequisite, or at least a favourable condition, for parole.

A post-sentencing concern for victims is a lack of input into decisions regarding the early release of offenders and the conditions of that release. In 1990, the National Parole Board affirmed the rights of victims:

> (w)e recognize that for victims, offenders, and their respective families our decisions are
> of critical importance. We will therefore strive to exercise the highest degree of sensitivi-
> ty and respect in our dealings with those primarily affected by our processes and deci-
> sions. (p. 6)

Consistent with meeting this goal, the Board undertook to increase the sharing of information between the Board and victims. As such, they welcome victims' opinions regarding both policies and risk assessment of offenders. Under normal circumstances, however, it is the obligation of the victim to submit any information; the Board will not pursue the input of victims unless absolutely necessary. Similarly, if victims wish to attain information regarding parole decisions, they must apply for it. The provision of information varies depending on the type of information requested. Policy information is readily available. The Corrections and Conditional Release Act allows certain information regarding offenders to be provided to victims (Griffiths & Verdun-Jones, 1994). This information includes: the offender's name, the offence for which the offender was convicted, the date of commencement and length of sentence, the eligibility dates and review dates applicable to the offender for unescorted temporary absences and parole. In addition, victims may receive information regarding the location where the offender is serving the sentence, the date of any hearing, and the details of any conditions attached to any form of release. Aside from these provisions and others (detailing the openness of parole hearings to victims), there have been few attempts to integrate the effective participation of victims in parole decisions.

COMMUNITY MEDIATION

A final major program based on restorative justice principles is the use of community mediation in conflict resolution. Since the community is also affected by the incident, their participation can be beneficial. A representative from the community can help the victim and offender come to a negotiated resolution. The community sees that the problem has been resolved and feels that justice has been served. As such, the majority of modern proposals involve the use of community mediation.

The first community mediation centre was started by Mark Yantzi and was known as the Kitchener VORP. By 1980, the program became centralized in terms of the people who took part and the goal they were trying to achieve. Dean Peachey (1989) described it as:

> The adversary nature of the legal system with its emphasis on determining guilt or
> innocence seemed particularly unsuited for handling cases between acquaintances,
> where both may have contributed to a disagreement leading to an assault or property

damage. By handling such conflicts through mediation it might be possible to resolve the dispute to the satisfaction of both parties, and prevent it from escalating to the point where a more serious offence might take place. (p. 20)

In 1982, the program began a slow decline due to an unfavourable ruling regarding restitution in the Ontario Court of Appeal (R. v. Hudson, 1982). Since that time, there has been strong revitalization of restitution within the justice system. By 1996, 26 jurisdictions across Canada had established VORP programs (The Church Council on Justice and Corrections, 1996).

As an alternative to the adversarial process, community mediation in VORP programs provides more power to the participants of the conflict and allows them to come to a mutually satisfactory solution. As opposed to working against each other, the victim and the offender need to work together in order to find a solution. Once the solution is agreed upon, everybody (victim, offender, and community) feels that justice has been served and that life will return to normal. The restorative criminal justice system provides a fair and adequate reaction to crime by reaffirming society's values, by instilling respect (as opposed to fear or contempt) for the law, by realizing just resolutions and by focussing on problem solving for the future rather than establishing blame for past behaviour (Umbreit & Carey, 1995).

THE FUTURE OF RESTORATIVE JUSTICE IN CANADA

The John Howard Society supports and promotes the concept of restorative justice. Consistent with the goal of preventing crime by developing and implementing new policies and techniques within the criminal justice system, this new ideology offers several alternatives. The development of a Community Reconciliation Centre by the John Howard Society of Manitoba (JHSM) has been one way in which restorative justice has been implemented.

The JHSM has four unique goals. First, they strive to "provide direct Restorative services that empower persons in conflict with the law" (John Howard Society of Manitoba, 1992). In addition, they advocate for the reform of the criminal justice system toward a restorative justice model, strive to make active use of volunteers and facilitate public awareness of criminal justice. Consistent with these goals, the JHSM was awarded government funding to implement a program known as Restorative Resolutions.

Restorative Resolutions is one of the most comprehensive restorative programs initiated across North America. The aim of Restorative Resolutions is "to provide selected offenders the opportunity to re-establish trust and acceptance with the individuals and community they have harmed" (The Church Council on Justice and Corrections, 1996, p.5). The project takes into account the need for reparations, the need to involve victims and the community, the need to educate all participants, as well as the need to reduce the costs of the criminal justice system. Beyond these main focusses, this project tries to "build bridges between Aboriginal and Non-Aboriginal cultures" (John Howard Society of Manitoba, 1992: p. 14).

Referrals to the program originate from lawyers (either Crown or defense), judges, community corrections officers, resource groups, and various other members of society (The Church Council on Justice and Corrections, 1996). Using established guidelines, the intake staff select offenders who are most likely to succeed under the framework. Techniques for selection include risk prediction scales, motivation testing interviews, and a willingness by offenders to accept responsibility.

Once selected, staff determine a case plan that is designed exclusively for the offender (The Church Council on Justice and Corrections, 1996). These plans are individually determined to best meet the needs of the offender and the associated victim. Potential plans might include compensation, restitution, community service work, counselling, mediation, education, employment, and crime-free behaviour. To determine the case design, meetings are held weekly and involve a team approach.

Beyond offender-oriented activities, the program also extends opportunities to victims (The Church Council on Justice and Corrections, 1996). These activities include participation in the form of mediation and victim impact statements, education, and information provision. There is strong emphasis on involving the victim in order to make reparations and to help the rehabilitation of the offender.

The project attempts to involve the community by making use of volunteers. Volunteers may be used in several areas including mediation, service delivery, and community education.

The Manitoba project encourages the federal and provincial correctional agencies to look at the restorative alternative quite carefully. With a growing need for fiscal responsibility and cost effective alternatives, the restorative model represents an appealing change.

Restorative justice principles can also be seen in the Aboriginal justice movement across Canada. In essence, traditional Aboriginal justice is based on the restorative model. The goal is to facilitate restoration, rehabilitation, and reintegration. Increasing numbers of Aboriginal groups are lobbying for a return to traditional justice. These reforms have gained the support of judges and politicians, and are gradually being put in effect. These movements will undoubtedly open the doors for new programs that attempt to incorporate restorative ideals.

CONCLUSION

Restorative justice is a new model for criminal justice. While some authors have criticized the model as unrealistic (Cragg, 1992), the movement is still gaining momentum. Restorative justice models emphasize the importance of holding offenders accountable for their behaviour while providing victims and community members every opportunity to participate in the justice process. The John Howard Society of Alberta supports the movement toward restorative justice. There are two ways in which this can be accomplished.

First, in evaluating any new programs that are created, it is helpful for groups to use five questions developed by Howard Zehr.

  a. Do victims experience justice?
  b. Do offenders experience justice?
  c. Is the victim-offender relationship addressed?
  d. Are community concerns being taken into account?
  e. Is the future being addressed?

By using these questions, every program can be evaluated in terms of its degree of restoration. The Society should seek to incorporate these principles in all its programs.

Second, the John Howard Society of Alberta should also actively pursue the creation of restorative programs. In order to prove the success of the principles, projects similar to Restorative Resolutions need to be developed.

REFERENCES

Ash. M. (1972). On witnesses: A radical critique of criminal court procedures. *Notre Dame Lawyer*. No. 48, 386–425.

Austin, J., & Krisberg, B. (1982). The unmet promise of alternatives to incarceration. *Crime and Delinquency: A Publication of the National Council on Crime and Delinquency, 28* (3), 374–409.

Bazemore, G., & Umbreit, M. (1995). Rethinking the Sanctioning Function in Juvenile Court: Retributive or Restorative Responses to Youth Crime. *Crime and Delinquency, 41* (3), 296–316.

Bridges, G.S., & Stone, J.A. (1986). Effects of criminal punishment on perceived threat of punishment: Toward an understanding of specific deterrence. *Journal of Research in Crime and Delinquency, 23*, 207–39.

Canadian Centre for Justice Statistics. (1996). Government spending on adult correctional services. *Juristat, 16* (3).

Canadian Sentencing Commission. (1987). *Sentencing reform: A Canadian approach*. Ottawa: Minister of Supply and Services Canada.

Chelimsky, E. (1981). Serving victims: Agency incentives and individual needs. In S. Salasen (Ed.), *Evaluating victim services*. Beverly Hills, California: Sage Publications Ltd.

Chupp, M. (1989). Reconciliation procedures and rationale. In M. Wright & B. Galaway (Eds.), *Mediation and Criminal Justice*. Newbury Park, California: Sage Publications Ltd.

Church Council on Justice and Corrections. (1996). Satisfying justice: Safe community options that attempt to repair harm from crime and reduce the use or length of imprisonment. Ottawa: Church Council on Justice and Corrections.

Christie, N. (1982). Conflicts as property. In C.L. Boydell & I.A. Connidis (Eds.), *The Canadian Criminal justice system*. Toronto: Holt, Reinhart, and Winston of Canada, Ltd.

Cragg, W. (1992). *The practice of punishment*. New York: Routledge.

Doob, A.N., & Roberts, J.V. (1983). *Sentencing: An analysis of the public's view of sentencing*. Ottawa: Department of Justice, Canada.

Galaway, B., & Hudson, J. (1991). Introduction: Towards restorative justice. In B. Galaway & J. Hudson (Eds.), *Criminal justice, restitution, and reconciliation*. New York: Willow Tree Press, Inc.

Griffiths, C.T., & Verdun-Jones, S.N. (1994). *Canadian criminal justice*. Toronto: Harcourt Brace.

Hudson, J., & Galaway, B. (1977). Introduction. In B. Galaway & J. Hudson (Eds.), *Offender restitution in theory and action*. Toronto: Lexington Books.

Hudson, J., & Galaway, B. (1981). Restitution and the justice model. In D. Fogel & J. Hudson (Eds.), *Justice as fairness*. New York: Anderson Publishing Co. Ltd.

Jacob, B. (1977). The concept of restitution: An historical overview. In J. Hudson & B. Galaway (Eds.), *Restitution in criminal justice*. Toronto: Lexington Books.

John Howard Society of Manitoba. (November, 1992). *Funding proposal for Restorative Resolutions*. Submitted to Solicitor General of Canada.

John Howard Society of Ontario. (April, 1985). *Brief to the Canadian Sentencing Commission*. (Available from The John Howard Society of Ontario. 46 St. Clair Avenue East, Third Floor. Toronto, Ontario, M4T 1M9.)

Knudten, R.D., Meade, A., Knudten, M., & Doerner, W. (1976). *Victims and witnesses: The impact of crime and their experience with the criminal justice system*. Washington, DC: Government Printing Office.

Martinson, R. (1974). What works? Questions and answers about prison reform. *The Public Interest, 34*, 22–54.

National Parole Board. (1990). *Victims and the National Parole Board: A discussion paper*. Government of Canada.

Peachey, D.E. (1989). The Kitchener experiment. In M. Wright & B. Galaway (Eds.), *Mediation and Criminal Justice*. Newbury Park, California: Sage Publications Ltd.

Reeves, H. (1989). The victim support perspective. In M. Wright & B. Galaway (Eds.), *Mediation and Criminal Justice*. Newbury Park, California: Sage Publications Ltd.

Rosenbaum, D.P. (1977). *Reactions to criminal victimization: A summary of victim community, and police response*. Evanston, Illinois: Evanston Police Department.

Sherman, L., & Barnes, G. (1997). Restorative Justice and Offenders' Respect for the Law. Canberra: Australian National University.

Symonds, M. (1980). The "second injury" to victims. In L. Kivens (Ed.), *Evaluation and change: Services for survivors*. Minneapolis, Minnesota: Minneapolis Research Foundation.

Umbreit, M.S. (1990). Violent offenders and their victims. In M. Wright & B. Galaway (Eds.), *Mediation and criminal justice*. Newbury Park, California: Sage Publications.

———. Having offenders meet with their victims offers benefits for both parties. *Corrections Today*, 53(4), 164–66.

Umbreit, M.S. & Carey, M. (1995). Restorative justice: Implications for organizational change. *Federal Probation*, 59(1), 47–54.

Umbreit, M.S. & Coates, R.B. (1992). *Victim offender mediation: An analysis of programs in four states of the U.S.*. Minnesota: Citizens' Council on Crime.

Van Ness, D.W. (1990). Restorative justice. In B. Galaway, & J. Hudson (Eds.), *Criminal justice, restitution, and reconciliation*. New York: Willow Tree Press, Inc.

Woolpert, S. (1991). Victim-offender reconciliation programs. In Duffy, K.G. et al. (Eds.), *Community mediation: A handbook for practitioners and researchers*. New York: The Guilford Press.

Zehr, Howard. (1990). *Changing Lenses: A New Focus for Crime and Justice*. Waterloo, Ontario: Herald Press.

SEVEN

Sentencing as a Gendered Process: Results of a Consultation

RENATE M. MOHR

INTRODUCTION

There is one striking feature of sentencing reform in Canada and other jurisdictions that has recently surfaced in the literature (Daly 1989; Morris 1988). Historically,

Source: Renate M. Mohr, "Sentencing as a Gendered Process: Results of a Consultation," *Canadian Journal of Criminology*, 32, 3 (1990): 479–85. Copyright by the Canadian Criminal Justice System. Reproduced by permission of the *Canadian Journal of Criminology*.

sentencing reforms, like all other law reform efforts, have been gender-neutral in form and substance (Boyle 1985; Gavigan 1983). Feminist literature critically examines the significance of gender-neutral research as it reveals itself in androcentricity, overgeneralization, and gender insensitivity (Eichler 1988). Symptomatic of gender-neutrality in sentencing reform efforts is research that consists of constructing our thinking around men rather than women and men, research that involves the gathering of information with regard to one sex and treating it as if it applied to both sexes, and, finally, research that ignores sex as "a socially significant variable in cases in which it is, in fact, significant" (Eichler 1988). This paper seeks to reveal ways in which gender-blindness in law reform efforts inevitably results in formal, rather than substantive, justice. As a recent consultation with a women's organization illustrated, understanding sentencing as a gender process is the beginning, not the end, of a new process of reform (CAEFS 1988: 32).

> There is much work to be done. Little has been written about the status of women in conflict with the law. Few people have been educated to understand how attitudes regarding gender, race and class influence decision-making on a daily basis. Sentencing data is inadequate at best, and little exists on women as a distinct group.

GENDER-BLIND REFORM EFFORTS

Gender-neutral research is necessarily blind to the reality that "[r]egardless of individual judge's commitment to the abstract values of fairness and impartiality, unconscious gender-based myths, biases and stereotypes can and often do influence judicial decision-making, fact-finding, and the conduct of a court room environment" (Wikler 1987). The role of gender in shaping decision-making is key in understanding the sentencing process, since, as Freda Steel (1987) writes of family law, "... the subject is essentially a fact-based arena of decision-making, where legal principles are merely guidelines to extraordinary amounts of flexibility granted to the judiciary." Blindness to the impact of gender biases, sex roles, and stereotypes on decision-making, law-making, and law reform has been re-enforced rather than challenged by law school training (Wikler 1987). It is not surprising, therefore, to learn that sentencing reform has long been guided by gender-blindness.

Interestingly, although gender bias has been overlooked, there has long been a recognition in the literature on sentencing that unconscious biases and personal characteristics of judge shape their individual approaches to sentencing. Over 200 years ago, Beccaria (1764: 10) expressed concern over the subjective nature of sentencing decisions and how, due to the judge's unbridled discretion, "... the spirit of the law would be the product of a judge's good or bad logic, of his [sic] good or bad digestion; it would depend on the influence of his passions, on the weakness of the accused, on the judge's connection with him [sic] and on all those minute factors that alter the appearance of an object in the fluctuating mind of man." Then, as now, although there was a concern with personal biases, the gender of the sentencer and the person subject to the sentence was left unquestioned.

In the last two decades, the relationship of social class and race to the exercise of judicial discretion has been studied in mainstream Canadian literature on sentencing (Hogarth 1971). Hogarth's study on the background characteristics of magistrates revealed that a number of "extra-legal" factors were central to their sentencing behaviour. These factors included political affiliation, social class, background, age, religion, and ethnic background. Gender is once again conspicuous in its absence. Although this study remains an important contribution to sentencing literature, its gender-blindness is revealed in the gender-neutral title of the text. Hogarth studied the sentencing behaviour of an almost (if not totally) exclusively male judiciary yet the book was given the title, Sentencing as a Human Process. To use the word human to describe what is almost exclusively a male process serves further to obscure the significance of the gender of those who sentence.

In their first major report on sentencing reform in Canada, the Law Reform Commission of Canada (LRCC) (1977) stated that their work was based on "the assumption that perceptions, attitudes, practices and expectations are the primary forces in shaping our approach to crime." Again, although the LRCC raised social class and race as personal attributes that affect attitudes and perceptions, their work too remained gender-neutral. That concern that the individual attitudes and perception of judges were largely responsible for unwarranted disparity in sentences was to be a guiding theme in the following law reform efforts (Canada 1984; Canadian Sentencing Commission 1987). The Canadian Sentencing Commission was created in 1984 with the broad mandate requiring it to address this issue of unwarranted disparity that was, according to the terms of reference, "inconsistent with the principle of equality before the law." Unlike previous reform efforts that continued to propose that multiple rationales should guide the sentencing of judges (Canada 1984), the Commission proposed the imposition of a single rationale to structure the decision-making process and ensure a "uniformity of approach" to sentencing. The Commission recommended that the paramount principle governing the determination of a sentence should be that the sentence be proportionate to the gravity of the offence and degree of responsibility of the offender. The just deserts solution proposed by the Commission was the first serious attempt to ensure that individual judges sitting in courts of different levels across the country would no longer sentence according to their personal rationales but would share a uniform approach.

In the next part of this paper, the limitations of the just deserts rationale will be explored as they were revealed in a recent consultation that raised the significance of gender, in form and substance. The consultation revealed, as feminist literature asserts, that legislative change must be accompanied by change at the personal level if it is ever to achieve goals of substantive equality. Just deserts may be the rationale that will ultimately lead to a more just process of sentencing, but so long as it remains gender-neutral (as well as colour-blind and class-less), it will remain on the level of the abstract. As feminists have long agreed, and as the consultation reveals, treating un-equals equally will not result in equality. Rather than neutralise gender, race, and class, a sentencing rationale must ensure that, like in the development of equality rights under the Charter, unequals are treated "in proportion to the inequality existing between them" (Bayefsky 1987).

RESULTS OF THE CONSULTATION

To assert that sentencing is a gendered process is to suggest that the gender of both the sentencer and the subject of the sentence is a crucial element in understanding and defining the roots of unwarranted disparity. In January 1988, the Department of Justice provided funding to a national women's organization to respond to the report of the Canadian Sentencing Commission (1987). The Canadian Association of

Elizabeth Fry Societies (CAEFS) represents 19 community-based agencies across the country that work with and on behalf of women involved in the justice system. As an organization structured to work with women, CAEFS was uniquely situated to raise issues of gender so long ignored in the sentencing reform process. As the title of one of the first books on Canadian women in conflict with the law suggests, to date, the criminal justice system has considered women "too few to count" (Adelberg and Currie 1987). As the results of a consultation that drew from the experiences of women and men working with women reveal, when women are counted, both the form and substance of the approach to sentencing reform changes.

As set out in the consultation document (CAEFS 1988: 8), the purpose of the consultation was not simply to gather responses to the Sentencing Commission's lengthy report, but rather to build on concerns and issues raised by the participants who had a wealth of first-hand knowledge of the impact of current sentencing practices and laws on women.

> Although the Commission's report has many worthy proposals, we do not set out in this consultation to deal with the proposals in the order and framework established by the Commission. Again, the reason for this is simple. If we are to take context seriously, then we must first uncover the experiences of women in conflict with the law. It is those experiences that will provide us with a framework for reform proposals, if they are truly to address the daily sources of inequities experienced by women.

This has been described as a feminist methodology because it takes "the experiences of women as the initial starting point for the formulation of legal critiques and political agendas" (Boyle 1985; Greshner 1987; Lahey 1985). Although neither the methodology nor the results of the consultation can be described fully, some of the results of the interviews will be highlighted below.

Eighteen of the 19 member societies located in communities from Sydney, Nova Scotia to Prince George, British Columbia, participated in this consultation. Two telephone interviews were conducted with each of the participants (a staff member or society board member). In order to facilitate preparation for the first interview, each participant received a list of open-ended questions to consider. The questions sought to uncover the views and perceptions as to the problems that — in their particular community — were the greatest source of unwarranted disparity and inequity in sentencing (CAEFS 1988: Appendix B).

As a result of the first telephone interviews, a clear picture of issues and problems of greatest concern to women in conflict with the law emerged. In spite of the regional differences, the differences in size of the community, etc., there was a general consensus on all of the major issues raised by participants coast to coast.

The second telephone interviews were to draw on the context or picture that emerged as a result of the first interviews. In the second set of interviews, participants were asked to respond to reform proposals that would address the concerns they raised. If the Sentencing Commission proposed a recommendation that was relevant to a particular concern raised, it was presented to the participant as a suggested reform. Again, just as the context painted by participants came through with remarkable clarity, so did their suggestions for the directions of sentencing reform. Social services, education, and communication were the primary concerns repeated in the conversations. Many participants stressed that before legislators, judges, lawyers, and other actors in the criminal justice process can be educated as to the "realities of women and crime," they must first understand something about the inequalities women suffer in Canadian society generally. The report sets the context for understanding the status of women in Canada through citing Statistics Canada figures that show women's wages in 1985 remained at 64.9 percent of their male counterparts.

> Unfortunately, the majority of the poverty-stricken are women, the phenomenon becoming known as the feminization of poverty. Families headed by women are 4.5 times more likely to be poor than families headed by men. A full 44 percent of female-headed households are poor. In 1981, women as single parent headed almost one in every ten Canadian families.

In addition, the consultation document listed other "realities" of women's lives raised by participants, including violence, in pornography or in fact, and other "historical barriers which go far beyond issues of choice in reproduction." The consequences of sentencing reform efforts that overlook the "realities of women's lives" were far-reaching in the eyes of the participants:

> Commonly-held social values and attitudes to women are not in touch with the real life experiences of women, nor are the social institutions established to provide services to them. Despite billions of dollars of federal and provincial programming, women have still had to establish their own separate institutions such as interval houses for battered women and their dependents, health-care collectives, child care centres, and multi-service facilities for aboriginal women, immigrant women, and other identifiable social groups in need of support. While some of this may be anticipatory planning by women's groups, much of it stems from the "reality gap" — the difference between services provided to women by traditional institutions and the real life requirements of women.

One question that emerged from a discussion of the significance of gender to sentencing practices and laws was a question that would never have been raised in the course of a traditional consultation. The question asked by one participant was the following: given these realities, why do law makers ask "why" women come into conflict with the law instead of questioning how it is that so few women come into conflict with the law? The very fact that this question is never asked, should give great hope to critical scholars — for if it is taken seriously, it suggests that there may be answers in this "different voice" to which we have just begun to listen.

The problem facing women in conflict with the law that was most often raised by participants was the lack of social services available to women. Interestingly, the lack of social services was raised in response to the question about what it is that causes the most unwarranted disparity.

> The answers to this question were very revealing as to the context which would ultimately unfold. The answers did not focus on issues like unreasonably high maximum penalties or on the need for presumptive guidelines for judges. Instead, the answers read as follows. Poverty. Race. Socialization. Power imbalance. Class bias. Violence. Access to legal representation. Attitudes. Lack of knowledge about the context of women's lives.

These answers have never emerged in the course of traditional consultations on state reform efforts. The reason, once again, is that once in print the structure of the reform efforts themselves is so powerful that their foundation is rarely questioned. Meaningful reform requires that the form itself be challenged. It requires an understanding of women in conflict with the law that very few people have. The reason for this is that very few women and men have an understanding of the social significance of gender in Canada today. Significantly, education and communication were the two major areas raised by participants as areas of priority to be addressed in any re-thinking of sentencing. Stereotypes and other biases that are shared by many Canadians were also cited as causes of unwarranted disparity.

The proposed solution to this problem was not that "a uniformity approach" to sentencing be imposed on judges, but that "... the agendas of continuing education seminars for lawyers and judges give priority to issues of gender, race and class." The report stressed that "[u]ntil judges are taught about the violence and poverty that exists in homes across the country, we cannot expect them to understand the 'impact' of their decisions on the lives of the women they sentence daily." The call for education was overwhelming. All those who work in the criminal justice process were singled out as in need of attention, given the decision-making power that goes along with their roles. A broad recommendation was made urging "... the Department of Justice to meet with provincial departments of education and to call upon them to provide education, at all levels of schooling, on the operation and limitations of the criminal law and criminal justice system."

The issue of communication was invariably raised whenever sentencing was discussed as a "process." Participants agreed that there was no sense of process, either as experienced by the women they worked with or by themselves as court workers. Currently, the report acknowledges, few decision-makers get feedback "as to either the impact or the effectiveness of their decisions." The importance of good communication between the volunteer court workers and the judge was stressed by many participants and those communities that reported a good relationship between the volunteer court-worker and the judge had the greatest success in using community-based sanctions. An interesting observation was made by one of the participants regarding how simple it would be to improve communication between the community and the actors in the "process." In her particular community, a committee had been set up to discuss renovations of the new court house. The committee includes judges, lawyers, court workers, police officers, and a variety of community representatives. If it is possible to get these people talking to one another about the renovation of a building, she suggested, it should be possible to get them together to discuss the work they do every day. Once again, this is a small but significant example of the creative recommendations that spring from a form of consultation that listens to and values experience.

CONCLUSION

The essential connection between gender and the criminal law was perhaps best summarized in the conclusion of the CAEFS report. (1988: 20)

> The criminal law has never been "our" criminal law, if "our" is to reflect the lives of women and men. It has been drafted, enforced, and reformed primarily by men, for

men. Although beyond the purview of this consultation, the substantive criminal law is in need of reform efforts that take issues of gender, race and class seriously.

Although this is but a brief description of a women-centred consultation, it is evident that the issues central to the reform of sentencing laws and practices, as seen by women and as felt by women, are different from those that have been raised in previous reform efforts. The popular just deserts sentencing rationale proposed by the Sentencing Commission as a solution to unwarranted disparity was felt by participants to leave too many questions unresolved and too many attitudes unchecked.

If we are ever to achieve the goal of proportionality—that the "punishment fit the crime," we need contextual information about not only the crime but also the punishment. Judges must be aware of the pains of imprisonment that cannot be measured in time alone. (CAEFS 1988: 21)

Although it was conceded that the just deserts rationale may be the best solution to unwarranted disparity in a society where there is true equality, until we attain that goal, we must continue to search for an approach that requires judges and law reformers to uncover, rather than cover-up, gender, race, and class differences.

REFERENCES

Adelberg, E. and Claudia Currie. 1987. *Too Few to Count*. Vancouver: Press Gang Publishers.
Bayefsky, Anne F. 1987. Defining equality rights under the Charter. In Sheilah Martin and Kathleen Mahoney (eds.), *Equality and Judicial Neutrality*. Toronto: Carswell.
Beccaria, Caesar. 1764. *On Crimes and Punishments*. New York: Bobbs-Merrill.
Boyle, Christine. 1985. Criminal law and procedure: who needs tenure? *Osgoode Hall Law Journal* 23: 427.
Canada. 1984. *Sentencing*. Ottawa: Government of Canada.
Canadian Association of Elizabeth Fry Societies. 1988. Sentencing in Context: Revealing the Realities of Women in Conflict with the Law. Ottawa: Unpublished Consultation document.
Canadian Sentencing Commission. 1987. *Sentencing Reform: A Canadian Approach*. Ottawa: Ministry of Supply and Services.
Daly, Kathleen. 1989. Rethinking judicial paternalism: Gender, work-family relations, and sentencing. *Gender & Society* 3: 9.
Eichler, Margrit. 1988. *Nonsexist Research Methods: A Practical Guide*. Boston: Allen & Unwin.
Gavigan, Shelley. 1983. Women's crime and feminist critiques: A review of the literature. *Canadian Criminology Forum* 6: 75.
Greshner, Donna. 1987. Judicial approaches to equality and critical legal studies. In Sheilah Martin and Kathleen Mahoney (eds.), *Equality and Judicial Neutrality*. Toronto: Carswell.
Hogarth, John. 1971. *Sentencing as a Human Process*. Toronto: University of Toronto Press.
Lahey, Kathleen. 1985. Until women themselves have told all that they have to tell. *Osgoode Hall Law Journal* 23: 519.
Law Reform Commission of Canada. 1977. *Guidelines: Dispositions and Sentences in the Criminal Process*. Ottawa: Minister of Supply and Services.
Morris, Allison. 1988. Sex and sentencing. *The Criminal Law Review*: 163.
Steel, Freda M. 1987. Alimoney and maintenance orders. In Sheilah Martin and Kathleen Mahoney (eds.), *Equality and Judicial Neutrality*. Toronto: Carswell.
Wikler, Norma J. 1987. Identifying and correcting gender bias. In Sheilah Martin and Kathleen Mahoney (eds.), *Equality and Judicial Neutrality*. Toronto: Carswell.

EIGHT

The Role of Sentencing in the Over-Representation of Aboriginal People in Correctional Institutions

CAROL LaPRAIRIE

INTRODUCTION

For the past two decades, virtually, everything written and discussed in the area of aboriginal people and the criminal justice system has used as its starting point the over-representation of aboriginal people as inmates in federal, provincial, and territorial correctional institutions. Rarely, however, has there been any concerted attempt to analyze this issue in any systematic way.[1] There are assumptions that sentencing accounts for a significant part of the problem, but the relationship between sentencing and over-representation has not been explored systematically. The politicization of criminal justice issues within the agendas of land claims, self-government, and constitutional matters has created the prevailing discourse. The lack of attention to the issue in the academic criminology world has permitted continuation of the political rhetoric. This article seeks to address some of the outstanding questions by focusing on sentencing and examining the over-representation phenomenon within the context of criminal justice processing at two critical points, i.e., police and judicial decision-making.

1. THE MEANING OF OVER-REPRESENTATION

Over-representation has been used to describe the percentage of aboriginal people in federal, provincial, and territorial correctional institutions as compared to their percentage in the general population.[2] For example, aboriginal people comprise approximately 1.5–2 percent of the Canadian population but make up approximately 8–10 percent of the federal correctional institutional population and considerably more in provincial and territorial institutions, particularly in northwest Ontario and the western provinces, although the exact percentages are unclear.[3] It is apparent, as well, that for certain aboriginal groups such as women and juveniles, the rates may be even more extreme (LaPrairie 1987).

Reliance on the standard of aboriginal population ratios, i.e., inmate versus general populations, has obscured other ways of understanding over-representation. For example, if one changed the standard to aboriginal and non-aboriginal *age distributions* in the general population, the "over-representation" picture might look quite different. Higher birth rates and lower life expectancy suggests a relatively larger aboriginal 14–25 year old age group. The aboriginal percentage of this group is higher than the aboriginal percentage of the general population. This is also the group with the highest participation rate in the criminal justice system; so it would not be surprising to see high aboriginal representation among offenders from this age group. Whether this group would be disproportionately represented is another question. One of the few researchers to address the age distribution issue analyzed the characteristics of a large cohort of aboriginal and non-aboriginal inmates in B.C. and concluded that:

> The distribution of age for the offender population, for example, seems to have a greater correspondence with the native population at large than it does with the general population at large. The increased number of native offenders may prove to partially be a function of the age distribution within the general native population.[4] (Muirhead 1981)

Similarly, if one follows the theoretical approach of the critical criminologists and uses class (based on socio-economic level) as the standard and predictor of who goes to jail, aboriginal people may well be statistically *under*-represented. Given the same economic reality, non-aboriginal offence rates would no doubt be much higher. There are, then, different ways to look at the over-representation issue and relying solely on population ratios may limit the analysis.

2. THE CAUSES OF OVER-REPRESENTATION

Simply put, there are three competing but not mutually exclusive explanations for the disproportionate representation of aboriginal people in correctional institutions. There are:

a. *Differential treatment by the criminal justice system* [i.e., something different is happening to aboriginal people than to non-aboriginal people in their contacts with the criminal justice system, at police, charging, prosecution, sentencing, and parole decision-making points];
b. *Differential commission of crime* [i.e., aboriginal people are committing more crimes as they have "non-racial attributes placing them at risk for criminal behaviour." (Bonta 1989: 49) These attributes could be related to socio-economic marginality and, concomitantly, alcohol abuse].
c. *Differential offence patterns* [i.e., aboriginal people commit crimes that are more detectable (more serious and/or more visible) than those committed by non-aboriginal people].

These explanations are self-explanatory and there is little need to discuss them further. There is, however, a need to provide a context within which to locate them. The issues of incidence of crime and offence patterns of aboriginal people have been largely ignored in discussions of over-representation. The willingness to focus on criminal justice processing serves a number of agendas, not the least of which is political, in both aboriginal and non-aboriginal terms. For aboriginal political goals of self-government, it directs attention to the need for a "parallel" system of justice if the system of the majority group can be shown to be irrelevant or unsatisfactory to the indigenous minority; for non-aboriginal, dominant interests, it allows attention to focus on the criminal justice system rather than on disparities in society, the solution to which would be economic re-structuring.

Attention to incidence of crime or offence patterns would require an examination of fundamental social structure and economic disparity. This paper is an attempt to demonstrate how fragile the criminal justice processing explanation is and to argue the need for the criminal justice system to redirect the issue to where it more properly belongs — in the social, political, and economic spheres. The first step in this process is to examine the state of research knowledge in the sentencing of aboriginal people.

DIFFERENTIAL CRIMINAL JUSTICE PROCESSING

Decision-making is inherent to each component of criminal justice processing but the most critical points, i.e., police charging and sentencing, are usually targeted in discussions of aboriginal over-representation, even though there is often inconsistent or uneven information about the nature and scope of this involvement.

1. POLICE DECISION-MAKING

Considerable anecdotal data exist with regard to police/aboriginal contacts and police decision-making, but few empirical data have been collected because of methodological difficulties in participant observation research. In addition, examining practices in one jurisdiction would not necessarily allow the generalization of findings. Reserve policing varies from band constables to band police force to general police services; rural policing varies from RCMP to provincial police forces, and, municipal policing varies from RCMP to provincial forces to municipal forces. As a result, it is difficult to explicitly point to differential police charging and arrests as the basis for the disproportionate incarceration rates. However, Bienvenue and Latif in their study of arrests in Winnipeg showed a disproportion of aboriginals and attributed it to the over-surveillance of aboriginal people by police (Bienvenue and Latif 1974).

Although empirical data are lacking, assumptions about the existence of differential, racist charging practices abound.[5] The acceptance of these assumptions has led to the implementation of initiatives designed to reduce the cultural conflict between aboriginal people and police. These include cross-cultural training and the indigenization of policing, i.e., the addition of aboriginal people as special constables to forces such as RCMP and Ontario Provincial Police.

Police decision-making in criminal justice processing remains the most critical information gap in accounting for the disproportionate presence of aboriginal people in the system. It is essential to know if aboriginal people receive different police treatment from non-aboriginals. For example, are they being differentially arrested and charged? Are they over-policed (i.e., the "more police more crime" syndrome)? Are they investigated differently (i.e., more or less comprehensively)? Are there differences between and among types of police forces (e.g., urban/rural) in their contacts with aboriginal people? And is there geographic variation in police response to aboriginal people? The above questions raise the need to understand better the exact nature and scope of the problems that face aboriginal people in their contacts with police. This is not to minimize the seriousness of the issue of over-representation but to reiterate concern about the use of rhetoric in the absence of knowledge.

2. JUDICIAL DECISION-MAKING (SENTENCING)

The most critical and controversial area of criminal justice processing of aboriginal people is sentencing. There is considerable rhetoric about overt racism and unwarranted disparity in the conviction and sentencing of aboriginal people. In one of the most recent and widely reported papers, "Locking Up Natives in Canada" by Michael Jackson, under the auspices of the Special Committee on Imprisonment and Release of the Canadian Bar Association, the author states that "one reason why Native inmates are disproportionately represented in the prison population is that too many of them are being unnecessarily sentenced to terms of imprisonment" (Jackson 1988: 212). No data are presented to support the implication that racial bias leads to imprisonment. In a similar way, Morse and Lock support the view of aboriginal offenders that "virtually the entire justice system as a system ... is biased against native people" (Morse and Lock 1988: 48), and appear to base this belief, at least in part, on aboriginal inmates' perceptions that they receive harsher sentences than do non-aboriginals. The Morse and Lock study does not compare aboriginal inmate perceptions with those of a non-aboriginal control group of inmates, and Jackson gives no data to support his claim. These are examples of the limited methodologies and levels of analysis that have prevailed to date. In order to examine the sentencing of aboriginal offenders, it is necessary to identify the sentencing issues. For purposes of this paper these are:

a. *Unwarranted disparity in dispositions* — are aboriginal people incarcerated for offences for which non-aboriginal offenders receive non-carceral sentences, controlling for seriousness of offence, prior record, and other legally-relevant variables?

b. *Unwarranted disparity in sentence length* — do aboriginal offenders receive longer sentences (of incarceration, probation, and community service orders) than non-aboriginal offenders, controlling for seriousness of offence and prior record?

To date, there have been few empirical attempts to address these questions. This may be changing. Recent research by Scott Clark (1989), sponsored by the federal Department of Justice, and the draft terms of reference for the proposed Task Force on the Criminal Justice System and its Impact on Indian and Metis People in Alberta[6] (Alberta Task Force 1989) suggest that research activity in this area may increase significantly.

Clark's review of sentencing literature and empirical research in aboriginal criminal justice (Clark 1989) provides no conclusive evidence to support or reject the existence of unwarranted disparity or overt racial bias in the sentencing of aboriginal people. He points out that the lack of a solid empirical base has inhibited any real understanding of whether bias exists in the conviction and sentencing of aboriginal accused. It is clear from Clark's account that there have been few attempts in Canada to examine the sentencing of aboriginal people within the standard "individual-processual" theoretical approach much less in the broader "structural-contextual" approach envisioned by Hagan and Bumiller (1983). The former approach explains sentencing in the context of legal and extra-legal factors; the latter in the social, economic, and political context. The utility of the emphasis on criminal justice processing as the cause of over-representation explains the reluctance to promote a more fundamental context to sentencing.

A. UNWARRANTED DISPARITY IN DISPOSITIONS

Two of the first Canadian attempts to examine the issue of disparity in dispositions were undertaken by Dubienski and Skelly (1970), using Winnipeg arrest data, and by John Hagan (1977), using a sample of incarcerated offenders and a sample of offenders for whom pre-sentence reports had been written. Hagan's 1977 work followed his earlier research on factors affecting judicial decision-making where he found that judicial reliance on a law and order model of society explained more variance in sentencing than did race (Hagan 1974). Dubienski and Skelly found relatively fair treatment of Indian accused except in the area of regulatory offences where fines were disproportionately imposed. This was a form of discrimination because the Indian group was less able to pay fines. Hagan's 1977 research revealed more severe sentencing of aboriginal people in rural areas; he attributed this to the lack of bureaucratization in courts resulting in greater discretion in the criminal justice system.

Contrary to Hagan's urban/rural court findings were those of Boldt, Hursh, Johnson and Taylor (1983: 269) in the Yukon where no evidence of harsher or more lenient sentencing was revealed, and legal factors (particularly prior record) explained sentence variance. In addressing the concern that aboriginal people are less likely to receive probation to the same degree as do non-aboriginal offenders, the Research Group's study for the Correctional Sentences Project using national data on custodial, fine default, and probation admissions is informative (The Research Group 1987). For the year 1984–85, for the jurisdictions where data were available, the highest number of custodial admissions for aboriginal offenders were for murder, aggravated assault, and manslaughter. The lowest number of custodial admissions for aboriginal offenders for the same period were for extortion. The highest number of *fine default* admissions for aboriginal offenders were for public mischief and obstruct justice; the lowest for trafficking in drugs. The highest number of *probation* admissions were for aggravated assault and possession under; the lowest for theft of credit cards.

Aggregating the data (although limited because all jurisdictions are not represented) is useful in challenging the belief that aboriginal people receive probation for serious offences less often than do non-aboriginal people. Variations by province and territory or by race of victim may exist; but the fact that the numbers of probation admissions for a serious offence such as aggravated assault are higher for the aboriginal than the non-aboriginal accused might suggest less prejudicial treatment than is generally supposed. Moyer's research on comparative dispositions for aboriginal and non-aboriginal people accused of homicide provides some interesting findings (Moyer 1987). The Canadian Centre for Justice Statistics, Homicide Project, provided native and non-native victim, suspect and court procedure data for the period

1962–84. However, from 1962–73, only murder offences are included; from 1974, murder, manslaughter, and infanticide offences are included.

Moyer's analysis revealed that Natives were less likely to be convicted of first or second degree murder and more likely to be convicted of manslaughter than were non-natives — 76.3 percent and 73.7 percent of native men and women respectively as compared to 45.6 percent and 56.4 percent non-native; only 4.0 percent of native men were convicted of first degree murder as compared to 13.5 percent of non-native men; one-half as many native suspects were convicted of second degree murder as were non-native. It is important to keep in mind that Moyer's data did not include information on victims and alcohol involvement so the application of the findings is limited.

A recent study in B.C. under the auspices of the Legal Services Society, examined the effect of sentencing practices in summary conviction courts for the single charge offences of common assault and theft under $1,000, for a 9 month period in 1988. The sample consisted of Legal Services Society cases — a total of 1,772, of which 409 involved Common Assault and 1,363 Theft Under. Aboriginal people comprised 29.3 percent of the common assault cases and 21 percent of the theft under cases. In general, the findings showed that:

> ... individuals of Native ancestry with prior criminal convictions were acquitted less frequently and found guilty more often (of theft under one thousand dollars category only — author's note) than non-Native individuals in similar circumstances. Individuals of Native ancestry free of prior criminal convictions are granted stay of proceedings more frequently, and found guilty less often than individuals of non-Native ancestry. Single, unemployed individuals of Native ancestry residing off-reserve were sentenced to jail time more often than those of non-Native ancestry[7] (or than those of Native ancestry living on reserve seems to be the assumption in the paper although it is not specified). (Lewis 1989: 15)

The study included variables such as education, sex, age, employment, and residency (on/off reserve); but the relationship of these factors to sentence outcome for the aboriginal and non-aboriginal groups is unclear, except as previously noted for employment and residency. More sophisticated analysis using regression or other techniques with larger sample sizes would be necessary to clarify the effect of these variables.

Taken together these findings provide no definitive answers to the question of racial bias or unwarranted disparity in the sentencing of aboriginal people, but highlight some of the contradictions that exist.

B. DISPARITY IN SENTENCE LENGTHS

Better data on sentence lengths for aboriginal and non-aboriginal accused allow for a more focused discussion on whether unwarranted disparity exists. Early work by Schmeiser (1974), Hagan (1974), Hylton (1981), concluded that the shorter sentence lengths given aboriginal accused reflected the fact that they received custodial sentences for the less serious offences. The issue of disparity in disposition is still unclear but recent work suggests that aboriginal accused may be receiving shorter sentence lengths even when controlling for type of offence. Missing from the analysis are the effects of socio-economic and cultural factors upon judicial decision-making.

The findings from Moyer's homicide data are interesting and raise questions for further research (Moyer 1987). About one-half of the non-aboriginal persons convicted of homicide received life sentences as compared to one-fifth of the aboriginal persons; nearly 50 percent of the aboriginal accused received periods of detention less than five years as compared to less than 25 percent of the non-aboriginal group. The sentences for aboriginal women were particularly light as 29 percent were placed on probation or given a suspended sentence as compared to only 10 percent of the non-aboriginal women (Clark 1989: 24). Although Moyer was unable to present the findings in terms of offence category by sentence length, her findings suggest that aboriginal homicide offenders receive less severe sentences than do non-aboriginals for the same offence categories. Again, it should be stressed that data on alcohol involvement and race of victim were not available for consideration in the analysis.

The research by Canfield and Drinnan (1981), using 5 years of federal admissions data from 1976–80, shows disparity in sentence length that favours aboriginal accused.[8] When examining offence type by sentence length, the native groups almost consistently received shorter sentences than did the non-native groups for the same offences. For example, 55.1 percent of the natives received sentences of 4 years or less for attempted murder as compared to 23.2 percent of non-natives; 34.4 percent of the natives received sentences of 6 years or more as compared to 60.2 percent of the non-natives. For manslaughter the figures were 43.4 percent (native) and 22.2 percent (non-native) for sentences of 4 years or less, and 26.7 percent and 51.3 percent respectively for 6 years or more. Similar disparities were found for break and enter, theft, assault, robbery, and sexual offences as well. In general, these findings were supported in a later study by Moyer, Billingsley, Kopelman and LaPrairie (1985) using 1981–82 data.

The Moyer et al. research examined sentence length by offence type for aboriginal and non-aboriginal admissions to federal, provincial, and territorial correctional institutions. Admissions to the provincial and territorial institutions revealed few differences between the two groups in terms of sentence lengths for Criminal Code and provincial/territorial offences. (Moyer et al. 1985) However, Correctional Services, Canada data showed aboriginal sentenced admissions to be generally shorter than non-aboriginal sentenced admissions in 1982.

The most recent research on sentence lengths (Bonta 1989) found no significant differences between average sentence lengths for native compared to non-native offenders even after controlling for criminal history.

DISCUSSION

The data concerning the role of judicial discretion in causing the alleged statistical over-representation of aboriginal people in correctional institutions remain contradictory and unclear. On the one hand, there are suggestions of unwarranted disparity recurring throughout the aboriginal criminal justice literature and in media reports emanating from the three Inquiries presently underway in Canada.[9] In addition, where there appears to be some empirical basis to the question of disparate sentencing in terms of sentence type, the contributing factors range widely from rural court procedures, as suggested by Hagan (1977: 597), to the over-imprisonment for minor offences explanation put forward by Dubienski and Skelly (1970). More comprehensive data are required, however, on sentencing patterns for both aboriginal and non-aboriginal offenders for a range of offences controlling for legal and extra-legal factors as much as possible in order to determine whether unwarranted disparity in sentence types causes disproportionate incarceration of aboriginal persons. It is quite clear that more aboriginal people in Canada are in correctional institutions than would be expected given their numbers in the general population (if that is even the most appropriate standard to be using as discussed earlier). The exact role of sentencing in creating over-representation is still unknown.

Sentence length data, however, tell a different story. Canadian data are limited, but they suggest the possibility of shorter sentences for aboriginal offenders for some offences. There are some international data that parallel the Canadian findings. Recent and relatively comprehensive data from Australia show shorter sentence lengths for aborigines for virtually all offence categories. Using 1984 aggregated average sentence length data (excluding Queensland where ethnicity is not recorded), the author found that:

> In only two significant categories are the Aboriginal average sentences greater than the equivalent for non-Aboriginals — despite the gross disparities in prior imprisonment records. Even though 81.1 percent of Aboriginal prisoners have previously been in prison under sentence, compared with only 57.5 percent of non-Aboriginal prisoners, the average sentence for Aboriginal prisoners is only 42.6 months compared with 74.9 months for non-Aboriginals. This cannot be entirely attributed to the different types of offences committed by Aboriginals since the sentencing disparity is roughly consistent across the whole range of offences. (Walker 1987: 111)

The Australian findings contradict what is generally known about sentencing decision-making from the available Canadian research, i.e., seriousness of offence and prior record are the most significant variables. If shorter sentence lengths for aboriginal offenders are confirmed in future research, it will be necessary to determine if judges rely more on incarceration when aboriginal offenders cannot meet the criteria for probation but balance incarceration decisions with shorter sentence lengths. There may be important consequences to such a practice. For example, does the combination of incarceration and shorter sentence lengths result in higher recidivism rates and longer prior records? Do longer records make incarceration more likely in the event of a subsequent conviction?

Hogarth (1971) examined sentencing decisions with respect to aboriginal people. More recently, a study by Patricia Brantingham, Daniel Beavon, and Paul Brantingham (1982) analyzed sentencing decisions for 2,000 legally aided cases (not necessarily aboriginal people) initiated in two Canadian communities. We can derive from these studies the message that research into the sentencing of aboriginal people must account for factors (cultural, historical, political, social, economic, and geographic) that have created a particular identity and environment for aboriginal groups in Canada. The complexities that result with respect to who appears in the criminal justice system and how they are perceived by decision-makers may require different theoretical and methodological approaches than those normally adopted by researchers. Indeed, the need to take a broader view has been identified by Hagan who suggests that "consensus and conflict theories do not provide sufficient attention to the structural relationships that emerge from a joining of organizational and political forces in the direction of criminal justice operations" (Hagan 1989: 116–135).

The findings of Brantingham *et al.*[10] question some of the "sacred cows" in the aboriginal over-representation discourse. For example, is it valid to state generally that aboriginal people plead guilty more often and are more likely to be sentenced to periods of incarceration as a result of so pleading? Similarly, can it generally be said that aboriginal people suffer more adverse effects in their dealings with the criminal justice system because they have legal aid representation rather than lawyers from the private bar? The Brantingham *et al.* findings suggest the need for comparative research to determine if their findings based on research in non-aboriginal communities apply to an aboriginal sample.

It is clear that understanding the sentencing of aboriginal offenders is like trying to complete a jigsaw puzzle without all the pieces. Even where data are available, they often raise more questions than answers. Perhaps what is required at this point is the presentation of three possible explanations, i.e., overt racism, systemic discrimination, and/or preferential treatment, as a way of identifying the parameters for further exploration.

RACISM, SYSTEMATIC DISCRIMINATION, OR PREFERENTIAL TREATMENT?

As previously discussed, accusations by aboriginal people and others of overt racism in the criminal justice system have played an important role in the "over-representation" discourse to date. The fact that solid data on the relationship between criminal justice processing and the over-representation of aboriginal people as inmates in correctional institutions are limited at best does not inhibit the wide-spread use of this explanation. Perhaps the adoption of this perspective fulfils both real and perceived, i.e., symbolic, needs in ways that other explanations could not accomplish — the illuminating of contemporary aboriginal life as marginalized, resulting from the historical processes of colonization, dislocation from homelands, and erosion of traditional activities. This position also supports certain political agendas (such as self-government development) that require the treatment of aboriginal people by dominant systems to be such that aboriginal specific systems would be the only logical solution to the "problem."

That is not to say that no racism exists in the criminal justice system. Anecdotal material suggests that racism (both real and perceived) is a major concern to aboriginal people and warrants attention by those charged with criminal justice policy responsibilities. A commitment to research, which examines races as an explanation for disparities in criminal justice processing, is required (Zatz 1987). In the absence of sound empirical data, one is left to speculate about the anomalies identified above.

If aboriginal people are indeed at greater risk of incarceration than non-aboriginal accused for the same offences, explaining this phenomenon solely in racism terms may be simplistic and misleading with respect to finding real and long-lasting solutions to the over-representation problem. Some theorists have recently raised the issue of systemic discrimination as a means of accounting for disparity in sentencing dispositions (Archibald 1989; Clark 1989; LaPrairie 1988). It would undoubtedly be useful to explore this approach further.

SYSTEMIC DISCRIMINATION OR
PREFERENTIAL TREATMENT?

In short, systemic discrimination as defined by Archibald, Clark, and others points to the significance of "treating unequals equally"; that is, applying the same criteria to all offenders in disposition considerations. This phenomenon may have more adverse consequences for aboriginal accused if, for example, judges make disposition decisions and/or probation officers make recommendations regarding dispositions based on the presence or absence of certain structural factors such as employment, education, or family and community supports. As researchers such as Petersillia (1985) have noted in analyzing the criminal justice processing of blacks in the U.S., the granting of probation is based on certain risk factors, in part, and that providing the court with more complete background information may prejudice judges against granting probation. The recognition that aboriginal people reside at the lowest socio-economic level in Canadian society and that perceptions of marginality may affect judicial decision-making should not be ignored in understanding and explaining the phenomenon of differential sentencing.

Archibald, in his discussion of systemic discrimination in sentencing, suggests that a social responsibility model of crime causality, which locates crime in social and economic marginality and inequality, should be taken into account at sentencing. (Archibald 1989) Adopting such an approach implies institutionalizing the practice of "treating unequals unequally" to reduce the impact of social and economic disparities between groups. If some of the findings indicating less severe sentences for aboriginal accused are verified in further research, this may be evidence that some judges are aware of the realities facing aboriginal people in everyday life and that this is reflected in length of sentences. In short, there may be some evidence of "treating unequals unequally." What remains a greater problem for the criminal justice system is the "over use" of incarceration for aboriginal people when criteria for existing options for sentencing cannot be met.

SENTENCING REFORM

Existing data, although limited and incomplete, would suggest the disproportionate sentencing of aboriginal people to periods of incarceration in the absence of other sentencing options. This situation makes one of the most compelling arguments for sentencing reform. Nowhere else is the use of the criminal justice system to address a major social and economic problem so potentially problematic as it is in relation to aboriginal people. It is this group that appears to be incarcerated for less serious offences because its members do not qualify for probation, and few options but incarceration are available to judges. Their deprived socio-economic situation acts against aboriginal people at sentencing and against communities in the development and maintenance of community-based alternatives. The geographic location of the majority of reserves makes access to universal sentencing alternatives difficult and often impossible.

The sentencing of aboriginal people to shorter periods of incarceration as a way of "balancing" harsher dispositions has a long-term revolving door effect in addition to the short-term unpleasantness of being put in jail. Over time, the revolving door syndrome creates a large group of aboriginal people with long records of incarceration that act against them in subsequent court appearances.

Clearly, if many aboriginal people are incarcerated for relatively minor offences (an issue for provincial institutions only, as federal inmates are in for more serious offences) for which few options are available, it is imperative to examine other avenues for dealing with the problems they present. The social and economic marginality of aboriginal people in Canadian society is the fundamental problem and their involvement in the criminal justice system as offenders is a vivid testimonial to it. The criminal justice system is not a vehicle for social restructuring; neither should it be a storage receptacle for social problems. The criminal justice system could divert those to be handled outside it, and develop options to incarceration for those who require handling within it. Incarceration should be used only as a last resort.

The social distintegration, economic deprivation, and geographic location of the majority of reserves (resulting from colonization, cultural dislocation, and marginalization) often present a poor prognosis for the implementation and maintenance of community-based diversion and/or sentencing options. Criminal justice policy and program decision-makers must be committed to developing, evaluating, and institutionalizing justice programs, where required and feasible. This is necessary to ensure that community-based criminal justice initiatives become entrenched and do not suffer the "here today gone tomorrow" syndrome of so many activities in aboriginal communities dependent on outside funding. Creative planning and commitment is also required in urban areas to provide alternatives to imprisonment.

Adequate training of community-based workers and monitoring and assistance from provincial professionals have been identified by Clark as integral to the success and stability of programs. (Clark 1989) Serious consideration must also be given to the "access" problem, i.e., aboriginal people being excluded from universal alternative programs because of where they live. Perhaps the most critical element is the necessity for criminal justice programs to reflect the real needs in reserve, rural, and urban communities as well as the ability of the communities to develop and sustain them.

NOTES

1. One of the few exceptions is the work by James Bonta (1989), where risk assessment scales were administered to Native and non-Native inmates in three northern Ontario jails and the issue of over-representation was related to criminal justice processing.
2. Over-representation figures emerge from information collected routinely on admissions to correctional institutions and based on self-identification. Because information is collected routinely only at the corrections admission level, it is the one consistent source of data.
3. Normally, admission data are used to describe the over-representation phenomenon. However, the difficulty with admissions to provincial institutions is that it can count the same person more than once, if an individual is serving numerous short sentences over a 2-year period. As well, it has been suggested that in some provinces fine defaulters, upon sentence to a correctional institution, are admitted to the institution and immediately released to fine option programs. What this means is that they could appear in admissions data but are not serving actual custodial time.
4. Statistics Canada data on the age distribution of the B.C. native population show the under-20 native group to be 50.18 percent as compared to 29.83 percent for the non-native group.

5. Kanai News, June 23, 1989 pp. 4, 11. While only one reference is provided here, there is an abundance of material that refers to the racial nature of police decision-making. The assumption of overt racism on the part of police was very much at the root of the three inquiries into the treatment of aboriginal people by the criminal justice system — the Donald Marshall, Manitoba, and Alberta (Blood Reserve) Inquiries. In a recent presentation to the Western Judicial Conference, June 24–29, 1989, Brian Thorne of the First Nations of South Island Tribal Council stated that non-Indian Policing is "filled with subtle and sometimes blatant racial prejudice." (Western Judicial Education Centre 1989)

6. The term that refers specifically to the sentencing disparity research issue is as follows: "determine whether and to what extent differences exist in sentencing practices as (sic) between Indian and Metis people."

7. Aboriginal participation rates are difficult to interpret in the offence categories because it is not necessarily a random sample; as the Legal Services Society was established to provide assistance to groups with special needs, in this case aboriginal people. The analysis also limits findings, for example, number and type of prior convictions are important factors in sentencing dispositions; single variables were analyzed in relation to sentence outcome for the aboriginal and non-aboriginal groups rather than looking at them in combination, so that it is impossible to determine how much explanatory value each variable has. Finally, there is no information provided for sentence lengths.

8. Sentence lengths were calculated by the author from the tables provided.

9. Royal Commission on the Donald Marshall Jr. Prosecution, the Manitoba Public Inquiry into the Administration of Justice and Aboriginal people, and the Alberta Public Inquiry into Policing on the Blood Reserve.

10. Case facts, aggravating and mitigating circumstances, and prior record were most strongly related to sentence type decision-making. Entering a guilty plea, although statistically significant, was weakly related to sentence type — guilty pleas were associated with higher probation and lower fine rates, but were not associated with incarceration rates. Individuals represented by a public defender received fewer jail sentences than private counsel clients. Sentence length decisions were strongly associated with prior record, use of weapons, and length of criminal career.

REFERENCES

Alberta Task Force. 1989. Terms of Reference: Task Force on the Criminal Justice System and Its Impact on the Indian and Metis People of Alberta. Alberta: Ministry of the Attorney General Alberta.

Archibald, Bruce P. 1989. Sentencing and visible minorities: Equality and affirmative action in the criminal justice system. Paper presented at the Sentencing Now and in the Future Conference, March 3–4, Halifax, Nova Scotia.

Bienvenue, Rita M. and A.H. Latif. 1974. Arrests, dispositions and recidivism: a comparison of Indians and Whites. *Canadian Journal of Criminology*, 16: 105–116.

Boldt, Edward, Larry Hursh, Stuart Johnson and Wayne Taylor. 1983. Presentence reports and the incarceration of Natives. *Canadian Journal of Criminology* 25: 269–276.

Bonta, James. 1989. Native inmates: institutional response, risk and needs. *Canadian Journal of Criminology*, 31: 49–61.

Brantingham, Patricia, Daniel Beavon and Paul Brantingham. 1982. Analysis of Sentencing Disparity in Two Canadian Communities. Ottawa: Department of Justice, Canada.

Canfield, Carolyn and Linda Drinnan. 1981. Comparative Statistics: Native and Non-Native Federal Inmates — A Five Year History. Ottawa: Ministry of the Solicitor General.

Clark, Scott. 1989. Sentencing Patterns and Sentencing Options Relating to Aboriginal Offenders. Ottawa: Department of Justice, Canada.

Dubienski, Ian and Stephen Skelly. 1970. Analysis of arrests for the year 1969 in the City of Winnipeg with particular reference to arrests of persons of Indian descent. Unpublished.

Hagan, John. 1974. Criminal justice and native people: A study of incarceration in a Canadian province. *Canadian Review of Sociology and Anthropology Special Issue*: 220–236.

———— 1977. Criminal justice in rural and northern communities: A study of the bureaucratization of justice. *Social Forces* 55: 597–612.

———— 1989. Why is there so little criminal justice theory? Neglected macro- and micro-level link between organization and power. *Journal of Research in Crime and Delinquency*, 26: 116–135.

Hagan, John and Kristin Bumiller. 1983. Making sense of sentencing: A review and critique of sentencing research. In Alfred Blumstein, Jacqueline Cohen, Susan Martinaud and Michael Tonry (eds.), *Research on Sentencing: The Search for Reform*. Washington, DC: National Academy Press.

Hogarth, John. 1971. *Sentencing as a Human Process*. Toronto: University of Toronto Press.

Hylton, John. 1981. Locking up Indians in Saskatchewan: Some recent findings. *Canadian Ethnic Studies*, 13: 144–151.

Jackson, Michael. 1988. Locking Up Natives in Canada — A Report of the Special Committee of the Canadian Bar Association on Imprisonment. Ottawa: Canadian Bar Association.

LaPrairie, Carol Pitcher. 1987. Native women and crime: A theoretical model. *Canadian Journal of Native Studies*, 1: 121–137.

———— 1988. Aboriginal youth and the YOA. In Joe Hudson, Joe Hornick and B. Burrows (eds.), *Justice and The Young Offender in Canada*. Toronto: Wall and Thompson.

Lewis, Dave. 1989. An Exploratory Study into Sentencing Practices in Summary Convictions Court in British Columbia, Vancouver: Legal Services Society. Unpublished.

Morse, Brad and Linda Lock. 1988. Native Offenders' Perceptions of the Criminal Justice System. Research Reports of the Canadian Sentencing Commission. Ottawa: Department of Justice Canada.

Moyer, Sharon. 1987. Homicides Involving Adult Suspects 1962–1984: A Comparison of Natives and Non-Natives. Ottawa: Ministry of the Solicitor General.

Moyer, Sharon, Brenda Billingsley, Faigie Kopelman and Carol LaPrairie. 1985. Native and Non-Native Admissions to Federal, Provincial and Territorial Correctional Institutions. Ottawa: Ministry of the Solicitor General.

Muirhead, Greg. 1981. An Analysis of Native Over-representation in Correctional Institutions in B.C. Vancouver: Ministry of the Attorney General.

Petersillia, Joan. 1985. Racial disparities in the criminal justice system: A summary. *Crime and Delinquency*, 31: 15–34.

Research Group (The). 1987. Research Reports on Sentencing. Reports of the Correctional Sentences Project. Ottawa: Department of Justice Canada.

Schmeiser, Douglas. 1974. The Native Offender and the Law. Ottawa: Law Reform Commission of Canada.

Walker, John. 1987. Prison cells with revolving doors: A judicial or societal problem? In Kayleen Hazelhurst (ed.), Ivory Scales: Black Australia and the Law. Australian Institute of Criminology.

Western Judicial Education Centre. 1989. Introduction to Aboriginal Law, The Western Workshop Proceedings, June 24–29, Vancouver, B.C.

Zatz, Marjorie S. 1987. The changing forms of racial/ethnic biases in sentencing. *Journal of Research in Crime and Delinquency*, 24: 69–92.

NINE

Should Victims Participate in Sentencing?

WAYNE N. RENKE

An innocent voice cut through the rank atmosphere of the Bernardo sentencing proceedings. Eleven-year-old Ryan Mahaffy wept as he addressed Bernardo: "Because you murdered my sister, you have changed my life in so many ways.... Because of you I am an only child.... some people have called you a monster and evil and I agree."

Some might wonder whether Ryan's evidence should have been admitted. Why should the impression of victims — those who have been harmed or their survivors — form any part of sentencing proceedings?

Victim participation in sentencing seems objectionable on many grounds. It opens up another front against which an offender must defend. It compromises judicial independence — how could a judge resist the emotional and political pressure exerted by victims before the bench? It yields evidence irrelevant to offenders' culpability. "Punishment," wrote George Fletcher in *With Justice for Some: Victim's Rights in Criminal Trials*, "responds to the wrong the offender commits, but not to the particular wrong as measured by victims willing to testify.... It hardly makes sense to think of life as sacred if its value is a function of how much others love or need the person killed," or, one might add, if it is a function of the eloquence of a survivor or his or her family. Victim participation is prejudicial to offenders since victims may encourage excessive sentences to achieve vengeance, typically not an accepted purpose of sentencing. It is unfair to offenders since those who have harmed eloquent victims may face stiffer sentences.

But despite these objections and despite the high value accorded offenders' interests in the criminal law, victims like Ryan Mahaffy should have the right to participate in sentencing hearings. Victim participation promotes both the accountability of sentencing proceedings to the public and the accountability of offenders to their victims. Current governing legal rules permit restrained victim participation while preserving offenders' procedural protections. Nor does victim participation seriously compromise the equal treatment of offenders.

THE BURDEN OF PROOF

As a matter of policy, even apart from Charter concerns, the interests of accused or offenders should have presumptive priority over competing interests in the criminal justice process. A trial is not a rally, public inquiry, or parliamentary committee hearing. A trial determines guilt or innocence. Punishment is imposed on the offender

Source: Wayne N. Renke, "Should Victims Participate in Sentencing?" *Policy Options*, 17, 1 (1996): 13–17. Reproduced by permission of *Policy Options*.

and none other. Generally, the state, with its large aggregations of power, should not be permitted to limit individuals' liberties without justification. Therefore, advocates of measures that limit offenders' interests through state power should bear the burden of proof.

Victim participation in sentencing may be considered a form of state action since the state facilitates it through both legislation and assistance programs. It may also be considered to limit offenders' interests by, at least, increasing offenders' legal and practical burdens and by threatening increased sentences. Nevertheless, compelling interests are served by victim participation in sentencing, and offenders' interests are not necessarily impaired unduly by the promotion of these interests.

INTERESTS SERVED BY VICTIM PARTICIPATION IN SENTENCING

The practical result of victim participation in sentencing is that a victim is permitted to speak for himself or herself. The victim may make a statement in writing, in accordance with a victim impact statement program, or orally, upon the ruling the sentencing judge. The victim's words are not words of a lawyer but the words of ordinary experience. Why, one might wonder, is this recovery of the victim's voice important? It might benefit a victim personally by providing catharsis but what public interests does it serve?

Victim participation promotes the openness, intelligibility, and accountability of criminal processes to the public. Victim participation reinscribes sentencing in ordinary experience. When a victim is permitted to describe the effects of an offence in his or her own words, private grief is expressed in ordinary language. The words used, the emotions conveyed, and the message given to the offender are comprehensible. The victim's speech opens the court room. The victim's speech does matter to sentencing; this shows that the criminal justice process reflects, to a degree, the perspectives of citizens. the victim's speech is a small sign of the court's accountability. Victim participation, then, should enhance the public's regard for the administration of justice, itself a worthy objective.

Moreover, victim participation takes back victimhood and punishment from their professionalized redefinitions. Legal discourse is not necessary to define or comprehend victims' injuries, and the pursuit of remedies for criminal injuries does not require the substitution of legal professionals for victims. We should keep in mind that the appropriation of criminal prosecutions by the legal profession is a relatively recent (19th century) development in Anglo-Canadian law. Victim participation in sentencing is also a small sign that the criminal law is not the sole province of an autonomous guild. But if sentencing is open to victim participation and if victims wish to see that justice is done, they cannot rely only on lawyers. They must act, they must participate. Sentencing becomes accountable to the public in the sense that the public bears some responsibility for its functioning; it becomes more the public's institution.

One might suggest that a crime, in contrast to a private wrong, harms society rather than the individual. Punishment, then, should reflect the social significance of the crime, not its impact on the victim. This suggestion is too baldly put. Evidence concerning the magnitude and impact of a crime on a victim has traditionally been considered in the calculation of sentences.

A benefit of the legislative and policy focus on victims might be the increased awareness and use of such evidence. Victim participation of the type we are considering, however, seems to serve some further purposes; it is not merely a new or improved version of what was always previously admissible. A further interest victim participation promotes is the accountability of offenders.

According to Bill C-41, one of the objectives of sentencing is "to promote a sense of responsibility in offenders, and acknowledgement of the harm done to victims and to the community." Accountability moves in two directions — from the offender to the community and from the offender to the victim. This point turns on the rejection of the view that crime is only a violation of the relation between the offender and society. An offence is also, primarily and directly, a violation of the relation between the offender and his or her victim. Without victims, there would be no crimes. Outside the law, a common technique for encouraging an offender to take responsibility is to show the offender the precise consequences of his or her actions, to show how others have been hurt, to show the losses caused by those actions. Victim participation imports this technique into sentencing. Exposing an offender to the harm he or she has inflicted on another person may elicit remorse and accountability more effectively than advising an offender that he or she has transgressed against some abstract community.

If victim participation is understood within the framework of accountability, it has no necessary connection to increased punitiveness. Accountability is concerned less with the quantity of the sentence than with the quality of the sentencing procedure, less with the judge's impression of the gravity of the offence than with communication between the victim and offender. Understood in this way, victim participation in sentencing avoids many of its criticisms. It does not provide a measure of injury that varies with victims' literary skills. A compelling statement should not be an aggravating factor in sentencing; a poorly written statement or the absence of a statement should not be a mitigating factor in sentencing. Rather, an expression of victim impact exposes the meaning of the criminal act to the offender ("look, this is what you have done").

Even if one concedes that victim participation in sentencing serves compelling interests, its governing legal rules must not unduly impair offenders' interests.

CURRENT LAW

Victims may put statements before sentencing courts pursuant to legislation or judges' rulings. Under current legislation, for the purpose of determining a sentence, the judge may (not must) consider an unsworn statement prepared by a "victim" in a provincially prescribed form. "Victim" means the person to whom harm was done or who suffered physical or emotional loss as a result of the commission of the offence; or, where this person is dead or incapacitated, the spouse or any relative of that person, anyone who has custody of that person or anyone who is responsible for the care or support of that person or any of that person's dependants. The statement is to describe the harm done to or the loss suffered by the victim as a result of the offence. The statement is filed with the court and a copy is provided to the accused and the prosecutor.

Victims' participation through this procedure is circumscribed. The statement is to concern only a victim's loss, not other matters such as sentencing recommendations or the victim's reflections on the substantive offence. The statement is reduced to writing, so the court is guarded against emotional outbursts during viva voce testimony. The judge has the ordinary power to disregard any prejudicial or scandalous portions of the statement. The judge has the discretion to disregard the statement entirely.

The offender maintains due process protections. The mere fact that the statement is unsworn should cause no alarm. Sentencing hearings tend to be relatively informal and evidence is frequently accepted simply through the unsworn submissions of counsel. If the offender challenges some allegation in the statement, he or she may call evidence to contradict the allegation. The victim may be called as a witness for the Crown, provide sworn testimony and be subject to cross-examination.

The victim impact statement provisions do not exhaust the means by which victims may participate in sentencing. Victims generally lack standing in criminal cases, though, and so cannot claim to be heard as of right. If Crown counsel cooperates, the victim may be called as a witness so that he or she may testify; or, as in the Bernardo case, the Crown may proffer videotaped or other documentary evidence prepared by the victim. The offender may or may not challenge the admissibility of the evidence. Generally, the judge is entitled to consider any credible and trustworthy evidence.

The last and overriding protection for the offender is the judiciary. Judges are subject to myriad influences and pressures, yet are generally considered to maintain their independence and impartiality. If judges are not swayed by pickets, editorials, or condemnations by hostile politicians, they should be expected to maintain their independence in the face of victims and determine fit sentences. Furthermore, a judge's sentence is reviewable by the provincial Court of Appeal (in practice, the court of last resort in most sentencing matters), which can correct a sentence falling outside the established range of punishment.

The law as it now stands adequately constrains victim participation in sentencing. Victim participation, however, could be modestly enhanced without diminishing offenders' protections.

PROSPECTIVE DEVELOPMENTS

The law might be developed in two directions. First, victims could be extended the right to make oral unsworn statements respecting the impact of the offence. This would be the equivalent of the offender's ability to offer unsworn evidence at sentencing. If the victim were properly briefed, his or her evidence would not stray into improper areas; the judge, in any event, could maintain control over the proceedings. The oral statement would give the victim a greater sense of participation in the sentencing. A victim might also find an oral statement advantageous if he or she has difficulty expressing himself or herself in writing. Oral statements pose advantages and disadvantages for the offender. The offender may obtain less complete disclosure of the contents of the oral statement before the hearing; but if the statement is contentious, the victim will be present to be called as a witness. Otherwise, the oral statement would be on the same footing as a written statement. The oral statement appears to be an acceptable development.

Second, the scope of statements could be expanded. Victims could be permitted to make sentence recommendations or to reflect on the circumstances of offences. Victims, I suggest, should not make sentencing recommendations. The purpose of victim participation is to inject ordinary experience into the court, not to transform victims into another set of lawyers with another set of legal submissions. Crown prosecutors, not victims, may best oppose offenders' positions on sentence. Furthermore, insofar as offender accountability is the target of victim participation, sentence quantum should not be the concern of victims. Victims should also not comment on the circumstances of offences. Again, it is the prosecutor's job to marshal this evidence. The victim should be given no special forum in which to provide an unsworn version of what may well be controversial facts. The victim's version of events should be adduced in the ordinary course of trial or sentencing proceedings. To permit this evidence to be given unsworn in sentencing proceedings would violate the offender's due process rights.

EQUALITY ISSUES

The mere fact that different offenders face different types of victim participation does not raise equality concerns. Offenders embrace contingency when they engage in crime. Some victims die; others miraculously survive. Some victims attend trial; others may not. Some victims give compelling testimony; others may not. Harming an eloquent victim is simply one of the risks run by the offender. Moreover, if, as I have suggested, the focus of victim participation is offender accountability rather than sentence increase, offenders may not be materially prejudiced by even eloquent victim participation.

In any event, the distinction between eloquent and non-eloquent victims is frequently exaggerated. Money and a higher education are not prerequisites for expressing pain. Witness Ryan Mahaffy's remarks: they would not have been improved by a ghost-writer.

The real equality issues in the victim participation context concern the information provided to victims and the assistance available to them. All victims should be informed of the ways in which they may participate in sentencing and should have access to assistance if they desire to participate. Provincial victims' assistance programs, police departments, RCMP detachments, and victim assistance units attached to policing services do attempt to inform and assist victims. Unfortunately, limited resources in our difficult economic times leave the scope of victim assistance programs at less than an ideal level. Not all victims receive the information or assistance they might need. This, however, is a political grievance of victims, not a ground for eliminating the good that the present system can accomplish.

CONCLUSION

Sentencing should become neither spectacle, nor occasion for the Crown and victims to "gang up" on offenders, nor space for the displacement of law by emotion. The interests of victims may be recognized in sentencing, however, without producing these results. In sentencing, legal reality and victims' reality should merge; victims should be allowed to reach offenders through ordinary language, and show offenders that reality of the effects of their acts. Perhaps the belief that offenders will be prompted to take responsibility for their actions is unrealistically optimistic. This belief, I suppose, is no more unrealistically optimistic than the beliefs that offenders will be rehabilitated or that prospective offenders will be deterred by punishment.

PART THREE
Policing Communities

A good deal of policy change and debate characterizes the field of policing today. Policing is said to be in transition from the traditional law enforcement model toward a community-based approach. Many of the issues confronting Canadian policing are related to how police departments provide services to the community, the limits of traditional policing strategies, and the need for a new model of policing in which there is a partnership between the police and the community (Griffiths and Verdun-Jones, 1994).

In 1990 the Solicitor General of Canada issued a discussion paper that contributed to this debate by laying out a vision of policing in the future when police departments are accountable to the community they serve (Normandeau and Leighton, 1990). Citizens, as the ultimate consumers of police services, will contribute to the setting of police priorities. The dominant emphasis in this vision is one of police–community partnership in trying to solve underlying neighbourhood problems rather than merely dealing with crime incidents after the fact. The phrase "community policing" represents this change in focus, when once again the police are close to their primary resource: ordinary citizens.

Data on policing in Canada presented in the discussion paper show that the number of officers per capita increased steadily from 1962 to 1975, and then levelled off. Meanwhile, the number of offences recorded per police officer increased fairly steadily over the same period. The discussion paper then notes that the use of police forces to maintain peace, order, and security is one of the most valued yet costly services for Canadians.

Furthermore, a variety of socio-demographic trends are projected to have far-reaching consequences for the nature of police work by the year 2000 (Normandeau and Leighton, 1990). These include an aging population that should reduce overall crime rates, while increasing victimizations related to the quality of life of the elderly, as well as fear of crime. Policing in an increasingly multicultural Canada will be challenged by racial tension, and a transformed family structure will mean higher rates of female crime, and more unsupervised children and youth on the street. Technological changes will increase opportunities for some types of property crime as well as emerging forms of crime associated with business, the environment, and communications. At the same time a growing fiscal crisis will limit police force budgets, forcing choices over limiting service and requiring proof of efficiency and effectiveness. Greater public participation in policing will emerge. While changing cultural values will be reflected in greater permissiveness toward "consensual" crimes, there will be even less public tolerance of violence against women and children.

This document claims that there is a growing consensus that "community policing" is the most appropriate response to the crime and disorder problems of modern Canadian society. While at first glance community policing seems a relatively recent development in policing, in many ways it represents the re-emergence of the original approach to urban public policing. The main historical trend has been a shift of responsibility for maintaining order away from the community to formal agencies of social control, with a corresponding decrease of community involvement. This has pressured police to play a variety of roles and pursue a number of objectives, including law enforcment/crime control, order maintenance, and service provision (Griffiths and Verdun-Jones, 1994). The crime control model of the police responding to citizen reports of crime incidents and patrolling randomly in an attempt to deter crime came to dominate police organization. This distanced the police from the community, a development enhanced by technological changes such as two-way radios, patrol cars, and on-board computers, as well as the invention of randomized motorized patrol and rapid response to calls from the public (Normandeau and Leighton, 1990).

However, this crime control model of policing has been called into question by research evaluating preventive patrolling and rapid response. For example, the Kansas City experiment (Kelling et al., 1974) examined the effect of different levels of patrol on criminal activity and citizen perceptions of police protection. Three different patrol strategies were randomly allocated to beats as similar as possible on a number of variables that might affect the level of crime. The experiment found that the level of patrol activity had no effect on reported victimizations or public perceptions of crime and the police. Research on response time (Spelman and Brow, 1984) found that delay by victims in calling the police renders police response time irrelevant to catching an offender. Police response time made a difference in only about 3 percent of all crime calls.

The marginal effectiveness of the crime control model of policing, along with the loss of community assistance and support in dealing with crime and disorder problems, has stimulated the re-emergence of community policing as represented in police–community partnership (Normandeau and Leighton, 1990). This discussion document identifies twelve ingredients of this "new" approach:

- the role of the police is fundamentally one of peace officers rather than merely law enforcers
- the key strategy in police-community partnership is community consultation
- the police adopt a pro-active approach by identifying local crime and disorder problems with input from the local community
- a flexible problem-oriented policing strategy is developed that will address the crime and order problems and their underlying causes
- broader police responses to underlying causes of problems are also introduced, particularly crime prevention activities
- these prevention activities involve a branching out to other service delivery agencies to form strategic partnerships fostering inter-agency cooperation
- police operate as information managers who engage in interactive policing by reciprocal formal and informal information exchange with community members
- tactics are developed to reduce the unfounded fear of being victimized
- most police officers become career generalists responsible for a broader range of activities
- front-line officers have greater responsibility and autonomy to undertake neighbourhood policing tactics
- the organizational structure is changed from the hierarchical, para-military model to a flatter profile
- there is a degree of accountability to the community in terms of a review of progress on priorities supported earlier by the community.

The consultation document claims that this "new" approach has become part of the conventional wisdom in most progressive urban police services in Canada and that there is growing consensus that community policing is the most appropriate policing approach. However, implementing this approach in a systematic way remains an issue. Bayley (1988) argues that community policing is a paradigmatic rather than a mere technical shift in police practice. It has profound implications for how police organizations are structured, how resources are allocated, and for the recruitment, training, and role of patrol officers (Griffiths and Verdun-Jones, 1994). While some innovative pilot projects have been developed, these are often grafted on to existing police operations (Kennedy, 1991). Murphy (1988) has argued that these community policing initiatives remain in most cases isolated strategies, an adjunct to the core crime control/rapid response to calls for service model. Implementation of community-based policing has been quite limited and its impact modest, at least in part due to resistance from the police themselves (Clairmont, 1991). The police culture and the dominance of the crime control model make it difficult to implement community policing as an all-embracing organizational change in service delivery. In fact, some critics have suggested that the adoption of community policing is more a matter of rhetoric than reality (Klockars, 1988).

An issue of continuing importance in the policing of communities concerns the extent to which police should vary their practices according to the expectations of different communities or different segments within a community. Research suggests that police do vary their enforcement practices according to neighbourhood characteristics (Sherman, 1986). However, this issue becomes even more salient with the move toward community-based policing. Communities may be divided and it may be unclear with whom the police should form partnerships. Communities of consensus may be a fiction since communities are, in fact, complex, ambiguous, diverse, and highly stratified (Mastrofski, 1988). This issue has special relevance in Canada for the policing of Aboriginal communities.

READINGS

The first reading of this section by Leighton takes a critical look at the concept of community policing. Leighton claims that community policing has received wide support despite lack of agreement on what it is and weak evidence for its effectiveness. He identifies a full partnership between the community and their police as the central principle of community policing and contrasts it with the traditional, "professional" model of policing. Leighton then describes some of the community policing initiatives in Canada and identifies nineteen unresolved issues that may challenge the viability of these initiatives. He concludes with a call for a critique of community policing as the dominant vision of progressive policing and for the development of a better theory about community policing.

The next paper is an impact evaluation of a neighbourhood foot patrol program, one form of community-based policing. The authors describe this Edmonton program and present the results of a quasi-experimental evaluation of how successful the program was in achieving a reduction of repeat calls-for-service, improvement of public/user satisfaction with police, and increased job satisfaction of foot patrol constables. The findings indicate success in achieving all three objectives.

The final paper of this section focusses on the policing of Aboriginal communities. Harding identifies four main approaches to reforming policing to redress problems faced by Aboriginal people: cross-cultural training programs for police; legal education for Aboriginal people; native constables; and tribal policing programs. Harding discusses each approach, linking their development to certain underlying political and ideological assumptions. He then reviews the implications of Aboriginal urbanization for urban policing, including the development of independent processes for dealing with citizen complaints. Harding asserts that Aboriginal justice is not possible without a political resolution to the problems arising from colonialism. He concludes by considering some of the issues involved in the development of a parallel Aboriginal justice system.

QUESTIONS FOR DISCUSSION

1. Why has community policing become so popular? What factors have influenced its adoption as a public policy?
2. What constitutes the "community" for community policing? With whom should/could the police form partnerships? How does this affect the establishment of local policing priorities? Can/should the police and the community be co-equal partners?
3. Are the police capable of dealing effectively with the underlying causes of crime? What do they have to contribute to inter-agency cooperation in dealing with underlying causes?
4. Do the characteristics of Aboriginal communities suggest that they may be more or less amenable to community policing?
5. Discuss the potential benefits and problems of a parallel Aboriginal justice system.

REFERENCES

Bayley, David. 1988. "Community policing." Pp. 225–38 in J.R. Greene and S.D. Mastrofski (eds.), *Community Policing: Rhetoric or Reality*. New York: Praeger.

Clairmont, Don. 1991. "Community-based policing." *Canadian Journal of Criminology* 33: 469–84.

Griffiths, Curt T. and Simon N. Verdun-Jones. 1994. *Canadian Criminal Justice*. Toronto: Harcourt Brace Canada.

Kelling, George L., T Pate, D. Dieckman, and C.E. Brown. 1974. *The Kansas City Preventive Patrol Experiment*. Washington, D.C.: Police Foundation.

Kennedy, Leslie W. 1991. "The evaluation of community-based policing in Canada." *Canadian Police College Journal* 15: 275–89.

Klockars, Carl B. 1988. "The rhetoric of community policing." Pp. 239–58 in J. R. Greene and S. D. Mastrofski (eds.), *Community Policing: Rhetoric or Reality*. New York: Praeger.

Mastrofski, Stephen D. 1988. "Community policing as reform." Pp. 47–67 in J. R. Greene and S. D. Mastrofski (eds.), *Community Policing: Rhetoric or Reality*. New York: Praeger.

Murphy, Christopher R. 1988. "The development, impact, and implications of community policing in Canada." Pp. 177–89 in J.R. Greene and S.D. Mastrofski (eds.), *Community Policing: Rhetoric or Reality*. New York: Praeger.

Normandeau, André and Barry Leighton. 1990. *A Vision of the Future of Policing in Canada*. Ottawa: Minister of Supply and Services Canada.

Sherman, Lawrence W. 1986. "Policing communities: What works?" Pp. 343–86 in Albert J. Reiss, Jr. and Michael Tonry (eds.), *Crime and Justice: A Review of Research*, Volume 8. Chicago: University of Chicago Press.

Spelman, William and Dale K. Brown. 1984. *Calling the Police*. Washington, D.C.: Government Printing Office.

TEN

Visions of Community Policing: Rhetoric and Reality in Canada

BARRY N. LEIGHTON[1]

INTRODUCTION

Community policing, sometimes referred to as community-oriented policing, community-based policing, or problem oriented policing, is currently presented by academic observers of policing as characterizing "modern," "progressive," or "contemporary" policing (Skolnick and Bayley 1986, 1988 a,b; Kelling 1987; Murphy 1988a; Greene and Mastrofski 1988; Trojanowicz and Bucqueroux 1990; Sparrow, Moore, and Kennedy 1990). While many of these commentators have also actively influenced the direction of community policing, it has been the prevailing wind of change among North American police leaders for the past few decades and a key ingredient of the public and professional discourse on policing reform. Canadian police professionals have also adopted as their conventional wisdom the view that community policing represents the most progressive approach to contemporary policing (Normandeau and Leighton 1990 a, b). Indeed, the majority of police leaders consulted during a series of federal government consultations during 1990 laid claim to their own police force as the most progressive in Canada, if not amongst police forces in the western world, on the grounds that they had adopted or had always been pursuing a community policing approach (Leighton 1990). Obviously, they cannot all be the leading police agency. Further, community policing appears to be in the eye of the beholder, especially when the beholder is a police executive, major, or other stakeholder in a local effort to establish community policing or to motivate change in policing.

Despite this conventional wisdom, it is not clear why community-based policing has recently become so popular in North America and elsewhere as the generic, all-purpose police solution to crime and disorder problems, especially given the weak empirical support for its effectiveness. In many ways it is like oat bran: there is general agreement that it has some beneficial effect and it has many devotees, but scientists are not quite sure how or why it works. Indeed, police executives claiming success for their own community-based policing project without a rigorous evaluation is like prematurely announcing a cure for colon cancer. Like oat bran, community policing may have more to do with bulky rhetoric and process; that is, an indirect effect rather than the direct effect of its substance on the desired outcome.

Source: Barry N. Leighton, "Visions of Community Policing: Rhetoric and Reality in Canada," *Canadian Journal of Criminology*, 33, 3–4 (1991): 485–522. Copyright by permission of the Canadian Criminal Justice Association. Reproduced by permission of the *Canadian Journal of Criminology*.

The question posed by Greene and Mastrofski (1988) as to whether community policing in Canada is "rhetoric or reality" is obscured by unrestrained support for the approach. This immense support flies in the face of a lack of agreement over what it means in theory and practice, and presents the problematic for this discussion. Accordingly, this paper attempts to present a clear and meaningful definition or description of community policing. It then sketches out some of the community policing initiatives taken by selected police forces across Canada. A number of unresolved issues are raised that may challenge the viability of community policing or, if responded to, may assist in improving its chances for greater effectiveness. Finally, an explanation for the popularity of this approach is sought in a brief review of its apparent origins and an attempt is made to place this policing paradigm within a broader theoretical context.

2. DEFINITION

What is community policing? As has been observed, the concept has a wide range of meanings (Manning 1984), resulting in little agreement over even its general nature. Indeed, it could be said that, like the concept of "community," the concept of "community policing" is in the eye of the beholder. However, while it is generally considered to be the "new" approach to policing that has recently begun to sweep through North America, Europe, and common law countries such as Australia and New Zealand, community policing might be more correctly referred to as a re-emergence, renewal, or revitalization of a former philosophical, organizational, and operational approach to urban policing developed last century in Metropolitan London by Peel and his associates. The current version of this approach may be summarized by a central principle followed by a family of subsidiary value statements on the preferred police role, authority, managerial style, organizational arrangements, and an operational approach in terms of strategies and tactics.

The central principle underlying this style of urban policing is a full *partnership between the community and their police* in identifying and ameliorating local crime and disorder problems. It claims that crime and disorder problems are the *joint property* of the community as "client" as well as of the police as the local agency delivering public security services. Accordingly, the police and the community are *co-producers of order and civility* (Wilson and Kelling 1982; Murphy and Muir 1984) and "co-reproducers of order" (Ericson 1982). They achieve this remarkable symbiotic state through an interactive, cooperative, and reciprocal relationship (Short 1983) that, in practical terms, means that community members, as clients of the police, participate in shaping police policy and decision making. Underlying this partnership principle is the core assumption that the level of crime, disorder, and fearfulness in a community is inversely related to the level of public participation in policing. That is, public participation breathes life into the partnership principle.

This relationship of partnership and participation contrasts with the "professional, bureaucratic, or traditional" model of policing in which crime is the exclusive property of the police under this "professional policing" or "crime control" model, the police form a "thin blue line" against crime and, in practice, unfortunately also form a thin blue line against the community. In operational terms, the professional model can be characterized in a number of different ways but has been described succinctly by Kelling and Moore (1988) as a technology-driven, rapid response strategy coupled with random motorized patrol. It is as if police forces under the "professional model" operated like a hospital organized as a large emergency ward. Most of the staff would be sitting around waiting for those relatively rare, life threatening events when the public would call in to ask for a rapid response by ambulance. Ambulances would cruise the accident "hot spots" to be more readily available but also to deter high risk behaviour such as unsafe driving or driving under the influence of alcohol. Patients would arrive only by ambulance, the regular wards would be largely forgotten, and regular health care would be neglected. Certainly, no one would indulge in preventive health care. Community policing can also be portrayed through a medical model. But, rather than being like an emergency ward, community policing is seen as being more like preventive medicine, with an emergency response used for only a small proportion of health care cases. This approach involves promoting and maintaining good health — exercise, a balanced diet, a lot of fibre, and less red meat — in the same way as building safer communities that have less crime and disorder problems relies upon the elements of community policing and preventive policing or crime prevention.

This juxtaposition of "community policing" and "professional policing" (see Table 10.1) is largely a heuristic device, or perhaps a pedagogical technique, that sharpens the contrast at the expense of rigour in the presentation of past and present policing practices (as does the "three eras of policing" referred to later). The professional model, which currently serves as a useful straw man for proponents of community policing, nonetheless played an important part in the development of modern policing and meets one of the minimal conditions of public expectations for safety in the form of rapid, reliable response for those relatively rare life-threatening incidents.

While there are a variety of components to various visions of community policing, most of them proceed from the partnership principle that has far-reaching implications for the organization and operations of police forces. For example, the police-community partnership is often seen as providing new resources from the community that combine to form the symbol of a "broad blue line" against crime and disorder in the community or, as Sklolnick and Bayley (1986) characterize it, a "new blue line" that has a more general role than merely crime control. Their vision of community policing identifies four elements, in terms of police-community reciprocity, a real decentralization of command, reorientation of patrol and civilianization. Others' visions follow the seminal work of Goldstein (1979, 1987, 1990) by identifying it with problem-oriented policing that largely limits community policing to the problem solving ingredient. Some of the components of the broad blue line are principles or value statements while others represent the routine distinction between strategies (e.g., problem solving) and tactics (e.g., foot patrol, mini-stations, consultative committees).

There are perhaps sixteen subsidiary ingredients of "community policing" that summarize the conventional wisdom among many police leaders and academics. The following summary is an elaboration on one of this author's contributions to an "official vision" of community policing (Leighton 1989; Solicitor General 1990; Normandeau and Leighton 1990; Leighton 1990).

1. *The central objective or mission of the police* in Canadian society is to ensure peace, order, and civility, to provide related services to the community, and to facilitate a

sense of security among the public. In helping to maintain peace, order, and security in local communities, police officers exercise their side of the partnership with the community by being routinely — but not exclusively — responsible for the reduction and prevention of crime and the promotion of public order and individual safety. In the words of Sir Robert Peel's first two police commissioners, Sir Charles Rowan and Sir Richard Mayne, the new police follow the principle "... that the police are the public and that the public are the police..." (Reith 1975). Accordingly, the police official's role is fundamentally that of a peace officer. By contrast, the objective of the traditional or professional policing approach is more narrow: it is to enforce the criminal law, solve crime, and apprehend criminals. The police role is to serve as law enforcement officers responsible only for crime control; that is, anything else is mere "social work" and not "real policing."

2. *The police legal authority* and their mandate to police local communities is derived from democratic institutions and is delegated by elected representatives to police executives. Where "the community" voices, through one means or another, their public approval of the nature and scope of the policing arrangements, then they are reaffirming their approval of the police mandate as well as their direct consent to be policed. Conferring of consent contributes in no small way to the success of community policing and goes beyond both the legal authority to police as a minimal requirement and a police-community partnership as an operating principle. By contrast, legal authority under the professional model is formal, passing through a chain of clearly circumscribed responsibility to the chief and down in hierarchical, para-military fashion through the chain of command. This authority structure is exclusive and shuts the door on community participation of any kind, at any level.

3. Community police agencies are *service-oriented organizations*. Because police officers serve and protect the public and provide related services to the public for crime and disorder problems, the preferred title of their organizations is now a "police service." This service orientation is consistent with the interpretation of urban policing as another municipal service, along with health, education, etc., which are delivered as legal and social justice entitlements to local taxpayers. It is also a reflection of the growing tendency to view the public as clients of the police who consume their services, in much the same way as they consume other goods and services in the private sector. Hence, private sector standards are being introduced into policing, including performance values such as the "search for excellence" (Peters and Wasserman 1982; Kanter 1983) and the search for quality in those services, for "continuous quality assurance" and for continuous improvement (Sensenbrenner 1991). As a result, the corporate culture and subculture is transformed. The corporate culture becomes that of a service agency to the public, borrowing values from the private sector such as partnerships, search for excellence, continuous quality assurance, etc. The subculture becomes that of a white-collar profession that is responsible, responsive to community needs, and driven by a code of professional ethics. By contrast, policing under the former model primarily serves the limited outcome of police work focused largely on crime control. This emphasis is symbolically represented by the use of "police force" as the preferred term for their organizations.

4. *A community consultation* process is employed as a key strategy to help the police accomplish the important objective of *identifying policing priorities* for addressing

TABLE 10.1 *Approaches to Policing*

Issue	Traditional Approach	Community-Based Approach
Objective/Mission:	to enforce the criminal law, solve crime, and apprehend criminals	to ensure peace, order, and civility; provide services to the community; and facilitate a sense of security
Police Role: outcome orientation	law enforcement officers police work	peace officers client/consumer; service delivery
Authority/Mandate: source	delegated from elected representatives; exclusive	delegated from elected representatives and community; multiplex
accountability	exclusive; formal/legal; often co-opted by police chief	multiple; formal/legal and informal with community; usually independent by police governing authorities with community through consultations, etc.
priority setting responsibility for crime/order problems	exclusive property of police	shared/partnership with community as client
Main Strategy:	incident solving (of discrete incidents seen as unrelated to other similar incidents)	problem solving (of patterns among similar incidents and their underlying causes) and therefore of future similar incidents, i.e., crime prevention
Criteria for success: effectiveness	lower crime rates; higher clearance rates	absence of crime, disorder, and incivility; reduction in repeat calls for service from repeat addresses, offenders, and victims; reduced fear; greater community satisfaction
efficiency	more rapid response time	problem identification and solution, in partnership with the local community
Tactics/Police Response: style	reactive — uniform/standard tactics	proactive — flexible tactics that are tailored to community needs and the nature of crime or disorder problems
response to calls predominant tactic	undifferentiated; rapid response to all calls random, motorized, preventive patrol	differential response; target "hot spots" victims, places, offenses, offenders/recidivists tailored to community and problem type; e.g., dedicated neighbourhood foot and/or car patrol, directed patrol, zones, mini-stations, flexible shifts, integrated teams, civilianization, volunteers, community liaison committees, etc.

relationship to community	distant, few contacts (usually limited to victims, witnesses, and offenders)	close, many contacts (facilitated by the above tactics)
source of intelligence	internal; suspects, victims	public, community
use of technology (cars, radios, computers)	over reliance, technology driven	balanced, flexible, not technology driven (i.e., as a means to a tactic)
relationship to other community services	lead role	partnership; recognizes limits to police mandate and expertise; inter-agency links (e.g., housing, employment, education, victim support agencies)
Organization & Control:		
management style	para-military	participatory/democratic
authority/command structure	centralized; hierarchical	decentralized; flatter, more "horizontal"
scope of officer responsibility	narrow; little discretion	broad, delegated; wide discretion and autonomy
control	invisible to public; informal internal discipline and formal/bureaucratic control (rules and regulations)	visible to public; formal internal discipline and external/public complaints mechanisms
loyalty	to superior via chain of command (i.e., the "Brown" model)	to *Charter*, *Criminal Code*, common law, and the community (i.e., the "Blue" model)
functional units	specialized	integrated (includes investigation)
role definition	specialized, with many specialist roles/units	generalist constable, with minimal complementary specialist roles/units
human resources	generic police officer rotated through specialist positions	open to lateral entry, civilianization, part-time staff, career specialization, etc.
Corporate Culture:		
professional culture	blue collar (below officer rank); policing as a career	white collar (all ranks); policing as a vocation
sub-culture	police as separate from the community; self-image as being superior to clients	police as members of the community; self-image as partners with the community in crime and disorder control

crime and disorder problems in the community. This process may be done on an annual basis, usually with the assistance of a police governing authority (e.g., police board or commission) and establishes the relatively short-term priorities for the year, as well as providing community feedback on police performance over the past year. This process also assists community representatives to set their agenda for safety and security in their area and to better understand the problems associated with public policing. A variety of consultation mechanisms that facilitate a police-community dialogue are currently being explored by Canadian police forces, such advisory or consultative committees and meetings with local interest groups. This approach differs from the former "professional" model, which usually pursued "police-community relations" through a specialized unit rather than at all levels of police service through a variety of means.

5. Taking a *proactive* approach to crime and disorder problems is a key strategy with the community policing approach, although it may also stand alone as part of "problem oriented policing" (Goldstein 1979, 1990; Eck and Spelman 1987 a,b). Rather than passively waiting for the calls or randomly patrolling for a presumed deterrent effect, the police anticipate future calls by identifying local crime and disorder problems. A first step in a scanning and forecasting process that identifies problems based on demographic and other "social data," including information from other agencies. It also includes input from the local community. The scanning process is accomplished in part by "crime analysis" involving the analysis of patterns among similar crimes and calls for service. "Hot spots" of similar crimes are identified by time, place, and type of offence. These hot spots are brought to the attention of street constables at the neighbourhood level, and to police managers and the police commission for community- or city-wide problems. Input from the local community is received in terms of local crime and disorder priorities. A strategic plan may be developed that priorizes the competing crime and disorder problems at the community level and may be debated in public discussions. This problem-identification strategy contrasts with the "professional model" approach of a knee-jerk, undifferentiated rapid-response to the majority of calls for service that are treated separately, despite any commonalities and prior history. Once responded to, each incident is treated as an event that is closed when the case has been solved.

6. The main police response strategy to address local crime and disorder problems is a *problem-solving strategy*, which is developed with a focus on their underlying causes (Goldstein 1979, 1990; Murphy, 1991). The most appropriate proactive and reactive policing tactics are selected to address particular crime and disorder problems in each neighbourhood, reflecting the reality that crime and disorder problems are not unitary phenomena, nor are the solutions, and nor are neighbourhoods and communities. This "community specific" approach parallels "client-specific planning" in designing individual treatment within the "something works" paradigm in corrections. Accordingly, flexibility in the use of tactics from the full range is a central principle in this approach and no single tactic can be identified with community policing. Indeed, any means of increasing the level and quality of contact between citizens and the police can be used that will facilitate greater public participation. Tactics might include zone policing, neighbourhood foot patrol, officers dedicated to particular beats, mini-stations or store-front offices, differentially responding to calls for service, volunteers,

greater civilianization, flexible shifts, integrated teams (of foot patrol, motorized patrol, and investigative functions), and community advisory or liaison committees. Once the problem has been solved or significantly reduced, then an evaluation or assessment is conducted to determine the effectiveness of the tactics for the particular problem and type of neighbourhood. By contrast the professional policing model focuses on discrete incidents that are treated as unrelated to other similar incidents, such as those previously occurring at the same place or time or with the same offender or victim.

7. A careful *balance* is maintained between proactive (e.g., prevention, problem solving) and reactive tactics (e.g., emergency response). Community policing recognizes the reality of a continued requirement for those tactics commonly identified with the professional model, including in particular a rapid-response capability that remains a fundamental requirement for policing when occasional life-threatening incidents arise. It is also necessary to continue maintaining a few specialist units, including homicide investigation teams that might also have responsibility for family violence where most homicides occur. However, the principle of minimal specialization is observed and the number of specialized units is severely limited, with the functions of "grin-and-wave" or community relations squads transferred to generalist constable. Whereas the professional approach preferred the use of rapid-response and random patrol tactics over other tactics, community policing does not reject any tactics that are appropriate to the problem and the neighbourhood.

8. Police address the *underlying causes of problems* using a broader set on longer-term *responses*, particularly crime prevention activities. These include opportunity reduction tactics such as "target hardening," principally, "crime prevention through environmental design" (CPTED) techniques. As well, "crime prevention through social development" (CPTSD) is recognized as the long-term solution in which prevention strategies focus on the reduction of the motivation of potential offenders or recidivists to engage in criminality by removing the root causes of these motivations. Under this framework, prevention tactics address poverty, unemployment, poor education, and work skills, inadequate housing, poor health, and other underlying causes of crime. On the other hand, the professional model treated long-term prevention as not within the realm of policing and continued to merely plug the leaking dike on a leak by leak basis.

9. *Inter-agency cooperation* is a key strategy involving a branching out to other service delivery agencies to form strategic partnerships and a more cooperative and productive division of labour. This allows both types of prevention activities (CPTED, CPTSD) to be more efficiently and effectively undertaken. Inter-agency cooperation recognizes the limits of policing beyond what they do extremely well, which is providing a round-the-clock, first rapid-response to crime and related crises. It also recognized the complementarity of police and those other agencies that are better able to provide a longer-term response for victims and to undertake crime prevention by removing the underlying causes of crime. This cooperative response places the police within a service network of agencies addressing urban safety and, more generally, the "healthy cities" approach. On the other hand, the former policing model often over-extended police organizations for many functions better provided by other agencies and presented an "iron agency curtain" by failing to link up with or cooperate with these other

agencies. Where police did cooperate with other agencies, then police professionals usually insisted on taking the lead role.

10. *Information management* is emphasized, relying on people-contacts within the
community as a major but not exclusive source of information and intelligence.
Much of the success of policing depends on how well its personnel operate as
information managers who engage in "interactive policing" by routinely exchang-
ing information on a reciprocal basis with community members through close
formal contacts and numerous information networks. While much of the police
work is often seen as not being "real" police work because it involves providing
services and information unrelated to crime, community police do so on the
grounds that, not only is policing a service to the public, but it allows the public
to become more familiar with their police service and the police to become more
knowledgeable about their community. Closer ties with community members are
a good investment because they can become sources of valuable information or
police "intelligence" when crime problems later arise. By contrast, while some
specialized units emphasize human sources of intelligence, the professional
model generally exhibits an over reliance on technology, such as cars, radios, and
computers. Indeed, the professional model tactics appear to be technology-driven rather than technology being used as a means to enhance the efficiency and
effectiveness of preferred tactics. Contacts with the community are not only
inhibited by a reliance on technology, but distance police from the community. In
many police forces contact with the public was once prohibited unless they were
explicitly for crime-related business involving victims, witnesses, and offenders.
Intelligence sources were therefore largely internal to police agencies.

11. The composition of community police services is shifting towards a better
reflection of the demographic and social composition of the communities they
serve, particularly through the recruitment of women, visible and ethnic minorities, and Aboriginal police officers. Positions that are not directly related to
crime control are increasingly being civilianized. Community volunteers are also
being used in mini-stations and other community policing tactics although it is
interesting to note that, in the logical extension of the Peelite vision of community policing, it is the police who are the true volunteers, being paid full-time to
assist the community to control crime and disorder. These trends facilitate an
improved understanding of community views by police professionals.

12. More relevant *criteria for success* of police service effectiveness or performance are
now being established. These criteria are now reaching a more appropriate balance between those stressing community policing processes and those stressing
its impact. Some of these new indicators of effectiveness include: (1) identifying
local crime and disorder problems through a police-community consultation
process; (2) solving local crime and disorder problems through a police-community consultation process; (3) higher reporting rates for both traditional crime
categories and for non-traditional crime and disorder problems; (4) reducing the
number of repeat calls for service from repeat addresses; (5) improving the satisfaction with police services by public users of those services, particularly victims
of crime; (6) increasing the job satisfaction of police officers; (7) increasing the
reporting of information on local crime and disorder problems by community
residents, and increasing the knowledge of the community and its problems by
local beat officers; and (8) decreasing the fear of personal victimization. The

reduction of the unfounded fear of crime and of being victimized is a legitimate objective within the new approach, including fear reduction tactics directed towards the elderly, children, and other vulnerable groups in society. Typically, those with the lowest statistical risk have the greatest fear of being victimized, particularly elderly. The police now have a responsibility to ensure that this fear has constructive rather than debilitating effects so that those who are vulnerable or view themselves as vulnerable may take reasonable crime prevention measures and then enjoy a safe environment. The professional model, by contrast, sees fear reduction as being outside established police responsibilities and accepts as legitimate the established criteria of (1) response time, (2) charges cleared, (3) others that stress the efficiency rather than the effectiveness of policing, and (4) popularity polls on how much community members like their local police force.

13. There is a *transformed organizational structure* in two ways, resulting in *greater responsibility and autonomy* for front-line, street constables to apply community policing strategies and tactics in neighbourhoods. First, the hierarchical, paramilitary organizational model that exists in many large police services is changed into a flatter profile in which the front line of policing, where police services are provided, is the most important part of the organization. A great deal of responsibility is shifted down a rank, making some levels redundant. In designing a more efficient police service delivery organization, there is therefore a "de-layering" of the authority structure. Second, there is a geographical decentralization of many functions including management and resource deployment so that those with responsibility are closer to the consumers of their services. Similarly there is a "temporal decentralization," with service delivery being based on neighbourhoods rather than on shifts. Resources are justified mainly on how well they serve the front-line police officers responsible for neighbourhood policing, problem solving, and rapid response to the rare life-threatening calls or for incidents in progress. Decentralization may result in the dispersal of headquarters specialists, if not the complete break-up of many headquarters specialized units, with their duties assumed by generalist constables. In larger police services, there may still be a need for a few headquarters specialists (e.g., one victims specialist, one crime prevention specialist, etc.), but only in a support role for the front-line officers. In this way, headquarters staff in larger police services might be reduced by perhaps half its former numbers, thus releasing further resources to front-line policing. This police organization with minimal specialization is in sharp contrast to the complex, specialized, centralized, hierarchical police agency of the past.

14. Most police officers are permitted to become *career generalists (i.e., the generalist constable model)* rather than specialists and are responsible for a broader range of activities than permitted under the "professional" model, including solving neighbourhood crime and disorder problems. In many respects, the generalist constable is as much a specialty as is a physician serving as a general practitioner who has specialized in family medicine. The balance between generalist duties and emergency response duties has not been settled, however, nor has an appropriate proportion of officers pursuing generalist duties and other specialties duties been established. While many officers may still be rotated through specialties as part of career advancement, those who prefer to continue as street constables pursuing community policing may do so and be recognized within the

reward structure, with this generalist constable role as a possible life-long career option. Rather than being the "dirty work" of policing where street officers apply as soon as possible to transfer to non-street duties or specialized units, this is now an honourable status. Accordingly, community policing street constables are treated as highly trained, relatively well-paid, white-collar professionals who have the respect of their colleagues and the local community. By contrast, they were treated generally as "blue-collar workers" under the "professional" model, at least until they reached the respectability of commissioned officer rank.

15. As a result of organization transformation and the re-emergence of the generalist constable model, the *loyalties of officers* working under a community-policing regime, or the "blue" model (Guth 1987), is primarily towards the *Charter*, the *Criminal Code*, the common law, and the community. While this "blue model" raises the historically suspect and romantic concept of the autonomous English "village bobby" maintaining the King's Peace in hamlets across the land, it is a more appropriate reflection of legal status of Canadian police officers as peace officers. A significant outcome is the fostering of a "new police professionalism" that is supported by a code of ethics and many of the other attributes of professions, with one obvious exception being the lack of a self-governing status. By contrast, the loyalties of police officers under the para-military or "brown" model is to the chain of command, working within a narrow range of responsibilities and limited autonomy. These loyalties have created an organizational culture of strict control over its members and a resilient sub-culture characterized by authoritarianism and conservatism.

16. Given the priorities supported earlier by the community, there is a degree of *accountability to the community* in terms of a review of progress on those priorities, possibly conducted through public consultations. To avoid entanglement with established accountability structures, police misconduct is discussed publicly in the form of explanatory accountability. Hence, informal accountability complements legal accountability that is exercised through formal external oversight or review bodies whose authority is delegated from elected officials. This combination of legal and public accountability provides a great measure of protection from misconduct for both the public and the police. Unlike the earlier "professional model," under which police officers in close contact with the local community were regarded with suspicion and as potentially corruptible, the protection of legal and public scrutiny frees the police from the public's fear of police corruption, allowing them to become close to the communities they serve and to direct the most appropriate community policing strategies and tactics towards specific crime and disorder problems in each neighbourhood.

3. COMMUNITY POLICING IN CANADA

How well do community policing projects in Canada fulfil the above description of community policing? In other words, how well is it implemented or operationalized to fulfil these sixteen elements and objectives? The performance of Canadian police services under community policing framework is difficult to assess because there are few evaluations of community policing, most police forces have implemented only a few of the tactics, there is little consensus on the criteria for community policing, and the methodology for evaluation has not been agreed upon. Moreover, unlike the

U.S. where a rather forthright article by Greene and Taylor (1988) critically reviewed eight major evaluations, Canadian reviewers have yet to provide similar constructive criticisms of the few evaluation studies that have been undertaken so far. Yet, it is towards these U.S. studies that Canadian researchers and police professionals turn when assessing their own projects and designing their evaluations. Like Rosenbaum's (1988) rejection of all but one evaluation study of crime prevention projects, Greene and Taylor (1988) conclude that "nothing works" because nothing has been scientifically proven to work in community policing on the grounds that none of the studies they reviewed met basic criteria for sound, rigorous evaluations. Other commentators have similarly high standards that seldom seem to be met (Sherman 1986; Weatheritt, 1983).

To date there are only three published reports of evaluations of community-based policing in Canada. The first evaluation, conducted by Lambert (1988), describes the history and development of Metro Toronto Police Force's mini-stations and found them well received by local residents (see also Murphy and de Verteuil 1986; Murphy 1988b). The second study is an evaluation of the City of Victoria Community Police Stations (Walker 1987 and Walker 1989) in which a community survey showed that the majority of respondents were aware that a neighbourhood community station existed and a significant proportion of them had also contacted the local station. Perhaps one of the most rigorous evaluations of a community policing program conducted anywhere (Hornick, Burrows, Tjosvold, and Phillips, 1990; Hornick, Burrows, Phillips and Leighton 1991; Koller 1990) is of the City of Edmonton Police Service Neighbourhood Foot Patrol Project. This was a pilot project involving 21 constables working mainly on foot out of mini-stations strategically located in selected neighbourhoods. The study reported that the project (a) significantly reduced the number of repeat calls for service in the beat neighbourhoods with foot patrol; (b) improved user satisfaction with police services; (c) improved constables' job satisfaction; and (d) increased constables' knowledge of the neighbourhoods and their problems. As well, Edmonton police plan to evaluate a planned service-wide implementation as a further step towards becoming (in the words of the chief) the "Mayo Clinic of community policing in Canada."

While there do not appear to be any other evaluations currently underway, there is still a significant number of descriptive and analytic studies of community policing, mainly in municipal police services. As well, there is a surprisingly large number of police forces whose community policing initiatives have yet to be studied or even described, despite the fact that they may be characterized as "police forces of excellence in community policing" (Leighton, forthcoming). A few of these initiatives deserve to be highlighted.

Over the past three years, the Halifax Police Department has significantly reorganized its traditional structure and operations to become more community oriented, including implementation of zone-based team policing, decentralization of criminal investigation, crime analysis and direct patrol, the expansion of crime prevention, and the expansion of foot patrol in core urban areas and the establishment of a "village constable" program (Clairmont 1990). Fredericton police have also introduced an innovative, inter-agency storefront office (the Devon Storefront) in a low income housing project (Dixon 1990). In late 1986, Le service de police de la communauté urbaine de Montréal (Montreal Urban Community Police) implemented the first stage of a zone community police service designed to prevent crime by getting closer to the residents of communities with high crime rates (Cartier, Grenon and Rizkalla 1987). Halton Regional Police Force, near Toronto, is another police force of excellence that has introduced community policing innovations, including zone and beat policing, mini-stations, and "Village constables" (Loree 1988). In Winnipeg, four experimental beat patrols were introduced during 1988 in the city core as its first component of community policing, with at least one beat constable working out of a mini-station (Linden 1989). Community-based policing has been a stated objective of the Metropolitan Toronto Police Department since the early 1980s (Lambert 1988) and one notable achievement is the annual airing for public discussion of policing priorities by the Toronto Police Commission. While zone policing was implemented in Calgary and in Ottawa police services and a mini-station was established in Vancouver during the 1970s, these initiatives appear not to have been consolidated until recent years. For example, the Ottawa Police Force has just established the first few of at least five mini-stations, re-organizing around zones and beats once again, and establishing community consultation committees, possibly along focus-group lines.

Turning to provincial policing, Ontario has adopted community policing principles in the preamble to the *Ontario Police Services Act* of 1990 and Ontario Ministry of the Solicitor General, and the Ontario Provincial Police are actively promoting community-based policing, particularly in small towns. An Action Plan has been implemented (Ontario Provincial Police 1990) and monitoring of progress has produced feedback, revealing an impressive range of activities (Ontario Provincial Police 1991). At the same time, in a 1989 annual Directional Statement, the Commissioner of the Royal Canadian Mounted Police (RCMP) directed that all detachments above a certain size should establish community advisory or consultative committees. As well, a community policing implementation committee is now working with a strategic planning framework to review and enhance the implementation of community policing operational practices (RCMP 1990). As a police service predominantly serving rural and small-town constituencies, the typical RCMP response is that it has always done community policing, is currently doing community policing, and plans to continue to do community policing in the future in a systematic way across Canada.

It is interesting to note that the role the Canadian federal government department responsible for policing has played in promoting community policing is the vision of appropriate policing. This vision is found in policy papers (Murphy and Muir 1984; Linden, Barker and Frisbie, 1984), conferences (Loree and Murphy 1987), and research funding (Hornick et al. 1990). Solicitor General Canada, together with its Ontario provincial government counterpart, has also produced a series of reports on community policing that have been designed to serve the information, training, planning, and management needs of Canadian police departments implementing community policing (Mitzak and Leighton 1991). The Canadian Police College, an RCMP service to Canadian police forces, has an ongoing series of dedicated seminar and regional training sessions on community policing and includes this in the content of more general executive-level courses. Finally, the federal department recently distributed a public discussion paper (Normandeau and Leighton 1991 a,b) that was intended to shape the rhetoric of community policing and, in doing so, increase the likelihood that a community policing approach will be implemented in police agencies across the country. This paper argues that community policing is the most appropriate police response to current and future trends in Canadian society and it is noteworthy that it is the first time a Solicitor General of Canada has endorsed a particular approach to policing.

This sketchy, selective review of community policing in Canada shows that the approach is fast becoming part of the operational framework in most progressive police services and that there is a growing number of police departments planning for, experimenting with, or implementing community policing programs. There are also some very promising experiments and innovations: some police services have implemented at least part of the core strategies, such as some form of foot patrol, have attempted to decentralize some police activities by establishing storefront offices and zone policing, and have facilitated regular contact with the community through advisory committees or other mechanisms. As a result, while some still seek legitimacy for local initiatives by touring the key U.S. community policing sites and soliciting the views of a favoured U.S. academic, there is no longer any need for police professionals to look towards examples of community policing outside Canada for lessons and insights. Nonetheless, some issues and concerns remain. While police executives have got the rhetoric of community policing, there is still a need to bridge the gap between the philosophy and strategies of community policing and the tactics of community policing. As well, while community policing has been widely accepted by Canadian police executives, there is a lack of consensus over its definition as well as considerable variation in both the application of its principles and on its implementation. As a result, few programs resemble each other in more than some core tactics. At the same time, some police executives responsible for these programs claim unqualified success and a national stage to proselytise their approach, despite the lack of a rigorous evaluation. As is the case elsewhere, one of the main issues facing Canadian police executives at this time is how to implement community policing in a systematic way and on a department-wide basis. Further, police leaders need to discover how to obtain feedback on their efforts, i.e., by monitoring followed by a comprehensive impact evaluation. So that others can learn from the more promising of these experiments, there is also an urgent need for these initiatives to be well documented. Despite these drawbacks, one prominent U.S. academic recently found that, not only is there no crime or policing crisis, but community policing is alive and well in Canada (Bayley 1991).

4. ISSUES IN COMMUNITY POLICING

While the many drawbacks to community policing and many outstanding issues have been addressed elsewhere (Manning 1984; Waddington 1984; Greene and Taylor 1988; Bayley 1988; Murphy 1988a; Riechers and Roberg 1990; Goldstein 1990; Skolnick and Bayley 1986, 1988a,b), they are summarized here as issues that need to be addressed over the next decade by those police services seeking to implement a community policing approach. The first group relate to more operational policing or issues surrounding the implementation of community policing while the second half refer to more fundamental and theoretical issues.

1. From an operational policing point of view, there is the need to distinguish between the tactics of community policing and the overall strategies of problem-solving and a police-community partnership. Both foot patrol and mini-stations are

just two tactics that may or may not be appropriate for some neighbourhoods and for some crime problems. Foot patrol is usually inappropriate in low crime areas with less dense populations while mini-stations must do more than serve traditional public relations and crime prevention objectives. The main strategies of community policing are problem solving and community participation in priority setting.

2. Placing an emphasis on a particular tactic runs the risk of community policing being regarded as an "add-on" program that is just another specialized and, therefore, marginalized unit rather than being seen as a department-wide program with implications for most policing operations. Police mini-stations, in particular, are often used merely as public relations out-posts, as a stationary "grin-and-wave" squad, especially when they do not handle even the low priority centralized calls for service. Police-community consultative or advisory committees can also become a marginalized tactic, especially when used to divert public attention from the real issues of policing priorities. Nonetheless, it may be necessary to test or demonstrate a program on a partial basis before adopting a program throughout a police service. Whatever approach is used, the introduction of innovation by police executives needs to be supported as a risk-taking exercise that may run the chance of failure.

3. A definition of "community" must be developed that identifies a practical way in which a local community or neighbourhood can be recognized and related to by the police to make possible useful dialogue on local crime and disorder. This presents the question of how "community" can be operationalized in terms of who represents that community and through what means or structure (Murphy 1988a). Attempts at developing a working definition of "community" have generally failed largely because community is in the eye of the beholder (Leighton 1988). Previous attempts at operationalizing "community" have struggled with democratic representation in neighbourhoods. However, Stenning (1981) found that police committees are generally inadequate ways of representing local communities. One of the reasons for this failure is that communities are not usually homogeneous social units characterized by a consensus of values, norms, and agreements on crime problems (Waddington 1984; Riechers and Roberg 1990). More recent suggestions have given up democratic representation at the local level as being too problematic, preferring instead to use existing local interest groups and leaders (Goldstein 1990).

   As well, it is clear that there is a revisionist history about the nature of communities in the past that romanticize them (Manning 1984; Leighton 1988) as well as romanticizing Peel's London Bobbies (Cain 1973; Miller 1977). The so-called "three eras of policing" (Kelling and Moore 1988) are reminiscent of the three eras of community that have been characterized as the "community lost, community saved and community transformed" models (Wellman 1979; Wellman and Leighton 1979; Leighton 1988). However, there are obvious ways in which communities have changed which explains why the romantic version of Peel's policing cannot be reconstructed in North American cities. These reasons include urbanization, post-industrialization, technological change, transformations in communications and transportation, and legal changes, to name but a few of the most obvious societal changes (Mastrofski 1990).

4. The issue of what community policing means in a rural and small-town context has yet to be explored and examined to show how policing in this context differs

fundamentally from urban policing (Murphy 1985, 1988a). This examination should include: (1) the differences in policing between large municipal forces and both small-town and rural forces, (2) problems facing small police services with limited resources that are implementing community policing, (3) the criteria for successful implementation of this approach, and (4) the methods for evaluating small forces. It has been argued that community policing is merely an urban application of small-town policing principles.

5. Because it is not yet clear what impact community policing actually has on crime, it has yet to be proven to "work." While it may be successful in addressing disorder problems and in reducing fear of crime, it has yet to be demonstrated scientifically that it actually reduces crime itself. Part of this problem is that community policing generates new clients and "new" types of crime that the public would not otherwise bother reporting to the police. It is also not clear what impact, if any, that community participation (as a key component of community policing) actually has on community policing. This question raises further issues regarding whose criteria are accepted as the appropriate measures of effective policing in a community. Accordingly, "success" depends upon who "owns" crime and disorder issues, whether it is the exclusive property of the police, of police governing bodies, or shared by police and the community. As well, the assessment should be scientifically evaluated by an independent agency. But the failure of the old "professional" policing model is partly demonstrated by the failure to sufficiently address "non-traditional" crimes, such as sexual assault, spousal assault, child sexual abuse, and so on (Braiden 1986). It was only when these categories of crime were secured as legitimate targets for formal police activities that the success or failure of different policing models could be more realistically assessed. Consequently new measures of police service effectivness or performance must be developed that stress its impact rather than the processes and structures for accomplishing community policing. These criteria must contrast with those of the "professional" model, which included such measures as the police response time and the proportion of charges cleared. On the other hand, some of the "new" measures are not without fault. For example, community "satisfaction" with the police has been shown to be practically useless as an indicator of police effectiveness, although it is not yet clear what it does demonstrate (Clairmont and Murphy 1990). Indeed, popularity polls are becoming far too popular with police chiefs as a way of managing public opinion rather than crime.

Perhaps one of the most difficult tests of this "new" approach to policing is its ability to ameliorate problems associated with disadvantages or vulnerable groups in Canadian society, including police relationships with aboriginal peoples in an urban environment, new Canadians, ethnic and visible minorities, women, the elderly, and children and youth at risk. Equally as difficult a question is whether community policing would have helped at Oka in the summer of 1990. The answer is likely to be that it might have beforehand and it might be relevant over the next ten years, contingent on the resolution of land claims and self government issues. This answer is a reminder that the reality of policing a complex, diverse, largely urban society characterized by structured inequality occasionally presents police agencies with situations when they are likely to resort to the techniques of "hard policing," such as those associated with riot control, homicide, etc. Accordingly, the strengths and limitations of community policing must be recognized, including the fact that it cannot be a panacea that will solve all crime and disorder problems.

6. New criteria must be developed for evaluating police officers working in a police service operating on community policing principles. When the criteria for police service performance change, then the formal position descriptions, performance criteria, and rewards (e.g., promotion) must also be changed to reflect these changes. Unless the reward structure is changed in accordance with the new criteria and principles, then community policing strategies and tactics will not be implemented in other than a cosmetic manner.

7. Greater community involvement with policing might be interpreted by police executives as providing additional or supplementary resources through volunteers, neighbourhood watch, and other forms of community surveillance. But by providing a legitimate link with other service delivery agencies, community policing may result in an attempt by police agencies to exploit other agencies to fill the gap created by a fiscal crisis. However, it may be equally found that other agencies might look to the police to fill their own underfunded needs. On the other hand, co-operation with human service and social service agencies provides additional resources to policing through the pooling of their respective scarce resources. As well, local crime and order problems become joint responsibilities, with the consequent sharing of both successes and of failures or limitations. It is not yet clear whether police co-operation with human service and social service agencies actually results in a bigger bang for the collective buck in delivering urban services to targeted groups and victims. Nor is it clear whether police executives are equipped to enter into inter-agency co-operation with highly competitive voluntary sector partners.

8. As a traditionally reactive agency primed for the key function of providing rapid response to the relatively rare emergency incident, the capacity of policing to shift to a more balanced, proactive stance has yet to be demonstrated. Nor is it clear whether private sector or some other service delivery agencies are an appropriate model for police agencies when, with the exception of health care, they lack this key emergency function. Consequently, it may be inappropriate to import the standards of service, quality, efficiency, and effectiveness from private industry into human service delivery professions.

9. By advocating a police-community partnership, community policing seeks to empower the community to bring it onto a more equal footing with the police in terms of joint "ownership" of local crime and disorder problems and as "co-producers" of peace, order, and security at the local level (Murphy and Muir 1984; Wilson and Kelling 1982, 1989). On the one hand, there is the possibility that the community will acquire greater control over local crime and disorder matters (Kinsey, Lea and Young 1986). More plausible is the prospect, as Bayley (1988) warns, of transforming the community into an interest group on behalf of the police. After all, it is the community side of the "partnership" that is least likely to have the expertise and resources to take advantage of any empowering opportunities. This is particularly relevant when public advocacy is encouraged by establishing police-community consultative committees. As well, public participation through this and similar mechanisms may be a diversionary device used by police leaders to defuse potential criticism from the community. Indeed,

involvement in these committees often appears to degenerate into fundraising and organizing for already established crime prevention programs. As a result, the police rather than the community are likely to be further empowered by a community policing regime (Savage 1984).

10. One aspect of problem-solving can get out of control. The logical extension of the "hot spot" approach also covers "hot-persons," being victims or groups sharing individual characteristics (of their residences) of statistically at-risk victims, as well as "hot places" and "hot offenders" or potential offenders, with the latter consisting of recidivists or offenders at statistically high risk of re-offending and of potential offenders fitting a profile of offenders (e.g., drug interdiction activities). But an "aggressive order maintenance" or "intensive policing" approach that targets people, times, and places can also get out of hand, leading not just to mindlessly focusing on the "signs of crime" or on crime as a surface symptom, thereby ignoring the root causes, but it may also lead to harassment and bias in the delivery of police services.

11. As with most crime prevention programs in practice, community policing exhibits a class bias by finding fertile ground in neighbourhoods and communities where it is needed least in comparison with lower socio-economic areas (Rosenbaum 1986, 1988). That is, if it could be shown that community policing "works," then there is likely to be a bias in its impact. Consequently, further research is necessary on the exact nature of class bias, and community policing must be tested in neighbourhoods and communities where it is really needed rather than just in those neighbourhoods in which its success can be guaranteed because of the lack of need or because of the availability of resources.

12. Community policing is a useful rhetorical tool for police chiefs to solicit additional funds. During the 1960s and 1970s, when crime rates were increasing rapidly, chiefs could argue for more officers and resources on the grounds of a crime wave. With overall crime rates settling down, chiefs have had to shift their argument from "quantity" policing to a "quality policing" argument. That is, in order to deliver high quality policing services, as represented by community policing, then they require additional officers and resources.

13. Police services are being asked to perform schizophrenic responsibilities, as both "green berets" and "peace corps." On the one hand, they are asked to serve as an armed force permanently at red-alert status to provide a rapid response to the relatively rare life-threatening incidents. At the same time they are now being asked to serve as a "peace corp" by becoming a "partner" with the community to address crime and disorder problems, ranging from mediating domestic disputes to solving the underlying causes of crime. But how can police forces designed for an emergency response with a para-military organization be transformed into a more "democratic" one exhibiting the characteristics of participatory management? Indeed, it sometimes appears that the public present the police with contradictory demands by "wanting it all," despite the inherently conflicting nature of their requirements, including the bottom line of a rapid response, seeing the police "on the job" even when most preventive patrol activities largely serve as public relations, as well as reduced crime rates. Unfortunately, when the full brunt of the fiscal crisis is felt (hastened at the local level by down-loading of police and other human service delivery costs from federal and provincial governments to the municipal level), then the emergency response function may

emerge again as the predominant tactic of policing. Perhaps the only positive side to this outcome is that there may be greater local control over an emasculated police service.

14. The local focus of community policing generates "sand-box policing" in terms of a bias towards defining problems as local ones, ignoring the regional, national, and international nature of many problems, such as drugs, organized crime, corporate and white collar crime, and environmental crime. In many ways, community policing trivialises some of these major crime problems by interpreting or stressing them as local problems with local solutions. Instead, attention is focused on local issues that tend to be disorder problems rather than crime problems. Hence, decentralized community policing runs the risk of becoming localized or "going native" by being directed by local values, norms, culture, and concerns in contrast to those articulated in the *Charter*, the *Criminal Code*, and the common law. The former are community, collective, or corporate rights while the latter are primarily individual rights. While it may be justifiable in certain circumstances to allow collective rights to override individual ones, when these collective rights are local ones, then, they run the risk of great variations in the meaning and practice of justice between communities (Waddington 1984; Bayley 1988; Murphy 1988a; Klockars 1986; Sykes 1986). In the extreme, localization of policing can run amok by expanding police practice beyond the legal boundaries as well as supporting vigilantism by community members (leading to the next point, below).

15. It is not yet clear whether community policing results in tighter or loser "handcuffs" on the community. On the one hand, it may further weaken any control the police now have on crime at the local level. On the other hand, community policing may further penetrate the community to introduce even more intrusive techniques of formal social control. It seems that community policing does widen the net of control beyond crime control by legitimizing an expanded role for the police in terms of the type of behaviour that is addressed, particularly order maintenance problems such as street nuisance behaviour and other "non-crimes" that do not traditionally or technically fall within the legal realm of policing (Manning 1984; Klockars 1985; Walker 1984; Wilson and Kelling 1982). As Bayley (1988) points out, the distinction between public and private becomes increasingly blurred. In rare instances, the police might take community involvement as providing a mandate for additional powers that would otherwise be inconsistent with routine policing practices.

16. A corollary issue arises over how far in a free and democratic society the police should go in performing their role (Klockars 1985). This is a particularly acute question when there is an over-increasing demand for expanded police services. The police are in danger of becoming far too politically involved with the community affairs (Goldstein 1987) and of surrendering their professional neutrality (Sykes 1986). The question should be addressed as to whether the police should engage in community development activities, as "community catalysts," to create local initiatives and, indeed, to fabricate community where it is weak, not readily apparent to outsiders, or is lacking.

17. In light of the more prominent role played by the community, a further issue surrounds whether there is a greater or lesser accountability at the local level. Local partnership in policing may be understood as providing local communities with

a direct oversight role over their police at the expense of established accountability mechanisms.

18. Increased police officer autonomy may lead to systematic under-performance. While community police services are being increasingly characterized by a growing formalization of internal regulations and disciplinary procedures and by a "new professionalism" typical of self-governing, white-collar professions, it is too soon to assess whether this trend reduces the likelihood of police taking advantage of the greater professional freedom afforded them. As well, the growing tendency for police services to adopt a code of ethics or professional conduct is likely to have only a long-term impact on the police professional culture and sub-culture.

19. Police leaders can use community policing as a strategy to avoid criticism for not reducing crime by claiming that, given one new criteria for success in the reduction of the public's fear of crime, this approach can at least reduce the fear of crime. This is akin to looking for a lost coin under the street lamp because that is where the light is shining. As well, the question arises as to how far the police can go in reducing the fear of crime by persuading particular segments of the community, such as the elderly, that their fear is largely unfounded when the statistical risk of them being victimized is considered. Although unlikely, it is not clear whether the police, as a government agency, incur civil liability for "guaranteeing" public safety.

5. ORIGINS OF COMMUNITY POLICING

Why is community policing so popular and whose interest does it serve? One explanation may lie not so much in its appeal but in the growing recognition that the established policing paradigm has become recognized as exhausted in light of its clearly demonstrated inefficiency and ineffectiveness. Hence, the answer might lie in its origin through the history of policing.

While some commentators see the history of community policing in the U.S. as the direct result of crises occurring during the 1960s, which led to national-level attempts to provide solutions during the 1970s (German 1969; Walker 1983; Riechers and Roberg 1990). The current rhetoric of community policing is often associated with the packaging of American police history into three eras (Kelling and Moore 1988). But despite criticism that these three eras of policing and the linear progression of U.S. policing through these eras is somewhat revisionist (Walker 1984; Hartman 1988), it is nonetheless a useful and compelling heuristic device, complete with ideal types pushed to their extreme to present an overly simplified typification and therefore simplistic historical account of the development of policing. Further, this scheme provides an intriguing parallel to Cohen's (1985) "master patterns" in social control that apply more appropriately to correctional control, with limited application to the course of policing history.

As the party line of community policing would have its genealogy, the origins of public urban community policing lie in both American and British policing, with Sir Robert Peel's Metropolitan London police established over 150 years ago providing the first paradigm. But, beginning about the 1930s onwards, the "professional policing" paradigm became established within North American urban police forces, assisted by the efforts of police leaders such as W.O. Wilson and Volmer. This development was largely in reaction to the close ties that police established with their local communities, which were understood to have facilitated the widespread, systemic corruption of police agencies by local political party organizations. In order to minimize corruption in American police forces, they intentionally distanced themselves from the community they served. Tactics were developed to ensure this distancing occurred, assisted by technological developments such as the telephone, then the patrol car and two-way radio, followed by on-board computers. While these new technologies permitted tighter control over individual police officer behaviour, two further policing strategies were even more powerful influences in distancing the police from the local community. These strategies were the invention of random motorized patrol as a presumed deterrent to potential criminals, and the invention of rapid response as the uniform response to all calls to the police from the public. Under this "professional" policing model, the two main criteria for police force performance then became (1) the proportion of charges laid of offenses reported to the police and (2) the response time to calls for service made to the police by the public. However, U.S. evaluations of these two strategies have shown that they are marginally effective in preventing or containing crime and hardly worth the loss of positive police-community relations (Young and Cameron 1989; Ellickson, Petersilia, Caggiano, and Polin 1983).

While there appear to have been other failures of the "professional model" in the U.S.: a failure of funding as a result of the fiscal crisis, a failure of public confidence, and a failure of legitimacy (Klockars 1988), they do not seem applicable to the Canadian experience. Nonetheless, as a result of a number of profound failures in the existing paradigm, the U.S. experiment in professional policing eventually revealed its own contradictions and limitations, bringing about a crisis within the paradigm. But, rather than being compelled towards a new paradigm, the crisis returned policing to an earlier one. This "new" paradigm turned out to be a romanticized one from the past, in the form of a re-emergence of, and renaissance in, community policing.

How well does this revisionist history and the conveniently packaged paradigms fit the history of policing in Canada? Unfortunately, there has been little rigorous scholarship on the historical development of Canadian policing, from the colonial period to the present. Nothing compares, for example, with the history of New Zealand colonial policing by Hill (1986, 1989). Indeed, the Hollywood version of RCMP visions of order (Walden 1982) and the popular myth of order preceding settlement and cultural values regarding a "deference to authority" (Friedenberg 1980) are an enduring element of Canadian popular culture. But what little is known about the history and development of Canadian policing suggests a number of tentative conclusions.

First, Canadian police are held in high regard and there does not appear to be a crisis in public support for the police. Second, Canadian police are relatively well financed and are currently not experiencing a deep fiscal crisis. Third, the reasons for exerting tighter control over police officers in the U.S., as prescribed by the "professional model," were not as applicable to their Canadian counterparts. In the present century at least, there has been a marked absence of routine political influence over Canadian police forces. By comparison with the U.S., there has also been a lack of widespread corruption and systemic individual misconduct within Canadian police forces. Of course, there have been exceptions: the use of the police to break up the

Winnipeg Strike, the involvement of the RCMP in national security abuses, individual corruption within forces of some of the major municipalities and in many small municipalities that ended largely over a decade ago. In recent decades, other cases involving individual officers and made known to the public have been relatively isolated, although recent commissions of inquiry suggest otherwise, especially with respect to systemic bias in the delivery of police services to Aboriginal people and discrimination against visible minorities. Nonetheless, it might be concluded that the means for exerting tighter control over routine street policing were, in the Canadian context, largely misplaced.

If there were no discernible crisis within public policing in Canada, the question arises as to why there has been a return to community policing in this country. As Murphy (1988a) presents the issue, the lack of internal and external pressures for reform of Canadian policing is a curious phenomenon that demands an explanation and he interprets this situation as being due to the lack of a national police research institutional framework that can critically examine current practices, new developments, and innovations in policing. As a result, Canadian police are more vulnerable to trends from the U.S. Much more should be made of the ideological imperative of the academic criminal justice and policing enterprise from the U.S. While there are outstanding individual academics in Canada who contribute to a body of relatively critical research on the police, there is no "critical mass" of academics who are routinely involved in an American-style criminal justice approach with police operational activities. In some respects, police researchers get only one kick at the cat because if they earn the displeasure of the police executive of the police force they studied, they will not only have muddied the local waters for their own colleagues but they are unlikely to have access to other police forces. Accordingly, there is an urgent need to marshall a healthy critique of community policing as the dominant vision of progressive policing and, because this critique must be an independent one that can only be provided by neutral academics, there is also a requirement for independent funding. This requirement is critical because most research on Canadian police services is funded by federal and provincial governments of their agencies that largely set the agenda of police research generally (Brickey 1989).

6. CONCLUSIONS: TOWARD A THEORY OF COMMUNITY POLICING

Is there now or can there ever be a community policing theory? The "signs of crime" or "broken windows" thesis of Wilson and Kelling (1982, 1989) is usually identified as the theory underlying community policing (Greene and Taylor 1988; Riechers and Roberg 1990; Skogan 1990). This thesis focuses on the cognitive conclusions of potential offenders based on their perceptions of the physical deterioration of neighbourhoods and has the flavour of environmental determinism. It follows W.I. Thomas's sociological dictum on the self-fulfilling prophecy by arguing that if a neighbourhood is defined as being in decay and disorder then it will inevitably become characterized by disorder and crime. However, reviewers such as Greene and Taylor (1988) have found this thesis unsatisfactory on a number of theoretical and empirical grounds. One explanation may be that the "broken windows" notion applies almost appropriately to order maintenance and that attempts to expand it to cover crime control generally are simply beyond its capacity. If so, then it could serve only as one part of a broader theory of community policing. Indeed, it hardly addresses the underlying causes of crime, whether as offender motivations or as the foundations of these motivations in structured inequalities, and therefore falls far short of an adequate explanation of crime or of a theory of community policing. Nonetheless, Skogan (1990) presents comprehensive, compelling evidence of a clear link between disorder and crime in American cities. It would appear, therefore, that until a competing theory of community policing is developed, the "broken windows" view is by default the current theory of community policing.

In the face of this conclusion, it is still suggested here that a comprehensive theory of community policing has yet to emerge and that community policing, as it is currently constructed, is a theoretically undeveloped set of policing principles and practices that at best is a "theory sketch" (Dumont and Wilson 1967). At its core is the principle or "strategy" of a police-community partnership and the hypothesis that the effectiveness of community policing is directly related to the degree of involvement by the community it serves. While these do not constitute a theory, at least they provide the elements of a theory about policing, including at least two fundamental aspects of the approach, much of which were addressed earlier in one form or another. First, a theory about community policing should raise questions over the role of community in policing and social control generally (Duffee 1990). Second, a theory about community policing should raise questions over the role of policing in the social control of the community.

Concerning the first aspect, the role of formal community participation in public urban policing has had a chequered career, from community relations programs through to crime prevention activities. Beyond participation in these fairly circumscribed programs, how far can community members go in participating in major decisions that govern policing? Does it make sense to argue that police and community can become equal partners in policing, as "co-producers" of order? Or does it make sense, as Kinsey, Lea, and Young (1986) suggest, to argue that the community — in the guise of the local state — can possess exclusive authority over local police and can control police policies and priorities? Further, is the conferring of local "consent" on policing (Morgan 1989) — even if a "community consensus" is possible — merely a masking of vested interests, raising the same issues associated with all claims of consensus? "Legitimate" consensual agreements might only be possible at such a micro-neighbourhood level so as to be quite impractical for policing arrangements. And, as mentioned earlier, exclusive local authority and "consensus" might remove the neutrality of the police and relegate policing to an arm of local politics and vested interest. Further, it might reduce local policing to local concerns or "sand-box policing." And how "local" does the local state have to become before it loses its legitimacy on the grounds of being undemocratic or out of touch with the common law, the *Criminal Code* and the *Charter*? The question remains, then, about the independence or relative autonomy of the police with respect to the local, regional, and national state and about whose interests are served at each of these levels. If the relative autonomy of the police has any meaning, then it is about a type of control over policing resources that is independent of the local community the police serves. On the other hand, it is precisely the local autonomy of police forces that led to the "professional model" of policing and the distancing of the police from local concerns and priorities. These and other questions demonstrate the need to locate a theory about community policing, and policing generally, within a broader theory of the state (Ratner and McMullan 1987).

Regarding the role of the police in social control of the local community, questions arise as to whether it makes sense to restrict policing to crime control so that, as Brogden (1982, 1989) suggests the penetration of the community by the police will be arrested. After all, as Chapman (1979) warns, the encroachment of policing on the traditional responsibilities of other agencies, such as those covered by order maintenance, the underlying causes of crime, inter-agency co-operation, and other community policing objectives, could lead down the slippery slope towards the police state (Gordon 1984). On the other hand, should the community abandon state sponsored policing, as Taylor (1981) suggests, going it alone as the sole source of order maintenance and crime control? In any event, it is clear that the role of police under a police-community partnership as proposed by the vision of community policing demands critical examination.

In conclusion, this paper has attempted to summarize the rhetoric and reality of the dominant vision of community policing in Canada. It finds that the future of community policing in Canada is probably well assured and will easily survive these and other criticisms. While it may be viewed by some as merely going back to the basics of traditional Peelite policing, the implementation of community policing strategies and tactics will nonetheless have a profound and far-reaching impact on Canadian police services that pursue the approach. By raising some critical issues and identifying a theoretical space that needs to be occupied, the need for a theory about community policing has been demonstrated. There is a need for further research on the working of community policing tactics, such as consultative committees, in order to examine such issues as whether the "broad blue line" of community policing co-opts the community or whether the community co-opts policing. However, an even more urgent need is to set the agenda for a critical discourse on the role and impact of community policing in Canadian society.

NOTE

1 The views presented in this article are those of the author.

REFERENCES

Bayley, David H. 1991. Managing the Future: Perspective Issues in Canadian Policing. (User Report No. 1991-02) Ottawa: Ministry of the Solicitor General.

———. 1988. Community policing: A report from the devil's advocate. In J.R. Greene and S.D. Mastrofski (eds.), *Community Policing: Rhetoric or Reality*. New York: Praeger.

Braiden, Chris. 1986. Bank Robberies and Stolen Bikes: Thoughts of a Street Cop. (User Report No. 1986-04) Ottawa: Ministry of the Solicitor General of Canada.

Brickey, Stephen. 1989. Criminology as social control science: State influences on criminological research in Canada. *Journal of Human Justice* 1(1): 43–62.

Brogden, Michael. 1982. *The Police: Autonomy and Consent*. London: Academic Press.

———. 1989. Social accountability and police power — Squeezing the discretionary space. Paper presented at the Society for Reform of the Criminal Law Conference on Police Powers. Sydney, Australia, March.

Cain, Maureen. 1973. *Society and the Policeman's Role*. London: Routledge.

Cartier, Benard, Sylvie Grenon et Samir Rizkall. 1987. *Prévention communautaire du crime: Les citoyens visités et les policiers non-intervenant s'expriment sur le programme.* Montréal: Société de Criminologie du Québec.

Chapman, B. 1970. *Police State.* London: Pall Mall.

Clairmont, Donald. 1990. *To the Forefront: Community-Based Zone Policing in Halifax.* Ottawa: Canadian Police College, RCMP.

Clairmont, Donald and Chris Murphy. 1990. Rural victims survey. Draft paper for Ministry of the Solicitor General of Canada.

Cohen, Stanley. 1985. *Vision of Social Control.* Cambridge: Polity Press.

Dixon, Carol. 1990. The Resident Perspective: An Evaluation of the Fredericton (Devon) Storefront. Report written in partial fulfilment of M.A. Carleton University, School of Social Work.

Duffee, David E. 1990. *Explaining Criminal Justice: Community Theory and Criminal Justice Reform* Prospect Heights, IL: Waveland Press.

Dumont, Richard G. and William J. Wilson. 1967. Aspects of concept formation, Explication and theory construction in sociology. *American Sociological Review* 32: 985–995.

Eck, John E. and William Spelman. 1987a. Who ya gonna call? The police as problem busters. *Crime and Delinquency* 33(1): 31–52.

———. 1987b. Problem-solving: Problem-Oriented Policing in Newport News. Washington, DC: U.S. Department of Justice, National Institute of Justice.

Ellickson, Phyllis, Joan Petersilia, Michael Caggiano, and Sandra Polin. 1983. *Implementing New Ideas in Criminal Justice.* Washington, DC: U.S. Department of Justice, National Institute of Justice.

Ericson, Richard V. 1982. *Reproducing Order: A Study of Police Patrol Work.* Toronto: University of Toronto Press.

Friedenberg, Edgar Z. 1980. *Defence to Authority: The Case of Canada.* White Plains, NY: M.E. Sharpe.

Germann, A.C. 1969. Community policing: An assessment. *Journal of Criminal Law, Criminology and Police Science* 60(1): 89–96.

Goldstein, Herman. 1979. Improving policing: A problem-oriented approach. *Crime and Delinquency* 25: 236–258.

———. 1987. Towards community-oriented policing: Potential, basic requirements and threshold question. *Crime and Delinquency* 33(1): 6–30.

———. 1990. *Problem Oriented Policing.* New York: McGraw-Hill.

Gordon, P. 1984. Community policing: Toward the local police state. In P. Scraton (ed.), *Law, Order and the Authoritarian State.* (Reprinted 1987). Milton Keynes: Open University Press.

Greene, Jack R., and Stephen D. Mastrofski (eds.) 1988. *Community Policing: Rhetoric and Reality.* New York: Praeger.

Greene, Jack R. and R.B. Taylor. 1988. Community-based policing and foot patrol: Issues of theory and evaluation. In J.R. Green and S.D. Mastrofski (eds.), *Community Policing: Rhetoric or Reality.* New York: Praeger.

Guth, DeLloyd J. 1987. The common law powers of police: The Anglo-Canadian tradition. Paper presented at the Canadian Law in History Conference (8-10 June). Ottawa: Carleton University.

Hartman, Francis X. (ed.) 1988. Debating the Evolution of American Policing. Perspectives on Policing, No. 5. Washington, DC: U.S. Department of Justice, National Institute of Justice and Harvard University, John F. Kennedy School of Government.

Hill, Richard S. 1986. *The History of Policing in New Zealand. Policing the Colonial Frontier.* Vol. 1. Wellington: Government Printer.

———. 1989. *The History of Policing in New Zealand. The Colonial Frontier Tamed.* Vol. 2. Wellington: GP Books.

Hornick, Joseph P., Barbara A. Burrows, Ida Tjosvold, and Donna M. Phillips. 1990. An Evaluation of the Neighbourhood Foot Patrol Program of the Edmonton Police Service. Ottawa: Ministry of the Solicitor General of Canada. (User Report No. 1990-09).

Hornick, Joseph P., Barbara A. Burrows, Donna M. Phillips, and Barry Leighton. 1991. An impact evaluation of the Edmonton neighbourhood foot patrol program. *Canadian Journal of Program Evaluation* 6(1): 47–70.

Kanter, Rosabeth Moss. 1983. *The Change Masters*. New York: Simon and Schuster.

Kelling, George L. 1987. Acquiring a taste for order: The community and police. *Crime and Delinquency* 33(1): 90–102.

Kelling, George L., and Mark H. Moore. 1988. From political to reform to community: The evolving strategy of police. In J.R. Greene and S.D. Mastrofski (eds.), *Community Policing: Rhetoric or Reality*. New York: Praeger.

Kinsey, Richard, John Lea, and Jock Young. 1986. *Losing the Fight Against Crime*. New York: Basil Blackwell.

Klockars, Carl B. 1985. *The Idea of the Police*. Beverly Hills, CA: Sage.

———. 1986. Street justice: Some micro-moral reservations: Comments on Sykes. *Justice Quarterly* 3(4): 513–516.

———. 1988. The rhetoric of community policing. In J.R. Greene and S.D. Mastrofski (eds.), *Community Policing: Rhetoric or Reality*. New York: Praeger.

Koller, Katherine. 1990. *Working the Beat: The Edmonton Neighbourhood Foot Patrol*. Edmonton: Edmonton Police Service.

Lambert, Leah R. 1988. Police mini-stations in Toronto: An experience in compromise. *Royal Canadian Mounted Police Gazette* 50 (6): 1–5.

Leighton, Barry. 1988. The concept of community in criminology: Toward a social network approach. *Journal of Research in Crime and Delinquency* 25 (4): 351–374.

———. 1989. Community policing. Brief presented at the European and North American Conference of Mayors on "Safer Cities." Montréal, October.

———. 1990. The future of policing in Canada. Paper presented at the Annual Meeting of the American Society of Criminology. Baltimore, November.

———. 1991. *Community Policing in Canada: A Review*. Ottawa: Ministry of the Solicitor General of Canada. (Forthcoming).

Leighton, Barry and Joseph Hornick. 1990. Evaluating community-based policing: Lessons from the Edmonton project. Paper presented at the Canadian Evaluation Society annual meeting. Toronto, May.

Linden, Rick. 1989. *A Report on the Winnipeg City Police Community Officer Program*. Winnipeg: University of Manitoba, Criminology Research Centre.

Linden, Rick, I. Barker, and D. Frisbie. 1984. *Working Together to Prevent Crime: A Practitioner's Handbook*. Ottawa: Ministry of the Solicitor General of Canada.

Loree, Donald J. 1988. Innovation and change in a regional police force. *Canadian Police College Journal* 12(4): 205–239.

Loree, Donald J. and Chris Murphy (eds.) 1987. Community Policing in the 1990s: Recent Advances in Police Programs. Ottawa: Ministry of the Solicitor General of Canada and Ministry of Supply and Services Canada.

Manning, Peter K. 1984. Community policing. *American Journal of Police* 3 (2): 205–227.

Mastrofski, Stephen D. 1990. The prospects of change in police patrol: A decade in review. *American Journal of Police* 9(3): 1–79.

Miller, W.R. 1977. Cops and Bobbies: Police Authority in New York and London, 1830–1870. Chicago: University of Chicago Press.

Mitzak, Marsha and Barry Leighton (eds.). 1991. *Community Policing: Shaping the Future*. Ottawa and Toronto: Solicitor General Canada and Solicitor General Ontario.

Morgan, Rod. 1989. Policing by consent: Legitimating the doctrine. In R. Morgan and D.J. Smith (eds.), *Coming to Terms with Policing: Perspectives on Policy*. New York: Routledge.

Murphy, Chris. 1985. The social and formal organization of small-town policing: A comparative analysis of RCMP and municipal policing. Unpublished doctoral dissertation. Toronto: University of Toronto.

————. 1988a. The development impact and implications of community policing in Canada. In J.R. Greene and S.D. Mastrofski (eds.), *Community Policing: Rhetoric or Reality*. New York: Praeger.

————. 1988b. Community problems, problem communities, and community policing in Toronto. *Journal of Research in Crime and Delinquency* 25(4): 392–410.

————. 1991. *Problem-Oriented Policing*. Ottawa: Ministry of the Solicitor General, Federal-Ontario Community Policing Report Series.

Murphy, Chris and Jacques de Verteuil. 1986. *Metropolitan Toronto Community Policing Survey*. Ottawa: Ministry of the Solicitor General of Canada.

Murphy, Chris and Graham Muir. 1984. *Community-Based Policing: A Review of the Critical Issues*. Ottawa: Ministry of the Solicitor General of Canada.

Normandeau, André and Barry Leighton. 1990a. *The Future of Policing in Canada*. Ottawa: Ministry of the Solicitor General of Canada. Discussion Paper.

————. 1990b. *The Future of Policing in Canada*. Ottawa: Ministry of the Solicitor General of Canada. Background Paper.

Ontario Provincial Police. 1990. *Community Policing Strategy Implementation: 12 Month Action Plan*. Toronto: Field Support Division.

————. 1991. *Field Superintendents Workshop: Community Policing and Crime Prevention*. Toronto: Field Support Division.

Peters, Thomas J. and Robert Wasserman. 1982. *In Search of Excellence*. New York: Harper & Row.

Ratner, Robert S. and John L. McMullans (eds.). 1987. *State Control: Criminal Justice Politics in Canada*. Vancouver: University of British Columbia Press.

Reith, Charles. 1975. *The Blind Eye of History: A Study of the Origins of the Present Police Era*. Montclair, NJ: Patterson-Smith.

Reichers, Lisa M. and Roy R. Roberg. 1990. Community policing: A critical review of underlying assumptions. *Journal of Police Science and Administration* 17(2): 105–114.

Rosenbaum, Dennis P. (ed.). 1986. *Community Crime Prevention: Does It Work?* Beverly Hills, CA: Sage.

————. 1988. Community crime prevention: A review and synthesis of the literature. *Justice Quarterly* 5(3): 323–395.

RCMP. 1990. *Strategic Plan*. Ottawa: Royal Canadian Mounted Police, Corporate Services Branch.

Savage, Steve. 1984. Political control of community liaison? *Political Quarterly* (Jan.–Mar.)

Sensenbrenner, Joseph. 1991. Quality comes to city hall. *Harvard Business Review* (March–April): 64–75.

Sherman, Lawrence. 1986. Policing communities—What works? In A. Reiss, Jr. and M. Tonry (eds.), *Communities and Crime: Crime and Justice*. Vol. 8. Chicago: University of Chicago Press.

Short, C. 1983. Community policing—Beyond slogans. In T. Bennet (ed.), *The Future of Policing*. Cambridge: University of Cambridge.

Skogan, Wesley G. 1990. *Disorder and Decline: Crime and the Spiral of Decay in American Neighbourhoods*. Toronto: Collier Macmillan Canada (New York: The Free Press).

Skolnick, Jerome H. and David H. Bayley. 1986. *The New Blue Line: Police Innovation in Six American Cities*. New York: Free Press.

————. 1988a. Theme and variation in community policing. In M. Tonry and N. Morris (eds.), *Crime and Justice: A Review of Research*. Chicago: University of Chicago Press.

————. 1988b. *Community Policing: Issues and Practices Around the World*. Washington, DC: U.S. Department of Justice, National Institute of Justice.

Solicitor General of Canada. 1990. The Future of Policing in Canada: Discussion Paper. Ottawa: Ministry of the Solicitor General of Canada (Prepared by André Normandeau and Barry Leighton).

Sparrow, Malcolm K., Mark H. Moore, and David M. Kennedy. 1990. *Beyond 911: A New Era for Policing*. New York: Basic Books.

Stenning, Philip C. 1981. The role of police boards and commissions as institutions of municipal government in organizational police deviance. In C. Shearing (ed.), *Organizational Police Deviance, Its Structure and Control*. Scarborough, ON: Butterworths.

Sykes, Gary W. 1986. Street justice: A moral defense of order maintenance theory. *Justice Quarterly* 3(4): 497–512.

Taylor, Ian. 1981. *Law and Order: Arguments for Socialism*. London: Macmillan.

Trojanowicz, Robert and Bonnie Bucqueroux. 1990. *Community Policing: A Contemporary Perspective*. Cincinnati: Anderson.

Waddington, P.A.J. 1984. Community policing: A sceptical appraisal. In Philip Norton (ed.), *Law and Order and British Politics*. Aldershot, England: Gower.

Walden, Keith. 1982. *Visions of Order: The Canadian Mounties in Symbol and Myth*. Toronto: Butterworths.

Walker, Christopher R. 1987. The community police station: Developing a model. *Canadian Police College Journal* 11(4): 273–318.

Walker, Christopher R. and S. Gail Walker. 1989. *The Victoria Community Police Stations: An Exercise in Innovation*. Ottawa: Canadian Police College.

Walker, Samuel. 1983. *The Police in America*. New York: McGraw Hill.

———. 1984. Broken windows and fractured history: The use and misuse of history in recent police patrol analysis. *Justice Quarterly* 1(1): 75–90.

Weatheritt, Mollie. 1983. Community policing: Does it work and how do we know? In T. Bennet (ed.), *The Future of Policing*. Cambridge: University of Cambridge, Institute of Criminology.

Wellman, Barry. 1979. The community question: The intimate ties of East Yorkers. *American Journal of Sociology* 84(5): 1201–1231.

Wellman, Barry and Barry Leighton. 1979. Networks, neighborhoods and communities. *Urban Affairs Quarterly* 14(3): 363–390.

Wilson, James Q. and George Kelling. 1982. Broken windows. *Atlantic Monthly* (March): 29–38.

———. 1989. Making neighbourhoods safe. *Atlantic Monthly* (Feb.): 46–52.

Young, Warren and Neil Cameron (eds.). 1989. *Effectiveness and Change in Policing*. Wellington, New Zealand: Victoria University of Wellington, Institute of Criminology (Studies Series No 3).

ELEVEN

An Impact Evaluation of the Edmonton Neighbourhood Foot Patrol Program

J.P. HORNICK, B.A. BURROWS, D.M. PHILLIPS, AND B. LEIGHTON

In 1987 the Edmonton Police Department made it a departmental objective to incorporate the philosophy and implement the practice of community-based policing. As

Source: J.P. Hornick, B.A. Burrows, D.M. Phillips, and B. Leighton, "An Impact Evaluation of the Edmonton Neighbourhood Foot Patrol Program," *Canadian Journal of Program Evaluation*, 6, 1 (1991): 47–70. Reproduced by permission of the *Canadian Journal of Program Evaluation*.

a result, the Neighbourhood Foot Patrol Program (NFPP) was developed and imple-mented in 21 neighbourhood beat areas. This innovative policing program was based on the principle that policing must be based within the community rather than the criminal justice system. That is, crime is dealt with in terms of its impact on the community rather than its legal status, and police constables provide ongoing foot patrol services in the neighbourhoods where recurring problems originate. Since foot patrol constables are highly visible, citizens may observe them performing their daily duties. This approach also allows constables to learn more about their beat and to adapt to the community they serve (Alpert & Dunham, 1986).

The Edmonton Police Department's decision to implement a community-based policing program coincides with pervasive reform of policing policy and programs in Canada, the United States, and other western countries (e.g., Green & Mastrofski, 1988; Lambert, 1988; Trojanowicz & Bucqueroux, 1990; Walker, 1987). A common feature of the revised programs is their emphasis on greater interaction with the community, with the goal of resolving underlying community problems that lead to crime and disorder.

In the United States, the impetus for reform of policy has come from at least three factors: (a) increasing crime rate, (b) increasing fear of crime and victimization on the part of citizens, and (c) the assumption that communities are dissatisfied with police performance. Community policing has also been widely adopted in Canada, possibly because the U.S. tends to be a stimulus and source of innovation for the Canadian criminal justice system. The negative effect of this dependence on U.S. police innovation, technologies, and research knowledge has been a lack of research and development focusing specifically on innovative community policing programs in Canada (Murphy, 1988).

Recognizing the need to document and evaluate innovative community policing programs in Canada, the Edmonton Police Department contracted with the Canadian Research Institute for Law and the Family to conduct a comprehensive process-and-impact evaluation of the NFPP during its first year of operation. This article presents the findings of the impact component of the evaluation. Specifically, findings are presented on how successful the program was in achieving reduction of repeat calls-for-service, improvement of public/user satisfaction with police, and increased job satisfaction of NFPP constables.

THE PROGRAM

The NFPP is best described by examining its goals, objectives, strategies, and struc-tural components.

GOALS

The primary goal of the NFPP is to prevent crime and create a better community. This requires some consideration of the quality-of-life issues that surround crime, such as poverty, racism, and anger, and leads to the NFPP's second goal: to provide proactive policing services aimed at solving problems rather than simply reporting incidents. The third goal of the NFPP is to provide a service that is based within the community rather than the criminal justice system, that is, one that involves the community in identifying and solving problems. Thus, NFPP police constables "act as community team leaders in identifying problems that damage the quality of life, then work through the community as a whole to find and apply solutions to those problems" (Cassels, 1988).

OBJECTIVES

The NFPP was designed to achieve the following objectives:

1. Reducing the number of repeat calls-for-service. Achievement of this objective involves reducing the number of repetitive calls arising from, and subsequent dispatches to, a particular address as well as reducing the overall number of repeat addresses in a beat area.
2. Improving public satisfaction with the police. This objective involves increasing the positive attitude of citizens toward the police constable and the service he or she provides to the community.
3. Increasing the job satisfaction of participating constables. The program was designed to promote both a sense of commitment to the neighbourhood and a sense of ownership of the neighbourhood's problem on the part of the foot patrol constables. This sense of ownership, combined with the autonomy and opportunity to try new approaches to policing, is intended to increase job satisfaction.
4. Increasing the reporting of information on crime in the community. The foot constables spend many working hours getting to know the people in their foot patrol areas. It follows that they would have greater access to information about suspects and suspicious activity on a day-to-day basis than would constables providing more traditional, intermittent motor patrol service to that area.
5. Solving community problems. A substantial variety of community problems exist in the foot patrol areas, including prostitution, substance abuse by minors, parking problems, juvenile crime, family disputes, theft, break-and-enter, and alcohol- and drug-related violence. It was hoped that foot patrol would reduce the severity and occurrence of such problems.

STRATEGIES

The program strategies include the following:

1. Targeting police services to "hot spots." Selection of the 21 foot patrol areas involved a lengthy procedure to identify hot-spot areas. The computer information system was used to identify areas that experienced high volumes of crime/incident occurrences, repeat addresses, dispatched calls, and dispatched units.
2. Decentralizing the service. Each constable operates out of a storefront office located within the beat area. Storefronts were established to promote constable autonomy and identification with the community.
3. Increasing police visibility. Increasing police visibility enables community members to become used to having a foot patrol constable in their neighbourhood. It should increase community involvement in identifying and solving specific problems and facilitate the gathering of intelligence. Foot patrol constables walk large portions of their beats virtually every working day.

4. Increasing constables' autonomy and problem-solving ability. The more autonomous the foot patrol constables are, the more likely they are to depend on community members rather than fellow constables for support. They are also likely to spend more time interacting with community members.

5. Involving the community in defining problems. The constables have day-to-day contact with neighbourhood residents and business people. This promotes communication about issues of concern to these people. For example, a business owner is more likely to tell a foot patrol constable whom he sees daily about a suspicious group of juveniles that have been loitering outside of his business than he is to make a formal complaint to the police department, which may or may not result in the dispatch of a regular police constable.

6. Involving the community in solving problems. The resources of community members are assumed to be beneficial to the foot patrol constable in solving problems. Involving the community in problem-solving gives citizens the message that some of the responsibility for crime prevention rests with them.

7. Increasing constables' knowledge of the community. This strategy goes hand-in-hand with many of the others. Once constables become familiar with their foot patrol area, they should be better able to identify community members to help in the problem-solving process. Constables should also become more knowledgeable of who does what in their communities.

STRUCTURAL COMPONENTS

The structural components of the NFPP program were developed to put the above strategies into effect. They include the following:

1. A constable assigned to patrol a small geographic area on foot. Foot patrol is intended to promote police visibility, to increase the constable's knowledge of and adaptation to the community, and to promote community involvement in problem-solving.

2. A storefront office in each foot patrol area. Storefront offices are intended to decentralize police service, promote community involvement, provide a place for volunteers to work, and make the constable accessible to the community.

3. Community liaison committees. The committees are composed of key players in the community and are organized to promote community ownership of problems.

4. Volunteers. Volunteers are recruited both to encourage community involvement and to share some of the constables' workload.

5. Use of a specific problem-solving strategy by the constable. Problem-solving involves problem identification, identification of various alternatives for long-term solutions, and implementation of the most appropriate solutions.

METHODS

DESIGN

The impact evaluation consisted of numerous quasi-experimental designs to test various aspects of the program using multiple data sources. In some components, data were collected from both foot and motor patrols and comparisons between the two groups were made.

REPEAT CALLS-FOR-SERVICE ANALYSIS

Prior to commencement of the NFPP in April 1988, police computer services was requested to produce a listing, for all 21 beat areas, of all addresses for which at least two calls-for-service had been made between March 1, 1987, and February 29, 1988. A similar request was later made for the period May 16, 1988, to May 15, 1989, which corresponds closely to the NFPP's first year of operation.

The printouts generated by the police department's computer database (OSCAR) provided the following data for each call-for-service: address, atom, date, case number, complainant name, offence code, and offence description.

Data for the May 1988–May 1989 period were used to generate a report that tallied the number of calls per address. Likewise, the March 1987–February 1988 printouts were used to tally the number of calls per address for the previous year. The frequency of repeat calls per address was then analyzed to see whether any significant changes in the numbers of repeat calls occurred within the 21 beat areas.

SURVEY OF SERVICE USERS

A list of potential contacts was generated consisting of citizens who had contact with either foot or motor patrol constables during the course of the process study (not reported on here). The variables listed for each citizen were constable study ID, date of contact, contact name, contact type, address under investigation, type of address under investigation, and offense code. Research assistants then examined the information and identified persons who could probably be contacted at the address noted. This procedure involved considering the completeness of name and address data, in conjunction with the contact type code, location code, and offense code, when available.

Contact with certain types of individuals was avoided. For example, it would have been inappropriate to contact any suspects or offenders. Therefore, the list of potential contacts included only complainants/victims, witnesses, professionals, general citizens, or business persons. Contact with any young offender witnesses and with victims under the age of 18 was also avoided.

After potential contacts were identified, their telephone numbers were sought using the telephone directory and the Harrison's Directory. Interviews were conducted by telephone between May 24 and June 10, 1989, five to six months after respondents' contact with police. The service user survey questionnaire was used in these interviews.

PERSONNEL SURVEY

The attitudes of constables toward various aspects of policing were measured by the personnel survey. All foot patrol constables ($N = 21$) and a random sample of motor patrol constables ($N = 80$) were asked to complete the survey shortly after the inception of the NFPP (May 1988) and again one year later (May 1989). The baseline instrument, based on the previous work of the Police Foundation, Washington, DC, measured constables' attitudes toward the following issues: general (i.e., motor patrol) police function, police performance issues, job satisfaction, personal motivation and job involvement, and personal feelings toward work. At the posttest, attitudes toward the following two issues were added to the original instrument: foot patrol function and resource allocation. These topics relate directly to foot patrol and therefore could not be investigated during baseline testing, when the program had not yet been fully implemented.

Before the baseline study began, a sample of 80 motor patrol constables was randomly drawn. Personnel surveys and stamped, self-addressed return envelopes were forwarded to these constables and to all 21 foot patrol constables. The return rate was 100 percent for the foot patrol constables and 92.5 percent (74/80) for the motor patrol. In May 1989 the follow-up questionnaires were sent to only those constables who had returned the questionnaire at the pretest. Again, the foot patrol had a 100 percent response rate, but the motor patrol response rate dropped to 81 percent (60/74).

Data from the completed surveys were entered, and the degree of attitude change on subscales from pretest to posttest was calculated for both groups. Further, t-tests were conducted to determine whether there was a significant difference between the two groups in terms of the amount of change exhibited on subscales. For all remaining items not belonging to subscales, the mean scores for the two groups were simply compared for the pretest and posttest.

FINDINGS: PROGRAM IMPACT

REPEAT CALLS-FOR-SERVICE

As discussed earlier, data on repeat calls-for-service for the 21 beat areas were obtained from the Edmonton Police Department computer system. The objective of this analysis is to determine whether there was any significant decrease in the number of calls per repeat address from the pretest (March 1, 1987–February 29, 1988) to the posttest period (May 16, 1988–May 15, 1989).

There are two principal variables in this analysis: the number of repeat addresses (defined as addresses accounting for at least two calls in the course of the year) and the number of repeat calls per address. It would be inconclusive to consider either variable alone when attempting to assess changes in the number of calls per repeat address. However, before examining the interplay between the two variables, it is necessary to understand how each of them changes from pretest to posttest. Therefore, the following discussion considers changes in the number of repeat addresses from pretest to posttest, changes in the number of calls from pretest to posttest, and, finally, changes in the number of repeat calls per address from pretest to posttest.

NUMBER OF REPEAT ADDRESSES

The number of repeat addresses declined slightly from 4,014 during the pretest to 3,918 during the posttest, representing a decrease of about 2.4 percent. Of course, these figures alone do not reveal much about the patterns of change in the number of repeat addresses.

Improvement is considered to have occurred if the number of repeat addresses declined or a greater number of repeat addresses disappeared than appeared at the posttest. 14 of the 21 (66.6 percent) beats improved by virtue of having had decreases in the percentages of repeat addresses, and 12 of the 21 beats (57.1 percent) improved because more repeat addresses had disappeared than appeared at the posttest. Overall (all beats considered together) improvement was also noted on both criteria. It must be emphasized, however, that the number of repeat addresses alone indicates little. Conclusions may be drawn only when the number of calls per repeat address is analyzed.

NUMBER OF CALLS
The number of calls decreased from 21,001 at pretest to 19,612 at posttest, representing a decrease of 6.6 percent. Again, however, it must be emphasized that data on the total number of calls alone does not explain much.

NUMBER OF CALLS PER REPEAT ADDRESS
Of the 21 beats, 7 (33.3 percent) exhibited a significant decrease from pretest to posttest, and 2 (9.5 percent) exhibited a significant increase from pretest to posttest. A significant decrease was observed overall. At the pretest, the average number of calls per repeat address ranged from 1.87 to 9.36; at the posttest they ranged from 1.76 to 7.89.

Some improvement was made from pretest to posttest in terms of the average number of calls per repeat address. However, it is necessary to know whether similar changes were experienced in nonbeat (i.e., motor patrol) areas before attributing this moderate success to the NFPP. Unfortunately, this information is not available.

USER SATISFACTION WITH FOOT AND MOTOR PATROL

As mentioned above, the service user survey was conducted in May and June 1989 to assess whether the foot and motor patrol contacts differed in their attitudes toward the police service. At the same time, some of the demographic data were collected to ensure that there were no significant demographic differences between the two groups.

Analysis of the data revealed no significant differences between the foot and motor patrol contacts in terms of age, gender, marital status, education levels, or length of time in neighbourhood. However, there were some differences in the occupational structures of the two groups. Almost 68 percent of the foot patrol contacts were engaged in white-collar occupations, compared to 39.8 percent of motor patrol contacts. Further, only 32.4 percent of the foot patrol contacts were engaged in clerical, technical, skilled, or semi-skilled labor, or were students, homemakers, retired, unemployed, or self-employed, compared to 60.2 percent of the motor patrol contacts. The impact of socioeconomic status on satisfaction with the police is not known. It may influence attitudes toward the police to some extent, but is probably less significant than factors associated directly with respondents' experience during and in the aftermath of the crime.

Analysis of the data obtained through the service user survey revealed numerous significant differences between the motor and foot patrol contacts. Overall, the foot patrol contacts exhibited generally higher levels of satisfaction with the police. Specific attitudinal differences between the two groups are discussed below.

NEIGHBOURHOOD ATTITUDES

Foot patrol contacts had a more positive and optimistic attitude toward their neighbourhoods. Significant differences were found between the foot and motor patrol contacts on all three items designed to measure attitudes toward neighbourhood. However, the general wording of these questions, without direct reference to policing, makes it difficult to draw a direct link between the responses given and the presence/absence of foot patrol.

ATTITUDES TOWARD THE INCIDENT AND INVESTIGATING CONSTABLE

Before levels of satisfaction with the investigating officer were gauged, respondents were asked if they could recall the specific incident that prompted the contact and the officer who came to investigate. There were significant differences between the two groups on both items. First, significantly more motor patrol contacts (96 percent, compared with 87 percent of foot contacts) recalled the specific incident that led to contact with the officer. This may be due to the greater tendency of foot patrol officers to converse with the public, resulting in some blurring of these meetings in the minds of citizens. Second, significantly more foot respondents (89 percent, compared to 77 percent of motor patrol respondents) recalled the specific investigating officer. These two differences are complementary, reflecting the increased contact between citizens and foot patrol constables. However, it should be noted that the degree of recall is very high in both cases, suggesting that they do not compromise the validity of the study.

Foot patrol constables received significantly more positive ratings than their motor patrol counterparts on virtually all items in Part 2 of the service user survey that are suitable for statistical tests of difference. Specifically, the foot patrol constables were perceived more favorably than the motor patrol on the following items:

- Officer clearly explained action to be taken
- Officer was helpful
- Officer was polite
- Citizen was confident that conflict would be resolved
- Officer understood citizen's feelings toward the crime
- Officer's manner helped citizen feel comfortable about reporting complaint
- Officer's manner helped citizen feel relaxed after incident
- Same officer returned to tell how problem was resolved (54.5 percent of foot patrol contacts, compared to 30.8 percent of motor patrol contacts, answered "yes" to this question)
- Citizen was satisfied with follow-up contact with police
- Citizen heard whether incident was resolved (65 percent of foot patrol contacts and 48.6 percent of motor patrol contacts answered "yes" to this question)
- Citizen was satisfied that justice had been served
- Citizen was satisfied with how officer responded

The motor patrol was not rated more favorably than the foot patrol on any Part 2 items to the extent that statistical significance was achieved. However, responses to question 10 (feelings about the incident) indicate that the motor patrol contacts were significantly more frightened about the crime incident than were the foot patrol contacts. This higher level of fear among the motor patrol respondents may indicate that this group experienced generally more serious offenses than the foot patrol group, and that motor patrol constables tend to receive more higher priority calls than do foot patrol constables.

Several items in Part 2 refer to follow-up by the police. As mentioned above, foot patrol contacts more frequently reported that the same officer returned to tell them how the problem was resolved, that they heard whether the incident was resolved, and that they were significantly more satisfied with the follow-up contact provided. A higher proportion of foot patrol contacts also reported follow-up as helping them to feel better about reporting the crime. All of these data point to more diligent follow-up on the part of the foot patrol constables. 66.2 percent of foot patrol contacts and 48.1 percent of motor patrol contacts reported that the police officer returned to inform them. Again, this points to more follow-up on the part of foot patrol constables.

ATTITUDES TOWARD GENERAL POLICE SERVICE AND EFFECTIVENESS

Part 3 of the survey asked seven questions about general police effectiveness; the findings indicate higher levels of satisfaction with the foot patrol than with the motor patrol. Statistical significance was observed for six of the seven items, with foot patrol receiving more positive ratings on all six. These items were police effectiveness in working with the neighbourhood to solve local problems, dealing with problems of concern to the neighbourhood, preventing crime, keeping order on the streets, and treating people politely and fairly. There was no statistically significant difference in the perceived effectiveness of foot and motor patrol in helping victims of crime.

Finally, it should be noted that while the foot patrol received more positive ratings from the public, the ratings given to the motor patrol were also fairly high, tending to center on "good" (a 2 on the 5-point scale). Therefore, many aspects of the results should be considered when drawing conclusions, and a narrow preoccupation with "who is better" should be avoided.

JOB SATISFACTION

As explained above, foot patrol constables ($N = 20$) and a sample of motor patrol constables ($N = 60$) completed the personnel survey in May 1988, shortly after the inception of the NFPP, and again in May 1989. Some demographic data were collected during the pretest to ensure that the two groups were generally similar and to obtain background information. That data indicated that the two groups were very similar in terms of age, marital status, age at which they joined the Edmonton Police Department, number of years they had been with the department, and education level. However, the motor patrol sample reported having been with their unit significantly longer than the foot patrol sample. Also, a considerably higher proportion of motor patrol respondents (91.7 percent compared to 45 percent for foot patrol) had been with the patrol division during the previous six months, whereas a greater proportion of the foot patrol had been on beat detail (40 percent) or in some other area (15 percent) of the police department.

Differences between foot and motor patrol respondents were apparent in terms of certain job satisfaction subscales and personal motivation, and job involvement subscales for each group and subscale.

From the pretest to the posttest, the foot patrol became significantly more satisfied than the motor patrol on the following subscales: compensation, organization policy and procedures, growth and satisfaction, and internal work motivation. In addition, the foot patrol was significantly more satisfied with physical working conditions at both pretest and posttest than were the motor patrol constables. However, both groups experienced only minimal change on this subscale from pretest to posttest.

In contrast, the motor patrol showed no significant improvement in satisfaction on any subscale, in terms of either within-group pretest-top-posttest change or changed scores in comparison to foot patrol.

CONCLUSIONS

The findings of the impact evaluation indicated that the Edmonton NFPP achieved three major program objectives: reducing repeat calls-for-service, achieving a high degree of user satisfaction with police services, and increasing job satisfaction of the NFPP constables.

The total number of repeat calls-for-service in the foot patrol areas decreased by 6.6 percent during the first year of the project. There was also a decrease in both the number of repeat addresses per beat area and the average number of calls per repeat address.

The survey of users of police services provided the strongest evidence for the success of the program. Data collected from users of foot patrol and motor patrol services, indicated that the foot patrol was generally perceived more favourably than the motor patrol. Foot patrol constables were viewed as more helpful, polite, able to resolve conflict and understand feelings, and prone to provide follow-up material than the motor patrol constables. Finally, the job satisfaction of the foot patrol constables also improved over the period of the study, adding to the evidence that the program was successful.

The success of this program seems to be attributable to a number of key factors. First, the program was well planned, well documented, and implemented on a relatively small scale. Second, the constables who volunteered for the program were experienced and respected by their fellow officers. Third, the program was targeted for specific areas that had been identified as hot-spot areas. Finally, ownership of the program was transferred to the department as a whole during the first six months of the program. This was conducive to integrating the program with the regular policing activities of the department, and also led to acceptance of the program by constables and higher rank officers throughout the department.

REFERENCES

Alpert, G.P., & Dunham, R.G. (1986). Community policing. *Journal of Police Science and Administration, 14*, 212–222.

Cassels, D. (1988). *The Edmonton Police Department Neighbourhood Foot Patrol Project: Preliminary report.* Edmonton: Edmonton Police Department.

Green, J.R., & Mastrofski, S.D. (Eds.). (1988). *Community Policing: Rhetoric or Reality.* New York: Praeger.

Lambert, L.R. (1988). Police mini-stations in Toronto: An experience in compromise. *Royal Canadian Mounted Police Gazette, 50*, 1–5.

Murphy, C. (1988). The development, impact, and implications of community policing in
    Canada. In J.R. Greene & S.D. Mastrofski (Eds.), *Community Policing: Rhetoric or Reality*
    (pp. 177–189). New York: Praeger.
Trojanowicz, R., & Bucqueroux, B. (1990). *Community Policing: A Contemporary Perspective.*
    Cincinnati, OH: Anderson.
Walker, C.R. (1987). The community police station: Developing a model. *Canadian Police
    Journal, 11,* 273–318.

TWELVE

Policing and Aboriginal Justice

JIM HARDING

OVERCOMING DENIAL

Since the 1960s, we have witnessed a change from widespread denial of systemic
discrimination in policing of Aboriginal people to the pondering of fundamental
alternatives to the traditional organization and role of peace officers as law enforcers.
To say this is not to scapegoat police forces, since in some ways they are reflections
of the larger society. The same negative stereotypes of Aboriginal people existing
within police forces have been found in other strata as well (Hylton 1979, 1980). In
a general sense, then, the RCMP Assistant Commissioner is right that

> ... it should not be surprising that we have racial intolerance within the force because,
> as products of a larger Canadian society, we enter its ranks with all the usual bias, preju-
> dice, and racism baggage that this society generates (Head, 1989: 25).

If police forces truly wish to professionalize in the best sense then, this will not
be taken as an excuse for the shortcoming. Rather, it will act as a challenge to change
and possibly advance beyond other sectors of Canadian society. Because some people
who plan to be doctors hold vestiges of pre-medical myths about the body is no
excuse for graduating medical students who would constitute a risk to their patients.
Racism in policing is no less a risk to the targeted citizenry than would be a surgeon's
stereotypes of body functioning to a patient on an operating table.

Nor is this mirroring of racism within policing necessarily any greater than
within other parts of the criminal justice system. Racial as well as class and gender
discrimination within the Canadian legal process has been documented by several
people (Comack 1990; Samuelson and Schissel 1991). As was written in one of
Prairie Justice Research's major research reports on Aboriginal justice:

Source: Jim Harding, "Policing and Aboriginal Justice," *Canadian Journal of Criminology*, 33, 3–4 (1991):
363–83. Copyright by the Canadian Criminal Justice Association. Reproduced by permission of the
Canadian Journal of Criminology.

It is not difficult to illustrate the extent to which both the substantive law and the law enforcement system discriminate against the poor of whom Indigenous people make up a disproportionately large group (Havemann, Couse, Foster and Matonovitch 1985: 20).

The fact that it took the $7,000,000 Commission of Inquiry into the wrongful conviction of Donald Marshall to confirm this to a broader, somewhat skeptical public only shows how deep the denial of systemic discrimination has been.

WHY FOCUS ON POLICE

There remains a strategic reason for putting extra attention on overcoming racism within Canadian policing. As the front-end of the criminal justice system, discriminatory discretion in policing shapes everything that follows. If any significant change is to be made in the steady trend to overincarcerate Aboriginal people, something must change in policing itself. Furthermore, policing is the most powerful part of the criminal justice system, utilizing about two-thirds of the funds used for criminal justice in Canada in the 1970s, when charges of racism against police in Canada first became pronounced.

There is another related reason for focussing on policing. Research in the mid-80s suggested that the deployment of both police and police budgets was greater on a per capita basis in the hinterland areas of Canada where Aboriginal people are in greater numbers. This was particularly the case for the North, where police per 100,000 were more than twice the Canadian average (4.9 to 2.2 in 1980), and where policing expenditures were 171 percent to 244 percent higher than the Canadian average. Also, with the highest incarceration rate of Aboriginal people in Canada, Saskatchewan had the highest per capita rate of police (2.8) (Havemann et al. 1985: 23–24). Other research suggests that the growth of private and public police in the North came with the expansion of corporate development that was itself dislocating to Aboriginal communities (Harding 1978; Schriml 1985).

Research on private policing raises another dimension. Though Stenning focusses on urban private policing of mass corporate property, his analysis raises pertinent questions about accountability and Aboriginal justice. He notes that:

> Agreeing that what they do is not "real policing" is ... a naturally attractive public position for private policing spokespeople to adopt, since it allows them to get on with what they are doing without attracting the unwanted public scrutiny and constraints which are being applied with increasing intensity to the public police (1989: 181).

He reiterates that "If agreeing that they do not do 'real policing' turns out to be an effective way of avoiding these kinds of accountability and constraints, one can hardly be surprised to find them doing so" (1989: 183).

Stenning sees private policing as an alternative, less criminalizing model for public policing to consider. But we also have to recognize that private police are part of the social control system that separates most Aboriginal (and other poor strata) from the dominant, corporate society. Aboriginal youth are already in greater conflict with private police, as seen in some urban shopping malls. This, in part, is because their high unemployment and relative impoverishment makes them less attractive for profitable consumerism. As urbanization and demographics converge, this could prove to be a source of systemic discrimination that is more invisible than is the public policing, which is presently being scrutinized by various judicial inquiries. From this perspective, private policing shouldn't be confused with community-based policing alternatives.

A variety of studies confirm that:

> ... in the hinterland there is a greater chance of contact between Indigenous peoples and police officials, given the higher ratio of police to general population and the role of the police as "gatekeepers" to the criminal justice system (Havemann et al. 1985: 25).

And the exact same structural predisposition to arrest and incarceration exists for Aboriginal people migrating to the more intensely policed inner-city areas.

The extent of denial of such systemic discrimination should not be overlooked. Such denial was quite typical among researchers looking at the increasing incarceration of Aboriginal people in the 1960s. In the influential *Indians and the Law* (1967), the Canadian Corrections Association wrote:

> The constant surveillance sometimes required by the Indian and Metis people can, under these circumstances, harden into open dislike on the part of the police ... It is obvious that the Indian people, particularly in the cities, tend to draw police attention to themselves, since their dress, personal hygiene, physical characteristics and location in run-down areas make them conspicuous. This undoubtedly results in more arrests (1967: 36–37).

Such "reasoning" reflects ethnocentrism at best, and racism at worst. Such seemingly white supremacist thinking was not that uncommon at the time. In an inquiry in the N.W.T. (Morrow 1968: 22–23), a denial of racial discrimination was cloaked by its acceptance of rationalizations for such discrimination. Nor was there any mainstream political encouragement to question the ethnocentric or racist notions that helped cloak the systemic discrimination against Aboriginal people. We only have to remember that it was in 1969 that Jean Chretien, then Minister of Indian Affairs in Trudeau's government, introduced the White Paper that rejected all Aboriginal rights and declared an assimilationist policy for Aboriginal people.

REFORM AS TECH-FIX

There are no short cuts if policing is to respond to the growing pressures for Aboriginal justice in Canada. It is quite enlightening to look back with a critical eye at the way reforms in policing, which were to take Aboriginal people into account, were first conceptualized in the 1970s.

There have been four main approaches to reforming policing to redress the problems being faced by Aboriginal people in the criminal justice system. The first two, an emphasis on cross-cultural training programs for police forces, and legal education for Aboriginal people, both assumed that enhanced attitudes and information would help correct injustices. The last two, often confusedly linked together as "indigenization of policing" included the creation of native constable and tribal policing programs. Native constable programs have been the preferred strategy over the last 15 years. Pressure, however, continues to grow for the transfer of more policing to autonomous tribal programs.

It is important to recognize how police and program-related research usually reinforces underlying political and ideological assumptions. If the assimilation of Aboriginal people is desired, then certain approaches to research, policy, and program will tend to follow. Since fundamental Aboriginal rights were not widely accepted within Canadian politics or the dominant society in the 1970s, when the first stab at police reform was taken, it is not too surprising that the approaches tended to contradict fundamental Aboriginal justice.

All the four above approaches, especially the grouping of the tribal policing along with Native constable programs, tended to assume and pronounce that the problem was one of correcting the use of police discretionary powers. None of them, not even a narrowly conceived tribunal policing, complemented the notion or demands for self-government among Aboriginal people.

CROSS-CULTURALISM

Cross-culturalism training was embraced as some sort of panacea that would not require any fundamental rethinking of policing, or for that matter, anything else. It was usually envisioned in terms of the dominant culture, not in terms of two historically distinct cultures. One criminological analysis of cross-culturalism stated:

> The criminal justice system exists to preserve the basic values of our culture. If properly understood, those of the native are not basically different. Insofar as the current cultural manifestations of the two value systems appear in conflict, these must be resolved based on the core values underlying both (James 1979: 461–462).

French social historian Michel Foucault would have a field day with this analysis, for the criminologist continues:

> Perhaps it is the fact that the prison represents the ultimate failure to succeed in the dominant society that forces some natives to face the option of becoming successful natives, better able to face with pride the challenge of surviving in today's world (1979: 457).

No one will deny that the prison plays a role in disciplining Aboriginal (and minority groups) to live within the dominant society. But that hardly suggests or, for that matter, promotes any underlying harmony of cultures. From such a perspective you do not have to do much guessing which normative system will be the integrating and, hence, dominating one.

The cross-cultural approach to reforming policing sometimes gets explicitly linked to the notion of multi-culturalism that emerged in Canada in the late 1970s. This did no more to affirm Aboriginal culture than the kind of neocolonist perspective reflected above. This reduction of Aboriginal culture to the notion of multiculturalism was all too common:

> ... while some countries have tried to assimilate minority groups so that there is only one set of values and traditions, in Canada we have traditionally fostered and encouraged ethnic pluralism (Hylton, 1981: 9–10).

A somewhat similar treatment is offered by Linden who deals with Aboriginal people as part of a changing ethnic and racial structure in Canada, and concludes:

... The effects of racism combined with the social and economic deprivation which faces some minority groups can lead to over-involvement in crime ... some parts of the country may face more crimes as the minority population increases unless these underlying problems are dealt with (1989: 119).

Though this notion of ethnic pluralism sounds great, it obscures the fundamental difference between Aboriginal and immigrant peoples. In reducing both to multiculturalism, it totally ignores the problems of self-determination peculiar to colonized peoples.

Furthermore, without a workable system of legal pluralism such as suggested by the Canadian Bar Association (Jackson 1988), cultural pluralism is rather meaningless when it comes to issues of policing and criminal justice. There remains a vast amount of conceptual, policy, and political confusion in our country as presently pulled between bilingualism and multiculturalism. It might be more accurate and helpful to talk of the need for multi-nationalism, not to be confused with the corporate version. Certainly until the two founding nations of Canada (1867) agree to a responsible social contract with the Aboriginal nations, or first peoples, the confusion will persist.

The same underlying problems exist with the thrust for legal education for Aboriginal people. It is noteworthy, however, that the Native courtworkers program in Saskatchewan — one of the few programs that might have provided concrete legal information to Aboriginal people at risk of incarceration — was cut early in the term of the present Conservative government. Backlogs and fees in legal aid have just further exacerbated the situation. Without effective legal counsel and legal education for Aboriginal people, particularly youth at risk of incarceration, it is unlikely that cross-cultural awareness would make much difference.

NATIVE CONSTABLES

A neocolonial and/or multicultural view of policing reforms predominated in the Native constable programs launched in the 1970s. Though it acknowledged the need to bring policing closer to the community, the Indian Affairs Task Force on Policing on Reserves (Department of Indian Affairs and Northern Development 1973) saw problems of Aboriginal people as those of a minority group (1973: 5–6). And, though it considered two options for indigenizing policing (the so-called options 3 (a) and 3 (b), it rejected the first option of autonomous Aboriginal police forces, as advocated by Indian groups in Saskatchewan and New Brunswick, purportedly due to a lack of police experience in Aboriginal communities. Instead it embraced option 3 (b), or the Native Special Constable program.

It is worth considering why it took until the mid-70s for "indigenization of policing" to be taken seriously as an option in Canada. Though lip-service was given to this as a step towards more Aboriginal self-government, it seems clear that the need for a more effective social control system was the paramount consideration. Certainly, this was the case in the United States, where one review of the use of Indian police concluded:

It provided that they should be employed also "for the purposes of civilization of the Indians" which eventually was to inspire some of the most interesting, if debatable, duties of the Indian police (Hagan 1966: 69).

Like cross-cultural training, Native constable programs were primarily con cerned with making policing more effective. They were not fundamentally concerned with reducing incarceration rates of Aboriginal people, though the supporters of the program would likely prefer this to happen. If it didn't, however, the program would not be seen to have failed. Social control, not self-determination, was the main concern.

Though the federal government adopted option 3 (b), most Aboriginal authors remained critical of the program. A summary of the critique by Brass (1979) stated:

> ... special constables are recruited from the "affluent" elements in the band population, not the traditional or poor families, and yet it is mostly these latter groups of Indigenous peoples who are in conflict with the law ... peer pressure to identify with white fellow officers is likely to occur and thus defeat the purpose of the special constable program ... the "special" status with lower pay and entry qualifications will promote a double standard and reinforce cultural relativism and stereotyping (Havemann et al. 1985: 33–34).

It is not too surprising that

> ... most studies done by or for Indigenous organizations approve of autonomous policing while those done by or for government agencies appear to prefer policing by special constables (Havemann et al. 1985: 37).

One Ontario evaluation of option 3 (b) found a definite increase in reported crime, and hence an increased involvement of Aboriginal people within the criminal justice system (Harris 1977). This is not necessarily to suggest that any more conflict existed with the involvement of the special Native constables. It is quite likely that these Native police were intervening in real problems in Aboriginal communities. But the outcome was more criminalization of Aboriginal people, and not necessarily the strengthening of the community to address these problems. A higher proportion of arrests in Aboriginal communities appear to be for assaults, and a lower proportion for property crimes. As such, special constables may just be furthering the systemic discrimination that already has Aboriginal people doing more time for less serious offenses than the norm.

Nevertheless, government evaluations tended to encourage continuation of the special constable programs. As Justice Kirby of Alberta remarked:

> Not only does it afford an opportunity for Indians to assume greater responsibility in law enforcement on reserves, it can also be a means of solving the problem of communications between Indians and the RCMP (1978: 28).

It should come as no big surprise that very few Aboriginal people were consulted in this or other government inquiries of the time. Furthermore, you don't have to be cynical to see that the criteria of success are self-serving for the police.

Meanwhile, an Aboriginal evaluation of the same Alberta special constable program by Native Counselling Services came to a very difficult conclusion:

... Option 3b cannot now be regarded as a viable program for most reserves. Although it was conceptually solid and there was potential for its constructive development, the program has become politically defunct. The current trend is clearly towards autonomous Indian policing (1980: 25).

TRIBAL POLICING

Support for tribal policing has clearly increased as the limitations of these piece-meal approaches to police reform have become more apparent. An alternative to crime-control policing is essential if overincarceration is to be averted while community-based problems are addressed in a preventive manner. This unified approach is not realistic for policing, which is controlled by authorities outside the emerging processes of Aboriginal self-government.

There are now several tribal policing programs that allow more in-depth consideration of a fundamental alternative to traditional policing. These include the Dakota Ojibway Tribal Council (DOTC) in Manitoba, the Amerindian Police Force in Quebec, the Louis Bull Police Force in Alberta, the Aboriginal Peace Keeper Force in British Columbia, and the Mohawk Police Keeper Force in Ontario. All of these involve, to some extent or another, the devolution of traditional policing. They all involve the creation of Aboriginal police who are as much human service and community development workers, and play a role as conflict resolvers, as they are classical peace officers. From the start the DOTC program describes its reserve police officer as "... part social worker, taxi driver, alcohol worker, ambulance driver, peace keeper and dog catcher" (Sinder and Moyer 1981: 20).

As Havemann et al. wrote: "... policing issues have lesser significance if social problems are dealt with by methods other than the criminal justice system" (1985: 45). What is needed in most Aboriginal communities is more help to local people, and not criminalization of the underlying social, economic, and political problems. Mediation is much more crucial than prosecution.

We know that this objective is not always met, nor is it easy to meet. Increases in reported crime can occur with tribal policing, in part because the Aboriginal community lacks the infrastructure and resources to directly deal with the problems criminalized. As such, the tribal police face the same dilemma as federal and municipal police. By consequence they too contribute to the net-widening process that community policing and community corrections has sometimes been found to create.

Part of this net-widening likely results from the emphasis on law enforcement in police training. But it is also necessary to consider the part played by the growing role of social class within Aboriginal communities. An evaluation of the RCMP Native Special Constable program found that officers were recruited from upper socio-economic and educational levels of the reserve population. This may also be occurring with tribal policing. Even if tribal programs have more direct community accountability, the dilemma remains that Aboriginal people are increasingly stratified in terms of both poverty and economic and political power. And this will shape the kinds of interests that influence policing priorities and methods.

Granted the opportunity exists within Aboriginal communities to establish a broader-based network of community accountability than is typical or very realistic in the rest of society. This potential, reflected in the growing use of elders, clearly grows with a resurrection and revitalization of Aboriginal cultural approaches to conflict resolution. However, this depends greatly on a political and constitutional resolution of outstanding historical grievances. And even if the role of stratification can be downplayed in Aboriginal policing in Aboriginal communities, the issues cannot be ignored in the urban areas. It is the steady urbanization of Aboriginal people that constitutes the greatest challenge to the viability and effectiveness of tribal policing.

URBAN POLICING

With the highest per capita Aboriginal population of any province, it is not surprising that Saskatchewan's cities also have the highest per capita Aboriginal population. The extent of urbanization in the last few decades is rather astonishing, akin to the pattern seen in some third world countries.

Sine the mid-60s the registered Indian population in Saskatchewan has more than doubled to 68,000. Combined with Metis and non-Status Indians, the total Aboriginal population is now about 170,000. With the existing birthrate, it is likely there will be one-quarter of a million Aboriginal people in the province by 2000, which would amount to about 25 percent of the total population.

With present trends, the vast majority of Aboriginal people will live in urban areas. At present it is estimated that 50 percent or more of all Aboriginal people live in cities and towns. Approximately 35,000 people of Aboriginal background live in Regina alone. The population of the city of Prince Albert could be 75 percent Aboriginal by 2000 according to one researcher (Elliot 1989: 12–14).

Because the birth rate of Aboriginal people remains higher than the Canadian, there will be an overall increase in young Aboriginal people. With the Canadian population aging, there remains the possibility of enhanced generation conflict between young, relatively poor Aboriginal youth and an older, mainstream population. As Elliot has written:

> High unemployment, low education levels, a political will for nationalism, unsettled land claims and a weak and inconsistent aboriginal political leadership will probably be the key factors leading to aboriginal youth discontent (1989: 8).

Though generational differences would contribute to any tension or conflict, there is always the chance that the differences would be interpreted in terms of racism, which would just further aggravate the problems.

Furthermore, the breakdown of the Aboriginal extended family in rural and northern areas may be even more exaggerated in urban areas. It was estimated in 1981 that one-third of all Aboriginal families were headed by a single parent and 90 percent of these single-parent homes lived below the poverty line. Two-thirds of two-parent Aboriginal families were also thought to live below the poverty line (Elliot 1989: 14). Urban poverty, like rural poverty and family breakdown, will continue to contribute to the well known vicious circle. It becomes a vicious cycle of social problem, conflict with the law, penalty, retribution, social problem" (Elliot 1989: 17).

Urbanization and heightened disadvantage and conflict may already be reflected in a shift in urban criminalization rates for Aboriginal people. Elliot argues that incarceration of Aboriginal people used to be fairly evenly split between rural and reserve areas, on the one hand, and urban centres, on the other. Now she says "... the breakdown is 15 percent reserve based and 85 percent off-reserve, predominantly urban based, which points to a near epidemic of aboriginal justice and crime issues in the urban area" (1989: 18). Clearly, there is need for research to explore and confirm this trend. It could have devastating implications for the attempt to address the overincarceration of Aboriginal peoples through a parallel Aboriginal justice system.

At the same time, it must be recognized that the high rate of criminalization of urban Aboriginal people, particularly youth, reflects the systemic discrimination and outright racism that persists in many police forces. It is no accident that the largest grouping of recommendations from the Marshall Commission (37 of 82) had to do with policing. These highlight the need to "improve the professionalism among municipal police departments," to consider whether to "regionalize municipal policing," to establish "minimum policing standards," "to ensure the independence" of the process of handling citizen complaints, and for municipal forces to "develop official policies on racial discrimination." (Royal Commission on the Donald Marshall Jr., Prosecution 1989: 16–17) All of these relate to making policing more accountable.

This line of reasoning has some direct implications for other jurisdictions— especially on the Prairies—where contact between police and Aboriginal people is even higher than in Nova Scotia. If we are to reduce and ultimately prevent the kind of racism and wrongful conviction reflected in the Marshall case, public accountability will have to be strengthened in all police forces across Canada. And it is well known that resistance to a fully independent process of citizen complaints persists within many police forces. One can only hope that there is no longer an outright rejection of the notion, as was reflected in a police conference on police accountability in the early 1980s in Saskatchewan (Harding 1981: 9–10).

An underlying resentment towards police and the criminal justice system clearly persists among Aboriginal people. Elliot says Aboriginal people

> ... see police services as perpetuators of oppression and insensitive to cultural etiquette and social values. Concerns ... centre around policing styles, intimidation in policing and court process ... (Specific complaints include) ... police assaults, the need for an unbiased complaints mechanism, how police handle themselves when searching a home or vehicle ... how people are handled in the cell blocks ... (1989: 16–17).

In Regina there are some signs of improvements since the late 1970s and early 1980s. In that period, a short-lived and financially insecure Race Relations Committee was not designed nor resourced to address the underlying reasons for serious maltreatment of some Aboriginal people by the police. The matter came to a head with the City's Inquiry into its use of police dogs (Couse, Geller, Harding and Havemann 1982). Our discussion of this Inquiry and its findings noted that

> The Review found that the use of dogs in Canada is most common west of the Lakehead, precisely in these urban areas in which the urban migration of Indigenous people has occurred. The use of dogs also began when this migration was on the rise (Harding and Matonovitch 1985: 147).

Some people at the time referred to Regina as the Apartheid city of Canada.

Since the Inquiry, the blatant and discriminatory use of police dogs has receded. In the last few years, however, there has been one death of a distressed Aboriginal youth in the midst of a SWAT team action (by suicide, according to an inquest), and another death of an Aboriginal adult while under police arrest (police officers were charged and acquitted). These events—along with the provincial judicial inquiries underway—have helped refocus the attention of the media on perceptions and problems of racism within the city and police (Appleby, Cernetig and York 1990).

It is not surprising that Aboriginal organizations are beginning to think seriously about the problems of survival let alone self-government in an urban era. The Federation of Saskatchewan Indian Nations (FSIN) is considering extending its mandate to the cities where over one-half of Treaty Indians already reside. Indian-controlled programs and services in the cities are now on the political agenda. At the same time, differences among Aboriginal political organizations—themselves partly rooted in colonial distinctions and jurisdictional disputes—make consolidated services and programs to meet the immense needs of urban Aboriginal people highly problematic. There are now four major different Aboriginal organizations in Saskatchewan: one of Treaty Indians (FSIN), one for Metis (Metis Society), another not excluding Non-Status Indians (Assembly of Aboriginal Peoples), and an Aboriginal Women's Council.

All these groups face serious contradictions rooted in history, conditions, and policy. How, for example, do Treaty Indian groups establish administrative centres in cities when the federal government, which directly pays for many of their services of Treaty Indians no longer considers them federal wards after one year off the reserve? Formal but largely meaningless self-government could end up being granted when resources to an urbanized Aboriginal people are drying up.

Unless Aboriginal rights are acknowledged in the Canadian constitution and substantial resources are ensured, the prospects for most urban Aboriginal people do not look good, going into the next century. It could be said that the alternative to substantive self-determination could be urban ghettoization. At just the time that policing is becoming more sensitized to the need for new approaches on reserves and in other rural areas, urban trends are converging in such a way that without social justice for Aboriginal people the likelihood is that the criminal justice system and a law and order politics will continue to dominate.

THE POLICE RESPONSE

Canadian police forces are clearly caught between the apparent lack of political will on the part of the federal government to resolve a social contract with Aboriginal people (Kly 1990) and the powerlessness, impoverishment, and strife persisting within many Aboriginal communities and families. (This is a variation of the predicament whereby police often see themselves as the filling in the social sandwich.) Though there is some sensitivity among police forces to the desires for both Aboriginal self-determination and self-government, there also remains a deep ambivalence towards the kind of legal pluralism that would be required to enable this to occur.

Some senior federal police officials seem more astutely aware of the need for changes in policing. RCMP Commissioner Inkster has recently stated:

I think that providing a policing service for the native community in this country is the single largest challenge of police officers in this country today. It is my hope that, while we have not always given that community the highest priority, we can turn that around (Head 1989: 15).

In his Directional Statement for 1989 he indicated:

We must all consider a new policing approach for aboriginal people. Our emphasis must be policing of native people rather than for native people. We must have imagination to truly understand their culture and problems so that we can adjust our approach to provide a service that is fair and sensitive to their needs (Head, 1989: 14).

A recent speech by the Assistant RCMP Commissioner (also Director of Aboriginal Policing Services) shows both an underlying sympathy, but also ambivalence towards Aboriginal justice. Certainly Assistant Commissioner Head recognizes that Aboriginal people

... have been held out of the mainstream since we began our interpretation of the Treaties and very simply they are seeking their place in the larger society (1989: 13) ... (For him the) ... number one priority between Canada's aboriginal people and elected government would quite frankly be an early settlement of outstanding land claims.

He has expressed some urgency about this, saying "I am afraid that if these land claim settlements are not soon reached the frustrations will boil over into the streets and roadways" (1989: 33). A similar warning has come from George Erasmus, President of the Assembly of First Nations. The Oka crisis and confrontation between warriors and the Quebec police and Canadian army in the summer of 1990 clearly shows how right both men were.

With all this apparent concern for better cross-cultural relations and land settlements, ambivalence remains about an Aboriginal-controlled parallel justice system. It can even be argued that cultural sensitivity may, in part, be seen as necessary for institutional survival, for the Assistant RCMP Commissioner stated:

We will either adapt and change or we will be out of the policing business as we know it, for there are many tribal groups who are looking for alternative methods. The opportunity for us is now and the time is relatively short (1989: 19).

As pressure for Aboriginal justice grows from revelations from various judicial inquiries, the RCMP seems intent on integrating the remaining constables of Aboriginal background into the regular forces. According to Assistant RCMP Commissioner Head's statistics, there are already more Native constables in the regular RCMP, than operating under the Special Constable program started in the 1970s. (He indicated about 180 are in regular service compared to 165 in the latter program. Furthermore there are another 55 Special Constables employed under provincial contracts.) RCMP policy now seems to be that:

The Special Constable program served us well until 1989 but it is now time to move on to eliminate the stigma of the "Special Constable" category and to look at affirmative action in its full context (Head, 1989: 18).

For me the most telling statement by Assistant Commissioner Head was when he said, referring to Aboriginal people coming into the RCMP: "We want them to understand us because we want them to become part of us" (1989: 34).

This policing model is not one inclined towards a parallel Aboriginal justice system, though some views exist that could still encourage moving in that direction. Assistant Commissioner Head perceptively comments that

... where we have municipal contracts with towns and cities, we sit with the police committees in developing goals, objectives and strategies. Surely the native communities, where we police, should have the same opportunity (1989: 22).

But this is not intended to reinforce Aboriginal-controlled community-based policing so much as to say that native communities deserve the same treatment as "other" municipalities.

TOWARDS LEGAL PLURALISM

Very little is presently being written that considers the issues of policing and Aboriginal people in their full political context. Yet, without a fully political resolution to the problems arising from colonialism, Aboriginal justice is not possible. The question that everyone working within the criminal justice system must ask is whether the moves towards a parallel justice system present any way to prevent the kind of future urban conflict and aggravated racism projected above.

One way that this may happen is through the courts, through *Charter of Rights* challenges. As Cohen has stated:

Proposals previously dismissed out of hand for such novel initiatives (as) the creation of alternative court systems are now receiving a respectful audience. However, significant attention has not yet been paid to the equality dimensions of the nostrums that have been proposed (1989: 40).

One concern is that formal equality, i.e., using the same justice system, may take precedence over substantive equality, which recognized the need for alternatives due to differential treatment and need in Supreme Court decisions. Certainly this kind of judgment has become typical of the Supreme Court since the Charter (Mandel 1989). However,

... questions involving the adequacy of the delivery of police and court services in aboriginal communities in Canada may be brought before the courts in Canada for early consideration. If they are, it is quite possible that these issues will find their way onto the legislative agenda as well (Cohen 1989: 62).

The Canadian Bar Association report on Aboriginal Justice also raises the constitutional issues about equality before the law. It states:

... one of the principal reasons for considering aboriginal justice systems is that the existing criminal justice system has created a condition of disadvantage, particularly in terms of the number of native people in Canada's prisons (Jackson 1988: 49).

But to achieve an Aboriginal justice system we must learn from the past attempts at cultural as well as legal domination of Aboriginal people. Jackson advances the notion of legal pluralism:

The idea of native justice systems requires us to address the place that legal pluralism should play in Canada, particularly in the context of criminal law (1988: 46).

We can, perhaps, even turn colonialism on its head. He notes that the first basis for an "Aboriginal" court was created in Section 107 of the Indian Act in 1881, by which the Indian agent also became a justice of the peace. Obviously

The creation of Section 107 Indian Act justices of the peace did not spring from the federal government's concern to maintain the distinctiveness of Indian societies and communities within a pluralist Canada; quite the reverse (1988: 36) ... (He continues) ... Given the repressive antecedents of Section 107 courts and their association with the power and authority of Indian agents, they hardly appear to be an appropriate model for justice mechanisms which further native self-determination. However, if Indian communities wish to pursue the early implementation of some form of tribal court system, the enabling provisions of section 107 may be of some significance (1988: 37–38).

The Marshall Inquiry has followed this legal argument by recommending a parallel justice system based on this precedent in the Indian Act. However, there are several questions that should be raised about this legal strategy. For one thing this "parallel" system would not extend beyond reserves covered by the Indian Act. And we have seen what accelerating urbanization is doing to undercut the viability of the reserve system as a basis for self-government. Furthermore, this "parallel" system would only apply to status Indians, and so would not only exclude other groups of southern Aboriginal people but also the vast majority of those in the NWT, including all Inuit. The applicability of such a system, as a basis for community-based alternatives to incarceration, would therefore be greatly restricted, especially in view of the high overall rate of incarceration of urban Aboriginal people.

Then there is the added fact that a parallel indigenous criminal justice system could still constitute a form of cultural oppression for some Aboriginal people as Jackson notes:

... in Dene and Inuit communities, the designation of an individual with unilateral powers of decision-making over others runs counter to deeply held concepts of egalitarianism and social structures which are built upon complex diffusion rather than concentration of authority (1988: 41).

When the limited view of a parallel justice system such as recommended by the Marshall Commission is scrutinized, it reveals many of the same shortcomings we noted about police reforms in the 1970s. Jackson himself comments that

In Saskatchewan, where native justices of the peace were introduced in the 1970s and operated for several years, the system was bedevilled by the lack of adequate training for justices, little or no support staff, inadequate facilities for holding hearings and a lack of consensus among native communities on the appropriateness of a native justice of the peace holding court on the reserve in which he was residing (1988: 41–42).

This sounds much like the limitations noted above for the Special Constable program.

Limited or not, it is clearly time to begin to make changes that will enable Aboriginal people to take control of their lives in fundamental ways. And this must occur in the criminal justice system. As Jackson himself concludes:

> The task of accommodating aboriginal justice systems with individual rights is a necessary part of the recognition of legal pluralism in the particular context of the criminal justice system. It should not be beyond our legal imagination to reach such an accommodation. The tension between collective and individual rights in the criminal justice system is not new.... It is not unrealistic to anticipate that models of aboriginal justice systems can be worked out in a Canadian context which, cognizant of the experiences of other jurisdictions, can reflect the accumulated wisdom of both aboriginal law and the common law (1988: 51).

There is presently a political opening to begin such changes. Opportunities for change in the pursuit of fundamental justice do not occur that frequently. Encouraging the creating of processes and resources for Aboriginal justice is in the fundamental interest of Canadians, and perhaps more so, of those who work within the criminal justice system. As the front end of that system, the police — especially urban police — have much to gain. We can only hope that more policing officials will provide positive leadership on this in the coming years.

To not move in this positive, transformational direction will be to guarantee further Okas. We eagerly await the perspective and recommendations of the Manitoba Aboriginal Justice inquiry in this regard.

REFERENCES

Appleby, Timothy, Miro Cemetig, and Geoffrey York. 1990. Policing the Prairies, Parts 1–3. Toronto: *The Globe and Mail*, April 20–21, p. A1.

Brass, Oliver, J. 1979. Crees and Crime: A Cross-Cultural Study. Regina: University of Regina, mimeographed.

Canadian Corrections Association. 1967. Indians and the Law. Ottawa, Ontario: Canadian Corrections Association.

Cohen, Stanley A. 1989. Human rights and criminal justice in the 1990s. In Donald J. Loree (ed.), *Future Issues in Policing and Symposium Proceedings*. Canada: Ministry of Supply and Services.

Comack, Elizabeth (ed.). 1990. Race, class, gender and justice. Vancouver: *The Journal of Human Justice*. Vol. 1, No. 2. Spring.

Couse, Keith, Gloria Geller, Jim Harding, and Paul Havemann. 1982. Brief submitted to the Public Hearing for the Review of the City of Regina Police Canine Unit. Regina, SK: School of Human Justice, University of Regina.

Department of Indian Affairs and Northern Development. 1973. Report of the Task Force: Policing on Reserves. Ottawa, ON: Indian and Northern Affairs.

Elliot, Maxine. 1989. *Policing in the 1990s: Environmental Issues for the Prairies*. Regina: Mebas Consulting Ltd.

Hagan, William T. 1966. *Indian Police and Judges: Experiments in Acculturation and Control*. New Haven, CT: Yale University Press.

Harding, Jim. 1978. Development, underdevelopment and alcohol disabilities in Northern Saskatchewan. *Alternatives* 7: 4.

———. 1981. Policing the Police: Conference Defends Self-Control Method. *Briarpatch* 10(10): 9–10.

Harding, Jim and Rae Matonovitch. 1985. Self-Study of Justice Research About Indigenous People: 1981–1984. Regina: Prairie Justice Research, University of Regina.

Harris, R.E. 1977. Evaluation of the Indian Policing Program. Ontario Provincial Police, Planning and Research Branch.

Havemann, Paul, Keith Couse, Lori Foster, and Rae Matonovitch. 1985. *Law and Order for Canada's Indigenous People*. Regina: Prairie Justice Research, University of Regina.

Head, R.H.D. 1989. A speech to the Canadian Association of Chiefs of Police and Federal Corrections Services. Banff, AB: R.C.M.P., mimmeographed, Nov. 10.

Hylton, John. 1981. Policing in a Multicultural Society: Some Implications for Police Educators. Presented at Eighth Annual Police Educators Conference, Thunder Bay, ON: May 18–22.

Hylton, John and Rae Matonovich. 1980. *Public Attitudes About Crime and the Police in Moose Jaw*. Regina, SK: Prairie Justice Research, University of Regina.

Hylton, John, Rae Matonovich, James Varro, Bijal Thakven, and Dave Broad. 1979. *Public Attitudes About Crime and Police in Regina*. Regina: Prairie Justice, University of Regina.

Jackson, Michael. 1988. Locking up Natives in Canada. A Report of the Committee of the Canadian Bar Association on Imprisonment and Release.

James, J.L.T. 1979. Towards a cultural understanding of the Native offender. *Canadian Journal of Criminology* 21(4): 453–462.

Kirby, W.J.C. (Chairman). 1978. Native People in the Administration of Justice in the Provincial Court of Alberta. Edmonton: Alberta Board of Review, Provincial Courts, Report No. 4.

Kly, Yussuf. 1991. Native people and the criminal justice system: Racism in an international context. In L. Samuelson and B. Schissel (eds.), *Criminal Justice's Sentencing Issues and Reforms*. Saskatoon, SK: Social Research Unit, University of Saskatchewan.

Linden, Rick. 1989. Demographic change and the future of policing. In Donald J. Loree (ed.), *Future Issues in Policing and Symposium Proceedings*. Canada: Ministry of Supply and Services.

Mandel, Michael. 1989. *The Charter of Rights and Legalization of Politics in Canada*. Toronto: Wall and Thompson.

Morrow, William G. 1968. Inquiry Re: Administration of Justice in the Hay River Area of the North West Territories, Ottawa, ON: The Privy Council.

Native Counselling Services of Alberta. 1980. Policing on Reserves: A review of Current Programs and Alternatives. Edmonton: Native Counselling Services of Alberta.

Royal Commission on the Donald Marshall, Jr., Prosecution. 1989. Digest of Findings and recommendations: Province of Nova Scotia.

Samuelson, L. and B. Schissel (eds.). 1991. *Proceedings: Criminal Justice: Sentencing Issues and Reforms*. Saskatoon: Social Research Unit, University of Saskatchewan.

Schriml, Ron. 1985. Public and private policing: The accountability debate. In Jim Harding (ed.), *The Politics of Social Policy: The Blakeney Years in Saskatchewan*, unpublished.

Singer, Charter and Sharon Moyer. 1981. *The Dakota-Ojibway Tribal Council Police Program: An Evaluation*, 1979–1981. Ottawa, ON: Ministry of Solicitor General, Research Division.

Stenning, Philip C. 1989. Private police and public police: Toward a redefinition of the police role. In Donald J. Loree (ed.), *Future Issues in Policing and Symposium Proceedings*. Canada: Ministry of Supply and Services.

PART FOUR
Guns, Drugs, and Prostitution: Attempts at Control

Recent Canadian crime control policy debates have included such topics as gun control, drug strategy and enforcement, and street prostitution. This section includes articles examining each of these issues.

Of these three issues, gun control probably generated the most public attention. During the first half of the decade of the 1990s gun ownership and gun control legislation were highly contentious, with proponents and opponents seeking to influence public opinion and government legislation. However, gun control in Canada has evolved over a long period of time, dating back to at least 1892 when the first nation-wide permit system for the carrying of small arms was established. Early legislation focussed primarily on the registration of firearms. But by the 1970s the debate over legislation shifted to its ability to control firearm use by criminals (Scarff, 1983). Bill C-51 was passed in 1977 as the most comprehensive revision of the Criminal Code regarding firearms since 1892, with the objectives of reducing access to firearms by potentially dangerous or irresponsible users, reducing criminal use of firearms, and promoting proper handling and storage of firearms. In addition to stricter controls on the acquisition, registration, and conveyance of firearms, this legislation also created the offence of using a firearm during the commission of an indictable offence and provided more severe penalties for criminal use of firearms by creating minimum mandatory penalties. A statistical evaluation of the effects of the 1977 legislation on the incidence of firearms offences over time (Department of Justice, 1996) yielded somewhat inconsistent results. Firearm homicides, suicides, and robberies have all declined in the post-legislation years, although some of these downward trends preceded the legislation. However, controlling for variables that could influence the occurrence of such offences, the results suggested that the 1977 legislation reduced the rate of homicide but not the incidence of suicides involving firearms. Other research (Scarff, 1983) has suggested that other weapons may to some extent replace firearms in the commission of robbery. Scarff's (1983) evaluation of this legislation concluded that subsequent to its implementation the courts did impose more severe sentences for firearms offences.

Marc Lepine shot fourteen women to death in 1989 in Montreal. This resulted in a number of women's groups and other organizations calling for even stricter gun control legislation. In 1990 the Government introduced Bill C-80, later replaced by Bill C-17 that was proclaimed in 1991. This legislation broadened the categories of prohibited and restricted firearms and established new criteria for granting a Firearms Acquisition Certificate. Interest groups such as the Coalition for Gun Control and the Canadian Bar Association lobbied for even stricter gun control while the National Firearms Association opposed tougher firearms legislation as a means of crime control. This controversy intensified with the introduction of Bill C-68, the Firearms Act, given assent in December 1995. This act establishes a universal firearms registration system and requires a licence to own, acquire, or borrow firearms and buy ammunition. Individuals who pose a threat to public safety are not eligible to hold a licence. This legislation also increases the mandatory minimum sentence to four years plus a lifetime prohibition against possession of a restricted or prohibited firearm upon conviction for any of ten specific violent offences involving firearms.

Current legislative approaches to gun control represent a combination of supply and demand reduction. Through registration and licencing restrictions the law attempts to limit the supply of firearms, particularly for use in the commission of crimes, while tougher sanctions for the criminal use of firearms aim to reduce demand through deterrence and incapacitation of offenders. However, the effectiveness of such policies remains contentious (see, for example, guns and violence symposium in the *Journal of Criminal Law and Criminology* 86(1), Autumn 1995; commentary and debate on guns and violence research in the *Journal of Quantitative Criminology* 11(4), December 1995; comments and rejoinder in *Canadian Journal of Criminology* 35(1), January 1993).

READINGS

The first two readings in this section discuss various aspects of recent Canadian firearms legislation. The first article by Gabor considers two assumptions of recent legislation: whether reducing gun availability will reduce gun-related crime, and whether increased penalties for misuse of firearms are a deterrent. He first discusses whether the legislation can reduce access to firearms before turning his attention to the research on the relationship between gun availability and crime. A number of studies show a positive relation between levels of firearm ownership and homicide rates, but not other crimes. Gabor also argues that firearm attacks have the highest probability of producing a serious injury or death, and some firearms are more damaging than others. Concerning deterrence, mandatory penalties may have an impact if they are consistently applied, which is unlikely. But while doubtful that the gun legislation will have a significant impact on public safety, Gabor concludes by applauding the symbolic function of such legislation in denouncing violence.

Reading Fourteen by Stenning argues that current gun control policies are unlikely to succeed because they offer a too simplistic solution to a complex problem, and they are based upon faulty assumptions. He distinguishes among three types of firearms abuse, arguing that effective measures will vary from type to type. Stenning then critiques the assumptions of the several theories used to justify gun control and concludes that there is little evidence of their validity. He cautiously concludes that some kinds of gun control may be effective in relation to some kinds of firearms abuse but not others, that even effective measures do not have unlimited effectiveness, and that a serious examination must be made of the costs and benefits of proposed legislation compared to possible alternative responses.

In contrast to this gun control legislation, a recent major revision of Canada's drug legislation, the Controlled Drugs and Substances Act (Bill C-8, given assent in June 1996), passed with much less public discussion and debate. This may, in part, reflect the absence of well-organized, opposing interest groups to bring the issue to media and public attention. This bill was initially proposed (as C-85) in 1992 by the previous Conservative government and reintroduced with similar provisions as Bill C-7 by the subsequent Liberal government. One commentator labelled this bill as "little more than a genuflection in the direction of the U.S. (Boyd, 1994:27)." The Government claimed that this legislation is required by Canada's international commitments under United Nations conventions, although others such as Boyd (1994) have disputed this. This bill maintains a punitive approach towards those convicted of possession of marijuana, despite evidence of little judicial enthusiasm, police support, or public interest in such a response (Boyd, 1994). Boyd argues that this approach results in selective enforcement, therefore leading to disrespect for the law and the police, while also diverting energy and money from more serious crime problems. He also claims that studies of countries where marijuana possession has been decriminal-ized suggest no change in consumption as a result of greater toleration.

Over the long term, the evolution of Canada's drug laws has been in the direc-tion of increased criminalization and punishment of drug users (Giffen et al., 1991). This law enforcement approach to drug use persisted in spite of contrary recommen-dations from the Le Dain Commission, which was established to investigate drug use in Canada and make policy recommendations. In its final report the Commission recommended a gradual withdrawal from the use of the criminal law against non-medical users of drugs (Commission of Inquiry into the Non-Medical Use of Drugs, 1973). However, subsequent policy-making has not followed the Commission's rec-ommended approach (Erickson and Smart, 1988).

Several policy alternatives toward drugs can be identified. The two basic strate-gies have been supply reduction and demand reduction (Moore, 1993). Supply reduction attempts to reduce the availability of illegal drugs through aggressive law enforcement, while demand reduction seeks to reduce or eliminate the desire for drugs among potential or current consumers through education, treatment, and gen-eral deterrence. Aggressive law enforcement is generally ineffective against a product or service many people desire, and there is no evidence that drug education pro-grams, by themselves, substantially reduce drug use (Walker, 1994). Drug treatment can be effective for those users who want to quit (Currie, 1992). Critics of current drug policy have suggested an alternative approach, harm reduction, which sees drug use as a public health rather than crime control issue. Such an approach would include the removal of criminal penalties for the possession and sale of some cur-rently illegal drugs and their replacement by a system of regulation (see, for example, Karel, 1991).

The article by Erickson reviews recent trends in Canadian drug policy, offering comparisons with policy in the United States. Illicit drug use in Canada is lower and Canadians appear to be less concerned about illicit drugs than Americans. Yet strict enforcement and punishment has traditionally been Canada's primary strategy on illicit drugs, according to Erickson. She traces the decline of this dominant policy from 1969–1986, but then notes the renewed spirit of prohibitionism in the new Canadian Drug Strategy announced in 1987, at least partly attributable to the drug panic imported by American media. Although Canada did not adopt an all-out drug war comparable to that in the U.S., Erickson detects an ambivalence concerning the priority between demand and supply reduction measures. While previously there appeared to be a balanced approach, she concludes that the scales of influence have now tipped disproportionately towards the enforcement sector with a focussing of both demand and supply reduction efforts in the police. In concluding this article Erickson briefly outlines an alternative, harm-reduction approach to substance use.

Street prostitution resurfaced as a policy problem in Canada in the mid-1970s with various legal strategies designed to suppress it proving to be ineffective (Lowman, 1991a). For example, vagrancy statutes, municipal bylaws, and various provisions of the Criminal Code had all been used at different times. But in 1978 the Supreme Court ruled that soliciting for the purposes of prostitution was only an offence if it was pressing and persistent (Hutt v. The Queen, 1978). Police forces blamed this decision for the sudden increase in street prostitution in many large cities (Larsen, 1996). In the early 1980s two committees were set up by the federal government to investigate aspects of prostitution and recommend policy changes. The Badgley Committee was asked to examine youth prostitution, while the issue of adult prostitution was assigned to the Committee on Pornography and Prostitution (Fraser Committee). Although the latter recommended that most prostitution activities be decriminalized, in 1985 the federal government enacted instead Bill C-49, which criminalized all public communication for the purposes of prostitution (Larsen 1996). An evaluation of the first few years of this legislation concluded that it was not effective in removing the street prostitution trade (Fleischman, 1989).

In 1995, 92 percent of all prostitution incidents reported by police in Canada involved communicating to buy or sell the services of a prostitute; only 5 percent involved the procuring of persons to become prostitutes and 3 percent were for participation in the operation of a common bawdy-house (Canadian Centre for Justice Statistics, 1997). This supports Lowman's (1991a) claim that law enforcement is mainly geared to keeping prostitution out of sight. However, since December 1985 when the communicating law replaced the soliciting law, there has been a shift towards more males being charged. Between 1986 and 1995 almost half (47 percent) of all persons charged with communicating were male, compared with 36 percent of those charged with soliciting between 1977 and 1985. This increase may reflect changes in enforcement policy towards clients (Canadian Centre for Justice Statistics, 1997). But Lowman (1991b) shows how enforcement practices toward prostitutes and clients vary within and between police departments, reflecting practical considerations, policing philosophies, and administrative decisions.

Nick Larsen argues in Reading Sixteen that it's time to legalize prostitution. While Canadian legislation in effect criminalizes all public communication for the purpose of prostitution, he claims that it is ineffective as a control. Larsen provides several reasons why he believes strict criminal laws will not work and offers four recommendations for a non-criminal approach to controlling prostitution.

QUESTIONS FOR DISCUSSION

1. What purpose(s) does current Canadian gun control legislation aim to accomplish? What assumptions concerning the causes of violent crime does this legislation make? Are there alternative assumptions?
2. Discuss Gabor's opinion that no aspect of Bill C-68 is likely to have a significant impact on the safety of Canadians.
3. What costs are associated with a prohibitionist policy regarding drug use?
4. What purpose(s) of punishment are in dispute in debates concerning decriminalization of drugs and prostitution?

REFERENCES

Boyd, Neil. 1994. "The Liberals on drugs." *Policy Options* 15(8):26–28.
Canadian Centre for Justice Statistics. 1997. "Street prostitution in Canada." *Juristat* 17(2):1.
Commission of Inquiry into the Non-Medical Use of Drugs. 1973. Final Report. Ottawa: Information Canada.
Currie, Elliott. 1992. *Reckoning: Drugs, the Cities, and the American Future*. New York: Hill and Wang.

Department of Justice. 1996. *A Statistical Analysis of the Impacts of the 1977 Firearms Control Legislation*. Ottawa: Minister of Supply and Services Canada.

Erickson, Patricia G. and Reginald Smart. 1988. "The Le Dain Commission Recommendations." In Judith C. Blackwell and Patricia G. Erickson (eds.), *Illicit Drugs in Canada*. Scarborough, ON: Nelson Canada.

Fleischman, J. 1989. Street Prostitution: Assessing the Impact of the Law: Synthesis Report. Ottawa: Department of Justice Canada.

Giffen, P.J., Shirley Endicott, and Sylvia Lambert. 1991. *Panic and Indifference: The Politics of Canada's Drug Laws*. Ottawa: Canadian Centre on Substance Abuse.

Karel, Richard B. 1991. "A model legalization proposal." Pp. 80–102 in James A. Inciardi (ed.), *The Drug Legalization Debate*. Newbury Park, CA: Sage.

Larsen, E. Nick. 1996. "The effect of different police enforcement policies on the control of prostitution." *Canadian Public Policy* 22(1):40–55.

Lowman, John. 1991a. "Prostitution in Canada." Chapter 4 in Margaret A. Jackson and Curt T. Griffiths. *Canadian Criminology*. Toronto: Harcourt Brace Jovanovich Canada.

_____. 1991b. "Punishing Prostitutes and Their Customers." Chapter 15 in Les Samuelson and Bernard Schissel (eds.), *Criminal Justice*. Toronto: Garamond Press.

Moore, Mark H. 1983. "Controlling criminogenic commodities." Chapter 8 in James Q. Wilson (ed.), *Crime and Public Policy*. San Francisco: ICS Press.

Scarff, Elisabeth. 1983. *Evaluation of the Canadian Gun Control Legislation*. Ottawa: Minister of Supply and Services Canada.

Walker, Samuel. 1994. *Sense and Nonsense About Crime and Drugs*. Belmont, CA: Wadsworth.

THIRTEEN

The Proposed Canadian Legislation on Firearms: More Symbolism than Prevention

THOMAS GABOR

The Canadian Government is currently endeavouring to pass its second major package of legislation dealing with firearms in the last three years. While such legislation may serve the symbolic function of communicating our collective condemnation of violence, its primary purpose is to foster public safety through the prevention of firearm-related violence.

The proposed legislation is designed to curb criminal violence and other harms in two ways. First, it elevates the risks of using firearms for criminal purposes, for smuggling, or for failing to comply with safety storage and other requirements through mandatory penalties, enhanced border controls, and the establishment of a

Source: Thomas Gabor, "The Proposed Canadian Legislation on Firearms: More Symbolism than Prevention," *Canadian Journal of Criminology*, 37, 2 (1995): 195–213. Copyright by the Canadian Criminal Justice Association. Reproduced by permission of the *Canadian Journal of Criminology*.

national registration system. Second, it proposes to limit the availability of certain handguns, assault, and replica weapons. Reducing availability is assumed to decrease the amount of firearm-related violence and crime, independent of any deterrent effect of enhancing penalties for the misuse of firearms.

In this commentary, I will address both assumptions of the proposed law; that is, that violence can be prevented both by limiting access to firearms and by increasing the penalties associated with the criminal misuse or trafficking of firearms. With respect to availability, one must show not only that decreasing gun ownership levels leads to a reduction of violence, but that banning certain types of firearms will, in fact, reduce ownership levels.

WILL REDUCING FIREARM AVAILABILITY ENHANCE PUBLIC SAFETY?

Currently, about seven million firearms are owned by Canadians (Department of Justice 1994; Gabor 1994). The proposed legislation includes provisions for banning various models of handguns and military-type long guns. These bans, given full compliance on the part of those currently in possession of these weapons, would reduce the overall inventory of firearms in Canada by approximately half a million providing the volume of all other categories of firearms remained unchanged. Full compliance, of course, is unrealistic and so is the idea that the number of other firearms would remain static. There is no evidence, for example, that the introduction of certification for firearm owners (FAC's) in 1979 led to a reduction in the national firearm inventory. Quite the contrary, this inventory seems to have risen in volume as indicated by:

• the number of FAC's obtained since 1979 (Mundt 1990; Hung 1992; RCMP 1992);
• increases in the cumulative number of restricted firearm registrations as well as in their rate of acquisition from 1982–1990 (Hung 1992);
• a 250 percent increase in the number of permits issued to carry restricted weapons from 1979 to 1990; and
• an increase in the annual number of firearms imported into Canada since the early 1980s (Hung 1992).

Thus, banning certain firearms offers no guarantee of a shrinking inventory, if the demand for other firearms increases. It is possible, though, that the demand for firearms may be more successfully curtailed by the proposed registration system, as all firearms (not just owners) will require registration as of January 1, 1998. Owners will be charged a small fee for each firearm transaction that takes place. This additional fee may reduce firearm purchases to some extent.

If the firearm inventory in Canada can be reduced through the prohibition of additional categories of firearms and enhanced border controls, the evidence then suggests that there may be a beneficial effect on public safety. Although there is some strong evidence linking availability and certain social harms such as violent crime, suicide, and accidental death, a caveat needs to be made about the concept of availability. Only a minority of studies have used direct measures of availability drawn from a survey of gun ownership in a given jurisdiction. Firearm availability in an area is often inferred from such things as firearm sales and production, the proportion of offences committed with firearms, and the accidental death rate due to firearms.[1]

Surveys of firearm ownership have tended to yield estimates of the proportion of households with firearms, rather than the total number of firearms in circulation. Studies relying on these surveys have sometimes found a positive correlation between the proportion of households with firearms and the homicide or suicide rate. Technically, these studies merely suggest that homicides and suicides increase with the number of households possessing firearms. They tell us little about the impact of the total volume of firearms on crime or suicide rates. Nor do purely correlational studies inform us about causal direction: that is, whether increasing rates of gun ownership produce increases in various social harms or whether increases in criminality and suicidality create a greater demand for firearms.

Since few studies have investigated the impact of changing volumes of firearms on rates of violence and other harms, research provides little guidance for policy in terms of whether reducing the inventory of firearms will have a beneficial effect. It might be argued that the accessibility of firearms is as important as their volume. Thus, whether a household has one firearm or ten may be inconsequential in terms of a potential domestic homicide or suicide. All that is required to achieve one's objectives is access to one firearm — accessibility, of course, would be enhanced by a poorly stored (loaded and unlocked) firearm.

The implication is that the proposed banning of certain military-style firearms may reduce access to these highly lethal weapons, but their owners may still have access to other firearms, albeit less dangerous ones. Simply reducing the number of firearms in circulation, therefore, may not be sufficient to reduce the number of misuses. Thus, the success of the proposed legislation hinges, to some degree, on whether some households make the decision to get rid of their firearms altogether. Nothing in the proposals directly attempts to convince at least some Canadian families to surrender all their firearms.

Assuming that the legislation does succeed in reducing the access to firearms of some Canadians, what does the research literature tell us about the relationship between firearm availability and violent crime, suicide, and accidental death?

VIOLENT CRIME

Does the presence of firearms contribute to violent crimes? There are three issues here (Reiss and Roth 1993). First, there is the issue, just mentioned, as to whether firearm availability contributes to the volume of violent crimes. The second issue is whether, once a crime occurs, the presence of a firearm affects the probability of an attack on the victim, bearing in mind that violent offences (especially robbery) do not always involve physical contact between offender and victim. The third issue relates to the impact of the presence of firearms on the severity and lethality of assaults. Thus, once an attack takes place, is the use of a firearm more often lethal and injurious than the use of other weapons or no weapons at all?

This third issue gets at the weapon substitution argument so often used by opponents of gun control. The notion that "guns don't kill, people do" assumes that the instrument used by the perpetrator of violence is merely a dispensable tool, which, if unavailable, can be replaced by a more accessible weapon. Even if such substitution were to take place in every instance in which a violent crime was contemplated and no firearm was available, those opposing controls on firearms must address the respective dangerousness of firearms versus potential replacements.

The likelihood of weapon substitution in every potential violent incident is, in my view, profoundly exaggerated by opponents of gun control. Recent social science research stresses situational as well as dispositional factors in human behaviour (Clarke 1992). Criminologists studying the dynamics of violent crimes have observed that to understand the outcomes of these crimes, one has to look at situational factors as well as the proclivities of the perpetrator. The outcomes of offences are not simply predetermined by the characteristics and motives of the perpetrator; they are also linked to factors such as the physical setting, victim behaviour, the presence of bystanders, the influence of alcohol and illicit drugs, and the presence of lethal weapons. Consider the following statements by armed robbers regarding their selection of targets:

> It was a Sunday. I didn't know where to get some money. I had a gun but no bullets ... I saw a convenience store. On Sunday, you don't have much choice. I didn't look at the risks. I needed money ... (Gabor, Baril, Cusson, Elie, LeBlanc, and Normandeau 1987: 57)

> I hit the first bank I ran into because I didn't have much time; not much time to look around ... (Gabor *et al.* 1987: 57).

These two cases show that many robberies are committed fairly spontaneously, rather than in the premeditated fashion suggested by opponents of gun control. The presence or absence of firearms and ammunition, among other circumstantial factors, will shape decision-making; including, perhaps, the decision to commit a robbery in the first place. Firearms are not simply tools that perform predetermined tasks (crimes); they are tools that may affect, in their presence or absence, the task itself.

1. FIREARM AVAILABILITY AND VIOLENT CRIME RATES

A number of cross-national and American studies show a positive correlation between levels of firearm ownership and homicide rates (Killias 1993; Cook 1979; Cook 1987; Block 1977; McDowall 1991). Other crimes, however, do not appear to vary with firearm ownership levels (Cook 1979; McDowall 1986; Kleck 1991). These findings present the hypothesis that firearms may not affect the decision to commit a crime as much as their gravity. More will be said below about the manner in which the presence of firearms may affect the outcome of an offence.

One of the most sophisticated methodologies brought to bear on the question of firearm availability and homicide, the case-control study, has been used by medical researchers. Kellermann and his associates (1993) examined 388 domestic homicides that took place in three American counties. A control group of 388 individuals were matched with the homicide victims on sex, race, age, education, socioeconomic status, and type of dwelling. The investigators found that firearms were more likely to be kept in the homes of the homicide victims than the controls. They found that the presence of firearms significantly increased the risk of homicide in the home, even after employing the aforementioned controls *and* statistically controlling for such factors as previous violence and use of drugs in the home.

Some of the hypothesized reasons for the apparent link between firearm availability and homicide include:

1. Firearms are more lethal than other weapons and hence more likely to transform assaults and robberies into homicides (this point will be explored below);
2. Firearms provide an impersonal and antiseptic means of killing at a distance for people who are too squeamish to stab or beat others (Kleck and McElrath 1991);
3. Firearms can serve as an equalizer for the physically vulnerable, permitting violence on the part of people otherwise incapable of inflicting serious damage upon others (Cook 1981; Kleck and McElrath 1991);
4. Firearms facilitate violent attacks on heavily-guarded and armed targets, ranging from political figures to police officers, banks, and armoured trucks (Cook 1981). For example, nearly all murdered police officers have been shot;
5. Bystanders are far more likely to be injured or killed in a firearm attack than in an attack with any other weapon (Colijn, Lester, and Slothouwer 1985; Larson 1993);
6. Drive-by-killings are almost always committed with a firearm (Gabor 1994);
7. Some experiments indicate that the mere presence of a firearm at the time of an altercation may elicit an impulsive aggressive response due to a learned association between firearms and aggression, a phenomenon referred to as a "weapons effect" (Berkowitz and LePage, 1967).

2. PRESENCE OF FIREARMS AND THE PROBABILITY OF ATTACK

Having established that the availability of firearms may affect the volume of homicides, what do studies tell us about the impact of the presence of firearms on the likelihood that a victim will be physically attacked during some other criminal offence?

The offence of robbery is instructive here as it is a "violent" offence that only occasionally involves physical harm or injury. Does the possession of a firearm in the hands of the perpetrator(s) affect the likelihood of a violent attack upon the victim?

In this case, there is considerable consensus among students of robbery that robbers armed with guns are *less likely* to attack and injure their victims than those with other weapons or no weapons at all (Normandeau 1968; Conklin 1972; Feeney and Weir 1975; Block 1977; Luckenbill 1981; Gabor *et al.* 1987). The apparent reason for this stimulation of violence is that the presence of firearms makes victim resistance, and the subsequent use of the weapon to gain his/her compliance, less probable. On the other hand, any weapon that makes victim compliance and, hence, offender success more likely may be said to reinforce the offender's behaviour, as he can expect a more successful outcome at lower risk to himself with the help of a firearm (Skogan 1978).

3. FIREARM ATTACKS AND THE PROBABILITY OF
SERIOUS INJURY AND DEATH

Once an attack has occurred, do those involving a firearm produce more serious consequences? In this writer's view, the evidence dealing with this question is the most consistent and compelling in the firearms literature. Studies repeatedly indicate that weapons can be located on a continuum in terms of their lethality.

Without exception, firearm attacks have the highest probability of producing a fatality or serious disability. The most conservative finding has been that firearm attacks are twice as likely to result in death as are knife attacks (Reiss and Roth 1993). In the most meticulous and influential study of this issue, Zimring (1968) found that firearm attacks were between two and a half and five times as likely to cause death as knife attacks, depending on various assumptions about the perpetrators' motives. Cook (1987), in his study of robbery in 43 American cities, found that the firearm robberies had a lethality rate three times greater than that of knife robberies which, in turn, had three-fold the fatality rate of robberies using other weapons. Unarmed robberies were least likely to end in death.

Not only is there a hierarchy in terms of the lethality of various weapons, with firearms at the top, but firearms differ among themselves in terms of their dangerousness. Arthur Kellerman, a specialist in emergency medicine, and his colleagues (1991: 30) have made the following observations about the impact of a number of variables pertaining to the properties of firearms and projectiles on the human body:

> ... the specific capacity of a firearm to cause injury depends on its accuracy, the rate of fire, muzzle velocity, and specific characteristics of the projectile ... Because the kinetic energy of a moving object increases with the square of its velocity, weapons with high muzzle velocities, e.g., hunting rifles, generally cause greater tissue damage than weapons with lower muzzle velocities, e.g., handguns. However, the size, shape, and nature of the projectile also play a powerful role in determining the severity of the resultant injury. A nonfragmenting bullet travelling at high speed will penetrate and exit a body with little damage outside the bullet path. A lower caliber rifle, designed to mushroom or fragment on impact, may damage a much larger amount of tissue ... Damage also increases in direct proportion to the mass of the projectile. Gunshot wounds caused by larger caliber guns are more than twice as likely to result in the death of the victim than wounds caused by small caliber guns. The number of projectiles striking the body also influences the expected severity of injury.

To its credit, the proposed legislation would ban several models of military-style firearms with rapid-fire capacity. The legislation would also ban low caliber pistols (Saturday night specials) that are easy to conceal and that have few functions other than criminal uses. The legislation would "backfire" if all those formerly carrying the banned small pistols would now switch to higher caliber weapons. Such a wholesale substitution would be unlikely because larger weapons are more visible and cumbersome to carry around. Furthermore, if a large-scale switch to larger firearms occurred, this situation would at least attest to the potential effectiveness of firearm bans in limiting the access of those at high risk to specified types of firearms.

SUICIDE

....

Three quarters of firearm deaths in Canada are suicides (Hung 1992). Suicide is the most common cause of unnecessary death among adolescents (Cheiffetz, Posener, LaHaye, Zaidman, and Benierakis 1987).

The evidence linking firearm availability with suicide is stronger than in relation to other social harms. Fifteen of sixteen studies have shown that countries or jurisdictions with higher firearm ownership levels had higher rates of firearm suicides than those with lower ownership levels (Gabor 1994). Half of these studies indicated that overall suicide rates, too, were affected by levels of ownership and half the studies showed no relationship, but no studies found that ownership levels and overall suicide rates were inversely related.

A number of case-control studies have revealed an influence of both firearm availability and accessibility on suicide. Brent and his associates (1991) compared a group of 47 adolescent suicide victims in Western Pennsylvania with a matched group — matched on age, gender, race, and social class — of 47 hospitalized suicide attempters, and another control group of 47 psychiatric inpatients who had never attempted suicide. The majority of the suicide victims had used a gun, whereas none of the attempters had used a firearm. Firearms were twice as likely to have been present in the homes of the suicide victims than in the homes of either of the control groups. Firearms in the homes of the victims were also stored less securely (loaded and unlocked) than were those in the homes of the control groups. Victims with guns in their home tended to use them even if they were stored securely. The authors concluded that the presence of a firearm in the home is a risk factor in suicide and is more important than its accessibility (manner of storage). This study also showed that firearm availability increases both the likelihood of suicide attempts and their lethality.

Kellerman and his colleagues (1992) also employed the case-control method to examine suicides occurring in the home in Shelby County, Tennessee and King County, Washington. A total of 438 controls were matched with 442 individuals who had committed suicide on the variables of sex, age, race, and neighbourhood of residence. Persons close to the suicide victim were interviewed to obtain the necessary information on the victim. The case subjects were more likely than the controls to have had a substance abuse problem, history of mental illness, to have lived alone, and to have had firearms in the home. The presence of a firearm was found to be a risk factor in suicide, even after these other risk factors were controlled statistically. In homes with firearms, a gun was the method chosen for suicide in 86 percent of the cases, whereas, in homes where firearms were not usually kept only 6 percent of suicide victims killed themselves with a gun. These investigators also found that improper storage elevated the risk of suicide.

These findings provide support for the safe storage provisions of the previous legislation and the ammunition controls currently being proposed. The presence of firearms and accessible ammunition (especially to those at higher risk) elevate the risk of suicide because few individuals obtain firearms specifically for the purpose of the suicide (Browning 1974; Kellermann et al. 1992) and every other method available to an individual has a lower lethality rate (Kleck 1991: 258).

The presence and accessibility of firearms are critical because of the impulsive nature of so many suicides, especially those of adolescents. Many suicides are not carefully calculated but are precipitated by stressful events (e.g., interpersonal conflicts) and facilitated by the consumption of intoxicants (Moyer and Carrington 1992: 34; Kimberley, Chapdelaine, Viau, and Samson 1991; Peterson, Peterson, O'Shanick, and Swann 1985; Brent *et al.* 1988; Hawton 1986: 98; Poteet 1987; Tonkin 1984). The occasional temporal clustering of adolescent suicide (Robbins and Conroy 1983) indicates that the recent suicide of a peer may be a key precipitating factor. Some studies also show that many adolescents who have committed suicide did not make a previous attempt, did not leave a suicide note, nor did they communicate their intention verbally (Tonkin 1984; Poteet 1987). These findings indicate that suicide, especially among the young, often is not the result of longstanding reflection and premeditation.

Perhaps the best evidence of the impulsive element in many suicides and of the often transient nature of suicidal ideation stems from three clinical studies of survivors of self-inflicted gunshot wounds—all the subjects in these studies had shot themselves in the head or some other critical region of the body (Peterson *et al.* 1985; Shuck, Orgel, and Vogel 1980; Kost-Grant 1983). Many of the subjects attributed these very serious attempts to an interpersonal crisis or intoxication. Many reported having suicidal thoughts for less than 24 hours. Follow-ups revealed that the majority were happy to have survived, adjusted well, and did not make further attempts at suicide.

The evidence presented here suggests that it is a dangerous myth to believe that only those with longstanding depression and other psychiatric disorders make serious attempts at suicide. To be sure, there are those who are committed, over the long-term, to kill themselves. No amount of gun and ammunition control or safe storage can stop these people from achieving their objective. Reducing the availability and accessibility of highly lethal, easy, and expeditious methods of self-destruction can make a difference, however, for those whose suicidal motivation is more ambiguous or transitory.

ACCIDENTAL DEATH

About four percent of firearm-related deaths in Canada (about 60 per year) are classified as accidents (Chapdelaine, Samson, Kimberley, and Viau 1991). Although this number is modest, there are probably ten-fold that number of cases that result in injury and disability (Todd 1991). One concern is that a quarter of accidental firearm death victims in Canada are under 15 years of age and another 30 percent are in the 15 to 24 age category (Chapdelaine et al. 1991).

Very few studies have probed the link between firearm availability and accidents. Some correlational evidence, though, is suggestive of such a link. Sweden, a country with very restrictive firearm legislation including strict licensing of owners had only 32 nonhunting fatalities arising from shootings from 1970–82, for an annual rate of .07/100,000 (Ornehult and Eriksson 1987). On the other hand, the United States, the least restrictive western country, has an annual fatality rate of .7/100,000. Canada, where ownership levels fall somewhere in between Sweden and the United States, has an annual accidental death rate by firearms that falls in between these two countries (.2/100,000).

American ownership levels are two to three times those of Canada, depending on whether these levels are measured by the proportion of households owning firearms or by the per capita volume of firearms. It is interesting that the accidental firearm fatality rate in the United States has been consistently twice to three times that of Canada (Mundt 1990).

Although the evidence is scarce, there seem to be few alternative explanations for such correlations other than that greater availability leads to a higher number of accidents. Some authors have advanced the far-fetched argument that accidents are not due to availability but to recklessness on the part of irresponsible users. The evidence clearly indicates, however, that the majority of firearm accidents are just that—hunters showing momentary lapses in judgment; children unaware that a firearm is loaded or real; and, others who accidentally discharge a firearm due to insufficient training or faulty product design (Gabor 1994).

The proposed legislation is not likely to have a major bearing on firearm accidents. The safe storage provisions of previous legislation are probably the best safeguard against accidents and the proposed registration system may increase compliance with safe storage requirements. The proposed ammunition controls may have some impact if they can limit access to loaded firearms of those (including the young) without a legitimate reason for such access. The banning of some military-style weapons may make it difficult for some zealots to engage in war games that might eventuate in accidents.

WILL INCREASING THE RISK OF FIREARM MISUSES ENHANCE PUBLIC SAFETY?

Apart from limiting the availability of certain models of highly lethal firearms through prohibitions and improved border controls, the proposed legislation is designed to raise the risks associated with firearm misuses of non-compliance.

One aspect of the proposed legislation is a mandatory four-year prison sentence for the use of a firearm or replica weapon in the commission of serious offences, such as attempted murder and robbery. Such a mandatory sentence is intended to circumvent the problem of enhanced sentences, whereby a minimum sentence of one year for the illegal use of a firearm is to be served consecutively to the sentence for the underlying offence. Although these enhanced sentences appear to have reduced firearm-related violence in some American urban areas (Reiss and Roth 1993: 275), they have also been plagued by the tendency of some judges to compensate for the additional penalty by reducing the sentence for the underlying offence (Lizotte and Zatz 1986).

The question, therefore, is whether the mandatory minimum penalty will increase the average sentence meted out for the offences under consideration and whether these mandatory sentences will be undermined by pleas negotiations. In any event, a four-year prison sentence may amount to only a third of that when parole and remission are taken into account.

The evaluation literature provides little guidance regarding the effectiveness of bans on assault weapons or of national registration systems. Such a system would undoubtedly foster increased accountability and care in firearm transactions and in their storage, thereby indirectly preventing some harm. The system would also enhance the tracing of registered firearms following a criminal offence. The number of criminal offences committed by legally obtained versus illegitimate firearms is still an unknown. Also, the system's effectiveness clearly hinges on the extent of compliance regarding registration by the population as a whole.

Non-compliance can be catastrophic if it leads to complacency on the part of police officers responding to a domestic dispute. One of the arguments for a registration system is that officers responding to a domestic call can determine expeditiously whether firearms are registered to that household. If that household has not registered any firearms, will the police be less prudent than they might have been in the absence of such a system? In the absence of a registry, they would likely assume that all households are armed.

Enforcing compliance is partly the responsibility of our Customs Service. Although the proposed legislation intends to enhance border controls, the porousness of the Canada–U.S. border is a major challenge, if the drug traffic is any indication. One interesting initiative is the proposed expansion of legislation governing the forfeiture of proceeds of smuggling to the firearms area. Also expanded would be powers regarding the forfeiture of vehicles used in the smuggling of unregistered firearms. Such legislation aims to create a major disincentive for smuggling and appears to have met with some preliminary successes in relation to the drug traffic, at least in terms of disrupting some major trafficking operations. Not enough is known about the effects of proceeds of crime legislation on the actual supply of illicit drugs. In any event, it may be the case that firearms smuggling operations are very different, perhaps smaller, than those dealing with drugs. Obviously, the more numerous and diffuse these operations, the more limited the potential impact of disrupting a few of them.

CONCLUSIONS

The proposed legislation is diverse and some of its elements may occasion modest reductions in firearm misuse. Levels of firearm ownership have been shown to influence homicide and suicide rates, as well as gun accidents. There is nothing in the legislation, however, that directly tackles ownership levels. Banning assault weapons among civilians is a reasonable move and may conceivably avert a mass murder, but such high-profile incidents are responsible for a miniscule proportion of violent crimes.

The proposed mandatory penalties may have an impact if the proposed amendments to the *Criminal Code* are applied consistently. Their potential deterrent and incapacitative effects may be diminished by the possibility that the resulting sentences, on average, are no longer than those presently imposed.

Enhanced border controls are a major challenge, given the porousness of the Canada–U.S. border and the probable diffuseness of the firearms traffic. We have insufficient knowledge about the extent of firearms misuse that is attributable to legitimately obtained versus smuggled firearms to speculate on the potential contribution of enhanced border controls on violent crime.

No aspect of this proposed package of legislation is likely to have a significant impact on the safety of Canadians. Legislation, however, serves more than just utilitarian concerns. Registering firearms, controlling the allocation of ammunition, and banning assault weapons and pocket pistols are reasonable measures in a society that wishes to denounce violence and to promote prudence and accountability in the handling of lethal products. There is nothing in these proposals that will keep people from maintaining a wide variety of firearms for legitimate purposes. Gun lobbyists, who claim to be concerned with violence and other misuses of firearms, ought to be pleased that the high-risk individuals who tend to purchase assault weapons and pocket pistols will no longer be able to obtain these products legitimately. After all, incidents such as the Montreal massacre and the carrying of concealable weapons on a large scale makes still more restrictive legislation more likely. The proposed mandatory penalties and enhanced border controls are also compatible with the agendas of most gun lobbyists.

Despite the limitations of the proposed measures, I commend the Minister of Justice for his courage in promoting such contentious legislation. Our country ought to be clearly distinguished from our neighbour to the south, where members of Congress are seriously considering the repeal of assault weapon bans. We have few lessons to learn from a country in which close to 40,000 people die each year from gunshot wounds.

NOTE

1. The use of the last two indices is, of course, circular as one cannot ascertain whether firearm-related deaths and accidents are influenced by availability when these events also serve as the measures of availability.

REFERENCES

Berkowitz, L. and A. LePage. 1967. Weapons as aggression-eliciting stimuli. *Journal of Personality and Social Psychology* 7: 202–07.

Block, R. 1977. *Violent Crime*. Lexington, MA: Lexington Books.

Brent, D.A., J.A. Perper, C.J. Allman, G.M. Moritz, M.E. Wartella, and J.P. Zelenak. 1991. The presence and accessibility of firearms in the homes of adolescent suicides: A case-control study. *Journal of the American Medical Association* 266: 2989–95.

Brent, D.A., J.A. Perper, C.E. Goldstein, D.J. Kolko, M.J. Allan, C.J. Allman, and J.P. Zelenak. 1988. Risk factors for adolescent suicide. *Archives of General Psychiatry* 45: 581–88.

Browning, C.H. 1974. Epidemiology of suicide: Firearms. *Comprehensive Psychiatry* 15: 549–53.

Chapdelaine, A., E. Samson, M.D. Kimberley, and L. Viau. 1991. Firearm-related injuries in Canada: Issues for prevention. *Canadian Medical Association Journal* 145: 1217–22.

Cheiffetz, P., J. Posener, A. LaHaye, M. Zaidman, and C. Benierakis. 1987. An epidemiological study of adolescent suicide. *Canadian Journal of Psychiatry* 32: 656–59.

Clarke, R.V. 1992. *Situational Crime Prevention: Successful Case Studies*. New York: Harrow and Heston.

Colijn, G.J., D. Lester, and A. Slothouwer. 1985. Firearms and crime in the Netherlands: A comparison with the United States of America. *International Journal of Comparative and Applied Criminal Justice* 9: 49–55.

Conklin, J.E. 1972. *Robbery and the Criminal Justice System*. New York: Lippincott.

———. 1979. The effect of gun availability on robbery and robbery murder. In R. Haveman and B. Zellner (eds.), *Policy Studies Review Annual*. Beverly Hills, CA: Sage.

Cook, P.J. 1987. Robbery violence. *Journal of Criminal Law and Criminology* 78: 357–76.

———. 1981. The effect of gun availability on violent crime patterns. *Annals of the American Academy for Political and Social Sciences* 455: 63–79.

Department of Justice. 1994. *The Government's Action Plan on Firearms Control*. Ottawa: Government Services Canada.

Feeney, F. and A. Weir. 1975. The prevention and control of armed robbery. *Criminology* 13: 1–19.

Gabor, T. 1994. *The Impact of the Availability of Firearms on Violent Crime, Suicide, and Accidental Death: A Review of the Literature with Special Reference to the Canadian Situation.* Ottawa: Department of Justice.

Gabor, T., M. Baril, M. Cusson, D. Elie, M. LeBlanc, and A. Normandeau. 1987. *Armed Robbery: Cops, Robbers, and Victims.* Springfield, IL: Charles C. Thomas.

Hawton, K. 1986. *Suicide and Attempted Suicide Among Children and Adolescents.* Beverly Hills, CA: Sage.

Hung, C.K. 1992. *Firearm Statistics.* Ottawa: Department of Justice.

Kellermann, A.L., F.P. Rivara, N.B. Rushforth, J.G. Banton, D.T. Reay, J.T. Francisco, A.B. Locci, J. Prodzinski, B.B. Hackman, and G. Somes. 1993. Gun ownership as a risk factor for homicide in the home. *The New England Journal of Medicine* 329: 1084–91.

Kellermann, A.L., F.P. Rivara, G. Somes, D.T. Reay, J. Francisco, J. Banton, J. Prodzinski, C. Fligner, and B.B. Hackman. 1992. Suicide in the home in relation to gun ownership. *The New England Journal of Medicine* 327: 467–72.

Kellermann, A.L., R.K. Lee, J.A. Mercy and J. Banton. 1991. The epidemiological basis for the prevention of firearm injuries. *Annual Review of Public Health* 12: 17–40.

Killias, M. 1993. International correlation between gun ownership and rates of homicide and suicide. *Canadian Medical Association Journal* 148: 1721–25.

Kimberley, M.D., A. Chapdelaine, L. Viau, and E. Samson. 1991. Prevention of firearm-related injuries in Canada. *Canadian Medical Association Journal* 145: 1211–13.

Kleck, G. 1991. *Point Blank: Guns and Violence in America.* Hawthorne, NY: Aldine de Gruyter.

Kleck, G. and E. McElrath. 1991. The effects of weaponry on human violence. *Social Forces* 69: 669–92.

Kost-Grant, B.L. 1983. Self-inflicted gunshot wounds among Alaska natives. *Public Health Reports* 98: 72–78.

Larson, E. 1993. The story of a gun: The maker, the dealer, the murderer — inside the out-of-control world of American firearms. *The Atlantic* 27: 48–78.

Lizotte, A. and M.S. Zatz. 1986. The use and abuse of sentence enhancement for firearms offences in California. *Law and Contemporary Problems* 49: 199–221.

Luckenbill, D. 1981. Generating compliance: The case of robbery. *Urban Life* 10: 25–46.

McDowall, D. 1991. Firearm availability and homicide rates in Detroit, 1951–1986. *Social Forces* 69: 1085–1101.

———. 1986. Gun availability and robbery rates: A panel study of large U.S. cities, 1974–78. *Law and Policy* 8: 135–48.

Moyer, S. and P. Carrington. 1992. *Gun Availability and Firearms Suicide.* Ottawa: Department of Justice.

Mundt, Robert J. 1990. Gun control and rates of firearms violence in Canada and the United States. *Canadian Journal of Criminology* 32: 137–54.

Normandeau, André. 1968. Trends and Patterns in Crimes of Robbery in Philadelphia. Doctoral dissertation. Philadelphia: University of Pennsylvania.

Ornehult, L. and A. Eriksson. 1987. Fatal firearm accidents in Sweden. *Forensic Science International* 34: 257–66.

Peterson, L.G., M. Peterson, G.J. O'Shanick, and A. Swann. 1985. Self-inflicted gunshot wounds: Lethality of method versus intent. *American Journal of Psychiatry* 142: 228–31.

Poteet, D.J. 1987. Adolescent suicide. *The American Journal of Forensic Medicine and Pathology* 8: 12–17.

R.C.M.P. 1992. Annual Firearms Report to the Solicitor General of Canada, 1992. Ottawa, Canada.

Reiss, A.J. and J.A. Roth. 1993. *Violence: Understanding and Preventing.* Washington, DC: National Academy Press.

Robbins, D. and R.C. Conroy. 1983. A cluster of adolescent suicide attempts: Is suicide contagious? *Journal of Adolescent Health Care* 3: 253–55.

Shuck, L.W., M.G. Orgel, and A.V. Vogel. 1980. Self-inflicted gunshot wounds to the face: A review of 18 cases. *Journal of Trauma* 20: 370–77.

Skogan, Wesley. 1978. Weapon use in robbery. In J. Inciardi and A. Pottieger (eds.), *Violent Crime*. Beverly Hills, CA: Sage.

Todd, A.R. 1991. Report on a Background Paper Concerning Firearm Storage Standards and Firearm Safety Training for the Department of Justice, Manitoba Natural Resources, 1985–90. Wininpeg, Manitoba.

Tonkin, R.S. 1984. Suicide methods in British Columbian adolescents. *Journal of Adolescent Health Care* 5: 172–77.

Ziring, F.E. 1968. Is gun control likely to reduce violent killings? *The University of Chicago Law Review* 35: 721–37.

FOURTEEN

Gun Control: A Critique of Current Policy

PHILIP C. STENNING

Governments have been inspired to re-enter the fray of gun control legislation by spectacular tragedies such as the "Montreal massacre," the "Just Desserts" killing and the drive-by shooting in Ottawa, rather than on the basis of any systematic and credible research. Just as lawyers know that "hard cases make for bad law," it is perhaps time for policy makers and legislators to give more recognition to the fact that highly unusual, sensational incidents do not provide the best basis on which to formulate sound policy and legislation.

There are essentially two reasons why current gun control policies and legislative proposals in Canada are unlikely to achieve significant success. First, they are too simplistic; second, they are typically based on some highly questionable (and wrong) assumptions. As I shall illustrate, these two flaws are closely related.

THE NATURE OF "THE GUN PROBLEM"

First, gun control proposals tend to be based on the premise that there is "a gun problem." Almost always, as in the U.S., this is characterized as a "crime problem." Almost always, there is talk about how to get firearms out of the hands of "criminals," while keeping them available to "legitimate users" (hunters, sportsmen and so on).

Yet anyone who knows the evidence knows full well that there is not one firearms abuse problem, but many, each of which is quite different from the others. Take, for instance, homicide, suicide, and robbery involving firearms. Firearms

Source: Philip C. Stenning, "Gun Control: A Critique of Current Policy," *Policy Options*, 15, 8 (1994): 13–17. Reproduced by permission of *Policy Options*.

homicides frequently involve offenders and victims who know each other (just over 45 percent of cases in 1991). They are committed roughly equally with handguns and long guns (rifles and shotguns) and involve an unkown mixture of legally and illegally owned firearms. At present, we have little systematic knowledge about how frequently firearms used in homicide have been recently acquired (legally or illegally) for the purpose. Firearms homicides account annually for about 33 percent of all homicides, and 15 percent of all firearms-related deaths. The proportions and rates of firearms homicide have been stable for many years; indeed the rate has declined slightly in recent years. There appears to be a trend toward handguns rather than long guns as the weapon of choice; we do not yet have an adequate explanation for this.

By comparison, firearms suicides account for the large majority (about 78 percent) of all firearms-related deaths in Canada, and about 32 percent of all suicides. Ninety percent of them are committed with long guns. We have no reliable data in Canada on whether the guns used in these cases were recently acquired specifically for the purpose of suicide. (Research suggests that in the U.S. this occurs in only about 10 percent of cases; however, there is good reason not to assume that the situation is necessarily the same here.) It appears likely that most of the weapons used in firearms suicides are legally owned. As with firearms homicide, the rate of firearms suicide has been stable for many years, showing a slight decline recently.

When it comes to firearms robberies, we know very little. A large proportion of firearms robberies (probably a majority) involve handguns, and these have been illegally acquired. We do not have clear evidence, however, as to what proportion of the "firearms" used in these offences are actually imitation, rather than real working firearms. (Imitation weapons are not covered by most gun control laws.) Police-generated statistics indicate that the proportion of all robberies committed with firearms has declined somewhat in recent years in Canada.

We do not currently have adequate profiles of the kinds of people who are likely to be involved as "offenders" in these three very different kinds of firearms abuse. Apart from the fact that most of them would be male, the profiles of the three kinds of firearms abusers are likely to quite different.

Even distinguishing among these three kinds of firearms abuse may not be adequate for the formulation of effective policy, however. For example, closer analysis of firearms homicides suggests that "domestic," "acquaintance," and "stranger" firearms homicide have quite distinctive characteristics, in terms of offender, victim, and weapon profiles. "Family" firearms homicides, for instance, occur relatively more frequently in non-urban areas, are more likely to involve legally owned long guns and are more likely to involve female offenders than is the case with other types of firearms homicides. Even accidental firearms deaths (which account for less than 5 percent of all firearms-related deaths in Canada) are mostly of two quite distinct kinds; those occurring outdoors (hunting accidents), involving adult "offenders" and legally owned long guns; and those occurring indoors, typically involving legally owned weapons, where the "offenders" are often young children and where handguns are more likely to be used.

Gun control proposals hardly ever directly address the specific characteristics of different kinds of firearms abuse, and are consequently unlikely to be successful in achieving reductions in the incidence of abuse. It does not require much mental agility to appreciate that effective measures to reduce firearms suicides are likely to be quite different from those aimed at reducing firearms homicides of various kinds or those targetting firearms robberies, etc. Almost all current gun control proposals, however, are of the "one-size-fits-all" variety, and are based on two sets of assumptions, both of which are inadequate.

GUN CONTROL THEORY

I. THE GENERAL AVAILABILITY THESIS

The first of these sets of assumptions has dominated both debate and research on gun control for many years, in Canada and elsewhere. It involves two related premises: (1) firearms abuse is directly related to firearms availability; (2) restrictive firearms control laws reduce firearms availability, and thus firearms abuse. The problem with both of these premises is that they are only partly true. We need to get a better understanding of the parts that are not true if we are to make any headway in reducing various kinds of firearms abuse.

The notion that firearms abuse is directly related to firearms availability is an extremely plausible one, and is undoubtedly partly true. Obviously, if there were no firearms available, there would be no firearms abuses. To be useful, however, the firearms availability thesis has to be considered in light of the fact that the total elimination of firearms in Canada (especially if this is not accomplished in the U.S.) is not a realistic goal. Even if possible, it would probably not be politically feasible, since it would entail a vast economic cost that would be disproportionately borne by poorer areas of the country, where hunting contributes to the local economy in a major way.

All the same, one only has to look, for instance, at the role of handguns in homicide in the US compared to the more limited role of handguns in homicide in Canada to suspect that there may be some relationship between availability and abuse (and between gun control and availability) in this case.

My own research on police officer suicides provides a very clear indication of such a relationship. Seventy-five percent of the police officer suicides I studied involved handguns (usually the officer's own service revolver). This compares with a figure of less than 10 percent in the general population. It is not unreasonable to assume that the easy availability of handguns to police officers probably has something to do with this result.

But it is a big intellectual leap from the proposition that firearms availability is so many times a critical factor in firearms abuse to the generalization that firearms availability is the critical factor in *all* firearms abuse. Yet this latter is the premise on which almost all gun control proposals are based. Unfortunately, it is empirically unsupportable. Two examples will suffice to illustrate why.

The highest concentrations of firearms in Canada are in rural communities. Data from the most recent study on this matter, produced by Angus Reid in 1991, indicate that approximately 60 percent of household firearms in Canada are in non-urban households. Yet most firearms abuses occur in urban areas; in recent years, for instance, urban areas have accounted for about 65 percent of firearms homicides. While almost every household in remote Aboriginal communities contains at least one firearm (and typically more), the proportion of homicides in these communities committed with firearms is no higher than the proportion in other rural and urban non-Aboriginal communities.

Thus the relationship between firearms availability and firearms abuse is neither straightforward nor universal, but rather contingent on various other important factors we have not yet adequately understood; further, the relationship will be more or less direct depending on what kinds of firearms abuse we are considering. For instance, the relationship may be quite strong for domestic homicide, suicide, and accidental firearms deaths in urban areas, and quite weak for other kinds of firearms homicides, and firearms robberies, in these same urban areas. It may be even weaker or non-existent in rural areas, perhaps because attitudes toward firearms are quite different there.

RATHER AMBITIOUS VENTURE

Basing gun control primarily on the general availability thesis involves quite a gamble, which is hard to justify in fiscal terms. We have no idea how many illegally owned guns there are in Canada, but it would not be beyond the bounds of plausibility to suggest that illegal guns (most of which are probably to be found in urban areas) may now account for as much as 10 percent of the household gun stock. On this (admittedly speculative) basis, and if the current Angus Reid estimates of the legally owned household gun stock are correct, we may expect that there are about 6.6 million firearms in legal and illegal household ownership in this country. Since there are an average of about 1,500 firearms-related deaths each year in Canada (1,471 in 1991), this suggests that approximately one in 4,400 of these guns is involved in a death each year — in some ways a surprisingly low figure, given the lethality of these instruments. (The ratio is probably actually somewhat lower, since some guns cause multiple deaths.) If, as seems likely, not all of these deaths are really preventable (the truly determined murderer or suicide will probably succeed no matter what controls are in place), the number of guns involved in hypothetically preventable deaths is probably lower still. Trying to prevent these few guns from getting into the hands of firearms abusers through the general regulation of all household firearms can be seen to be a rather ambitious (not to mention expensive) venture.

The second premise of the general availability thesis — that restrictive firearms laws will necessarily reduce firearms availability — is unfortunately also invalid. In 1976, just before major new restrictive firearms laws were introduced in Canada, the estimated household gun stock was approximately 5 million. Fifteen years later, the number is estimated to have increased by approximately 20 percent, to about 6 million. During the same period, the population of Canada increased by approximately 19 percent. Whatever else the 1977 gun control amendments achieved, therefore, they did not apparently lead to any significant reduction in household firearms availability.

It is arguable, of course, that mere numbers of household firearms are not an adequate measure of their availability (although this is the measure used in all the relevant studies). It might be argued, for instance, that although there are about as many household firearms per capita in Canada as there were 15 years ago, measures such as safe storage provisions (requiring firearms to be kept under lock and key when not in use) may still have reduced the availability (or at least the accessibility) of these weapons. At present, however, we have no way of knowing how adequately safe storage laws are actually being obeyed and enforced, and no way of knowing, if they are, whether this increased inaccessibility is actually resulting in any decline in the incidence of various kinds of firearms abuses. In the absence of any attempt at systematic evaluation of such measures, we are left with little more than a hope and a prayer.

II. THE SPECIFIC AVAILABILITY THESIS

While most gun control laws are ostensibly aimed at reducing the general availability of firearms, some (such as screening of applicants for certificates and permits) appear to be based on a notion of specific, rather than general, availability. The broad idea here seems to be that, even if reducing the general availability of firearms may not cause a reduction in the incidence of firearms abuses, it may be that measures aimed at reducing firearms availability to specific individuals who are likely to commit abuses could be effective. Thus through screening procedures, for instance, we attempt to deny firearms to people with criminal records or histories of violence or mental illness, hoping thereby to reduce the incidence of abuse. There are two fundamental problems with such reasoning, however.

First, it is assumed that potential firearms abusers will submit to such screening, rather than secure their firearms illegally. At present, we have no systematic information about what role legally and illegally owned firearms play in various kinds of firearms abuses. If, as seems likely, a significant proportion of firearms used in certain kinds of homicides and other crimes are obtained illegally, the efficacy of screening procedures in reducing such abuses is likely to be small. Secondly, even in cases where firearms abuses involve legally owned firearms, we presently have no way of knowing whether such screening procedures are likely to be effective. For instance, we do not know what proportion of people who commit homicide or suicide with legally owned firearms would have been subjected to screening procedures: presumably many of those who use firearms belonging to other people would not have been identified. Nor do we know how many people who commit firearms abuses have criminal records or recent histories of violence or mental illness; or whether, if they do, they would have been successfully identified. Marc Lepine, the perpetrator of the tragic "Montreal massacre" in 1989, apparently was not identified as potentially dangerous. Nor, apparently, was Valery Fabrikant, who shot four of his academic colleagues to death at Concordia University in 1993.

Without reliable profiles of the kinds of people who have easy access to firearms and the kinds of people who perpetrate various kinds of firearms abuses — information that can only be obtained through systematic research — we have no way of knowing whether the criteria used to identify potential firearms abusers in advance are actually effective. And without systematic monitoring of how the screening process is actually being implemented in practice, we have no way of knowing whether it is achieving the established goals.

III. OTHER THEORIES

Several other theories about how gun controls can work to reduce the incidence of firearms abuses can be detected in current Canadian gun control laws, but they play a relatively minor role compared to the general and specific availability theses. Thus, *deterrence* and *incapacitation* are both strategies used in the sentencing and other options (e.g., firearms prohibitions) available to the judiciary, although prohibitions can be regarded as yet another manifestation of the specific availability thesis. A "competency thesis," according to which firearms abuses are related to the incompetence of some people who have access to firearms, is also evident in firearms training requirements; but this theory could obviously only be applicable to a very small range of ("accidental") firearms abuses.

Finally, there is what one might call the "acceptability thesis," according to which the incidence of at least some kinds of firearms abuses may be related to the social acceptability or unacceptability of certain uses for firearms. Thus, for instance, handgun controls may be aimed at prescribing limited socially acceptable uses for such weapons (for instance, recreational target shooting, protection of large shipments of bullion or self-defence against animals in the bush, but not routine domestic home defence).

Unfortunately, we are about as much in the dark about the validity of these other theories of gun control as we are about the validity of the availability theses.

EVALUATING GUN POLICIES

At present, no identifiable goals have been established against which the success or failure of legislative gun control provisions can be measured. To date, evaluations have been inadequate, methodologically questionable, inconclusive, and contradictory. Gun control measures tend to be hailed as "successful" if the incidence of various kinds of firearms abuses can be shown to have diminished following their implementation. Yet typically, evidence that it was the gun control measures, rather than some other factor(s) that produced such reductions is either very weak or non-existent. The unfortunate result is that such research tends to encourage exaggerated and inflexible positions on both sides of the gun control debate. A failure to find significant benefits from a particular gun control package is paraded as proof that "gun control doesn't work," and evidence that the situation has improved somewhat following the introduction of such legislation is heralded as proof that more laws are needed.

It seems likely, however, that the truth lies elsewhere; that some kinds of gun control measures may be relatively effective in relation to some kinds of firearms abuse, but not in relation to others. It seems likely, too, that even "effective" measures do not have unlimited effectiveness, and that more is not necessarily better. Handgun controls in Canada probably provide a good example of this. It is plausible that existing controls have had some influence in saving Canada from the handgun scourge experienced in the U.S. But it is not at all clear that any tightening of the existing handgun controls (short of an outright ban on private handgun ownership) would achieve any commensurate additional benefits. In fact, such a measure might actually stimulate the illegal handgun market, leaving us worse off than before.

Control measures tend to be suggested by gun control advocates without any serious examination of the costs and benefits, or of the possible alternative uses to which the money could be put. Yet without such estimates, it is impossible to assess whether expenditure of public funds and resources on gun control is more beneficial than, say, improving counselling services for suicidal people or for those having domestic difficulties.

Firearms abuse, like cancer, crime, and pollution, is a complex, not a simple problem; to be successful, responses must be multi-faceted and sensitive to the complexities. This poses a substantial challenge to policy makers and legislators, who must present complex "packages" and programs to media and a public who are notoriously unreceptive to complexity.

To have any serious hope of enacting effective gun control laws, we must insist that such controls be introduced not just because they may seem plausible (as is typically the case now), but only on the basis of clear evidence that they have a good prospect of actually working. To marshall such evidence, we shall not only have to distinguish among different kinds of firearms abuse, and gain a fuller understanding of their key characteristics (by offender, victim, weapon, and situation), but also pay attention to identifying the actual costs and problems of implementing different kinds of controls.

While this may seem to be a demanding standard to justify further controls — and would undoubtedly require a substantial investment in research — it is one which, if met, would maximize effectiveness while minimizing wasteful expenditure of tax dollars and unnecessary erosion of liberty and civil rights.

FIFTEEN

....

Recent Trends in Canadian Drug Policy: The Decline and Resurgence of Prohibitionism

PATRICIA G. ERICKSON

During the era of alcohol prohibition in the United States, industrious Canadians were producers and exporters of this then forbidden drug across the world's longest undefended border.[1] By contrast, in the current illicit drug trade, Canada though sometimes a transshipment point for drugs destined for the United States,[2] is largely a partner in prohibition of illicit substances. Indeed, Canada, given its early legislative efforts in 1908 to control such substances, and its high profile when the first international treaties were signed, may be said to have led the way in forging modern drug prohibition, influencing the United States in its approach.[3] Since then, Canada and the United States have shared an overlapping history in regard to "narcotics."[4]

While this process of reciprocal influence over eight decades has resulted in many similarities, the outcomes have been different. Because levels of illicit drug use and associated problems are much lower in Canada than they are in the United States, Canada provides an interesting case control study for examining the American experience.

....

Source: Patricia G. Erikson, "Recent Trends in Canadian Drug Policy: The Decline and Resurgence of Prohibitionism." Reprinted by permission of *Dædalus*, Journal of the American Academy of Arts and Sciences, from the issue entitled, "Political Pharmacology: Thinking about Drugs," Summer, *121*, 3 (1992): 239–67.

Like most industrialized societies, their drug policies have relied heavily on the criminal law to control drug supplies and to punish offenders. The term "prohibitionism" includes the array of laws, criminal justice practices, and social evaluations that serve to suppress particular forms of drugs, forbidding their use, production, and sale. Most nations have an official policy of prohibiting narcotics; most are signatories of the United Nations treaty, the *Single Convention on Narcotic Drugs*. Yet implementation varies widely, from the ferocious policies of Malaysia and Singapore to the benign ones practiced by the Netherlands. Vigorous enforcement of drug prohibition involves substantial socioeconomic costs and the curtailment of individual personal freedoms. No democratic government can persevere in this approach unless it had wide support in the populace.

In 1986–1987, while the United States launched a newly invigorated drug war, Canada enunciated a very different federal drug strategy. Since repressive responses to illicit drug use had been the hallmark of drug policies in both countries from the early 1900s, this apparent divergence could be seen as an effort by Canada to distance itself from the legacy of its past policies, to forge a new direction. Was Canada's Drug Strategy something more profound than Canadians just saying "No Thank You" to drugs? The evidence suggests that Canada still has a distance to go if it wishes to distinguish itself from the more unequivocally aggressive American response.

A LAW ABIDING SOCIETY

A distinctive feature of Canadian society is the general lower rate of crime and violence, compared to the United States of America.[5] In 1988, the murder rate south of the Canada–U.S. border was more than three times that to the north, and the American robbery rate was over twice that of Canada's.[6] The total number of homicides in all of Canada in 1990 was 656,[7] comparable to that of either Detroit or Washington, D.C. Canada has much stricter gun control laws than the United States, and Canadian police officers were less likely to be killed on duty in the 1980s than in the two preceding decades.[8] American officers involved in drug related investigations have been increasingly at high risk.[9] Nor has Canada's history been marred to any marked degree by assassinations, civil unrest, and other forms of extreme political violence, leading William Kilbourn to refer to Canada as "the peaceable kingdom still."[10]

Anyone who doubts the uniqueness of Canada's culture, values, and identity need look no further than a recent issue of *Dædalus*.[11] Yet, both Canada and the United States resort to substantial punitive responses to criminal offenders. While the American incarceration rate is the highest in the world, and Canada's incarceration rate is one-fourth of that, it is still fifth in the world.[12] An increasing proportion of incarcerated Americans are drug offenders; they comprise close to half of all inmates in certain jurisdictions. In 1988, 6 percent of provincial and 11 percent of federal inmates in Canada were imprisoned for offenses against drug laws: approximately 7,000 in total.[13] If Canada no longer permits capital punishment, it provides the most severe sentence available, life imprisonment, for trafficking or importing cannabis, cocaine, heroin, and other "narcotics." Canada's rate of drug offenses (that is, those discovered and recorded by the police) peaked in the 1980–1985 period at nearly 300 per 100,000. The United Nations reported this to be the highest in the world during that period,[14] but it has apparently been surpassed by the United States since then.[15]

Still the use of illicit drugs in the two countries has been very different. Whatever substance or demographic group is considered, Canadian rates are lower.[16] For example, among cocaine users, the highest levels of use in the U.S. population have been reported in the age category, 18 to 25. In 1982, a year of peak use, 18.8 percent of these young adults were reported to have used cocaine. In the province of Ontario, the proportion of the young adult group using cocaine in 1984 was recorded as 7.1 percent. While 6.7 percent of Ontario high school seniors used cocaine in 1985, in the comparable American group, 13.1 percent had done so. Differences are also conspicuous for cannabis. While the most recent student surveys show 27.5 percent of US seniors using the substance in the past year, 21.6 percent of Ontario high school seniors used it in the same period. Nationally, 23.2 percent of all Canadian adults used cannabis at some time in their lives; only 6.5 percent were current users in 1989. Adult levels of cannabis use in the United States have been consistently higher.

While injection drug use, particularly of opiates, is notoriously difficult to determine, the Canadian estimates of an upper limit of about 25,000 users[17] are dwarfed by estimates of at least one million regular injection drug users in the United States.[18] The death rate in Toronto comprising cases in which heroin or cocaine is detected is from one-seventh to one-fourteenth lower than in the comparable American cities, New York and Philadelphia. Cases of AIDS and rates of HIV infection attributable to injection drug use as the sole risk factor are also much lower in Canada, at less than 5 percent,[19] though rates are substantially higher in imprisoned populations.[20] The difference may result, at least in part, from the legal availability of needles and syringes in pharmacies in Canada and the introduction of needle exchange programs in major Canadian cities by the end of the 1980s.

These differences do not necessarily reflect a more general difference in attitudes to *all* drugs. For example, licit drug use is comparable in the two countries. Per capita alcohol consumption is about the same, with Canada slightly higher; the same is true for cigarette smokers. Also, Canadians appear to be less concerned about illicit drugs than are Americans. When public opinion in both countries was surveyed in 1990 on their most important national problems, Canadians placed drugs eighth on their list; Americans placed it second from the top.[21] National attention in Canada has tended also to focus on issues of tobacco control, the overprescribing of pharmaceuticals, and alcohol problems. The Royal Commission of Inquiry into the Non-Medical Use of Drugs established in 1969 to examine increasing drug use — the Le Dain Commission — may have contributed to this broader perspective when it articulated a definition of "non-medical drug use" that encompassed both licit and illicit substances.[22]

While the prevalence of illicit drug use is considerably lower in Canada than in the United States and the magnitude of drug use differs substantially, the trends in illicit drug use in both countries have run a parallel course. Both countries experienced a marked rise in illicit drug use during the 1970s, followed by a levelling off, and a decline in the 1980s.[23]

HISTORY, CULTURE, AND POLICY PERSPECTIVES

There are two major ways of conceptualizing the differences in crime and illicit drug use as between Canada and the United States.[24] The "cultural lag" model assumes that the differences are only a matter of degree; it is simply a matter of time before Canada reflects the same level of such problem activities as its larger neighbor. This version, particularly popular with media commentators for whom each example of violent crime, drug bust, or cocaine overdose provides *further* evidence that Canada is destined to achieve American levels of urban disorder and decay, is very different from the "distinct society" view that holds that the two countries are fundamentally different in their attitudes, values, culture, and social institutions. These, in turn, are thought to shape the propensities for crime and deviance, including illicit drug use. In this latter view, Canada has traditionally valued social order over individual rights and freedoms, producing a more law-abiding populace, placing greater faith in the discretion of legal authorities. These contrasts are summarized by David Bayley:

> Compared with the U.S., Canada is very fortunate indeed ... Curiously, though, these striking differences in rates of criminality between Canada and the U.S. are not a source of congratulations among Canadians. Instead, they tend to wring their hands in the belief that Canada must inevitably follow the frightening example of the U.S. They do not pause to consider that there may be differences in socioeconomic structure as well as culture between the two countries that would make this unlikely.[25]

Indeed, the broader social net in Canada — more substantial public support for medical care, public schools, and social services[26] — may have helped reduce levels of poverty and deprivation, and may provide less fertile ground for drug use and crime. If Canadians have maintained lower levels of drug use, how is this connected to today's sociolegal responses to drugs and the more recent enunciations of a more vigorous drug policy?

In Canada, antinarcotic criminal laws were initiated in 1908, largely directed at opium smoking among Chinese laborers.[27] Subsequent modifications to the laws provided ever harsher penalties and fewer legal protections for suspected users and sellers.[28] This trajectory persisted until 1969. Then, for the first time, the vigor of the legal response diminished. More changes in the direction of greater leniency were expected in the 1970s, in the wake of the Le Dain Commission. Reform of the drug laws appeared to be an imminent possibility.[29] In the 1980s, however, the use of illicit drugs declined. Marijuana arrest activity and sentence severity diminished in Canada, as it did in the United States, where eleven states decriminalized possession, without refueling a new epidemic of marijuana use.[30] Concomitantly, public interest and political attention to drug issues waned.[31]

By the mid-1980s, however, the process of a qualified retreat from criminalization ended; a resurgence of antidrug sentiment and intensification of legal responses followed. What revived this prohibitionism? What factors contributed to this dramatic shift in social response?

THE LEGACY OF PROHIBITIONISM, 1908-1969

This era of drug policy, extensively analyzed elsewhere,[32] will be summarized briefly here. Canada may be unique in the extent to which centralized bureaucratic control characterized the formative period of Canadian narcotics law. The federal chief of the Division of Narcotic Control coordinated reports from the federal enforcers (the

Royal Canadian Mounted Police [RCMP]) and federal drug prosecutors, guaranteeing that most of their expressed need for greater powers were met legislatively. Because criminal law in Canada is under federal jurisdiction, all legal enactments related to the entire country.

During the heyday of the 1920s, when the fundamental structure was first established, provisions provided for the search of premises and their occupants without warrants, the creation and issuance of blanket search warrants, called writs of assistance, for dwellings, various restrictions on legal appeals, the whipping of the convicted, the sentencing of offenders to hard labor, mandatory minimum sentences, and the deportation of convicted aliens, regardless of the length of their domicile in Canada. These harsh provisions, possible because of the depth of anti-Asiatic sentiment, were enacted almost solely against the Chinese. Cannabis was added to the schedule in 1923 without parliamentary debate. In 1954, the severity of the penalties for trafficking was increased yet further; the reverse onus of proof, requiring the accused to establish his innocence, was applied to a new offense, possession for the purpose of trafficking.

As P. James Giffen and his colleagues have illustrated in great detail, the principal architects of drug policy in this period were those charged with its execution.[33] This bureaucratic partnership of social control agents remained virtually unchallenged until the 1950s when concern for providing treatment for opiate users broadened the range of players. This was yet further expanded by the marijuana controversy of the 1960s. The public appears to have accepted these broad powers of social control, and the police and courts used them effectively to process drug offenders in substantial numbers, resulting in high rates of criminalization and incarceration.

A reliance on strict enforcement and punishment has traditionally been Canada's primary strategy on illicit drugs. As the Le Dain Commission stated in 1972: "The law is the primary instrument of social policy ... The question is whether, and to what extent, the criminal law is a proper instrument for such a policy."[34] The Commissioners addressed this question by conducting a cost-benefit analysis with the not unreasonable assumptions (though rarely applied historically in drug policy matters) that the benefits of the policy should be demonstrable, not to be exceeded by its costs.

THE DECLINE OF PROHIBITIONISM: PENALTY REDUCTION AND MILD LIBERALIZATION, 1969–1986

A number of pressures arose in the 1960s, precipitating the questioning and modification of this dominant policy. There was an upsurge in youthful drug use, especially marijuana, and the overloading of the courts with these "cannabis criminals." Limited sentencing options led half of all cannabis possession offenders to be imprisoned, and the emergence of competing interest groups vying for the right to define "the drug problem" changed the picture.[35]

A different policy emphasis, manifested gradually in both real and contemplated law reform, the eventual reduction in enforcement activity, less severe sentences, and a new public awareness of individual rights of drug users was apparent. Actual legal changes were few compared to the many debated during this period. Major changes included the provision of a "fine only" sentencing option in 1969 as an amendment to the *Narcotic Control Act* and the provision of absolute and conditional discharge alternatives in 1972.[36] Such discharges, providing a finding of guilt but not a conviction, were new to the *Criminal Code*. Other proposals for legal changes were made but never implemented. For example, a major reform that attracted substantial political attention in 1968, 1970, 1974, and 1980, but not approved, was a proposal to move cannabis from the *Narcotic Control Act* to the less restrictive *Food and Drugs Act*.[37]

Declines in sentence severity for cannabis possession during this period, and greater efficiency of the courts in processing these offenders, helped reduce pressure for meaningful law reform.[38] Judges quickly utilized the fine and discharge options; fewer users were jailed. Convictions climbed dramatically in the 1970s for cannabis offenses (of which about 90 percent were for simple possession) to a peak of nearly 44,000 in 1981, but then declined to 22,510 in 1985. During this period, annual convictions for illicit drugs other than cannabis rarely numbered more than 1,000,[39] and Canada's drug policy was directed at, and dominated by, cannabis.

Another manifestation of some tempering of the earlier allegiance to prohibitionism was an increased recognition of individual rights in drug cases. The process began with critiques in the 1970s and culminated in the mid-1980s with the abolition of writs of assistance, the removal of mandatory minimum sentences for importing, and the elimination of the reverse onus clause in cases of possession for the purpose of trafficking. Although passage of the new *Charter of Rights and Freedoms* in 1982 was not prompted specifically by a concern with perceived injustices regarding drug offenders, its effect was to remove some of the procedural disadvantages that had been applied to suspected or accused drug users/sellers, but not to other categories of potential criminals.[40]

Even minor shifts in a well-entrenched social response to a particular form of deviance cannot occur without changes in the social evaluation of the unacceptable behavior.[41] The initial criminalization of illicit drugs was made possible by the development of strongly held fact beliefs concerning the pernicious effects of certain drugs, their ability to enslave users, and the evil and immoral qualities of those who distributed them.[42] A number of social influences in the 1960s and 1970s led to the discrediting of the more extreme forms of the "dope fiend" mythology of the earlier era.

One relevant factor was the narrowing of the social distance between drug users and the mainstream of society. Indeed, many in the mainstream gained personal familiarity with illicit drugs, as the use of marijuana, LSD, and cocaine (at a later date) became more prevalent in the adolescent and young adult population. It is difficult to maintain the seriousness of criminal behavior when the activity is engaged in by a substantial proportion of the population, by those in one's own family and social network. As well, these new users of cannabis and other drugs who were going to court in increasing numbers occupied a higher social status than that associated with the heroin addict stereotype. The law was widely assailed for making criminals of middle class youth. Prime Minister Pierre Trudeau, in a session with students in 1977, said: "If you have a joint and you're smoking it for your private pleasure, you shouldn't be hassled."[43] Also, health risks, physical and psychological dependency, and the progression theory of drug escalation (first marijuana, then heroin), were assessed repeatedly in government reports in many countries, and were deemed less serious than previously believed.[44]

Another influence was the contribution made by cost-benefit research to a more objective analysis of the prevailing policy of criminalization. Many studies documented the weakness of the deterrent effect of the law in preventing the initiation or continuation of drug use.[45] Also, increased evidence of the substantial costs of suppression efforts directed at trafficking, and the limited effectiveness of supply-side measures, had their effect.[46] Together, such studies led many to conclude that existing policy could be improved on, even if agreement on the best alternatives remained elusive.[47]

THE RESURGENCE OF PROHIBITIONISM: FROM MALIGN NEGLECT TO RENEWED REPRESSION, 1986-1992

As the 1980s advanced, most forms of illicit drug use declined; arrests for cannabis decreased, those for cocaine gradually increased; the courts continued routinely to process drug cases; the urgency of earlier drug policy debates was replaced by public and political indifference. Canada had, it seemed, learned to live both with drug use and prohibition.[48] Some imagined that illicit drug use, like abortion, gambling, homosexuality, and other previously criminalized acts would follow the cycles of diminished social concern, less intervention, greater toleration.[49]

In 1986, crucial events occured. First, the American President, Ronald Reagan, declared a new crusade against drugs, stating that "Drugs are menacing our society ... there is no moral middle ground." Within two days, Prime Minister Brian Mulroney departed from his prepared text to announce that "Drug abuse has become an epidemic that undermines our economic as well as our social fabric."[50] Bemused Canadian drug professionals and researchers, who knew that the problems had neither worsened nor gone away, were caught by surprise. Many, sought by the media for comment, challenged the Prime Minister's view of an "epidemic"; the more politically adept reiterated the requirement for resources to prevent and treat existing drug problems, *including* alcohol and prescription drugs. Even government officials were caught off guard, as was one high-ranking official in Health and Welfare Canada at that time, who described the events that followed: "when he [the PM] made that statement, then we had to make it a *problem*."[51] Thus drug issues returned to the social and political agenda.

In the aftermath of the Prime Minister's remark, events moved rapidly. The Canadian government created a federal drug secretariat, which consulted widely with community groups and agencies, and provided a new national focus on a drug strategy "with objectives of reducing the harm to individuals, families and communities from the abuse of drugs."[52] Formally announced in May 1987, the Strategy projected funding of $210 million over the next five years. The funds were to be unevenly allocated; 70 percent was to go for prevention and treatment; 30 percent for enforcement and control. Pressure from addiction agencies guaranteed that drug abuse comprised not only illicit drugs, but alcohol, licit pharmaceuticals, solvents, and, to a limited extent, tobacco. The new Strategy explicitly recognized the inadequacy of supply efforts; it made its focus the reduction of demand through education of the young, together with provisions for treatment. This initiative at first distanced itself from the American "War on [Illicit] Drugs" and its priority of enforcement over both prevention and treatment.[53]

Canada's Drug Strategy, as it is officially known, has now completed its first five year mandate; in 1992 it was renewed for a further five years.[54] It is timely, therefore, to assess its impact, to consider its likely future direction. Because the Strategy did not simply replace all existing policies and programs, and because public beliefs and attitudes towards drugs, and the social evaluations they entail, are a volatile and conflicting mix, the results have been contradictory.

In this period, manifestations of a renewed spirit of prohibitionism included the creation of new offenses and laws. In 1989, Bill C-61 gave the police new powers to seize and the courts to forfeit the assets of arrested drug offenders. Compared to the previous five years, when the antidrug profiteering program garnered only $51 million, $60 million was realized between 1989 and 1992.[55] Another law, Bill C-264, banning the sale of drug paraphernalia, was enacted in 1988.[56] Some prosecutions of "head shop" merchants followed; drug literature, such as the magazine *High Times*, was stopped at the border. The failure of the Canadian athlete to pass drug tests in the 1988 Olympics, and the resultant inquiry, increased public awareness and concern about the ready availability of performance-enhancing drugs.[57] In 1992 steroids were moved up a step in the legislative hierarchy, from Section F of the *Food and Drugs Act* (covering most prescription drugs) to join barbiturates and amphetamines in Section G, which provides more severe penalties for trafficking. Thus, the net of criminalization widened to include drug pipes, literature, and steroid dealers; more of the assets of those suspected of profiting from drug selling were confiscated.

Proposals to increase the surveillance and detection of drug users or sellers and to restrict their liberty became more common. Workplace drug testing of transport workers in order to match American practices, backtracked after trade unions, the Privacy Commission, and other groups protested.[58] A multinational corporation, Imperial Oil, initiated random drug testing of all employees in "safety sensitive" positions, and made urine testing mandatory for new employees.[59] Challenges to this policy from the Canadian Civil Liberties Association and the unions are now before the courts. A form of zero tolerance, tried by Canadian Customs officials for a period, was withdrawn after numerous public complaints and little demonstrable payoff in detection. A federal proposal to deny parole to serious violent offenders and *drug traffickers* has aroused little public reaction, to date, and is apparently under active consideration despite the government's commissioned research that showed first-time trafficking offenders were a low risk group for recidivism.[60] Since the *Narcotic Control Act* (1961) already provides life imprisonment for trafficking and importing, calls for tougher penalties must, by definition, either be symbolic or focus on actual sentencing and/or parole practices.[61]

This period of resurgence was marked also by substantial, renewed enforcement and harsher penalties.[62] Cannabis offenses, numbered about 41,000 in 1986 and 38,276 in 1990. Not only did high levels of enforcement continue, but cannabis remained the major component of antidrug activities. In 1990, 64 percent of the 60,039 drug offenses in Canada were for cannabis; the majority were for simple possession only. Total convictions for cocaine increased from 2,793 to 6,909 between 1985 and 1989, and those incarcerated for cocaine possession went up from 17 percent to 29 percent. Since convictions (as opposed to offenses) have not been compiled or published for cannabis since 1985, the reporting of actual conviction totals since that year has been dominated by cocaine, perhaps contributing to the misleading public impression that cannabis was no longer an enforcement priority.

Increased resources were put into local drug squads. In Toronto, for example, ninety-seven new officers were added in 1989, and $1.2 million was spent on drug buys. Enforcement activity was enhanced: seizures doubled; there was a 31 percent increase in all drug charges, a 53 percent rise in trafficking charges.[63] This led to the overloading of court dockets and of jail cells. In Ontario, the number sentenced to provincial correctional facilities for drug offenses rose from 1,812 in 1986–1987 to 3,137 in 1989–1990.[64] This represented an increase from 4 percent to 7 percent of all Ontario incarcerations. Federally, the proportion of inmates admitted under the *Narcotic Control Act* grew from 9 percent to 14 percent between 1986 and 1990.

The nature of federal police activity also changed during the latter half of the 1980s when cannabis and cocaine use were in fact declining or levelling off. The RCMP focused more and more on small-scale traffickers. While cocaine trafficking charges more than doubled from 1985–1989,[65] the proportion of traffickers in the smallest amount (less than one ounce or 28 grams) more than tripled, from 10 percent to 33 percent. At the same time, those investigated for the largest amount (one kilogram or more) declined slightly, while those involving intermediate amounts declined from 53 percent to 34 percent of the total. Although seizures of cocaine were reported to have increased by 268 percent in 1989 (to 712.4 kilograms), this was due principally to a single large seizure of 500 kilograms.

The search for small-scale traffickers was even more pronounced for cannabis. Despite steady declines in use in the population as a whole, and a large drop in seizures, the RCMP maintained an almost equivalent level of charges in 1988 and 1989.[66] From 1985 to 1989 the proportion of traffickers in the smallest amounts nearly tripled, rising from 25 percent to 72 percent, while investigations for the largest amounts decreased from 14 percent to 4 percent of the total.

These data for cocaine and cannabis trafficking illustrate a well-documented phenomenon in the study of crime rates in general, namely that recorded offenses will increase in direct proportion to police resources.[67] This is particularly true when an activity, like drug use and sale, depends on proactive police discovery rather than a citizen-initiated response.[68] Thus, the influx of resources to the police from Canada's Drug Strategy in 1987 enabled the police to demonstrate and maintain a high level of "productivity" in overall investigations, seizures, arrests, and charges. The additional funding was not contingent on the police operating any differently than they were accustomed to doing in drug matters.[69] The overall drug crime rate (offenses per 100,000) climbed from 221.9 in 1986 to 258.9 in 1989.[70] That the police were able to achieve this in a time of stable or declining drug use is a telling testament to their initiative.

Following the advent of the Drug Strategy in 1987, with more government funding for prevention, the police increased their involvement also in community-based alcohol and drug education, with the production of video and other such materials. About 1,000 local officers from 128 forces were trained to deliver these programs by the RCMP's special unit, PACE, Police Assisting Community Programs. In fact, according to the Strategy's own internal assessments, the majority of its prevention resources went to police-controlled educational programming.[71]

It is possible that the police officer is indeed the authority figure who can most effectively deliver the abstinence message to youth, urging them to stay away from drugs.[72] The police are perhaps filling a perceived need in the community. Still, the general lack of demonstrated effectiveness in school-based programs in changing actual drug use behavior[73] and the lack of systematic evaluation of the police programs,[74] in relation to the variety of needs and experiences of youth, raise doubts. One concern is that preoccupation with illicit drugs diverts attention from the "real killers," alcohol and tobacco.[75] Another worry is that while youthful substance use has declined overall, the proportion of heavier, more frequent users of alcohol, tobacco, and other drugs has not; the "problem" continues.[76] Programs to encompass less risky practices for those already using, or intending to use drugs, or who are experiencing substance-related difficulties, are perhaps not readily delivered by those whose primary role in society is identified with enforcement and punishment.[77] Nor is it at all clear that adequate programs exist to meet Canadian treatment needs when large numbers of Canadians seek alcohol/drug programs in the United States; 3,500 from Ontario did so in 1990.[78]

A key social influence that facilitated the renewal of prohibitionism was the image of the drug problem presented to Canadians by the American media.[79] Cocaine, especially in the form of crack, was portrayed as the drug that finally fulfilled all the expectations of the "demon drug" mythology. Represented unidimensionally as highly dangerous and addictive in virtually all popular media sources,[80] the drug scare message was delivered. Although levels of cocaine use and attendant problems undoubtedly increased in Canada during the 1980s, the national survey data indicated that prevalence remained low (current use by 0.9 percent in 1985; 1.4 percent reported use in 1989).[81] The province of Ontario, which has the most consistently recorded trend data, showed a decline in cocaine use in the student population after 1985 and a stable level of use for adults since then.[82] Other Canadian studies showed that most used the drug infrequently and had few serious problems; the headlines told a very different story.[83]

This "secondhand" or "borrowed" drug panic about cocaine and crack was imported from the United States as part of a larger cultural infiltration, with its highly negative evaluations of illicit drug use and users.[84] The feeling of threat helped justify increasingly repressive responses against those defined as the "enemy."[85] Fed by extreme views of "instant addiction," and fatal results followed by exposure to these all-powerful substances, such messages helped to build and maintain the consensus required to support the punitive and exclusionary responses to drug users.

Canada and the United States have begun to be less distinguishable in their media and other public imagery concerning drugs. A variety of antidrug messages have appeared on milk cartons, in bus shelters, on letters delivered by the post office, in children's cartoon programs, inserted into sports events on prime-time TV. Ben Johnson, after years of taking steroids and lying about it, returned in disgrace from the Seoul Olympics, repented publicly, and was soon recruited as an antidrug role model for the country's youth.[86] Two people navigated Niagara Falls in a barrel, itself an offense, to show young people that there were alternatives to drugs. Canadian journalists produced their own share of "drug scare" stories, but also offered more balanced accounts such as that provided by David Suzuki's *Nature of Things* special on CBC, "Dealing with Drugs." This program contrasted harm reduction approaches in Liverpool and Amsterdam with the drug war in New York, and examined Canadian efforts at grappling with drug problems.[87]

While Canada did not embrace an all-out drug war comparable to the American effort, its policy seemed beset by ambivalence regarding both priorities and objectives. This contradiction was suggested by the terminology used by federal officials in describing Canada's Drug Strategy. The focus on demand reduction over supply measures began to erode. Perrin Beatty, the Minister of Health and Welfare, struggling in 1990 to describe the Canadian policy, said: "We believe that the first course of action in *combatting* drug abuse is to *help* the drug user or *potential* drug user. While the *major priority* is demand reduction, curbing supply is *equally important*, especially as a *complement* to demand reduction efforts."[88] The 1990 RCMP drug report not only documented falling prices and greater purity of cocaine, but also projected easier availability of almost all illegal drugs in Canada in the next two years.[89] In this context, the Solicitor General, Pierre Cadieux, who was less restrained in the use of war-like imagery, remarked: "What we're saying is that the war has not been won yet but that we are making steady progress." One can only wonder what a "setback" would be.

It has been difficult to know who spoke for, or indeed who defined Canada's Drug Strategy. There are many players, including ministers sharing cabinet responsibility, police officials, federal and provincial civil servants, and all those from addiction agencies who participated in community consultations across the country. The leadership of the Canadian Centre on Substance Abuse (CCSA), created by the 1987 initiative, saw the Strategy as a tentative step in the direction of harm minimization.[90] As an example of this new direction for the future of Canadian drug policy, the Chief Executive Officer, Jan Skirrow, said:

> A successful attack on the harm associated with drug use will require comprehensive social policy ... every aspect of how human beings organize and govern themselves becomes an issue, because drug use is associated with nothing less than who we are as individuals, how we see our world and our place in it, and how we exercise our individual skills and abilities to live life as we wish.[91]

The annual report for 1990–1991 of the CCSA specifically speaks out against an American-style supply reduction focus; it emphasizes the need for "a humane and uniquely Canadian alternative to the punitive War on Drugs."

While it is premature to determine the shape drug policy will take for the rest of the 1990s, recent statements provide certain indications. Federal ministers announced the renewal of Canada's Drug Strategy in March 1992 for a further five-year period, with a budget of $270 million.[92] The Minister of National Health and Welfare remarked that while the "remarkable success" of the Strategy was illustrated by declines in illicit drug use, especially among young people, the problem of substance abuse still existed.[93] The aim was said to be harm reduction, and the key elements were prevention and health promotion; a number of high risk groups were targeted for future attention.

The Solicitor General highlighted specific funding of $33 million for three new units to specialize in the enforcement of the Proceeds of Crime laws. He confirmed plans for the RCMP and the Department of National Defense to extend their cooperative arrangement to include both coastal surveillance and assistance on land. Also included was a plan to share forfeited crime profits with the provinces, an apparent victory for those who have argued that these funds should return to local coffers rather than go into general federal revenues. The involvement of the military and the return of seized drug assets to the police characterize current American practices. The Strategy's emphasis on demand-side measures focused on continuing and strengthening the police role in drug education: "It's no exaggeration to say that now, Canadian police forces lead the western world in the police-delivery of the drug abuse awareness, the drug prevention message to youth."[94]

The pronouncements surrounding the renewal of Canada's Drug Strategy appear to represent a subtle shift of emphasis. While previous statements favored a "balanced" approach, the scales of influence have tipped disproportionately to the enforcement sector, focusing both demand and supply efforts in the police. What is not explicit in this, or in the first version adopted in 1987, is recognition that the dominant policy remains one of criminalization. Nor are the various costs and limitations of the effectiveness of this approach addressed.[95] Despite the care and concern expressed for young people, the fact is that adolescents and young adults are still arrested in large numbers (mainly for cannabis), go to court, get criminal records, and are often imprisoned. Indeed, the evidence demonstrates increased criminalization. With respect to drug policy, a recent all-too apt comment was: "Canada's bite is worse than its bark."[96]

A cynical view of the renewal of Canada's Drug Strategy might be that the catch phrase "harm reduction" is putting a new face on the established policies of prohibitionism. The downward trend in illicit drug use, already well established before the advent of the Drug Strategy, is heralded as its achievement. Personal testimony and "informed opinion" appear to be sufficient to declare the Strategy a success. If "policies are judged by their consequences but crusades by how good they make the crusaders feel," then Canada is still in search of a coherent and effective drug *policy*.[97]

An alternative, more charitable, view of recent developments in Canadian drug policy is that political leaders and other federal and provincial officials deserve credit for resisting an all-out drug war. Demand reduction was made a funding priority. Tangible benefits of the Drug Strategy included the direction of resources to treatment programs and other community projects, the training of addiction professionals, the greater involvement of Native communities in various programs, and the improved communication and coordination of addiction groups across the country.[98] The continuation of the Drug Strategy for another five years provides time to reshape the approach, perhaps redirecting enforcement efforts to more community-based ways of maintaining public order and supporting treatment efforts. The many voices involved in drug policy decisions would seem to ensure a more even-handed approach.

CONCLUSION

A Canadian, attending an international conference, recently asked an Australian what accounted for that country's greater success in taking innovative approaches to illicit drug problems. The Australian approaches, for example, have included early needle exchange programs, plans for a pilot heroin maintenance program, and a ticketing system for marijuana possession. The Australian reply was, "we're just lucky to be so far away from the United States."[99] Proximity may be one factor. The influence of the American media, and political and economic pressures, is felt more directly in Canada and perhaps in Mexico, than in many other countries. But other factors beyond the dominance of a smaller country by its larger neighbor also contribute. The inertia of Canada's own history, its tradition of repressive laws and criminal justice institutions and procedures, impede fundamental change in drug policy.

Canada's drug problems are considerably less serious than those in the United States, but the policies pursued in recent years reveal parallel trends. For a brief period, it appeared that a continued heavy reliance on criminalization as the dominant policy was waning, that Canada had learned from its own experiences with prohibitions, as well as those of its neighbor. For the past two decades, conflicts over the appropriate societal response to drugs in Canada have produced fluctuations ranging from great public interest, to increased tolerance during the newer wave of marijuana use, to less severity of penalties, followed by relative indifference, and then a return to increased public concern and heightened punitive responses. More recent antidrug sentiment and adverse social evaluations of drug takers may have been fostered by the drug scare over cocaine and crack use.

Twenty years ago, the Le Dain Commission (1972) set an overall goal of Canadian drug policy to achieve gradual withdrawal from criminal sanctions against the user, with the development of alternative means to discourage use and reduce harm. To continue to rely on criminalization of users and expanded enforcement activity impedes the development of less punitive interventions. The attempt to shape Canada's Drug Strategy in a new direction appears to have been compromised by a basic allegiance to prohibitionism, the perpetuation of established traditional approaches, and the further funding support for enforcement.

What elements could contribute to a more constructive drug policy, and what features could likely reduce the harmful consequences of drug use? A useful potential alternative could be rooted in a public health perspective and its harm reduction paradigm.[100] As a point of departure, public health-oriented thinking questions the supply-demand dichotomy as the only dynamic for the control of substance use. A principal societal goal in health care is to maximize the health and well-being of the populace through the treatment and prevention of illness and the minimization or elimination of exposure to factors that adversely affect health, especially of the young.[101] Elimination may be desirable, but if not completely attainable, effort can be focused on using regulatory controls to set standards of public safety and the minimization of risk.

For example, if one considers potentially dangerous activities voluntarily engaged in, a comparison of cocaine use and snowmobile use provides an interesting contrast in policy approaches. Deaths related to each of these activities are of similar magnitude in the province of Ontario;[102] both have been a matter of public concern, but the means sought to reduce the harm of snowmobiles include licensing, age restrictions, instruction on safe use, specific areas for use, and warnings about combining alcohol and snowmobile driving. There have been no efforts to ban snowmobiles or imprison their users or sellers. Essentially, in the public health model, society seeks to learn the least destructive ways to live with a certain level of activities — for example, alcohol and tobacco use, the driving of motor vehicles — and endeavors to minimize harm through a variety of less coercive means than criminal punishment. Criminal penalties, with respect to drug issues, are reserved for combining use with activities such as drinking and driving, that pose special risks to the safety and well-being of others. Restriction of availability is necessary for risk minimization and may involve a variety of strategies.

Harm reduction paradigms are a more recent elaboration of general public health principles that have been prompted, in part, by the AIDS epidemic among injection drug users in several countries. Several key concepts relevant to policy development have emerged as these approaches have been extended to other forms of individual and social harm related to drug use. One feature is that abstinence is not always the only appropriate objective of policy. Second, harm reduction strategies recognize that prohibition in and of itself can generate certain types of harms, at both the individual and societal levels, in direct proportion to the vigor of implementation. Third, the drug user is viewed as a member of society, and may need treatment and assistance to reintegrate into the community. Fourth, harm reduction is most often a community-based strategy and places as much or more responsibility for effectiveness on strategic partnerships than in formal institutional interventions. Fifth, some forms of legal controls and their enforcement may be essential for harm reduction but need to be integrated into an overall strategy.

A practical example of how this might apply in Canada concerns cannabis offenses. The addition of cannabis to the *Narcotic Control Act* in 1923, which has been described as a "law without a problem,"[103] may now create more problems than it solves. A new objective for the renewal of Canada's Drug Strategy might be for this country to *lose* its standing as one of the world's leaders in per capita drug arrests. This might be accomplished by stopping much of the cannabis possession enforcement activity and reducing the emphasis on small-scale traffickers. If enforcement against such offenders were curtailed, the results would likely be a net reduction in individual, social, and economic costs. Such measures could lead to significant savings of public resources, which could then be used to fund harm reduction strategies in the community, or directed to other pressing social problems. Similar arguments could be considered with respect to users of other illicit drugs, who may be in even greater need of treatment or support than cannabis users.

Observers of drug policy trends in Canada, looking towards the year 2000, consider several questions: Was the recent modest relaxation of prohibitionism merely a transient anomaly? Is the drug scare destined to be a permanent public feature that will support continuation of repressive policies? Will Canada chart a new course within the evolving model of harm reduction? Canada's prohibition policy was forged in a different era, in a very different Canada, and has dominated official response to drug use for about a century. Serious alternatives were first articulated by the Le Dain Commission. It is time to explore what a health-directed public policy for drugs could mean for Canada.

ACKNOWLEDGEMENTS

I wish to express my appreciation to Joan Moreau for the computer graphics and other assistance. I am also indebted to Bruce Alexander, Neil Boyd, the late Chet Mitchell, Eric Single, and Robert Solomon for many stimulating discussions about Canadian drug policy and to Yuet Cheung and Clifford Ottaway for their helpful comments on this paper. Any views expressed in this article are the author's and do not necessarily reflect those of the Addiction Research Foundation.

NOTES

1. Reginald Smart and Alan Ogborne, *Northern Spirits* (Toronto: ARF Books, 1986). For a work of fiction set in this era, see Mordecai Richler, *Solomon Gursky Was Here* (Markham: Viking, 1989).
2. RCMP, *National Drug Intelligence Estimate* (Ottawa: Minister of Supply and Services Canada, 1990), 5.
3. David F. Musto, "Foreword" to *The Steel Drug: Cocaine in Perspective*, by P.G. Erickson, E.M. Adlaf, G.F. Murray, and R.G. Smart (Lexington: D.C. Heath, 1987), xv.

4. P. James Giffen, Shirley Endicott, and Sylvia Lambert, *Panic and Indifference: The Politics of Canada's Drug Laws* (Ottawa: Canadian Centre on Substance Abuse, 1991); and David F. Musto, *The American Disease: Origins of Narcotic Control* (New Haven: Yale University Press, 1973).

5. John Hagan, *The Disreputable Pleasures: Crime and Deviance in Canada* (Toronto: McGraw-Hill Ryerson, 1991).

6. David H. Bayley, *Managing the Future: Prospective Issues in Canadian Policing* (Ottawa: The Solicitor General of Canada, 1991).

7. Statistics Canada, *Canadian Crime Statistics, 1990* (Ottawa: Canadian Centre for Justice Statistics, 1991).

8. Bayley, *Managing the Future*, 9.

9. "Police Deaths Rise in War on Drugs," reported in *C.J. the Americas* 2 (6) (December–January 1990): 5. See also Gary T. Marx, *Undercover: Police Surveillance in America* (Berkeley: University of California Press, 1988) for examples of stress and danger related to undercover narcotics work.

10. William Kilbourn, "The Peaceable Kingdom Still," *Dædalus* 117 (4) (Fall 1988).

11. "In Search of Canada," *Dædalus* 117 (4) (Fall 1988).

12. Correctional Services Canada, 1990–1991.

13. Statistics Canada, *Adult Correctional Services 1987–88* (Ottawa: Canadian Centre for Justice Statistics, 1988).

14. *Globe and Mail*, 17 April 1992, A1–A2. Based on the index published in the UN Human Development Report.

15. Bayley, *Managing the Future*, 9.

16. E.M. Adlaf, R.G. Smart, and M.D. Canale, *Drug Use Among Ontario Adults 1977–1991* (Toronto: ARF, 1991); E.M. Adlaf and R.G. Smart, "Drug Use Among Canadian Students," *Journal of Drug Issues* 21 (1) (1991): 51–64; L.D. Johnston, P.M. O'Malley, and J.G. Backman, "1990 National High School Senior Drug Abuse Survey," Press Release, 24 January 1991; National Institute on Drug Abuse, *National Household Survey: Main Findings 1990* (Washington, D.C.: DHHS, 1990); Health and Welfare Canada, *National Alcohol and Drug Survey: Highlights Report* (Ottawa: Queen's Printer, 1990).

17. Perrin Beatty, "Foreword" to "Drug Issues: A Canadian Perspective," *Journal of Drug Issues* 21 (1) (1991): 1–8.

18. P. Selwyn, D. Hartnell, W. Wasserman, and E. Drucker, "Impact of the AIDS Epidemic on Morbidity and Mortality among Intravenous Drug Users," *American Journal of Public Health* 79 (October 1989): 1358–62.

19. R.G. Smart, "AIDS and Drug Abuse in Canada," *Journal of Drug Issues* 21 (1) (1991): 73–82.

20. Susan Thorne, "Education the Main Weapon as Prison Officials Defend Against AIDS Threat," *Canadian Medical Association Journal* 146 (4) (1992): 573–80.

21. "The Two Nations Poll," *Maclean's*, 25 June 1990, 50–52.

22. Le Dain Commission, *Interim Report* (Ottawa: Information Canada, 1970), 3.

23. Adlaf et al., *Drug Use Among Ontario Adults, 1977–1991*; Adlaf and Smart, "Drug Use Among Canadian Students"; Johnson et al., "1990 National High School Senior Drug Abuse Survey"; National Institute on Drug Abuse, *National Household Survey*; Health and Welfare Canada, *National Alcohol and Drug Survey*.

24. Hagan, *The Disreputable Pleasures*, 221–29.

25. Bayley, *Managing the Future*, 10.

26. Robert G. Evans, "We'll Take Care of It For You: Health Care in the Canadian Community," *Dædalus* 117 (4) (Fall 1988): 155–89.

27. Robert Solomon and Mel Green, "The First Century: The History of Non-Medical Opiate Use and Control Policies in Canada, 1870–1970," in J. Blackwell and P.G. Erickson, *Illicit Drugs in Canada: A Risky Business* (Toronto: Nelson Canada, 1988), 88–116.

28. Giffen et al., *Panic and Indifference.*

29. Patricia G. Erickson, *Cannabis Criminals: The Social Effects of Punishment on Drug Users* (Toronto: ARF, 1980).

30. Eric Single, "The Impact of Marijuana Decriminalization: An Update," *Journal of Public Health Policy* 10 (4) (Winter 1989): 456–66.

31. E.M. Bryan, "Cannabis in Canada — A Decade of Indecision," *Contemporary Drug Problems* 8 (1979): 169–92; P.J. Giffen and Sylvia Lambert, "What Happened on the Way to Law Reform?" in Blackwell and Erickson, *Illicit Drugs in Canada*, 345–69.

32. Giffen et al., *Panic and Indifference*; and Solomon and Green, "The First Century: The History of Non-Medical Opiate Use and Control Policies in Canada, 1870–1970.

33. Giffen et al., *Panic and Indifference*, 534.

34. Le Dain Commission, *Cannabis* (Ottawa: Information Canada, 1972), 275.

35. Erickson, *Cannabis Criminals.*

36. Ibid., 24–28. Nevertheless, discharges were counted with convictions in official statistics.

37. Ibid., 28–29.

38. P.G. Erickson and G.F. Murray, "Cannabis Criminals Revisited," *British Journal of Addiction* 81 (1) (1986): 81–85.

39. Joan A.E. Moreau, "Selected Statistics on Convictions for Illicit Drug Use in Canada," in Blackwell and Erickson, *Illicit Drugs in Canada*, 449–55.

40. Robert M. Solomon and Sidney J. Upsrich, "Canada's Drug Laws," *Journal of Drug Issues* 21 (1) (1991): 17–40.

41. Jerome H. Skolnick, "The Social Transformation of Vice," *Law and Contemporary Problems* 51 (1) (Winter 1988): 9–29.

42. Giffen et al., *Panic and Indifference*, 149–62.

43. Quoted in Bryan, "Cannabis — A Decade of Indecision," 181.

44. See the Le Dain Commission, *Final Report* (1973); The US National Commission on Marijuana and Drug Abuse, *Marijuana: A Signal of Misunderstanding* (1972); The National Academy of Sciences Committee on Substance Abuse and Habitual Behavior, *An Analysis of Marijuana Policy* (1982); and in the United Kingdom, The Advisory Council on the Misuse of Drugs, *The Effects of Cannabis Use* (British Home Office, 1982).

45. See Erickson, *Cannabis Criminals*, 86–97.

46. E.M. Brecher, *Licit and Illicit Drugs* (Mount Vernon: Consumers Union, 1972); Daniel Glaser, "Interlocking Dualities in Drug Use, Drug Control and Crime," in J.A. Inciardi and C.D. Chambers, eds., *Drugs and the Criminal Justice System* (Beverly Hills: Sage, 1974), 39–56; P. Reuter and M. Kleiman, "Risks and Prices: An Economic Analysis of Drug Enforcement," in M. Tonry and N. Morris, eds., *Crime and Justice: An Annual Review of Research* (Chicago: The University of Chicago Press, 1986), 289–340.

47. This list could be very lengthy, but the point is well illustrated by the contributors to this special issue of *Dædalus*. For recent Canadian contributions to the development of drug policy alternatives, see Bruce Alexander, *Peaceful Measures: Canada's Way Out of the War on Drugs* (Toronto: University of Toronto Press, 1990); Neil Boyd, *High Society: Legal and Illegal Drugs in Canada* (Toronto: Key Porter, 1991); Chester N. Mitchell, *The Drug Solution: Regulating Drugs According to Principles of Efficiency, Justice and Democracy* (Ottawa: Carleton University Press, 1990); and Blackwell and Erickson, "Concluding Remarks: A Risky Business" in *Illicit Drugs in Canada*, 444–48.

48. Patricia G. Erickson, "Living with Prohibition: Regular Cannabis Users, Legal Sanctions and Informal Controls," *International Journal of the Addictions* 24 (3) (1989): 175–88.

49. Daniel Glaser, "The Criminal Law's Nemesis: Drug Control," *American Bar Foundation Research Journal* (1985): 619–26.

50. Patricia G. Erickson, "Past, Current and Future Directions in Canadian Drug Policy," *International Journal of the Addictions* 25 (3/A) (1990): 247–66.

51. Personal communication, February, 1991.

52. Erickson, "Past, Current and Future Directions," 260–61.

53. Office of National Drug Control Policy, *National Drug Control Strategy* (Washington, D.C.: US Government Printing Office, 1989). See also Eric Single, "Canada's Drug Strategy: Does It Matter?" presented at the World Congress of Therapeutic Communities, Montreal, 24 September 1991.

54. Minister of National Health and Welfare, *Canada's Drug Strategy* (Ottawa: Minister of Supply and Services Canada, 1992).

55. RCMP, *National Drug Intelligence Estimate*; Solicitor General of Canada, News Release, 6 April 1992.

56. S.J. Upsrich and R.M. Solomon, "Comment on Bill C-264," *The Journal* 18 (3) (March 1989): 7.

57. The Dubin Inquiry, *Commission of Inquiry into the Use of Drugs and Banned Substances* (Toronto, 1989).

58. The Privacy Commission of Canada, *Drug Testing and Privacy* (Ottawa: Minister of Supply and Services, 1990); "The Prospect of Compulsory Drug Tests," *Globe and Mail*, 31 March 1990, D5.

59. Richard Sutherland, "Mandatory Drug Testing: Boon for Public Safety or Launch of a Witch-Hunt?" *Canadian Medical Association Journal* 146 (7) (1992): 1215–18.

60. R.G. Hann and W.G. Harman, *Predicting General Release Risk for Canadian Penitentiary Inmates* (Ottawa: Solicitor General of Canada, 1992). For a rationale for less severe drug trafficking sentences, see N. Dorn, "Clarifying Policy Options on Drug Trafficking," in P.A. O'Hare, R. Newcombe, A. Matthews, E.C. Buning, and E. Drucker, eds., *The Reduction of Drug-Related Harm* (London: Routledge, 1992).

61. The severe penalties available in the Canadian narcotic laws have always been tempered by broad prosecutorial and judicial discretion to impose less serious charges or sentences. This potential expansion of the political role in lengthening time served in prison goes against this tradition. See also R. Solomon, E. Single, and P. Erickson, "Legal Considerations in Canadian Cannabis Policy," *Canadian Public Policy* 9 (4) (1983): 419–33.

62. P.G. Erickson and Y.W. Cheung, "Drug Crime and Legal Control: Lessons from the Canadian Experience," *Contemporary Drug Problems* (forthcoming); Bob Williams, K. Chang, and M.V. Truong, *Annual Sourcebook* (Toronto: ARF, 1992).

63. "Drug War Gains Credited to Undercover Squad," *The Globe and Mail*, 1 February 1990, A15.

64. Williams et al., *Annual Sourcebook*.

65. RCMP, *National Drug Intelligence Estimate*, 26.

66. Ibid., 53.

67. Hagan, *The Disreputable Pleasures*, 58–59.

68. Lois B. de Fleur, "Biasing Influences on Drug Arrest Records: Implications for Deviance Research," *American Sociological Review* (40) (1975): 88–103; Alfred R. Lindesmith, *The Addict and the Law* (Bloomington: Indiana University Press, 1965); and more recently, the Canadian Centre for Substance Abuse, *Annual Report 1990–91*, quoting Raymond Kendall, the Secretary General of Interpol: "If more resources are put into law enforcement, you will turn up more drugs," 5.

69. For accounts of alternative approaches for the police to adopt, see G. Pearson, "Drugs and Criminal Justice"; L. Zaal, "Police Policy in Amsterdam"; and A. Fraser and M. George, "The Role of Police in Harm Reduction," all in P.A. O'Hare et al., eds., *The Reduction of Drug-Related Harm*.

70. Williams et al., *Annual Sourcebook*.

71. Health and Welfare Canada, "Update of the National Drug Strategy," May 1989, mimeograph.

72. Others have noted that overall, police institutions in Canada have been marked by more professionalism, better salaries, better training, less corruption, and greater political legitimacy than their U.S. counterparts. The tradition of British-style, nonconfrontational policing has been strong in Canada. Law enforcement has not been undermined generally by concerns about disparity in policing and excessive violence. More recently, the growing multicultural composition of the larger cities, and some instances of police violence against minorities, have begun to raise questions about how well the police do represent the communities they serve. Nevertheless, the considerable respect accorded historically to the police has enhanced their credibility as spokesmen in the public discourse about the threat of drugs. See Bayley, *Managing the Future*; and "Canada's American Disease," *The Economist* (30 May 1992): 45.

73. M. Goodstadt, "School-based drug education in North America," *Journal of School Health* 56 (7) (1986): 278–81; John O'Connor and Bill Saunders, "Drug Education: An Appraisal of a Popular Perspective," *The International Journal of the Addictions* 27 (2) (1992): 165–85.

74. Some evaluations have been done, but deal with "knowledge" and "satisfaction" rather than behavioral impacts. See Sandra G. Walker, *Evaluation Report: Victoria Police Drug Abuse Resistance Program* [DARE], 1989, mimeograph.

75. Robert Solomon and Lisa Constantine, "The 'Miami Vice' View of Drugs: Identifying Canada's Real Drug Problems—Alcohol and Tobacco," *International Journal on Drug Policy* 3 (1991): 44–52.

76. R.G. Smart, E.M. Adlaf, and G.W. Walsh, *The Ontario Student Drug Use Survey: Trends Between 1977 and 1991* (Toronto: ARF, 1991), 120–21.

77. P.G. Erickson, "Should Police Teach About Drugs?" *The Sunday Star*, 7 May 1989.

78. E. Single, P.G. Erickson, and J. Skirrow, "Drugs and Public Policy in Canada"; Paper presented at the RAND Conference on American and European Drug Policies: Comparative Perspectives, Washington, D.C., 6–7 May 1991.

79. C. Reinarman and H.G. Levine, "The Crack Attack: Politics and Media in America's Latest Drug Scare," in J. Best, ed., *Images and Issues: Current Perspectives on Social Problems* (New York: Aldine de Gruyer, 1989); The New Yorker, 1 January 1990, 21–22.

80. R.L. Akers, "Addiction; The Troublesome Concept," *Journal of Drug Issues* 21 (4) (1991): 777–92.

81. Single et al., "Drugs and Public Policy in Canada"; and Erickson et al., *The Steel Drug*, 63.

82. Smart et al., *The Ontario Student Drug Use Survey*, 80–81; and Adlaf, et al., *Drug Use Among Ontario Adults*, 42–43.

83. P. Erickson et al., *The Steel Drug*; Y.W. Cheung and P.G. Erickson, "Crack Use in Canada: A Distant American Cousin," in C. Reinarman and H.G. Levine, eds., *Crack in Context: Myths, Realities and Social Policies* (forthcoming); and Y.W. Cheung, P.G. Erickson, and T.C. Landau, "Experience of Crack Use: Findings from a Community-Based Sample in Toronto," *Journal of Drug Issues* 21 (1) (1991): 121–40.

84. See E. Goode, "The American Drug Panic of the 1980s: social Construction or Objective Threat?" *The International Journal of the Addictions* 26 (9) (1990): 1083–98; and D.B. Heath, "Prohibition or Liberalization of Alcohol and Drugs," in M. Galanter, *Recent Developments in Alcoholism*, vol. 10 (New York: Plenum, 1992) 129–45.

85. Giffen et al., *Panic and Indifference*, 81–86; 576–77.

86. Judith Blackwell, "Discourses on Drug Use: The Social Construction of a Steroid Scandal," *Journal of Drug Issues* 21 (1) (1991): 147–64.

87. Originally broadcast on the CBC, 24 November 1991.

88. Beatty, "Drug Issues: A Canadian Perspective," 4, emphasis added.

89. RCMP, *National Drug Intelligence Estimate*, 4.

90. Single et al., "Drugs and Public Policy in Canada"; and Jan Skirrow, "A Lesson from the Thymus Gland," *The Journal* 21 (2) (April/May 1992): 9.

91. Jan Skirrow, "Epilogue," in Giffen et al., *Panic and Indifference*, 584–85.
92. The same budget that gave Canada's Drug Strategy a further five year lease on life also eliminated over twenty scientific and scholarly policy advisory groups funded by the federal government, including the Law Reform Commission of Canada.
93. Benoit Bouchard, Speech on the Renewal of Canada's Drug Strategy, 31 March 1992.
94. Doug Lewis, Speech on the Renewal of Canada's Drug Strategy, 6 April 1992.
95. Cost-benefit analysis and research findings in general seem most useful to politicians in buttressing the positions that they have already decided to take. Social science research seems destined to be ignored in the drug policy area, at least for the time being, much as it was in the arena of alcohol policy. See Robin Room, "Social Science Research and Alcohol Policy making," in Paul Roman, ed., *Alcohol: the Development of Sociological Perspectives on Use and Abuse* (New Brunswick: Rutger's Center of Alcohol Studies, 1991).
96. Robert McCoun, "What Harms Do Harm Reduction Strategies Reduce? A Cross-National Study of Heroin Addiction," keynote address presented at the Third Annual Conference on Harm Reduction, Melbourne, Australia, 23 March 1992.
97. Thomas Sowell, *Compassion v. Guilt and Other Essays* (New York: William Morrow, 1987).
98. CCSA, *Annual Report* 1990–91.
99. The exchange occurred in a plenary session of the Third International Conference on the Reduction of Drug-Related Harm, Melbourne, Australia, 23–27 March 1992. Various sessions at the meeting also highlighted these Australian examples.
100. John Ashton and Howard Seymour, *The New Public Health* (Milton Keynes: Open University Press, 1988); and P. O'Hare et al., eds., *The Reduction of Drug Related Harm*.
101. P.H.M. Lohman, K. Sankaranarayanan, and J. Ashby, "Choosing the Limits of Life," *Nature* 357 (21 May 1992): 185–86; and Patricia G. Erickson, "A Public Health Approach to Demand Reduction," *Journal of Drug Issues* 20 (4) (1990): 563–75.
102. B. Rowe, R. Milner, C. Johnson, and G. Bota, "Snowmobile-related deaths in Ontario: A 5-year Review," *Canadian Medical Association Journal* 146 (1992): 147–52; and Chief Coroner's Office of Ontario, 1991.
103. Giffen et al., *Panic and Indifference*.

SIXTEEN

....

Time to Legalize Prostitution

E. NICK LARSEN

The 1989 Supreme Court of Canada decision affirming the constitutional validity of Canada's prostitution law has proved to be somewhat of a legal non-event. Popularly referred to as Bill C-49, Canada's most recent street prostitution legislation developed out of the political furor surrounding the existence of rampant street prostitution in Canada's largest cities during the late 1970s and early 1980s. While the origins and extent of this prostitution problem are still debated by academics, politicians, and police officials, there is little doubt that Bill C-49 represents one of the toughest approaches to prostitution control in western societies. This legislation

....

Source: E. Nick Larsen, "Time to Legalize Prostitution," *Policy Options*, 13, 7 (1992): 21–22. Reproduced by permission of *Policy Options*.

effectively criminalizes all public communication for the purposes of prostitution whether it is verbal, written, or by gestures. Despite its tough provisions, however, there is little doubt that Bill C-49 is ineffective at controlling street prostitution, a fact that has been confirmed by the Ministry of Justice's own evaluation of the law, as well as by several independent assessments. This documented ineffectiveness of the law makes the question of its constitutional validity somewhat irrelevant. It also makes it imperative that Canada rethink its position on the legal status of prostitution one more time.

The most paradoxical aspect of Canadian prostitution law is the fact that prostitution itself is legal but that it is virtually impossible to carry it out without committing a criminal offence. This point has been noted repeatedly by academics and other socio-legal analysts, but for some inexplicable reason it has failed to be seriously addressed in the numerous attempts to amend Canadian prostitution laws over the past three decades (including the repeal of the vagrancy provisions in 1972). The illogicality implicit in prohibiting almost all aspects of a legal activity, including the practice of a legal occupation, constitutes sufficient reason in itself for conducting a serious re-assessment of exactly what we are attempting to accomplish with our prostitution laws. If our goal is the suppression of prostitution, then the continued legality of the activity cannot be justified.

On the other hand, if we merely wish to regulate prostitution so as to protect the "public interest," then we must consider whether there are better ways of doing so without resorting to the criminal law. In this respect, prostitution is one of the few "legal" occupations that is covered by the provisions of the Criminal Code.

The intent of this brief article is to outline some of the reasons why stricter criminal laws will simply not work and to discuss several recommendations for implementing a non-criminal approach to prostitution control.

The first point that is crucial to understanding why criminal laws are doomed to fail centres around the motivation of engaging in prostitution. Most of the research conducted on this issue indicates that the ranks of prostitutes are almost overwhelmingly comprised of economically deprived women and juveniles (both males and females) who have suffered a history of physical and sexual abuse. These people enter prostitution out of dire financial need and for many it represents their only real means of survival (in their eyes, at least).

Without being melodramatic, it can be argued that many prostitutes are so desperate that they are unlikely to be deterred by a summary conviction offence, and indeed most have long records for repeat offences. While many people in the recent prostitution debate advocated that the courts impose jail sentences on repeat offenders, this approach would likely simply increase jail populations without reducing prostitution levels to any significant degree. In any event, recent opinion polls cited in the media indicate that the Canadian public does not favor overly harsh penalties for prostitution.

Another argument against employing stricter criminal sanctions against prostitution is that they would likely force prostitutes to adopt potentially riskier working styles. While Bill C-49 has not been effective in reducing the levels of prostitution, there is some evidence to suggest that it has resulted in increased numbers of murders and serious assaults against prostitutes. This has occurred because prostitutes have moved off the main thoroughfares onto poorly lighted lanes and side streets, and in some cases have taken to hitchhiking as a means of attracting potential clients. Both alternatives have reduced their ability to screen potential clients before entering their cars where they are at most risk. In a similar vein, the law has been successful at deterring the more "respectable" customers from frequenting the prostitution strolls and the dearth of customers has forced some prostitutes to accept customers they would otherwise reject.

One final argument against stricter criminal sanctions revolves around the role played by male ancillary players in the prostitution trade. Historical research has reiterated time and again that crackdowns on prostitution have inevitably driven prostitutes underground and were accompanied by increases in pimping and procuring activities. Inasmuch as pimping and procuring involve exploitive relationships in which males dominate female prostitutes through violence and extortion, these activities ought to be discouraged as much as possible. In terms of the recent prostitution debate, pimping activities declined after the infamous Hutt decision prompted many prostitutes to turn their pimps in to the police. Unfortunately, pimping quickly resurged after Bill C-49 was implemented. This being the case, it seems obvious that even tougher laws aimed at prostitutes would simply exacerbate the current situation in which pimps control most of the prostitution activity in many Canadian cities.

In light of the above points, it appears that it is time for the federal government to seriously consider a non-criminal approach to controlling prostitution, and the following recommendations are made with respect to implementing such an approach. (It should be noted that these recommendations are also based on an independent evaluation of the implementation of Bill C-49 in Vancouver, Edmonton, Winnipeg, and Toronto.)

1. It is recommended that most prostitution-related offences be removed from the Criminal Code and dealt with by means of regulatory statutes similar to those used to control other businesses. This represents a general statement of principle and is intended to be qualified by the more specific points that follow.

2. It is recommended that the bawdy house provisions in the Criminal Code be repealed and that prostitutes be allowed to operate legally in fixed locations as long as their activities do not contravene other statutes, i.e., noise by-laws, etc. It is worth noting that a similar recommendation made by the Fraser Committee was rejected by Justice Minister John Crosbie, who argued that prostitutes would probably use their apartments to service clients picked up on the street, and thus it would do little to reduce the nuisance associated with street prostitution. It was also argued that bawdy houses are uncommon even though they are rarely prosecuted, and that this indicated that most prostitutes prefer to work on the street. These arguments are considered invalid because they neglect to consider the fact that prostitutes cannot currently advertise the location of bawdy houses to attract clients. In this respect, many prostitutes (interviewed in the independent evaluation referred to above) have suggested that they would prefer to be off the street if they could only be assured of a sufficient supply of customers. Thus, it is logical to suggest that bawdy houses might well become much more common if they were legal, and this would reduce the nuisance of street prostitution.

3. It is recommended that provincial and municipal governments be empowered to establish legal prostitution areas under the same zoning laws as are used to regulate land use in general. Opponents of this approach argue that legal "red

light areas" would be unwelcome anywhere, and that it would be impossible to find suitable areas for legalized street prostitution. They further argue that there would still be problems with prostitutes who refused to stay within the prescribed boundaries. While there is some validity to these concerns, the fact remains that this approach has been used successfully in several European countries for many years. In any event, there are ways of mitigating these concerns, including tax concessions and compensation to residents and business owners in designated areas. Further, it would be a simpler matter to deal with prostitutes who operate outside the legal area since it could be made a strict liability "civil" offence. The fact that the Calgary bylaw and the Vancouver injunction were so successful suggests that a civil approach to the problem would work as long as prostitutes are given areas where they can legally work. Once again, most of the prostitutes interviewed in the above mentioned research stated that they would be only too willing to obey zoning regulations as long as suitable areas were provided for their use.

4. It is recommended that cities that establish legal prostitution areas be required to establish prostitution committees comprised of representatives from residents, business owners, police officials, politicians, and prostitutes. The function of these committees would be to monitor the prostitution trade and liaise among the various groups to identify and resolve possible problems before they become serious. This approach was used successfully in the Strathcona area of Vancouver in the late 1980s, and to a lesser extent was practiced in Edmonton and Ottawa with good results. The key variable, however, is the inclusion of prostitutes. Similar police–citizen committees in Toronto and the Mount Pleasant area of Vancouver, which did not include prostitutes, were much less successful at solving the problem.

The above recommendations represent the minimum changes that are needed to successfully implement a non-criminal approach to prostitution.

There are areas that should remain subject to criminal sanctions, including pimping and patronizing juvenile prostitutes. In the latter case, decriminalizing adult prostitution might make it easier to identify and apprehend juvenile prostitutes, since there is some reason to expect that adult prostitutes might cooperate with police and child welfare authorities in order to remove juveniles from the strolls.

While many of the above recommendations have been advocated, and even experimented with in the past, they have yet to be implemented in a serious, systematic fashion.

In closing this discussion, it is important to reiterate the need to consult the prostitutes and encourage a process of dialogue between them and other affected groups. This approach, combined with the other changes recommended above, might well mean that Canada will not have to amend its prostitution laws again.

PART FIVE
Prison and Its Alternatives

Canadian corrections has undergone significant change in the last few years, at least partly as a result of growing concern over public safety fuelled by a number of serious crime incidents involving prisoners or offenders under community supervision (Adams, 1990). Various government reports, consultations (Solicitor General Canada, 1990), and legislative initiatives have led to changes in the structure and operations of the correctional system. Some victims' rights groups have lobbied hard for increased penalties, more stringent screening for conditional releases, and a greater emphasis upon public safety in the operation of the correctional system. There has also been a significant increase in the total correctional population (federal, provincial, probation, and conditional release), up 44 percent from a decade ago (Centre for Justice Statistics, 1997). Correctional agencies have been forced to become more accountable due to such factors as their large operational costs, rising crime rates, increased fear of crime, and the requirements of the Charter of Rights and Freedoms (Griffiths and Verdun-Jones, 1994).

A major source of the difficulties experienced by corrections is the conflicting goals of sentencing we reviewed in Part Two. The correctional service is charged with the task of carrying out the sentence imposed by the court, a sentence that may attempt to incorporate several diverse goals such as retribution, incapacitation, and rehabilitation. The challenge is stated explicitly in the major recent legislation governing corrections, the Corrections and Conditional Release Act of 1992. The Act states that the purpose of federal corrections is to contribute to the maintenance of a just, peaceful, and safe society by: carrying out sentences imposed by the courts through the safe and humane custody and supervision of offenders; and assisting the rehabilitation of offenders and their reintegration into the community as law-abiding citizens through the provision of programs in penitentiaries and in the community.

The same kind of tension concerning goals can be found with respect to conditional release programs. Most offenders serving sentences of imprisonment will eventually be released back into the community. Parole represents a gradual, controlled, and supported release of offenders to help them reintegrate into society as law-abiding citizens. However, the Corrections and Conditional Release Act states as the first principle applicable to boards of parole that protection of society is the most important consideration in any conditional release decision. Another of the six principles directs parole boards to make the least restrictive decision consistent with the protection of society.

Ekstedt and Griffiths (1988) identify six periods of correctional philosophy in Canada according to the relative emphasis upon different goals. In recent years a "rehabilitation era" (1938–70), in which a treatment orientation prevailed, was replaced by a "reintegration era" (1970–78), stressing the value of community corrections and concern for the effectiveness of treatment programs. These authors label the period since 1978 "reparation," which constitutes a return to the punishment objective, with an increasing emphasis on victims and offender responsibility.

The rehabilitative goal came under a general cloud of suspicion with the publication of Martinson's (1974) review of over 200 evaluations of correctional treatment programs. The conclusion that "nothing works" in correctional treatment contributed to the decline of the rehabilitation model in U.S. and Canadian correctional practice in the late 1960s and early 1970s (Griffiths and Verdun-Jones, 1994) and led to the shift back towards the increased use of sanctions as the means for crime control (Bonta, 1997). However, this conclusion remains controversial (Doob and Brodeur, 1989; Gendreau and Andrews, 1990; Lab and Whitehead, 1990). A recent report to Solicitor General Canada (Bonta, 1997) concludes that direct treatment services are more likely to reduce recidivism, and thus enhance community safety, than are criminal sanctions. The report claims that effective treatment programs are those that: match the intensity of treatment services to the risk of the offender; target the criminogenic needs of the offender; and use cognitive-behavioural interventions.

A federal Task Force (1977) proposed the opportunities model of correctional programs in which the Correctional Service provides programs and services for offenders but where it is the responsibility of the offender to take advantage of these. Several core programs have subsequently been developed since a majority of offenders have needs in one or more of such areas as: living skills (including parenting, anger and emotion control, and problem-solving); substance abuse intervention; sex offender treatment; family violence programs; literacy, educational, and vocational/trades training. In the 1990s federal correctional practice appears to be based on a mixture of providing program opportunities, control of offenders, with perhaps some remnants of the rehabilitation model (Griffiths and Verdun-Jones, 1994). Assisting offenders to live law-abiding lives in the community also contributes to the number one goal of the criminal justice system — the protection of society (Solicitor General Canada, 1996).

Current incarceration rates in Canada are high by international standards. At 133 per 100,000 population the Canadian rate is higher than most western democracies other than the United States (600 per 100,000) (Solicitor General Canada, 1997a). The federal inmate population has increased 27 percent since 1986–1987 and is expected to grow further in the next few years (Canadian Centre for Justice Statistics, 1997). The number of admissions to federal and provincial institutions in 1995–1996 declined 4 percent from the previous year but is still 25 percent higher than ten years ago. A number of factors have contributed to this increase, including longer sentences, an accumulation of "lifers" in penitentiaries since the abolition of capital punishment and the requirement to serve lengthy sentences before parole eligibility, and the increasing use, under the terms of the Corrections and Conditional Release Act of 1992, of detention for the entire duration of the sentences of certain offenders believed to be a danger to society. Subsequent legislation (Bill C-45 and Bill C-55) will likely also contribute to an increase in the federal inmate population by requiring all repeat offenders to serve at least one-third of any new consecutive sentence before parole eligibility, and requiring judges to give an indefinite sentence to those classified as a Dangerous Offender.

But incarceration is expensive. The average cost of keeping an offender in a federal penitentiary is nearly $46,000 per year. This compares to about $27,000 for a halfway house or $9,000 to supervise an inmate on parole (Solicitor General Canada, 1997a). As a consequence, the Federal Government has recognized that other methods of dealing with lower-risk offenders must be considered. "Building more prison cells to lock up more people for longer periods of time is not an effective response or a greater guarantee for safer communities (Solicitor General Canada, 1997a). This is recognized in Bill C-41, an Act to Amend the Criminal Code (Sentencing) proclaimed into law in the fall of 1996 where it is stated that a further objective of sentencing is to promote the use of alternatives to imprisonment where appropriate. This Act requires courts to consider all available options to imprisonment where appropriate, and to consider imprisonment if no other course of action will ensure the protection of society. It also allows the use of alternate measures such as restitution for minor offences.

In addition, Bill C-55 amended the Corrections and Conditional Release Act to allow for an earlier day parole review for low-risk, non-violent offenders.

In fact, the majority of federal and provincial offenders are under some form of community supervision — in 1995–96, 77 percent of the total correctional case-load — but only 12 percent of total correctional operating expenditures were for these services (Canadian Centre for Justice Statistics, 1997). The total community supervised population has increased by 50 percent since 1986–87. Community pro-grams include diversion and probation, as well as several forms of conditional release — the planned and gradual release of inmates back into the community. The Corrections and Conditional Release Act sets out five types of conditional release for federal offenders: temporary absences, work release, day parole, full parole, and statutory release (which allows most federal offenders not granted parole to serve the final one-third of their sentence in the community under supervision). Since almost all inmates will eventually return to the community, gradual release under supervi-sion reduces the likelihood of offenders committing another crime and provides a better environment for rehabilitation and reintegration of the offender. On average, approximately 72 percent of those released on full parole successfully complete their sentence in the community without committing a new offence or breaking the condi-tions of their release (Solicitor General, 1997b). However, the longer term effective-ness of community-based corrections programs in reducing recidivism is more diffi-cult to evaluate since usually the lower-risk offenders are selected for these programs. For example, many successful low-risk offenders placed in diversion programs or on probation would probably rehabilitate themselves on their own (Walker, 1994). Furthermore, there is controversy about whether such programs merely expand the net of social control by subjecting to official supervision low-risk, minor offenders who would otherwise have been screened out of the system or not given a sentence of incarceration.

As part of the effort to limit the use of imprisonment, a new set of community programs has been developed called intermediate sanctions. Examples of such pro-grams include intensive probation supervision, home confinement, electronic moni-toring, and shock incarceration. Since these programs emphasize restrictions on offenders to control their behaviour, it is questionable whether such sanctions consti-tute treatment. A recent review of such programs concluded that they are unlikely to deter criminal behaviour more effectively than regular probation or prison place-ments (Cullen et al., 1996).

READINGS

Female and Aboriginal offenders are two categories that have seen a good deal of policy discussion and change in recent years. In Reading Seventeen Moffat briefly identifies the different issues regarding female offenders, provides a statistical profile of them, and outlines the history of the Kingston Prison for Women. She argues that successive reports on incarcerated women in Canada have identified the same issues and solutions, but that the struggle for adequate programming and equal treatment has been met with apathy and neglect. She then focusses on the recommendations and conclusions of the 1990 report of the Task Force on federally sentenced women. This Task Force attempted to integrate the interests and concerns of a vari-ety of groups, including inmates at the Prison for Women. Moffat discusses how the research for the Report was driven by a "women-centered approach" and relied heavily upon qualitative information obtained from inmates. She outlines the Report's major recommendations, including the closure of the Prison for Women and the construction of four small regional facilities and an Aboriginal "healing lodge," and discusses some of the difficulties to be anticipated in their implementation. The article concludes by reiterating the fundamental sexism of our society reflected in the penal system and the need to recognize the distinctive life experiences of women prisoners.

In Reading Eighteen Nielsen analyzes changing correctional policies toward Aboriginal offenders using the concept of problem populations. She argues that Aboriginals were originally viewed as "social junk"—a costly yet relatively harmless burden to society. However, correctional staff have increasingly perceived them as "social dynamite"—those who have the potential to actively call into question established relationships. "Social dynamite" is more youthful, alienated, and politically volatile. This change in perception has led to changes in correctional control tactics. Nielsen discusses the various changes in correctional policy, programming initiatives, fact-finding task forces, and increased accuracy in inmate enumeration that she claims resulted from this changed perception. However, she concludes that the relations between Aboriginal inmates and correctional staff will remain volatile until the underlying social, economic, and political causes of Aboriginal involvement in the criminal justice system are addressed.

Reading Nineteen focusses on the overuse of imprisonment as a penal sanction and the substitution of community sanctions for many offenders currently imprisoned. Doob argues that in spite of the apparent consensus to de-emphasize imprisonment, we have not managed to substitute community sanctions due to the failure to develop a coherent sentencing policy. In considering this issue he reviews evidence that suggests that expanding the range of sentencing alternatives to include community alternatives is not inevitably only a supplement rather than a replacement for imprisonment, as some have claimed. However, it is necessary to adopt specific policies to ensure that alternatives to imprisonment work as alternatives rather than mere supplements. He suggests several necessary policy changes for community sanctions to become sanctions in their own right and not merely "alternatives": enactment by Parliament of a coherent sentencing policy that endorses the use of community sanctions; a method of providing authoritative and unambiguous guidance on sentencing to judges; and development of a program of well-run community sanctions.

The next reading examines one specific community sanction, house arrest with electronic monitoring, one of several so-called intermediate sanctions between imprisonment and probation/parole. Mainprize is concerned with two issues: the cost effectiveness of electronic monitoring and its potential for widening the net of social control. The two issues are closely connected since, to the extent that community sanctions do not divert offenders otherwise headed for terms of imprisonment, they broaden the net of social control and, in the process, increase correctional expenditures. While Mainprize concludes that it is premature to determine if offender net-widening has been occurring, the number of correctional personnel did increase, which raises doubts concerning cost effectiveness.

McMahon challenges the conventional critical literature on community corrections that claims that the development of community alternatives necessarily widens the net of penal control. She first reviews the development of the concept of net-widening in the critical criminology literature. This literature is pessimistic regarding the possibility of penal reform, arguing that it could have little impact on the inherently repressive tendencies of the criminal justice system. McMahon then subjects the Canadian research on community alternatives to critical analysis, challenging the contention that no decrease in imprisonment has accompanied the development of alternatives.

The final paper in this section examines the policy debates regarding the future of parole in Canada. Brodeur identifies two issues in this debate: the security issue of whether parole is detrimental to community safety; and the structural issue of the widening gap between how the criminal justice system appears in legislation and documents and the reality of what actually happens, undermining penal system credibility. The balance of the article deals with the latter issue. Brodeur first argues that the debate about parole raises real questions concerning whether we should have a determinate or indeterminate system of sentencing, and the meaning of custody. He claims the National Parole Board has tried to minimize the significance of these questions. He then states that the current rationale for parole — the need to protect the public — is at odds with parole's essential characteristic of early release of offenders. This discrepancy, in his view, contributes to a further widening of the gap between the theory and the reality of the criminal justice system. Thirdly, he contrasts sentencing with parole. Insofar as it gives priority to the pragmatic concern of risk assessment, which can legitimately take any factor into account, parole may conflict with sentencing, which rests on a moral foundation and is constrained by values and rights. The retention of parole may also unintentionally contribute to an acceleration of the movement towards an increased use of more punitive intermediate sanctions, e.g., placing all released inmates under intensive electronic surveillance. Brodeur concludes that the current alleged reform of parole is actually a strategy of slow attrition that will eventually amount to its abolition, but without any compensatory and comprehensive reform of sentencing.

QUESTIONS FOR DISCUSSION

1. What are the problems likely to be encountered in implementing the policies recommended by *Creating Choices*?
2. Should the penal system provide equal treatment for female and male inmates? Aboriginal and non-Aboriginal inmates?
3. Discuss Doob's claim that community sanctions should not be alternatives to imprisonment but sanctions in their own right. What obstacles are there to the adoption and implementation of this policy?
4. Discuss how the concepts of net-widening and cost effectiveness are closely connected in the new intermediate punishment programs.
5. Describe the methodological, theoretical, and political problems that lead McMahon to conclude that the concept of net-widening should be considered problematic.
6. What are some of the intended and unintended consequences of current policy and practice concerning parole? Should parole be abolished? If so, with what should it be replaced?

REFERENCES

Adams, M. 1990. "Canadian attitudes toward crime and justice." *Forum on Corrections Research* 2:10–13.

Bonta, James. 1997. Offender Rehabilitation. Ottawa: Public Works and Government Services Canada.

Canadian Centre for Justice Statistics. 1997. Adult Correctional Services in Canada, 1995–96. Ottawa: Minister of Industry.

Cullen, Francis T., J.P. Wright, and B.K. Applegate. 1996. "Control in the community." Pp. 69–116 in A.T. Harland (ed.), Choosing Correctional Options That Work. Thousand Oaks, CA: Sage.

Doob, Anthony N. and J.P. Brodeur. 1989. "Rehabilitating the debate on rehabilitation." Canadian Journal of Criminology 31:170–192.

Ekstedt, John W. and Curt T. Griffiths. 1988. Corrections in Canada. Toronto: Butterworths.

Gendreau, Paul and D.A. Andrews. 1990. "Tertiary prevention." Canadian Journal of Criminology 32:173–184.

Griffiths, Curt T. and Simon N. Verdun-Jones. 1994. Canadian Criminal Justice. Toronto: Harcourt Brace Canada.

Lab, Stephen P. and J.T. Whitehead. 1990. "From 'nothing works' to the 'appropriate works'." Criminology 28:405–416.

Martinson, Robert M. 1974. "What works? Questions and answers about prison reform." The Public Interest 35:22–54.

Solicitor General Canada. 1990. Directions for Reform: Corrections and Conditional Release. Ottawa: Minister of Supply and Services Canada.

———. 1996. "Offender rehabilitation." Ottawa: World Wide Web Home Page.

———. 1997a. "Prison overcrowding." Ottawa: World Wide Web Home Page.

———. 1997b. "Conditional release." Ottawa: World Wide Web Home Page.

Task Force on the Creation of an Integrated Canadian Corrections Service. 1977. The Role of Federal Corrections in Canada. Ottawa: Supply and Services Canada.

Walker, Samuel. 1994. Sense and Nonsense about Crime and Drugs. Belmont, California: Wadsworth.

SEVENTEEN

....

Creating Choices or Repeating History: Canadian Female Offenders and Correctional Reform

KELLY (HANNAH) MOFFAT

The treatment of women in the criminal-justice system has been scrutinized and vigorously debated over the last two decades. Authors have repeatedly argued that paternalistic and patriarchal attitudes have dominated criminological research and penal policy; one well-documented consequence of this dominance has been

....

Source: Kelly (Hannah) Moffat, "Creating Choices or Repeating History: Canadian Female Offenders and Correctional Reform," Social Justice, 18, 3 (1991): 1984–2003. Reproduced by permission of Social Justice.

inferior and sexist programming afforded to female inmates (Sargent, 1985; Edwards, 1989; Feinman, 1980; Berzins and Cooper, 1982; Carlen, 1988; Adelberg and Currie, 1987; Morris, 1987). It has also been argued that criminology, like most academic disciplines, is primarily concerned with the activities and interests of men and thus focused away from women and areas of concern to women (Morris, 1987: 1). Female offenders have been systematically ignored by criminological researchers and correctional planners who have focused their attention, money, and program efforts on male offenders. Correctional programs for women are largely unsatisfactory and inferior in quantity, quality, and variety to those for male offenders. However, the recent increase in women's involvement in correctional administration, criminology, and private organizations has resulted in greater acknowledgement and awareness of female offenders and their dilemmas.

In Canada, the struggle by women prisoners for adequate programming and substantive equality is entrenched in a history of apathy and neglect. Correctional planning for women has been categorized as an "afterthought," since women often represent only a small fraction of the total inmate population (Ross and Fabiano, 1985). Our knowledge of the female offender is inadequate and incomplete. Research on female offenders often reiterates the plight of imprisoned women without offering feasible and meaningful alternatives.

This article examines attempts to close the Canadian Federal Prison for Women in Kingston, Ontario, and the most recent attempt to restructure federal women's imprisonment. In so doing, my primary focus will be on the recommendations and conclusions of the 1990 report entitled *Creating Choices* by a Task Force on federally sentenced women. The research methods and the political uniqueness of the Task Force will be discussed. To put this analysis in context, I briefly outline the history of the Prison for Women, which demonstrates the primary problems and inadequacies of the current system. A statistical profile of Canadian female offenders is also included. Finally, practical difficulties with some of the Task Force recommendations are outlined along with areas for further research.

CANADIAN WOMEN IN CONFLICT WITH THE LAW

Women comprise a small minority of those who come into conflict with the law.[1] However, those who do offend tend to be young, poor, under-educated, unskilled, and drug or alcohol dependent. A large number of women in prison have reported that they have been victims of physical and sexual abuse,[2] and many are emotionally or financially dependent on abusive male partners (Adelberg and Currie, 1987). In Canada, the *Badgley Report* found an association between child sexual abuse and future prostitution. Similarly, an unpublished study shows that 52 percent of the women in a sample of inmates reported being sexually abused as children and estimates put the proportion as high as 80 percent to 85 percent (Axon, 1989: 25). In addition, an increasing number of women inmates tend to be single parents. Researchers suggest that 30 percent to 40 percent of convicted women are caring for children at the time of their incarceration, and that 50 percent to 70 percent of all incarcerated women have had at least one child.

A disproportionate number of these women tend to be Native. Native women make up about 20 percent of federally sentenced women although they represent only 3 percent of Canada's total female population. The types of offenses committed by Native women are different from those committed by non-Native women. The report of a recent Task Force (1990) on the criminal-justice system and its impact on the Indian and Metis People of Alberta indicates that violent offenses and offenses against persons accounted for a higher portion (67.4 percent) of Native female federal-offender admissions than of non-Native female federal-offender admissions (31.5 percent). Aboriginal offenders often experience racism, discrimination, and a devaluation of their culture that is intensified and complicated by their interaction with the law. It seems that the high rate of criminalization of Native women is clearly linked to their bleak socioeconomic profiles (Johnson, 1987: 39).

According to *Statistics Canada 1989*, women accounted for 15 percent of all criminal charges laid. If convicted and sentenced to a period of less than two years, women offenders would serve their sentence in a provincial correctional facility. According to Ontario Ministry of Correctional Services, in 1988–1989 approximately 8.5 percent of the people admitted to provincial jails and detention centers were female. If sentenced to two years or more, convicted women are required to serve their time in a federal penitentiary. Women who are sentenced to two years or more are sent to the Prison for Women in Kingston, Ontario — the only federal institution for women in Canada. Correctional Services Canada reports that as of March 1989 there were 285 women serving federal sentences in institutions, compared with 13,066 men, indicating that only about 2 percent of people serving federal time are women. It has been suggested that the lower rates of incarceration for women may be related to the comparatively minor nature of their offenses, their shorter criminal histories, and the often ancillary role that women play to men in serious crimes (*Ibid.*: 33–34). Likewise, the lack of alternatives to the Prison for Women may influence the length of women's sentences.

Federal/provincial exchange of service agreements allows some female inmates, while under federal jurisdiction, to serve their sentences in provincial institutions so that they may be closer to their families and community. Approximately 40 percent of all federally sentenced women use this option. Participation in exchange of service agreements is based on sentence length, severity of offense, and the personality of the offender. Some provinces refuse to take women serving more than five years (Saskatchewan, Manitoba) or more than 10 years (Alberta, British Columbia). Unfortunately, the programs and facilities available in provincial institutions are designed for short-term inmates, and as a result they cannot satisfy the needs of federally sentenced women. There is a wide gap between the level of services available at the Prison for Women versus that available at provincial facilities. Despite the inadequacies in programming, these agreements are the only alternative to the Prison for Women. The program location choices imposed by current exchange of service agreements is further complicated by the fact that most provincial jurisdictions have only one facility for women (*Creating Choices*, 1990: 78). Initially, these agreements were designed to accommodate Canada's unique geographical features, which include the enormous size of the land mass, and a relatively sparse and scattered population with significant cultural and language differences.

Another difficulty with these agreements is that they are not equally available to all federally sentenced women. MacLeod (1986: 54–55) notes that there is an uneven geographical distribution of these agreements, which puts women from certain parts of the country at a disadvantage. She further suggests that this imbalance in distribution has existed since the inception of exchange of service agreements.

Between 1975 and 1984, 60 percent of the female federal inmates serving their sentences in provincial institutions were serving them in Quebec, another one-third were in Alberta or British Columbia, and only one percent were incarcerated in the Atlantic provinces (*Ibid.*). One explanation for this inequity is the existence of a formal agreement allowing French-speaking federal female prisoners to reside at Maison Tanguary, in Montreal, Quebec, to ensure the provision of French-language staff and services (Hatch and Faith, 1990: 453).

This research, like most on incarcerated women in Canada, focuses on the federal system. Historically, there has been a major concern about what to do with federally sentenced women. Debates have generally concentrated on centralization of prisons for women in one institution versus the decentralization of services. Despite various recommendations for dispersion, a decision was made in the early 1920s to build one central institution for women (Berzins and Cooper, 1982: 402). Since the construction of this facility, several task forces and Royal Commissions have indicated a preference for decentralized services for federal women prisoners. Likewise, there seems to be continuing confusion and disagreement among correctional administrators, community organizations, and the government concerning the needs of the female offender. Not until the most recent Task Force *Creating Choices* (1990) has anyone seriously bothered to investigate women prisoners' perceptions of their needs. For the most part, reforms, methods, techniques, and ideologies of prison management in women's institutions have been predominantly associated with particular views as to women's "proper place" in society (Reid, 1985: 129). Increasingly, it is being recognized that women, although underrepresented in the criminal-justice system, are overrepresented in the welfare and mental-health system as well as in programs for victims of violence. As a result, penal regimes for women cannot function in isolation from other community and social services if they are to adequately evaluate and satisfy the needs of female offenders. The Task Force on federally sentenced women (*Creating Choices*, 1990) is one of the first formal government recognitions of these realities of women's lives. The members of this Task Force made a conscious effort to deal with the social circumstances that often contribute to women's criminal behavior. Their report states:

> Women in Canada, and in other Western nations, live in inequalities flowing from traditions and values which emphasize their dependency on men and institutions. As well, the discrimination within discrimination experienced by Aboriginal women in this social reality is also ignored in the past understanding of the problem (*Ibid.*: 73).

The Task Force supported the belief that:

> Women in prison have more in common with other women than they do with male inmates, and that programs and services should be designed to meet local needs and circumstances, or planned individually, not on the basis of some centralized blueprint (Shaw, 1989: 11, in *Creating Choices*, 1990: 82).

In the following discussion it will become increasingly evident that women prisoners have been, and continue to be, the victims of outright discrimination when it comes to providing them with meaningful services, programs, and accommodations. Consequently, it has been asserted that we must ensure that "the remedies formulated can be realistically expected to counteract, in substance, and over the long range, the conditions that discriminate against women in the federal prison system" (Berzins and Cooper, 1982: 400).

THE PRISON FOR WOMEN

Penal regimes for women have constituted a curious amalgamation of stereotypical views about women and both humane and inhumane treatments and reforms.[3] Canada's treatment of female offenders reveals a:

> fascinating mixture of neglect, outright barbarism, and well-meaning paternalism. Because of their small numbers and the insignificance attached to their crimes, women offenders have been housed wherever and in whatever manner suited the needs of the larger male population (Cooper, 1987: 127).

Before the construction of the Prison for Women, federal female offenders were usually held in temporary quarters in male prisons where they had little or no access to programs or services. Cooper (1987) indicates that such arrangements often led to abuse and mistreatment. The Brown Commission (1848–1849) noted in its report that the women housed in Kingston Penitentiary for men were often physically, emotionally, and sexually abused by both staff and other inmates, and that the women's section was overrun with insects.

> The sleeping cells were frightfully over-run with bugs, especially in the spring of 1846; women used to sweep them out with a broom. It was so very bad that on one occasion it was suggested to the warden to let the women sleep in the day room and [the matron] would sit up all night with them, and be responsible for them; the warden would not consent. The women suffered very much, their bodies were blistered with bugs; and they often tore themselves with scratching (Brown Commission Report, 1849: 34).

At that time there was growing public concern over the treatment of the women and children housed in the Provincial Penitentiary at Kingston.[4] However, "there was little agreement on how best to rehabilitate women prisoners, and the conflicting views tended to neutralize efforts to change the conditions of women offenders' confinement during the nineteenth century" (Cooper, 1987: 130). This apathy and neglect continued until 1913, when a female prison was finally erected within the walls of Kingston Penitentiary. At that time public concern was refocused and the dispersion of female inmates became a controversial and prominent issue. In 1914, the *Report of the Royal Commission on Penitentiaries* recommended that women prisoners be housed closer to their families and communities in provincial facilities. This concern over the geographic dislocation of federal female inmates is reiterated in the 1990 Task Force *Creating Choices*.

Despite many recommendations for dispersal of women prisoners, in 1934 the notorious Prison for Women was opened in Kingston, Ontario. This facility was designed to house all federally sentenced women and it was modeled on men's maximum-security facilities. Initial security planning hoped to be able to accommodate women with different security classifications. Unfortunately, the inflexibility of this design resulted in the overclassification of women, most of whom are best suited for less-secure settings. The construction of one centralized maximum-security facility prevented correctional administrators from using the technique of cascading. This technique allows correctional administrators to relocate inmates in different institutions with different security levels. Depending on the needs and behavior of the inmate, an inmate may be moved from a maximum-security institution to a medium- or minimum-security facility or vice versa.

Four years after the opening of the Prison for Women, the Archambault Report (1938) concluded that the prison should be closed and that women should be returned to their home provinces. Again, the major concern was geographical dislocation, and the possible repercussions of the alienation and isolation of women inmates from their communities and families. Since 1934, all but one of nine major government commissions and task forces[5] that have investigated the problems of federally sentenced women have recommended the closure of the Prison for Women. There have also been many private-sector reports that have repeatedly stated the necessity and exigency of closing the Prison for Women.[6]

A significant development in the history of women prisoners' struggles occurred in 1981, when the Canadian Human Rights Commission stated "that federal female offenders were discriminated against on the basis of sex, and that in virtually all programs and facility areas, the treatment of federal women inmates was inferior to that of men" (Cooper, 1987: 139). This decision was reached after a year-long investigation following a complaint launched on behalf of the inmates at the Prison for Women by "Women for Justice," an Ottawa-based group concerned with the needs of female offenders (Berzins and Cooper, 1982: 400).

Each successive report on incarcerated women in Canada clearly identifies the same issues and the same solutions that are being outlined today. One concern is the neglect of women offenders in terms of programming and adequate accommodation because of their small numbers. "Virtually every report since 1934 identified federally sentenced women as *correctional afterthoughts* in terms of programming quality and variety" (*Creating Choices*, 1990: 37). The application of programs and policies based on male-offender populations, particularly in terms of security, has further complicated the situation of women prisoners. The MacGuigan Report (1977) condemned the Prison for Women, arguing that it was "unfit for bears, much less women," and it further stated that most women are overclassified and that they did not need the impediments and restrictions of maximum-security supervision (p. 135). Furthermore, there is a lack of community centers and halfway houses for women to be moved to, and, as a result, there are several complications associated with discharge planning and parole. Another problem consistently outlined is that of geographical dislocation and isolation resulting not only from the immense size of Canada, but also because there has been only one federal institution for women. As a result, women are frequently separated from their families. There is strong concern over the hardships experienced by the separation of mothers and children during incarceration. A report of the Canadian Bar Association (1988: 239) argues that this family and community separation "not only makes the pains of imprisonment harder than is reasonable, but also undermines women's prospects for successful re-integration." The final major problem is the failure of women's prisons to provide satisfactory services for specific groups such as Aboriginal women or French-speaking women (Ouimet, 1969; Chinnery Report, 1978; Daubney, 1988: Task Force on Aboriginal Peoples in Corrections, 1990). Beyond the constant reiteration of these dilemmas, interchangeable solutions have been put forth with a monotonous regularity (Shaw, 1989: 22). These solutions include the closure of the Prison for Women, the development of new prisons for women, the transfer of all federal inmates to provincial facilities, and the dispersal of women to smaller regional facilities under federal authority.

PRISONERS' STRUGGLE FOR EQUALITY

Although the Prison for Women has been incessantly scrutinized and investigated, deplorable and inequitable conditions remain. Besides these inquiries, several legal challenges have graphically illustrated the injustices facing federally sentenced women. Most of these challenges, both past and present,[7] have occurred under the equality and other provisions of *The Canadian Charter of Rights and Freedoms*. These cases have revealed that:

> in certain institutions the rights of federally sentenced women have been breached by the failure of the system to provide equal means for women to serve their sentences within a reasonable distance from their home, to provide equal opportunities, to provide equal programming, and to provide equal standards of facilities both in comparison to men and in comparison to federally sentenced women serving their sentences in another institution (*Creating Choices*, 1990: 84).

When pursuing rights arguments, caution must be exercised. Federally sentenced women have discovered that although the state may concede a right, that does not mean that it will make the structural alterations that will allow for the exercise of that right. For example, in the case of the female offender, the courts have ruled that imprisoned women should be given the same rights as male prisoners; however, they do not require the funding and resource provisions necessary to implement and improve programs and treatment services.

Although the rhetoric of rights and equality has helped empower women prisoners in some cases, there is reason to be skeptical of any reform attempts that merely try to make women equal to men instead of addressing women inmates' unique experiences. Admittedly, litigation based on equality can improve conditions for women prisoners somewhat (e.g., educational and vocational opportunities). However, these legal arrangements are often poorly adapted to the specific realities of women, such as childcare and medical needs. In accord with this argument, Ross and Fabiano (1985: 123) argue in their report to the Solicitor General of Canada, *Correctional Afterthoughts: Programs for Female Offenders*, that there has been increasing pressure on the government to provide equal services for women. However, they feel that this demand for equality, although warranted, may serve to "limit female offenders to the quantity, quality, and variety of services which are available to men; services which may not meet the needs of either group." They further indicate that by focusing only on providing women the same services as men, we may inadvertently succeed in marginalizing them by providing them with services that are not designed to meet their needs.

Public awareness of these problems has resulted in government pressure for change. This pressure for change stems from a variety of sources. There are many individual crusaders (such as Claire Culhane) and groups concerned with women's rights (such as Women for Justice and the Elizabeth Fry Society) who advocate on behalf of incarcerated women. These individuals and groups have brought considerable attention to the treatment of women in the criminal-justice system. Similarly, the revelations of sensational cases and tragedies have exposed women's prisons to further public scrutiny. In Canada, the Marlene Moore case[8] and recent Native inmate suicides have been instrumental in revealing the deplorable conditions of women's prisons. For many, these cases symbolize the failure of our mental-health and penal institutions to respond to the problems and pain of women prisoners. Allegations that women have been mistreated and discriminated against in prisons have led to demands (and sometimes court orders) for equal opportunity in correctional facilities, programs, and services (Ross and Fabiano, 1985: 1). Considering these difficulties, there has been increased political pressure on the government and on correctional management to improve the availability of services and accommodations for female offenders.

TASK FORCE ON FEDERALLY SENTENCED WOMEN

One consequence of this pressure was *Creating Choices* (1990), the report of a Task Force on federally sentenced women in Canada. The Task Force was designed to remedy the problem of inadequate research on women's prisons and alternatives to incarceration. This project was fully supported by Ole Instrup, Commissioner of Correctional Services Canada, who made a clear commitment to reviewing the needs of federally sentenced women. Interest in developing a Task Force to address women prisoners' issues was shared by the Elizabeth Fry Society and Native groups. Likewise, trends and events such as feminist criticism of the existing system, Aboriginal demands for more control over justice for their people, Charter challenges, repeated recommendations for the closure of the Prison for Women, rethinking of Corrections Canada Mission Statement, and tragedies at the Prison for Women reinforced a ground swell of consensus that fundamental reform is urgently required. The mandate of the Task Force was:

> to examine the correctional management of federally sentenced women from the commencement of their sentence to the date of warrant expiry, and to develop a policy and a plan which would guide and direct this process in a manner that is responsive to the unique and special needs of this group (*Creating Choices*, 1990: 88).

For the most part, this report reiterates the same problems, perplexities, and recommendations as preceding reports and Task Forces. However, the response to this report has been more promising. The political alliances developed as a result of the Task Force are both unique and problematic.

The attempts made by the Task Force to integrate the interests and concerns of a variety of groups is commendable. For the first time in the history of Canadian women's corrections, several adversarial factions cooperated with each other to outline areas of concern and to produce a set of collective recommendations. The major participants were the federal government, Canadian Association of Elizabeth Fry Societies, Aboriginal Women's Caucus, and inmates at the Prison for Women. Interestingly, although the Task Force attempted to include a variety of perspectives, it appears to have omitted the perspectives of correctional officers and those individuals who work in the Prison for Women. One of the most striking features of the *Creating Choices* report is the extensive documentation of inmates' perspectives and the absence of staff input. For example, efforts could have been made to ascertain the correctional staff's perceptions and evaluations of existing programs and proposed programs, and they may also have been asked to outline problem areas with suggestions about how to better train staff and restructure the institution. This omission may have serious consequences when these recommendations of this Task Force are implemented. Admittedly, the Task Force is aware of the importance of staff training; however, there is no detailed account of staff concerns when dealing with federally sentenced women or the needs of correctional personnel.

The research completed for the Task Force was driven by a "women-centered approach" and its representatives were from women's groups and others "whose beliefs stressed that issues such as poverty, racism, wife battering, and sexual abuse are central to women's crime" (*Ibid.*: 83). Some research for the Task Force was completed by two Native inmates at the Prison for Women, Fran Sugar and Lana Fox. These women provided the Task Force with information from the first report about First Nations women in the Canadian federal prison system. The report provides anecdotal information on the lives and experiences of 39 Aboriginal women who have been incarcerated at the Prison for Women. Likewise, a survey of federally sentenced women, completed by Margaret Shaw (1989), outlines the views and experiences of federally sentenced women in Canada. The purpose of these research projects was to:

> provide the Task Force with information about the current population as a basis for its deliberations on future provisions for federally sentenced women. In particular it was designed to provide a broader picture of the federal population than is normally available, and the views of the women themselves on the experiences of imprisonment, their need for programs and services, and on where and under what conditions they might prefer to serve their sentences (*Ibid.*: 1).

The Task Force relied heavily on this qualitative information. Unfortunately, the reported views of federally sentenced women inmates are not balanced with the views of correctional personnel who interact with these individuals daily. The report could have benefited from more structured empirical studies and an integrated analysis of current literature and research on imprisoned women, especially the material on Native women.

The Third National Workshop on Female Offenders (Pittsburgh, Pennsylvania, in May 1989) was consistent with the ideologies underlying *Creating Choices*. The theme, "The Changing Needs of the Female Offender — A Challenge for the Future," was generally interpreted as "a call for the restructuring of corrections for women rather than the patch-working evident in so many correctional systems, which work against the objective of responsible self-sufficiency" (*Creating Choices*, 1990: 83). The second major influence on the thinking of the Task force was the Aboriginal struggle for self-determination. An awareness of this problem was essential since incarcerated Aboriginal women are often victims of cultural ignorance and deprivations. Similarly, the Task Force emphasized that "the achievement of equality for Aboriginal women in the correctional system is dependent on enhanced

Aboriginal participation and increased Aboriginal control over programs and services" (*Final Report*, Task Force on Aboriginal Peoples in Federal Corrections, 1990: 10). It was these trends and events within the correctional system and Canadian society that supported the Task Force's comprehensive approach to change. Although feminist perspectives and Aboriginal struggles were driving forces of the Task Force, these positions have not been explicitly integrated into all government thinking on corrections.

The findings and recommendations of the Task Force were based on the insights gained from extensive consultations and from the results of several research projects. Many of the previously mentioned problems of overclassification, geographical dislocation, separation from families, inadequate programs, and cultural ignorance were outlined by the Task Force. In addition to these findings, the Task Force also revealed the extent and severity of the high incidence of self-injurious behavior among the women at the Prison for Women. The relatively high incidence of substance abuse as a part of the offense or offense history of the women and their expressed need for more comprehensive substance-abuse and mental-health programs were also outlined. There was also a concern about the paucity of community-based services for federally sentenced women, and the need for educational and vocational programs that foster marketable skills. Finally, there was a recognizable need for culturally sensitive programs and services for women, especially Aboriginal and immigrant women.

The Task Force's recommendations are based on the belief that a "holistic" approach to the treatment of federally sentenced women is required to address the historical problems, and is predicated on principles of empowerment, meaningful choices, respect and dignity, supportive environments, and shared responsibility. The plan places high emphasis on the need for federally sentenced women to recover from past trauma and to develop self-esteem and self-sufficiency through programs and services designed to respond to their needs. It stresses the need for physical environments that are conducive to reintegration, highly interactive with the community, and reflective of the generally low security risk of federally sentenced women (*Creating Choices*, 1990: 125–135). Ironically, the Task Force advocates treatment and rehabilitative approaches after candidly stating that rehabilitation is incompatible with incarceration (*Ibid.*: 41).

The recommendations of the Task Force were presented in a report to the government in April 1990, and a few months later the federal government announced that they would implement the Task Force's recommendations. One recommendation to be implemented immediately is the elimination of transfers from provincial correctional institutions to the Prison for Women. In the past, provincially sentenced women who posed a security threat could be transferred from a provincial facility to a federal facility.

Other proposals were to recruit more feminist and Aboriginal counselors, and to establish a daily presence of an Aboriginal counselor at the Prison for Women. Also, there is a recommendation to admit prisoners who have self-injured to the prison or community hospital and return them to the general population as soon as possible instead of treating these individuals punitively. It has also been recognized that geographic dislocation can cause many hardships, and, as a result, it has been recommended that prisoners should have access to funded visits with family members and enhanced telephone contacts.[9]

The most significant long-term recommendation of the Task Force is for the closure of the notorious Prison for Women, and the construction of four small regional facilities and one Aboriginal "healing lodge." Each regional facility would be developed and operated under a program philosophy that approximates community norms, focuses on the use of community services and expertise, and is geared to the safe and earliest possible release of federally sentenced women. Programs available at each of these facilities are expected to be culturally sensitive and responsive to the needs of women. Programming will concentrate on individual and group counseling that would be sensitive to sexual, emotional, and physical abuse, and teach everyday skills and coping techniques. The primary programming will also include health care, mental-health services, addiction programs, family visiting, mother and child programs, spirituality and religion, Aboriginal programs, education, and vocational training. These facilities will also rely extensively on volunteer services. Many local community groups will be encouraged to interact with the inmates to foster a community responsibility for the facility and to provide important community connections for women about to be released (*Ibid.*: 138–147).

The Aboriginal healing lodge would allow federally sentenced Aboriginal women to serve all or part of their sentences in a culturally sensitive environment. The intention is that the physical space and programs for the healing lodge should reflect Aboriginal culture. This facility would address the needs of federally sentenced Aboriginal women through Native teachings, ceremonies, contact with elders and children, and interaction with nature (*Ibid.*: 147–150). Presently, the breadth of problems facing Aboriginal women in the criminal-justice system has not been adequately researched and analyzed. We do not have a clear understanding of the realities of Native women's lives.

Although the closure of the Prison for Women can be viewed as progress, the construction of five more women's prisons across the country raises serious concerns about the future of women's imprisonment. One curious aspect of this recommendation is the endorsement of the construction of these new "facilities" (prisons) by the Elizabeth Fry Society, which has historically supported the abolition of prisons. Rather than a shift in ideology, the Elizabeth Fry Society's participation in the Task Force and support of these recommendations may reflect increased private sector involvement in corrections. Griffiths and Verdun-Jones (1989: 592) note that in recent years:

> there has been an increase in the number of contracts between the federal and provincial governments and the John Howard Society, Elizabeth Fry Society, the Salvation Army, and other private non-profit agencies for the delivery of programs and services, particularly in the supervision of adult offenders.

Another difficulty with the construction of these new prisons is that it would not necessarily solve the problems outlined in the Task Force report. Two of the most serious difficulties facing federally sentenced women are geographic dislocation and overclassification. If the recommendations for the construction of these new facilities are implemented, there will be some improvement in geographic isolation, but the problem of security still exists. Depending on the location of these centers, and provided that they accept all inmates from the surrounding area, women will be permitted to be closer to their families and communities. However, due to practical and monetary constraints, some dislocation will remain. Furthermore, if an Aboriginal inmate wants to serve her sentence in the Aboriginal healing lodge, depending on the location of her home province, she must choose between services and proximity to her community and family. This problem is quite similar to those associated with previously mentioned exchange of service agreements. To further improve and reduce imprisoned women's isolation and alienation from the family, these new institutions must have improved visiting and family contact programs.

Classification and security concerns were not adequately dealt with in the Task Force report. The lack of proposals that deal with these issues is problematic. The assumption here is that each facility will be able to adapt to different levels of security needs. This assumption is problematic, and a similar mistake was made when the Prison for Women was constructed in 1934. Furthermore, past task forces and Royal Commissions have been skeptical of the effectiveness of housing offenders with diverse security needs in the same institution. The proposals for these regional facilities concentrate on women prisoners with low- to medium-security classifications and not the offender who poses a security risk. The Task Force recommends the use of dynamic security and unit management, which is based on the idea of integrating concepts of control, support, and assistance. However, the Task Force recognizes that "the full expression of such integration, because it is dependent on establishing stable, productive, personal relationships rather than institutional ones, will be difficult to achieve in traditional correctional environments" (*Creating Choices*, 1990: 107). Although the Task Force was aware of these complications, it still advocated a non-authoritative security structure and the creation of an environment "where relationships are based on role modeling, support, trust, and democratic decision-making can thrive between staff and federally sentenced women" (*Ibid.*: 108). Given that these facilities would still effectively be prisons, it will be interesting to see if this rhetoric is ever translated into correctional practice. Under the current system, and in any institution that limits inmate rights, the notion of truly democratic decision-making between inmates and guards is inconceivable.

Instead of traditional male-oriented and culturally specific classification systems, the Task Force favors development of a woman-centred and culturally relevant assessment system. The assessment system would be designed to look at the whole spectrum of a woman's needs from a holistic perspective, including needs relating to programming, spirituality, health, family, culture, and release plans. Through this assessment it is hoped that staff will be better able to respond to the needs of federally sentenced women (*Ibid.*: 112). The Task Force feels that an emphasis on security classification is nonproductive when dealing with the female offender and that it is not conducive to rehabilitation. However, the fact remains that these women are in prison and there are bound to be some complications with this approach, especially with "high need" or "high risk" offenders, where the protection of society is a paramount concern.

A final concern with the proposals for the expansion of women's prisons is the effect this might have on judicial attitudes and sentencing patterns. Presently there is a lack of good empirical research on the sentencing of women. Judges have been generally reluctant to give dispositions of federal time to women since there was only one institution for federally sentenced women. In some cases, judges have publicly indicated that the conditions at the Prison for Women are deplorable and, as a result, they are reluctant to issue sentences of two years or more. With these proposed changes, there is some concern that there may also be an increase in the number of women being sentenced to federal institutions who would have otherwise received a less severe sentence. There is a danger of a resurgence of paternalistic thinking and lengthy sentences for the "benefit of the offender." There is currently no attempt by the government to assess the likelihood of this problem. If this potential complication is not attended to, women's imprisonment may be affected by problems of over-crowding since the institutions being proposed would not be designed to hold large numbers of women.

The Task Force also recommended that the government develop a community-release strategy that would expand and strengthen residential and nonresidential programs and services for federally sentenced women on release. These facilities are to be developed by community groups and other interested agencies, including halfway houses, Aboriginal centers, satellite units, home placements, addiction-treatment centers, multi-use women's centers, mixed-group housing, and mother and childcare centers (*Ibid.*: 152–153). In response to this proposal, the Ministry of the Solicitor General recently opened a minimum-security institution for female offenders in Kingston to provide inmates with the opportunity to prepare for release into the community (Pale Green Paper on Correctional Reform, 1990: 39). A community approach allows women prisoners the use of services and programs available in the community, since it does not attempt to duplicate these costly services in the institution. This proposal would be particularly beneficial to women prisoners who have historically had a difficult time acquiring funding and resources for programming and treatment services. The mobilization of community resources provides the distinct advantage "in providing community-based services to offenders, including better access to community resources, a greater ability to involve the local community in program initiatives, and the capacity to provide services beyond those mandated by the government" (Ekstedt and Griffiths, 1988: 276). Overall, proposals with respect to women's imprisonment in Canada seem to be following the broader trend toward "community-based corrections."

The Ministry of the Solicitor General of Canada endorsed these proposals and announced that the Prison for Women shall be closed by 1994. According to the federal government and the Canadian Association of Elizabeth Fry Societies, these recommendations have received a tremendous amount of community support and enthusiasm. At this time, it is difficult to anticipate the response of the communities where the new facilities will be located. To date, there have been few attempts to ascertain the reactions of federally sentenced women, but there are indications that they are not as enthusiastic as others about the closure of the Prison for Women and the dispersal of the women across the county. Inmates fear that they will lose their collective power and that they will be further discriminated against.

If implemented, the Task Force's recommendations will have a tremendous impact on the Canadian correctional community, and there is hope that at last serious consideration is being given to the predicament of incarcerated women. However, this report and its recommendations merely scratch the surface of this topic; more in-depth and detailed research is necessary. In some cases, as presently articulated these proposals may further complicate and aggravate the situation of federally sentenced women. Before these ideas are firmly entrenched in correctional policy, some consideration should be given to the possible consequences of the development of the proposed facilities. Without advocating the preservation of the

Prison for Women and the continuation of the current situation of discriminatory and inadequate treatment and programming, a multi-dimensional investigation of the potential problems associated with the construction of new smaller "facilities" for women should be completed. Furthermore, the government and interested groups should develop a strategy for dealing with any problems that occur during the implementation of these proposals. A well-researched and predetermined plan of action will prevent impulsive reactions and ensure progressive and positive remedies.

A fundamental precondition for successful reform for women prisoners is the recognition that their life experiences are different from those of men. To effectively deal with the female offender, we must recognize and challenge our assumptions of punishment. Furthermore, we must be aware of the fact that the very

> structure and fabric of Corrections Canada, the basic definitions, working tools, mechanisms, and philosophies, policies, methodologies, and procedures that form the backbone and flesh of our penological system have all without exception been born, raised, and sometimes died, male (Berzins and Cooper, 1982: 405).

Not only is the structure of our penal system inherently male, it is also, to a great extent, culturally ignorant and intolerant. Penological reforms must acknowledge, without exploiting, the existence of gender and cultural differences that are defined by the social, political, and economic structures of our society. Only recently have attempts been made to address these crucial issues of women's imprisonment. In spite of the Task Force's recommendations, however, almost all of the problems facing Canadian women prisoners remain unresolved. If Correctional Services Canada again fails to convert the Task Force's proposals into a plan for action, the apathy and neglect that have characterized Canadian women's prisons for over a century will continue.

NOTES

1. See Hatch and Faith (1990: 432–456) and Johnson (1987) for more detailed statistical analysis of female offenders.
2. At present, research on the physical and sexual abuse of women prisoners is inconclusive. Most Canadian research in this area has used self-report data as a measure of abuse. No attempts have been made to independently verify and substantiate this research. As a result, current figures may underrepresent or overrepresent the extent of this tragedy.
3. A detailed history and comprehensive analysis of women's imprisonment in Canada is provided by Cooper (1987: 127–144), Strange (1985: 79–91), and Berzins and Cooper (1982: 399–416).
4. The Provincial Penitentiary in Kingston was built in 1835 and Confederation occurred in 1867. At that time, the institution was designated a federal facility and renamed Kingston Penitentiary.
5. These include: *Brief on the Woman Offender* (Ottawa: Canadian Corrections Association, 1968); Report of the Canadian Committee on Corrections (Ottawa: Queens Printer, 1969); Report of the Royal Commission on the Status of Women (Ottawa: Information Canada, 1970); Report of the National Advisory Committee on the Female Offender (Ottawa: Solicitor General Canada, 1976); Report to Parliament by the Sub-Committee on the Penitentiary System in Canada (Ottawa: Supply and Services, 1977); "Brief on the Female Offender" (Ottawa: Canadian Association of Elizabeth Fry Societies, 1978); "Brief to the Solicitor General" (Ottawa: Civil Liberties Association Canada, 1978); Report of the

National Planning Committee on the Female Offender (Ottawa: Solicitor General of Canada, 1978); Brief on the Woman Offender (Montreal: Canadian Federation of University Women, 1978); Report of the Joint Committee to Study Alternatives for the Housing of the Female Offender (Ottawa: Solicitor General Canada, 1978); Progress Report on the Federal Female Offender Program (Ottawa: Canadian Corrections Service, 1978); Ten Years Later (Ottawa: Canadian Advisory Council on the Status of Women, 1979); "Brief to the Canadian Human Rights Commission" (Ottawa: Women for Justice, 1980). The list is from Adelberg and Currie (1987: 143–144).

6. For the most part, these reports have been written by the Canadian Association of Elizabeth Fry Societies.

7. The most recent (1990) litigation involving federally sentenced women is the Saskatchewan Court of Appeal case between the Attorney General of Canada and Carol Maureen Daniels. This case was sponsored by LEAF (Women's Legal Education and Action Fund). Ms. Daniels is a Native woman convicted of murder. In the ruling of this case, the Court of Appeal overruled a lower-court order that placed a ban on imprisoning Saskatchewan women in the Prison for Women in Kingston. The lower-court ruling argued that sending women to the Prison for Women in Kingston was discriminatory, and cruel and unusual punishment. They further indicated that this prison constituted a threat to the lives of the women and that it deprived them of their cultural and family ties.

8. Marlene Moore committed suicide at age 31 while serving her sentence in the federal Prison for Women in Kingston, Ontario, after many previous self-mutilations and suicide attempts. Many women have killed themselves in this frequently condemned prison, but none of their deaths has struck the same degree of horror as that of Marlene Moore. The book entitled *Rock-a-Bye Baby* (1991) by Anne Kershaw and Mary Lasovich tells the story of Marlene Moore's life and death in Canadian prisons.

9. A more detailed and comprehensive discussion of the recommendations proposed by the Task Force on federally sentenced women can be located in *Creating Choices* (1990). For this article, I have only summarized what I believe are the most significant recommendations with respect to the problems outlined by the research for the Task Force.

REFERENCES

Adelberg, Ellen and Claudia Currie. 1987. *Too Few to Count: Canadian Women in Conflict with the Law*. Vancouver: Press Gang Publishers.

Archambault Report. 1938. "Report of the Royal Commission to Investigate the Penal System in Canada" (Archambault Report).

Axon, Lee. 1989. "Model and Exemplary Programs for Female Inmates: An International Review." Ottawa: Ministry of the Solicitor General.

Berzins, Lorraine and Sheelagh Cooper. 1982. "The Political Economy of Correctional Planning for Women: The Case of Bankrupt Bureaucracy." *Canadian Journal of Criminology* (October).

Brown Commission. 1849. "Report of the Royal Commission to Inquire and Then Report upon the Conduct, Economy, Discipline, and Management of the Provincial Penitentiary" (The Brown Commission Report).

Canadian Bar Association. 1988. "Justice Behind the Walls: Legislate to Compel Closure of Prison for Women." The Canadian Bar Association.

Carlen, Pat. 1988. "Women's Imprisonment: Current Issues." *Prison Service Journal* (April): 7–12.

Cooper, Sheelagh. 1987. "The Evolution of the Federal Women's Prison." In Adelberg and Currie (eds.), *Too Few to Count: Canadian Women in Conflict with the Law*. Vancouver: Press Gang Publishers.

Daubney Committee. 1988. "Report of the Standing Committee on Justice and Solicitor General on Its Review of Sentencing, Conditional Release, and Related Aspects of Corrections: Taking Responsibility" (Daubney Committee), Ottawa: Supply and Service.

DeCostanzo, Elaine and Janet Valente. 1985. "Designing a Corrections Continuum for Female Offenders: One State's Experience." *Prison Journal* 64, 1: 120–135.

Edwards, Anne. 1989. "Sex/Gender, Sexism, and Criminal Justice: Some Theoretical Considerations." *International Journal of Sociology of Law*.

Ekstedt, John and Curt Griffiths. 1988. *Corrections in Canada: Policy and Practice*. Toronto: Butterworths.

Evans, Maureen. 1989. "A Survey of Institutional Programs Available to Federally Sentenced Women." Ottawa: Ministry of the Solicitor General.

Feinman, Clairice. 1980. "An Historical Overview of the Treatment of Incarcerated Women: Myths, Realities, and Rehabilitation." In *Women in the Criminal Justice System*.

Griffiths, Curt and Simon Verdun-Jones. 1989. *Canadian Criminal Justice*. Toronto: Butterworths.

Hatch, Alison and Karlene Faith. 1990. "The Female Offender in Canada: A Statistical Profile." *Canadian Journal of Women and the Law* 3, 2: 432–456.

Johnson, Holly. 1987. "Getting the Facts Straight: A Statistical Overview." In Adelberg and Currie (eds.), *Too Few to Count: Canadian Women in Conflict with the Law*. Vancouver: Press Gang Publishers.

LaPrairie, Carol. 1987. "Native Women and Crime in Canada." In Adelberg and Currie (eds.), *Too Few to Count: Canadian Women in Conflict with the Law*. Vancouver: Press Gang Publishers.

MacGuigan, M. (Chair). 1977. "Report to Parliament by the Sub-Committee on the Penitentiary System in Canada" (MacGuigan Report). Ottawa: Supply and Services.

MacLeod, Linda. 1986. *Sentenced to Separation: An Exploration of the Needs and Problems of Mothers Who Are Offenders with Children*. Ottawa: Ministry of the Solicitor General.

Morris, Allison. 1987. *Women, Crime, and Criminal Justice*. Oxford: Basil Blackwell.

Moyer, Imogene. 1985. "Deceptions and Realities of Life in Women's Prisons." *Prison Journal* 64, 1: 45–56.

Ouimet, R. (Chair). 1969. "Report of the Canadian Committee on Corrections" (Ouimet Report). Ottawa: Queen's Printer.

Pale Green Paper. 1990. *Directions for Reform Corrections and Conditional Release*. Ottawa: Ministry of the Solicitor General.

Reid, Susan. 1985. "The Reproduction of Women's Dependence as a Factor in Treating the Female Offender." *Canadian Criminology Forum* 7 (Spring): 129–143.

Report by Cassey. 1991. "Report of the Task Force on the Criminal Justice System and Its Impact on the Indian and Metis People of Alberta" (Cassey Report). Ottawa: Supply and Services (March).

Report by Chinnery. 1978. "Report of the National Planning Committee on the Female Offender" (Chinnery Report). Ottawa: Solicitor General Canada.

Report of the Macdonald Commission. 1914. "Report of the Royal Commission on Penitentiaries" (The Macdonald Commission). Ottawa: Ministry of the Solicitor General.

Report of the Task Force on Federally Sentenced Women. 1990. "Creating Choices." Ottawa: Ministry of the Solicitor General (April).

Ross, Robert and Elizabeth Fabiano. 1985. *Correctional Afterthoughts: Progress for Female Offenders*. Ottawa: Ministry of the Solicitor General.

Sargent, John. 1985. "Evolution of a Stereotype: Paternalism and the Female Inmate." *Prison Journal* 64, 1.

Shaw, Margaret et al. 1989. "Survey of Federally Sentenced Women." Prepared under contract for the Ministry of the Solicitor General Canada. Ottawa: Ministry of the Solicitor General.

Smandych, Russell. 1991. "Beware of the Evil American Monster: Upper Canada Views on the Need for a Penitentiary, 1830–1834." *Canadian Journal of Criminology* (April): 125–147.

Strange, Carolyn. 1985. "The Criminal and Fallen of Their Sex: The Establishment of Canada's
First Women's Prison." *Canadian Journal of Women and the Law* 1: 79–92.

Sugar, Fran and Lana Fox. 1990a. "*Nistum Peyako Seht'wawin Iskwewa*k: Breaking Chains."
Canadian Journal of Women and the Law 3, 2: 465–483.

————. 1990b. "Survey of Federally Sentenced Aboriginal Women in the Community."
Prepared for the Native Women's Association of Canada for submission to the Task Force
on Federally Sentenced Women (January).

Task Force on Aboriginal Peoples in Federal Corrections. 1990. *Final Report*. Ottawa: Ministry of
the Solicitor General.

Women for Justice. 1980. "Brief to the Canadian Human Rights Commission." Ottawa: Women
for Justice.

EIGHTEEN

....

Canadian Correctional Policy and Native Inmates: The Control of Social Dynamite[1]

MARIANNE O. NIELSEN

INTRODUCTION

Native[2] offenders are currently the subject of more organizational activity than any
other minority group found within Canada's correctional[3] system. From a situation in
the 1960s in which there were no policies or programs addressing the needs of
Native inmates, a change has occurred so that, since the early 1980s, a number of
new initiatives have been introduced; however, it has been remarked that these
actions are "uncoordinated, haphazard and reactive" (Newby, 1981: 35). While the
lack of coordination is important, the real key, in analytical terms, is the word "reactive." Frideres and others have pointed out that governments only act on Native
issues when forced to and then have "invariably done so in White interests" (1988:
257). The questions that arise are: What has prompted the Canadian government,
specifically the correctional branch of the government, to change its response to
Native inmates? And more significantly, whose interests are being served?

NATIVE CORRECTIONAL POLICY

Newby (1981: 44–45) suggests three purposes for Native correctional policy:
(1) guaranteeing Natives equality of treatment, (2) responding to political pressure,

....

Source: Marianne O. Nielson, "Canadian Correctional Policy and Native Inmates: The Control of Social
Dynamite," *Canadian Ethnic Studies*, 22, 3 (1990): 111–21. Reproduced by permission of *Canadian Ethnic
Studies*.

and (3) solving the management problems caused by the existence of a large minority with special needs. Social organizational theory would suggest that there are more factors than just these in play, that indeed there are many environmental conditions (Hall, 1987: 219–25) that could influence changes in organizational structures and operations, including policy development. The impact of these factors may be direct or indirect, through intervening mechanisms. It is argued that where environmental influences impinge upon correctional policy towards Native inmates, there is at least one important intervening mechanism that must be taken into account. This variable is the changing perception of Native inmates by correctional staff. Because of space limitations, only the intervening mechanism will be dealt with in this paper.

Using a conceptional framework suggested by Spitzer (1975), it is argued that as Native inmates, originally seen as "social junk," are redefined as "social dynamite" (primarily as the result of outside conditions) more effective control strategies are sought, resulting in changing policies and procedures.

NATIVE INMATES AS A "PROBLEM POPULATION"

Hagan discusses the regulation and management of problem populations, groups that "threaten the social relations of production" by calling into question the key components of the capitalist system, such as the capitalist modes of appropriating the products of human labour, the social conditions under which capitalist production takes place, the patterns of distribution and consumption, the process of socialization for production and the ideology that supports society (Hagan, 1984: 138–39). Spitzer (1975) in his analysis looks at these populations at the level of class, focussing on the threat to the ruling class posed by a relative surplus population of unemployed and underemployed that, ironically, is necessary for maintaining the functioning of the system by providing labour power and consumers. He divides this problem population into two sub-categories: "social junk" which, from the point of view of the dominant class, is a costly yet relatively harmless burden to society, and "social dynamite," which is characterized by its potential actively to call into question established relationships. He describes the social junk population as passive and unable or unwilling to compete in the social order. It includes groups such as the aged, mentally ill, handicapped and mentally retarded. Social dynamite is more youthful, alienated, and politically volatile. Whereas social junk is usually administered through welfare and social service agencies, social dynamite is usually administered by the criminal justice system, although there is overlap, for example, in the case of alcoholics, the welfare poor, and problem children (Spitzer, 1975: 645–6).

Where Spitzer is more concerned with the structure of control and deviance in society as a whole, this discussion is concerned with one component of a smaller system. Despite criticisms that Spitzer's analysis "suffers from a crudeness at the level of understanding of the multifarious phenomena involved in social control" (Rodger, 1988: 566), his conception is useful at the level of organizational analysis where there are a smaller number of factors to consider. It is also appropriate to an environmental perspective because of his conception that:

> our understanding of punishment in a class society must be forged from an examination of the entire framework of material relationships, conditions, and conflicts, within which ... arrangements and interests emerge (Spitzer, 1979: 225).

Within Corrections, correctional staff and inmates are the dominant and subordinate groups involved in the social relations of production. What they supposedly produce are rehabilitated individuals and a safer society through a temporary warehousing of bodies, i.e., "short-term social protection and long-term recidivism reduction" (Haley and Lerette, 1984: 86). An effective organization meets these two goals as demanded by the standards set by outside organizations; an efficient organization is measured by a low ratio of resources consumed to output produced (Pfeffer and Salanchik, 1978: 11). Any group that threatens the effectiveness or efficiency of this process through its behaviour, personal characteristics, or status (Hagan, 1985: 221) is a problem population.

The Native population in general can be classified as a problem population for society, characterized by low income, lack of work skills, high unemployment rates, low levels of education, high suicide rates, high rates of death by violent death, and high crime rates (Frideres, 1988). If it is often the case, as Frideres suggests, that the primary concern of service organizations dealing with Native people, including Corrections, is regulating and controlling their clients so that they conform to "middle class criteria" (1988: 253), these conditions are indicative of the massive task being faced.

In addition, by their very existence, Native people present the federal government with a management problem because of the government's special historical obligations to them. As well, in dealing with Native offenders, it is necessary to take two cultures into account — that of the dominant non-Native society and that of Native peoples. It is a situation made more complex by the fact that there is not just one Native culture but many and that these vary, not only in content but in degree of integration with the dominant culture (Frideres 1988: 150).

NATIVE INMATES

Returning to the organizational level, it is frequently stated that Native people are over-represented in the criminal justice system. In Corrections they make up about ten percent of the male federal inmate population and 13 percent of the female federal inmate population whereas Native people make up two percent of Canada's total population (Correctional Law Review, 1988: 3). In most provincial institutions their proportions are higher so that, for example, Native people comprise 60 percent of the Saskatchewan provincial correctional institution admissions (Jackson, 1989: 216). The Native population is particularly over-represented in the Prairies (Task Force on Aboriginal Peoples, 1988: 23; Correctional Law Review, 1988: 3). What is seldom mentioned in these descriptive reports is that Native people are the single largest ethnic minority group found in Canada's correctional institutions. The proportion of Native offenders has grown from 1983 to 1987 and indicators are that the proportion is still climbing (*Forum*, 1989: 6). Because of the high birth rate among native people and the declining birthrate among other Canadians, a large number of Native young people will be entering the "at risk" age group in the next few years, with the trend continuing well into the future unless conditions change (Perreault et al., 1985: 36). This makes them a force to be reckoned with for correctional planners, and thereby defines them as the primary problem population for Corrections.[4]

Early descriptions of Native inmates such as that provided by the Canadian Corrections Association (1967: 23–28) emphasized that alcohol abuse was one of the main reasons that Native people were in jail, and that Native inmates might be more appropriately dealt with through treatment programs instead of incarceration. In addition, it was "universally reported that the Indian people are model prisoners and are well-liked by the custodial staff. In general, their morale is superior to that of the non-Indian inmates, and it seems that Indians chafe less at prison routines and are more amenable and less demanding than non-Indians." (Canadian Corrections Association 1967: 47). Model prisoners are also described as those that "cause little or no trouble in the institution" (Correctional Law Review, 1988: 8). This conception of Native prisoners, reinforced by socio-demographic characteristics and popular stereotypes (Jackson, 1989: 218) is in keeping with the description of Spitzer's social junk population. Also in keeping with Spitzer's conception, Native inmates, and Native people in general, have suffered from a myth of needing protection (Adams, 1989: 147). Havemann et al. (1985: 159) describe the "blaming the victim" explanation for Native criminality as focussing on differences between people, rather than on the operation of the system. The causal factor is the individual offender's behaviour and therefore presenting no danger to the system.

Native inmates are seldom called "model prisoners" any longer (Correctional Law Review, 1988: 8). Newby (1981: 39) suggests that the "existence of a noticeably large racial minority from a different and underprivileged background within a prison system has traditionally been a source of tension and security risk; in other words, a serious management problem." The problem exists from the point of view of Native offenders as well; Morse and Lock (1988: 54) report that:

> In all correctional institutions ... the policies continue to be made by non-Natives for non-Natives. Management is for the most part non-Native; classification officers are non-Native; living unit officers and security staff are all non-Native. In addition, most of the non-Native staff are unaware of and possibly unsympathetic toward Native culture. These factors all contribute toward polarization between Native inmates and non-Natives in the institutions. (1988: 54).

Newby (1981: 39–40) suggests that if the proportion of Native inmates continues to grow, accompanied by "increased political demands and disappointed expectations by Native groups in the community," a confrontation scenario becomes more possible. The possibility of a management problem can be seen in the potential for violence that Native inmates represent: 73 percent of Native inmates are incarcerated for violent offences compared to under 60 percent of non-Natives (Task Force on Aboriginal Peoples, 1988: 26). They are also more frequently involved in incidents of prison violence, at the rate of 168.9/1000 compared to 111.8/1000 for Whites and 124.2/1000 for others (Campbell et al., 1985: 13).

Based on a longitudinal analysis of inmate records, complemented by interviews with inmates and Native community members, McCaskill (1985: 69) reports that Native inmates have become more heterogeneous in their personality characteristics. They are younger and more intelligent, but: 'The most striking change has occurred in what might be considered the stereotypical image of the Native inmate, i.e., "passive/withdrawn/shy" and "inferior/immature/dependent."' Taken together — McCaskill notes that the percentage of Native inmates who exhibited these traits has dropped from 56 percent in 1970 to 28 percent in 1984. Nevertheless, McCaskill has identified three types of Native offenders in the correctional institutions:

1) passive, traditionally-oriented; 2) socially and politically active inmates; and 3) inmates assimilated to the dominant culture. Each of these groups calls for a different program response (1985: 79–80), thereby creating problems.

NATIVE SELF-HELP GROUPS IN CORRECTIONAL INSTITUTIONS

The low rate of participation by Native inmates in general rehabilitative programs (Standing Committee, 1988: 211; Correctional Law Review, 1988: 5) means that Native inmates are not assisting Corrections as an institution to accomplish one of its two main purposes, that of rehabilitation.[5] The high Native recidivism rate (Schmeiser, 1974: 81) also calls the effectiveness of Corrections into question. At the same time, their increasing involvement and cohesiveness (McCaskill, 1985: 74) in inmate groups, gives them an organizational basis from which to make demands, as does the support of outside criminal justice and political oganizations. Inmates as individuals are in a position of weakness when faced with the power of Corrections in its capacity as a component of the State (Haley and Lerette, 1984: 67); however, organized in groups they have more power.[6] Pressures from inside the institutions originate with Native self-help groups such as the Native Brotherhoods and Sisterhoods. These organizations are run by Native inmates, often with the assistance of outside criminal justice agencies. Native self-help groups serve as the focus of cultural and spiritual activities in most provincial and federal correctional institutions (Task Force on Aboriginal Peoples, 1988: 21) and in many ways parallel the growth of political activism in Native communities outside the institutions (Jackson, 1989: 292). They do not have the power to shape programming, but are an effort to "create order out of disorder, to develop self-respect and pride where now only alienation and bitterness prevail" (Jackson, 1989: 290, 292). As a result of their efforts, these groups have been recognized as having a rehabilitative impact and have been endorsed by various government task forces (Standing Committee, 1988: 214).

These self-help organizations have created fears among correctional staff so that: "In some cases these [Brotherhood] initiatives have been perceived by correctional administrators as exercises in "red power" and as such potentially undermining of institutional good order and security." (Jackson, 1989: 290). Native inmates can therefore be seen to be challenging the social relations of production within Corrections. Native inmates challenge the mode of production with high recidivism rates; threaten the social conditions of production through involvement in violent incidents; exist as an example of the distribution and consumption system gone wrong; refuse to participate in socialization processes, i.e., institutional programming; and challenge through increasing political activity the ideology that supports Correctional functioning.

Within Corrections, the alternatives for handling a problem population of inmates, following the four categories of Spitzer's model, are: 1) normalization, i.e., reducing the scope of deviance processing by creating "invisible deviants" who are not visible in the system. In the case of offenders, this means decarceration; preventing them from entering the system through crime prevention or diversion programs; processing them through the system as fast as possible by using day parole and full parole; or putting them in the care of private agencies. 2) A second strategy is conversion, that is, encouraging the direct participation by potential trouble-makers in control efforts. In Corrections this means hiring members of the problem population to work as front-line staff to use their knowledge and life experience to assist in the control of their fellows. 3) A third strategy is containment, that is, classifying the population as homogeneous and using geographic segregation and informal and formal sanctions to administer it. In Corrections this means the establishment of separate services to compartmentalize and segregate problem inmates from the mainstream. 4) The final strategy is providing support for criminal enterprise so that greater power is given to organized crime allowing it to create a parallel opportunity structure (Spitzer, 1975: 648–9). Of these four options only the fourth has not been tried as a means of controlling Native inmates (although with the recent happenings on the Akwesasne Reserve and the accompanying allegations of smuggling, illegal gambling, and violence, this point could be debated).

Corrections has used all of the above strategies although they have been embodied as new policy, programming initiatives, fact-finding task forces, and increased accuracy in inmate enumeration. Regardless of what they are called, they are procedures used as means of controlling Native inmates. In order to clearly identify the various procedures used by Correctional officers, a more detailed discussion of these control processes will be presented.

Policy: In 1981 the federal Solicitor General declared its dealing with Native people to be one of seven major areas for policy change. Its primary objectives for Native inmates became: to reduce the number of imprisoned Natives; to increase the number of Native staff employed in the criminal justice system; to establish more Native consultation in policy-making; to respond to Native policing, institutional and after-care needs; and to encourage improved federal/provincial coordination (Newby, 1981: 13). This approach was rooted in a general policy encouraging the provision of special services to all offenders with special needs, including the mentally or physically handicapped, Francophones, "lifers" and others. Native inmates, therefore, were not singled out for special attention because of their status as Aboriginal peoples, but as one of a number of problem populations. By 1983 changes in policy were proposed to allow special Native spiritual programs (Couture, 1983), but it was not until two years later that Native spiritual programs were implemented, although no specific mention was made of Native inmates, as such. An "Action Plan" for hiring more Native staff was also put into effect that year (Correctional Law Review, 1988: 37). In 1987, a specific policy outlining Native programming was declared (Task Force on Aboriginal Peoples, 1988: 18). The current mission statement of the Correctional Services of Canada specifically refers to Native inmates in strategic objective 2.2, which is: "To ensure the special needs of female and native offenders are addressed properly" (Native Advisory Committee, 1989: 5).

Programming: Before 1970, there were few or no programs or services provided by any level of correctional services in Canada that were designated specifically for Native inmates (Canadian Corrections Association, 1967: 48). Twenty years later, Correctional Services of Canada provides or facilitates: a Native Advisory Committee, Native Liaison Workers, Spiritual Elder Services, Native Brotherhood/Sisterhood Groups, Native Cultural Programs, Native Alcohol and Drug Counselling Programs, Native Conditional Release/Parole Supervision, Native Halfway Houses, Native Academic Upgrading Programs, Native Awareness Training for Staff, and Employment

Affirmation Action Programs (Correctional Services of Canada, 1989: 7). These are the services offered at the federal level; more programs are available at the provincial level. Alberta, for example, contracts with Native Counselling Services of Alberta to operate a minimum security correctional institution, to provide Parole supervision and, until recently, to operate a forestry Camp and offer Native Liaison services in provincial correctional institutions. Native organizations are also on contract to provide correctional services in B.C., Ontario, Saskatchewan, Quebec, and Manitoba (Task Force on Aboriginal Peoples, 1988: 18). Many of these programs are designed specifically to speed inmates through the system, convert Native people into staff, or segregate inmates.

The Correctional Law Review (1986: 35) states,

> There is a growing recognition that imaginative programming as well as the active involvement in programming of all correctional staff, is not only appropriate from a rehabilitative perspective, but is also effective to reduce tension levels in institutions and the risk presented by offenders.

Concerns have been raised about the intent of some aspects of this social control strategy. For example, Havemann (1988: 85, 91) suggests that hiring programs aimed at increasing the number of Native staff may have a "benign intent" but will actually increase oppression against Native people because these Native staff are used to increase the legitimacy of the dominant society's values. As well, this strategy brings into question the personal identities of the staff and the traditional methods of social control used by the community.

Fact-finding task forces: There has been an increase in the number of government initiated or funded task forces and committees mandated to investigate, in whole or in part, the problems presented by Native inmates. The first report to mention the special needs of Native inmates was the Ewing Report in 1936; but the first one recognized as having real impact on government strategies was *Indians and the Law* by the Canadian Corrections Association in 1967. Reports have appeared periodically since then with ten appearing in just over 22 years, but the frequency has increased sharply in the last few years. For example, in 1988, there were four reports that dealt directly with residential and post-release services for Native inmates (see Task Force on Aboriginal Offenders, 1988; Correctional Law Review, 1988; Standing Committee, 1988; and see Jackson, 1989). Recommendations made by these reports have covered a wide range of strategies including improvements to record-keeping, inmate assessments, staff training, and security arrangements. In terms of Spitzer's model, these recommendations encompass conversion strategies, for example, increasing the number of Aboriginal community members on the National Parole Board (Task Force on Aboriginal Peoples, 1988: 82); normalization strategies, for example, increasing the access of Native offenders to information on release preparation (Task Force on Aboriginal Peoples, 1988: 87); and containment strategies, for example, contracting more services for Native inmates to Native groups active in the criminal justice system (Advisory Committee, 1984: 27).

Enumeration: Increased efforts are being made in Corrections to enumerate the number of Native offenders. The Canadian Corrections Association in 1967 (p. 62) made particular mention of the difficulty of finding statistics concerning Native offenders, as did Schmeiser in 1974 (p. 1). In 1982, Co-West commented on the lack of statistics everywhere in the Alberta criminal justice system, with the exception of Corrections (pp. 130–8). Changes, therefore, had occurred in Alberta, as they had throughout Canada in that eight year period. Several years later, Corrections is still one of the few components of the system to count its Native population, although concerns are raised occasionally about the accuracy of these counts.

In summary, a change has occurred in correctional policy towards Native people. Native inmates have gone from being insignificant entities within the system to being a group needing enumeration, investigation, services — as a means of control.

Despite these initiatives, however, there are still problems in the Correctional Services of Canada's operational policy. In terms of Spitzer's conceptualization: 1) although Native offenders often receive shorter sentences (LaPrairie, 1990: 434), the normalization strategy in general has had problems. For example, Native offenders are released less frequently on parole (Hann and Harman, 1986: 5.15), and other components of the criminal justice system have exhibited a lack of cooperation (NCSA, 1982). 2) Conversion efforts have suffered from problems in hiring and keeping Native staff due to high educational requirements and conflicting demands from inmates and co-workers (Solicitor General Canada, 1975: 54; Task Force on Aboriginal Peoples, 1988: 38–9). The alternative of training non-Native staff to better handle Native inmates through cross-cultural awareness courses is still not carried out systematically (Task Force on Aboriginal Peoples, 1988: 44). 3) Containment is being tried through contracts with Native criminal justice agencies and seems, so far, to be the most frequently used strategy (see, for example, NCSA, 1981 and 1989).

CONCLUSION

It is necessary to remember that when studying the relations between any minority and a dominant group, the minority group is concerned with changes to improve its position. In general, the dominant group will respond positively to these demands up to a critical point at which the status quo is seriously endangered (Frideres, 1988: 407). Native inmates, a "social dynamite" population, are making demands. But, how seriously are they endangering the status quo within Corrections? How much change has really happened?

Indicators show a significant increase in the control strategies being used on the Native problem population, but the results in terms of a lowered recidivism rate, for example, are not evident. As Newby (1981: 14) so succinctly argued: "Progress is not to be measured in miles, or even feet, but in inches." Why is this the case?

While the number of control strategies are multiplying as the perception of Native inmates changes, the approaches being tried are not new, as Newby and others have pointed out. Countless studies have concluded that only wide-ranging changes in the social, economic, and political foundations of Canadian society will have any real impact on Native involvement in the criminal justice system. This means that the very existence of a problem population such as Native inmates calls into question the fundamental economic, political, and social relationships within Canadian society.

Control strategies do not work because they are not addressing the real causal factors that are found in the long history of Native/non-Native relations (Newby,

1981: 14), that is, in the environment external to the correctional system. As Spitzer might have said, the needed changes would have to affect the social relations of production in Canadian society. Just as these causal factors are ultimately found in the environment, so, too, will change have to occur in the environment. It must be remembered that Corrections, like many service organizations, has only limited power to affect solutions in its environment.

Until changes in the wider environment occur, Corrections will have to continue to control its problem population of Native inmates, all the while recognizing that the situation has the potential to become more and more explosive as time goes on.

NOTES

1. An earlier draft of this paper was presented at the Annual Meeting of the Canadian Sociology and Anthropology Association, Victoria, May 26–30, 1990. Financial assistance from the Faculty of Graduate Studies and Research, the President, the Vice-President (Research) and the Alma Mater Fund of the University of Alberta, is gratefully acknowledged.
2. According to Morse (1985: 1), the term "Native" includes people "who trace their ancestors in these lands to time immemorial" and so includes Status, Non-Status, Metis, and Inuit. The words "Native," "indigenous," and "Aboriginal" will be used synonymously.
3. "Corrections" is defined as "that aspect of government services which are responsible for supervising sentenced offenders" (Newby, 1981: 8). The differences among the various jurisdictions will be mentioned only when relevant.
4. It should be noted that from the point of view of many Native people, they are not a problem population. Their "problem" activities are based on "the daily struggle and passive resistance on which we have survived the colonialism of the past four centuries." (Manuel and Posluns, 1974: 182).
5. The only main purpose is the custody and control of inmates (Advisory Committee, 1984: 17–18).
6. See, for example, Irwin (1980) concerning the impact of organized inmate groups on an institution and on Corrections in general.

REFERENCES

Adams, Howard. 1989. *Prison of Grass, Revised Edition*. Saskatoon: Fifth House.

Advisory Committee to the Solicitor General of Canada on the Management of Correctional Institutions (Carson Committee). 1984. *Report*. Ottawa: Solicitor General Canada.

Campbell, Gayle, Frank J. Porporino and Len Wevrick. 1985. *Characteristics of Inmates involved in Prison Incidents, Phase I*. Ottawa: Solicitor General Canada.

Canadian Corrections Association. 1967. *Indians and the Law*. Ottawa: Canadian Welfare Council.

Correctional Law Review. 1988. *Correctional Issues Affecting Native Peoples*. Ottawa: Solicitor General Canada. (Working Paper No. 7).

———. 1986. *Correctional Philosophy*. Ottawa: Solicitor General Canada. (Working Paper No. 1).

Corrections Services Canada. 1989. "Update on Native-oriented programs for: Native Offenders." *Let's Talk*. 14/5: 6–7.

Couture, Joseph. 1983. "Traditional Aboriginal Spirituality and Religious Practice in Federal Prisons." (photocopy)

Co-West Associates. 1981. *A Program Review and Evaluation Assessment: Criminal Courtworker Program, Native Counselling Services of Alberta*. Ottawa: Department of Justice.

Ewing Commission. 1936. *Report*. Edmonton: n.p.

Forum in Corrections Research. 1989. 1/2: 6.

Frideres, James S. 1988. *Native Peoples in Canada: Contemporary Conflicts, 3rd ed.* Scarborough: Prentice-Hall.

Hagan, John. 1984. *The Disreputable Pleasures: Crime and Deviance in Canada, 2nd ed.* Toronto: McGraw-Hill.

———. 1985. *Modern Criminology: Crime, Criminal Behavior, and its Control.* Toronto: McGraw-Hill.

Haley, Hugh J. and Peter Lerette. 1984. *Correctional Objectives, the First Step to Accountability.* Ottawa: Canada Solicitor General.

Hall, Richard H. 1987. *Organizations: Structures, Processes and Outcomes, 4th ed.* Englewood Cliffs, NJ: Prentice-Hall.

Hann, Robert G. and William G. Harman. 1986. *Full Parole Release: An Historical Descriptive Analysis.* Ottawa: Solicitor General Canada.

Havemann, Paul. 1988. "The Indigenization of Social Control in Canada." In Bradford W. Morse and Gordon R. Woodman (eds.) *Indigenous Law and the State.* Dordrecht: Foris.

Havemann, Paul, Keith Couse, Lori Foster and Rae Matonovich. 1985. *Law and Order for Canada's Indigenous People.* Regina: School for Human Justice, University of Regina.

Irwin, John. 1980. *Prisons in Turmoil.* Toronto: Little-Brown.

Jackson, Michael. 1989. "Locking up Natives in Canada." *University of British Columbia Law Review,* 23/2: 215–300.

LaPrairie, Carol. 1990. "The Role of Sentencing in the Over-Representation of Aboriginal People in Correctional Institutions." *Canadian Journal of Criminology,* 32/3: 429–440.

Manuel, George and Michael Posluns. 1974. *The Fourth World: An Indian Reality.* Don Mills, ON: Collier-Macmillan.

McCaskill, Don. 1985. *Patterns of Criminality and Correction Among Native Offenders in Manitoba.* Saskatoon: Correctional Services of Canada.

Morse, Bradford W. 1985. "Aboriginal Peoples and the Law." In Bradford W. Morse (ed.) *Aboriginal Peoples and the Law.* Ottawa: Carleton University Press.

Morse, Brad and Linda Lock. 1988. *Native Offenders' Perceptions of the Criminal Justice System.* Ottawa: Supply and Services.

Native Advisory Committee. 1989. *Response to the Report of the Task Force on Aboriginal Peoples in Federal Corrections.* n.p.

Native Counselling Services of Alberta (NCSA). 1981. "Private Sector Alternatives to Corrections: The Role of NCSA." Edmonton: NCSA (photocopy).

———. 1982. "Creating a Monster." *Canadian Journal of Criminology,* 24/3: 323–328.

———. 1989. *Annual Report, 1988-89.* Edmonton: NCSA.

Newby, Liz. 1981. *Native People of Canada and the Federal Corrections System: Development of a National Policy — A Preliminary Issues Report.* Ottawa: Correctional Service of Canada.

Perreault, J., L. Paquette and M.V. George. 1985. *Population Projections of Registered Indians, 1982 to 1996.* Ottawa: Indian and Northern Affairs.

Pfeffer, Jeffrey and Gerald R. Salanchik. 1978. *The External Control of Organizations: A Resource Dependency Perspective.* New York: Harper & Row.

Rodger, John J. 1988. "Social Work as Social Control Re-Examined: Beyond the Dispersal of Discipline Thesis." *Sociology,* 22/4: 563–581.

Schmeiser, Douglas. 1974. *The Native Offender and the Law.* Ottawa: Law Reform Commission.

Solicitor General Canada. 1975. *Native Peoples and Justice.* Ottawa: Solicitor General Canada.

Spitzer, Steven. 1979. "Notes Toward a Theory of Punishment and Social Change" In Rita J. Simon and Steven Spitzer (eds.) *Research in Law and Sociology, Vol 2.* Greenwich: JAI Press.

———. 1975. "Toward a Marxian Theory of Deviance." *Social Problems,* 22/5: 638–651.

Standing Committee on Justice and Solicitor General (Daubney Commission). 1988. *Taking Responsibility.* Ottawa: House of Commons.

Task Force on Aboriginal Peoples in Federal Corrections. 1988. *Final Report.* Ottawa: Solicitor General Canada.

NINETEEN

Community Sanctions and Imprisonment: Hoping for a Miracle but Not Bothering Even to Pray for It

ANTHONY N. DOOB[1]

BACKGROUND TO THE PROBLEM

It is unlikely that many readers of the report of the Canadian Sentencing Commission (1987) were surprised to find that the Canadian Association of Elizabeth Fry Societies, the John Howard Society of Canada, and the Quaker Committee on Jails and Justice were quoted as saying, in effect, that, in Canada, we should be more sparing in our use of imprisonment as a sanction. But belief that we overuse imprisonment is not limited to groups such as these. A case can be made that there is a consensus in Canada that more people are being imprisoned than should be. In a national poll carried out in the mid-1980s, about 70 percent of Canadians indicated that they would rather put tax money into the development of community sanctions than into building more prisons (Doob and Roberts 1988). This opinion is not new. One can find numerous statements in official Canadian reports suggesting that dispositions other than imprisonment for our offenders should be developed.

More than half a century ago, the Report of the Royal Commission to Investigate the Penal System of Canada (the Archambault Report 1938: 100) stated that:

> The undeniable responsibility of the state to those held in its custody is to see that they are not returned to freedom worse than when they were taken in charge. This responsibility has been officially recognized in Canada for nearly a century but, although recognized, it has not been discharged.

In the 1956 report of the Committee appointed to inquire into the principles and procedures followed in the remission service of the Department of Justice of Canada (the Fauteux Report 1956: 14, 18), readers are told:

> In addition, it goes without saying that, from a financial point of view, a great saving of public moneys can be achieved by the use, in proper cases, of probation rather than

Source: Anthony N. Doob, "Community Sanctions and Imprisonment: Hoping for a Miracle but Not Bothering Even to Pray for It," *Canadian Journal of Criminology*, 32, 3 (1990): 415–28. Copyright by the Canadian Criminal Justice Association. Reproduced by permission of the *Canadian Journal of Criminology*.

imprisonment as a means of rehabilitation ... The trend in England ... appears to be "imprisonment as a last resort." This new approach ... has probably resulted from the success of probation and parole and has not, so far as we can ascertain, resulted in any general increase in crime in that country.

In its 1969 report "Toward Unity: Criminal Justice and Corrections," the Canadian Committee on Corrections (the "Ouimet Committee") recommended an approach that should have minimized the use of imprisonment:

> The existence of [certain] restrictions upon the power of a court to sentence otherwise than to imprisonment all too frequently leads to a practice of imposing a sentence of imprisonment in the absence of mitigating factors. (Canada, Canadian Committee on Corrections 1969: 191)
>
> In conclusion the Committee maintains that imprisonment or confinement should be used only as an ultimate resort when all other alternatives have failed, but subject to its other recommendations concerning different types of offender and different categories of dispositions. (Canada, Canadian Committee on Corrections 1969: 204)

The Law Reform Commission of Canada, in its first report to Parliament urged that we make less use of imprisonment. It argued that even in the case of:

> hard core real crimes needing traditional trials and serious punishments ... we need restraint. For one thing, the cost of the criminal law to the offender, the taxpayer and all of us — must always be kept as low as possible. For another, the danger with all punishments is simply that familiarity breeds contempt. The harsher the punishments, the slower we should be to use it. This applies especially to punishments of last resort. The major punishment of last resort is prison. This is today the ultimate weapon of the criminal law. As such it must be used sparingly.... (Law Reform Commission of Canada 1976: 24)
>
> Restricting our use of imprisonment will allow more scope for other types of penalties.... Positive penalties like restitution and community service orders should be increasingly substituted for the negative and uncreative warehousing of prison. (Law Reform Commission of Canada 1976: 25)

Perhaps more surprising than these statements by non-parliamentary bodies is the endorsement of the increased use of community sanctions in the August 1988 "Report of the Standing Committee on Justice and Solicitor General on its Review of Sentencing, Conditional Release and Related Aspects of Corrections" (commonly known as the "Daubney Committee"). It suggested that Canada overuses imprisonment and should make more use of community sanctions.

> The Committee reached a consensus early in its deliberations about the desirability of using alternatives to incarceration as sentencing dispositions for offenders who commit non-violent offences. Using incarceration for such offenders is clearly too expensive in both financial and social terms.... Too many people are sentenced to incarceration for non-violent offences and non-payment of fines — this creates over-crowding and results in violation of the proportionality principle in sentencing. Moreover, the growth in prison populations does not appear to have reduced crime. In the Committee's view,

expensive prison resources should be reserved for the most serious cases. (Daubney Report 1988: 49–50)

Though not explicitly stating his disapproval of the relatively high level of use of imprisonment in Canada, the then Minister of Justice, Mr. Ray Hnatyshyn, in August 1988, told the Canadian Bar Association in the context of announcing plans for the reform of sentencing that,

Many sources have documented the reliance on imprisonment in this country. While this is changing, Canada still incarcerates a comparatively large number of individuals. This is costly to the individual and to society at large, and has been the target of criticism by academics and practitioners alike. (Hnatyshyn 1988: 5)

An earlier government document, published in 1982 over the signature of the then Minister of Justice, Jean Chrétien, "sets out the policy of the Government of Canada with respect to the purpose and principles of the criminal law" (Preface to "The Criminal Law in Canadian Society"). As the then Minister notes,

As such, it is unique in Canadian history. Never before has the Government articulated such a comprehensive and fundamental statement concerning its view of the philosophical underpinnings of criminal law policy. (Canada 1982: Preface)

Consistent with previous documents, the policy of the Government of Canada, apparently was (and presumably still is) that,

in awarding sentences, preference should be given to the least restrictive alternative adequate and appropriate in the circumstances. (Canada 1982: 64, 65)

The policy statement goes on to note that this principle, read together with others implies that

a hierarchy of sentencing options, from the least to the most serious, should be available, (at least potentially) for most offences, and that in effect the use of the more serious alternatives must be justified on grounds of necessity.

A bit later in this statement of Government of Canada policy, the reader is told that guidelines applicable to sentencing should "establish that imprisonment should be used only when lesser sanctions are inadequate or inappropriate...."

If Canada were the only country where these kinds of concerns were being expressed, one might not be surprised to find that change had not been implemented. But Canada is not alone. In Britain, at about the same time as the Daubney Committee was making its final recommendations, a Green Paper was released with a clear anti-imprisonment tone. Entitled "Punishment, custody, and the community," the paper introduced the topic in the following way:

Last year 69,000 offenders were sentenced to custody for indictable offences in England and Wales. For many of them, this was the right punishment, because their offences were very serious.... But for other, less serious, offenders, a spell in custody is not the most effective punishment. Imprisonment restricts offenders' liberty, but it also reduces their responsibility.... Punishment in the community would encourage offenders to drop out of crime and to develop into responsible and law abiding citizens. (United Kingdom 1988: 1)

After noting that most inmates of British prisons were not convicted of violent offences, it points out that most are there for burglaries that are often "opportunist thefts from houses with open doors or windows, with no damage to the house or threats to the people living there. Nearly half the burglaries reported are of offices, shops and other buildings, not houses." In this context, the Green Paper asks (rhetorically, one might suggest):

"Are we sending too many people to prison? Is imprisonment the best, or only, way to deal with recidivist burglars and thieves....?" (United Kingdom 1988: 9)

In February 1990, the Government of the United Kingdom answered its own question. Using harsh law-and-order language, Mrs. Thatcher's government's White Paper states that:

The Government believes that more offenders should be punished in the community.... The Government believes that a new approach is needed if the use of custody is to be reduced. Punishment in the community should be an effective way of dealing with many offenders, particularly those convicted of property crimes and less serious offences of violence.... (United Kingdom 1990: 18)

Though it points out the financial savings to be realized if the Government is successful in shifting people from prison to the community, the paper concludes that:

The proposals in this White Paper are put forward on their merits because punishment in the community is likely to be more suitable and effective than custody for offenders who have not committed the more serious offences. The proposals should increase punishment in the community and reduce the use of custody. Punishment in the community also imposes a lesser burden on the taxpayer than custody. (United Kingdom 1990: 47)

In another part of the Commonwealth, one only has to read the table of contents to infer the position being taken. The title to Chapter 3 of the 1988 report on sentencing of the Australian Law Reform Commission — "Reducing the emphasis on imprisonment" — gives the flavour of Australian (federal) concerns and approaches. That Commission notes that

... the emphasis which the criminal justice system presently places on imprisonment as a punishment for offences must be reduced. Instead more emphasis needs to be placed on non-custodial sanctions, particularly the community based sanctions such as the community service order ... (Australia, Law Reform Commission 1988: 20)

Later in the report, it is noted that

All Australian governments, including the federal government, are committed to reducing the emphasis on imprisonment as a sanction. This was underlined when corrections Ministers, meeting in Melbourne in 1987, endorsed a public statement that said, in part "in each jurisdiction, a review and rationalization of sentencing legislation, policies and practices should promote diversion from imprisonment and should reduce the maximum and average lengths of imprisonment. (Australia, Law Reform Commission 1988: 27)

Finally, a recent United Nations report prepared by representatives of about a dozen countries representing all parts of the world recommended that

A range of sanctions should be available to enable the sentencing judge to choose the most appropriate one, bearing in mind [that] sentences involving imprisonment should be imposed only if there are demonstrable grounds for believing that community sanctions would be inappropriate.... Imprisonment should be used as a last resort.... None but the most serious offences should be excluded from the application of community sanctions.... (United Nations 1988: 8)

Apparently almost alone in its view of imprisonment is the United States Sentencing Commission. In its "Introductory Commentary" on probation, for example, the Commission notes that under U.S. federal law "probation is a sentence in and of itself." It then goes on to note that:

Probation may be used as an alternative to incarceration, provided that the terms and conditions can be fashioned so as to meet *fully* the statutory purposes of sentencing, including promoting respect for law, providing just punishment for the offence, achieving general deterrence, and protecting the public from further crimes by the defendant. (U.S. Sentencing Commission 1988: 5.5; emphasis added)

One does not have to be too cynical to suggest that it is unlikely that probation (or any other disposition) will ever "meet fully" all of these purposes. In any case, there are few offences covered by these guidelines where a convicted offender could completely escape custody.

Indeed, even the most trivial offences committed by someone with no criminal record include, within the guideline range, at least some time in custody. Those slightly more serious do not contain the possibility of a community sanction if sentenced within the guideline range. Under the U.S. Sentencing Commission's guidelines, a break and enter of an unoccupied store where the total loss was minimal committed by a person with no criminal record would result in a sentence of between 10 and 16 months. Had it been a dwelling that was broken into, the guideline indicates that the sentence (for the first-time offender) should be between 24 and 30 months.

In Canada, of course, accurate sentencing statistics are not available, but it is likely that most such cases — especially where it was a non-dwelling that was burgled — would result in a community sanction. Under the guidelines proposed by the Canadian Sentencing Commission, the presumptive sentence would be a community sanction for a first offender who committed a minor burglary of either a dwelling or a non-dwelling.

In the context of most civilized countries, the various recommendations made by the Canadian Sentencing Commission for a de-emphasis on imprisonment can hardly be seen as anything but the current Canadian and world wisdom. Few, then, would be expected to argue against the restrictions placed on imprisonment included in the Commission's "Principles of Sentencing":

> A term of imprisonment should be imposed only (a) to protect the public from crimes of violence, (b) where any other sanction would not sufficiently reflect the gravity of the offence or the repetitive nature of the criminal conduct of an offender, or adequately protect the public or the integrity of the administration of justice, (c) to penalize an offender for willful non-compliance with the terms of any other sentence that has been imposed on the offender where no other sanction appears adequate to compel compliance. (Canada, Canadian Sentencing Commission 1987: 154)

Why then is it that we do not have the kind of increased use of community sanctions that we apparently, like much of the world, have wanted? As is implied by the sub-title, the thesis of this paper is that in many jurisdictions — and certainly in Canada — we should not have been surprised when we began creating "alternatives" to find that the efforts were not as we might have wanted. We should not have been surprised if we were to find that the use of incarceration was not diminished by these new alternatives. Similarly, we would have no valid reason to be smug if we had found that incarceration levels had decreased as a result of these new sentencing alternatives. In fact, we had no reason to expect any particular outcome because we did almost nothing to determine how community sanctions would be used.

PURPOSE OF THIS PAPER

I will attempt in this paper to accomplish three broad tasks. First, I will call attention to some of the evidence, in particular the Canadian evidence, on the impact of new, non-carceral "alternatives" to imprisonment. In this review, I will be relying largely on some recent work suggesting that, at least in Canada, the notion that community sanctions are simply add-ons to imprisonment is inaccurate or at least over-simplified.

Second, I will suggest that part of the problem with "alternatives" to imprisonment is that we often do little to ensure that alternatives work as alternatives rather than as mere supplements to imprisonment. Their effect will be determined by a number of factors, not the least of which is whether there is a meaningful policy on the matter.

Finally, I will outline what I see as the necessary steps to be taken to devise a system of punishments that decreases our use of imprisonment. I will use, as an illustration of what such a policy might look like, the 1987 report of The Canadian Sentencing Commission.

ARE ALTERNATIVES REALLY ALTERNATIVES?[2]

In Canada, the conventional (but now revised) wisdom about the effect of community sanctions on imprisonment is based in large part on studies by Hylton (1981, 1982) in Saskatchewan, and by Chan and Ericson (1981) in Ontario. The conventional (but now revised) wisdom of the 1970s and 1980s about community corrections can be summarized by extracting one sentence from Stanley Cohen's 1985 book *Visions of social control: Crime, punishment and classification*: "Community control has supplemented rather than replaced traditional methods" (Cohen 1985: 44).

McMahon (1988) identified some of the deficiencies in the data bases that were being used and, as well, identified some of the questionable assumptions being made in assessing what sentences were actually being handed down at the time when "alternatives" to incarceration were being implemented in these locations. For example, Hylton essentially ignored *federal* inmates in his analysis. Although, relatively speaking, their admission *numbers* are small (as compared to those serving provincial sentences of less than two years), their impact on prisoner *counts* (i.e., number of people in prison on a given day) is relatively large. Thus, in order to know whether overall imprisonment increased or decreased or stayed the same during a period, it is important to know whether increases in one part of the system coincided with decreases or increases or stability in another. An increase in the number of provincial inmates could be due to something as simple as a *decrease* in the number of people getting sentences of two years or more.

Other problems beset the analysis in Ontario by Chan and Ericson. McMahon carefully explores these problems noting, among other things, difficulties that occurred due to inconsistent, or at times, inappropriate indicators of social control. This is an area in which it is easy either to sink into a quagmire of statistics or to fly blindly through clouds of figures picking and choosing from among those that are easily available. One has to be mindful not only of the differences between rates and numbers, counts and admissions, sentenced admissions and all admissions, but one also must consider carefully exactly what one's question really should be. Thus, for example, as McMahon points out, certain forms of use of "alternatives" can *inevitably* lead to an increase in the total number of people under "social control" at any given point.

Following her example, imagine a hypothetical jurisdiction where 50,000 people were being sentenced to serve 30 days in prison each year. The average daily prison population would then be 1/12 of 50,000 or 4,167. If, instead of sentencing them all to one month of imprisonment, half of these 50,000 (or 25,000) were given a year of probation, the average prison population would reduce to 2,084 but the total *penal* population would rapidly rise to 27,084 (25,000 on probation plus the 2,084 in prison). More people would, therefore, be under some form of state control on any given day, but fewer would be in prison. Such an "effect" would, of course, be different from any effect that the existence of the alternatives might have in increasing the amount of overall social control by adding such punishments as a Community Service Order to a simple term of probation.

In any case, without wanting to get too far into the details of McMahon's analysis, it is clear that during the period of time when "alternatives to imprisonment" were being introduced and encouraged in Ontario (from 1951 to 1983), Ontario total imprisonment *rates* (per 100,000 in the population) were, if anything, decreasing. The same holds for total (federal and provincial) counts. McMahon points out that the decrease in indicators of imprisonment in Ontario is not uniform across different sentence lengths. There is an indication that long sentences may be getting longer. However, at the low end (sentences under 30 days) — where presumably one might reasonably expect "alternatives" to be used as alternatives — there is evidence of substantial decarceration. Overall, during the thirty year period that she studied, the net result is that the total imprisonment rates (measured in admissions or prisoner counts) declined.

It may well be that a miracle occurred without prayer. The lesson, however, is quite clear. We do *not* automatically have to assume that if a penal system expands the range of sentencing alternatives available to the sentencing judge to include punishments that take place in the community (the so-called "alternatives"), these will inevitably have no effect on the use of imprisonment.

WHAT SHOULD WE EXPECT FROM "ALTERNATIVES"

It appears that "alternatives to imprisonment" are often instituted for a very simple reason: there is a feeling among some associated with the criminal justice system — often administrators rather than judges or legislators — that the sanction of imprisonment is used more than it should be. The underlying assumptions behind such administrative changes seem to be as follows:

1. In the absence of a wide range of alternatives, judges are reluctantly imprisoning offenders.
2. Those offenders who are presently being given community sanctions are receiving sentences that involve, from the judges' perspective, sufficient control, punishment, or rehabilitative opportunities.
3. Judges will automatically see the new community sanction as appropriate for a wide range of offenders who, previously, were predominantly receiving sentences of imprisonment.

Each of these assumptions can be questioned. The important thing, however, is that each of these assumptions concerns the beliefs, opinions, and decisions of judges. They do not relate to the beliefs, opinions, and decisions of policy people, legislators, or administrators. In the absence of some other kind of guidance, decisions about sanctions are going to be made by judges.

HOW DO DECISION MAKERS VIEW "ALTERNATIVES"?

It is perhaps worthwhile to relate an anecdote at this point. A few years ago, I was doing some work on community service orders as a disposition for young persons (in this case those under sixteen years old under the *Juvenile Delinquents Act*). I knew the literature and the rhetoric about community service orders. In a number of different settings I spoke to judges about their views of community service orders for juveniles. Two responses stand out in my mind. I had asked a judge, now that a community service order programme was in place in his community, whether he imposed community service orders instead of putting the young person in custody. He looked at me rather incredulously and explained that he only considered custody in the absolutely most serious cases and a community service order would be completely inappropriate for young persons of that sort.

A second judge also, I expect, saw me as a rather naive academic to think that the "alternative" disposition of a community service order was an "alternative" to imprisonment. He patiently explained to me that community service orders were really a good way of keeping a particular youth out of trouble. He told me that he determined the number of hours of work that a young person should be forced to do by figuring out how many hours (per week) he needed to assign to keep the youth busy (and, according to this theory, out of trouble). Thus, if a young person was stealing things after school or on Saturdays, his hours of court-ordered work would be set to make sure that he was working instead of stealing. Community service orders were, for this judge, a form of more effective probation supervision than simple probation.

I have suggested that for the most part we tend to put "alternatives" in place with the hope that they will be used instead of imprisonment, yet typically we do not go one step more and do something to ensure that this is the case. In Ontario, the Ministry of Correctional Services has, to its credit, been trying to expand its range of alternatives for quite some time. A few years ago, because of concern that the judges were not seeing "alternatives" as alternatives to imprisonment, they commissioned a study (Jackson 1982) to find out how judges viewed "alternatives" to imprisonment.

There was evidence in Ontario that community service orders, intended by the Ministry that had set them up as an alternative to their prisons were, in fact, being used largely for "low-risk offenders convicted of non-serious crimes" (Jackson 1982: 14). The study's author notes that in her interviews with judges

> a majority of the judges did not view community service orders as alternatives to incarceration. A notable exception to this was in one [location] where it had been made explicit policy more forcefully by the senior judge that community service orders were to be implemented as alternatives.

The main point seems to be that in a system like that in place in Canada — where sentencing is supposed to accomplish a number of often contradictory purposes — sentences of incarceration and "alternatives" to incarceration are usually seen by judges as accomplishing different functions. As Jackson's (1982: 44) report notes:

> Therefore it should not be surprising that [judges] do not use [incarceration and alternatives] for similar cases. Unless there is an explicit effort to alter these perceptions, it is predicted that alternatives will continue to be used as offshoots of probation, for individuals perceived to be in need of rehabilitation and not considered dangerous nor likely to recidivate.... But those offenders destined for prison are not likely to be those destined to the community in the present process because judges ... perceive the risk for public safety in terms of the offence as a more important consideration than the offender's needs.

Although there was certainly a lot of variability across judges on what they considered in sentencing an individual, there were also some regularities in how they viewed imprisonment compared to community sanctions. The considerations that judges were most likely to list for sentencing someone to prison were different from those that the judges considered when sentencing someone to an "alternative." For incarceration those considerations that were endorsed by at least a quarter of the judges were as follows (in the order of the likelihood of being mentioned):

- It is a serious, violent crime, where protection of the public is needed against the offence.
- Offender has a prior criminal record and/or the offender's age makes imprisonment a sensible disposition.
- Nature of the offence (i.e., degree of physical harm to public; prevalence of it in the community).
- Offender is seen to be likely to commit other offences in the future.
- No other alternative than jail is appropriate to achieve general deterrence because of seriousness of the crime.
- The offender is dangerous. (Jackson 1982: 8)

As an example of how these same judges saw community sanctions, we can look at what they said they considered for community service orders:

- Ability and availability of the offender to do the work (perceived to have a high likelihood of completing the work).
- Normally an offence not involving violence.
- Young, first offenders. (Jackson 1982: 8)

One can hardly be surprised that for some offenders, community service orders are not being used as alternatives to imprisonment. These views from the bench suggest that this particular community sanction is not being thought of as being appropriate for somewhat less serious cases that otherwise would go to prison. It is for a qualitatively different kind of case.

Norval Morris (1988: 3) has suggested other necessary conditions for community sanctions to be effective sanctions. Under the heading "Some dogmatic propositions concerning intermediate punishments and their imposition" he lists, among other things:

> Intermediate punishments must be rigorously enforced; if they are to be effective and credible sanctions, adequate resources for their enforcement are essential.
>
> Breaches of conditions of intermediate punishments must be taken seriously by the supervising authority and, in appropriate cases by the sentencing judge, if these punishments are to become credible sanctions.

SUMMARY: WHAT DOES ALL THIS MEAN?

Imagine that it was late one evening and a restaurant was serving more wine than usual. The supply of red wines was low. The owner then realized that he had just received a shipment of rosé wines. He then added the rosé to his wine list. Should we assume that he would be successful in inducing his customers who otherwise would order red to order his "alternative" rosé? Or would the customers who normally would not drink wine now order the rosé alternative? Or, would customers ignore the new choice and simply act as they would have without the new choice? On the basis of the information I have provided, is there any way that anyone should be able to predict what would occur?

My point, then, about "alternatives to imprisonment" is that simply providing the alternative, in the absence of any other change, is not enough. More effort is needed to ensure that an "alternative" is truly an "alternative" to one particular option.

What do we need to do to ensure that "alternatives" to imprisonment are really used as "alternatives" and not as supplements to (sometimes already high rates of) imprisonment?
In Canada, we have almost no effective sentencing policy. Unfortunately, we are not unique in this defect in our criminal justice system. It seems that sentencing policy is something that a number of countries would like to leave ambiguous. To the extent that we do have a policy on sentencing in Canada, it derives not from Parliament, but from appointed judges. Judges in Canada may not be enthusiastic about creating public policy, but in the area of sentencing, we have left them no choice.

The policy that judges have created in Canada is better described as the absence of a policy. It says, like many such "non-policies," that sentences are to accomplish a number of different purposes: rehabilitation of this offender, deterrence of this offender, incapacitation of this offender, deterrence of others, and denunciation of criminal behaviour. The only problem is that the policy, such as it is, does not indicate how these different purposes are to be blended, or which is to dominate the decision in particular cases. For the most part, sentencing judges are on their own in deciding how to reconcile these disparate purposes. Most importantly, the non-policy under which sentencing decisions are made at the moment gives almost no meaningful guidance to the judge on when to incarcerate and when to use community sanctions.

We haven't told our judges what would normally be expected as a sentence for a particular kind of case, nor have we even told the judges what principles should govern the sentencing process. This is really a remarkable state of affairs given that sentencing offenders for criminal matters is usually the most intrusive action that the state takes against its members.

How we sometimes make it easier to imprison people than to use other sanctions.
Lack of a policy for the allocation of sentences is, then, the first problem. A more subtle problem is administrative. A judge can sentence a person to prison without having to enquire, or even consider, whether such a sentence is appropriate for the person or even if there is space in the prison for this offender. The presumption is that it is the responsibility of the government to find a space for *any* offender sentenced to imprisonment.

This is not the case with some community sanctions. For example, a judge must normally see not only whether a community service order programme exists in a community before sentencing an offender to a number of hours of community service, but also whether an offender is an appropriate candidate for a community service order.

For young offenders in Canada, a community service order *cannot* be made unless, among other things, "the youth court is satisfied that the person or organization for whom the community service is to be performed has agreed to its performance" (Young Offenders Act, s.21(9)(b)). From a practical point of view, this may make some sense. However, no parallel requirement is in place for custody: the correctional administrators have no choice about receiving a person for custody.

Imprisonment is the "standard" sanction: others are "alternatives."
Our thinking and sometimes our laws reflect a presumption in favour of imprisonment. Our penalty structure for criminal offences is uniformly stated in terms of the maximum sentence of imprisonment that can be imposed. Other sanctions, then, become "alternatives." This is not true of the Young Offenders Act where a number of different dispositions are listed (in S.20(1) of the Act), the final one being custody. The problem is that even our language tends to encourage us to think first of imprisonment, and then of "alternatives."

It was in part for these reasons that the Canadian Sentencing Commission, in its 1987 report, used the term "community sanctions" instead of the more common terms such as "non-custodial" or "non-carceral" sanctions or "alternatives" to imprisonment. The Commission wanted to get away from the dichotomy between custody and all other sanctions, and wished to emphasize that it does not view imprisonment as the pivotal sanction with all other possible sentences being measured against it.

The linguistic distinction between the term "alternatives" and some term like "community sanctions," which emphasizes the independent status of the sanction is important beyond the symbolic point that it makes. It leads one to ask the obvious and critical questions: If we have "community sanctions," when should they be imposed?

This in turn forces us to ask a series of other questions including the following:

• How should sentences — community sanctions included — be allocated?
• What purpose or purposes should sentencing serve?
• What principles should govern the determination of sentences?
• What kinds of offenders convicted of what kinds of offences should normally receive community sanctions?

An example of an attempt to increase the use of community sanctions: The report of the Canadian Sentencing Commission.
The formal Declaration of Purpose and Principles of Sentencing proposed by the Canadian Sentencing Commission need not be reproduced here (see Canada 1987: 152–155). For the purposes of this paper, it is sufficient to consider the following aspects of it:

a. The paramount principle determining the sentence is that the sanction be proportionate to the gravity of the offence and the degree of responsibility of the offender for the offence.
b. There is a presumption in favour of the least onerous sanction.
c. Imprisonment is to be imposed only for specific purposes.

The implications of this policy are important. First of all, since the severity of the sentence is supposed to be proportionate to the seriousness of the offence, it follows that the less serious offences — in particular the very common but less serious property offences — should predominately receive less severe sentences. Given that the Commission also endorsed the principle of restraint in the use of imprisonment, this statement could be operationalized as meaning that there should be an increased use of community sanctions.

But a statement of purpose and principles is not enough. It may tell judges what principles to follow and may give judges a fairly good idea for a particular case of the appropriate levels of sanction *in relation to* other cases. But on its own, such a statement does not tell the judge explicitly what kinds of sanctions should be imposed for particular kinds of cases. Thus a "proportionality" model such as that recommended by the Canadian Sentencing Commission is neither harsh nor lenient on its own; without further elaboration, it does not imply either an increased use of community sanctions nor an increased use of imprisonment. Principles are necessary, but they do not provide sufficient guidance for the sentencing judge.

The Canadian Sentencing Commission went one step further in suggesting that explicit policy be made. It recommended that guidelines—created by a Commission, but assented to by Parliament—be made part of our sentencing law. Guidelines, under its recommendations, could consist of two separate parts. For all offences, there would be an explicit presumption of custody or community sanction. If the presumptive disposition were a sentence of imprisonment, the guideline would indicate the presumptive range. If it were not, then, a community sanction would be imposed. Furthermore, the Commission recommended that specific guidance—presumably in the form of guidelines—be developed for the use of community sanctions. As von Hirsch, Wasik, and Greene (1989) have noted, explicit guidance for community sanctions can be given that is consistent with an over-riding sentencing rationale.

CONCLUSION

In the context of the theme of this paper, then, community sanctions should not be "alternatives," but should become sanctions in their own right. More importantly, they should be sanctions that would be described in appropriate legislation as appropriate for certain kinds of cases. In other words, they wouldn't be add-ons to the system, but would be, presumptively, the correct sanction for many offences.

According to the Canadian Sentencing Commission, community sanctions should often be used instead of imprisonment and should be designated as the appropriate sentence for many common offences. Many very common property offences (for which a sizable number of offenders are currently imprisoned) would have, as the presumptive sentence, a community sanction. It is expected that, if the Canadian Sentencing Commission recommendations were implemented, the number of people incarcerated would drop because of the increased use of community sanctions.

Clearly, however, there can be no guarantee of success. There is a good deal of evidence that the criminal justice system is quite resistant to change. Changes cannot be made at one level of the system—in this case in the law governing sentencing—with an assurance that the changes would be implemented exactly as intended. It was for that reason, among others, that the Canadian Sentencing Commission recommended that a permanent sentencing commission be created. It would have as one of its major responsibilities the monitoring of sentencing to ensure that desired changes occurred. It would be able to recommend—and implement—changes quickly to eliminate unanticipated problems should they occur.

In Canada it would appear that a number of conditions must be met to be confident that there will be increased use of community sanctions, or "alternatives." These would include:

- The presence of well-run community sanctions;
- A policy that endorses the use of them;
- Legal and administrative procedures that put community sanctions on an equal footing with imprisonment as sentencing choices;
- Guidance to decision makers on the appropriate use of community sanctions.

Obviously it is possible to have successful "alternatives" without the policy changes I have suggested just as it might happen, to use the analogy I made earlier, that adding a third type of wine to a menu will shift customers away from the wines in short supply. However, if we want to ensure success, we probably have to work a little harder to achieve the changes we want. Those who believe in the effectiveness of prayer might try that. But Parliamentary action would seem to be a more sure bet.

NOTES

1. An earlier version of this paper was prepared for the Interregional Meeting of Experts for the Eighth United Nations Congress on the Prevention of Crime and the Treatment of Offenders, 30 May to 3 June 1988, in Vienna. Funds received by the Centre of Criminology, University of Toronto, from the Contributions Programme of the Solicitor General, Canada, to the Canadian Criminology Centres aided the preparation of this paper. I would like to thank Maeve McMahon, Mr. Justice Archie Campbell, and David Faulkner for their helpful comments on earlier drafts of the paper.
2. I am relying in this section on a recent, as yet unpublished, Ph.D. thesis by Maeve McMahon at the University of Toronto.

REFERENCES

Australia. 1988. The Law Reform Commission: Report No. 44: Sentencing. Canberra: Australian Government Publishing Service.

Canada. 1987. Canadian Sentencing Commission. Sentencing Reform: A Canadian Approach. Ottawa: Supply and Services, Canada.

———. 1976. Law Reform Commission of Canada. Our Criminal Law. Ottawa: Supply and Services, Canada.

———. 1969. Canadian Committee on Corrections (The Ouimet Committee), Toward Unity: Criminal Justice and Corrections. Ottawa: The Queen's Printer.

———. 1956. Report of the Committee Appointed to Inquire into the Principles and Procedures Followed in the Remission Service of the Department of Justice Canada. (The Fauteux Report). Ottawa: The Queen's Printer.

———. 1938. Report of the Royal Commission to Investigate the Penal System of Canada. (The Archambault Report). Ottawa: The Printer to the King's Most Excellent Majesty.

———. 1988. Report of the Standing Committee on Justice and the Solicitor General on its Review of Sentencing, Conditional Release and Related Aspects of Corrections. Taking Responsibility. (The Daubney Report). Ottawa, Queen's Printer for Canada.

———. 1982. The Criminal Law in Canadian Society. Ottawa: Government of Canada.

Chan, Janet and Richard V. Ericson. 1981. Decarceration and the Economy of Penal Reform. Toronto: Centre of Criminology, University of Toronto.

Cohen, Stanley. 1985. Visions of Social Control: Crime, Punishment and Classification. Cambridge: Polity.

Doob, Anthony N. and Julian V. Roberts. 1988. Public punitiveness and public knowledge of the facts: some Canadian surveys. In Nigel Walker and Mike Hough (eds.), Public Attitudes to Sentencing: Surveys from Five Countries. Aldershot, England: Gower.

Hnatyshyn, Ray. 1988. An Agenda for Reform of Sentencing. Speech to the Canadian Bar Association Annual Meeting. Montreal (August 24, 1988).

Hylton, John H. 1981. Community corrections and social control: The case of Saskatchewan, Canada. *Contemporary Crises* 5: 193–215.

———. 1982. Rhetoric and reality: A critical appraisal of community corrections programs. *Crime and Delinquency* 28: 341–373.

Jackson, Margaret. 1982. Judicial attitudes towards community sentencing options. Toronto: Ministry of Correctional Services, Ontario.

McMahon, Maeve. 1988. Changing penal trends: Imprisonment and alternatives in Ontario, 1951–1984. Unpublished Ph.D. thesis, University of Toronto.

Morris, Norval. 1988. Alternatives to custody. Notes accompanying a talk given to the meeting of the Society for the Reform of the Criminal Law. Ottawa: August 3, 1988.

United Kingdom. 1988. Punishment, Custody, and the Community. (Presented to Parliament by Command of Her Majesty, July 1988). London: Her Majesty's Stationery Office.

———. 1990. Crime, Justice and Protecting the Public. The Government's Proposals for Legislation. (Presented to Parliament by Command of Her Majesty, February 1990). London: Her Majesty's Stationery Office.

United Nations. 1988. Report of the Interregional Preparatory Meeting for the Eighth United Nations Congress on the Prevention of Crime and the Treatment of Offenders on Topic II: "Criminal Justice Policies in Relation to Problems of Imprisonment, Other Penal Sanctions and Alternative Measures." Vienna 30 May–3 June 1988.

United States Sentencing Commission. 1988. Guidelines Manual. Washington: The United States Sentencing Commission.

von Hirsch, Andrew, Martin Wasik, and Judith Greene. 1989. Punishments in the community and the principles of desert. *Rutgers Law Journal* 20: 595–618.

TWENTY

Electronic Monitoring in Corrections: Assessing Cost Effectiveness and the Potential for Widening the Net of Social Control

STEPHEN MAINPRIZE[1]

INTRODUCTION

Since the advent of the use of electronic monitoring (EM) in correctional programming — dating from 1984, in Florida, where programmatic use was first inaugurated

Source: Stephen Mainprize, "Electronic Monitoring in Corrections: Assessing Cost Effectiveness and the Potential for Widening the Net of Social Control," *Canadian Journal of Criminology*, 34, 2 (1992): 161–80. Copyright by the Canadian Criminal Justice Association. Reproduced by permission of *Canadian Journal of Criminology*.

(Petersilia 1987a; Schmidt 1989) — two significant issues have been articulated in the literature in connection with this new development. Criminal justice policy analysts and academics have been concerned about the *cost effectiveness* of EM, as well as the potential that programs involving EM will "widen the net of social control," (Fox 1987; Berry 1985, 1986; Griffiths 1978; Petersilia 1988; Ball and Lilly 1988).

Despite the interest and concern shown in the literature, there are as yet no detailed empirical studies of the impacts of this fast-spreading correctional policy in terms of cost effectiveness and net-widening (Blomberg, Waldo, and Burcroff 1987). Significantly, evidence from studies of previous community-based correctional programs suggests that alternatives to incarceration actually cost more in the long run, as well as expanding the base of the population subjected to correctional supervision — widening the net of social control (Cohen 1979; Hylton 1982; Austin and Krisberg 1981; Greenberg 1975; Chan and Ericson 1981).

The question that needs to be addressed in the case of the new programs employing EM is this. Are these programs following the same course as the earlier community-based sanctions? The programmatic and evaluation literature has provided little or no detailed evidence to assess this question beyond conveying per diem comparison figures for various correctional programs. These comparison figures indicate that community-based programs employing EM are generally less costly than secure custody programs (Petersilia 1987a). Unfortunately, per diem costs are more often than not taken in isolation from overall system contexts and do not reflect "true" cost assessments (Petersilia 1987a; Schmidt and Curtis 1987). The present paper attempts to remedy this weakness by addressing some points of evidence and related conceptual issues concerning the cost effectiveness and net-widening issues.

This paper will examine these two issues in both general and specific terms. Since most reports of the use of EM in community-based punishment programs has been in U.S. jurisdictions, it is necessary to draw on and analyze these materials. The paper will also examine a specific program in order that some of the conceptual issues and evidential materials can be elaborated and grounded in a more concrete manner. To this end, materials from the B.C. EMS program will be examined in light of the two-fold interest in the issues of cost effectiveness and the potential for net-widening.

THE NEW INTERMEDIATE PUNISHMENT PROGRAMS AND THE REFORM RHETORIC OF COST SAVINGS

The introduction and use of "alternatives to incarceration" in the 1960s and 1970s — such as the expanded use of fines, community service orders, and restitution — was based on a recurring set of rationalizations that have paved the way for program developments (Cohen 1985). Chan and Ericson (1981) refer to these rationalizations as a "holy trinity of penal reform," which include claims of "cost effectiveness," "efficiency,"[2] and "humaneness."[3] These rationales are *again* evident in the reform discourse associated with the new community-based punishment programs of house arrest and intensive probation supervision (IPS), which are conceived either as alternatives to incarceration or alternative *forms* of incarceration (McCarthy 1987; Petersilia 1987a; Burkhart 1986; Byrne 1986).

These new sanctions are referred to as "intermediate punishment" programs (Rush 1987; McCarthy 1987; Petersilia 1987a) because they fit along the continuum of punishments somewhere between imprisonment and probation/parole.

Surveillance, punishment, and control are chief program objectives. In the new intermediate punishments, the "controlee" is given more freedoms than prison, but the experience of house arrest and IPS is more onerous than a simple term of probation where "supervision" tends to be more infrequent and is based on therapeutic intervention models. In house arrest and IPS programs, the chief concern of staff is that of surveillance/policing or ensuring the prisoner/probationer is adhering to prescribed program rules. This program meets conservative demands for punitive treatment of offenders, as well as symbolically conveying a sense of the achievement of community protection (Burtch 1988).

Intermediate punishment program advocates and correctional reformers have consistently based their recommendations for the development and use of these programs on the claim that they are cost effective (in addition to claims of efficiency and humaneness). If programs are to be cost effective, "they must be able to act as competing alternative sanctions for a significant percentage of the custodial population" (Berry and Matthews 1989). Therefore, to the extent that these new punishment programs do not absorb offenders headed for terms of imprisonment, they are broadening the net of social control and, in the process, increasing expenditures for corrections. Thus, the concept of cost effectiveness is closely connected to that of net-widening.

While some correctional administrators claim programs are cost effective and are not leading to net-widening (Flynn 1986), more critical investigators (Johnson, Hauger, Maness, and Ross 1989) are less persuaded that this is the case. Clearly, the issue of cost is crucial to assessing systemic expansion (as follows).

In the following section, the connection between net-widening and cost effectiveness is analyzed by differentiating two kinds of net-widening. Subsequently, the interest in net-widening or system expansion is examined by way of preliminary evidence from the B.C. EMS program. Finally, some concluding, speculative comments will be offered concerning an interpretation of these materials.

NET-WIDENING

It is usually believed that widening the net of social control is bad; however, there are practical policy objectives on the basis of which system expansion could be lauded. I do not propose to answer the question of whether net-widening is good or bad here. Suffice it to say that efficiency and humaneness are sanctified objectives of penal reform (Chan and Ericson 198). Their achievement alone may offset political or administrative fallout resulting from increased costs associated with system expansion. Whatever the reality of program costs turns out to be, the fact remains that these programs have mainly been promoted on the basis of their alleged fiscal efficacy.

First, there are two related but distinct varieties of net-widening: offender net-widening and correctional personnel or systemic net-widening.

OFFENDER NET-WIDENING

Berry and Matthews (1989: 21) propose some variations on the fish net metaphor when they suggest that "much of the genuine concern about net-widening has arisen from situations where attempts have been made to reduce the range or intensity of intervention and inadvertently other clientele have been hauled in." This type of net-widening is offender-focused inasmuch as attention is directed to assessing whether an offender processing organization is bringing more offenders into the correctional system or whether the new "alternative" sanction is being used to supplement existing sanctions (such as probation and parole).

As suggested above, if offenders classified or adjudicated into the new intermediate sanctions are "true" prison diversions (and this in itself is not always easy to determine), then correctional costs ought to be lower when gauged over the longer term. This would be the case because prison diversion substitutes a less expensive sanction for one that is more costly. It may also be forestalling the expensive capital costs associated with prison construction. The central question here is whether the existence and use of the intermediate sanctions has been absorbing offenders other than those bound for prison, thus producing some significant incidence of offender net-widening and increasing correctional costs as a consequence. Evidence in this area is not encouraging.

Referring to Florida's Community Control program and the Florida Department of Corrections evaluation of that program (where only about 1/3 of offenders are monitored by EM), Petersilia (1987a) states that 70 percent of offenders subject to house arrest in the community control program are likely bona fide prison diversion, whereas 15 percent of offenders in the "community control" house arrest program are cases of offender net-widening, where probation is being enhanced by greater supervision and hence is costing more.

There are good reasons to suspect the reliability of these figures. Johnson et al. (1989) critically evaluate the above data that Petersilia appears to accept as prima facie evidence of cost and diversionary efficacy. In referring to the program evaluation, Petersilia draws her conclusions from Johnson et al. (1989: 155) who state:

> a three year study of Florida's House Arrest program by the Florida Department of Corrections (1987) concludes that house arrest is economically justified due to the dollar savings gained in comparison to prison costs. However, a review of their study creates doubts as to whether the savings were realized. The group for which electronic monitoring was being used consisted of offenders that in many cases would otherwise have been placed on probation. In addition, new sentencing guidelines were introduced by the state after the first year of the study period. Under these new guidelines, it appears only those persons who would normally have been eligible for probation could be sentenced to an optional program such as community control.

In reviewing the evaluation report of Florida's Community Control program (a component of which is house arrest), Johnson et al. (1989: 156) conclude

> that it is virtually impossible to verify how many offenders were actually diverted from prison. Based on Florida's sentencing guidelines, they estimate that 66.9 percent of community controlees were "bona fide" prison diversions.
>
> It is our contention that the 66.9 percent diversion rate is inflated. The report seems to treat probation and Community Control as very similar sentencing alternatives. In fact the report states that "probation and Community Control are intertwined and are an integral part of each other" (p. 12). While in one sense probationers can be viewed as prison diversions, many view probationers as anything but prison diversions.

If in fact Community Control in Florida deals with individuals who would otherwise be placed on probation, one wonders if it is a "bona fide" prison diversion. According to Petersilia (1987a) probation supervision is by far the cheapest form of corrections. If offenders in Florida are being put on electronic monitoring when they would otherwise have been placed on probation, the state of Florida is paying more rather than less.

These same authors then turn their attention to Petersilia's Rand monograph, *Expanding Options for Criminal Sentencing* (1987a), in which she reviews five different studies of programs involving EM, Johnson *et al.* (1989: 156–157) state that these studies indicate

> that the target populations did not consist of prison-bound offenders, but instead were comprised of those offenders currently on probation or work release programs. With few exceptions, participants in the program had only been convicted of misdemeanors. Given the "hand-picked" makeup of the target population, it would seem obvious that little or no economic impact could be felt due to the fact that individuals convicted of misdemeanors do not ordinarily receive prison sentences. Consequently, electronic monitoring in these five studies did not save money or relieve overcrowded prison conditions.

Clear, Flynn, and Shapiro (1987: 35) express similar kinds of concerns for intensive probation supervision programs in U.S. criminal justice jurisdictions. Despite great efforts to screen only prison-bound offenders for the much lauded Georgia IPS program, these researchers find:

> Georgia's Department of Corrections' (DOC) evaluations show that IPS cases look, on the whole, very similar to regular probation cases in Georgia, particularly when it comes to the risk of new criminal behavior. IPS cases have somewhat more serious criminal records, including the current offense, and discriminant function analyses have suggested that as many as half the IPS cases may be true diversions from prison. Nevertheless, a profile of IPS clients is not much different from a profile of regular probation cases (statewide), yet is remarkably dissimilar from a profile of imprisoned offenders. In addition, over half of the IPS cases fall into the two lowest risk categories (out of four) of Georgia's risk assessment instrument.

Clear *et al.* (1987: 47) suggest that it is fairly easy to compute the prospects of added costs in this case (of apparent net-widening). "If about one-half of the intensive clients are true diversions, and one-third of those fail and the failures receive sanctions double the original term or longer, then the actual savings in person-incarceration days are negligible."

As part of their investigation of the use of EM, Johnson *et al.* (1989: 162) conducted a survey of probation officers and prosecutors in various American criminal justice jurisdictions. They asked respondents to convey their attitudes and report their practices regarding the use of EM. In conclusion, these researchers state: "[o]ur survey indicates that probation officers and prosecutors are quite reluctant to consider many prison-bound offenders for electronic monitoring." Having examined various case studies pertaining to programs incorporating EM, Johnson *et al.* (1989:

157) conclude that "there seems to be little support for the argument that electronic monitoring saves money...."

Some efforts are being made to ensure that prison-bound offenders do make up the target offender population for house arrest. One tactic is demonstrated by the B.C. Corrections Branch, an agency that has dealt with the problem of offender net-widening — and the increased costs associated with it — by ensuring that its EMS program is not a *sentencing option* of the court, that it is a *correctional classification option*. B.C. EMS program personnel select and screen offenders who are on their way to secure custody, rather than those offenders given probation or some other community-based program (Corrections Branch 1989). Exactly what effects this correctional administrative discretion is having on judges' sentencing practices is not clear. Judges in B.C. may be compensating for their inability to employ the EMS program as a direct sentencing option by meting out harsher sentences to offenders who might otherwise be given shorter jail terms, probation, community service, or restitution sentences. Experience in the U.S., in fact, shows that judges tend to *triple* sentences as a compensation for viewing house arrest with EM as equivalent to prison (Clear 1988; Petersilia 1987a: 42). Research into judicial sentencing practices in B.C. is required in order to settle this question.

CORRECTIONAL PERSONNEL SYSTEM NET-WIDENING

The other distinction pertaining to net-widening is based specifically on assessment of budgetary expenditures and staffing increases. This is a system vantage-point rather than one that checks the intricacies of processing offenders in order to determine bona fide prison diversion cases, then comparing and assessing per diem rates. Since it is evident that many of the intermediate punishment programs are not being applied to a prison-bound offender population, the per diem cost comparison method in these cases is largely irrelevant.

What this points to is that per diem comparisons between programs are insufficient by themselves and need to be viewed within a larger systemic framework (Petersilia 1987a). Thus, Schmidt and Curtis (1987: 146) point out that

> [t]he cost of a monitoring program cannot be directly compared to per diem costs of incarceration. The largest component of per diem costs is staff salaries. Therefore, until the number of released inmates is large enough to affect staffing of the facility, the only savings achieved are in marginal categories such as food.

The metaphor of the fish-net is limited to offenders and neglects the possibility that program counts may be stabilized or reduced; however, the social control apparatus may well be expanding in the process. The metaphor that takes account of this system expansion is that of social *networks*, meaning the organized system of correctional personnel. This distinction focuses attention on system features like number of additional personnel, added costs, and evidence of structural or systemic expansion. Expansion can be assumed to be occurring where increases in level and intensity of regulation provided by the new punitive options are expanding the networks of social control and there is no evidence that reductions are occurring in other parts of the system as a result. Essentially, what occurs in this type of net-widening is that more correctional personnel are necessary for the new program entities that mutate out of the punitive apparatus. Along with this added system capacity are produced increases in the intensity and level of regulation of offenders (Austin and Krisberg 1981). New and different nets, but additional nets nonetheless.

In social net(work) expansion, system enlargement occurs even when (apparently) successful efforts are made to restrict intermediate sanctions like house arrest to prison-diverted offenders who otherwise appear to be prison-bound, as in B.C. It would seem that for many of the American programs, at least, efficiency in administrative regulation and control is enhanced (Ball and Lilly 1988) through the further rationalization and differentiation of punishment techniques. The prison crowding and fiscal crisis impacts on correctional personnel caseloads are eased. Dangerously large probation caseloads are reduced through the new intermediate punishment programs, to the point that adequate supervision is again feasible (Petersilia 1987a).

In both kinds of systemic expansion — whether due to more offenders being hauled in or to the addition of system personnel and program "service delivery" capacity — correctional costs increase. Ironically, this is being accomplished under the banner of "cost-effectiveness."

One of the chief reasons American intermediate punishment programs are deemed to be cost effective is because, in most cases, offenders themselves are contributing significantly in fees toward the cost of their house arrest or IPS programs (something that does not happen in the B.C. EMS program). In reference to programs of house arrest with EM, Renzema and Skelton (1990: 14) point out in their recent program survey that

> approximately two-thirds of all programs collect fees. When fees are collected, they average $200 per month. There are significant variations according to program type in both the proportions which charge fees and in the fees. For example, only 23 percent of programs serving parole or community confinement populations charge fees while 86 percent of those whose clients are inmates (work furlough, in most cases) charge fees. When fees are charged, probationers pay an average of $155 per month while inmates pay an average of $228 per month. A few programs charge clients as much as $15/day for monitoring. The vast majority of programs that charge fees have a sliding scale in order to avoid discriminating against indigent offenders.

The "privatization" of these kinds of corrections services may be one of the main reasons intermediate punishment programs have diffused so rapidly in American criminal justice jurisdictions. It may also account for why the phrase "cost effective" in connection with these programs is bandied about so readily. What proportion the fees represent compared to the total cost of program supervision is not clear. Petersilia (1987a: 82), however, points out that "Georgia's IPS program ... is totally supported by probation supervision fees." The electronically monitored house arrest program in Palm Beach County, Florida — run by the non-profit corporation PRIDE, Inc. — is also completely funded by offender-paid fees (Rogers and Jolin 1989: 146).

The intermediate sanctions vary considerably in cost depending on the level of correctional supervision, whether EM is used, and how sophisticated the EM information system happens to be (Petersilia 1987a: 83). Petersilia's figures show that intensive probation may cost between $1,500–$7,000 annually, while house arrest ranges between $1,350–$7,000 (without electronics) and $4,500–$8,500 (with the more expensive continuous signalling EM system) annually. With program fees averaging approximately $6.70 per day (as per Renzema and Skelton's figure of $200 per month), it means two-thirds of program offenders are contributing annual fees of $2,445. Thus, in the case of some programs this falls within range where the total costs of program are covered by fees, whereas for other programs additional revenues would be required from local, state, or federal sources.

The issue of offender-funded program through fees raises the disturbing prospect that offenders are not equal before the law in terms of sentencing. Economic status clearly eliminates many indigent offenders from being considered for such programs. In the absence of reliable data, we can only speculate about the screening decisions of programs that rely heavily on offender fees, even though most programs claim to accommodate less financially able offenders through sliding fee scales that reduce offender contributions according to their ability to pay. Regardless of the latter policy fears exist that current programs may "foster a two-track system of justice that favors the haves over the have-nots" (Petersilia 1987b: 8).

Whether programs are partially or completely supported by offender fees, it is not clear how much staffing of corrections has been affected by the existence of these programs. Renzema and Skelton (1990: 15) provide the results of the recent program survey in regard to this issue. They state:

> [o]f 173 agencies reporting employment data, 88 had added employees, 12 had lost employees (although not positions) and the remainder were unchanged. Among the 88 agencies which had added employees since adopting EM, 56 attributed a total increase of 274 employees to the demands of EM. Of the 12 agencies losing employees, two agencies reported losing a total of five employees due to EM.

Irrespective of the public or private locus of staff funding, it is clear from these figures that programs involving EM are expanding the networks of correctional personnel. More new correctional positions are being created by these intermediate punishment programs.

THE B.C. EMS PROGRAM: FUTURE PROGRAM DEVELOPMENT, PROGRAM COSTING, AND EXPANSIONARY DRIFT

From the fall of 1987 until spring of 1989, the B.C. Corrections Branch's Electronic Monitoring System (or EMS program) was pilot tested. This program employs EM to "verify" the curfew compliance of offenders on home confinement or house arrest. A pilot project evaluation report was subsequently produced that essentially rationalizes and legitimizes the practice of house arrest accompanied by the place verification capability provided by remote electronic monitoring. A new institutional entity has been borne whose (subsequently) confirmed budget has lifted to "program" status (Corrections Branch 1989).

Throughout the pilot period and up to the present, offenders headed for short jail terms (less than 3 months sentence) have been screened according to various criteria for participation in the EMS program. In addition to voluntary participation, one noteworthy criterion excludes violent offenders.[4] Offenders voluntarily sign a contract specifying the conditions of the house arrest program and the obligations and expectations under which they are held accountable by correctional personnel.

When offenders are not engaging in some approved activity such as work, hospital visits, religious services, and/or treatment, they are strictly confined inside their residences.

By late 1990, approximately 900 offenders have served their sentence of imprisonment on this house arrest program. The program has expanded out from the Lower Mainland Region to the Fraser Region of the province of B.C. and is supposed to commence operations in the Vancouver Island Region in the spring of 1991. Eventually, the Corrections Branch wants to extend the EMS program throughout the entire province.

Though it is too early to conduct a thorough cost assessment of the EMS program, it is important to review what little evidence there is in regard to program costing and systemic expansion. "Cost effectiveness" has been a significant rationale for developing the EMS program (Corrections Branch 1987, 1989). Claims of cost effectiveness need to be examined closely in order to gauge where and/or to what extent net-widening/system expansion is occurring.

The earlier discussion paper (Corrections Branch 1987) and the EMS Pilot Project Evaluation (Corrections Branch 1989) report formulate the EMS program as a potentially important programmatic response in the context of a changing carceral configuration. This changing configuration of secure centres involves three new correctional facilities that will soon replace the Lower Mainland Regional Correctional Centre (referred to as LMRCC or Oakalla Prison), which also handles a substantial portion of the "intermittent offenders" who serve their sentences on weekends. Both documents identify the intermittent population as a chief target group for the EMS program. The new facilities are more specialized and, hence, the intermittent sentenced population — mainly low risk offenders — are not projected to be managed in those new locations since this would defeat one of the problems that these offenders pose, namely employing excessively expensive and unnecessary means of incapacitation for those who do not need it. This is a poor economy of punishment, then, in the eyes of Corrections Branch officials. Exactly what proportion of all low risk offenders EMS can manage is very much open to question at this point in time.

It is noteworthy that the evaluation report submitted to the Branch Management Committee by the Pilot Project Director states that "it is anticipated that a total 70 percent reduction in the intermittent population can be made within a year and a half of implementation" (Corrections Branch 1989: 40). It makes sense that the lower this percentage becomes the more problematic is the achievement of the fiscal objective as set out in the discussion paper. Failure to meet this objective would seem to imply either one or a number of the following options: building the minimum security facilities for which the Branch wants to avoid allocating capital costs; revamping other correctional centres; devising and implementing another set of "alternative alternatives"; or employing Sheriff's holding cells (all of which defeats the initially stated purpose of the EMS program).

In the course of research during the pilot period, the interviewing of Pilot Project staff indicated that there had been much dispute about the 70 percent calculation. It was disclosed that Regional Directors of the Corrections Branch had concerns about this figure and how reliable it might be. The Local Director indicated that he and a Program Analyst had done a more detailed investigation, actually attending LMRCC so as to interview a sample of offenders on a case-by-case basis, with application of actual EMS program screening criteria. Results showed the estimate to be approximately 42 percent, rather than the optimistic 70 percent figure. A 42 percent displacement of the intermittent population suggests that the anticipated elimination of capital costs may not be feasible or not as substantial as initially estimated (Corrections Branch 1987). It is noteworthy that in the report submitted in January (Corrections Branch 1989: 59) to the Branch Management Committee pursuant to its decisions about the future of the EMS program, it is stated:

> How the Branch will accommodate intermittents is still undecided. Use of a mothballed facility (such as the Chilliwack Security Unit), expansion of existing CCC's, and use of the Sheriff's holding cell are some of the alternatives that have been discussed.

The upshot of this is that, as the population of intermittents grows larger and cannot be handled by the EMS program, the more problematic becomes the prospect of forestalling capital construction costs (either in renovations or in new construction); unless, of course, sufficient bedspace is available in community correctional centres. If local *Sheriff's* holding cells are employed for some of the intermittents who are not suitable for the EMS program, this would reintroduce the problem of incarcerating low risk offenders in higher security facilities and at greater cost — in other words, a false economy — something that already occurs, but whose elimination the Corrections Branch would like to achieve (Pilot Project Director, Interview: May 24, 1989).

The original projection of staffing and program costs in the discussion paper estimated that 150 offenders could be supervised with long-term leased equipment and that five correctional officers would be required to accomplish this. The projected annual budget in the discussion paper for this staffing level was $400,000, which involved equal expenditures on staff and equipment. Subsequent budget figures provided by the program analyst indicate that approximately $625,000 is necessary annually for ten correctional staff managing 50–70 offenders.

In the post-pilot period (summer, 1989), an operational director and five correctional officers were managing the system capacity of 25 offenders, though numbers (summer, 1989) fluctuated between about 10 offenders and system capacity (25 offenders). The EMS Pilot Project Evaluation report (Corrections Branch 1989) proposed that the province-wide implementation of the program could be substantially put into place near the end of 1991, though this estimate conflicts significantly with operational expansion as of March 1991, which has been limited to the Lower Mainland and Fraser Valley regions. It appears that expansion into rural regions of the province entails problems related to the provision of cost effective supervision.

The evaluation concludes that "[w]ith an average daily population of 40, the EMS program would require about 10 full-time positions to operate, made up of two probation officers, six institutional officers and two administrative support staff" (Corrections Branch 1989: 40). These latter estimates appear to be more in line with current staffing levels. The evaluation estimates that by 1993–1994 the daily program count will be about 175 offenders. Thus, based on the figure of a 1-to-4 staff-inmate ratio, this will mean the need for about 44 new correctional and support staff also. This is a far cry from the earlier estimate that five correctional officers could supervise 150 offenders on the EMS program. In a recent interview with one agency official, it was disclosed that startup of the EMS program actually entailed the provision of new positions rather than redeployment of correctional officers from other areas of this local correctional system.

However sincere and thorough the planning for the program happened to be, nonetheless, a substantial underestimate of the labour requirements accompanying the use of EMS has occurred. Since this researcher was not permitted to re-interview the author of the initial discussion paper (Corrections Branch 1987), it is not possible to obtain any official accounting for this great disparity between what was projected (i.e., 5 FTE's to manage 150 offenders) and what the evaluation determined to be necessary (i.e., 10 FTE's to manage 40 offenders and, extrapolating on the basis of this, 40 FTE's to manage 160 offenders). This means that approximately *eight times* the initially projected staffing level is necessary to manage offenders on the EMS program. This is without considering the likelihood that more staff will be necessary for rural regions of the province.

Rural implementation of the program will likely mean additional costs because monitoring will be done "long-distance." Exactly how the local supervision will operate in geographically larger areas and how this will affect staffing are questions that are not altogether clear at this point. This could well prove to be another place wherein the underestimation of staffing occurs, in which case the program will, again, cost more to administer — in terms of staffing — than had been projected.

A question that crops up here is whether the EMS program can prevent additional capital costs. In the event that the program leaves a substantial portion of the intermittent offender population still in need of facilities, it suggests that it may not prevent additional capital expenditures, perhaps only limit them somewhat. It appears to be the case that the great efforts that went toward promoting the program (e.g., with judiciary, with other justice system personnel, and with the general public) have achieved an initial integration of this new punishment technique within this local correctional system.

Whether the EMS program achieves the level of success suggested by the discussion paper in regard to managing the intermittent sentenced population at reduced costs seems very questionable at this point. Nonetheless, the evaluation states that cost savings will be realized from the program, eventually.

More recently, the Corrections Branch has adopted a new strategy in expanding the EMS program, which has until now exclusively focused on intermittent offenders (those serving 90 days and less on weekends in community and regional correctional centres). Whereas currently short-term sentenced offenders assessed as appropriate candidates for EMS go straight into the program ("front-end" use of EMS), the shift in intake policy implied in the new direction taken by the program means that EMS will become part of a graduated system of controls applied to prison-based offenders assessed as appropriate ("back-end" use of EMS).

The new direction envisioned for the EMS program anticipates it as a viable substitute for outmoded or costly community correctional centres: two such centres have been suggested for closure thus far. Substitution of EMS for offenders serving lengthier terms of secure custody is proposed as a way to bypass the expensive capital cost outlays associated with new facilities that would be required in the absence of the EMS program option. Since there are many obstacles in attempting to evaluate cost effectiveness when comparing prison and community-based programs (Ekstedt and Griffiths 1984: 267), we should not be surprised to find mixed and/or inconclusive results (Boyanowsky and Verdun-Jones 1977a, b).

Earmarking the EMS program for offenders who are serving lengthier sentences — those completing sentences of up to two years in some cases — poses various problems that need to be noted. Many offenders who might otherwise be transferred to the community correctional centres slated for closure may not be suitable candidates for placement on the EMS program, in which case it may be necessary to maintain them in more costly facilities.

Moreover, the prison-based offenders who become eligible for this program tend to represent a "riskier" clientele. This implies either that community safety may be compromised by having such offenders on the program or that elevated levels of supervision will be required. The latter, of course, means increased staffing costs.

A fairly high level of discipline and/or maturity/responsibility is necessary in order for offenders to adjust successfully to home confinement terms exceeding two months (Mainprize 1990). Offenders are otherwise expected to go about their scheduled (and preferably *structured*) business, albeit within the framework of EMS program rules and behavioural expectations. Apart from the curfew compliance monitoring provided by the EMS program, the correctional officer supervision tends to be "hands-off," with the focus of supervisory attention being on curfew and program rule compliance (e.g., insuring no alcohol or illegal drugs are being ingested; insuring attendance for "approved" activities like work, educational training, treatment programs, medical appointments).

Important elements of ongoing programming and supervision provided by direct, continuing interaction with correctional personnel in community correctional settings will clearly be lost. This may prove to be detrimental to offenders' integration into the community after a stint of incarceration. It is an empirical question whether the reintegrative and rehabilitative needs of offenders serving lengthier sentences can be met by the current EMS program emphasis on surveillance. Corrections classification policy will clearly have important consequences for program technical violations and recidivism rates.

CONCLUSIONS

The evidence presented above suggests the new community-based intermediate punishment programs in general and the EMS program in particular produce systemic expansion. At this point in time, it is not altogether clear how the EMS program fits into this pattern of apparent expansion. The pilot project evaluation asserts that "cost savings" will accrue from the 1992–93 fiscal year onward however, no detailed specification of costing methods is supplied. This renders any future assessment of the impact of the program more difficult since there are no clearly spelled out financial parameters in terms of which comparisons over time can be made.

In any case, all of the suggestive evidence reviewed previously concerning staffing of the EMS program indicates that, whatever happens regarding the offender-side of net-widening/expansion, the correctional-side of network-widening/expansion appears to be occurring. There is no reason to believe that this trend is going to reverse directions in the future since provincial correctional policy is not informed by a "deep-end" strategy of systemic reduction. A deep-end strategy is based on the premise that if system capacity is available, it will — one way or another — get used. The latter refers to fundamental reductions in penal system capacity (such as shutting prisons and cutting programs of incarceration). This usually requires broad-based political and criminal justice system consensus. The probable result of the failure to adopt such a policy is an expansionary drift (Rutherford 1984).

What are we to make of correctionalists' claims of cost effectiveness against the backdrop of this evidence? One avenue of explanation may be provided by way of Foucault (1978, 1979, 1980, 1983). Rather than examining the concordance of programmatic designs, their institutional embodiments, and subsequent outcomes, Foucault proposes an alternate hypothesis, namely that there is a non-correspondence of penal designs (discourse), practical institutional organization (practices), and outcomes (effects) (Gordon 1980; Smart 1983). This hypothesis is related to the foregoing insasmuch as evidence suggests systemic *expansion* of the penal apparatus and the concomitant regulatory bureaucracy.

This *non*-correspondence of discourse-practices-effects at the programmatic or service delivery level (i.e., corrections ends up costing more rather than less), belies a *correspondence* at the level of the strategic operation of power: between outcomes (the "multiplication of power") and the latent objective of the penal system, which is that of growth. Ironically, this takes the form of the productivity of punitive power carried out within the practical organization of the reform strategy of "decarceration" (Cohen 1985; Hylton 1981, 1982; Chan and Ericson 1981; Scull 1977). Preliminary evidence from this particular program would seem to suggest that the policy of electronically monitored house arrest is a species of "community-based alternatives to incarceration" and part of a reform strategy that facilitates system expansion, otherwise referred to as widening the networks of social control.

NOTES

1. Although the author is responsible for the contents and interpretation of the present paper, he wishes to thank Bob Ratner for helpful comments and suggestions made during previous discussions of ideas contained herein.
2. "Efficiency" can be understood as referring to processes of rationalization in the achievement of "external" and "internal" organizational goals. External organization goals would include the punitive objectives of *incapacitation*, *punishment*, *deterrence*, and *rehabilitation*. Internal organizational goals are more difficult to define precisely, but can be generally and abstractly conceived as the rational organization of available resources involved in the attainment of external goals.
3. Two elements go into defining the humaneness of a punishment. A punishment is humane to the degree that it permits or facilitates offenders' choosing lawful courses of action (rather than coercing a course of action through fear): referred to as the principle of voluntary action. Humaneness can also be defined by the extent to which it limits debilitating effects on offenders: referred to as the principle of minimization of negative impacts.
4. Program criteria include: voluntary participation, sentence of 90 days or less, "non-violent," no outstanding charges.

REFERENCES

Austin, James and Barry Krisberg. 1981. Wider, stronger and different nets: The dialectics of criminal justice reform. *Journal of Research in Crime and Delinquency* 18 (1): 165–196.

Ball, Richard A. and J. Robert Lilly. 1988. Home incarceration with electronic monitoring. In Joseph E. Scott and Travis Hirschi (eds.), *Controversial Issues in Crime and Justice* (*Studies in Crime, Law and Justice*, Volume 1). Beverly Hills, CA: Sage.

Berry, Bonnie. 1985. Electronic Jails: A New Criminal Justice Concern. *Justice Quarterly* 2: 1–24.

————. 1986. More questions and more ideas on electronic monitoring: Response to Lilly, Ball and Lotz, *Justice Quarterly* 3 (5): 363–70.

Berry, Bonnie and Roger Mathews. 1989. Making the Right Connections: Electronic Monitoring and House Arrest. Unpublished manuscript, University of Washington.

Blomberg, Thomas G., Gordon P. Waldo, and Lisa C. Burcroff. 1987. Home confinement and electronic surveillance. In Belinda R. McCarthy (ed.), *Intermediate Punishments: Intensive Supervision, Home Confinement and Electronic Surveillance* (*Issues in Criminal Justice*, Volume 2). Monsey, NY: Criminal Justice Press.

Boyanowski, Ehor O. and Simon N. Verdun-Jones. 1977a. A Pilot Study of Community Correctional Centres in British Columbia. Part I: Literature Review. Burnaby, BC: School of Criminology, Simon Fraser University.

————. 1977b. A Pilot Study of Community Correctional Centres in British Columbia. Part II: Report on Community Correctional Centres in British Columbia. Burnaby, BC: School of Criminology, Simon Fraser University.

Burkhart, Walter R. 1986. Intensive probation supervision: An agenda for research and evaluation. *Federal Probation* June: 75–77.

Burtch, Brian E. 1988. State Control, Technology, and Community: The politics of electronic monitoring of offenders. Unpublished manuscript, School of Criminology, Simon Fraser University.

Byrne, James M. 1986. The control controversy: A preliminary examination of intensive probation supervision programs in the United States. *Federal Probation*. June: 4–13.

Chan, J.B.L. and R.V. Ericson. 1981. Decarceration and the Economy of Penal Reform. Toronto: Centre of Criminology.

Clear, Todd R. 1988. A Critical Assessment of Electronic Monitoring in Corrections. Unpublished manuscript. Newark: Rutgers University.

Clear, Todd R., Suzanne Flynn, and Carol Shapiro. 1987. Intensive supervision in probation: A comparison of three projects. In Belinda R. McCarthy (ed.), *Intermediate Punishments: Intensive Supervision, Home Confinement and Electronic Surveillance* (*Issues in Criminal Justice*, Volume 2). Monsey, NY: Criminal Justice Press.

Cohen, Stan. 1979. The punitive city: Notes on the dispersal of social control. *Contemporary Crises*. October: 339–363.

————. 1985. *Visions of Social Control: Crime, Punishment and Classification*. Cambridge: Polity Press.

Corrections Branch. 1987. Electronic Monitoring System for Offender Supervision. Province of British Columbia, Ministry of Attorney General [Discussion Paper, April].

————. 1989. Electronic Monitoring System for Offender Supervision. Province of British Columbia, Ministry of Solicitor General [EMS Pilot Project Evaluation, May].

Ekstedt, John W. and Curt T. Griffiths. 1984. *Corrections in Canada: Policy and Practice*. Toronto: Butterworths.

Flynn, L.E. 1986. House arrest: Florida's alternative eases crowding and tight budgets. *Corrections Today* July: 64–68.

Foucault, Michel. 1978. *History of Sexuality*. Volume I: *An Introduction*. Translated by Robert Hurley. New York: Vintage/Random House.

————. 1979. *Discipline and Punish: The Birth of the Prison*. New York: Vintage Books.

————. 1980. *Power/Knowledge: Selected Interviews and Other Writings by Michel Foucault, 1972–77*. (Edited by Colin Gordon) New York: Pantheon Books.

————. 1983. The subject and power. In H.L. Dreyfus and P. Rabinow (eds.), *Michel Foucault: Beyond Structuralism and Hermeneutics* (2nd Edition) Chicago: University of Chicago Press.

Fox, Richard G. 1987. Dr. Scheitzgebel's machine revisited: Electronic monitoring of offenders. *Australian & New Zealand Journal of Criminology* 20: 131–147.

Gordon, Colin. 1980. Afterword. In Colin Gordon (ed.), *Power/Knowledge: Selected Interviews and Other Writings by Michel Foucault, 1972–77*. New York: Pantheon Books.

Greenberg, David F. 1975. Problems in community corrections. *Issues in Criminology* 10: 1–33.

Griffiths, Curt T. 1987. Electronic Monitoring of Offenders: The Application of High Technology to Corrections. Tokyo: United Nations and Far East Institute for the Prevention of Crime and the Treatment of Offenders.

Hylton, J.H. 1981. The growth of punishment: Imprisonment and community corrections in Canada. *Crime and Social Justice* 15: 18–28.

———. 1982. Rhetoric and reality: A critical appraisal of community correctional programs. *Crime and Delinquency* 28: 341–373.

Johnson, B.R., Linda Haugen, Jerry W. Maness, and Paul P. Ross. 1989. Attitudes toward electronic monitoring of offenders: A study of probation officers and prosecutors. *Journal of Contemporary Criminal Justice* 5 (3): 153–164.

Krisberg, B. and J. Austin. 1982. The unmet promise of alternatives to incarceration. *Crime and Delinquency* 28: 374–409.

Mainprize, Stephen. 1990. Incorporating Electronically Monitored House Arrest into British Columbia Corrections: The processes of power, knowledge, and regulation in the debut of a punishment technique. Unpublished Doctoral Dissertation. Department of Anthropology and Sociology, University of British Columbia.

McCarthy, Belinda R. (ed.). 1987. *Intermediate Punishments: Intensive Supervision, Home Confinement and Electronic Surveillance* (*Issues in Criminal Justice*, Volume 2), Monsey, NY: Criminal Justice Press.

Petersilia, Joan. 1987a. Expanding Options for Criminal Sentencing. Santa Monica, CA: The Rand Corporation, R–3544–EMC.

———. 1987b. House arrest is worthy innovation—If it's not just for the well-off. *Perspectives*. Fall: 8–9.

———. 1988. House Arrest. National Institute of Justice/Crime File, Study Guide.

Renzema, Marc and David Skelton. 1990. Trends in the use of electronic monitoring: 1989. *Journal of Offender Monitoring* 3 (3): 12, 14–19.

Rogers, Robert and Annette Jolin. 1989. Electronic Monitoring: A Review of the Empirical Literature. *Journal of Contemporary Criminal Justice* 5 (3): 141–152.

Rush, Fred L. 1987. Deinstitutional incapacitation: Home detention in pre-trial and post-conviction contexts. *Northern Kentucky Law Review* 13 (3): 375–408.

Rutherford, Andrew. 1984. *Prisons and the Process of Justice: The Reductionist Challenge*. London: Heinemann.

Schmidt, Annesley K. 1989. Electronic Monitoring of Offenders Increases. NIJ Reports (No. 212), January/February: 1–5.

Schmidt, Annesley K. and Christine E. Curtis. 1987. Electronic monitors. In Belinda R. McCarthy (ed.), *Intermediate Punishments: Intensive Supervision, Home Confinement and Electronic Surveillance* (*Issues in Criminal Justice*, Volume 2). Monsey, NY: Criminal Justice Press.

Scull, Andrew. 1977. Decarceration: Community Treatment and the Deviant. New Jersey: Prentice-Hall.

Smart, Barry. 1983. On discipline and social regulation: A review of Foucault's genealogical analysis. In D. Garland and P. Young (eds.), *The Power to Punish*. London: Heinemann.

TWENTY-ONE

"Net-Widening": Vagaries in the Use of a Concept [1]

MAEVE McMAHON

During the 1980s, critical analyses of trends in the use of imprisonment and alternatives repeatedly pointed to the occurrence of "net-widening." It has been contended that although sentencing alternatives such as probation were intended to reduce the use of imprisonment, in practice they have not had this effect: prison populations have been maintained and increased, while so-called "alternatives" have proliferated. The conventional wisdom of the critical literature on community corrections is that the development of alternatives has been synonymous with a widening "net" of penal control (Austin and Krisberg 1981; Chan and Ericson 1981; Cohen 1985; De Jonge, 1985; Ericson and Baranek 1982; Hylton 1981, 1982; Lerman 1975; Lowman, Menzies, and Palys 1987; Mathiesen 1983; Matthews 1979; McCullagh 1988; Scull 1983, 1984; Warren 1981).

While the relevant literature is both extensive and influential, in this paper I challenge some core contentions about the nature and occurrence of "net-widening." Both the concept of "net-widening" and the uses to which it has been subject may have obscured as much as has been revealed about trends in the use of imprisonment and alternatives. As net-widening is an important analytical component of broader critical theorizing of developments in penal and social control, this paper also embodies a questioning of the theoretical and methodological frameworks characteristic of much critical criminological analysis.

How did ideas about net-widening develop? A full account of the intellectual career of this concept is beyond the present scope, but some observations can be made of changing critical understanding of trends in the use of imprisonment and alternatives.

It is hardly surprising that critical criminologists should have turned their attention to questions of decarceration. The development of distinctively new and critical criminologies from the late 1960s roughly coincided and intersected with the rapid demise of the ethos of rehabilitation in penal policy, and with the ensuing emphasis on community corrections and alternatives.

Initially, critical criminologists appeared uncertain about how to read the significance of community corrections, both in their traditional form of probation, and in the rapidly expanding range of community service orders, half-way houses, victim-offender reconciliation, diversion, temporary absence, and other programmes. It was acknowledged that "our information is imprecise and open to multiple interpretations"

Source: Maeve McMahon, "'Net-Widening': Vagaries in the Use of a Concept," *British Journal of Criminology*, 30, 2 (1990): 121–49. Reproduced by permission of *The British Journal of Criminology*.

(Cohen 1977: 217). Nevertheless, it was advocated that a critical stance be taken as a point of departure. As Cohen (1979: 343) questioned:

> Why should community corrections itself, not be subjected to suspicion about benevolent reform? A large dose of such skepticism, together with a much firmer location of the new movement in overall structural and political changes, is needed for a full scale critique of community corrections.

An important step toward such an analysis had already been taken with the publication of Andrew Scull's (1977) *Decarceration: Community Treatment and the Deviant—a Radical View*. According to Scull, (a) the threat of fiscal crisis of the state had prompted the shift toward decarceration and community corrections; (b) deinstitutionalization was actually occurring; and (c) probation and community corrections were being used in lieu of sentences to imprisonment.

Critical responses to Scull's thesis about penal populations[2] were pivotal in the development of themes of "net-widening." In addition to castigating Scull for his economism and functionalism, critics charged that he had posited community programmes as *alternatives* to prisons when they should more accurately be seen as *complements* to the institutions (Chan and Ericson 1981: 9; Cohen 1979: 361; Matthews 1979: 101, 109). Swayed by such critiques, Scull himself took up similar themes. In his later writing on decarceration he has highlighted "striking increases in prison populations," the "widening of the net phenomenon," and the "expansionist direction" in criminal justice generally (Scull 1984: 177, 178). In short, Scull modified his story of decarceration so that where alternatives were earlier seen by him as representing neglect of deviants, they were later seen as involving more control of offenders; where prison populations had earlier been seen as decreasing, they were later presented as more subject to increase.

By the mid-1980s, a critical consensus about the nature of contemporary trends in imprisonment and alternatives had become evident. For example Cohen, in his state-of-the-art summary of what is really going on "inside the system," argues that "all the evidence here indicates failure—that in Britain, Canada and the USA rates of incarceration are not at all declining and in some spheres are even increasing. Community control has supplemented rather than replaced traditional methods" (Cohen 1985: 44). Similarly, Lowman, Menzies, and Palys (1987: 211) summarize the situation of alternatives by stating that although

> designed originally to provide a community *alternative* to incarceration ... these programmes have become a supplement to them. Instead of *fewer* individuals going to prison, there are now more than ever. And instead of directing individuals out of the criminal justice system, the new programmes have directed more people into it ... The bottom line, therefore, is that more and more individuals are becoming subject to the scrutiny and surveillance of criminal justice personnel.

The tendency to express the empirical basis of arguments as much through metaphors and evocative images as through specific statistical statements about identifiable penal populations is a notable characteristic of the critical literature. Through this analytical strategy the language of net-widening has become prominent in depicting the scenario whereby community alternatives become add-ons to pre-existing prison populations. It has been claimed that the introduction of probation, parole, and recent community programmes has "invariably" contributed to loss of liberty and introduced many new people into the "control net" (Matthews 1979: 115). As "widening the net" is accompanied by "thinning the mesh," the predominant image is of a system in perpetual expansion, with deviants continually subject to new, more intrusive forms of social control which are woven into, and beyond, traditional institutional networks of penal control (Austin and Krisberg 1981; Blomberg 1980; Chan and Ericson 1981; Cohen 1979, 1983, 1985; Lowman, Menzies, and Palys 1987; Scull 1984; Van Dusen 1981).[3]

The metaphor of net-widening is typically allied with those of "stronger" and "different" nets. The most adroit specification of the empirical substance of these images has been provided by Cohen. According to him, with the development of alternatives,

> (1) there is an increase in the total number of deviants getting into the system in the first place and many of these are new deviants who would not have been processed previously (wider nets);
> (2) there is an increase in the overall intensity of intervention, with old and new deviants being subject to levels of intervention (including traditional institutionalization) which they might not have previously received (denser nets);
> (3) new agencies and services are supplementing rather than replacing the original set of control mechanisms (different nets). (Cohen 1985: 44)

In turn, it can be seen that two kinds of expansion are said to be involved in the evolution of wider, denser, and different nets. Firstly, it is contended that a *quantitative* form of expansion is occurring: with the development of community corrections, more and new people are being subject to penal processing. Secondly, it is contended that *qualitative* transformation of control is occurring: with the development of community corrections, people are being subject to more intensive and pervasive forms of penal processing.

In this paper it is the *quantitative* rather than the qualitative aspects of "net-widening" which are primarily at issue. This is because there is little doubt that with the growth of community corrections and other new forms of penal control, the qualitative nature of social control and regulation has indeed been changing (see Bottoms 1983; Cohen 1985; Ericson, McMahon, and Evans 1987; Garland and Young 1983; Lowman, Menzies, and Palys 1987; Mathiesen 1983; Peters 1986; Shearing and Stenning 1981, 1984, 1987). The question is, how should these new forms of control be interpreted, and how do they compare with prior situations? Where the growth of community corrections is concerned, the critical literature sees them as not simply different, but as more ominous than earlier forms of control. The portrait is of an oppressive situation that appears to be becoming worse. Evidence for this is often drawn from observations that the new programmes are add-ons to imprisonment: if alternatives "really" were alternatives, and if prison population were declining, the qualitative contentions would lose much of their analytical force. In other words, arguments about the occurrence of *quantitative* forms of "net-widening" often underlie, and always reinforce, critical arguments about the increasingly sinister nature of penal control.

POLITICAL AND ANALYTICAL RATIONALES
FOR CHALLENGING NET-WIDENING

Why should critical criminologists be sceptical and cautious in adopting the discourse and perspective of net-widening? The argument has been influential and apparently definitive. In contrast, for example, to critical ambiguity about the role of unemployment in affecting imprisonment rates (e.g., Box 1987; De Haan 1989; W. Young 1986), that of alternatives in expanding penal control has been taken as clear. Moreover, given that alternatives are better understood as "add-ons" to pre-existing prison populations, official and reformist discourse about the virtues of community corrections in terms of costs, effectiveness, and humaneness can be incisively deconstructed. Finally, the net-widening argument has critical theoretical appeal as it demonstrates that analyses of contemporary penal developments reaffirm the penetrating observations of influential revisionist historians such as Foucault (1979), Ignatieff (1978), Rothman (1980), and Scull (1979).

Political and analytical rationales underlie the need for a re-examination of net-widening. In terms of praxis, the critical literature on community corrections is pessimistic and conservative. Although critical analysts have sought to reject the empiricism, correctionalism, and positivism of mainstream criminologists (Sim, Scraton, and Gordon 1987), their logic is often similar. For example, critical analysts sought to supersede the concern with issues of "success" and "failure" characteristic of earlier positivist effectiveness literature on rehabilitation, but their own critique of penal trends has arguably merely broadened, rather than actually changed, the parameters of criminological debate. The conclusion associated with Martinson (1974) that "nothing works" has been adopted and generalized by critical analysts: where the "nothing works" argument was initially applied by positivists observing that correctional programmes had a limited impact in rehabilitating offenders, it was later critically argued that penal reform in general could have little impact on the predominantly repressive tendencies of the criminal justice system itself. In effect, critical criminologists substituted the recalcitrant criminal justice system for the recalcitrant offender of the positivist criminology that they sought to critique.

For mainstream criminologists and penal policy-makers, the belief that "nothing works"—particularly in rehabilitation—has contributed to the genesis of primarily administrative and regulatory approaches to dealing with crime and criminals (Melossi 1979; Bottoms 1983; Peters 1986; J. Young 1986). Community alternatives (and related processes of privatization) have played an important part in the evolution of this managerial approach to criminal justice. By contrast, for more critical criminologists, the perception that "nothing works"—particularly in reform of the criminal justice system—has contributed to the emergence of a political and policy-making void. Critical criminology, as in the "net-widening" argument, appears restricted to developing ever more penetrating critiques of contemporary trends. Participation in reform activity seems counter-productive. Rather, their findings often involve critical criminologists in the depressing task of advising and informing well-meaning reformers that they are doing "no good" (Cohen 1985).

The use of net-widening arguments by penal authorities should also be considered politically problematic. For example, in the Canadian province of Ontario, government officials proposed in 1984 to terminate a bail programme which had sought to divert accused persons awaiting trial from custodial to non-custodial supervision.

In doing so, the correctional minister was able to "emphasize our concern that the program may be expanding the net of social control" (Ontario *Hansard*, 1984, J-166). In actuality, the major reason for attempting to terminate the bail programme was to release funding for the province's rapidly expanding community service order programme. Moreover, while internal Ministry evaluations were uncertain whether the bail programme was net-widening or not, from the outset the minister of corrections acknowledged that "we have nothing under our act to deal with the Community Service Order in lieu of incarceration" (Ontario *Hansard*, 1978, 2998–9). In short, officials used the net-widening argument towards the diminution of a programme whose net-widening effects were questionable in favour of one where such effects were clear.

The service of the critical literature in the political interests of correctional officials, and particularly conservative ones, was also indicated in an interview with Donald Evans, formerly executive director of the Community Programmes Division, Ontario Ministry of Correctional Services. Apparently Stanley Cohen's writings provided a language particularly amenable to being "captured" by correctional officials. As Evans explained:

> I always kept up on the literature — I began to discover all the people using nice phrases [e.g., "decarceration"]. Cohen, of course, turned out to be *great* from a management point of view because he's a great categorizer ... You'd do things in chart form, and stuff that you could easily translate and use and make [into] management presentations if you wanted to. They looked good on overhead transparencies!

According to Evans, the critical literature was "read in a political sense, in a managerial sense" whereby the ideas and analyses "were decontexted [sic] from their theoretical bases" and "rhetoric was easily entered into Ministry speeches." Further, while the literature was originally used by those such as himself who, although sensitive to potential pitfalls, fostered the development of community programmes in the hope that they could be alternatives, it was later most forcefully used by those in the Ministry who sought a renewed emphasis on imprisonment. As Evans explained:

> And then what happened was *institutional* people [within the Ministry] would discover the articles in the journals I had circulated, photocopy them, and use them for their own arguments internally ... community corrections programmes were not solving their overcrowding problem, so they should *stop getting money*.
> Police also became aware of this claim. You would go to your conferences with local police, and they would stand up and say—"you guys, you're not doing anything, all you're doing is churning out people and your programs don't work ... It would be better if these people were at least incapacitated, they wouldn't commit any crimes."

Over time, according to the former director, officials' use of critical arguments about community corrections, coupled with a growing emphasis on "risk management," resulted in a situation whereby "community corrections caseload profiles [have] become an argument for prison building" (see McMahon 1988a). Clearly, the net-widening argument is amenable to use by correctional authorities whose interests and objectives can be at odds with those of the critical criminologists who developed the argument in the first place.

So far, such usurpations of the net-widening argument have been little discussed in the critical literature. But there are signs of a growing sensitivity to questions of the relationship of critical analyses of community corrections to strategies for a more progressive penal politics. The inherent pessimism, and related conservatism, of the perspective have now been acknowledged by some authors. For example, Roger Matthews has highlighted what he describes as the "impossibilism" of much of the decarceration literature, focusing on Scull's gloomy remarks in the "Afterword" to the second edition of *Decarceration*. Here, Scull accorded with the conventional wisdom in his statement that

> only a confirmed Pangloss can view the realities of a traditional penal system with equanimity, but what I have learned about the community corrections movement simply reinforces my conviction that tinkering around with the criminal justice system in a radically unjust society is unlikely to advance us very far toward justice, equity or (come to that) efficacy. Perhaps the best I can do is to persuade others to share my sense of discomfort. (Scull: 165, quoted in Matthews 1987*a*: 351)

For Matthews (ibid. 351–2): "This is the impossibilist stance in a nutshell. Prisons are a disaster, community corrections are invariably worse, realistic reform cannot be achieved without a fundamental transformation of the social structure, which is unlikely to occur in the foreseeable future, so there is nothing that can be done."

While Matthews' summary critique may be considered unduly harsh by some — particularly as Matthews himself earlier identified alternatives as "invariably" associated with a greater loss of liberty and net-widening (Matthews 1979: 115) — the proposals he advances toward countering impossibilism merit serious consideration. This is because rather than focusing only on what political and policy stances should be taken, Matthews identifies and addresses problematic aspects of the *analytical* perspective embodied in studies of community corrections and net-widening.[4] He argues that "impossibilism" reinforces, and is reinforced by, the "globalism" and "empiricism" of the literature. Globalism involves the tendency to overgeneralize from the particular, and especially when the instance lends support to the broader argument. Empiricism involves the juxtaposition of trends in different areas, and the use of one to explain the other, rather than trying "to decipher underlying relations" (Matthews 1987*a*: 347).

For Matthews, the impossibilism of Scull and others stems from "commitment to a functionalist metaphysic." In place of this, he recommends that analysts pay greater attention to the role of progressive reforms, and particularly to the contradictory aspects of capitalist social relations and the state: "any comprehensive theory of social control must take these tensions and contradictions as its point of departure" (ibid. 352, 354).

Cohen (1985: 241) has similarly pointed to the "analytical despair" and "adversarial nihilism" of much of the literature. He has further observed that "the results of the destructuring movements were indeed complicated, ambiguous, contradictory — and dialectical. But it was only the dark side of the dialectic that was exposed" (Cohen 1987: 364). Cohen has also been more frank than others in acknowledging the shifting critical perspectives and affiliations involved in the entrenchment of the conventional wisdom:

The proponents of the original destructuring/abolitionist ideas were not always "them"; that is, the people whom the theories were criticizing: the managers, bureaucrats, technicist criminologists, the powerful. They were us. We were the ones who wanted to abolish prisons, to weaken professional monopolies, to find forms of justice and conflict resolution outside the official system, to undermine the power of the centralized state, to create possibilities for real community and social justice. Critical scholarship has very well exposed the problems of this critical agenda — but the very effectiveness of this demystification job is a little embarrassing. You have to distance yourself from those original ideas and reforms, dismiss your enthusiastic support for them as matters of false consciousness or perhaps a product of over-enthusiastic youthful exuberance. Life seems more complicated as you get older; about that early love you say "well, yes, I wasn't really in love at the time, I only thought I was." (ibid. 366)

In seeking a way out of such pessimism, Cohen suggests a reaffirmation, albeit cautious, of the original destructuring values. Adopting a position of "moral pragmatism," he has advocated that programmes and developments be politically assessed in terms of their potential for realizing preferred values (ibid.; 1985). Analytically, Cohen has also made some important suggestions: there should be a "*slightly different reading* of the literature on social control," and one that would include "first, a sensitivity to success (however ambivalent), and second, an experimental and inductive attitude" (1987: 368, 369; emphasis added).

It is precisely the endeavour of "a slightly different reading" of the critical literature on community corrections that is being undertaken here. Rather than taking statements about net-widening at face value, their underlying framework of analysis is considered a core problematic to be explored. Re-examination of the assumptions and arguments of the literature reveals the discursive and analytical tactics that have fostered nihilism, globalism, and impossibilism. In particular, a disproportionate attention to themes of destructuring, deinstitutionalization, and to trans- and decarceration has resulted in the topic of *incarceration* being shifted to the periphery of analysis. Although contentions about trends in imprisonment are fundamental to the quantitative argument of net-widening, documentation of these trends has often been unsatisfactory. Crucial differences in the nature of imprisonment data compared to those on probation have been obscured. Incompatible forms of data on penal trends have been juxtaposed. Finally, with their assimilation into the international literature, problematic aspects of individual studies have been exacerbated. As in other social science areas, "ambiguities and qualifications are expressed, but then ignored as conclusions are drawn, and forgotten as they reach other arenas and other transmitters. A fact is not a near-fact, maybe-fact or convenient fact. It becomes reality" (Gusfield 1981: 59). These observations can be illuminated in the first instance through a re-examination of Canadian critical literature on decarceration.

A RE-EXAMINATION OF CANADIAN DECARCERATION LITERATURE

In the international literature on community corrections and their relationship to imprisonment rates, the Canadian experience has been posited as paradigmatic. Specifically, research by Hylton (1981) and by Chan and Ericson (1981) has frequently been drawn on in studies associating growing populations in community programmes with the maintenance and increase of prison populations. Reference to Canadian data as confirming the tendency of community programmes to widen the net rather than to decrease prison populations has been made by authors from countries including the United States, Britain, Australia, Israel, and Norway (e.g., Austin and Krisberg 1982; Bottoms 1983; Chan and Zdenowski 1986; Cohen 1985; Mathiesen 1986; Scull 1984).

That the work of Hylton and of Chan and Ericson is frequently cited in the literature is not surprising in light of their critical approaches and unequivocal conclusions. Hylton presents a case study of the province of Saskatchewan from 1962 to 1979, when a "number of so-called alternative programs were developed and implemented on a broad scale in order to reduce reliance on correctional institutions." He states that "throughout the period steady increases in the number and rate of admissions to prison and in the number and rate of persons incarcerated on any given day were observed" (Hylton 1983: 345, 367). In his analysis there is no doubt that the penal control apparatus expanded in conjunction with the province's commitment to community corrections.

Chan and Ericson are similarly unambiguous. They follow other critics in positing community programmes as *complements* to, rather than *substitutes* for, institutions. They argue that the population of community programmes, as well as that of prisons, is increasing. "Not only are more people coming under the system, more are being sent to prison as well." Having provided provincial and national empirical support for these assertions, Chan and Ericson (1981: 9, 45, 59) state that their study "confirms Rothman's observation that 'innovations that appeared to be substitutes for incarceration became supplements to incarceration' (Rothman 1980: 8) and Cohen's (1979) notion of 'thinning the mesh and widening the net.'"

Clearly, the Canadian version of the community corrections story accords with the critical conventional wisdom. An important theme of the account has been that no decrease in imprisonment has occurred with the development or alternatives. But although these arguments have been influential, a re-examination of the work of Hylton and of Chan and Ericson reveals serious flaws in their methods, data, and analytical frameworks. Their conclusions overgeneralize from the data and are conducive to misinterpretation by others. That misinterpretation of the basis and scope of their findings has occurred in practice is evident, for example, in the use of their work by Cohen (1985) in his state-of-the art analysis of contemporary penal trends.

A RE-EXAMINATION OF HYLTON'S RESEARCH[5]

According to Cohen (1985: 49), "Hylton's data on one province in Canada are a microcosm of the trend to expand in systems committed to community control." He also describes Hylton's work as "exemplary" in involving "a detailed follow-through of the overall dispositional patterns of one correctional system over time." Summing up Hylton's findings, Cohen states that "institutions now process more offenders than at any time in the province's history and *all trends indicate* that this expansion is increasing" (ibid. 47, 49; emphasis added).

One of the reasons for the frequent use of Hylton's research in the literature is that the quantitative inquiry it provides is far superior to that of most other studies. Indeed, as Austin and Krisberg (1982: 377) observe, following their careful review of the literature on alternatives to incarceration and on net-widening, "while the research on alternatives offers important information on policy, the quality of the research is, in general, poor. We reviewed scores of studies, but found only a few employing rigorous methods." Addressing the specific question of whether community programmes have reduced imprisonment, they report that "only one study was found that attempted to evaluate the effects of community correctional programs on the institutional population" (ibid. 386). Naming Hylton, they go on to summarize his conclusions about the relationship between the expansion of community correctional and institutional populations in Saskatchewan.

Given this dearth of rigorous quantitative studies, it is all the more important to realize that there are important omissions in Hylton's analysis. In particular, Hylton has only identified partial trends in the prison population, and his conclusions about overall expansion in the correctional system must be treated with caution.

Hylton's (1981) analysis includes both count and admissions data for the province's correctional system.[6] Specific to the prison population he states that "the average daily count per 100,000 in Saskatchewan institutions increased from 55.23 [in 1962] to 84.87 in 1979—an increase of some 54 percent in 18 years." Meanwhile, the "number of admissions per 100,000 population increased from 434.85 in 1962 to 688.72 in 1979—an increase of some 58 percent" (ibid. 196, 197). From these figures there appears to be no doubt that the prison population has grown considerably.

One of the crucial lacunae of Hylton's research is his exclusion of "Saskatchewan offenders under supervision of the federal correction authority, that is, those sentenced to a period of incarceration for two years or more." His focus is on "correctional programmes administered by the provincial correctional authority" (i.e., persons sentenced to periods of under two years).[7] According to Hylton, the omission of offenders incarcerated in federal institutions is "not difficult to justify" since these offenders "made up only a small fraction of the total offender population in Saskatchewan." He goes on to explain in a footnote that "admissions to the sole federal penitentiary in Saskatchewan represent less than one percent of the total admissions to the provincial correctional system in Saskatchewan" (Hylton 1981: 202, 214).

Although *admissions* to federal institutions may represent only a small fraction of total admissions to institutions, a very different distribution prevails with respect to *counts*. For example, Chan and Ericson's (1981: 77) national data for 1955 to 1977 show that the federal portion usually accounted for about a third, and on occasion for nearly a half, of the total inmate population in Canada. Thus Hylton's data on trends in the "average daily count in institutions" omits a substantial component of the Saskatchewan inmate population.

Hylton's omission of federal inmates in Saskatchewan must be considered serious. Preliminary inquiry into an alternative data source reveals that (a) in 1962, the first year Hylton examined, the count of federal inmates in Saskatchewan actually *exceeded* that of provincial ones; (b) subsequently, during some periods when the provincial prison population was increasing, the federal one was decreasing; and (c) in general, during the period of Hylton's study, the federal prisoner population in Saskatchewan appears to have been proportionately larger than is typically the case in Canadian jurisdictions (see Statistics Canada, *Correctional Institutions Statistics*). While the complexities of Canadian justice administration are pertinent here, the crucial question remains: can one claim to have studied the effect of community programmes on imprisonment when apparently upward of 40 percent of the standing prison population have been excluded?

Even if one were to accept Hylton's dubious proposition that information on the provincial prison population, and thereby only on imprisonment for less than two years, is adequate for a study of decarceration, there are still important omissions from his data. Most notably, Hylton omits consideration of remand and other non-sentenced admissions to prison. Arguably, non-sentenced admission should form an important component of an analysis of the prison and community programme populations. The length of time spent on remand can affect both the nature and length of sentence chosen by judges. Moreover, non-sentenced admissions can constitute a substantial and variable proportion of total admissions to prisons. In Ontario, for example, non-sentenced admissions constituted 34 percent of total admissions to prison in 1971, but only 14 percent in 1982. As Hylton's data are limited to sentence admissions, the reader is given no idea of the size of the remand sector of the prison population in Saskatchewan either at a specific point in time or longitudinally.[8]

The omission of non-sentenced admissions also obscures the meaning of the category "average daily count in institutions" as presented by Hylton and the inferences he draws about the length of sentences longitudinally. Based on his observation that sentenced admissions increased by 58 percent between 1962 and 1979, and that average counts increased by 54 percent, Hylton states that "on average, individuals were retained in correctional institutions for about the same length of time in 1962 as in 1979" and the system therefore "expanded by institutionalizing more offenders for about the same period of time" (Hylton 1981: 199). What Hylton has apparently done here is to juxtapose data on sentenced admissions only with data on average counts, which seem to include all inmates, sentenced and non-sentenced, in the institutions.

Hylton's interpretation of his own observation that the "system expanded by institutionalizing more offenders for about the same period of time" is also problematic. He goes on to say that "this finding is all the more remarkable when it is recalled that a number of programmes (including the CTR [Community-Training Residence] program) were developed in part to *reduce* the length of time offenders remained institutionalized" (Hylton 1981: 199, emphasis added). In fact, assuming that alternative programmes would be used primarily for those who would have shorter prison sentences in the first place, the effect of a "successful" use of alternatives should be rather to *increase* the proportionate length of time served by those remaining. This is because only those receiving longer sentences should still be going to prison in such a situation. Although individuals transferred to alternatives would experience a reduction or elimination in the length of time served in prison, if the development of alternatives was the only reform taking place, average prison sentence lengths would increase.

In summary, Hylton's analysis of the prison population in Saskatchewan is incomplete. While he documents the growth of community programmes in the province, the nature of their relationship to traditional institutions is by no means clear. Indeed, in a footnote that discusses institutions in the United States, Hylton points out that "decreases in one part of the [prison] system may be compensated for by increases in the other parts, but this may not become evident if only part of the social control apparatus is examined" (Hylton 1981: 213). Conversely, *increases* in one part of the prison system may be compensated for by decreases elsewhere. In the case of Saskatchewan, to what extent was the increase in the provincial system accompanied by a decrease in the federal one? Were there times when sentenced admissions were increasing and non-sentenced admissions were decreasing? Perhaps the complex research needed to answer these questions would demonstrate that Hylton is correct in his statement that the "utilization of correctional institutions did increase in the period from 1962 to 1979" (ibid. 207). However, in the absence of more detailed documentation of the process, his assertion remains propositional rather than factual.

In light of these methodological problems, the adoption of Hylton's conclusions by other analysts must also be considered problematic. Statements such as Cohen's (1985: 47) that Saskatchewan "institutions now process more offenders than at any time in the province's history and *all trends indicate* that this expansion is increasing" (emphasis added) represent an overgeneralization from limited data.

A RE-EXAMINATION OF CHAN AND ERICSON'S RESEARCH

Chan and Ericson's (1981) research has also been a frequent source for analyses of net-widening. Having pointed to the growth of alternative programmes in the province of Ontario, and in Canada as a whole, the authors contend that this has not been associated with any decrease in imprisonment: "none of the evidence appears to support that fewer people are being imprisoned today" (p. 42).

Chan and Ericson also obfuscate trends in the prison population. One way in which this occurs is through their making observations based on absolute numbers that do not accord with those based on stronger indicators of rates. They report that "in Canada, both federal and provincial prison populations are at an all-time high" (p. 39). This is true in terms of *absolute numbers*. However, the data for the Canadian prison population from 1955 to 1977 that they cite in support of this statement show that it clearly does not apply in terms of *rates per 100,000*, where the total stood at 95.9 in 1955, reached a high of 105.5 in 1962, and was 98.4 in 1977 (p. 77). Indeed, in terms of rates per 100,000, the imprisonment rate for Canada as a whole was higher in about a third of the years under consideration than it was in 1977. While increases in absolute numbers are an important concern for policy-makers and administrators, for analysts of penal trends — particularly in a country such as Canada, which has experienced significant post-war population growth — a better indication of changes in the relative size of prison population is provided through rates.

Specific to the Canadian provincial imprisonment rate (i.e., sentences of less than two years), Chan and Ericson go on to say that the "incarceration rate appears to have dropped in the early seventies but is now climbing rather steeply back to the late 1960 level" (p. 39). But their data indicate (p. 77) that the rate per 100,000 was higher in over half of the earlier years than that in 1977. Only in the federal prison population (i.e., sentences of two years and over) is an overall trend of increase evident. Although Chan and Ericson emphasize stability and growth of the prison population in their narrative, their data equally support the finding that the Canadian prison population per 100,000 was lower overall in 1972–7 than in 1955–60, with the decrease in the provincial prison population being greater than the increase in the federal one.

Further obfuscation has occurred as other writers, who accept the conventional wisdom of the continuance and growth of prison populations, have made statements based on Chan and Ericson's analysis, which go far beyond the data presented by them. According to Cohen (1985: 46), in Canada, "after a slight drop in the early seventies incarceration *rates* began to climb back to the late sixties level, and, by 1982, *rates* (in federal *and* provincial prisons) were showing an all-time high, both in the standing population and those flowing through the system" (emphases added).

Chan and Ericson's statement was specific to the provincial population, but Cohen generalizes it to the total prison population. He also makes a statement about an "all-time high" in terms of *rates*, although the similar statement made by Chan and Ericson was on the basis of absolute numbers. Cohen likewise overgeneralizes the situation of "those flowing through the system." The relevant data presented by Chan and Ericson (1981: 41–2, 78) are again in terms of absolute numbers, not rates, and only apply to the federal population, with no equivalent admission and release data being presented for the provincial population.[9] In addition, Cohen's phrase "by 1982" is perplexing, as he cites no Canadian data source other than Chan and Ericson, and their data do not go beyond 1978.

More fundamental confusion — with implications for understanding and use of the concept of net-widening more generally — arises in the context of Chan and Ericson's discussion of the comparative size and growth of prison and probation populations. Chan and Ericson's analysis is based on the graph reproduced here as Figure 21.1

The data in Figure 21.1 are central to Chan and Ericson's argument as this figure is the only one in which they present imprisonment and alternative community programme data in tandem. Clearly the graph illustrates a phenomenal growth in probation in Ontario between 1972 and 1978, with probation appearing to be far more significant numerically than imprisonment. Quantitatively, Chan and Ericson

FIGURE 21.1 *Ontario: Adults under probation supervision and average daily prison population, 1972–1978 (rate per 100,000 population)*

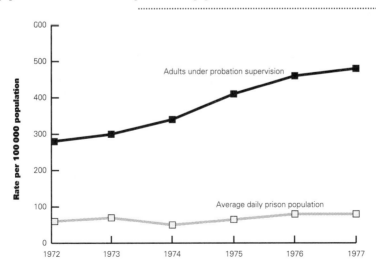

Source: Chan and Ericson (1981:44).

observe that "the rate of adult persons under probation supervision has risen from 275.4 to 503.7 per 100,000 population from 1972 to 1978," and that, during the same period, "the rate of incarceration has risen from 52.1 to 71.1 per 100,000 population" (pp. 42, 45).

When the statistical tables underlying Chan and Ericson's graph are examined (pp. 80–1), it can be seen that they are not comparing similar categories. Specifically, the category "adults under probation supervision" in their graph includes both counts *and* admissions. However, their category "average daily prison population" includes only counts.[10]

Despite inherent methodological problems (to be explained in a moment), it is interesting to observe that, when the corresponding information on prison admissions is tabulated, and graphed (Fig. 21.2), a very different picture emerges. Where Chan and Ericson's graph of probationers and prisoners suggests that probationers are numerically greater, the opposite situation is evident here. Further, while Chan and Ericson's graph suggests an overall trend of *increase* in prison population (being 36 percent greater in 1978 than 1972), presenting the data in a consistent manner suggests a trend of *decrease* from 1972 to 1976. Although there is some increase in the last two years, the 1977 figure of 772 counts and admissions per 100,000 is somewhat lower than that of 905 in 1972 (a 15 percent decrease for these years). Thus, when the imprisonment data are presented through the same counts and admissions categorization as used by Chan and Ericson for the probation data, the results can be used to challenge the assertion that the prison population had remained stable or increased as probation expanded.

This incorporation of prison admissions data to Chan and Ericson's presentation of trends is primarily of heuristic interest: as count and admissions data denote

FIGURE 21.2 *Ontario: prison counts + admissions; probation counts + admissions; and (provincial) prison counts, 1972–1978*

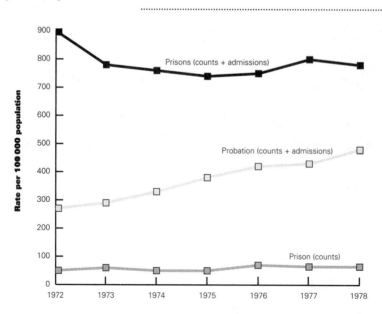

substantively different phenomena, their summation is methodologically questionable. Nevertheless, it is precisely the lack of recognition of the differing nature of firstly, admissions and count data, and secondly, probation count as compared to prison count data, which have contributed to the obfuscation of trends in corrections in the literature more generally. Some of this confusion can be clarified through addressing basic methodological questions, which in turn have crucial implications for the broader tenets of arguments about net-widening. Specifically, what are the ways in which data on probation and imprisonment can be compared? Is the manner in which probation and imprisonment data have usually been compared in the net-widening literature methodologically acceptable?

THE VAGARIES OF COMPARING DATA ON PROBATION AND IMPRISONMENT

Any comparison of probation and prison data requires careful attention to the nature of admissions and count data for each of these categories. This necessity can be illustrated by further considering the Ontario data for the period 1972–8 dealt with by Chan and Ericson. When the respective count and admissions statistics for probation and imprisonment are separated, some of the basic differences between these two dispositions become clearer.

Most notably, while there is little difference during these years between probation admissions and counts (indicating that the average probation term was approximately one year in duration), there is a vast gap between admissions and counts in the case of imprisonment (indicating that a substantial proportion of admissions are for very short periods). To support the argument of net-widening coupled with a stable or increasing imprisonment rate, the most effective way (and in this instance the only way) to recognize the data is to present the counts of those on probation and in prison.

The methodological strategy of combining probationer and prisoner counts facilitates the most dramatic statement about penal expansion made in the critical literature. It enables Hylton (1981: 203), for example, to state that "the rate per 100,000 population under supervision of the Saskatchewan correctional system increased from 85.46 in 1962 to 321.99 in 1979 — an increase of 277 percent in 18 years." However, given the differing nature of prison and probation dispositions, it is dubious that such juxtaposition is methodologically appropriate.

The differing lengths of sentences associated with probation and prison have important consequences in any attempt to examine count data. In particular, the fact that the average length of a probation sentence is longer than that of the average prison sentence must be considered crucial. One way of illuminating this is to consider the effect of alternative community programmes on the correctional population (i.e., probation plus imprisonment) in a hypothetical jurisdiction. In this hypothetical jurisdiction I shall assume that initially only the disposition of imprisonment exists, that there are 50,000 admissions a year, and that admissions are evenly distributed throughout the year. Then, reform takes place whereby probation is introduced as an alternative, and used precisely as intended by reformers seeking to reduce the use of imprisonment: that is, in such a way as to *replace* the disposition of a prison sentence in 50 percent of all cases, and without being used at all for people who would not have gone to prison in the first place. I shall also assume that in this hypothetical jurisdiction, the average prison sentence (both before and after reform) is 31 days, or about a month, while the average probation term (when introduced) is 365 days or a year. I shall further assume, for the purpose of this analysis, that there is a constancy over time in the conviction rates, in the number and types of offenders subject to a penal disposition, and in the population of the jurisdiction.

What I wish to point out is that net-widening, in terms of correctional population counts, is *by definition* a feature of alternatives to imprisonment. In this case, if the jurisdiction were to set out by sentencing 50,000 offenders a year to imprisonment, the average daily prison population (i.e., count) would be about 4,247. But subsequent to the first year of reform, when deinstitutionalization had been *successfully* accomplished in 50 percent of sentencing dispositions, with the other half now being sentenced to the newly introduced alternative of probation, the average daily penal population would increase to 27,123. Specifically, there would be about 25,000 probationers and 2,123 inmates in the system on any given day. In such a situation, in order to reduce the prison population by 50 percent through the use of probation as an alternative, it would be necessary to increase the penal population by 539 percent. Meanwhile, despite this enormous increase not one "extra" person would have been brought into the system. In what sense *numerically* does this result reflect net-widening? Would critical community corrections analysts argue that in such a situation reform had not been accomplished in practice?

The growth of the penal population even in this hypothetical case is due to the fact that the "average" probationer has about 12 times the probability of the average prisoner of showing up in the count statistics. In order to get a representative picture of the decarceration that was occurring, it might be more reasonable to divide the probationer counts by 12. One of the few ways in which deinstitutionalization through the use of probation could occur *without* net-widening in terms of counts would be if the judges, for every new probation sentence imposed, actually sent only 1 out of every 12 prison candidates to prison and let the other 11 convicted offenders go free. Another way would be for the probation disposition itself to be radically restructured, such that probation terms would become equivalent in length to prison terms: the "average" probation term imposed in lieu of imprisonment would be reduced to about a month. This, of course, would have enormous implications for other probation dispositions. One could hardly give one-month probation terms to probationers who would otherwise have gone to prison, while continuing to impose far longer probation terms on other probationers convicted for lesser offences and who are unlikely to be imprisoned at all.

Moreover, it should be recognized that in the hypothetical case described, I have, for purposes of clarity, been conservative in assuming that "average" prison sentence would remain at about one month after reform. Specifically, by assuming a continued average prison sentence of one month, I have implied that not only did the jurisdiction substitute probation for imprisonment in 50 percent of cases, but that it also *shortened* the sentence lengths of the remaining prisoners. As previously alluded to, a more realistic expectation is that the average length of sentences would *increase*, given that those with the shortest prison sentences would be more likely to receive the alternative of probation. In fact, if 50 percent of inmates prior to the hypothetical reform had average sentences of 20 days, and the other 50 percent an average of six weeks (yielding an overall average sentence length of about a month), the average inmate count after reform would be 2,877 inmates, and the total correctional count would 27,877. Therefore, in this case, resting on more plausible assumptions, securing only a 32 percent decrease in the prison population would entail a 556 percent increase in the penal population overall.

Even this second hypothetical case makes conservative assumptions. Bottomley and Pease (1986: 107) have estimated, on the basis of actual sentencing and imprisonment data for England and Wales in 1983, that sentences "up to and including six months account for 51 percent of receptions but only 17 percent of population." Therefore, "to attempt to reduce the sentenced prison population by a mere 17 percent, over half the custodial decisions of the courts would have to be substituted by non-custodial decisions." Meanwhile, the overall correctional population count would have to increase substantially.

Documentation and analysis of trends in corrections must include two fundamental points. First, even without any new people coming into the system, relatively small reductions in prison population necessitate large changes in sentencing practices. Second, expansion of correctional count populations is by definition a feature of even "true" alternatives to imprisonment. Critical analysts have assumed that the phenomenon of net-widening as illustrated through count data means that more people are actually coming into correctional systems. For example, Chan and Ericson (1981: 55) summarize their findings as they relate to other studies on community corrections—Greenberg (1975), Blomberg (1977), and Cohen (1979: 349):

> No doubt the picture presented here is still somewhat sketchy. More data on the use of community alternatives would have been useful to illustrate the extent of decarceration in this country. Statistics on sentencing patterns over the years would have helped to clarify the influx of prisoners. However, regardless of how many more details we add to the present picture, its central message is unlikely to change: people are not directed *from*, but *into* and *within* the system.

Whatever might be discovered about the movement of people *within* the system (as for example with the use of day release passes), the contention that community alternatives are invariably associated with more people coming *into* the system is problematic. When the detail of admissions to prisons is considered in relation to Chan and Ericson's Ontario data, the picture does change somewhat. The increase in probation admissions per 100,000 population was accompanied by some decrease in prison admissions.

Furthermore, when the data on prison *plus* probation admissions in Ontario are considered, the total for 1978, at 961, is lower than the 1972 figure of 986 per 100,000 population. Given that there is a decline in the overall rate of people coming into prison and probation when these two years are compared, in what sense *quantitatively* can the net-widening hypothesis be supported in Ontario for this period?

In summary, re-examination of Canadian critical literature on community corrections reveals two interrelated sets of problems in analyses of net-widening. First, it has been too readily assumed that prison populations are predominantly subject to maintenance and increase. Evidence of growth in sectors of the prison population has been generalized to the whole prison population. Indicators of decrease in imprisonment have been glossed over in favour of supporting the theme of expansion. Both the size of the prison population and longitudinal trends within it require closer attention in future studies.

Second, questionable approaches have been taken in juxtaposing data on probation and imprisonment. Quite apart from the dubious method of taking these penal dispositions in tandem without considering trends in court and sentencing data more generally (Bottoms 1983; Matthews 1987a), the substantive differences between imprisonment and probation data, notably with respect to counts, have received insufficient attention. That a growth in correctional counts reflects a growth in the numbers of people coming into the correctional system is one of the problematic impressions fostered by this omission. There is a need for greater precision in the mundane task of documenting quantitative penal data that is a prerequisite to their analysis and explanation.

CHANGING PENAL TRENDS: FROM PESSIMISM TO PRAXIS

This re-examination of the conventional wisdom of the critical literature on community corrections has identified various problems. Although contentions about stable and increasing prison populations are fundamental to net-widening arguments, documentation of trends has been unsatisfactory. Issues of incarceration require greater attention in future studies of decarceration or the lack thereof.

The very concept of net-widening should be considered problematic: aspects of net-widening, notably with respect to counts, are by definition a feature of community alternatives to imprisonment. If the implementation of alternatives, even in the ideal-typical form of a substitute for imprisonment, must lead to net-widening, how can its occurrence be used as an indicator of the failure of penal reform? The inherent conceptual obfuscations involved in net-widening suggest that the problems in the literature are not merely methodological ones of mis- or inadequate counting. Rather, there are deeper theoretical and political matters to be considered.

In identifying deeper problems I have pointed to the political pessimism characteristic of critical literature on community corrections. It is in the disjuncture between the pessimistic academic analyses and the progressive political aspirations of many authors that the nub of related problems may rest.

One of the ironies of critical analyses is that, while Foucault's historical work has been influential in the development of such gloomy perspectives, his remarks about more recent events caution against unreflexive pessimism. For example, Foucault has pointed to "a widespread facile tendency, which one should combat, to designate that which has just occurred as the primary enemy, as if this were always the principal form of oppression from which one had to liberate oneself" (1984, quoted in Cohen 1987: 369). In a similar vein, he has stated that he is "not easily convinced when told that today liberties are infringed upon, that there is a disintegration of rights and that we are becoming increasingly restricted. I wager that twenty years ago, or even a century ago, criminal justice was neither better organized nor more respectful [respectueuse]. It is pointless to dramatise the present, to lengthen its shadows by the imaginary glow of the setting sun" (Foucault 1988: 159–60).

The dramatic tendency toward seeing current developments as somehow worse than previous ones aptly sums up the stance of many critical analysts. Not only are new forms of penal control identified and ominously depicted, but previous ones are seen as continuing without modification. As encapsulated by Downes (1988: 60): "we end up with the worst of both worlds: an unreconstructed *ancien régime pénal* and a new-style carceral society." Modern society is characterized by an "overarching tendency" toward "more social control" (Cohen 1989).

Current pessimistic beliefs have also become futuristic. Where imprisonment is concerned, the conventional wisdom suggests dismal prospects. Here, as observed by Downes (1988: 187), the "bleakest view" is "offered by Cohen's depiction of a remorseless increase in the extent of and correlation between the length, depth, and breadth of imprisonment." But this vision of imprisonment has also come to overlook cautionary observations by Foucault: although the prison has experienced "extreme solidity" and resistance to transformation, this "does not mean that it cannot be altered, nor that it is once and for all indispensable to our kind of society" (Foucault 1979: 305). Rather, in the face of other transformations in penal control, Foucault has suggested that "the specificity of the prison and its role as a link are losing something of their purpose" (ibid. 306). While the possibility of the demise of imprisonment was given some attention in early analyses of decarceration (e.g., Cohen 1977; Scull 1977), such considerations have largely been displaced in favour of an emphasis on net-widening and expansion.

Gloomy assumptions and conclusions have become confused in the critical literature. The concepts of "wider," "stronger," and "different" nets are effective in directing attention *towards* trends in the expansion and extension of penal control. However, these concepts also serve to direct attention from any moderation of penal control that might have taken place, and from the superseding of some previous forms of penal control by preferable ones. Ability to recognize any reduction of penal control is limited. Any diminution can analytically be quickly overshadowed by the discovery of other, new forms of control considered of more significance in their sinister potential.

At the same time, just as perceptions of net-widening are becoming entrenched, critiques — including autocritiques — of analyses of decarceration and the dispersal of discipline thesis, as well as of uses of the concept of social control more generally, have been emerging (e.g., Bottoms 1983; Chunn and Gavigan 1988; Cohen 1987, 1989; Matthews 1987a; Rodger 1988). The challenge should be not only to deconstruct previous literature, but to develop more satisfactory analytical frameworks that will correspond with, rather than undermine, critical political and philosophical preferences. In this, an important task is to develop concepts that facilitate analysis of modification, emancipation, and progress that may have occured despite, within, and sometimes even because of modern penal developments. There is also a need to clarify developments that would be considered desirable in the penal realm, the values they reflect, and the sociological indicators of their accomplishments. In other words, in addition to refining sociological approaches to the analysis of penal trends, critical criminologists need to address philosophical and moral questions more directly than they have been prone to do (Bottoms 1987b; De Haan 1989).

More consideration of the experiences of those subject to imprisonment and alternatives is also required. As Downes (1988: 64) has commented, "what one wants to know is whether the pedlars of 'social control talk' so tellingly catalogued by Cohen (1985: ch. 5 and app.) make the same sort of impact on people's lives as the 'cruelty man' (officers for the National Society of the Prevention of Cruelty to Children) in late Victorian and Edwardian England." The views of those with whose interests critical criminology more generally has wished to identify have been rarely expressed in the decarceration literature.

These analytical tasks should be undertaken as part of the broader one of taking "penality" seriously. As David Garland (1985: 10) has elaborated, our concern must be with the whole of the penal complex, "including its sanctions, discourses, and representations." While critical criminologists have been incisive in exploring the interplay of conservative, official, and reformist discourses with the penal exercise of power, they have often overlooked the situation of critical discourse itself. Although usually in oppositional stance, critical research and discourse must also be recognized as part of the phenomenon of "penality."

In conclusion, the ability of critical criminology to supersede the circumscriptions of more traditional criminological knowledge and its part in the ominous exercise of penal power has yet to be specified. Is critical criminology, along with sociology and other social scientific knowledge, bound to remain an "ideological practice" (Smith 1974, 1984), and an ultimately conservative one? Hopefully not. Perhaps what is needed is a greater sensitivity to wider issues of social theory, and of political struggle, in the course of research on penal trends. Such sensitivity might further ability not only to criticize, but also to challenge and change penality. It might also transcend the reproduction of sociological pessimism through the advancement of critical praxis.

NOTES

1. Special thanks to Richard Ericson for his ongoing assistance and support. Thanks also to Keith Bottomley, Anthony Bottoms, Janet Chan, Stanley Cohen, Anthony Doob, Donald Evans, David Garland, Lorna Marsden, Roger Matthews, Robert Menzies, Diane Sepejak, Dorothy Smith, to *British Journal of Criminology* reviewers and others who have also read and/or discussed various aspects of this work with me. Preparation of this article was facilitated by a postdoctoral fellowship from the Social Sciences and Humanities Research Council of Canada tenable at the Centre of Criminology, University of Toronto. It was additionally facilitated by a Council of Europe criminological research fellowship, tenable at the universities of Oslo and Cambridge.

2. Scull's thesis also applied to mental health populations, where it has been comparatively better received and substantiated (see Scull 1984: 161–75).

3. The tendency toward supporting arguments as much through the use of metaphors, evocative images, and analogies as through statistical and empirical statements is characteristic of the critical correctional literature more generally. The prison, for example, is described as the "hard end" of the system, with the boundaries between it and other control institutions becoming increasingly "blurred." Community and private institutions such as the family, school, neighbourhood, and workplace are depicted as subject to "penetration" and "absorption" by formal modes of social control. As the "hard end" gets harder and the "soft end" gets wider, "bifurcation" is said to be occurring, with the processing of deviants undergoing "acceleration." In light of these developments, the "holy trinity" of reform rhetoric about the cost, effectiveness, and humaneness virtues of community corrections is revealed as a myth. Progressive "dreams" are better understood as "nightmares." Overall, contemporary penal trends are portrayed as involving a "dispersal of discipline": the prison retains its institutional strength, and is interwoven with, and dependent on, a "carceral continuum" which powerfully pervades social life in ever more subtle, complex, and effective ways (see Blomberg 1977; Bohnstedt 1978; Chan and Ericson 1981; Cohen 1979, 1983, 1985; Ericson and Baranek 1982; Greenberg 1975; Hylton 1981, 1982; Lerman 1975; Mathiesen 1983; Matthews 1979; Scull 1981, 1983, 1984; Warren 1981).

Here I am focusing on net-widening as (a) the trends it suggests are empirically identifiable; and (b) the analytical force of many of these other concepts often rests on the contention that net-widening is occurring.

4. Matthew's theoretical proposals in the analysis of decarceration are not explicitly linked by him to his more general project of advancing the cause of "left realism" in critical criminology (Matthews 1986, 1987*b*). Suffice to say here that I find the left realist approach discomfiting, as it usually leads in the direction of increased policing, criminalization, and victimization (McMahon 1988*b*). It is difficult to see how Matthew's (1987) decarceration article "fits" with the broader left realist endeavour, particularly where issues of penal policy are concerned.

5. The analysis in the following sections draws from Ericson and McMahon (1987) and McMahon (1988*b*).

6. *Count* data refer to the number of people on a given day. *Admissions* data refer to the number of committals in a given year. As will be elaborated, the necessity of identifying the differences between count and admission data, with respect both to imprisonment and other penal dispositions, is crucial in analysing and comparing the populations of correctional programmes.

7. In Canada, remand prisoners and those with sentences of less than two years come under the jurisdiction of provincial governments and their correctional agencies. Prisoners with sentences of two years and over come under the jurisdiction of the federal government and its correctional agency. Documenting prison population in any given province therefore requires examining both provincial and federal prisons in the province.

8. Hylton does mention the exclusion of inmates in "local police cells," which he estimates as rarely exceeding 20 or 30 (p. 22), but Canadian provincial correctional institutions normally also accommodate remand and other non-sentenced prisoners.

9. Chan and Ericson (1981: 43, 79) do present data on temporary absences from Ontario provincial prisons from 1974–8. These data are pertinent to the flow of inmates within the system rather than through it.

10. Chan and Ericson (1981: 80–1) specify the category "probation supervision" as "total under supervision at start of fiscal year [counts] and those placed under supervision during the fiscal year [admissions]." Their category "average daily prison population" refers only to prisoner counts at the end of the fiscal year.

Similar to Hylton, their Ontario prison count data include only provincial inmates, and not federal inmates in the province. In 1972 there were 29.3 inmates per 100,000 population in Ontario federal institutions. In 1978 the figure was lower, at 25.5.

REFERENCES

Austin, J., and Krisberg, B. (1981), "Wider, Stronger and Different Nets: the Dialectics of Criminal Justice Reform," *Journal of Research in Crime and Delinquency*, 18: 165–96.

———— (1982), "The Unmet Promise of Alternatives to Incarceration," *Crime and Delinquency*, 28: 374–409.

Biles, D., and Mulligan, G. (1983), "Mad or Bad? The Enduring Dilemma," *British Journal of Criminology*, 13: 275–9.

Blomberg, T.G. (1977), "Diversion and Accelerated Social Control," *Journal of Criminal Law and Criminology*, 68: 274–82.

———— (1980), "Widening the Net: An Anomaly in the Evaluation of Diversion Programs," in M.W. Klein and K.S. Teilman, eds., *Handbook of Criminal Justice Evaluation*, 572–92. Beverley Hills: Sage.

Bohnstedt, M. (1978), "Answers to Three Questions about Juvenile Diversion," *Journal of Research in Crime and Delinquency*, 15: 109–23.

Bottomley, K., and Pease, K. (1986), *Crime and Punishment: Interpreting the Data*. Milton Keynes: Open University Press.

Bottoms, A.E. (1983), "Neglected Features of Contemporary Penal Systems," in D. Garland and
  P. Young, eds., *The Power to Punish*, 166–202. London: Heinemann.

——— (1987a), "Limiting Prison Use: Experience in England and Wales," *Howard Journal*, 26:
  177–202.

——— (1987b), "Reflections on the Criminological Enterprise," *Cambridge Law Journal*, 46:
  240–9.

Box, S. (1987), *Recession, Crime and Punishment*. Basingstoke: Macmilan Education.

Chan, J., and Ericson, R.V. (1981), *Decarceration and the Economy of Penal Reform*. Research
  Report. Centre of Criminology, University of Toronto.

Chan, J. and Zdenowski, G. (1986), "Just Alternatives. Part I: Trends and Issues in the
  Deinstitutionalization of Punishment," *Australian and New Zealand Journal of Criminology*,
  2: 67–90.

Chunn, D.E., and Gavigan, S.A.M. (1988), "Social Control: Analytical Tool or Analytical
  Quagmire?" *Contemporary Crises*, 12: 107–24.

Cohen, S. (1977), "Prisons and the Future of Control Systems: From Concentration to
  Dispersal," in M. Fitzgerald *et al.*, eds., *Welfare in Action*. London: Routledge and Kegan
  Paul (in association with the Open University Press).

——— (1979), "The Punitive City: Notes on the Dispersal of Social Control," *Contemporary
  Crises*, 3: 339–63.

——— (1983), "Social Control Talk: Telling Stories About Correctional Change," in D. Garland
  and P. Young, eds., *The Power to Punish*, 101–24. London: Heinemann.

——— (1985), *Visions of Social Control: Crime, Punishment and Classification*. Cambridge: Polity.

——— (1987), "Taking Decentralization Seriously: Values, Visions and Policies," in J. Lowman
  et al., eds., *Transcarceration: Essays in the Sociology of Social Control*, 358–79. Aldershot:
  Gower.

——— (1989), "The Critical Discourse on 'Social Control': Notes on the Concept as Hammer,"
  International Journal of the Sociology of Law, 17: 347–57.

Cottle, T.J. (1979), "Children in Jail," *Crime and Delinquency*, 25: 318–34.

Davies, M.F. (1985), "Determinate Sentencing Reform in California and its Impact on the Penal
  System," *British Journal of Criminology*, 25: 1–30.

De Haan, W. (1989), *The Politics of Redress: Crime, Punishment and Penal Abolition*. London:
  George Allen and Unwin.

Deichsel, W. (1988), "Divert Young People from the Criminal Justice System, but Don''t Divert
  Attention from its Implications, Risks, and Dangers: Reflections on the Hamburg Model of
  Diversion." Paper presented at the 10th International Congress in Criminology,
  International Congress Centre, Hamburg.

De Jonge, G. (1985), "Community Service in Holland: A Penal Sham Success." Paper presented
  at the Second International Conference on Penal Abolition (ICOPA), The Free University,
  Amsterdam, The Netherlands.

Downes, D. (1988), *Contrasts in Tolerance: Post-War Penal Policy in The Netherlands and England
  and Wales*. Oxford: Clarendon Press.

Ericson, R.V., and Baranek, P.M. (1982), *The Ordering of Justice: A Study of Accused Persons as
  Defendants in the Criminal Process*. Toronto: University of Toronto Press.

Ericson, R.V., and McMahon, M.W. (1987), *Re-thinking Decarceration: Sentencing Trends in
  Ontario, 1951–1984*. Report to the Ontario Ministry of Correctional Services. Toronto:
  Centre of Criminology, University of Toronto.

Ericson, R.V., McMahon, M.W., and Evans, D. (1987), "Punishing for Profit: Reflections on the
  Revival of Privatization in Corrections," *Canadian Journal of Criminology*, 29: 355–87.

Foucault, M. (1979), *Discipline and Punish: The Birth of the Prison*. New York: Vintage.

——— (1984), "Space, Knowledge and Power," interview in *Skyline*, Mar. 1982, repr. in P.
  Rabinow, *The Foucault Reader*, 239–56. New York: Pantheon.

——— (1988), "The Catch-all Strategy," trans. Neil Duxbury, *International Journal of the
  Sociology of Law*, 16: 159–62.

Galvin, J. (1983), "Prison Policy Reform Ten Years Later," Introduction to special issue on prisons and sentencing reform. *Crime and Delinquency*, 29: 495–503.

Garland, D. (1985), *Punishment and Welfare: A History of Penal Strategies*. Aldershot: Gower.

——— (1986), "Foucault's *Discipline and Punish*: An Exposition and Critique," *American Bar Foundation*, 4: 847–82.

Garland, D., and Young, P., eds. (1983), *The Power to Punish: Contemporary Penality and Social Analysis*. London: Heinemann.

Grabosky, P.N. (1980), "Rates of Imprisonment and Psychiatric Hospitalization in the United States," *Social Indicators Research*, 7: 63–70.

Greenberg, D.F. (1975), "Problems in Community Corrections," *Issues in Criminology*, 10: 1–33.

Greenberg, D.F., and Humphries, D. (1980), "The Cooptation of Fixed Sentencing Reform," *Crime and Delinquency*, 26: 206–25.

Gusfield, J. (1981), *The Culture of Public Problems: Drinking-Driving and the Symbolic Order*. Chicago: University of Chicago Press.

Home Office (1988), *Punishment, Custody and the Community*. London: HMSO.

Hylton, J.H. (1981), "Community Corrections and Social Control: The Case of Saskatchewan, Canada," *Contemporary Crises*, 5: 193–215.

——— (1982), "Rhetoric and Reality: A Critical Appraisal of Community Corrections," *Crime and Delinquency*, 28: 341–73.

Ignatieff, M. (1978), *A Just Measure of Pain: The Penitentiary in the Industrial Revolution 1750–1850*. London: Macmillan.

Lerman, P. (1975), *Community Treatment and Social Control*. Chicago: University of Chicago Press.

Lowman, J., Menzies, R.J., and Palys, T.S., eds. (1987), *Transcarceration: Essays in the Sociology of Social Control*. Aldershot: Gower.

McCullagh, C. (1988), "A Crisis in the Penal System? The Case of the Republic of Ireland," in M. Tomlinson, T. Varley, and C. McCullagh, *Whose Law and Order? Aspects of Crime and Social Control in Irish Society*, 155–66. Belfast: Queen's University Bookshop (distributors).

McMahon, M.W. (1988a), "Changing Penal Trends: Imprisonment and Alternatives in Ontario, 1951–1984," Ph.D. thesis, Department of Sociology, University of Toronto.

——— (1988b) "Confronting Crime: A Review Essay," *Critical Sociology*, 51: 111–22.

Martinson, R. (1974), "What Works? Questions and Answers About Prison Reform," *The Public Interest*, 35: 22–54.

Mathiesen, T. (1983), "The Future of Control Systems: The Case of Norway," in Garland and Young (1983): 130–45.

——— (1986), "The Politics of Abolition," *Contemporary Crises*, 10: 81–94.

Matthews, R. (1979), "Decarceration and the Fiscal Crisis," in B. Fine, R. Kinsey, J. Lea, S. Picciotto, and J. Young, eds., *Capitalism and the Rule of Law*. London: Hutchinson.

——— (1986), "Beyond Wolfenden? Prostitution, Politics and the Law," in R. Matthews and J. Young, eds., *Confronting Crime*. London: Sage.

——— (1987a), "Decarceration and Social Control: Fantasies and Realities," in Lowman *et al.* (1987).

——— (1987b), "Taking Realist Criminology Seriously," *Contemporary Crises*, 11: 371–401.

Melossi, D. (1979), "Institutions of Social Control and the Capitalist Organization of Work," in B. Fine, R. Kinsey, J. Lea, S. Picciotto, and J. Young, eds., *Capitalism and the Rule of Law*. London: Hutchinson.

Michalowski, R.J., and Pearson, M.A. (1987), "Crime, Fiscal Crisis and Decarceration: Financing Corrections at the State Level" in Lowman *et al.* (1987): 248–71.

National Institute of Justice (1980), *American Prisons and Jails*, vol. i. Washington, DC: US Department of Justice.

Pease, K. (1985), "Community Service Orders," in M. Tonry and N. Morris, eds., *Crime and Justice: An Annual Review of Research*, 51–94. Chicago: University of Chicago Press.

Pease, K., and McWilliams, W. eds., (1980), *Community Service by Order*. Edinburgh: Scottish Academic Press.

Peters, A.A.G. (1986), "Main Currents in Criminal Law Theory," in J. van Dijk *et al.*, *Criminal Law in Action*. Antwerp: Kluwer.

Rodger, J.J. (1988), "Social Work as Social Control Re-examined: Beyond the Dispersal of Discipline Thesis," *Sociology*, 22: 563–81.

Rothman, D.J. (1980), *Conscience and Convenience: The Asylum and its Alternatives in Progressive America*. Boston: Little, Brown.

Rutherford, A. (1984), *Prisons and the Process of Justice: The Reductionist Challenge*. London: Heinemann.

Scull, A.T. (1977), *Decarceration: Community Treatment and the Deviant — a Radical View*. Englewood Cliffs, NJ: Prentice-Hall.

—— (1979), *Museums of Madness: The Social Organization of Insanity in Nineteenth-Century England*. New York: St. Martin's Press.

—— (1981), "Progressive Dreams, Progressive Nightmares: Social Control in Twentieth Century America," *Stanford Law Review*, 33: 575–90.

—— (1983), "Community Corrections: Panacea, Progress or Pretence?," in Garland and Young (1983): 146–65.

—— (1984), *Decarceration: Community Treatment and the Deviant — A Radical View*, 2nd edn. Cambridge: Polity.

Shearing, C.D., and Stenning, P.C. (1981), "Modern Private Security: Its Growth and Implications," in M. Tonry and N. Morris, eds., *Crime and Justice: An Annual Review of Research*, iii. 193–245.

—— (1984), "From the Panopticon to Disney World: The Development of Discipline," in A.N. Doob and E.L. Greenspan, eds., *Perspectives in Criminal Law*, 325–59. Aurora, Ontario: Canada Law Book.

—— (1987), *Private Policing*. Newbury Park: Sage.

Sim, J., Scraton, P., and Gordon, P. (1987), "Introduction: Crime, the State and Critical Analysis," in P. Scraton, ed., *Law, Order and the Authoritarian State*, 1–70. Milton Keynes: Open University Press.

Smith, D. (1974), "The Ideological Practice of Sociology," *Catalyst*, 2: 39–54.

——. (1984), "Textually-Mediated Social Organization," *International Social Science Journal*, 36: 59–75.

Sparks, R.F. (1971), "The Use of Suspended Sentences," *Criminal Law Review*, 384–401.

Statistics Canada (1962–79), *Correctional Institutions Statistics* (catalogue 85–207). Ottawa: Statistics Canada.

Steadman, H.J., and Morrissey, J.P. (1987), "The Impact of Deinstitutionalization on the Criminal Justice System: Implications for Understanding Changing Modes of Social Control," in Lowman *et al.* (1987): 227–48.

Sutherland, E.H. (1934), "The Decreasing Prison Population of England," *Journal of Criminal Law and Criminology*, 24: 880–900.

Van Dusen (1981), "Net-Widening and Relabeling: Some Consequences of Deinstitutionalization," *American Behavioral Scientist*, 24: 801–10.

Vass, A.A. (1986), "Community Service: Areas of Concern and Suggestions for Change," *Howard Journal*, 25: 100–11.

Warren, C.B. (1981), "New Forms of Social Control: The Myth of Deinstitutionalization," *American Behavioral Scientist*, 24: 724–40.

Young, J. (1986), "The Failure of Criminology: The Need for a Radical Realism," in R. Matthews and J. Young, eds., *Confronting Crime*, 4–30. London: Sage.

Young, P. (1986), "Review of S. Cohen, Visions of Social Control," *Sociological Review*, 34: 222–4.

Young, W. (1979), Community Service Orders: *The Development and Use of a New Penal Measure*. London: Heinemann.

—— (1986), "Influences Upon the Use of Imprisonment: A Review of the Literature," *Howard Journal*, 25: 125–36.

TWENTY-TWO

The Attrition of Parole

JEAN-PAUL BRODEUR

Since 1986, the National Parole Board of Canada (NPB) has issued a significant number of policy papers. A mission statement was followed by parole guidelines and by numerous booklets intended for the general public. In its November 1987 Briefing Book (Canada, National Parole Board 1987a) for the Standing Committee on Justice and the Solicitor General (The Daubney Committee), the NPB stated its core values, principle and strategic objectives. To this date, there are three core values, 22 principles and 28 strategic objectives. In May 1988, the NPB issued a document drafted for consultation on the Standards for Conditional Release supervision: the draft formulates 69 standards and two guidelines. The NPB has also commissioned numerous studies of early release and has developed, with consultants, a new risk-prediction scoring system. Finally, the Solicitor General of Canada has recently issued a series of proposals intended to curtail the use of early release in Canada.

This intense activity was sparked first by the murder of a young woman named Celia Ruygrok. She was an overnight supervisor in an Ottawa half-way house and was killed by a resident on parole. The murder was followed by a public inquest, which resulted in several recommendations to the NPB. The flurry of policy papers from the NPB was also a response to a recommendation by the Canadian Sentencing Commission (1987) to abolish full parole, granted on a discretionary basis. These two events, a murder and publication of the report of a commission appointed to study the sentencing process, are quite different and suggest that there are two separate issues involved in the debate over parole. On the one hand, there is a security question: is the existence of parole detrimental to the safety of the community?

On the other hand, there is what we may call a structural issue. Narrowly defined, this issue is concerned with the consonance of parole with the other components of the criminal justice system and more particularly with the principled process of sentencing. On the broadest level, the structural issue can be formulated in this way: there is now a widening gap between what appears to be the criminal justice system—as perceived through legislation and government documents—and what actually happens. This divorce between appearance and reality generates numerous problems, such as the practice of double-guessing, which pervades every level of the system. Every actor in the process tries to pre-empt what he or she believes will be happening at the next step by modifying his or her own decision (for instance, doubling the sentence to compensate for the possibility that parole is going to cut it down by one half). More fundamentally, this split between the criminal law and its application undermines the credibility of the whole penal system, because

Source: Jean-Paul Brodeur, "The Attrition of Parole," *Canadian Journal of Criminology*, 32, 3 (1990): 503–10. Copyright by the Canadian Criminal Justice Association. Reproduced by permission of the *Canadian Journal of Criminology*.

justice rests on its claim to make appearance and reality coincide. One is often reminded that justice must not only be done but must be seen to be done.

Although the security and structural issues interface in several ways, I shall be mainly concerned with the second one in this article. First, I will argue that the debate on the abolition of parole is an authentic one and that it cannot be reduced to a superficial misunderstanding stemming from a lack of information. Second, I will examine whether the rationale for parole as it is presently formulated in this country is not bound to widen the gap between the theory and the reality of the criminal justice system. Finally, I will contrast certain key features of sentencing with the practice of parole, as it is now evolving. This discussion will, I hope, also shed some light on the current predicament of early release in other countries.

THE DEBATE ON THE ABOLITION OF PAROLE

One of the most effective ways of intensifying a crisis is to deny its existence, thus avoiding any inquiry into its causes and its remedies. The gap between reality and perception is never wider than when we act as if the gap did not exist. In Canada, the NPB has responded to security issues by a series of measures intended to minimize the risk of releasing dangerous individuals and to placate public opinion. However, it has tried to play down the significance of the structural issue. One of the basic objections to parole is that it thwarts the meaning of custodial sentences and undermines the credibility of the criminal law. The NPB's answer to this objection is deceptively simple. In his presentation[1] to the Daubney Committee, the Chairman of the NPB stated the following:

> The judge determines the maximum length of incarceration. Parliament decides which portion of a sentence must be served in an institution in order to ensure that sentences meet their general objectives, and, finally, only when that portion of the sentence has been served under institutional control, the National Parole Board will determine whether the offender may continue to serve his/her sentence under parole. (Canada, National Parole Board 1987b: 8)

The explicit reference to Parliament is intended to remind us that the NPB only applies what is the law of the land and that it should not be decried for doing so. This answer misses the issue. First of all, wherever the abolition of parole is debated — in the U.S., in Sweden and in a great number of Commonwealth countries — the legality of parole is not what is challenged. What is alleged is that the statutes governing parole are not consistent with the sentencing statutes. For instance, section 83 of the *Canadian Criminal Code* provides a minimum term of imprisonment for the use of a firearm during the commission of an offense. It reads thus: "Everyone who uses a firearm ... (while committing an offence) is liable to imprisonment (in the case of a second or subsequent offence) for not more than 14 years and not less than three years."

If a judge were to give a second offender the minimum sentence of three years in jail as provided by section 83 and apply the law according to the argument advanced by the Chairman of the NPB to the Daubney Committee, this judge would have to formulate the sentence in a way similar to this: "I sentence you to a maximum three years of imprisonment, which is the minimum provided by the law."

This sounds awkward. One might reply that this awkwardness only stems from our insistence that words mean what they say, namely that imprisonment means incarceration. In a 1987 booklet entitled "Some people say ..." (foolish things), the NPB proposes an alternative to this semantic priggishness. Attempting to refute the assertion that "parole reduces the sentence imposed by the courts," the NPB presents the following argument:

> The court sets the length of the sentence. Parole affects only the ways of serving the sentence; it does not shorten or lengthen the sentence imposed by the court. Once the sentence is handed down it is up to the correctional agencies to determine the level of control they will impose on the offender. (Canada, National Parole Board 1987c: 3)

This argument takes us to the heart of the matter. It assumes that, with regard to sentences implying a deprivation of physical liberty, the court does not determine the *nature* of the sentence; it only specifies the period of time during which the offender is going to be under the control of the correctional agencies. Hence the sentence is indeterminate in two respects. First, with regard to imprisonment, the court sets only a maximum length; the minimum length is determined by the law on early release. Between the minimum and the maximum, the fate of the offender is left undecided by the sentence. Second, the level of control that is going to be imposed on the offender under a custodial sentence is largely unspecified. An analogous situation would be the determination of a fine in terms of numerical units, without an explicit specification of the currency in which it would be paid (that would be left to a "fine administration board").

Once they are spelled out, the implications of parole become very significant. It cannot be claimed that those who oppose parole have raised a cloud of dust only to complain afterwards that they cannot see. The question of whether we should have a determinate or an indeterminate system of sentencing and the question of the meaning of custody are real ones and cannot be resolved by waiting for the dust to settle.

A RATIONALE FOR PAROLE

Parole is a complex concept. Its core feature is release of an offender from prison before he has served his full custodial term. This release can be more or less automatic. In most countries practicing the early release of offenders, parole is granted on a selective and discretionary basis. The authority that grants parole—generally, a parole board—acts as a filter between prison and society. Finally, released offenders can be subjected to various degrees of supervision. Parole, then, normally has three features: time remission, discretionary selection, and supervision. Only the first feature is truly indispensable.

One has to ask whether providing a rationale for the filtering action of a parole board is equivalent to formulating a rationale for the early release of inmates. In other words, is justifying the existence of a parole board the same as justifying the existence of parole itself? Referring to recent developments in Canadian criminal justice, I shall argue that these are two quite separate issues.

In 1986, the NPB issued a public statement of its mission. It is clear that the board believes that by stating its mission, it is also justifying the existence of parole. The Mission Statement of the NPB reads thus: "... The Board, *by* facilitating the timely reintegration of offenders as law abiding citizens, contributes to the protection of society." (emphasis added) (Canada, National Parole Board 1987a: 4). However, in the NPB briefing book for the Daubney Committee, the Mission Statement is re-interpreted in the following manner: "The Board, *in* providing opportunities for rein-tegration, contributes to the protection of society *by* setting conditions suitable to each individual and, if required by returning the offender to custody or reducing the constraints imposed." (emphasis added) (Canada, National Parole Board 1987a: 4). The difference between these two statements is significant. According to the first, the Board protects society *by* facilitating the reintegration of offenders. This formulation puts emphasis on rehabilitation. However, according to the second version, the Board protects society mainly by supervising the released offenders, the accent being thus put on control.

This shifting of emphasis is easy to explain. In responding to the security issue, the NPB has based its Mission Statement on the need to protect the public. Now, in both the general literature on sentencing and in Canadian jurisprudence, the protec-tion of society is just another name for the traditional sentencing goal of incapacita-tion. I do not deny that the notion of protecting society can be construed as a crown-ing objective, compared to which other traditional goals such as deterrence or rehabilitation only appear as different means to achieve that one end. However, in order to justify measures as contradictory as putting someone *in* prison and releasing the person from prison earlier than was decided by the court, the protection of soci-ety has to be stripped of any precise content. No doubt one could build an elegant argument to the effect that the concept of national security is the foundation for the preservation of civil liberties. These exercises are usually futile, because miscon-strued notions eventually re-assert their original meaning.

That is what is happening in this country with regard to the protection of soci-ety. Section 10 of the Parole Act, which was proclaimed in 1959, sets forth three cri-teria for granting parole to an inmate, namely that he has benefited enough from prison, that parole will aid his rehabilitation, and thirdly, that his release on parole would not constitute an undue risk to society. The NPB has recently re-interpreted the Parole Act to mean that risk is the paramount consideration. Hence, in his pre-sentation[1] to the Daubney Committee, the Chairman of the NPB declared:

> The wording of Section 10 lends itself to an interpretation focused on risk and the pro-tection of society. It is natural to read criterion 3 as the most important criterion and criteria 1 and 2 as supportive of criterion 3. In other words, risk is the overriding factor. (Canada, National Parole Board, 1987b: 9)

The statement immediately associates risk assessment with the protection of society. Under our assumption that the protection of society is basically a rationale for incapacitation, this re-interpretation of the Parole Act was to be expected. Most, if not all the research literature on incapacitation focuses on risk assessment and on the prediction of behaviour. The recent proposal of the Solicitor General of Canada, which would curtail parole and abolish earned remission, lends additional weight to our assumption that the protection of society is a rationale for incapacitation.

In the short run there may be no real inconsistency in anchoring the filtering action of a parole board in such a rationale. Furthermore, incapacitation is fully con-sistent with supervision. It is difficult to see, however, how one can justify the core feature of parole—the early release of offenders—on the joint basis of the need to protect the public and the need to incapacitate offenders. Basing early release on the protection of society is like trying to run wearing armour: it is no way to win either a race or a battle.

There is no great difficulty in finding a rationale germane to parole. Such a rationale can focus on clemency, rehabilitation, or the provision of a safety net to ease the pressure generated by the growth of prison populations. Unfortunately, none of these purposes can be publicly proclaimed. Clemency would not fit the present mood of public opinion and, in any case, was rejected long ago in favour of rehabilitation. Rehabilitation, after an eclipse of ten years, is gathering new support. This notion, however, is much too controversial to be the cornerstone of a penal policy. The use of parole to reduce the prison population has been repeatedly disclaimed by the NPB. This use of early release is open to criticism both on the grounds that it is unprincipled with regard to justice and that it may endanger the safety of the public. It is nonetheless occurring, sometimes on a massive scale.

It would appear, then, that any rationale that reflects some of the reality and the effects of parole cannot be officially endorsed. On the other hand, the mission statement palatable to public opinion (and the pressure that it exerts on politicians to get tough on crime) is at odds with the essential characteristic of parole, namely that it is a form of early release. The fundamental discrepancy between parole and its proclaimed rationale to protect the public only widens the gap between the apparent legitimation of the criminal justice system and its true operation. Whatever else can be said of parole, it is surely the weakest link in the chain that is supposed to protect the public. By putting the focus on the reliability of risk assessment and on the need to protect society, the advocates of parole only compound the most damaging error of the criminal justice system: making promises that it cannot possibly fulfill.

SENTENCING AND EARLY RELEASE

There are many ways to address the issue of whether early release is consonant with a principled system of sentencing. The Canadian Sentencing Commission (1987) raised several relevant questions. The most troubling of these questions concerns the alleged relationship between the length of a custodial term and the likelihood of being released on parole. If it were proven that the probability of being released on parole increased with the length of the sentence, we would be compelled to draw the conclusion that the sentencing and the paroling authorities apply conflicting standards of proportionality between the seriousness of the offence and the severity of the sanction. The empirical evidence supporting a correlation between sentence length and the probability of being granted parole remains controversial.

I now want to discuss briefly two questions that are connected with some of the points I previously made. We have already seen that under the current interpretation risk assessment was the primary concern of releasing authorities such as the NPB. There is one basic difference between the determination of a sentence and the assessment of the risk of re-offending. Risk assessment is a pragmatic attempt to use science in order to predict future behaviour and, as such, can be said to be neutral in terms of moral values (value-free). Sentencing, on the other hand, is bound by a set of moral values. This contrast between *predicting* and *sentencing* is reflected in the guidelines that were developed to structure both of these processes respectively. All sentencing guidelines, whether *presumptive* or *merely advisory in nature*, state that certain offender characteristics are not relevant for sentencing or, at the very least, should not be considered grounds for greater severity. Gender, race, national origin, religion, socio-economic status, and employment history are among a list of factors that are generally excluded. It must be pointed out that these factors are said to be irrelevant on the basis of a value judgment asserting that discrimination is morally wrong. The situation is markedly different, however, with regard to risk assessment. For instance employment history was a legitimate consideration according to the U.S. federal parole guidelines. It is now taken into account by the pre-release decision policies recently issued by the Canadian NPB. Of course, it can be claimed that race and gender are not in fact used in assessing the risk that an applicant for parole will re-offend. However, the important point to be made here is that nothing rules out in principle the use of such factors, if they are shown to be good predictors. If you discriminate against the unemployed, you may eventually discriminate on the basis of race or national origin, risk assessment being a process that is value-free. Sentencing, however, is bound up with the values defining justice and is not, at least in principle, compatible with discrimination and violations of the principle of proportionality. I am not in any way suggesting that sentencing is the incarnation of virtue, where early release is a technical exercise. In certain cases the reverse may in fact be true. Nevertheless, it is crucial to realize that risk assessment belongs to the field of pragmatic knowledge and can legitimately take into account any factor that proves to be a good predictor. Insofar as it gives priority to risk assessment, parole may in this way conflict with sentencing that rests on a moral foundation and is constrained by values and rights. It may actually also conflict with its proclaimed core values and principles.

The second question that I shall address also relates to a point that was made previously. The NPB denies that parole reduces the length of a custodial sentence. Rather, it re-defines custody as a continuum of different levels of control, which extends from imprisonment in a maximum security penitentiary to conditional release. This re-definition has crucial implications.

During the last 15 years two kinds of sentencing reforms have been launched. The first kind has a high profile and consists in the transition of fully determinate systems of sentencing. In several cases, this transition was effected by the appointment of a sentencing commission and by the development of sentencing guidelines. The most important feature of these sentencing guidelines was to provide guidance on whether or not to incarcerate an offender. One of the basic assumptions of this high profile reform is that there is a clear-cut difference being embodied in the so-called "in/out line" drawn across sentencing grids.

There is, however, another kind of sentencing reform that is now quietly gathering steam and that has the potential to introduce drastic changes in the sentencing system. It is the development of new sentencing options (such as house arrest with electronic monitoring and intensive surveillance probation that are punitive but do not involve incarceration). This movement towards "intermediate" sanctions was sparked by prison overcrowding and by the prohibitive cost of building new facilities. It rests on the assumption that custody (being "in") is not separated from non-custody (being "out") by a strong dividing line but by a wide band that comprises many sentencing options half-way between being "in" and being "out." This assumption is fully consistent with the NPB re-definition of sentencing as a continuum of different levels of control, in which the in/out line becomes completely blurred. This is not the only common feature between parole and the move towards intermediate sanctions. Under a new rationale such as the protection of society, parole may eventually be transformed into a program that is both punitive and cost-effective. This change can be introduced by submitting prisoners on conditional release to electronic monitoring. Canada has so far resisted the use of anklets and other devices to monitor parolees. It is unclear whether the NPB will be able in the long run to withstand the mounting pressure to place all released inmates under intensive electronic surveillance.

The retention of parole is usually seen as a way to resist changes that are felt to be undesirable. The point of the preceding remarks is to suggest that the retention of parole can also be viewed as an unintended way to accelerate the movement towards an increased use of intermediate sanctions. What is troubling in this other reform scenario is that implications of intermediate sanctions have never been as thoroughly assessed as the consequences of abolishing parole. Hence, we may find ourselves ushered into a situation that will trigger a new escalation in control without having ever contemplated whether or not we wanted to go in this direction.

CONCLUSION

The point that I have been trying to make throughout this paper can be summarized in the following way. Not only is it too late to reform parole, but what is now proclaimed to be a reform of parole is no more than a strategy of attrition. Because of the politicization of the debate on the use of incarceration, the alleged reform of parole amounts to a transformation of early release into release at the latest possible point, into an environment that shortly may be electronically monitored. Indeed, the more forcefully that a parole board claims to make accurate risk assessment, the more the public will be shocked when the board is shown to have made a mistake. It is absolutely inevitable that some violent recidivists will succeed in slipping through the net of the parole board. The result will be renewed pressure for stiffer criteria of release and for more rigid supervision in the community, until early release mutates at last into "zombie" parole.

The slow attrition of parole will be fraught with all the disadvantages of the abolition of parole, without enjoying any of its benefits in terms of sparking a comprehensive reform of the criminal law. Being an incremental process, the attrition of parole will thwart any project to reform sentencing as a whole, and borne down by its own weight, the criminal justice system will keep on stumbling in circles. Even if parole is drastically curtailed the mere fact that it still exists in name will fuel the public perception that the system is too lenient towards offenders.

Most important of all, the fact that parole is withering from within instead of being abolished from the outside will foster the illusion that no change is occurring and that the *status quo* is preserved. Consequently, the need to assess the impact of the curtailment of early release on other parts of the criminal justice system will not be apparent. In this regard, it is significant that the 1988 proposals of the Solicitor General of Canada to increase the period spent in jail before parole eligibility for certain offences and to drastically cut down remission for good behaviour were made without any information whatsoever as to their impact on prison populations.

It has been alleged that the abolition of parole would make the criminal justice system more honest and that it would enhance its credibility. It may produce these effects. One thing at least is indisputable. The abolition of parole cannot be disguised as a minor adjustment within a structure that is basically sound. This structure is now collapsing and has to be replaced as a whole. If the abolition of parole makes us appreciate the urgency of a comprehensive reform of the criminal justice system and if it is a step in addressing this issue in a complete and responsible way, then we should proceed with it. Simply abolishing parole without re-ordering the rest of the system would be unwise. I have tried to argue that the *attrition* of parole that is now taking place will eventually amount to the *abolition* of parole, and without any compensatory reform of sentencing.

NOTE

1. It seems that two versions of this document exist. In this paper, I am quoting from what appears to be the first one publicly-released.

REFERENCES

Canada, National Parole Board. 1987a. Briefing Book for members of the Standing Committee on Justice and Solicitor General. Ottawa: National Parole Board.
———. 1987b. Chairman's Presentation to the Standing Committee on Justice and Solicitor General. Ottawa: National Parole Board.
———. 1987c. Some People Say .... Ottawa: Ministry of Supply and Services Canada.
Canadian Sentencing Commission. 1987. Sentencing Reform: A Canadian Approach. Ottawa: Ministry of Supply and Services.

PART SIX

Crime Prevention: The Impact of the Community, the Family, and the Situation

There has been a growing recognition that reactive methods of crime control, such as law enforcement and attempts at rehabilitating offenders, are ineffective and expensive means for providing public safety. Consequently, the proactive approach of crime prevention has begun to receive more attention. Of course, crime prevention programs are nothing new; the Chicago Area Projects were begun in the 1930s in an effort to get neighbourhood residents to do something about delinquency (see Short, 1969). However, rising rates of crime and increased fear expressed by citizens, as well as the high costs of traditional crime control methods, have combined to give crime prevention policy a higher priority and greater public visibility. This is particularly the case in several Western European countries, but Canada has also begun to move in this direction (Tonry and Farrington, 1995).

In the 1980s prevention programs such as Neighbourhood Watch and Block Parents were given wide publicity. In 1989 Canada hosted the European and North American Conference on Urban Safety and Crime Prevention, which adopted The Agenda for Safer Cities, a program of action to prevent crime and decrease feelings of insecurity in cities. Specific strategies were proposed based largely on the concept of crime prevention through social development (Canadian Council on Social Development, 1990). This Agenda concluded that crime prevention must be community-based and bring together those responsible for housing, social services, recreation, schools, policing, and justice to tackle situations that breed crime. Growing out of this conference, the Federation of Canadian Municipalities has initiated an Urban Safety and Crime Prevention Program with priority given to strategies that aim to reduce offences that cause the most trauma. The cornerstone of these strategies is to establish interagency networks and increased community collaboration. While the Federation will provide models and resources, initiatives must be generated locally by municipal leaders (Canadian Council on Social Development 1990). A number of communities across Canada have developed local safer communities initiatives (Hastings and Melchers, 1990).

Organizations such as the Canadian Council on Social Development, the Canadian Criminal Justice Association, and the Canadian Council on Children and Youth produced documents to stimulate public awareness and encourage policy-makers and practitioners to recognize the crime prevention through social development perspective (Canadian Council on Social Development, 1990). The Canadian Council on Social Development and the Canadian Criminal Justice Association had previously initiated the development of a National Social Strategy for Crime Prevention for Canada in 1989 emphasizing the importance of a comprehensive approach to preventing crime and the critical need for social programming (Canadian Council on Social Development, 1990).

Crime prevention policy was given a further boost when in 1993 the Common's Standing Committee on Justice and the Solicitor General issued a report urging establishment of a national crime prevention council, the development of a national crime prevention strategy, and that at the end of five years, 5 percent of the current criminal justice budget should be spent on crime prevention (Standing Committee on Justice and the Solicitor General, 1993). While the Federal Government created a twenty-five member national advisory crime prevention council in 1994, it has not implemented the recommended budget. The National Crime Prevention Council's focus is on crime prevention through social development, finding ways to help society deal with the underlying factors that undermine community safety and result in crime. Children and youth are the Council's immediate concern and it has prepared four fact sheets providing background information to communities to help create better opportunities for children from the prenatal stage to six years of age (National Crime Prevention Council, 1995).

The Federal Government did incorporate crime prevention in a small way into Bill C-41, An Act to Amend the Criminal Code (Sentencing). In Section 718 concerning the purpose of sentencing, the Act states that the fundamental purpose of sentencing is to contribute, *along with crime prevention initiatives*, to respect for the law and the maintenance of a just, peaceful and safe society .... However, it remains to be seen what this statement of principle or purpose will mean in practice.

Crime prevention has been defined as any action designed to reduce the actual level of crime and/or the perceived fear of crime (Lab, 1992). Crime prevention attempts to eliminate crime prior to the initial occurrence or before further activity, while crime control implies the management of an existing level of crime (Lab, 1992). Crime prevention thus encompasses a wide range of activities.

These activities have been classified in several different ways. For example, some have used the public health typology of disease prevention that classifies activities into primary, secondary, and tertiary prevention (Last, 1980). Each of these types addresses the problem at different stages of development (Brantingham and Faust, 1976). Primary prevention refers to actions taken to avoid the initial development of the problem. Attention is focussed on conditions of the physical and social environment that provide opportunities for or precipitate criminal acts, such as environmental design, neighbourhood watch, general deterrence, and public education about crime prevention. Secondary prevention focusses on those individuals or situations exhibiting early signs of the problem. Early identification of high-risk individuals or communities is essential, followed by interventions prior to the commission of illegal activity. But it is not always easy to clearly differentiate secondary from primary prevention. Tertiary prevention consists of actions at the stage where the problem is already manifest. Most of this type of prevention occurs within the criminal justice system, intervening with actual offenders seeking to prevent recidivism.

Tonry and Farrington (1995) have developed an alternative framework to classify crime prevention initiatives into developmental, community, and situational prevention. Tonry and Farrington recognize that there is some overlap at the borders of these types but argue that the scheme encompasses a broad range of crime prevention activities from many disciplines and agencies. Developmental prevention refers to interventions designed to prevent the development of criminal potential in individuals, especially those targeting risk and protective factors discovered in studies of human development. A recent review of prevention experiments with children targeting the development of antisocial behaviour concludes that prevention of later juvenile delinquency is more likely when interventions are aimed at more than one risk factor, last for a relatively long period of time (at least one year), and are implemented before adolescence (Tremblay and Craig, 1995). Early childhood interventions focussing on the three most important risk factors of socially disruptive behaviour, cognitive deficits, or parenting can have a positive effect in preventing later delinquency.

Community prevention is intervention designed to change the social conditions that influence offending in residential communities. Evidence of the effectiveness of community prevention is less convincing than for situational or developmental prevention (Tonry and Farrington, 1995). It has proven difficult to initiate community organization against crime in high-crime areas and difficult to sustain involvement in low-crime areas (Hope, 1995). Furthermore, both the development of community crime problems and community-based responses to them are affected by the operation of the wider urban housing and employment markets (Hope, 1995).

Finally, by situational prevention Tonry and Farrington mean interventions designed to prevent the occurrence of crimes, especially by reducing opportunities and increasing risks (Clarke, 1995). Although debate continues about whether situational approaches prevent or displace crimes to other times, places, and targets, it appears that some situational methods are effective in some circumstances (Tonry and Farrington, 1995). Situational measures may result in some diffusion of benefits to crimes/areas not directly targeted and thus achieve net preventive effects after displacement is taken into account (Clarke, 1995).

READINGS

In 1989 the Canadian Criminal Justice Association, in association with five other organizations, proposed a national strategy to make crime prevention through social development a matter of urgent and pressing concern in Canada. Reading Twenty-three is an edited version of this strategy and begins with a brief overview of the problem of crime in Canadian society, identifies the major social factors contributing to this crime, and claims that the traditional criminal justice system approach is no longer working. Rather, a nationally coordinated, systematic strategy for tackling the social situations that cause crime is required. This social development approach to crime prevention is complementary to opportunity-reduction approaches. The major recommendations in this strategy address five critical areas of social development: parents and families, schools, social housing and neighbourhoods, employment, and substance abuse, the media, and health.

The second reading in this part continues this focus on crime prevention through social development. Farrington discusses the implications of research on the development of delinquent and criminal careers for the social prevention of crime. From the results of several longitudinal investigations he identifies a number of factors that predict such careers and briefly suggests their policy implications in terms of social crime prevention programs. Farrington emphasizes the need for longitudinal research that includes experiments aimed at prevention of the development of delinquency and crime from these social factors.

An example of such longitudinal research incorporating a social prevention experiment is provided by the next reading by Tremblay and associates. This study followed disruptive kindergarten boys to mid-adolescence. A sample of boys identified as disruptive in kindergarten were selected and randomly assigned to a preventive intervention and control condition. Those assigned to the intervention condition received a two-year prevention program that included both a home-based parent training component and a school-based social skills component. The follow-up investigated the impact of these interventions on school adjustment and delinquent behaviour for six years following completion of the intervention. The results indicated that the interventions had a positive impact on school adjustment during the elementary grades, but that this impact disappeared in high school. Intervention did not have a significant impact on official delinquency (juvenile court records), although those boys who received intervention did self-report less delinquency. The authors discuss the policy implications of these results for further prevention efforts targeted at young, at-risk children and their parents.

A different type of crime prevention focusses on the immediate situations in which crime occurs. This approach analyzes the specific characteristics of given crime problems for ways to eliminate or reduce their magnitude. The reading by Brantingham and Brantingham places this situational form of crime prevention within the context of different types of crime prevention efforts, including legal prevention (deterrence), social prevention, community development, and neighbourhood watch. In contrast to these types, situational approaches argue that specific crime problems have unique characteristics that can be used in looking for solutions. Analyzing offenders' decision processes leading to an offence at a particular time and place is an important aspect of situational crime prevention. The article concludes with several examples of this approach, noting its applicability to high-volume property offences and nuisance behaviour, and the potential for crime displacement.

QUESTIONS FOR DISCUSSION

1. Describe some examples of potential crime prevention programs suggested by longitudinal research on the development of delinquent and criminal careers.
2. Should crime prevention through social development programs (e.g., job training and placement) be directed only to those individuals at high risk for crime or should they be made more generally available to all those in a category of presumed high-risk persons? How does the "prediction problem" relate to this issue?
3. Is early intervention with high-risk children likely to be more cost-effective, all things considered, than later intervention with adolescents and young adults? What problems need to be considered before adopting such a policy?
4. What distinguishes situational crime prevention? Is it more suitable for some types of crime than others?

REFERENCES

Brantingham, P.J. and F.L. Faust. 1976. "A conceptual model of crime prevention." *Crime and Delinquency* 22: 284–96.

Canadian Council on Social Development. 1990. Safer Communities: An Emerging Canadian Experience. Ottawa: Canadian Council on Social Development.

Clarke, Ronald V. 1995. "Situational crime prevention." Pp. 91–150 in Michael Tonry and David P. Farrington (eds.), *Building a Safer Society*, V. 19, *Crime and Justice*. Chicago: University of Chicago Press.

Hastings, Ross and R. Melchers. 1990. "Municipal government involvement in crime prevention in Canada." *Canadian Journal of Criminology* 32: 107–23.

Hope, Tim. 1995. "Community crime prevention." Pp. 21–90 in Michael Tonry and David P. Farrington (eds.), *Building a Safer Society*, V. 19, *Crime and Justice*. Chicago: University of Chicago Press.

Lab, Steven P. 1992. *Crime Prevention*. Cincinnati: Anderson Publishing Company.

Last, John M. 1980. "Scope and methods of prevention." In John M. Last (ed.), *Public Health and Preventive Medicine*. New York: Appleton-Century-Crofts.

National Crime Prevention Council. 1995. A Message to those Working with Children and Youth. Ottawa: National Crime Prevention Council.

Short, Jr., James F. 1969. *Juvenile Delinquency and Urban Areas*. Chicago: University of Chicago Press.

Standing Committee on Justice and the Solicitor General. 1993. *Crime Prevention in Canada*. Ottawa: Canada Communication Group.

Tonry, Michael and David P. Farrington. 1995. "Strategic approaches to crime prevention." Pp. 1–20 in Michael Tonry and David P. Farrington (eds.), *Building a Safer Society*, V. 19, *Crime and Justice*. Chicago: University of Chicago Press.

Tremblay, Richard E. and Wendy M. Craig. 1995. "Developmental crime prevention." Pp. 151–236 in Michael Tonry and David P. Farrington (eds.), *Building a Safer Society*, V. 19, *Crime and Justice*. Chicago: University of Chicago Press.

TWENTY-THREE

Safer Communities: A Social Strategy for Crime Prevention in Canada

CANADIAN CRIMINAL JUSTICE ASSOCIATION

INTRODUCTION

Canadians seek peace and security. The safety of our homes and streets helps define us as a people, particularly in contrast to the United States. Our constitutional ideals at Confederation were peace, order, and good government; uniquely in the Western world, one of our national symbols is a police force.

Yet polls suggest that the fear of crime is becoming a more significant factor in the quality of life of Canadians, whether or not it is justified by the actual number of criminal offences. In a 1988 Decima poll, two out of three Canadians felt that by the year 2000, it would not be safe to walk around in our cities. Government surveys in urban areas show that one in two women and two in three elderly Canadians are afraid to go out in their own neighbourhoods after dark.

The fear of crime can have many causes beyond the actual level of crime. Newspaper articles and television reports on sensational exceptional crimes create an impression of omnipresent criminals. The growing size of the communities with which we identify gives us a feeling that we are more vulnerable to these events. An offence reported on a transit system, for example, makes all users of that system feel at risk. The 1988 Report of the Standing Committee on Justice and Solicitor General noted, "discounting fears does not dispel them." Thus, while acknowledging the existence of fear, this paper concentrates on actual crime rates.

Source: Canadian Criminal Justice Association, "Safer Communities: A Social Strategy for Crime Prevention in Canada," *Canadian Journal of Criminology*, 31, 4 (1989) 359–401. Copyright by the Canadian Criminal Justice Association. Reproduced by permission of the *Canadian Journal of Criminology*.

What are the documented facts about crime in Canada? When compared to its neighbour to the south, Canada emerges as a relatively safe country, although compared to many other industrialized countries, our levels of violent crime are higher. There exists some concern that unless a comprehensive crime prevention strategy is put into place, our society and its crime rate may take on more and more of the attributes of American society.

While violent offences that result in loss of life are probably the most feared, murder has actually decreased in the last decade. Common assaults account for more than one-third of all violent offences. Of the robberies where the threat of force was used to obtain valuables, approximately one in four involved firearms; actual physical injury, however, is infrequent. Sexual assaults—aggravated or with a weapon—are now reported more openly and cause major trauma to the victims. In addition to reported crimes, many others are unreported, especially the assault of women, children, and elderly people in their own homes by family members.

Nearly one in six of all property offences is a residential break-and-enter crime. The average loss exceeds $1,000, and each year many of these crimes result in lasting and serious emotional trauma for the victims. Fortunately less than 2 percent of offences that start as break-ins escalate into attacks on the residents. Simple thefts and willful damage or vandalism each account for a similar number of offences.

The reported levels of crime are substantially higher now than in the 1960s and early 70s. The numbers of crimes recorded recently have increased approximately 20 percent for violent offences over the average for the early 1980s, a 50 percent increase from 1979, and close to 100 percent from 20 years earlier. The number of property offences has been approximately the same since 1981, although over 200 percent higher than in the 1960s.

What are the contributing factors to crime in Canada? While increases in the crime rate are partly due to better and more comprehensive methods of reporting and to greater opportunities for crime, studies point to a number of significant social factors, such as:

- an increase in the population of young males between the ages of 15 and 25 (a factor becoming more important as the population of Canada ages)
- inadequate parenting
- increases in family breakdown
- blocked life opportunities in school and employment for the young and minorities
- difficulties in housing
- the availability of firearms
- media programming depicting violence and the happiness that supposedly accompanies the acquisition of goods
- alcohol and drug use, and
- increasing urbanization and the resulting personal isolation and indifference.

Efforts to reduce crime have increasingly centred on these social factors. Crime prevention through social development is not a new idea, but the experience of other countries has revealed a number of significant new approaches to grappling with the issue. Social and economic policies are more and more concerned with crime prevention, and crime prevention is substantially more concerned with social and economic policy.

The United States affords an example of how traditional methods of fighting crime — the "cops, courts, and corrections" approach — are no longer working effectively. In the 1960s, the assassinations of John Kennedy, Martin Luther King, and Robert Kennedy precipitated three extensive Presidential Commissions to study crime, violence, and civil disorder in the U.S.A. Each commission recommended sweeping changes in social and economic policies to attack the situations that breed crime, yet few of their recommendations have been implemented. The levels of common crime have doubled or tripled since the 1960s, while the number of persons incarcerated has doubled in the last two decades, both in relation to the total population.

During this time, however, several American projects — such as the community crime prevention program in Seattle — have demonstrated that crime can be reduced when the appropriate methods are used. And the Eisenhower Foundation has demonstrated remarkable success in generating community-development approaches to tackling the causes of crime.

In Europe, recent crime prevention initiatives are characterized by a strong and visible sense of national leadership, by one of a variety of national councils or committees, and by permanent secretariats to support their objectives.

In France, for example, the Prime Minister stimulated the creation of more than 500 local city-level crime prevention councils. These councils bring together local elected officials, municipal administrators, and representatives of a broad range of local organizations. Guided by senior city officials and the terms of legal crime prevention contracts, the local councils are responsible for analyzing the crime problem as it affects their area, for reviewing and realigning existing programs to cope with crime, and for proposing new activities. They also coordinate local programs to prevent crime directly, through street workers and the police, as well as indirectly, through urban renewal and employment programs, among others.

England and Wales have established a joint national committee to promote crime prevention, again with leadership from the Prime Minister, and created a dedicated secretariat within the Home Office to promote crime prevention through policy and research. The committee is spending significant sums of money, particularly for job creation, to reduce situational opportunities for crime. A plethora of local groups is involved in crime prevention, although with little strong coordination. The committee has increased the extent to which its programs are directed toward the situations that breed crime by forming Crime Concern, a national organization with private-sector funding.

In Canada, several provinces have recently initiated crime prevention strategies with a focus on community involvement and social development. Quebec's Department of Public Security, for instance, supports a series of regional crime prevention committees throughout the province, each responsible for identifying priorities, planning activities, and mounting special programs for crime prevention at the regional level.

Manitoba is actively considering the creation of a provincial crime prevention council, building on a high level of interest and participation among a province-wide network of social services, businesses, unions, educators, seniors, and legal, community, ethnic, and cultural groups. The province has publicly committed itself to the concept of community and neighbourhood-based crime prevention.

For several years British Columbia has had a provincial Crime Prevention Association, which brings together representatives from police forces and community organizations to promote various social and physical approaches to crime reduction.

Several provinces have also established youth justice committees of citizens, following the implementation of the federal *Young Offenders Act*, which among other activities promote crime prevention at the local level.

As well, Canadian municipalities have become more involved in crime prevention through socially focused approaches such as developing recreational programs as alternatives to truancy, and addressing race relations to restore a better sense of community. Many municipalities have already established local committees for crime prevention, or have created working groups to study specific problems such as drug consumption among the young, the sexual abuse of children, and violence against women.

As all levels of government are realizing, however, crime prevention has been approached throughout Canada in a piecemeal fashion. Many people are wrestling with the problem, but in uncoordinated programs, committees, and groups of active and concerned citizens and professionals.

The Canadian Criminal Justice Association, one of Canada's oldest organizations concerned with the problem of crime, believes that the time has come for a new coordinated approach throughout the country. Building on the pioneering efforts of thousands of Canadians in past decades, we believe that Canada is ready for a national strategy for crime prevention. What we propose is a coherent, systematic strategy for effective crime prevention by tackling the social situations that cause crime.

The emphasis on crime prevention in the past has been on the role of the courts, police, and correctional systems to apprehend and limit an offender's opportunity to commit further crime. During the last two decades support has increased for public participation, particularly in opportunity-reduction programs such as Neighbourhood Watch and through the securing of personal property.

More recently, interest has grown among those responsible for crime prevention in understanding and addressing the social causes of crime: crime prevention through social development. Research has suggested that many chronic criminals display personal, familial, and social experiences and characteristics predisposing them to participate in criminal behaviour. It is assumed that various social interventions may alleviate these predisposing factors. This approach seeks action through the various policies, programs, and services already present in the social development field — social housing, education, health, income security, and social services — which, if directed to those most vulnerable, may lessen the factors predisposing an individual to crime.

In this paper, we emphasize social development as one major component in a comprehensive crime prevention strategy. Our recommendations are complementary to, not in competition with, opportunity-reduction approaches, the value of which we recognize. Nor do we ignore white-collar crime and new areas of criminal behaviour when we stress the need for the coordination of services to those most susceptible to becoming chronic criminals.

We are conscious that a growing number of offenders are being identified in relation to family violence or computer crimes for example, and that several of them do not systematically emerge from what we have described as the "at risk of becoming persistent delinquents" category. We acknowledge that measures to prevent these types of crimes should be considered also. We are putting forth a document that admittedly does not address all areas and patterns of crime but that nonetheless attempts to go as far as possible using existing knowledge and research findings.

As stated above, we also recognize that fear exists, and we are concerned about this very real feeling. Some of our recommendations concerning education and the media may contribute to the reduction or elimination of the fear of crime. At the same time, it is not the main object of this paper. What we propose goes deeper: to the causes of crime itself. The coordinated strategy we recommend would reduce crime rates and diminish the actual danger to Canadians.

Our strategy will require a concerted effort at all levels of government. It will mainly require the maintenance of currently successful social programs, the reallocation of certain existing human and financial resources toward redefined objectives, and perhaps a small investment in previously untouched territory.

By urging that we refocus some of our existing social programs and attitudes, we hope to prompt Canadians to action, to halt any trends toward increased crime, and to maintain our society as essentially peaceful.

Crime will never go away entirely, but we can make enormous progress in preventing it. We owe it to ourselves, and our quality of life in Canada, to make our communities as safe as they can be.

WHAT NEEDS TO BE DONE IN CANADA?

This chapter presents our major recommendations for crime prevention through five critical areas of social development.

A. PARENTS AND FAMILIES

If we expect children to become healthy, productive, contributing members of society, we must provide them with the nurturing and assistance they need. By supporting children early in their lives, we may be able to identify and deal with certain problems before they become more serious and expensive. Evidence increasingly suggests that, as well as benefitting the children, early investment programs can be cost-effective in lowering the costs of special education, public assistance, and criminal justice services for these children.

We recommend that:

1. Governments at all orders initiate a comprehensive review of the impact of policies and programs on disadvantaged families, and on their opportunities to escape lives of dependency on the state.
2. Programs be established to help disadvantaged families obtain enriched child care, while encouraging them to take employment training programs that would enhance their self-esteem and improve their opportunities for rising above the poverty line.
3. Family support and crisis intervention services be readily available and expanded to areas where they do not exist.

4. Positive parenting programs be developed, including respite care, parenting information services, toy resource centres, and preventive programs aimed at recognizing and assisting parents at risk of abusing or neglecting their children.
5. High-quality early childhood education programs be established.
6. Increased efforts be made to prevent unwanted pregnancies, particularly among teenagers, through more sex education and provision of family planning in schools, health clinics, and appropriate accessible settings.
7. Special efforts be made by all television networks to provide positive programming for children, particularly targeted to those who are disadvantaged.

B. SCHOOLS

Students from a wide variety of backgrounds and life styles attend our schools. Given the proper perceptual tools, teachers and administrators are able to recognize the underlying problems of most students before those problems lead to delinquency. Thus, schools are on the front line of crime prevention through social development.

We recommend that:

1. Priority be given to the early identification of children likely to have behavioural problems, and to the remedy of these problems through the coordinated work of parents, social services, housing, health, and school officials.
2. Remedial support programs directed to socially and economically disadvantaged children and youth continue to be developed.
3. Curricula be developed that focus on life skills, including parenting, sexual behaviour, and other areas of social development, and be implemented for all children.
4. Programs to prevent crime that focus on peer pressure and personal commitment — such as Students Against Drunk Driving — be developed and encouraged.
5. Schools take the initiative in increasing children's chances of successfully finishing school by promoting parent involvement in both home learning and school.

C. SOCIAL HOUSING AND NEIGHBOURHOODS

The social development and planning of neighbourhoods, including social housing, is a necessary element in the reduction and prevention of delinquency, and social priorities should be given at least equal weight with economic considerations.

We recommend that:

1. Social housing programs continue to emphasize increased integration of public and non-public housing, thereby diminishing the high concentration of disadvantaged young persons in one area.
2. The community and social development of neighbourhoods, including social housing, involve the close participation of all residents, particularly in programs for local environmental improvement, the planning, staffing, and development of public services, and local job-creation programs.

3. More challenging and relevant recreational programs be created for disadvantaged young persons, particularly those at high risk of committing crime.
4. Social housing organizations assist in the empowerment of tenants by involving them in the affairs of each housing project through tenants' associations and meetings, and by providing them with full knowledge about how to seek out the services of social agencies.
5. Community agencies give priority to people in social housing by bridging the geographical gap between social housing projects and the agencies, and by acknowledging the mixture of multiple problems faced by social housing tenants.

D. EMPLOYMENT

Although the relationship between unemployment and crime has not been established clearly, there are a number of factors—such as low income, low self-esteem, and truancy—that are influenced by employment, and whose combined presence can predispose to crime. Hence, recommendations aimed at improving employability, particularly for disadvantaged youth, are likely to improve social conditions and to reduce the likelihood of delinquency.

We recommend that:

1. Through the cooperation of government and the private and voluntary sectors, secondary-school drop-outs be provided with opportunities to acquire the skills necessary to obtain and retain gainful employment.
2. Employment preparation programs available to disadvantaged youth be continued and enhanced.
3. Economic policies be developed to reduce long-term unemployment and to encourage fulfilling alternatives for those who are unemployed.
4. All employers from the private and public sectors put into place within their organizations employment entry programs for disadvantaged youth.

E. SUBSTANCE ABUSE, THE MEDIA, AND HEALTH

The debate is still open as to whether or not substance abuse, the media, and health care are indeed contributing factors to delinquency. Nevertheless enough evidence suggests their relevance to warrant recommendations to monitor and promote research on their real impact.

We recommend that:

1. Authorities promote research on and evaluate programs oriented toward children and youth to prevent substance abuse, particularly programs stressing personal commitment and peer pressure.
2. Authorities responsible for regulating mass media monitor the research on crime in the media to reduce the undesirable effects of programming on levels of violence.
3. Research be undertaken to determine the effect of health factors, such as diet, on influencing criminal behaviour.

TWENTY-FOUR

Implications of Longitudinal Studies for Social Prevention

DAVID P. FARRINGTON

THE NEED FOR THE SOCIAL PREVENTION APPROACH

Our existing methods of controlling crime are not notably successful. Rehabilitative treatment, mostly based on counseling, has not reduced offending in well designed experiments, although it may be successful with some types of offenders: the young, anxious, verbal, intelligent, and neurotic, according to J.Q. Wilson. Deterrence, also, has not been proven effective in general, although it may work in some cases, e.g., driving offence, if the probability of being caught is increased.

Incapacitation, as an approach, is also ineffectual. It seems that huge increases in the prison population only have a small effect on the crime rate. In the United States, there is a great deal of interest in selective incapacitation, or targeting imprisonment for the small minority of frequent and serious offenders who account for a substantial proportion of all crimes. However, the effectiveness of this approach has not yet been demonstrated.

There is a need to look at new methods of controlling crime. In the public health arena, prevention is often more effective than treatment and the same may be true with crime. This paper is concerned with the scope for reducing crime through social prevention. It is not concerned with physical crime prevention through reducing opportunities for crime, but rather with ways in which people might become more law-abiding citizens.

THE NEED FOR LONGITUDINAL RESEARCH

Our ability to deal effectively with crime is greatly limited by our lack of knowledge about the history and development of criminal careers. We need to know what kinds of children develop into the most frequent and serious offenders. We need to know why people start committing crimes, why they continue, why their crimes change in frequency and seriousness, and why they stop committing crimes. We need to know how the course of criminal careers can be changed, and at what point it is best to intervene. We need to know the effects of early preventive, rehabilitative, deterrent, and incapacitative measures on the course of development of delinquency and crime.

For these kinds of questions, the best method of investigation is the longitudinal study, in which a sample of people are followed up from childhood, through

Source: David P. Farrington, "Implications of Longitudinal Studies for Social Prevention," *Justice Report*, 3, 2 (1986). Reproduced by permission of the *Justice Report*.

adolescence, into adulthood. Most of our knowledge about the course of criminal careers comes from studies of this kind — classic American studies by Marvin Wolfgang, Joan McCord, and Lee Robins in particular. Sadly, no Canadian study of this kind has been carried out, although there is a great need for one. An English longitudinal survey currently under my direction, shows the kind of knowledge that can be gained by using this technique.

THE CAMBRIDGE STUDY IN DELINQUENT DEVELOPMENT

This is a prospective longitudinal survey of 411 males. Data collection began in 1961–1962 when most of the boys were aged 8 to 9. We are currently attempting to interview the whole sample at age 31 to 32. At the time they were first contacted in 1961–1962, the boys were all living in a working class area of London. The vast majority of the sample was chosen by taking all the boys then aged 8 to 9 who were on the registers of six state primary schools within a one-mile radius of our research office. Almost all the boys were white, most had parents who had themselves been brought up in the United Kingdom or Ireland, and most were from working class families. The boys were interviewed and tested in their schools when they were aged about 8, 10 and 14, by psychologists. They were then interviewed in our research office at about 16, 18, 21, and 24, by young male social science graduates, and they are now being interviewed in their homes at about 31. Up to and including age 18, we tried to interview the whole sample on each occasion, and we always managed to interview a high proportion. For example, at age 18, 95 percent of the original sample were interviewed. We are now trying to interview nearly 90 percent of those who are not dead or abroad, for a total of about 350 interviews. At ages 21 and 24, we did not try to interview the whole sample but only selected subgroups.

In addition to the interviews and tests, we also interviewed their parents about once a year as long as the boy was at school. The primary informant was the mother although the father was also seen in most cases. We also had peer ratings completed by the boys when they were 8 and 10, and ratings by their teachers completed when they were 8, 10, 12, and 14. We have also been able to make repeated searches in the central Criminal Record Office in London to locate convictions of the boys, their parents, their brothers and sisters, and their wives and cohabitees up to the present day. Up to age 30, 146 of our 411 men have been convicted of criminal offences.

AGE AND CRIME

One of the most interesting results of the survey is the relation between age and crime. Generally, the prevalence of offending (the number of persons involved in crime) increases to a peak in the teenage years and then declines in the 20s. This is true not only of official convictions but also of self-reports of offending, although it does vary with type of offence (e.g., shoplifting tends to peak earlier and fraud later.) Interestingly, while the number of offenders varies dramatically with age, the rate of offending (the number of offences per offender) does not vary much. Generally, those first convicted at the earliest ages tend to have the longest criminal careers, suggesting again that early prevention could be particularly effective.

Why does prevalence peak in the teenage years? The most likely reason with boys is they (especially the lower class school failures, who are particularly at risk) have high desires for excitement, material goods, and status during this period, little chance of achieving these aims by legal means, and little to lose (since legal penalties are lenient and their intimates — male peers — often approve of offending). In contrast, after age 20, their desires become attenuated or more realistic, they have more chance of achieving their more limited goals legally, and the costs of offending are greater (legal penalties are harsher and their intimates — wives and girlfriends — often disapprove of offending).

Another interesting result of the longitudinal survey was that the reasons people committed offences varied with age. During the teenage years, many offences were said to be committed for excitement, enjoyment, or to relieve boredom, especially vandalism, joyriding, and shoplifting. As the boys grew older, more rational or utilitarian reasons predominated. One possible explanation is that the peak age is made up of relatively trivial offenders and normal boys who commit crimes for excitement, especially in groups. They have short criminal careers, from about 14 to 20. In contrast, those who start at the earliest ages (10 to 13) tend to commit offences for rational reasons, have long criminal careers persisting into their 20s, and are more likely to commit offences alone.

THE CHRONIC OFFENDER

Longitudinal studies show that a small proportion of boys commit a large proportion of all offences. Wolfgang first popularized this idea, showing that 6 percent of his sample accounted for 52 percent of all arrests. Similarly, in the Cambridge Study of Delinquent Development, about 6 percent of the boys accounted for about 50 percent of all the criminal convictions. Even more startling, 4 percent of the families accounts for about 50 percent of all convicted people, when fathers, mothers, sons, and daughters are included. The chronic offenders and chronic families are clearly prime targets for early prevention.

CONTINUITY OF OFFENDING

A major result in longitudinal studies is the demonstration of remarkable continuity in offending. Generally, the worst offenders during one age group tend to be the worst offenders during another. The best predictor of offending in one age group tends to be offending in the immediately preceding age group. Furthermore, troublesome and daring behaviour (as rated by teachers, peers, and parents) at age 8 predicts later offending, again showing the possibility of intervention in the most vulnerable group preventing crime. Teachers' ratings of aggressiveness at age 8 significantly predict convictions for violent offences, and self-reports of violence at age 18. American longitudinal studies have also found that behaviour problems in the first grade predict later persistent serious offending.

WHAT ARE THE CAUSES?

The major problem of interpretation in longitudinal surveys is establishing which factors are merely correlated with offending and which are actual causes. Researchers have shown that certain factors are predictors of offending (measured by official records or self-reports) independent of other factors. However, to prove that any factors are causes of offending, preventing experiments must be done in which certain factors are systematically varied and their effects on crime studied.

What should be the target of prevention experiments in the light of longitudinal research?

ECONOMIC DEPRIVATION

In the Cambridge Study of Delinquent Development, later offending was predicted by indices of economic deprivation. Similar results were obtained by Lee Robins. She found that children from poor families, in slum housing, and with parents or guardians with low status occupations, tended to become offenders. These results suggest that economic deprivation might be a target for early prevention. Delinquency might be reduced if the poorest families were given more social resources.

No study has yet demonstrated this, but there are a number of hopeful signs in research of released prisoners. In the "LIFE" project in Baltimore, Rossi and colleagues arranged for released prisoners to be allocated randomly to receive either unemployment benefit payments or no payments. The payments were reduced if the ex-prisoner obtained a job. They found that those who received the payments had significantly lower recidivism rates. Unfortunately, this hopeful result was not obtained when the program was replicated on a larger scale in two states. Those who received payments had recidivism rates that were no different from the remainder. However, the researchers were able to show that the payments acted as a disincentive to getting a job, and that unemployment tended to be associated with crime. They argued that, on the one hand, the payments caused a decrease in crime, but on the other hand they caused an increase in unemployment, which in turn caused an increase in crime. Hence, the two factors tended to cancel each other out to produce the overall result of no difference. Rossi and colleagues concluded that unemployment benefit payments to ex-prisoners could be beneficial in reducing crime, but only if they did not have the work disincentive effects. Similar conclusions might apply to social payments to deprived families.

LOW INTELLIGENCE

In the Cambridge study, low intelligence was one of the best independent predictors of later offending. Nonverbal IQ was highly related to all other measures of attainment, such as reading ability, verbal comprehension, vocabulary, and junior school grade results. Furthermore, low intelligence was especially characteristic of those first convicted at the earliest ages (10 to 13) and of the most persistent offenders. Wolfgang also found that low intelligence and attainment in the first six grades were significantly related to juvenile offending. One possible implication of these results is that measures to improve the intelligence and attainment of the lowest achievers might reduce their offending actions.

One of the most hopeful prevention experiments to improve cognitive and intellectual abilities is the Perry preschool project by Schweinhart and Weikart. This is a variation of the well known Head Start program. Lower class, lower intelligence black children were allocated more or less at random to experimental and control groups. The experimental group received a daily preschool program, backed up with weekly home visits over two years (ages 3 to 4). Over 120 children in the two groups were followed up to age 19. The experimental group showed shortlived gains in intelligence, but they were significantly better in elementary school motivation, school achievement at age 14, teacher ratings of classroom behaviour at 6 to 9, self-reports of classroom behaviour at 15, and self-reports of offending at 15. Up to age 19, 51 percent of the control group had been arrested or charged in comparison with only 31 percent of the experimental group, a statistically significant difference. We have known for a long time that delinquency is correlated with school failure. This project confirms the expectation that decreases in school failure will be followed by decreases in delinquency.

PARENTAL CHILD-REARING BEHAVIOUR

Loeber and Dishion, in their research on the early predictors of male delinquency, concluded that the best predictors were parental child-rearing techniques — even better predictors than early anti-social behaviour. In her follow-up study, Joan McCord found that cruel, passive, or neglecting parental attitude; harsh, or erratic parental discipline, and poor supervision all predicted later offending. Lee Robins also showed that harsh, or erratic parental discipline, and poor parental supervision predicted later offending in her two projects. Similar results were obtained in the Cambridge study. Harsh or erratic parental discipline, cruel, passive, or neglecting parental attitudes, poor supervision, and parental conflict, all predicted later offending when measured at age 8.

The implication of all this is that offending might be decreased if parents were trained to use more appropriate child-rearing techniques, especially discipline and supervision. One of the most hopeful approaches is the behavioural parent training pioneered by Gerry Patterson in Oregon. In this, parents are trained to notice what children are doing — to monitor child behaviour over long periods, to clearly state house rules, make rewards and punishments contingent upon behaviour, and negotiate disagreements so that conflicts do not escalate. The success of this approach has not been evaluated in a large scale longitudinal experiment, but this is clearly warranted.

SEPARATIONS AND BROKEN HOMES

Joan McCord found that the incidence of offending was high for boys reared in broken homes (caused by the loss of the natural father) without affectionate mothers, and for boys reared in united homes characterized by parental conflict. The incidence of offending was low for those reared in broken homes with affectionate mothers or in united homes without conflict. This and other longitudinal surveys suggest that it is not broken homes that cause offending, but parental conflict. The Cambridge study found that boys from homes broken by death were not particularly likely to become offenders later, whereas boys from homes broken by parental separation or desertion were likely to become offenders. Hence, it is not so much the break that is associated with offending as the conflict that causes the break.

The results suggest that parental conflict is a prime target for prevention efforts. More attempts should be made to help couples live together in harmony. Perhaps school children should receive instruction in how to achieve more harmonious marriages or cohabitations, emphasizing the desirability of not rushing into liaisons at an early age (since conflict is more acute for those who marry early,) and backed up by training in parenting and resolving conflicts.

CRIMINAL PARENTS

Both Robins and McCord found that criminal parents tended to have delinquent sons, and the Cambridge study obtained similar results. Interestingly, having criminal parents was more related to later offending than early offending (age 10–13). The interesting question is why. The possible explanations found for why criminal parents tend to have delinquent sons, is that criminal fathers tended to supervise their children poorly. Also, criminal mothers tended to have poor parental child-rearing behaviour, characterized by the factors mentioned above — harsh and erratic attitude and discipline. A major preventive implication of this longitudinal research is that it would be desirable to target training methods on criminal parents and that, if the methods were successful, the link between criminal parents and delinquent sons might be lessened.

DELINQUENT PEER INFLUENCE

Del Elliott, in his national American longitudinal study, concluded that bonding to delinquent peers was the most important independent correlate of self-reported offending. Similarly, the Cambridge longitudinal survey found that having delinquent friends at age 14 was an important predictor of convictions as a young adult. One possible implication of these results is that delinquency might be prevented by reducing delinquent peer influences and increasing prosocial peer influences. In St. Louis, Feldman and colleagues placed boys who were referred for antisocial behaviour into peer groups of about twelve. The groups consisted either of twelve antisocial boys or of one to two antisocial boys and ten to eleven prosocial boys. They found that the antisocial boys behaved significantly better if they were with prosocial peers than if they were with other antisocial peers. More research is clearly needed on peer influence, especially investigating the effectiveness of modeling as a technique.

SECURING CO-OPERATION

One of the most important results of the Cambridge longitudinal survey was that boys from unco-operative families were especially likely to become delinquents. One possible implication of this is that the families who are most in need of preventive treatment may be the most resistant to it. Therefore, it is important to find ways of overcoming unco-operativeness. In general, delinquency prevention programs need to appeal to the families and children who are most in need of them, so that they will participate wholeheartedly.

AN INTERRELATED SYNDROME

Longitudinal studies have demonstrated that offending is only one element of a larger syndrome of deviant or antisocial behaviour. In her follow-up of child guidance children, Robins found that as children these people stole, truanted, ran away from home, were aggressive, enuretic, disciplinary problems in school, pathological liars, etc. As adults, these people tended to be arrested, placed in mental hospitals, alcoholic, sexually promiscuous, divorced, vagrants, bad debtors, poor workers, etc. Similarly, the Cambridge study concluded that a constellation of adverse family background factors led to a constellation of socially deviant factors in adolescence and adulthood. Therefore, attempts to prevent offending, if they are successful, may have a much more general payoff in preventing a whole range of social problems.

IDENTIFYING CHRONIC OFFENDERS

About one-third of the 400 Cambridge study boys were convicted up to age 25, but just 23 people accounted for half of the convictions. To investigate the possibility of predicting these chronic offenders at their tenth birthday, a scale was developed to predict juvenile offending based on troublesome behaviour, social deprivation, having convicted parents, low intelligence, and poor parental child-rearing behaviour. The scale was constructed on half of the sample and validated on the other half. The 55 youths scoring highest on this scale included the majority of the chronic offenders (15 out of 23), 22 other convicted youths, and only 18 who were unconvicted. Therefore, to a surprising degree, many of the chronic offenders could have been predicted on the basis of background factors by age 10. In other words, early background factors can be used to identify children who are at risk of becoming frequent and serious offenders.

WHAT KIND OF RESEARCH IS NEEDED?

There is a great need for Canadian longitudinal research to trace the development of delinquency and crime in Canadian populations, and to see if the kinds of factors that predict offending in England and the United States are valid in Canada. There is also a great need for social prevention experiments in Canada.

One possible experiment would be to build on the Perry preschool project and Patterson's research as follows: Children born to convicted parents are a high risk group. Free day-care facilities could be offered to the parents of such children. They are likely to find this offer quite attractive. The day-care program would aim to provide an intellectually stimulating environment, consistent and loving caretakers, desirable parental role models, and training in desirable social skills. The women who accept the offer would be randomly assigned to receive the day-care program (or specific elements of it), a control program, or no program. The children would have to be followed up from the time of the program (possibly age 3 to 4) into school at age 6 to 8. The program will be a success if it improves school behaviour at age 6 to 8, since we know that bad behaviour at that age predicts later offending. We do not need a 20-year project. The day-care program could be backed up by parent training and followed at 6 to 8 by a home-school program designed to improve school attendance, academic achievement, the constructive use of leisure, etc., on an experimental basis. Canada needs longitudinal research that includes prevention experiments. By this means, important steps could be taken toward achieving crime prevention through social development.

TWENTY-FIVE

A Bimodal Preventive Intervention for Disruptive Kindergarten Boys: Its Impact Through Mid-Adolescence

RICHARD E. TREMBLAY, LINDA PAGANI-KURTZ, LOUISE C. MÂSSE, FRANK VITARO, AND ROBERT O. PIHL

It has been well established that an entrenched, disruptive behavioral pattern during the early school years markedly increases the risk for later antisocial behavior (e.g., Ensminger, Kellam, & Rubin, 1983; Farrington, 1991; Huesmann, Eron, Lefkowitz, & Walder, 1984; McCord, 1991; Robins, 1966; Stattin & Magnusson, 1989; Tremblay et al., 1992; Tremblay, Pihl, Vitaro, & Dobkin, 1994; White, Moffitt, Earls, Robins, & Silva, 1990). Hence, a consistently deviant antisocial pathway across development becomes apparent (Moffitt, 1993; Patterson, DeBaryshe & Ramsey, 1989).

The search for "the cause" of antisocial behavior has often resulted in an etiological debate regarding the influence of individual versus parent factors (e.g., Dodge, 1990; Lytton, 1990; McCord, 1993; Rowe, 1993). Some studies suggest that ineffective parenting may lead to antisocial disorders (Loeber & Stouthamer-Loeber, 1986), whereas others indicate that genetic and perinatal factors influence the risk of criminality (e.g., Duyme, 1989; Mednick, Gabrielli, & Hutchings, 1987; Plomin, Nitz, & Rowe, 1990). However, parental characteristics before the birth of a child remain strong predictors of both child-rearing practices and behavioral dispositions in children (Huesmann et al., 1984; Frick et al., 1992; Lahey et al., 1988; Serbin, Peters, McAffer, & Shwartzman, 1991), supporting the bidirectional nature of adult-child relationships in the parenting process (Belsky, 1984; Shaw & Bell, 1993). The conclusions drawn from these developmental studies have important implications for the nature, timing, and focus of intervention programs (e.g., Dodge, 1993; Kazdin, 1993; Reid, 1993).

In the past several decades, a multitude of parent effectiveness and social skills training programs have been developed, based on the assumption that either parental practices or children's social skills determine the course of disruptive disorders. Although such training programs appear promising, the preponderance of evidence suggests that single-focus programs achieve a low level of efficacy (Dumas,

Source: Richard E. Tremblay, Linda Pagani-Kurtz, Louise C. Mâsse, Frank Vitaro, and Robert O. Pihl, "A Bimodal Preventive Intervention for Disruptive Kindergarten Boys: Its Impact through Mid-Adolescence," *Journal of Consulting and Clinical Psychology*, 63, 4 (1995): 560–68. Copyright © 1995 by the American Psychological Association. Reprinted by permission.

1989; Kazdin, 1987, 1993). It is now generally proposed that interventions aiming to change the course of disruptive behavior must focus on modifying the different sources of influence that affect the development of antisocial behavior (Coie & Jacobs, 1993; Dodge, 1993; Reid, 1993). From this perspective, parent-focused and child-focused programs would be considered essential components of any multimodal approach (Dodge, 1993; Kazdin, 1993; Reid, 1993).

The timing of preventive interventions with youths at high risk for antisocial behavior remains an important issue. Because antisocial behavior problems are most salient during adolescence, this period has traditionally been the focus of most efforts. Numerous experimental interventions have also been implemented with prepubertal disruptive children, because it is at this period that troublesome behavior begins to appear as less manageable by adults (Coie & Jacobs, 1993). However, Eron (1990; Eron, Huesmann, & Zelli, 1991) has suggested that aggressive behavior crystallizes at approximately 8 years of age. It logically follows that interventions aiming to reduce antisocial outcomes should focus on at-risk children before this developmental period.

In light of current developmental theories of antisocial behavior, one would expect that a parent-and-child focused intervention, administered at a theoretically crucial point in development with an adequate level of intensity and duration should alter not only the short-term but the long-term developmental trajectory of young disruptive boys as well (Dodge, 1993). However long-term effects of treatment are not easily discernible. Kazdin (1993) has underscored the fact that the majority of child treatment studies have not collected follow-up data and that even a follow-up assessment as short as 1 year has been infrequent. Clearly, studies without extended follow-up preclude the assessment of the impact of interventions directed at modifying the developmental course of antisocial behavior. When interventions are conceptualized from a developmental perspective, one can easily imagine that effects that cannot be seen at the end of treatment (because they were not or could not be assessed) could be transformed into developmentally meaningful effects over the long term. Such delayed effects can be positive, as shown by the Perry Preschool Program (Schweinhart, Barnes, & Weikart, 1993), but they can also be negative, as shown by the Cambridge-Somerville study (McCord, 1978, 1992). Thus, the repeated longitudinal assessment of the impact of an intervention on children's lives remains essential from a scientific, clinical, and ethical perspective.

The nesting of experimental interventions within longitudinal studies is one way of ensuring the rigorous assessment of long-term effects of treatments while remaining cost efficient (Farrington, Ohlin, & Wilson, 1986; Tonry et al., 1991). The Montréal Longitudinal-Experimental Study represents such a design. Its general aim was to prospectively examine the development of a large sample of inner-city kindergarten boys, with a particular focus on antisocial behavior. From this sample, a subgroup of boys identified as disruptive in kindergarten was selected to test the effects of a preventive intervention program. Previous studies have noted beneficial effects during the elementary school years, (McCord, Tremblay, Vitaro, & Desmarais-Gervais, 1994; Tremblay et al., 1992; Vitaro & Tremblay, 1994). This article investigates the impact of the intervention on school adjustment and the development of delinquent behavior to age 15 (i.e., 6 years after the completion of the 2-year bimodal intervention program), a time when boys are most at risk for delinquent behavior (Farrington, 1986).

METHOD

....

PARTICIPANTS

....

Kindergarten teachers from schools in lower socioeconomic areas of Montréal, Québec, Canada were asked to rate the behavior of their male students at the end of the 1984 school year. Ratings were obtained from 87 percent of the teachers, for a total of 1,161 boys from 53 schools.

Of the total sample, the boys with a disruptive score above the 70th percentile ($n = 366$) on the Social Behavior Questionnaire (SBQ; Tremblay et al., 1992; White et al., 1990), 319 of which were randomly allocated to one of three groups (i.e., treatment, attention-control, or control; see Tremblay et al., 1992, for further elaboration regarding the characteristics of each group). A telephone interview with each mother permitted the verification of whether the family met two important criteria for eligibility: (a) ethnicity (only boys with Canadian-born parents whose first language was French were included) and (b) education (only boys whose parents had 14 years or less of schooling were included). Boys were excluded from the study if the family did not meet these criteria. In total, 904 boys met these selection criteria, 259 of which had been rated above the 70th percentile on the disruptive score. Of these, 16 were excluded from the analyses because they could not be located or they refused to answer the pertinent questions.[1]

The first of the three at-risk groups experienced the treatment condition for experimental study of the preventive intervention. The attention-control group represents the sensitization-contact condition. These boys participated in an intensive (school-based, home-based, and laboratory-based) observational study (Charlebois, LeBlanc, Gagnon, Larivée, & Tremblay, 1995; Lavigueur, Tremblay, & Saucier, 1995). Every second year (ages 7, 9, 11 or ages 8, 10, 12), the families were visited during four evenings. Families also came to the university laboratory for a 3-hr session on a Saturday. In addition, the child was observed at school for half a day on four occasions and spent a whole day in the university laboratory during the summer. Each family was assigned a resource person who made frequent contacts to plan the observation sessions and to collect questionnaire and interview data. Over the years, the mothers established trusting relationships with their resource persons. When the families asked for help they were referred to local mental health service professionals. A third group of boys from the at-risk population was created to act as a control group for assessing effects of the prevention experiment and also for evaluating the effect of the intensive observation condition. To ensure equivalence with the other two groups, each of which required consent, parents of children assigned to the control group were asked if they would participate in the activities required for the observational group if the research team was able to include them.

The three groups of disruptive boys were compared with a population-based random sample of kindergarten boys from French public schools in the province of Québec, Canada in 1986–1987 ($N = 1,000$). Families participating in this study were found to be significantly more socioeconomically disadvantaged than the representative sample of their same sex peers, as the occupational socioeconomic status (SES) and level of education of both parents were consistently lower. Moreover, they were consistently younger at the birth of their son, and the total family income was lower. The average family income was between $20,000 and $25,000 (Canadian dollars) for families of the disruptive boys compared with $30,000 and $35,000 (Canadian dollars) for families from the population-based random sample, $t(681) = -6.18$, $p < .001$.

TREATMENT PROCEDURE

On reviewing the literature addressing early intervention with aggressive children before 1984, two foci of treatment were selected: (a) parent training in effective child rearing and (b) social skills for the children (Bertrand, 1988). Both components were implemented by a multidisciplinary team, consisting of two university trained child-care workers, one psychologist, and one social worker. Working full time and being supervised by a half-time project coordinator, each case worker was responsible for providing individualized home-based training sessions to parents of 12 families and school-based group social skills sessions for 12 boys from 12 other families. This arrangement created a team approach, where two professionals coordinated their efforts with one family (i.e., one with the parents at home, the other with the child at school).

The parent-training component was based on the Oregon Social Learning Center Model (Patterson, 1982; Patterson, Reid, Jones, & Conger, 1975). The training procedures included giving parents a reading program, teaching parents to monitor their children's behavior, and to give children positive reinforcement for prosocial behavior, training parents to discipline effectively without using abusive punishment, teaching parents family crisis management techniques, and encouraging parents to transfer their new knowledge to new situations. The professionals followed this sequence and used as many sessions needed for the parents to master the skills (Bertrand, 1988). The maximum number of sessions given to families was 46, with the mean number of sessions for the duration of the program being 17.4, including parents that refused to continue participation. Teachers were contacted periodically to discuss the child's progress, the parents' involvement, and other issues the teacher would find pertinent.

For the disruptive boys receiving the intervention, it was reasoned that training in social skills would change their behavior toward peers, lead to more social acceptance, making them less inclined to turn to more antisocial activities. Two types of social skills training were administered by the professionals during lunch time within the context of a small group of four to seven prosocial peers from school, with the ratio being three prosocial peers for each disruptive boy. Prosocial peers were nominated by teachers. A prosocial skills training curriculum was implemented in the first year, consisting of nine sessions based on previous work (e.g., Cartledge & Milburn, 1980; Michelson, Sugai, Wood, & Kazdin, 1983). In the second year, 10 sessions were given to enhance children's problem solving and self-control in conflict situations, on the basis of previous work (Camp, Blom, Hebert, & Van Doorninck, 1977; Goldstein, Sprafrin, Gershaw, & Klein, 1980; Kettlewell & Kausch, 1983; Meichenbaum, 1977). The duration of the intervention program was 2 school years, from September 1985 to June 1987. Boys were 7 years old when the treatment was initiated and 9 years old when it ended.

MEASURES

School adjustment. It was expected that if disruptive behaviors were reduced, academic adjustment would likely show improvement. Being placed out of a regular classroom appropriate for their age served as an indicator of severe school maladjustment (Tremblay et al., 1991). No significant group differences had been observed for performance in mathematics and French when the boys were in first grade, the year before the intervention started.

Teacher ratings of disruptive behavior. We obtained these ratings from 10- to 15-year-old boys using the SBQ (Tremblay et al., 1991), which had been used to select the disruptive boys in kindergarten (age 6). From age 10 to age 12, the boys were in elementary school and had one main teacher for the whole day. From age 13 to age 15, most boys had more than one teacher every day. Math and French teachers were used as raters because they had the most contact with the boys. The mean internal consistency alpha for that scale between ages 6 and 15 years was .91 (range, .89 to .93). Scores ranged from 0 to 26 (13 items scored 0, 1, or 2).

Self-reported juvenile delinquency. The boys completed a self-report questionnaire addressing their involvement in antisocial behavior from ages 10 to 15 (a) Eleven questions were asked about theft (kept objects worth $10 or more, stole something from a store, stole $100 or more, entered without paying admission, stole money from home, stole something worth $10, stole something worth between $10 and $100, stole a bicycle, bought a stolen article, broke down a door to take something, been in an unauthorized place), (b) three questions about alcohol and drug use (consumed alcohol, has been drunk, consumed marijuana), and (c) six questions about vandalism (destroyed instruments, intentionally destroyed other's property, intentionally broke parts of school property, purposely broke something belonging to a family member, intentionally destroyed part of an automobile, set fire). At age 10, the boys were asked to report if they had ever misbehaved in the specified ways. From age 11, they were asked whether they had engaged in such behaviors in the previous 12 months. The response format for each question was never, once or twice, often, very often (scored 1, 2, 3, and 4) providing a range of total scores between 20 and 80. The mean internal consistency alpha between 11 and 15 years of age is .91 (range, .87 to .93).

Juvenile court records. Juvenile court files were used to identify boys who had been placed under the Juvenile Offenders' Act between ages 12 to 15 (this Canadian law does not apply before age 12). Youths are placed under this act if they are arrested by the police, charged, and found guilty of having broken a Canadian law. As such, they are officially designated as "delinquents." From the entire sample of 901 boys that met the criteria, 30 boys were placed under the Juvenile Offenders' Act. Between ages 10 and 15, these boys reported more delinquent acts than those who were not placed under the law, $t(1,N = 872) = 2.67$, $p = .01$. Interestingly, 6.7 percent of the disruptive kindergarten boys were placed under the Juvenile Offenders' Act between ages 12 and 15, compared with 1.7 percent for the nondisruptive kindergarten boys, $x^2(1,N = 901) = 15.82$, $p < .001$.

Perceptions of parenting behavior. Boys' perceptions of their parents' child-rearing practices were annually assessed from ages 10 to 15, with questions specifically probing parental supervision and punishment during the previous 12 months. Supervision describes to what extent the parents monitored their son's activities. The variable is composed of two questions: (a) Do your parents know about your whereabouts when you go out? and (b) Do your parents know with whom you are spending time when you go out? The boy answered by choosing "never," "sometimes," "often," or "always." The greater the score on supervision, the more the child is supervised. Cronbach's alpha for the supervision score has a mean of .74 between ages 10 and 15. The two questions that assessed the variable of parental supervision were accidentally omitted at age 13. The punishment variable represents the total of the following five questions: (a) Do your parents punish you by slapping or hitting you? (b) Do your parents punish you by not letting you do things you would like to do? (c) Do your parents punish you by arguing? (d) Do your parents punish you by saying that you cause them distress? and (e) Do your parents punish you by calling you names? The choices range from "never," "sometimes," "often," and "always." The greater the score on punishment, the more the boy is punished. Cronbach's alpha for the punishment score has a mean of .62.

RESULTS

Because no significant between-group differences were observed between the control and attention-control group on any of the measures of interest, these two conditions were combined to form a comparison group for the analyses that follow.

TEACHER-RATED DISRUPTIVENESS

To test the effect of the treatment on the development trend of disruptive behavior, we used an unbalanced repeated measures model with an unstructured covariance matrix. The 5V procedure in BMDP was used to analyze teacher-rated disruptiveness. An unstructured model was chosen because the repeated measures did not satisfy the univariate criterion of circularity and sphericity. The resulting unstructured analysis is actually the incomplete data analog of a multivariate analysis of repeated measures. For this procedure, the level of teacher-rated disruptiveness from ages 10 to 15 was compared between the groups. The level of disruptiveness was adjusted using the boys' kindergarten disruptiveness score on the SBQ. For this analysis, the covariate was judged to be adequately reliable for covariance analysis.

As shown in Figure 25.1 the results revealed an overall significant difference in the level of teacher-rated disruptiveness over time, $G^2(5,N = 164) = 49.30$, $p<.05$, confirming a decrease in the level of disruptiveness over time. However, the between-group difference in teacher-rated disruptiveness, $G^2(5, N = 164) = 2.60$, $p>.05$, was not found to be significantly different, nor was the between-group teacher-rated Disruptiveness × Time interaction, $G^2(5,N = 164) = 3.44$, $p>.05$. Although no significant main effect was found, a trend toward between-group differences for teacher-rated disruptiveness was evident; that is, the participants in the treatment group tended to be evaluated by the teachers as less disruptive than the comparison group from age 10 to age 13. It can be observed in Figure 25.1 that the level of disruptiveness of the total sample also decreased with age.

SELF-REPORTED DELINQUENCY

The longitudinal effects of the treatment on boy's self-reported delinquency were analyzed using an unbalanced repeated measures model with an unstructured covariance matrix. Again, the 5V procedure in BMDP was used. The long-term effects of the treatment on the boys' overall delinquency scales were compared from age 10 to age 15. In this analysis, boys' delinquency scores were adjusted by their

FIGURE 25.1 *The level of teacher-rated disruptiveness from age 10 to age 15.*

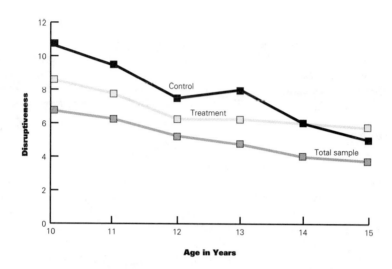

level of disruptiveness in 1984 (age 6). The covariate was not found to be significant and, consequently, it was removed from the analysis.

The self-reported delinquency patterns for the three groups of disruptive boys (as well as the pattern for the total sample) are shown in Figure 25.2. The curvilinear effect is partly due to the fact that the questions at age 10 requested a report of delinquent behavior up to age 10, whereas older boys were asked to report delinquent behavior in the past 12 months. The statistical analysis indicated that the boys' delinquency level significantly changed over time, G^2 $(5,N = 159) = 45.84$, $p<.05$. This effect was somewhat expected, as the delinquency level was more likely to increase over time. There was no Group × Time interaction, $G^2(5,N = 159) = 0.92$, $p>.05$, however there was a significant between-group difference, $G^2(5,N = 159) = 4.18$, $p<.05$, indicating that the treated group was reporting significantly less delinquent behaviors 1 to 6 years after the end of the intervention. No significant differences were observed between the treated and untreated groups when the total self-reported delinquency score was broken down into the stealing, vandalism, and drug use subscales.

JUVENILE COURT RECORDS

The juvenile court records provided an opportunity to verify official sanctions of extreme delinquent behavior. A total of 30 boys (3.3 percent of the total sample of 901 boys) were found to have been placed under the young offenders' act between ages 12 and 15. Of the disruptive boys who received treatment, 9.3 percent ($n = 4$) were placed under the Juvenile Offenders' Act, in contrast to 7.4 percent ($n = 9$) for the disruptive comparison group. This difference was not found to be significant, $x^2(1,N = 165) = .162$, $p>.05$.

FIGURE 25.2 *The self-reported delinquency patterns for the three groups of disruptive boys (as well as the pattern for the total sample).*

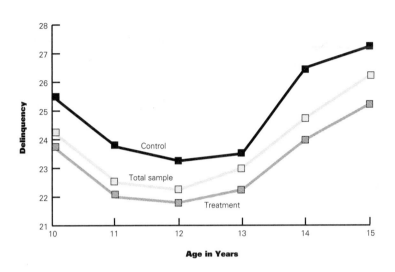

PARENTING

Because the intervention included a parent-training component, it was expected that a successful treatment would have changed parental behavior to the extent that the boys would perceive this change. Figure 25.3 shows that boys perceived they were being punished less and less as they became older, $G^2(4,N = 159) = 38.65$, $p<.05$. Surprisingly, there were no significant differences between the treated and untreated groups, $G^2(1,N = 159) = 0.11$, $p>.05$. The evolution of boys' perceptions of parental supervision are shown in Figure 25.4. Between ages 13 and 15, the treated boys tended to perceive more supervision from their parents than the untreated boys. Here too, the statistical analyses did not reveal any significant between-group differences.

DISCUSSION

The purpose of this article was to report the impact of a bimodal preventive intervention on the subsequent development of boys that exhibited a disruptive behavioral pattern in kindergarten. These boys were considered at high risk for later antisocial behavior. Development was examined by comparing treated boys with an appropriate control condition on a number of outcomes at prepubertal age, pubertal age, and again at mid-adolescence. The development of the treated and untreated disruptive kindergarten boys was presented against the backdrop consisting of the total original sample of disadvantaged urban boys. Such comparisons revealed that the disruptive kindergarten boys were indeed more at risk for antisocial behavior than their nondisruptive peers (see also Dobkin, Tremblay, Mâsse, & Vitaro, in press; Pulkkinen & Tremblay, 1992). The parent-and-child-oriented intervention

FIGURE 25.3 *Boys' perception of punishment by parents.*

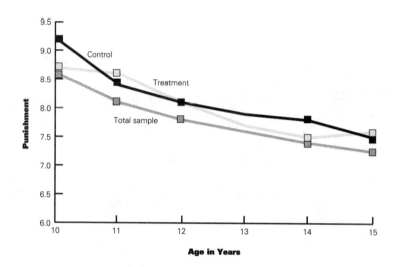

Figure 25.4 *Boys' perception of supervision by parents.*

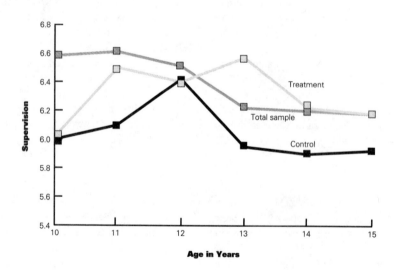

administered between 7 and 9 years old appeared to have a different beneficial influence on the boys' development, depending on age, domain, and data source.

With respect to global school adjustment, measured by being in an age-appropriate regular classroom, the intervention appeared to have a positive impact during the elementary school years; however, that impact disappeared by age 15, when the boys should have been in their third year of high school. This result is somewhat disappointing. It was intuitively expected that success in elementary school would have a positive effect on success in secondary school. However, when consideration is given to the level of success for the whole sample of boys who were in the low-SES kindergarten classes, it can be seen that a majority (59.3 percent) were not in an age-appropriate regular classroom by age 15. Given that poor school adjustment appears to be the norm for this sample of boys from low-SES environments, it becomes improbable that an intervention directed at disruptive behavior would have enabled disruptive kindergarten boys to have more success in high school than the majority of their peers. It is important to note that this phenomenon could not have been observed if the experiment had not been nested within a longitudinal study of a population-based age cohort.

The importance of the beneficial impact on elementary school adjustment should not be overlooked. The boys who remained in an age-appropriate regular classroom during elementary school were in a very different social and intellectual environment, compared with those who were held back or placed in special classes or schools. The quality of that environment may have had beneficial effects on other aspects of their development during high school (e.g., self-esteem, delinquency; Coie & Jacobs, 1993). Because being placed out of an age-appropriate regular classroom in high school appears to be normative for this cohort of boys, it is reasonable to speculate that being out of an age-appropriate classroom may not have the negative psychosocial impact that it could have if it happened during the elementary school years.

Similar results were obtained for teacher-rated disruptiveness, although in this case, the differences did not reach statistical significance. It is important to comment on this trend, because it suggests a different story from the previous results. The differences between the treated and untreated groups were observed during elementary school and disappeared during high school, as did the difference in global school adjustment. However, in this case the disruptive boys appeared to become better adjusted (i.e., teachers progressively giving lower disruptive ratings). Either most of the boys were becoming decreasingly disruptive or high school teachers were less able to observe these behaviors. Whatever the reason, it becomes less likely with time that adolescent boys will be evaluated as highly disruptive by their teachers. Hence, teacher-rated disruptive behavior in high school may not be an adequate indicator for the outcome of some preventive interventions.

Delinquency was assessed both with self-reports and court records. The latter did not reveal any significant differences between the groups. It was hoped that an intensive early intervention with disruptive boys would have reduced the number of boys who were put under the Juvenile Offenders' Act. Clearly, such a procedure is costly both in terms of social resources and human suffering for the boys and their families. It can also be seen that it is not a negligible phenomenon; 1.7 percent of the kindergarten boys from the low-SES schools and 6.7 percent of the disruptive kindergarten boys from that cohort were placed under the Young Offenders' Act between ages 12 and 15. However, because of the small number of treated participants, the power to detect a significant impact of the treatment on this variable was very low.

Thus, from the perspective of official delinquency, it is not clear to what extent this type of intervention with these at-risk boys has achieved its aim. However, from the perspective of self-reported delinquency the intervention has reduced the number of delinquent behaviors from age 10 to age 15. Taken together, these results could be an indication that the intervention did not have an impact on the worst cases (i.e., those with official juvenile delinquency records) but had an impact by significantly reducing the frequency of delinquent behaviors for a group of high-risk boys. This could be a meaningful effect, because each delinquent behavior is a socially meaningful event for a number of individuals (e.g., the victim, the delinquent, the families involved, the social control agents). It may be a meaningful effect for the development of the disruptive kindergarten boys as well, if reducing the frequency of their delinquent behavior from age 10 to age 15 has an impact on key developmental issues such as how they perceive themselves and who they associate with when they enter the period of young adulthood. This should be the focus of future assessments. The fact that the difference between the treated and untreated groups was maintained up to age 15 is especially encouraging, because one could have expected that the difference would disappear when delinquent behavior becomes more widespread in mid-adolescence (Farrington, 1986).

The findings suggest that the comparative changes in delinquent behavior and the significantly higher levels of academic adjustment observed in youngsters from the experimental groups may be attributable to the treatment. Improving parental practice and children's social competence does appear to influence their risk outcomes over the long term, supporting the hypotheses that parent effectiveness and social skills training are related to delinquent behavior. However, data from the boys' perceptions of parental supervision and punishment do not support the hypothesis that the parent training intervention had a significant impact on those particular child-rearing behaviors. Because boys' reports of parental supervision and punishment have been linked to self-reported delinquency (Hirschi, 1969), it was expected that boys' perceptions of their parents' child-rearing practices could be shown as mediators of the differences in self-reported delinquency. These counterintuitive results show how difficult it is to find clear causal paths in the development of deviant human behavior. The absence of a control group that received only parent training or only social skills training precludes more elaborate theoretical conclusions regarding which component of the bimodal intervention contributed the most variance in the boys' behavioral development. Nevertheless, there is sufficient literature suggesting the low level of efficacy when each component is used as the sole ingredient of treatment (Dumas, 1989; Kazdin, 1987, 1993). One can speculate that parent training could have indirect effects on boys' adjustment. The training could change some behaviors of the parents (e.g., more parent initiated contacts with teachers) without changing their discipline and monitoring behaviors to the point of significantly influencing the child's perception.

It would be surprising to find that a single intervention during elementary school, albeit multimodal and intensive, would change the developmental trajectories of disruptive boys and their families to the extent that they would never be in need of further support. The impact of such early interventions could possibly be increased by booster sessions with the boys and their parents before delinquency peaks in mid-adolescence. Ideally, a 2-year booster program could be implemented during the last year of elementary school (preparing for the transition to high school) and then during junior high school (immediately after the transition). In terms of content, booster treatments could involve enhancing problem-solving skills, life skills, and study skills to improve the participants' communication, conflict resolution, self-control, and academic abilities when faced with the less structured academic setting of high school and increased peer pressure. It would be equally important to offer a booster program for parents. This would be most needed during the junior high year, when parents must improve their monitoring and communication skills with their young adolescent, who is striving for more autonomy.

A number of limitations must be kept in mind. First the study was limited to French-speaking disruptive kindergarten boys living in low socioeconomic areas of a large metropolitan city in Canada. Disruptiveness was defined to include the 30 percent most disruptive boys in a population of disadvantaged urban boys. Although these boys were clearly more at risk for later delinquent behavior than those below the cutoff point, risk varied within this group. The relatively small number of treated participants precluded an analysis of treatment effects according to the risk level in kindergarten.

Understanding the impact of the intervention is also limited by the fact that no dose-response analyses could be performed. The professionals were instructed to give as many parent training sessions as needed by the families within the 2-year period. As such, families with the worst prognoses received more treatment. This is sound practice from a clinical and ethical perspective, but it obviates the study of dose response. A larger number of participants would be needed to study dose response and level of initial risk.

One can argue that these results may not be clinically meaningful. Nevertheless, the present study shows that an intensive intervention with disruptive kindergarten boys can have statistically significant positive results over the long term. The results also suggest that this impact varies with time. We believe that only larger studies with repeated booster sessions could show a clear impact on serious juvenile delinquency and adult crime. It may well be that this aim can be achieved only by intensive interventions with at-risk children before they enter kindergarten. This would mean more investment in prevention during pregnancy and infancy, as well as a firm commitment to follow these participants into adolescence and adulthood.

NOTE

1. In Tremblay et al. (1991b), 249 participants were reported to have met the criteria for inclusion. Recent verification of the demographic information obtained from the families revealed that six of these participants had one parent (five fathers and one mother) with more than 14 years of schooling. These participants were not included in the analyses reported here.

REFERENCES

Belsky, J. (1984). The determinants of parenting: A process model. *Child Development, 55,* 83–96.

Bertrand, L. (1988). Projet pilote de prévention du développement de comportements antisociaux chez des garçons agressifs à la maternelle: Guides d'intervention. [Pilot project for the prevention of antisocial behavior with aggressive kindergarten boys: Intervention Guide]. Montréal: Research Unit on Children's Psycho-Social Maladjustment, University of Montréal.

Blishen, B.R., & McRoberts, H.A. (1976). Revised socioeconomic index for occupations in Canada. *Canadian Review of Sociology and Anthropology, 13,* 71–79.

Camp, B.W., Blom, G.E., Hebert, F., & Van Doorminck, W.J. (1977). Think aloud. A program for developing self-control in young aggressive boys. *Journal of Abnormal Child Psychology, 5,* 157–169.

Cartledge, G., & Milburn, J.F. (1980). *Teaching social skills to children. Innovative approaches.* New York: Pergamon Press.

Charlebois, P., LeBlanc, M., Gagnon, C., Larivée, S., & Tremblay, R.E. (1995). Teacher, mother and peer support in the elementary school as protective factors against juvenile delinquency. *International Journal of Behavioral Development, 18,* 1–22.

Coie, J.D., & Jacobs, M.R. (1993). The role of social context in the prevention of conduct disorder. *Development and Psychopathology, 5,* 263–275.

Dobkin, P.L., Tremblay, R.E., Mâsse, L.C., & Vitaro, F. (in press). Individual and peer characteristics in predicting boys' early onset of substance abuse: A 7-year longitudinal study. *Child Development.*

Dodge, K.A. (1990). Nature versus nurture in childhood conduct disorder: It is time to ask a different question. *Developmental Psychology, 26,* 698–701.

———. (1993). The future of research on the treatment of conduct disorder. *Developmental Psychopathology, 5,* 311–319.

Dumas, J.E. (1989). Treating antisocial behavior in children: Child and family approaches. *Clinical Psychology Review, 9,* 197–222.

Duyme, M. (1989). Antisocial behaviours and postnatal environment: A French adoption study. *Journal of Child Psychology and Psychiatry, 7,* 285–291.

Ensminger, M.E., Kellam, S.G., & Rubin, B.R. (1983). School and family origins of delinquency: Comparisons by sex. In K.T. Van Dusen & S.A. Mednick (Eds.), *Prospective Studies of Crime and Delinquency* (pp. 73–97). Boston: Kluwer-Nijhoff.

Eron, L.D. (1990). Understanding aggression. *Bulletin of the International Society for Research on Aggression, 12,* 5–9.

Eron, L.D., Huesmann, L.R., & Zelli, A. (1991). The role of parental variables in the learning of aggression. In D.J. Pepler & K.H. Rubin (Eds.), *The development and treatment of childhood aggression* (pp. 169–188). Hillsdale, NJ: Erlbaum.

Farrington, D.P. (1986). Age and crime. In M. Tonry & N. Morris (Eds.), *Crime and justice: An annual review or research* (pp. 189–250). Chicago: University of Chicago Press.

———. (1991). Childhood aggression and adult violence: Early precursors and life outcomes. In D.J. Pepler & K.H. Rubin (Eds.), *Development and treatment of childhood aggression* (pp. 5–29). Hillsdale, NJ: Erlbaum.

Farrington, D.P., Ohlin, L.E., & Wilson, J.Q. (1986). *Understanding and controlling crime: Towards a new research strategy.* New York: Springer-Verlag.

Frick, P.J., Lahey, B.B., Loeber, R., Stouthammer-Loeber, M., Christ, M.A.B., & Hanson, K. (1992). Familial risk factors to oppositional defiant disorder and conduct disorder: Parental psychopathology and maternal parenting. *Journal of Consulting and Clinical Psychology, 60,* 49–55.

Goldstein, A.P., Sprafrin, R.P., Gershaw, N.J., & Klein, P. (1980). *Skill streaming the adolescent: A structural learning approach to teaching prosocial skills.* Champaign, IL: Research Press.

Hirschi, T. (1969). *Causes of delinquency.* Berkeley, CA: University of California Press.

Huesmann, L.R., Eron, L.D., Lefkowitz, M.M., & Walder, L.O. (1984). Stability of aggression over time and generations. *Developmental Psychology, 20,* 1120–1134.

Kazdin, A.E. (1987). Treatment of antisocial behavior in children: Current status and future directions. *Psychological Bulletin, 102,* 187–203.

———. (1993). Adolescent mental health, prevention and treatment programs. *American Psychologist, 48,* 127–141.

Kettlewell, P.W., & Kausch, D.F. (1983). The generalization of the effects of a cognitive-behavioral treatment program for aggressive children. *Journal of Abnormal Child Psychology, 11,* 101–114.

Lahey, B.B., Hartdagen, S.E., Frick, P.J., McBurnett, K., Connor, R., & Hynd, G.W. (1988). Conduct disorder: Parsing the confounded relationship to parental divorce and antisocial personality. *Journal of Abnormal Psychology, 97,* 334–337.

Lavigueur, S., Tremblay, R.E., & Saucier, J.F. (1995). Interactional processes in families with disruptive boys: Patterns of direct and indirect influence. *Journal of Abnormal Child Psychology, 63*, 359–377.

Loeber, R., & Stouthamer-Loeber, M. (1986). Family factors as correlates and predictors of juvenile conduct problems and delinquency. In M. Tonry & N. Morris (Eds.), *Crime and justice: An annual review of research* (pp. 29–149). Chicago: University of Chicago Press.

Lytton, H. (1990). Child and parent effects in boys' conduct disorder: A reinterpretation. *Developmental Psychology, 26*, 683–697.

McCord, J. (1978). A 30-year follow-up of treatment effects. *American Psychologist, 33*, 284–289.

———. (1991). Family relationships, juvenile delinquency, and adult criminality. *Criminology, 29*, 397–417.

———. (1992). The Cambridge-Somerville Study: A pioneering longitudinal-experimental study of delinquency prevention. In J. McCord & R.E. Tremblay (Eds.), *Preventing antisocial behavior: Interventions from birth through adolescence* (pp. 196–206). New York: Guilford Press.

———. (1993). Conduct disorder and antisocial behavior: Some thoughts about processes. *Development and Psychopathology, 5*, 321–329.

McCord, J., Tremblay, R.E., Vitaro, F., & Desmarais-Gervais, L. (1994). Boys' disruptive behavior, school adjustment, and delinquency: The Montreal prevention experiment. *International Journal of Behavioral Development, 17*, 739–752.

Mednick, S.A., Gabrielli, W.F., & Hutchings, B. (1987). Genetic factors in the etiology of criminal behavior. In S.A. Mednick, T.E. Moffitt, & S.A. Stack (Eds.), *The causes of crime: New biological approaches* (pp. 74–91). New York: Cambridge University Press.

Meichenbaum, D. (1977). *Cognitive-behavior modification: An integrative approach.* New York: Plenum Press.

Michelson, L., Sugai, D., Wood, R., & Kazdin, A.E. (1983). *Social skills assessment and training with children.* New York: Plenum Press.

Moffitt, T.E. (1993). Adolescence-limited and life-course persistent antisocial behavior: A developmental taxonomy. *Psychological Review, 100*, 674–701.

Patterson, G.R. (1982). *Coercive family process.* Eugene, OR: Castalia.

Patterson, G.R., DeBaryshe, B.D., & Ramsey, E. (1989). A developmental perspective on antisocial behavior. *American Psychologist, 44*, 329–335.

Patterson, G.R., Reid, J.B., Jones, R.R., & Conger, R.R. (1975). *A social learning approach to family intervention: Families with aggressive children (Vol. 1).* Eugene, OR: Castalia.

Plomin, R., Nitz, K., & Rowe, D.C. (1990). Behavioral genetics and aggressive behavior in childhood. In M. Lewis & S.M. Miller (Eds.), *Handbook of developmental psychopathology* (pp. 119–133). New York: Plenum Press.

Pulkkinen, L., & Tremblay, R.E. (1992). Patterns of boys' social adjustment in two cultures and at different ages: A longitudinal perspective. *International Journal of Behavioural Development, 15*, 527–553.

Reid, J.B. (1993). Prevention of conduct disorder before and after school entry: Relating intervention to developmental findings. *Development and Psychopathology, 5*, 243–262.

Robins, L.N. (1966). *Deviant children grown up.* Baltimore: Williams & Wilkins.

Rowe, D.C. (1993). *The limits of family influence: Genes, experience, and behavior.* New York: Guilford Press.

SAS Institute, Inc. (1989). *SAS/STAT user's guide* (4th ed.) Gary, NC: Author.

Schweinhart, L.L., Barnes, H.V., & Weikart, D.P. (1993). *Significant benefits. The High/Scope Perry School Study through age 27.* Ypsilanti, MI: High/Scope Press.

Servin, L.A., Peters, P.L., McAffer, V.J., & Shwartzman, A.E. (1991). Childhood aggression and withdrawal as predictors of adolescent pregnancy, early parenthood, and environmental risk for the next generation. *Canadian Journal of Behavioural Science, 23*, 318–331.

Shaw, D.S., & Bell, R.Q. (1993). Developmental theories of parental contributors to antisocial behavior. *Journal of Abnormal Child Psychology, 21*, 493–518.

Stattin, H., & Magnusson, D. (1989). The role of early aggressive behavior in the frequency, seriousness and types of later crime. *Journal of Consulting and Clinical Psychology*, 57, 710–718.

Tonry, M., Ohlin, L.E., Farrington, D.P., Adams, K., Earls, F., Rowe, D.C., Sampson, R.J., & Tremblay, R.E. (1991). *Human development and criminal behavior: New ways of advancing knowledge*. New York: Springer-Verlag.

Tremblay, R.E., Loeber, R., Gagnon, C., Charlebois, P., Larivée, S., & LeBlanc, M. (1991). Disruptive boys with stable and unstable high fighting behavior patterns during junior elementary school. *Journal of Abnormal Child Psychology*, 19, 285–300.

Tremblay, R.E., Mâsse, B., Perron, D., LeBlanc, M., Schwartzman, A.E., & Ledingham, J.E. (1992). Early disruptive behavior, poor school achievement, delinquent behavior and delinquent personality: Longitudinal analyses. *Journal of Consulting and Clinical Psychology*, 60, 64–72.

Tremblay, R.E., McCord, J., Boileau, H., Charlebois, P., Gagnon, C., LeBlanc, M., & Larivée, S. (1991). Can disruptive boys be helped to become competent? *Psychiatry*, 54, 148–161.

Tremblay, R.E., Pihl, R.O., Vitaro, F., & Dobkin, P.L. (1994). Predicting early onset of male antisocial behavior from preschool behavior. A test of two personality theories. *Archives of General Psychiatry*, 51, 732–738.

Tremblay, R.E., Vitaro, F., Bertrand, L., LeBlanc, M., Beauchesne, H., Boileau, H., & David, H. (1992). Parents and child training to prevent early onset of delinquency: The Montreal longitudinal-experimental study. In J. McCord & R.E. Tremblay (Eds.), *Preventing antisocial behavior: Interventions from birth through adolescence* (pp. 117–138). New York: Guilford Press.

Vitaro, F., & Tremblay, R.E. (1994). Impact of a prevention program on aggressive-disruptive children's friendships and social adjustment. *Journal of Abnormal Child Psychology*, 22, 457–475.

White, J.L., Moffitt, T.E., Earls, F., Robins, L., & Silva, P.A. (1990). How early can we tell? Predictors of childhood conduct disorder and adolescent delinquency. *Criminology*, 28, 507–533.

TWENTY-SIX

Situational Crime Prevention in Practice

PATRICIA L. BRANTINGHAM AND PAUL J. BRANTINGHAM

INTRODUCTION

The term crime prevention is used to cover a broad range of activities by individuals, groups, institutions, and governments. Some crime prevention activities try to reduce crime, fear, and nuisance problems directly by dealing with immediate situations.

Other crime prevention activities address crime indirectly by trying to alter general social background conditions that are thought to cause crime, with the intent of eventually reducing the likelihood of crime, nuisance behaviour, and fear (Brantingham and Brantingham, 1988; Lab, 1988; Brantingham and Faust, 1976).

Most crime prevention efforts tend to be generic in form and general in scope, grounded on standardized approaches or programs aimed at altering one or two factors believed to be related to criminality or crime. For example, mass media campaigns and public education programs are aimed at large numbers of people under the assumption that changing the general public's knowledge about crime will beneficially alter both victim and offender behaviour. Neighbourhood Watch and the more recent Block Watch programs tend to look the same across the continent, following a well-defined standard format in trying to increase local informal surveillance practices, a strategy assumed to be effective in reducing crime. (See, e.g., National Crime Prevention Institute, 1986; 133 *et seg.*; Crime Prevention Unit, 1989). Community crime prevention and social crime prevention programs are usually aimed at all the residents of a particular area or at all the members of a presumed class of "at risk" people. The same program, aimed at changing one or two presumed "causes" of criminality or crime, is directed at everyone.

The success of generic and generalized crime prevention programs is mixed at best. Media campaigns appear to have little demonstrable impact on crime rates or public behaviour (Rily and Mayhew, 1980; Sacco and Silverman, 1981), although, occasionally, claims for high impact are made (Monaghan, 1988). Watch-type programs often make claims for substantial impact on crime rates (Titus, 1984), though careful examination suggests far more modest results (Bennett, 1988; Skogan, 1988). Community and social crime prevention programs are popular and can often claim substantial social impact (Schlossman, et al., 1984; Lab, 1988), but just as often have little measurable effect on crime or criminality (Lundman, 1984; Skogan, 1988).

The mixed successes and failures experienced by generic and generalized crime prevention programs should not be surprising. Crime is not uniform. Shoplifting by a tourist in a record store is different from theft by a salesperson working in that same store. Robbery from a centre-city bank is different from theft of a motorcycle by a teenager. A sexual assault in a subway is different from abuse of a foster child by a foster parent. The people committing these diverse crimes cannot reasonably be considered as identical. Generalized approaches, while popular, are unlikely to have a substantial impact on crime rates because they cannot address the diversity of criminal behaviour.

There are, however, other ways to approach crime prevention by focusing closely on the specific characteristics of specific crime problems and looking for ways to eradicate or at least reduce the magnitudes of those problems. Approaches that focus on specific crimes fall into a category called Situational Crime Prevention (Clarke, 1980; Clarke and Mayhew, 1980; Cornish and Clarke, 1986). This paper will describe, in some detail, how situational crime prevention works, how it has been used, and what impact on crime is likely if it is accepted as a crime control policy.

TRADITIONAL APPROACHES TO CRIME PREVENTION

As a preface to our discussion of situational approaches, a short review of traditional crime prevention programs is necessary since situational crime prevention is, in part, a reaction to the difficulties experienced in trying to produce preventive results through traditional approaches. If traditional approaches worked well, of course, there would be little pressure to find new forms of crime prevention. If traditional approaches worked well, few people would possess criminal motivation and fewer still would actually commit crimes.

Perhaps the most common crime prevention activities could be placed under the categories of "legal prevention," "social prevention," and "Neighbourhood/Block Watch." Criminology frequently focuses on trying to understand why people commit crimes and to use that understanding to manipulate both their motivation and their actions.

LEGAL PREVENTION

Criminal legal theory assumes utilitarian motivation on the part of potential offenders. Criminal laws proscribe specific forms of behaviour and prescribe specific punishments for those who ignore the proscriptions. The assumption is that most citizens will comply with the law, some others will be deterred by the *threat* of punishments, and a few difficult people will require special deterrence through punishment for violation of the law. (See generally, Packer, 1968.)

It hardly needs comment that traditional legal crime prevention works imperfectly. Present crime rates are near their highest recorded historical levels (Brantingham and Brantingham, 1984) despite, or perhaps because of, a vast proliferation of criminal laws. Research on offender decision-making suggests that few offenders ever consider potential legal consequences seriously when deciding to commit an offence. (See, e.g., Bennett & Wright, 1984; Gabor, et al., 1987; Kube, 1988.)

Recent Canadian experience with the utility of criminal sanctions to control street prostitution is instructive. Tough new criminal sanctions, combined with new procedural rules making it easier for police to establish a case, were proclaimed in the mid-1980s. The new law resulted in more arrests and convictions, but had virtually no effect on the volume of street prostitution in major Canadian cities (Lowman, 1989). We are inclined to agree with Lab (1988: 94) that this traditional form of crime prevention holds out few promises for major additional preventive gains.

SOCIAL PREVENTION PROGRAMS

Contemporary mainstream criminological theories try either to explain why some people commit crimes and others do not, or to explain why some groups are more likely to get into trouble than others. This "offender-centred" criminology often involves a search for motives for criminal behaviour in offenders' social environments. This approach to criminology frequently tries to identify, often through attempts at theory construction,[1] some general cause of criminal (or deviant) behaviour. At one extreme, an absolute or complete determinant of criminal behaviour is sought. At the other extreme, criminal behaviour (in the aggregate) is seen to be partially caused by many factors.[2] Social prevention programs try to manipulate particular "causes" in order to reduce people's motivation to commit crime.

Independent of the identified "cause" of crime, the preventive program interest is frequently based on an image of some particular social environment associated with criminal behaviour. The image of the social environment considered in traditional social crime prevention seems often to be limited to social conditions associated with poverty or economic inequality; or to behavioural effects ascribed to school and workplace associations, friendship networks, and families.

COMMUNITY DEVELOPMENT PROGRAMS

Perhaps the most heralded, but least evaluated, form of social prevention program in North America is the neighbourhood development program embodied in the Chicago Area Projects [CAPs] and their progeny. Initiated in many of Chicago's high delinquency neighbourhoods by Clifford Shaw and his associates in the 1930s and 1940s, they aimed at reducing delinquency by rekindling informal social controls through revitalization of the weakened social and communal institutions in those neighbourhoods. Stressing self-help centred on resident leaders (such as Catholic parish priests), the CAPs provided professional staff to help the formation and operation of a local community committee that would, in turn, carry out three primary programs: a youth recreation program; a neighbourhood improvement campaign; and a detached youth worker program staffed by local adults (Lundman, 1984: 59).

Where there was a strong latent institutional structure such as the Catholic parish in the Polish dominated "Bush" at Russell Square in south Chicago, the CAPs were clearly successful in revitalizing neighbourhood institutions and in engaging residents in community activities (Schlossman, et al., 1984). Some CAPs also had substantial success in reducing the number of juvenile arrests in their areas by mediating between adolescents and police and by running information diversion programs. It is not so clear, however, that they had much impact on the criminality or criminal behaviour of neighbourhood residents. No evaluations were conducted and published during the original implementation of the CAP idea. Subsequent retrospective evaluations conducted in the early 1980s suggest that the CAPs did not work well in less homogeneous neighbourhoods or in neighbourhoods that lacked the latent, but powerful, social institutions that had been present in the showpiece CAP in the "Bush" (Schlossman, et al., 1984).

The CAP model seems not to have travelled well, either. As pointed out by Lundman (1984: 68–71), the Boston Mid-City project can be viewed as a relatively solid, if serendipitous, effort at replication of the CAP model during the 1950s. The project evaluator's conclusion is one of the bluntest in North American criminology: "Was there a significant measurable inhibition of law-violating ... behaviour as a consequence of Project efforts? The answer ... is 'No'" (Miller, 1962: 10). Similarly, the Mobilization For Youth program on the lower east side of Manhattan, which utilized CAP principles in passing, showed little in the way of measurable impact on the main goal: prevention of delinquency (Marris and Rein, 1969; Moynihan, 1969).

Although the results of these American projects suggest that such programs are too general in focus and too simplistic in operation[3] to effect measurable crime reduction, community based social crime preventions efforts abound in Canada. The YMCA, church groups, schools, park boards, volunteer groups and local governments are all strongly committed to the idea that strengthening community institutions is a good way to prevent crime; and they constantly look for additional ways to alter social conditions that are commonly associated with criminal activity. (See Brantingham, 1986, for a discussion of general trends in Canadian crime prevention and the Safer Communities issue of the Canadian Journal of Criminology [October, 1989] for recent group policy statements.)

These local Canadian social prevention programs are rarely evaluated, but when they have been, they have shown mixed results. Some programs have claimed considerable success, while others have had little effect (Hackler, 1978; Hiew, 1981; LeBlanc and Frechette, 1986).

That the results of such attempts are mixed should not be surprising. These programs typically attempt to do one of two things: either develop attractive activities that will keep high risk individuals (usually juveniles) so busy that criminal activity becomes less attractive; or reinforce the general social norms and local informal social controls that hold people back from crime. These programs often have implementation problems. They may not be situated near very many "high risk" people. They may not be attractive to those most likely to commit crimes. They may not be able to operate 24 hours a day, and may not be available to people when they are most likely to get into trouble. It may be that they reach their target groups, but not strongly enough to become a dominant preventive force; they may be the right medicine, but given in inadequate dosage (Bennett, 1988: 56; Rosenbaum, 1986).

SOCIAL COUNSELLING PROGRAMS

Social counselling for the high risk juvenile and his or her family has long been a social crime prevention strategy of choice. The results have been depressingly meager. The Cambridge-Somerville project, which provided long-term counselling to an experimental group of "pre-delinquents" and compared their subsequent criminal and social careers with those of a matched group of untreated "pre-delinquents," had long-term negative effects: the treated boys had worse criminal careers, higher suicide rates, and worse social success than boys in an untreated control group (Powers and Witmer, 1951; McCord and McCord, 1959; McCord, 1978). Similar programs working in other cities with both males and females seem to have produced the same disquieting results (See, Lundman, 1984: 42–44; Lab, 1988: 130; Krisberg, 1981).

POLICY ATTRACTIONS OF SOCIAL PREVENTION

While social crime prevention programs seem to have little measurable impact on crime occurrence, from a policy perspective, these programs are attractive because they appear to be trying to do something about the crime problem in ways that are intended to be beneficial to people with problems, both those who commit offences and those who do not, as well as to whole neighbourhoods. They hold out the promise of delivering their benefits to large numbers of people. The provision of new leisure and work opportunities as well as social and psychological support may indeed help many people. Not everyone with a social, psychological, or economic difficulty, or who feels or experiences some lack of institutional support is drawn to crime, but everyone who is in one of these positions is a potential beneficiary of help offered through social prevention programs.

NEIGHBOURHOOD WATCH/BLOCK WATCH

Neighbourhood Watch or Block Watch programs are now widespread across North America. In the United States, about 20 percent of all families live in a neighbourhood with a Watch-type program; about 8 percent of all families actually participate actively in such programs (Garofalo and McCleod, 1988). In Canada, the seven city

Canadian Urban Victimization Survey[4] estimated that 42 percent of residents were aware of Neighbourhood Watch and that 15 percent had actually participated in a related property marking program (Solicitor General Canada, 1984).

Organized by the police, Watch-type programs aim to stimulate neighbourhood cooperatives that will actively watch for and report suspicious behaviour in and around the neighbourhood. They are generic programs that are adopted "off-the-shelf" usually with only minor local modifications.[5] They are tied to the development of new community surveillance practices and other informal social control activities in the context of improved community organization. In a sense, Watch-type programs bridge the gap between the traditional community organization aims of many social prevention strategies and situational prevention approaches described in the next section.

Watch-type programs typically feature periodic neighbourhood meetings and crime prevention newsletters that provide residents with a picture of the current neighbourhood crime problem along with crime prevention and security tips. Modern Watch programs feature police-appointed Block Captains who are in direct contact with the local police crime prevention office and who sit at the apex of a telephone fan-out system that can reach every neighbourhood resident to provide information on recent crimes or to control rumours. Many of these programs supplement informal neighbourhood surveillance with other activities: property marking schemes such as Operation Identification; home security surveys; crime tip hotlines; street lighting improvement campaigns; block parenting programs; and citizen neighbourhood patrols.

These programs have been widely accepted as "off-the-shelf" prevention activities. They are based on the idea that crime can be reduced, without changing potential offenders' basic motivations, by making the apparent risk of being caught greater. They begin to move away from programs aimed at altering the offender's motivation, towards an approach that tries to make the site-specific decision to commit a particular crime more difficult — to deter individual site choices.

Watch programs are based on the assumption that surveillance indicators should make potential offenders believe the risk to getting caught would be high if they were to try to commit the offence. It is also obvious that Watch programs assume that police patrol cannot provide sufficient levels of surveillance and that residents (or workers) must become the "watchers."

Research on the effectiveness of these forms of surveillance programs is mixed. "Neighbourhood" surveillance may work in some "neighbourhoods" but not in others. The weight of evidence accumulated through evaluation studies conducted in North America and Britain now suggest that Watch programs may substantially improve participants' general attitudes about their neighbourhoods and may reduce participants' fear levels, but may not have much impact on crime (Worrell, 1984; Rosenbaum, 1986; Rosenbaum, 1987; Bennett, 1988; Skogan, 1988; but consider Titus, 1984).

This should not be surprising. In the urban mosaic (Timms, 1971), there is a high level of variability between residential areas. Why should a neighbour surveillance system work where "neighbours" do not know each other? Why should the system work in areas that are relatively transient, where residents rent and move frequently? Why should it work in high rise structures where people do not know who lives above or below them or even on the same floor? Why should it last very long in low crime areas, where "watching" has little purpose since the things that are being watched for rarely occur? Residential areas vary. Residential surveillance programs should vary with the socio-physical characteristics of the area, and with the potential crime sites and situations in the areas.

SITUATIONAL APPROACHES TO CRIME PREVENTION

Situational crime prevention is quite different from traditional approaches and is based on criminological assumptions quite different from the ones described in the previous section. Situational crime prevention looks at the criminal event itself. It is based on theoretical and research approaches that look at the intersection of potential offenders with the opportunity to commit offences (Brantingham and Brantingham, 1981, 1984; Cohen and Felson, 1979; Hirschi and Gottfredson, 1987; Jeffery, 1977; Sherman, et al., 1989) and at offenders' decision to commit particular offences at particular times and places (Brantingham and Brantingham, 1978; Carter and Hill, 1979; Cornish and Clarke, 1986; Taylor and Gottfredson, 1986).

Situational crime prevention is based on the idea that specific crime problems have unique characteristics that can be analyzed, understood, and utilized in looking for solutions. The approach was pioneered in England (Clarke, 1980; Clarke and Mayhew, 1980; Heal and Laycock, 1986). Instead of looking for a crime prevention technique that can be applied generically to a broad range of problems, situational prevention focuses on specific problems and looks for solutions that reflect the nature of those specific problems.

Situational crime prevention also assumes that to find solutions to crime problems, crime and the decision to commit a specific offence should be viewed as having a complex etiology and highly varied characteristics (Brantingham and Brantingham, 1978; Brantingham and Brantingham, 1981; Cornish and Clark, 1986; Taylor and Gottfredson, 1986).

The first step in situational crime prevention is crime analysis. What are the detailed characteristics of the problem? What is happening? Where and when is the problem occurring? Who might be committing the offences or causing the difficulty and why? What elements in the socio-physical background environment could be contributing, in an immediate way, to the observed crime pattern?

While the crime analysis must sometimes be based on estimates in the immediate absence of sufficiently detailed information, the analysis usually makes potential preventive intervention points apparent. It is the specificity of the analysis that makes possible prevention approaches stand out.

Understanding the offenders' decision to commit an offence at a particular time and place is crucial to interpreting and using the results of a specific crime analysis exercise. Current research supports the idea that the decision to commit an offence is complex and opportunities to commit offences are widespread. The decision to commit a crime is dependent on many factors. Those factors vary with the type of offender and the type of crime.

Cornish and Clarke (1986) use a processual model for understanding the decision to commit a particular offence. They identify seven conditions and sets of factors that influence such decisions:[6] background factors; previous experience and learning; generalized needs; perceived solutions to immediate needs; personal evaluations of perceived solutions; readiness; and reaction to chance events. (See Clarke and Hope, 1984; and Cornish and Clarke, 1986; for supporting research.)

Research into the decision processes of robbers and burglars makes it clear that opportunistic amateurs, journeymen who search for targets, and professionals who carefully plan their offences appear to use difference decision models (Maguire, 1983, 1988; Gabor, et al., 1987; Bennett and Wright, 1984; Walsh, 1978, 1980).

In reporting on the motivation of Oakland, California, robbers, Feeney (1986: 58) demonstrated high variability by quoting several robbers on why they committed the offence:

Robber 1: "I was mad and I had to do something to get it out of my system...."
Robber 2: "I don't know. It sounded easy and I guess I needed the money. We didn't really need it but we wanted to do something...."
Robber 3: "Because he asked me to help him out. He done a favor for me before. I didn't really want the money...."
Robber 4: "Just to cause some trouble. Well, we just wanted to try that...."

In an extensive analysis of a set of Quebec robbers' motives, Gabor, et al. (1987) found their primary motives were straightforward and utilitarian (1987: 63):

"It's the fastest and most direct way to get money."
"... with burglary you have problems selling goods like televisions and stereos ... [in] armed robbery you don't have problems; you get the money right away."
"... one armed robbery pays about as much as 20 burglaries ..."

The robbers' secondary motives focused on the thrill of the crime, feelings of power, and a desire for new experiences (Gabor, et al., 1987: 63):

"I wanted to try it. It was something fast, also easy perhaps and dangerous too...."
"... when I have a gun in my hands nothing can stop me."
"It's funny to see the expression of people when they have a .38 in their face ..."

Among the most interesting findings in the Quebec robbery studies are those relating to planning and target choice. Knowledge about this is central to effective situational crime prevention. Some robbers rely on tips or engage in systematic search and planning in picking a target, yet it is startling how critical immediate situational variables seem to be:

"... It was Sunday. I didn't know where to go to get some money. I had a gun but no bullets ... I saw a convenience store. On Sunday, you don't have much choice." (Gabor et al., 1987: 57)
"... I hit the first bank I ran into because I didn't have much time.... (Gabor et al., 1987: 57)
"... There must be a small street close by to park a car and to remove the disguises afterward.... (Gabor et al., 1987: 58)
"... luck put in an ideal spot. In passing in front of a place we saw an armored truck parked. It was a perfect corner for it, an ideal spot for the getaway.... (Gabor et al., 1987: 58)

These immediate situational motives are conditioned by the social and economic background situations commonly found in the criminological literature:

unemployment and personal economic problems, drug and alcohol use, association with criminal friends. Spending patterns and interpersonal grudges also contribute background motivation (Gabor et al., 1987: 64–67).

Burglars' decision-making, particularly in terms of target search and target choice, is more thoroughly researched and presents similar pictures. This research confirms the importance of the situational aspects of the criminal event and lends additional support to situational crime prevention approaches (See e.g., Rengert and Wasilchick, 1985; Bennett and Wright, 1984; Maguire, 1982; Waller and Okihiro, 1978.)

EXAMPLES OF SITUATIONAL PREVENTION

Situational crime prevention is perhaps best explained by giving examples. In British Columbia, RCMP crime prevention officers receive training in situational prevention during a course on Crime Prevention Through Environmental Design (Brantingham and Brantingham, 1988). In their municipalities, they work with local officials to reduce existing problems and to try to avoid constructing new problems as the municipality grows.

Before giving examples, it is perhaps important to pause and consider the types of behaviour that constitute crimes. Criminology often seems to focus on the study of serious or complex or glamorous crimes — murder, stock fraud, and other "white collar" crimes, prostitution and other "victimless" crimes — because they are interesting and uncommon.

Crime prevention should deal with the mundane behaviours that actually comprise the overwhelming volume of crime. The Canadian Urban Victimization Survey, for instance, found just over 60 percent of all incidents in its survey set were personal theft, household theft, or vandalism. About 60 percent of these were not reported to the police — usually because the offence was too minor or because the victim made the judgment that there was nothing the police could do. The victim survey, of course, misses offences where the "victim" is a business or an official organization. Vandalism is a school and park problem. Shoplifting is one of the most common forms of theft. Even in the rare and glamorous "victimless" crime area, most offences are rather minor. For example, in the mid-1980s over 95 percent of all drugs prosecutions in Canada were for cannabis possession (Brantingham and Brantingham, 1987). Situational crime prevention has been used most commonly to address high volume problems such as mischief offences, theft, and break and enters.

SITE/SITUATION-SPECIFIC EXAMPLES

Example 1: In a large suburban municipality, there was a brewer's warehouse that experienced repeated problems with people breaking into their delivery vans at night. The vans were empty, but backed up to the loading bay doors and locked up over night as if they contained merchandise. Offenders, apparently in search of beer, repeatedly cut through a fence on the perimeter of the warehouse lot and broke into the vans. No beer was stolen, since the vans were empty, but there were continuous repair costs to fix the damaged fence and delivery vans. The crime prevention officer convinced the warehouse manager to keep the delivery vans away from the loading bay doors (which were themselves very secure) and *unlocked* over night. The vans were opened at night on a few subsequent occasions, but they were not damaged as before.

Example 2: At a convenience store, there was a less serious, but more common problem. A high school was located opposite a church. On the street behind the church there was a convenience store. As might be expected, students from the high school walked through the church parking lot to get to and from the convenience store. Lots of litter was left in the church parking lot, producing calls for police service and complaints. Church members were upset by the mess, but unable to stop either the trespassing teenagers or their littering. This was a limited incivility nuisance problem, perhaps the first step toward situations of the sort addressed by Wilson and Kellig (1982) and Hunter (1978). (See Taylor and Gottfredson, 1986, for an overall approach to crime prevention methods.)

The crime prevention officer found an effective, low cost solution. He convinced the church to dig a ditch across the front of its property (except for an entrance way) and arranged a direct pathway from school to convenience store to be built along one edge of the church property. The new pathway had a tall cedar fence (2.5 metres) on one side to separate it from adjacent houses and a chain link fence on the other side. Low shrubs were planted by the chain link fence to enhance its appearance. The littering on the church grounds stopped and, perhaps surprisingly, the student pathway stayed clear of litter and graffiti. General research on littering and graffiti finds that keeping the area "clean" is a deterrent to further problems.

Example 3: There is an international example of something that has happened in video stores. To eliminate shoplifting, video stores are switching how they display videos they have for rental. Early on, they tended to place the actual VHS or Beta rental cassettes out on the shelves. People selected a cassette and carried it to a central desk for rental. This is similar to the situation found in many smaller lending libraries. It has the virtue of reducing staff time spent on telling customers whether particular videos are still available for rental: if they are on the shelves they are available; if they are not on the shelves, they are not available.

The situation has now largely changed: most stores display the small empty boxes that the videos originally came in, or they display small plastic display cards with advertising material. The customer must go to a central desk to determine whether a particular video is available, and if so, rent it before actually taking possession of the cassette. This is similar to the controlled stacks situation found in major research libraries: it occupies more staff time, but cuts casual user pilferage.

Research conducted in England on similar problems experienced with music cassettes in records shops shows similar transformations in display practices in order to reduce the problem of shoplifting (Mayhew, 1987b).

Example 4: The introduction of motorcycle helmets in England has been shown to have, over time, a beneficial situational crime prevention effect as an unanticipated consequence of a change made for other reasons. The major reason for legislating mandatory use of a helmet when riding motorcycles was safety related: people wearing helmets suffer far less serious head injuries than those not wearing helmets in the event of an accident. Many motorcycle thefts are spontaneous, opportunistic thefts. The element of spontaneity is largely suppressed by the situation under the new legislation. Because of the mandatory nature of the law, an unhelmeted motorcycle rider is unusual, will be quickly noticed by police, pursued, and ticketed. Few motorcyclists leave their helmets accessible when away from their vehicles. Few people who are not already riding a motorcycle carry around a spare helmet. The result is that one factor, a crucial factor for many in the decision to engage in an opportunistic theft, has been changed. Motorcycle theft rates have dropped substantially, and without apparent displacement into alternative forms of theft such as car or bicycle theft (Mayhew, 1987a).[7]

PLANNING SITE/SITUATION EXAMPLES

Situational prevention techniques have also been used to avoid anticipated future problems by looking at proposed developments to see whether they are likely to create socio-physical environments that encourage crime or nuisance behaviour or are likely to increase fear of crime levels.

Such work falls into planning and architecture, but requires a good understanding of crime. Planning and architecture involves making decisions that influence many people. Where should the major road be placed? Where should shopping centres be located? Where should apartments and single family homes be built in a community? Where should schools and parks be located? Where should convenience stores be located? What should buildings look like? Should cars and pedestrians be separated? These decisions are made while considering traffic flows, pedestrian street safety, public demands and needs, and current architectural and planning standards. (We are in a period called "post-modern." Buildings and development standards and esthetics have changed substantially from those in effect during the "modern" period when buildings were frequently flat and modern.)

In most parts of Canada these decisions do not involve exploring whether development proposals will affect where and when and what crimes will occur. Yet planning and development decisions do influence a wide range of criminal activities by influencing where people who commit offences go and where their criminal activities occur. Planning and development decisions can also create socio-physical environments where crime is "easy" and attractive, where opportunistic offenders are drawn toward crimes. The general areas of research used in evaluating proposed developments include environmental criminology (Brantingham and Brantingham, 1981, 1984); the reasoning criminal perspective (Cornish and Clarke, 1986); and the routine opportunities and areal guardianship perspective (Cohen and Felson, 1979; Felson, 1987).

British Columbia is, perhaps, the most advanced of Canadian jurisdictions in applying the results of research in environmental criminology and in generally pursuing situational crime prevention practices. RCMP and police in many municipalities throughout the province work with local planners and architects in reviewing plans. In some municipalities, police sit on design review panels to ensure that crime and nuisance generation potential is considered in designing new developments. Municipal and police interest began in 1978. After a series of provincial meetings, the RCMP developed a training course that was first taught in 1982 (see Brantingham and Brantingham, 1988, for a complete chronology). The design/development use of situational crime prevention has not to date addressed all types of crimes, but has focused on property crimes and nuisance behaviour that appears to be avoidable. The focus of the analysis of development proposals is on site-specific characteristics of certain types of offences. For example:

Site 1: Significant changes were made to the design of a church that was built in a "difficult" part of town near pubs and bars. Another church and other buildings in the neighbourhood suffered break-ins and vandalism, and had graffiti problems. In particular, the windows of an existing church were frequently broken. The design for the new church was changed to put its large windows at an angle to the street. The windows were made from Plexiglass. To break windows or vandalize the church, an offender would have to make a major effort—walk across some open ground and attack Plexiglass. Drinking problems and related property crime problems continued in the area, though no problems occurred at the new church.[8]

Site 2: British Columbia is a major tourist destination. Situational crime prevention approaches have been used to address crime problems at tourist attractions in Victoria, Vancouver, Port Alberni, and Whistler, among other places. The Harbourfront Project in Port Alberni is worth noting. RCMP crime prevention officers, through detailed crime analysis and site plan analysis, made suggestions regarding crime reduction as a harbour side tourist centre was planned. Their recommendations were aimed at controlling traffic at nearby intersections; reducing vehicle danger to pedestrians, particularly children, on proposed piers; reducing vandalism, theft from automobiles, and break-ins; and increasing the security of the fireboat and police boat. Some of their design recommendations were also intended to reduce pedestrians' fear of crime and actual risk when walking in the area at night (Hest and Harrison, 1983).

Site 3: The final example involves design changes made to the development of a "new" coal town, Tumbler Ridge, in northwestern British Columbia. A design team[9] conducted potential crime analysis on the initial concept plans and integrated the results of the analysis into the final process of designing the new town. Crime, safety, and nuisance potentials were considered in residential, commercial, and institutional designs integrated into the full town plan. The crime potential of designs, of course, was only one of the considerations in the planning process and was not the consideration that "won out" in all cases in which there were conflicts between crime potential and other design considerations.

The situational crime prevention suggestions put forward for Tumbler Ridge included:

— A redesign of some pedestrian pathways and the introduction of some additional new pathways in order to create "natural" routes from home to school to city centre. Such pathways reduce the number of pedestrians cutting through private yards, apartment parking lots, and apartment buildings, as well as the number trail blazing unexpected paths in public spaces. Well designed path systems should reduce vandalism, nuisance behaviour, and possible theft by separating children and adolescents from trouble spots and "good" opportunities.

–— The inclusion of special attractors at the town's recreation centre, together with a reduction of attractors in the adjacent shopping area. The attractors, including a video arcade that was moved from the town shopping area to the recreation centre, were suggested to draw teenagers to the recreation centre and away from the town centre. Drawing teenagers away from a shopping area reduces potentials for shoplifting, vandalism, littering, and nuisance behaviour. It was further suggested that the arcade be located in a clearly visible area near the recreation centre office so that unofficial surveillance would always be present.

— The redesign of the layout for adjacent shoppers' and pub patrons' parking lots in order to segregate pub parkers from shoppers' automobiles. This should reduce car vandalism and theft from auto for the shoppers. The crime prevention team also suggested the use of canned rather than bottled beer to reduce assault dangers and dangerous litter. It was always noted by the design team that pub goers and people who get drunk at the pub would, at other times, be shoppers, but problems associated with pubs should not be allowed to expand unpredictably into surrounding areas.

Other suggestions included redesign of parks to reduce nuisance behaviour (that is, conflict between children and adolescents and adults); the straightening of streets in some locations to reduce drunk driving accidents; the introduction of several non-criminogenic attractors for teenagers; and numerous changes to reduce vandalism by changing the paths of kids. As with the Port Alberni project, not all recommendations were accepted.

The pattern of recommendations in Tumbler Ridge, Harbourfront, and in the small site examples are typical of the situational crime prevention planning/design recommendations made in British Columbia. The situational approach looks at how a space will be used, particularly by teenagers who are likely to commit crimes or engage in nuisance or uncivil behaviour, and tries to find ways of designing access routes and paths to reduce the likelihood of conflict and crime. The emphasis is on high volume property offences and nuisance behaviour where problems are likely to be eliminated or reduced without displacement; or, if necessary, the approach tries to displace potential criminal or nuisance behaviour into less serious forms of crime (e.g., reduce residential break-ins even if there is displacement into commercial breaking and entry) or to less vulnerable locations.

SUMMARY

Situational crime prevention is a new approach that has certain attractions. While crime is frequently studied at a general level where many types of criminal behaviour are lumped together or people who commit crimes for many different reasons are analyzed as a group, crime prevention appears to be much easier when specific crime situations are addressed. If bicycles are stolen when they are left out of view at the school, move the bike racks. If kids vandalize a church on the way to a convenience store, change their path. It appears to be much more difficult to teach kids not to steal or vandalize, or to alter a structural feature of society that is failing to inhibit theft or vandalism, than it is to find a situational prevention strategy.

On the other hand, there may be situations where displacement might occur when one specific element in the situation is changed. This is an area that needs more research, but one in which sound research is extremely difficult. Displacement may take place in time or in space—to a different time or to a different area—or displacement may be to a different crime or even to non-criminal behaviour (Brantingham and Brantingham, 1984b; Gabor, 1978; Lowman, 1983). The argument that displacement will always occur, however, is difficult to support. Not all crimes will continue to occur in all circumstances. Not all criminals continue to hunt for targets no matter what the targets are like. The process of deciding to commit a crime is the subject of on-going research.[10]

As a policy, however, even if more research is needed, situational crime prevention appears to offer a good way of starting to reduce many crime problems. If accepted as a good approach, the British Columbia experience is a good example of how planning, architecture, municipal interests, and crime analysis undertaken by the police can be merged to address problem areas.

NOTES

1. The range of theories with current adherents might make a handy catalog of fashions in social science thinking over the last century or so: social disorganization theories date from the 1920s; social learning theories date from the 1890s or the 1930s depending on whether one prefers to trace their roots to Tarde or to Sutherland; strain theories date from the 1950s; control theories from the 1960s; labelling and other reactive social conflict theories from the 1960s; and modern Marxian theories of crime from the 1970s. (See Vold and Bernard, 1986, passim.)
2. For an interesting flow of debate over general theories of criminality, see the contest between Hirschi and Gottfredson (1987, 1989) and Steffensmeier (1989) over the idea of "white collar" crime.
3. Despite occasionally having sophisticated underlying theoretical rationales.
4. St. John's, Halifax-Dartmouth, Montreal, Toronto, Winnipeg, Edmonton, and Vancouver were surveyed for the CUVS.
5. It should be noted that the "goals" of these programs are broadening beyond crime reduction and, in fact, in some areas have become diversified. See Canadian Criminal Justice Association, October, 1989: 487–506, for examples of the diversity of goals now found in such programs in the United States.
6. For an introduction to the question of why some people decide to stop committing offences, see Cornish and Clarke, 1986; Pinsonneault, 1984; and Cusson and Pinsonneault, 1986.
7. See Gabor [*Canadian Journal of Criminology*, 32, 1 (1990)] for a cogent general analysis of displacement.
8. It should be noted that problems in and around drinking establishments are of substantial interest in situation prevention (see Poyner, 1983, for British examples; Brantingham and Brantingham, 1988, for examples in British Columbia).
9. The design sub-team charged with exploring crime potential, centred on Jack Hest, who then worked for the RCMP "E" Division Community Policing and Crime Prevention unit; Richard Rabnett, one of the principal architects on the Tumbler Ridge design team; and Patricia Brantingham, professor of criminology at Simon Fraser University.
10. See Cornish and Clarke, 1986; Carter and Hill, 1979; Brantingham and Brantingham, 1978 on offender decision making; see Brantingham and Brantingham, 1984, for an analysis of criminal search areas.

REFERENCES

Bennett, Trevor. 1988. The impact of Neighbourhood Watch on residents and criminals. *Journal of Security Administration* 11: 52–59.

Bennett, Trevor and Richard Wright. 1984. *Burglars on Burglary: Prevention and the Offender*. Brookfield, Vermont: Gower Publishing Company.

Brantingham, Patricia L. 1986. Trends in Canadian crime prevention. In Kevin Heal and Gloria Laycock (eds.). *Situational Crime Prevention: From Theory into Practice*. London: HMSO.

Brantingham, Patricia, and Paul J. Brantingham. 1987. An Evaluation of Litigation Services in the Department of Justice Canada. Ottawa: Bureau of Review, Department of Justice.

———. 1988. Situational crime prevention in British Columbia. *Journal of Security Administration* 11: 18–27.

Brantingham, Paul J. and Patricia L. Brantingham. 1984. *Patterns in Crime*. New York: Macmillan Publishing Company.

———. 1984b. Burglary mobility and crime prevention planning. In R. Clarke and T. Hope, *Coping with Burglary: Research Perspectives on Policy*. Boston: Kluwer-Nijhoff.

———. 1981. *Environmental Criminology*. Beverly Hills, California: Sage.

———. 1978. A theoretical model of crime site selection. In M.D. Krohn and R.L. Akers, *Crime Law and Sanctions*. Beverly Hills, California: Sage.

Brantingham, Paul J. and Frederic Faust. 1976. A conceptual model of crime prevention. *Crime and Delinquency* 22: 284–296.

Canadian Criminal Justice Association. 1989. Safer communities: A social strategy for crime prevention in Canada. *Canadian Journal of Criminology* 31: 359–579.

Carter, Ronald L. and Kim Q. Hill. 1979. *The Criminal's Image of the City*. New York: Pergamon Press.

Clarke, Ronald V.G. 1980. Situational crime prevention: Theory and practice. *British Journal of Criminology* 20: 136–147.

Clarke, Ronald V.G. and Tim Hope. 1984. *Coping with Burglary: Research Perspectives on Policy*. Boston: Kluwer-Nijhoff.

Clarke, Ronald V.G. and Pat Mayhew. 1980. *Designing Out Crime*. London: HMSO.

Cohen, Lawrence E. and Marcus Felson. 1979. Social change and crime rate trends: A routine activity approach. *American Sociological Review* 44: 588–605.

Cornish, Derek B. and Ronald V. Clarke. 1986. *The Reasoning Criminal: Rational Choice Perspectives on Offending*. New York: Springer-Verlag.

Crime Prevention Unit, Surrey RCMP Detachment. 1989. Surrey Block Watch Program Overview—June 1989, presentation to Surrey 2000 Hearings. Surrey, British Columbia: RCMP Crime Prevention Unit. [mimeo]

Cusson, Maurice and Pierre Pinsonneault. 1986. The decision to give up crime. In D.B. Cornish and R.V. Clarke, *The Reasoning Criminal*. New York: Springer-Verlag.

Feeney, Floyd. 1986. Robbers as decision-makers. In D.B. Cornish and R.V. Clarke, *The Reasoning Criminal*. New York: Spring-Verlag.

Felson, Marcus. 1987. Routine activities and crime prevention in the developing metropolis. *Criminology* 25: 911–931.

Gabor, Thomas. 1978. Crime displacement: The literature and strategies for its investigation. *Crime and/et Justice* 6: 100–107.

Gabor, Thomas, Micheline Baril, Maurice Cusson, Daniel Elie, Marc LeBlanc and André Normandeau. 1987. *Armed Robbery: Cops, Robbers, and Victims*. Springfield, Illinois: Charles C. Thomas.

Garofalo, James and Maureen McLeod. 1988. Improving the Use and Effectiveness of Neighbourhood Watch Programs. Washington, D.C.: National Institute of Justice, U.S. Department of Justice. [NCJ 108618]

Hackler, James. 1978. *The Prevention of Youth Crime: The Great Stumble Foreword*. Toronto: Methuen.

Heal, Kevin and Gloria Laycock. 1986. *Situational Crime Prevention: From Theory into Practice*. London: HMSO.

Hest, J.J. and J.T.L. Harrison. 1983. Policing the Port Alberni Harbourfront Project. Port Alberni, British Columbia: Crime Prevention Unit, Royal Canadian Mounted Police.

Hiew, C.C. 1981. Prevention of shoplifting: A community action approach. *Canadian Journal of Criminology* 23: 57–68.

Hirschi, Travis and Michael Gottfredson. 1987. Causes of white collar crime. *Criminology* 25: 949–974.

———. 1989. The significance of white collar crime for a general theory of crime. *Criminology* 27: 3509–371.

Hunter, A. 1978. Symbols of Incivility. American Society of Criminology Annual Meetings, Dallas.

Jeffery, Clarence R. 1977. *Crime Prevention Through Environmental Design*, (2d ed.). Beverly Hills, California: Sage.

Krisberg, Barry. 1981. The National Evaluation of Delinquency Prevention: Final Report. San Francisco: Research Center, National Council on Crime and Delinquency.

Kube, Edwin. 1988. Preventing bank robbery: Lessons from interviewing robbers. *Journal of Security Administration* 11: 78–83.

Lab, Steven P. 1988. *Crime Prevention: Approaches, Practices and Evaluations*. Cincinnati: Anderson Publishing Company.

LeBlanc, Marc and Frechette, M. 1986. La prévention de la délinquance des mineurs: une approche intégrée et différentielle. *Annales de Vaucresson* 24: 87–99.

Lowman, John. 1983. Geography of Crime and Social Control. Vancouver: Unpublished Ph.D. thesis, Department of Geography, University of British Columbia.

———. 1989. Street Prostitution: Asessing the Impact of the Law — Vancouver. Ottawa: Department of Justice.

Lundman, Richard J. 1984. *The Prevention and Control of Juvenile Delinquency*. New York: Oxford University Press.

Maguire, Mike. 1988. Searches and opportunists: Offender behaviour and burglary prevention. *Journal of Security Administration* 11: 70–76.

———. 1982. *Burglary in a Dwelling: The Offence, the Offender and the Victim*. London: Heinemann Educational Books.

Marris, Peter and Martin Rein. 1969. *Dilemmas of Social Reform: Poverty and Community Action in the United States*. New York: Atherton Press.

Mayhew, Pat. 1987a. Palatable Prevention of Motorcycle Theft Through Crash Rather Than Police Helmets. American Society of Criminology Annual Meetings, Montreal.

———. 1987b. Environmental Measures Against Shop Robberies and Shop Theft. American Society of Criminology Annual Meetings, Montreal.

McCord, Joan. 1978. A thirty year follow-up of treatment effects. *American Psychologist* 33: 284–289.

McCord, Joan and William McCord. 1959. A follow-up report on the Cambridge-Somerville youth study. *Annals of the American Academy of Political and Social Sciences* 322: 89–96.

Miller, Walter B. 1962. The Impact of a "Total Community" Delinquency Control Project. *Social Problems* 10: 168–191.

Monaghan, Laurie. 1988. Anatomy of a Crime Prevention Publicity Campaign. *Journal of Security Administration* 11: 60–69.

Moynihan, Daniel P. 1969. *Maximum Feasible Misunderstanding*. New York: Free Press.

National Crime Prevention Institute. 1986. *Understanding Crime Prevention*. Boston: Butterworths.

Packer, Herbert L. 1968. *The Limits of the Criminal Sanction*. Stanford, California: Stanford University Press.

Pinsonneault, Pierre. 1984. L'abandon de la carrière criminelle. Montréal: Centre International de Criminologie Comparée, Université de Montréal.

Powers, Edwin and Helen Witner. 1951. *An Experiment in the Prevention of Delinquency: The Cambridge-Somerville Youth Study*. New York: Columbia University Press.

Poyner, Barry. 1983. *Design Against Crime: Beyond Defensible Space*. London: Butterworths.

Rengert, George and John Wasilchick. 1985. *Suburban Crime: A Time and a Place for Everything.* Springfield, Illinois: Charles C. Thomas.

Riley, David and Pat Mayhew. 1980. Crime Prevention Publicity: An Assessment. Home Office Research Study, No. 63. London: HMSO.

Rosenbaum, Dennis P. 1986. *Community Crime Prevention: Does It Work?* Beverly Hills, California: Sage.

Sacco, Vincent F. and Robert A. Silverman. 1981. Selling crime prevention: The evaluation of a mass media campaign. *Canadian Journal of Criminology* 23: 191–202.

Schlossman, Steven, G. Zellman and Richard Shavelson. 1984. *Delinquency Prevention in South Chicago: A Fifty-Year Assessment of the Chicago Area Project.* Santa Monica, California.: Rand Corporation.

Sherman, Lawrence W., Patrick R. Gartin and Michael E. Buerger. 1989. Hot spots of predatory crime: Routine activities and the criminology of place. *Criminology* 27: 27–55.

Skogan, Wesley G. 1988. Community organizations and crime. *Crime and Justice: A Review of Research* 10: 39–78.

Solicitor General Canada. 1984. Crime prevention: Awareness and practice. *Canadian Urban Victimization Survey Bulletin* 3. Ottawa: Research and Statistics Group, Programs Branch, Solicitor General Canada.

Steffensmeier, Darrell. 1989. On the causes of "White-Collar" crime: An assessment of Hirschi and Gottfredson's claims. *Criminology* 27: 345–358.

Taylor, Ralph B. and Stephen Gottfredson. 1986. Environmental design, crime and prevention: An examination of community dynamics. *Crime and Justice: A Review of Research* 8: 387–416.

Timms, D.W.G. 1971. *The Urban Mosaic: Towards a Theory of Residential Differentiation.* Cambridge: Cambridge University Press.

Titus, Richard M. 1984. Residential Burglary and the Community Response. In R. Clarke and T. Hope (eds.), *Coping with Burglary: Research Perspectives on Policy.* Boston: Kluwer-Nijhoff.

Vold, George B. and Thomas J. Bernard. 1986. *Theoretical Criminology* (3rd ed.). New York: Oxford University Press.

Waller, Irvin and Norman Okihiro. 1978. *Burglary: The Victim and the Public.* Toronto: University of Toronto Press.

Walsh, Dermot. 1980. *Break-ins: Burglary from Private Houses.* London: Constable.

———. 1978. *Shoplifting: Controlling and Major Crime.* London: MacMillan.

Wilson, James Q. and George L. Kelling. 1982. Broken windows: The police and neighbourhood safety. *Atlantic* 249 (3): 29–38.

Worrell, P.B. 1984. An Evaluation of the Neighbourhood Watch Program in Thunder Bay. Ottawa: Ministry of the Solicitor General.

READER REPLY CARD

We are interested in your reaction to *Canadian Crime Control Policy: Selected Readings*, by Timothy F. Hartnagel. You can help us to improve this book in future editions by completing this questionnaire.

1. What was your reason for using this book?

    ☐ university course ☐ college course ☐ continuing education course
    ☐ professional ☐ personal ☐ other _____
    development interest _____

2. If you are a student, please identify your school and the course in which you used this book.

    _____

    _____

3. Which chapters or parts of this book did you use? Which did you omit?

    _____

    _____

4. What did you like best about this book? What did you like least?

    _____

    _____

5. Please identify any topics you think should be added to future editions.

    _____

    _____

6. Please add any comments or suggestions.

    _____

    _____

7. May we contact you for further information?

    _____

    _____

Name: _____

Address: _____

_____

Phone: _____

E-Mail: _____

(fold here and tape shut)

- -

MAIL ➤**POSTE**

Canada Post Corporation / Société canadienne des postes

Postage paid
If mailed in Canada

Port payé
si posté au Canada

**Business
Reply**

**Réponse
d'affaires**

0116870**399**   **01**

0116870399-M8Z4X6-BR01

Larry Gillevet
Director of Product Development, College Division
HARCOURT BRACE & COMPANY, CANADA
55 HORNER AVENUE
TORONTO, ONTARIO
M8Z 9Z9